MYSTERY, INTRIGUE AND SUSPENSE

MYSTERY, INTRIGUE AND SUSPENSE

OCTOPUS BOOKS

Acknowledgements

The publishers wish to thank the following for their kind permission to reproduce the pictures used in this book:

The Mansell Collection 11, 21, 28, 37, 39, 75, 530, 577, 584, 618, 701, 711, 720, 724; Keystone Press Agency 31, 56, 69, 140, 166 left, 204-205, 240, 278, 281, 439, 464, 475, 546; Radio Times Hulton Picture Library 36, 360, 691, 707 below, 709, 723; Popperfoto Limited 43, 47, 59, 61, 63, 91, 96, 103, 109, 111, 114, 115, 117, 119, 224, 283, 290, 323, 327, 329, 531, 549; Donald McLeish Collection 101; N.A.S.A. Woodmansterne Ltd 71, 210, 246; John Topham Picture Library 77, 79, 128, 164, 166 above and below right, 167, 179, 207, 251, 353, 391, 401, 406, 423, 451, 458, 469, 477, 478, 485, 489, 494, 511, 544, 553, 555, 567, 571, 590, 592, 592-593, 627, 629, 667, 673, 681, 685, 688, 714, 717; Mary Evans Picture Library 87, 132, 192 above, 193 above left and right, 525, 589, 604, 607, 610, 621, 651, 694, 697, 704, 707 above, 728, 733; G. Lebat/Geos 146-147; Fortean Picture Library 151, 159, 187, 192-193, 193 below, 197, 215, 237, 649; Rex Features 154-155; Robert Estall 252, 325, 343; News of the World 227, 233; National Army Museum 280; Peter Newark's Western America 299; Colin Bord 342, 349; National Film Archive/Stills Library 357; Syndication International Ltd 369, 669; Fox Photos Ltd 507; Daily Star Picture Library 635; Wide World Photographs Inc 636; Circus World 654; Camera Press 727;

This edition published 1987 by
Octopus Books Limited
59 Grosvenor Street
London W1

© Octopus Books Limited 1987

ISBN 0 7064 3056 5

Made and printed in Great Britain by
The Bath Press, Bath, Avon

Contents

A popular image of a UFO occupant.

Introduction

Since time immemorial events have occurred that have caused mankind consternation and puzzlement. Inexplicable happenings, sightings of strange objects, and peculiar experiences – adding up to total mystery.

However rapidly man increases his knowledge and understanding of planet earth, things are constantly happening to outwit and mystify him. So, even with science and technology rolling back the frontiers of knowledge, there are still many questions that remain unanswered.

In this crowded volume, there are tales to taunt and terrify – ghoulies and ghosties and long-leggety beasties, and even things that go bump in the night! There are also strange tales from deserted corners of the globe, exasperating crimes that go unsolved, hidden secrets of the human mind and fearsome freaks of nature. These stories will undoubtedly challenge the reader's understanding of his terrestrial surroundings and give profound insight into the most bizarre and unusual phenomena.

Chapter one

EARTH, SEA AND SKY

Man has an insatiable thirst for knowledge and a desire to discover hidden secrets. Although he has long since conquered the earth, sea and sky, there are still endless mysteries to penetrate. Does the Loch Ness monster really exist? Was a holocaust that devastated part of Siberia caused by aliens from another world? Who was the Minnesota iceman? Will man ever know the answers?

The ghost ship 'Mary Celeste'

What caused her crew to vanish without trace?

There was a certain strangeness about the two-masted sailing ship that lurched through the Atlantic swell. Something was amiss, but it was not easy at first to discern what it was. The crew on the deck of the brigantine *Dei Gratia* had watched the erratic journey of the mysterious ship ever since it had emerged as a speck on the grey horizon. The *Dei Gratia* had gained steadily on it until, in the early afternoon, Captain David Morehouse took up a parallel course and began to study the ship's odd configuration through his telescope.

The strange ship was a square-rigged brigantine like his own, but it had only two sails set. The others were either furled or hanging in tatters. The ship veered to left and right in the lightly gusting wind as if the helmsman were drunk. But Captain Morehouse soon realized why the ship was not sailing straight and smooth. For as the *Dei Gratia* drew closer, he saw that there was no one at the wheel . . . no one on deck . . . in fact, no sign of life at all. . . .

Morehouse had a signal run up, but there was no answer from the ghostly stranger. He ordered a longboat to be lowered, and three men rowed across to the ship. As they approached, they shouted: 'Brig ahoy, brig ahoy.' There was no reply. They swung their boat around the stern of the ship and peered up at the name painted there: *Mary Celeste*, New York.

The last time anyone had seen the *Mary Celeste* had been a month earlier when, on 4 November 1872, it had sailed from New York bound for Genoa, carrying a cargo of 1,700 casks of crude alcohol. Aboard were the 37-year-old American master, Captain Benjamin Spooner Briggs, and his first mate, Albert Richardson, leading a crew of seven. Also on board were the captain's wife, Sarah, and their two-year-old daughter, Sophia. Briggs, an upright, God-fearing, bearded man, was making his first voyage in the *Mary Celeste*. His previous commands had been of a schooner and a barque, but he had leaped at the chance of commanding the *Mary Celeste* when the consortium that owned it offered him a third share in the ship. It had originally been called *The Amazon*, but the owners gave the ship a new name, along with a badly needed refit, before sending it off across the winter Atlantic.

The *Mary Celeste* sailed out of New York's East River and pointed its bow towards the Azores, which were sighted, according to the log, on 24 November.

The *Mary Celeste*.

The weather until then had been good, and Mrs Briggs had spent much of her days on deck. In the evenings she worked at her sewing machine or played on the melodeon which she had persuaded her husband to allow her to bring on the voyage.

However, once past the Azores, the weather changed for the worse. A moderate gale blew. It was hardly serious enough to worry an experienced captain, and Briggs ordered some of the sails to be furled. There was no panic and the ship's log recorded only the barest facts. The following day was 25 November, and that morning the ship's bearings were noted in the log.

It was the last entry ever made.

Ten days later the longboat from the *Dei Gratia* came alongside the *Mary Celeste*. First Mate Oliver Deveau and Second Mate John Wright clambered aboard, leaving the third man below to secure the boat. Deveau and Wright searched the ship, and what they saw deepened the mystery.

The rigging flapped loosely in the wind. The wheel swung noiselessly, water slurped in and out of the open galley door, a compass lay smashed on the deck, the ship's boat was missing. But below decks, things were very different. Everything seemed orderly . . . except that there was no one to be seen.

In the captain's cabin was Mrs Briggs' rosewood melodeon with a sheet of music still on it. The sewing machine was on a table. Little Sophia's toys were neatly stowed away. In the crew's quarters, the scene was equally ordered. Washing hung on a line. Clothing lay on bunks, dry and undisturbed. In the galley, preparations seemed to have been made for breakfast, although only half of it appeared to have been served.

Deveau and Wright clambered back into the longboat and reported their discoveries to Morehouse. He suggested that the *Mary Celeste* must have been abandoned in a storm. But why then, asked Deveau, was there an open and unspilled bottle of cough medicine along with the unbroken plates and ornaments in the captain's cabin? A mutiny, suggested Morehouse. But there was no sign of a struggle – and why should mutineers abandon ship along with their victims? Perhaps the ship had been taking water. Deveau confirmed that there was three feet of water in the hold and that a sounding rod had been found on deck, but three feet would be a normal intake over ten days for an old timber-hulled ship and could easily have been pumped out.

Morehouse decided to put the unanswered questions aside and concentrate for the moment on more important matters – salvage money, for instance. He sent some of his crew back across to the meandering *Mary Celeste* and within hours the hold was pumped dry. By the following day, the rigging was repaired.

The captain could spare only three of his seven-man crew to sail the *Mary Celeste*. He chose Deveau and seamen Augustus Anderson and Charles Lund. In an amazing feat of seamanship, the three sailed the *Mary Celeste* 600 miles to what was to have been her first port of call, Gibraltar, where the *Dei Gratia* was awaiting them.

The British authorities in Gibraltar impounded the *Mary Celeste* and ordered a public inquiry. Morehouse, Deveau and his men were closely questioned. A bloodstained sword was said to have been found under Captain Briggs' bunk – was this not proof of foul play? The sword was examined and the stains proved not to be blood. Nine casks of alcohol were found to be dry and a further cask had been breached – could not the crew have gone on a drunken rampage? Deveau patiently explained to the inquiry that below decks the ship had been in perfect order. Could Briggs have panicked during a storm and ordered the ship's boat to be launched? Little sign of this either – in the captain's cabin, everything had been as orderly as it should have been at a gentleman's breakfast table. The captain had even neatly cut the top off his boiled egg, which remained uneaten on his plate.

But the question the investigators found most baffling was: how was the *Mary Celeste* able to remain on course without a crew for ten days and 500 miles? When the *Dei Gratia* caught up with the mystery ship, Morehouse was sailing on a port tack. The *Mary Celeste* was on a starboard tack. It was inconceivable, the inquiry was told, that the *Mary Celeste* could have travelled the course it did with sails set that way. Someone must have been aboard for several days after the last log entry. . . .

The authorities in Gibraltar were certain that the *Mary Celeste*'s missing longboat and the crew would soon turn up to explain the unanswered questions. But they never did, and, on 10 March 1873, the court of inquiry awarded an ungenerous £1,700 salvage money to Morehouse and his men. It was about 15 per cent of the value of the 200-ton ship and its cargo.

The inquiry closed but the arguments raged on. The occupants of the *Mary Celeste* had all been captured by pirates, they had been seized by a giant squid, they had stepped off on to an iceberg, they had died from yellow fever, the captain had gone mad. But the most extraordinary explanation of all was suggested 40 years later, in 1913.

Howard Linford, headmaster of a school in Hampstead, London, claimed to have discovered a revealing manuscript among the property bequeathed to him by an old school servant as he lay on his deathbed. The servant, a much-travelled man named Abel Fosdyk, had written an account of how he had been an unrecorded passenger on the *Mary Celeste* – and the only survivor of the tragedy that befell her.

Fosdyk wrote that during the voyage Captain Briggs found his daughter playing precariously on the bowsprit – the spar that juts from the front of a sailing ship. He ordered the ship's carpenter to use an upturned table to make a safe platform for her to play there. In doing so, the carpenter cut deep notches in the woodwork on either side of the bow – mysterious marks that were indeed found on the *Mary Celeste*. One calm day, Briggs had an argument with his first mate over a man's ability to swim with his clothes on, and the eccentric captain leaped over the side to prove his point. All the occupants of the ship rushed to the makeshift platform to get a better view, and the wood-work collapsed, flinging everyone into the sea. Sharks soon appeared and polished off all but Fosdyk, who clung to the remains of the platform until he was washed up on the African coast.

The story captured the imagination of readers around the world, but has been rejected as being far-fetched.

So the mystery of what happened to the crew of the *Mary Celeste* remains to this day. But what of the ship itself?

When the *Mary Celeste* was released by the Gibraltar court of inquiry, sailors refused to serve on the ship. They believed it was cursed. The ship changed hands 17 times in the next 11 years until it was bought by a group of Boston businessmen in 1884. They over-insured the ship and sent it off to Haiti. There, on a clear day and in a calm sea, the captain ran on to a coral reef. The attempted fraud was detected, and master and owners were all brought to court. Meanwhile, the old wooden hulk of the *Mary Celeste* rotted away unseen on the remote Caribbean reef.

The civilization that sank beneath the sea

Still the search goes on for the lost kingdom of Atlantis

It was a rich land, blessed with lush vegetation and mines of valuable minerals, including silver and gold. Its people were cultured and scien-tifically advanced. At the centre of the island kingdom, on top of a small hill, was a palace and a temple, the hub of a vast city, 12 miles from end to end. Around the hill was a moat – indeed, more a canal – packed with sailing ships. Around that, in concentric circles, were more canals. These waterways were linked by yet further canals to the open sea via an extensive system of docks and harbours by which the nation's valuable produce was ex-ported to the rest of the known world. It was a prosperous kingdom and a famous one. For, although it vanished from the face of the earth many centuries before Christ, its name is today still better known than those of many of the surviving nations of the globe. The name of that fabled kingdom and its great city . . . Atlantis.

The only description left to us of Atlantis was written by the Greek philosopher Plato in about 347 BC. And even he was not speaking of it first-hand. He was repeating stories written down by the Athenian traveller Solon who, in turn, had heard them from Egyptian priests. The story Plato passed on was that Atlantis was a great nation in decline. Its people had fallen into corrupt ways – and they earned a dreadful punishment. 'In one day and one night' the entire island, 350 miles across, was overtaken by a catastrophe of unsurpassed magnitude. Atlantis was rent by a volcanic explosion, followed by a tidal wave, and within 24 hours had vanished beneath the sea.

Plato puts the tragic fate of Atlantis at a period we would now date as 9600 BC. And the place? 'Beyond the Pillars of Hercules' – what we now call the Straits of Gibraltar. That puts Atlantis somewhere in the Atlantic Ocean, a theory which, as geologists tell us, cannot be correct. For there is no major subterranean land mass on the bed of the Atlantic to justify Plato's story. So, did the celebrated philosopher get his facts wrong? Or did he simply make up the whole story as a cautionary tale? The answer, in all likelihood, is that Plato's epic tale is based firmly on fact – although both his date and his geography are badly out. The result has been a riddle that has puzzled man for centuries. These are some of the areas suggested over the years as the site of the lost civilization.

Mid-Atlantic. A vast ridge runs in the shape of the letter S along the seabed the entire length of the North and South Atlantic, from Iceland to Tristan da Cunha. It has been suggested that the highest region of this mountain range, around the area of the Azores, was once all above sea level, forming the land of Atlantis. Until the present century, this was the most popular theory. But it has now been debunked by scientists who point out that the Atlantic Ridge is – and has been for thousands of years – slowly rising from the depths, not sinking.

North America. As soon as Christopher Columbus returned to Europe with his tales of lands across the ocean, interest in the lost kingdom of Atlantis was revived. English philosopher Sir Francis Bacon firmly linked legend and fact in his work *The New Atlantis*. And historian John Swain wrote: 'It may be supposed that America was one time part of that great land which Plato calleth the Atlantick Island, and that the kings of that island had some intercourse between the people of Europe and Africa.' Such a theory must be discounted, however. The North American races never achieved a level of civilization equal even to that which existed in Plato's time.

The Land Bridge. Various theories have been put forward about land bridges which may at one time have linked Africa with South America, or have joined Europe – via Britain, Iceland and Greenland – to North America. But geologists now know that no such bridge could have existed within the last 50 millions years.

The Sargasso Sea. Sargasso is the Portuguese word for floating seaweed, and the Sargasso Sea is just that. It is a $1\frac{1}{2}$-million-square-mile mass of weed that drifts off the Florida coast. Mariners once thought that it covered vast shallows beneath which may have been a sunken Atlantis. In fact, the sea is up to 1,500 ft deep.

The Scilly Isles. Phoenician, Greek and Roman historians all referred to the 'tin islands' off the British coast. These islands off Cornwall, Britain's only tin-mining region, do not fit, however, Plato's lush description.

Bimini. Between 1923 and his death in 1945, an American commercial photographer named Edgar Cayce made a name for himself as a faith healer and visionary. Although he had never read Plato's works, he claimed to have looked back in time and mentally visited Atlantis, and he described it in much the same way as the Greek philosopher had done 2,300 years before. Cayce added that Atlantis had been destroyed by an atomic explosion (the inhabitants having mastered the science of nuclear fission) around the year 10,000 BC – close to the date set by Plato. And he gave the site of Atlantis as North Bimini,

---

PLATO'S ATLANTIS
At the centre of the island (of Atlantis) was a plain, said to be the most beautiful and fertile of all plains, and near the middle of this plain was a hill of no great size. Around the hill were two rings of land and three of sea, like cartwheels. In the centre of the hill was a shrine sacred to Poseidon and Cleito, surrounded by a golden wall through which entry was forbidden. There was also a temple to Poseidon, which was covered all over in silver, except for the statues, which were of gold. Two springs, hot and cold, provided limitless water supplies, and there were indoor heated baths for kings and commoners, for women and for horses. On the outer rings of land there were dockyards and harbours, surrounded by a wall which was densely built up with houses. From this crowded area rose a constant din of shouting and noise throughout the day and night. Beyond were the plains, which brought to perfection all those sweet-scented stuffs which the earth produces now, whether made of roots or herbs or trees or flowers or fruits. All these, that hallowed island, as it lay then beneath the sun, produced in marvellous beauty and endless abundance.

– *Critias and Timaeus*, by Plato.

a small island in the Bahamas, forecasting that 'a portion of the temples may yet be discovered' in 1968 or 1969.

It was a preposterous story. And yet, in 1968, veteran American zoologist and deep-sea diver Dr J. Manson Valentine discovered some strange structures beneath the sea off the coast of North Bimini. They could be made out clearly only from the air, but when he dived to investigate he found that they were the walls of what seemed to be an enormous harbour, enclosing quays and jetties. The walls, about one-third of a mile long, were of massive stone blocks more than 16 ft square.

Subsequent expeditions – and there have been many – have alternately supported and debunked Dr Valentine's assertion that the formation amounts to a man-made harbour. In 1970, Dr John Hall, professor of archaeology at Miami University, led a survey of the site and reported: 'These stones constitute a natural phenomenon called Pleistocene beachrock erosion. We found no evidence whatever of any work of human hand. Therefore, alas for those who believe in the old legend, another Atlantis is dismissed.'

But two later American expeditions to Bimini, in 1975 and 1977, came up with very different findings. The expeditions' leader, Dr David Zink, of California, brought to the surface a block of stone with a tongue-and-groove worked edge. The conclusion: 'On balance, we believe that the structure at Bimini is archaeological rather than geological in origin – but its purpose must remain a matter for speculation.'

So the Bimini mystery is yet to be solved. The possibility that it is the site of a lost city has not been disproved. Yet the most likely site of Atlantis so far suggested is nowhere near the Caribbean. It is not even in the Atlantic. For most archaeologists now believe that Plato made two remarkable mistakes when he wrote about his lost island.

Firstly, it is most likely that Atlantis, if it existed at all, was not 'beyond the Pillars of Hercules', but in the Mediterranean itself. Secondly, when Plato recorded the disaster as having happened 9,000 years before the Egyptian priests' account, he may have written 9,000 in error for 900. If so, that would put the date of the demise of Atlantis at approximately 1500 BC instead of 9600 BC. And in 1500 BC, there did occur one of the most appalling cataclysms of ancient times . . .

Archaeologists now know that the civilization of Atlantis described by Plato was very much like the highly developed Bronze Age Minoan culture which flourished on the islands of the Aegean Sea until the 15th century BC. It ended abruptly in about 1470 BC – and until recent years no one has understood why.

It is now known, however, that around that time a volcanic explosion, unimaginably destructive, tore out the entire centre of the Minoan island of

Kalliste – now known as Santorini – which lies midway between Crete and the Greek mainland. Sea rushed in to fill the crater that was left.

Archaeologists are now excavating the 100-ft-deep deposits of volcanic ash that cover what may once have been Plato's fabulous island. What they have so far uncovered has enabled them to build up a frightening picture of the events that occurred there almost 3,500 years ago.

Because of the scarcity of human remains, it is assumed that the inhabitants of the island had some warning of the impending disaster through earth tremors and a series of minor volcanic eruptions. What probably happened next was this. The citizens took to their boats and headed for Crete, some 70 miles south. But before they had a chance to reach their goal, Kalliste exploded in a holocaust of fiery lava.

Molten rock spewed into the air, and ash and pumice stone rained down on the overcrowded boats. Soon the sea was an unnavigable mass of floating pumice. The people in the boats, unable to flee, died a slow and hideous death as the torrent of burning, choking ash became ever thicker. For some, the agony was ended by a tidal wave, perhaps 200 ft high, which swept out from the island, smashing the boats to matchwood. The giant wave, travelling at more than 150 miles an hour, soon reached Crete, heart of the Minoan empire. It swept away all the towns and villages along the northern coastline and obliterated the harbour serving the capital, Knossos.

The wave travelled on to the North African coast, where its effects may have been responsible for the Old Testament story of Moses' parting of the Red Sea. It has also been suggested that the rain of ash, which covered more than 100,000 square miles, may have been the origin of the story of the Egyptian plagues.

Some idea of what must have been the scale of the devastation can be gained from the example of the explosion of the volcanic Indonesian island Krakatoa in 1883. About 300 towns on the neighbouring islands of Java and Sumatra were wrecked, and 36,000 people died. The blast was heard 3,500 miles away in Australia, shock waves went round the world three times, volcanic dust reached Africa and even Europe, and tidal waves crossed the Pacific Ocean and damaged boats on the coast of South America.

Such must have been the fate of Kalliste. Today, as Santorini, it stands fragmented and desolate under its barren covering of ash. It is made up of two main islands, Thera and Therasia, whose sheer 1,000-ft cliffs curve round a seven-mile-wide expanse of water, in parts 1,000 ft deep. This water covers the caldera, the dead heart of the volcano, formed when the cauldron of molten rock burned out and collapsed in upon itself.

In the centre of the great sea-covered crater – at the spot where the palace and temple of Atlantis may once have stood – are two islets which arose from the depths long after the original catastrophe. They are rocks of black lava. Sometimes smoke rises from them in lazy wisps – a faint but threatening reminder of the cataclysm that may have destroyed the legendary kingdom of Atlantis.

LOST GARDEN OF EDEN

Atlantis is not the only legendary land lost beneath the waves. Two entire continents are reputed to have vanished without trace - each vastly larger than Atlantis and each, in its time, described as the cradle of mankind.

The names of these two lost Gardens of Eden were Mu and Lemuria. Mu was supposedly situated in the Pacific Ocean and was twice the size of Australia. Lemuria, according to legend, filled up most of the Indian Ocean and linked Africa with Malaysia.

The Mu theory was raised in 1870 by Colonel James Churchward, who claimed that, while serving with the Bengal Lancers in British colonial India, he was told the secrets of the lost land by Hindu priests. He was shown some tablets, since lost, and was taught a forgotten language called Naacal. Churchward also said that he had found identical stone tablets in Mexico. According to the tablets, Mu sank into the ocean in a great natural catastrophe 12,000 years ago, wiping out its 64 million people. Remarkably, the story of Mu was taken seriously at the time.

A somewhat better-argued tale was told about the lost continent of Lemuria. The name was coined by the 19th-century British zoologist Professor Philip Sclater, who named his nation after the lemur. It was fossils of this and of other animals, found in both Africa and Malaysia, that led Sclater to support legendary tales of a lost continent in the Indian Ocean. The many supporters of his theory included eminent biologist Ernst Haekel and evolutionist Thomas Huxley.

Less fanciful evidence is used to support the legend of Lyonesse - a land off the south-west English coast, said to have been visited by King Arthur and his knights. The 15th-century chronicler William of Worcester quoted monastery scrolls which referred to '140 parochial churches, all since submerged, lying between Cornwall and the Isles of Scilly'.

The land is said to have sunk into the sea in a single day. This extravagant punishment, so folklore has it, was meted out by the magician Merlin to drown King Arthur's treacherous knight Mordred and his rebel followers.

MIRACLE OF SURTSEY

Sunken cities? Lost continents? The world was inclined to treat such legends lightly - until the remarkable events of November 1963. It was then that the forces which obliterated Atlantis were seen at work, but in reverse.

The skipper of a fishing boat off the south coast of Iceland radioed his base to report a vast cloud of black smoke rising from the sea. He and his crew watched in awe as explosion after explosion burst from the depths. Rocks were hurled 500 ft into the air and the smoke billowed to more than 10,000 ft.

Then the fishermen noticed waves lapping over a vast black form which was slowly emerging from the ocean. It was the summit of a volcanic mountain rising from the depths.

Within 24 hours, the island was higher than a housetop. Within the week, its peak was 200 ft above sea level. And by the time that volcanic activity ceased two years later, the island was more than 500 ft high and over a mile long.

The Icelanders named their new-born island Surtsey, after Surtur, the god of fire in Norse mythology. Today, colonized by birds, insects and plants, it still stands as proof that new land can emerge from the depths as quickly as an old one can sink into legend.

Sinking of the 'Lusitania'

'War plot' theory of torpedoed luxury liner

'Torpedo . . . torpedo on starboard side.' That was the startled cry from the look-out on the foc'sle of the British liner *Lusitania* as it sped through the waters off the south coast of Ireland on 7 May 1915. There was no time to take evasive action, and the underwater missile found its mark.

Eleven miles away on the Old Head of Kinsale, south of Cork, people on shore were admiring the passage of the giant Cunard liner. Those with binoculars were puzzled to see a faint plume of smoke rise over the ship. One man checked his watch – the time was 2.11 pm. Eighteen minutes later the *Lusitania* had sunk beneath the waves, taking with it 1,198 people, 124 of them Americans.

It was that last figure that changed the course of history. For the death of the Americans precipitated the entry of the United States into World War One – and ultimately ensured victory for the Allies.

But the sinking of the *Lusitania* was not only a momentous event in the course of the bloodiest war the world had ever known. It also presented historians with a mystery that has not been solved to this day. That mystery is – was the *Lusitania* a passenger ship or a warship? Was the liner carrying arms? And was it knowingly sacrificed to bring America into the war?

The *Lusitania* was designed to wrest the Blue Riband, awarded for the fastest Atlantic crossing, from the two German lines that had held it since 1897. The liner was subsidized by the Admiralty under secret agreements that have never been released. It was 670 feet long, could carry 2,300 passengers in extreme luxury, had a crew of 900, travelled at 25 knots – and was to be able to mount twelve 6-in guns.

The liner's final voyage, from New York to Liverpool, began on 1 May 1915. The Germans had warned passengers intending to travel on the *Lusitania* not to book aboard the ship, and made clear that every enemy passenger ship in war-zone waters was liable to be attacked, and that neutral governments 'should not entrust their crews, passengers or merchandise to such vessels'.

The German Embassy in Washington went so far as to place advertisements in American newspapers warning: 'Travellers planning to embark on the Atlantic voyage are reminded that a state of war exists between Germany and Great Britain and that vessels flying the British flag are liable to destruction. Travellers sailing in the war zone on ships of Great Britain or her allies do so at their own risk.'

Nevertheless, 188 Americans booked as passengers aboard the *Lusitania*, and more than 4,000 cases of ammunition for the war effort were added to the officially 'innocent' cargo manifest.

As the liner left New York, several people on the other side of the Atlantic had its future in mind. Winston Churchill, who was then first lord of the admiralty, met the first sea lord, Lord Fisher, along with naval intelligence experts who had earlier been asked to prepare a report on the effect of a liner being sunk with American passengers aboard. Coincidentally, the US ambassador in London, in a letter to his son, wrote: 'What will Uncle Sam do if a British liner full of American passengers is blown up?' And King George V granted an audience to President Woodrow Wilson's special envoy, Colonel Edward House, at which the King is reported to have inquired: 'What will America do if Germany sinks the *Lusitania*?'

The scene was set for disaster. The vessel approached the Irish coast on 7 May. The master, Captain William 'Bowler Bill' Turner, had received only one warning of the peril ahead. It was a radio message from Vice-Admiral Sir Henry Coke, whose headquarters were at Queenstown, Cork, and it read: 'Submarines active off the south coast of Ireland.'

One of those submarines was the U20, under the command of Kapitan-Leutnant Walter Schwieger. The U20 had been at sea since 30 April and was on its way back to base at Wilhelmshaven when the *Lusitania* was spotted on the horizon. Schwieger at first did not recognize the liner and could only describe it as 'a forest of masts and stacks' – in those days the *Lusitania* was the tallest ship in the world.

As it approached Kinsale Head, the liner changed course. 'She was now coming directly at us,' said Schwieger. 'She could not have chosen a more perfect course if she had deliberately tried to give us a dead shot.'

At a range of a mere 400 yards, Schwieger ordered the torpedo to be fired. It hit the *Lusitania* on the starboard side below the bridge. Water poured in at a pressure too strong to be contained by the 119 supposedly watertight compartments. The bow dipped beneath the calm sea, and at the same time, the liner began to list to starboard.

The bow hit the sea-bed 315 ft below, but the stern still hung in the air, the enormous propellors pointing skywards. Then the vast bulk of the liner slid, steaming and bubbling, to the bottom.

The sea was dotted with frantic figures. The *Lusitania* was well equipped with lifeboats, but there had been no time to launch them all. Of the 1,198 people who perished, 785 were passengers. They included 125 children. One expectant mother gave birth in the water, and she and her baby died.

Argument has raged ever since over whether the Germans were right to view the *Lusitania* as a legitimate target of war, over whether the liner was armed and carrying a military cargo, and over the biggest question of all – did the British government send the *Lusitania* on a suicide course through U-boat infested waters in order to force America into the war?

The mysteries surrounding the sinking of the *Lusitania* have been exhaustively argued by historians and authors, most notably by writer Colin Simpson, whose book on the subject* propounded several controversial theories about the tragedy – not least that the vessel was armed with twelve 6-in. guns and was carrying a large cargo of munitions and explosives. Simpson claimed that the *Lusitania* underwent modifications in a Liverpool dry dock in 1913, enabling the liner to take heavy guns if required and, in effect, turning it into an auxiliary cruiser. One of the boilers, it was claimed, had been converted into a magazine, and lifts had been installed to hoist the shells up to the decks.

More controversial is Simpson's allegation that the British admiralty – and that means Churchill – called off the *Lusitania*'s destroyer escort even though U-boats were known to be in its path. Captain Turner was never told that the warships which he had assumed were still in the vicinity had been diverted elsewhere. And Turner himself, who survived the sinking, claimed throughout his life that a message in naval code had directed him to change course towards the point where the U-boat was waiting.

During his years of researches, Simpson turned up hitherto-unpublished documents from Washington's national archives and from Cunard and the admiralty. They led him to believe, as many historians do, that a massive Anglo-American cover-up took place after the disaster. The cargo manifest was said to have been falsified, and both Sir Henry Coke's signal log and the official admiralty signal register had their entries removed for 7 May – the only pages missing for the entire period of the war.

The other main mystery that has intrigued researchers is why the *Lusitania* sank so swiftly. The German G-type torpedo which was fired from the U20
* *Lusitania* by Colin Simpson (Longman, 1972).

was neither powerful nor deeply penetrating. Yet it sank a mighty ocean liner in just 18 minutes. How?

It has been claimed that the liner had a dangerous design fault built into it. The engines and machinery took up too much space, so some of the coal carried had to be stored in compartments not intended for that purpose. The engineers chose for their coal stores the special buoyancy compartments that were a safety feature of the liner. The empty air traps that should have kept the ship afloat were, on that fateful voyage, loaded full of coal.

But a more sinister reason has been suggested for the swift demise of the *Lusitania*. Divers who have been down to the wreck report that the side and bottom of the ship were blown outwards by an internal explosion far more severe than could have been caused by a torpedo. What could have caused such a blast?

Could it have been that deep in the holds of the *Lusitania* were stacked more than butter, cheese, bully beef and brass rods, as the cargo manifest showed? More even than the 4,000 cases of ammunition that were later admitted to have been stowed aboard? Was the *Lusitania* in fact a virtual munitions ship hiding its identity behind 1,198 innocent, doomed people?

The world's best-loved monster

Does a shy but friendly freak called Nessie lurk deep in a Scottish Loch?

More than 10,000 years ago, the last of the Ice Age glaciers gouged out a vast crevice in the Highlands of Scotland. As the ice receded, the 24-mile-long crack that remained filled with water – and provided a home for one of the most mysterious yet best-loved creatures of all time, the Loch Ness Monster.

The legend of the monster – 'Nessie', as she has affectionately come to be known – has haunted Loch Ness ever since she made her first recorded public appearance in 565 AD. In that year, St Columba was travelling to Inverness on a mission to bring Christianity to the Picts. He ordered one of his followers to swim out into the loch and bring back a small boat which had drifted from the shore. As the man started out, 'a strange beast rose from the water', only a few yards from him. St Columba, the story goes, faced the creature and shouted: 'Go thou no further, nor touch that man.' The monster fled.

Ever since, the people of the Great Glen of Loch Ness have recognized Nessie and her forebears as shy, retiring and harmless creatures who rarely visit the surface of their mountain home. Although the locals have known about the inhabitants of their loch for centuries, it is only within the last 50 years that Nessie's fame has spread round the world.

On 14 April 1933, John Mackay and his wife were driving along a newly built road beside Loch Ness. The surface of the water, glass-smooth, mirrored the surrounding peaks. Suddenly Mrs Mackay clutched her husband's arm.

'John,' she gasped, 'what's that . . . out there?'

The sunlit water of the loch was foaming and bubbling as though a volcano had erupted beneath the surface. John Mackay, a local hotel owner, braked sharply. Then he and his wife watched with fear-tinged fascination as a gigantic creature emerged . . . a creature, with at least two humps or coils and a snake-like neck. The monster threshed the surface of the loch until the water was white with foam. Then it dived out of sight.

Since that day in 1933, Nessie has played a tantalizing game of hide-and-seek with scientists, naturalists and thousands of other monster-hunters. There have been more than 3,000 claimed sightings of the elusive creature.

The Mackays' remarkable experience was followed by a similar encounter in November of the same year. This sighting gave the impetus for the Nessie cult to start up in earnest – for it provided the first photograph of the monster. The photograph was taken by engineer Hugh Gray as he walked near his home in the village of Foyers after church one Sunday. The loch was like a millpond but, about 100 yards offshore, he noticed a strange disturbance.

'A rounded back and tail appeared,' he said later, 'and a 40-ft-long creature churned the water, throwing up a cloud of spray.'

NESSIE IDENTIKIT
Eyewitness reports have built up the following picture of Nessie:
Length: **More than 50 ft.**
Body: **At least 30 ft long with a 12-ft girth.**
Head: **Snail-like and very small compared with the body.**
Neck: **About 4-7 ft long, graceful, and as thick as an elephant's trunk.**
Tail: **Rather flat, blunt at the end.**
Flippers: **Two small ones at the front, two large ones at the back.**
Skin: **Snail-like – grey, silver and black.**

Gray's photograph of the monster was sent to Kodak for analysis. The firm agreed that the film had not been tampered with, but the shadowy image was unconvincing as evidence.

A photograph regarded by many experts as still the best was snapped in April 1934 by Robert Kenneth Wilson, a London surgeon of unquestioned character and veracity. Wilson and a friend were driving alongside Loch Ness at the start of a holiday during which they hoped to take wildlife photographs – but the pictures Wilson took that day were of a form of wildlife he had never dreamed existed.

The surgeon and his companion had driven through the night and decided to stop for a rest near Invermorriston. As Wilson stretched his legs beside the loch, he became aware of a small head peering out of the water. He dashed back to his car, grabbed his camera and took a series of snaps. They showed an elegant head and neck, with the faint outline of a body remaining beneath the surface.

These photographs – and the hundreds taken since – were inevitably dismissed by the debunkers of the Nessie legend as showing tree trunks, seals, birds, otters or upturned boats. But whatever the truth, those first reports and pictures of the Loch Ness Monster caused a world-wide sensation.

The loch was soon crawling with tourists, scientists, big-game hunters, schoolboys and hoaxers. Villagers did a roaring bed-and-breakfast trade. Circus-master Bertram Mills offered £20,000 to anyone who could deliver the monster to him alive. Questions were asked in parliament about Nessie's safety. Eventually, a law was passed protecting any creature in the loch from being 'shot, trapped or molested'.

The one thing lacking was a serious, scientific examination of the evidence pouring out of Loch Ness day by day. The main reason for this was that a series of hoaxes – phoney sightings, touched-up photographs and the like – were rapidly turning Nessie into a joke. The canny Scots, it was said, had found a great way of extracting money from the purses of gullible foreigners.

One of the earliest hoaxes involved big-game hunter Michael Wetherell, a Fellow of Britain's highly-respected Zoological Society. In December 1933, he found what appeared to be the monster's footprint on the shore of the loch. Wetherell said: 'It is a four-legged beast. It has feet or pads about eight inches across. I judge it to be a powerful animal about 20 ft long.'

Amid intense excitement, plaster casts of the footprint were sent to London's Natural History Museum. Experts there identified the print as 'resembling that of a hippopotamus'. And then it was found that a mounted, dried foot of a hippo was missing from the museum at Inverness, only a few miles from the loch.

Of the three most sensational sightings reported in 1933 and 1934, two were by locals, the third by a London businessman.

This is how Alexander Campbell, a local freelance journalist, described what he saw on a June day in 1934:

As I left my cottage close by the loch, the creature rose from the water like a prehistoric monster. It was 30 ft long with a long, snake-like neck and a flat tail. Where the neck and body joined there was a hump. The monster basked in the sunshine until the noise of a boat from the Caledonian Canal disturbed it. It lowered its neck and dived, leaving a minor tidal wave behind it.

A few weeks before Campbell's sighting, a monk, Brother Richard Horan, of St Benedict's Abbey, Fort Augustus, reported:

I saw the monster rise out of the waters of Loch Ness, and watched it for 20 minutes. The head and neck protruded from the water at an angle of 45 degrees. It had a thickset neck, the lower side of which was silvery in colour. It had a snub nose. When a motor-boat came within earshot the monster sank, slowly.

London company director George Spicer told of a somewhat different but equally fantastic encounter with the monster:

My wife and I were motoring along the loch-side when we saw an extra-ordinary animal crossing the road about 200 yards ahead. It had a long neck a bit thicker than an elephant's trunk and a large body about five feet high. It had dark skin of a loathsome texture and it moved in a jerky sort of way. I speeded up, but the creature vanished into the thick undergrowth.

Other monster-hunters reported seeing the beast open and shut its mouth. Some said it had a mane, like a horse's. One spotter claimed to have been close enough to see drops of water falling from scaly skin as the monster shook itself.

By the summer of 1934 Nessie's fame had spread far enough to interest John Earnest Williamson, an American who was a leading expert in under-water photography. He arrived at Loch Ness with a contraption he called a photosphere – a submersible, windowed globe, in which he sat in an arm-chair taking underwater photographs.

What Williamson did not know before he reached Loch Ness was that below 30 ft the water is first dark brown and then an inky black that dims the most piercing lights. This murkiness is caused by particles of peat which for many thousands of years have been washed down the mountains into the loch. Williamson abandoned his plan and went home.

Each year up to the outbreak of World War Two, scores of sightings were reported and many more photographs taken. But during the war years there were no tourists. The roads round the loch were used only by a few locals and the armed forces. Nessie stopped making news.

It was not until 1947 that she reared herself into the front pages again. In that year, the clerk to Inverness County Council and three of his friends reported that they had seen humps of a beast that was swimming in the loch. The monster-hunting season had opened once more.

In 1951, local woodsman Lachlan Stuart rose early and stepped out of his

The Loch Ness monster at Castle Urquhart.

croft door to milk his cow. He glanced towards the loch, stopped in his tracks, then dashed back into his croft to grab a camera. He ran with it down to the shore and took one picture before the shutter jammed. His photograph showed three huge humps sticking as much as four feet out of the water. Out of the frame, but described by Stuart, was a neck topped by a head like that of a sheep, except that it was blackish and had no hair, wool or scales. From his description, corroborated by a friend who also rushed to the water's edge, the monster must have been between 50 and 60 ft long.

Recorded sightings over the succeeding years included the following:

1953: Several men cutting timber by the side of the loch reported that they had watched the monster for two minutes.

1954: A fishing boat entering Loch Ness from the Caledonian Canal, the waterway which links the loch with the sea, received on its echo sounder the imprint of a huge creature moving through the water at a depth of nearly 500 ft. Its length was 'at least 50 ft'.

1959: Automobile Association patrolman James Alexander stopped his motorcycle and sidecar at a phone booth on the edge of the loch. Alexander, who had his back to the loch, suddenly got a creepy feeling that he was being watched. He turned – and there, he claims, was the monster's head and neck sticking seven feet out of the water. He flagged down a passing truck, and the driver confirmed his story.

1960: Torquil MacLeod and his wife were driving near Invermorriston when they saw a large creature basking on a beach on the opposite shore. MacLeod watched it through binoculars for nine minutes before it flopped into the water. He described it as having grey, elephant-like skin and large paddle-like flippers. He estimated its length as 60 ft.

1960: Aviation engineer Tim Dinsdale took the first movie film of the monster. The four-minute sequence showed a humped-back creature zigzagging through the water at ten miles an hour. Dinsdale was so convinced by what he filmed that he gave up his career to live by the loch and hunt for Nessie.

1961: More than a dozen guests at a loch-side hotel claimed to have watched a beast 30 ft long, with two humps, rise out of the water and remain in view for six minutes.

1962: World-famous British naturalist Peter Scott helped launch the Loch Ness Phenomena Investigation Bureau to organize a serious study of the mystery. For ten years, bureau volunteers and one or two full-time workers kept watch on the loch. Their cameras were at the ready round the clock. They logged many sightings of their own and put on record scores of eye-witness stories. But the only prize worth having for such an effort eluded them. They, too, failed to get the definitive photograph of Nessie.

Perhaps the most useful thing the bureau did was to send films of what was claimed to be the monster to the Joint Air Reconnaissance Intelligence Centre, for independent analysis. The centre reported that one film showed an object which was neither a boat nor a submarine but which appeared to be 'an animate object, 12 to 16 ft long, 3 ft high and 6 ft wide'. Another film showed a similar object 6 ft wide and 5 ft high.

But the Loch Ness Phenomena Investigation Bureau failed to grasp its greatest chance of solving the mystery. In 1971, Tim Dinsdale was directing a 100-strong bureau team when a black, snake-like creature reared from the water. Dinsdale had five cameras but was too astonished to use any of them.

Frank Searle is another of the small number of fanatics who have taken up monster-hunting as a profession. In 1969, this Cockney ex-paratrooper gave up his job as a grocery-store manager, bought some first-rate photographic equipment and went to live in a tent by Loch Ness.

Searle then sat watching and waiting for his chance to make a fortune. For he reckoned that if his patience was rewarded with the first totally convincing pictures of Nessie, they could be worth £250,000 in world-wide publication fees.

Searle claims to have seen the monsters – he estimates there is a colony of at least 20 of them – 24 times. He says: 'They're bulky, 12 to 16 ft long with a sheep-like head and a 7-ft neck. They have paddle-like flippers.'

In 1972 and again in 1976, Searle took photographs which he claims were of the monsters. They were published round the world and described as 'the most amazing yet'. But a Glasgow zoology professor said of them: 'My first impression is that this is the carcass of an animal which has been in the water for some time. Or a tree.'

Throughout the 1960s and the 70s, monster-hunting continued as a major British sport. And Nessie became the Scottish Tourist Board's biggest single asset.

A diver who went down to recover a drowned man's body from the loch reported an eerie sight. He had seen huge rock ledges piled high with eels 'as thick as a man's torso'.

A frogman working in the loch claimed that Nessie had surfaced only 30 yards away from him. He said: 'It was about 30 ft long, with a long neck, an otter-like tail and four fins. I shouted to my mate, and it dived out of sight.'

Various ways of cornering or enticing Nessie were suggested. Dragging the loch with steel nets at a cost of £200,000 was ruled out. So was a scheme to induce Nessie to bask in water warmed by giant hot plates sunk in the loch. Proving tests on a British mini submarine took it 450 ft below the loch's surface. Its occupants saw nothing. 'It's as black as hell down there,' they said.

In 1969 the American invasion of Loch Ness began. Dan Taylor, a former

US Navy submarine crewman from Atlanta, Georgia, had spent five years and £20,000 building a tiny yellow glass-fibre submarine which he named *Viperfish*. He planned to fire darts from it to remove a sliver of Nessie's flesh. Taylor claimed to have picked up Nessie on his echo sounder, but never for long enough to track her. He also said that *Viperfish* had been sucked into a 130-ft-deep hole. But he repeated John Williamson's mistake of 35 years earlier. He had not realized that the loch's waters are impenetrably dark below 30 ft. He packed up and went home.

In 1970 Dr Robert Rines, president of the Academy of Applied Science, in Belmont, Massachusetts, spent two weeks at Loch Ness. He headed a four-man team equipped with sonar gear, underwater cameras and a 'sex cocktail' made from the reproductive essences of creatures such as sea cows, eels and sea lions. The team also had tapes, to be played underwater, of the sounds made by a variety of water creatures mating, fighting and 'talking'.

Rines later claimed that the sex cocktail had enabled him to make contact with creatures 'one hundred times the size of any fish in the loch'. They lived, he said, on a shelf 200 ft from the loch's shore. Two years later, in Boston, Rines produced colour and black-and-white photographs taken in the loch and showing what appeared to be a very large flipper attached to a cow-shaped body.

Almost at the same time as Rines' expedition, another US team reached the loch. This one, sponsored by the Cutty Sark whisky firm, was led by Professor James Ullrich, of the Smithsonian Institute. Ullrich had taken the precaution of paying £15 to insure himself at Lloyds for £5,000 against being bitten or maimed by the monster. He said: 'The monster is no longer a myth, but a scientific reality.' And a member of his team was just as certain: 'There's no question. There is a monster. Nobody seriously believes, do they, that the thing is a drainpipe, eight tree roots, or a biscuit crumb on the lens of somebody's camera? Because if it is, I don't think I can stand it.'

Cutty Sark had arranged with Lloyds of London for payment of £1 million to anyone who caught the monster alive and unharmed before May 1972. There were no serious claimants, and Ullrich's team, using much the same techniques as the Rines expedition had employed, including sex lures, failed to get any better evidence than its predecessors to support or crack the legend.

Then the Japanese jumped on the Nessie bandwagon. In 1973, Yoshiou Kou, the 36-year-old showman who had brought Muhammad Ali and Tom Jones to Japan, led a 15-strong team to Loch Ness. A Japanese business consortium had raised the cash, and Kou announced that his team would use two submarines which would arrive soon from Tokyo. But when Kou's divers saw how inky the loch water was, they cancelled their mission.

Meanwhile, the amateur monster-watchers seemed to be having more success. In 1974, truck driver Andy Call and his mate Henry Wilson were driving alongside the loch when the water foamed and a creature surfaced. Call says: 'It was black, 50 or 60 feet long, with a horse-like head. We watched it for 15 minutes. It submerged three times.'

The following year, two female university graduates from Munich claimed to have seen several humps moving around in the water. Ten days later, four French girls reported a similar sighting. They were joined by a party of English tourists who supported their story.

In 1978, lorry driver Hugh Chisholm and his wife Mhairi were driving along the loch towards their home at Inverness when they saw the monster. Mrs Chisholm said: 'It was really huge, with the head and one hump clearly visible. When it vanished underwater, it left large waves behind.' She said that on a previous occasion her husband had claimed to have seen Nessie – and she had laughed at him.

However, perhaps the most convincing evidence of the existence of a monster in Loch Ness has come as a result of a second expedition to Scotland by Dr Rines. On 20 June 1975, his team lowered two underwater cameras into the loch near ancient Urquhart Castle. They were at depths of 40 ft and 80 ft and they took 2,000 pictures at intervals of 75 seconds, aided by immensely powerful strobe lights. The resulting photographs appeared to depict a reddish-brown beast with a fat body about 12 ft long and an arching neck about 8 ft long. The head of the creature was hideous, with gaping jaws and two tube-like protruberances on top of it.

It at last convinced veteran monster-hunter Sir Peter Scott of Nessie's existence. He said: 'There are probably between 20 and 50 of them down there. I believe they are related to the plesiosaurs.'

The plesiosaur has not been seen on earth for 7 million years. The monster-hunters believe, therefore, that Nessie's ancestors may have been cut off from the sea when the loch was formed at the end of the last Ice Age. Loch Ness is up to 1,000 ft deep – deeper than the North Sea – and its vastness and remoteness would have allowed the creatures to flourish undisturbed as survivors from another millennium.

But why the spate of sightings from 1933 onwards? The monster-hunters have an explanation for that, too.

The road that John Mackay and his wife were driving along when they first spotted Nessie on 14 April 1933 had only recently been built and was the first to skirt the loch-side. To construct it, thousands of tons of rock had been blasted into the loch, and dense vegetation which for centuries had shrouded its banks had been cut down. This blasting, the experts say, destroyed the monsters' primeval underwater lairs – and left them, for the first time, homeless wanderers in the loch.

Curse of 'The Flying Dutchman'

Many have sighted the ship doomed to sail on forever

What was – or is – *The Flying Dutchman*? And why has a seemingly far-fetched sailor's yarn maintained such a fascination over the centuries – even for those who don't go to sea? The cautionary tale of the ship's captain who made a pact with the Devil was well known to seamen long before Wagner's famous opera. A fanciful story, certainly, but every few years, even to this day, the legend reappears as a weird and frightening warning.

The legend originated in the 17th century, when an unscrupulously greedy Dutchman, Captain Hendrik van der Decken, set sail from Amsterdam to make his fortune in the East Indies. All went smoothly until his ship tried to round the Cape of Good Hope. A fierce storm blew up, ripped the sails to shreds and battered the ship's timbers day after day.

At this point in the story, legend becomes mythology – the Devil is reputed to have appeared before the captain and asked him if he were willing to challenge God's will and head straight into the storm. The impatient Dutchman agreed, and brought down upon himself the curse of the Almighty – that he and his ghostly ship should roam the seas ceaselessly until Judgement Day.

It is a tale that does not beg to be taken too seriously. And yet, over the centuries, there have been numerous sightings of strange, old ghostly ships resembling the battered East-Indiaman, many of them from the area where *The Flying Dutchman* originally disappeared. Not only that, but the mariners' belief that anyone who sees the phantom ship will soon encounter bad luck has regularly been fulfilled.

Some of the witnesses of the nautical apparition have been of the utmost respectability. On 11 July 1881, Prince George, a 16-year-old Royal Navy midshipman who was later to become King George V, made an historic entry in his log book aboard *HMS Inconstant* off the coast of Australia. He wrote:

At 4 am *The Flying Dutchman* crossed our bows. She emitted a strange phosphorescent light as of a phantom ship all aglow, in the midst of which light the masts, spars and sails of a brig 200 yards distant stood out in strong relief as she came up on the port bow, where also the officer of the watch from the bridge saw her, as did the quarter-deck midshipman, who was sent forward at once to the forecastle, but on arriving there no vestige nor any sign whatever of any material ship was to be seen either near or right away to the horizon, the night being clear and the sea calm.

It is obvious that the young prince was deeply impressed by the vision, which was seen by 13 other men aboard the *Inconstant* and two sister ships. Later that day, the seaman who had first sighted *The Flying Dutchman* fell to his death from a mast. The death of the admiral of the fleet followed shortly afterwards.

The Flying Dutchman has been logged by several ships off the Cape of Good Hope, but perhaps the most astonishing sightings have been made by people standing on dry land.

In September 1942, four people were relaxing on the terrace of their home at Mouille Point, Cape Town, when they spotted an ancient sailing ship heading into Table Bay. They followed its progress for about 15 minutes before it disappeared from view behind Robben Island.

Three years earlier, in March 1939, almost 100 people saw the phantom East-Indiaman. They were sunbathing on Glencairn beach in False Bay, south-east of Cape Town, when a fully rigged sailing ship appeared out of the heat haze. It passed across the bay with its sails full, although there was not a breath of wind. The ship seemed to be heading for a distant, isolated beach. But, as the crowd of excited witnesses looked on, *The Flying Dutchman* vanished as suddenly as it had appeared.

Other parts of the world also have their own 'Flying Dutchman'.

Britain's phantom ship haunts the Goodwin Sands, the sandbank in the English Channel that has claimed 234 wrecks. It was on the Goodwins that the *Lady Lovibond* ran aground on 13 February 1748. The ship had left London for Oporto, Portugal, with its newly married skipper, Captain Simon Peel, his bride and some of the wedding guests. But, according to legend, a jealous mate, who was also in love with the bride, killed Peel and steered the ship on a suicide course on to the Goodwins. The entire company was drowned.

On 13 February 1798 – 50 years later to the day – a three-masted schooner identical to the *Lady Lovibond* was seen heading for the Goodwins. The crew of a fishing boat followed and heard the sounds of a celebration and women's voices. The schooner hit the sands, broke up – and vanished.

The same vision was reported by another ship's crew exactly 50 years later. It was seen again, by a group of watchers near Deal, Kent, on 13 February 1898. Does the phantom appear every 50 years? Watchers were on the lookout on 13 February 1948. Visibility was poor and they saw nothing.

North America's 'Flying Dutchman' lurks off the coast of Rhode Island. Its name is the *Palatine*, and it left Holland in 1752, packed with colonists heading for Philadelphia. But a winter storm blew the ship off course, the

captain was lost overboard, and the panicking crew mutinied. The passengers spent Christmas Day in confusion and terror. Two days later, the *Palatine* ran aground on rocks off Block Island and began to break up. As the storm abated, the doomed ship began to slip back off the rocks, drawn out to sea again by the tide. But before it could do so, dozens of local fishermen descended on the *Palatine*, took off the passengers and looted the ship.

When their frenzied rampage had ended and they had stripped the *Palatine* of everything of value, the fishermen set it on fire and watched it drift, ablaze from bow to stern, to the open sea. But even the tough fishermen were struck with horror when they saw a woman appear from her hiding place on the *Palatine* and stand on the deck screaming for help until the flames engulfed her.

For more than two centuries since, the *Palatine* has reappeared off the New England coast, a battered sailing ship swept by blood-red flames.

Creatures of the deep

Serpents – or just fanciful seadogs' tales

For as long as mariners have sailed the oceans, they have returned with tales of sea monsters and devils of the deep. Most reports are befogged by time, faulty memory – and sometimes alcohol. But there are some that cannot be ignored. . . .

Long before the film *Jaws* made holidaymakers afraid to bathe along North America's Atlantic shoreline, there was a strange series of sensational sightings of terrifying monsters. As early as 1638 there was discussion in the Boston press about sea serpents living off Cape Ann. But it was in 1817 that the New England sea monster mania really got under way. In that year, several people reported sightings off the Massachusetts coast.

The monster was first seen on 6 August, and its activities appeared to be centred on the fishing port of Gloucester. An official inquiry was set up and no fewer than 11 eyewitnesses gave sworn testimony. The descriptions of the monster are therefore well documented. The creature, it appears, was 70 ft long, dark brown and snake-like. A sailor called Amos Story claimed to have seen the monster twice. He said: 'Its head was shaped like a turtle's and was certainly larger than the head of any dog I ever saw. It carried it 10 or 12 inches above the water, and it moved through the water very rapidly.'

The local fisherfolk made a strong net to try to catch the beast, without success. Some formed armed search parties, but only one man got a shot at the creature. He was Matthew Gaffney, a ship's carpenter, who fired twice as the serpent circled his boat. The monster disappeared beneath the surface and, a few days later, left the vicinity altogether. It was last spotted heading north-east off Cape Ann.

Perhaps the creature later changed its mind and headed south again, because, in 1819, there was a report of a giant sea serpent attacking the schooner *Sally* off Long Island. That same year, a second attack was reported on the coast – a small sailing ship was sunk and the survivors blamed a sea monster.

First-hand documentation to substantiate such reports is rare and rightly regarded as suspect by scientifically-minded men. One sighting that was taken seriously, however, occurred on 6 August 1848. The master and several of the crew of the British warship *Daedalus* saw a dark brown head, with a shaggy mane down its neck, peering at them from the waters off the West African coast. Back in his home port, Captain Peter McQuhae reported to his lords commissioners of the Admiralty:

It was an enormous serpent, with head and shoulders kept about four feet constantly above the surface of the sea and, as nearly as we could approximate, there was at the very least 60 feet of the animal. It passed rapidly, but so close under our lee quarters that, had it been a man of my acquaintance, I should easily have recognized his features with the naked eye. The diameter of the serpent was about 15 or 16 inches behind the head, which was, without doubt, that of a snake. It was never, during the 20 minutes that it continued in sight of our glasses, once below the surface. It had no fins, but something like the mane of a horse, or rather a bunch of seaweed, washed about its back. It was seen by the quartermaster, the boatswain's mate and the man at the wheel, in addition to myself.

A similarly described serpent was seen in the same vicinity later that year by an American brig, the *Mary Ann*. Its crew described the creature in much the same terms as Captain McQuhae had done.

Why should an experienced captain of the Royal Navy lie and risk ridicule by reporting the fictitious sighting of a sea monster? There would seem to be even less reason why two respected members of the Royal Zoological Society should do so. In 1905 the two men, Meade Waldo and Michael Nicholl, were on the deck of the steamship *Valhalla* off the coast of Brazil when a mysterious creature surfaced alongside them. It was seen not only by them but by three members of the ship's crew. Waldo recorded the event later:

I saw a large fin or frill sticking out of the water, dark seaweed brown in colour, somewhat crinkled at the edge. I could see under the water the shape of a considerable body. A great head and neck rose out of the water ahead of the frill. The neck was about the thickness of a man's body; the head had a turtle-like appearance, as had also the eye. It moved its neck from side to side in a peculiar manner. We were sailing pretty fast and soon drew away from the object.

New England, West Africa, Brazil – three sightings of similar sea creatures. Could there really be such relics of another age lurking in the depths of the oceans?

Many hundreds of people must believe so, for they claim to have seen them. And not just at sea, but in lakes.

COLL, *North-west Scotland:* In 1808, a clergyman fishing off the isle of

A gigantic squid found in 1861, 120 miles north-east of Teneriffe.

Coll encountered what he described as a hideous, long-necked sea monster. Thirteen local fishermen backed his claim and said that the creature was between 70 and 80 feet long.

PORT Fairy, Victoria: Australian settlers reported capturing a strange creature in a lake in 1848. It had a head like a kangaroo but with a long neck and shaggy mane. It was assumed to be a 'bunyip', a mysterious animal that was once believed to inhabit remote lakes and rivers in many parts of Australia. Its name is an aboriginal word meaning water devil.

GALAPAGOS ISLANDS, Pacific: Two American whalers from New Bedford were sailing alongside each other about 250 miles north-west of the Galapagos Islands in 1852. The captain of one of the ships, the *Monongahela*, sent three boats to tackle what he thought was a basking whale. The men harpooned and killed it – but not before it had sunk two of the boats. The crew of the second ship, the *Rebecca Sims*, watched the struggling creature and later described it as a grey-brown reptile about 150 ft long with gnashing jaws. The *Monongahela*'s captain had the monster's head cut off and preserved in a vat of alcohol on deck. Then he set sail for home with his prize. Neither his ship nor the crew were seen again.

ISLE OF LEWIS, Scotland: The Times of 22 March 1856 reported a sighting, in a loch on the Isle of Lewis, of a water creature that 'looked like a huge peat stack or a six-oared boat'. It swallowed a blanket left on the shore by a girl herding cattle, then vanished into the loch.

SOUND OF SLEAT, North-west Scotland: In 1872, two clergymen claimed to have encountered a sea serpent with seven humps or coils stretching 100 ft.

NORTH SEA: In 1881, a Scottish fishing boat, the *Bertie*, was attacked by a fierce, humped monster that almost capsized it. One crewman fired a rifle at the creature but it continued to dive round the boat for several hours before finally disappearing at dusk.

LLANDUDNO, North Wales: A solicitor and a justice of the peace saw 'a dark, undulating creature as big as a large steamer' crossing the bay in 1882. Pressed for a more precise estimate of size, they guessed at 200 ft.

CAPE TOWN, South Africa: The crew of the steamship *Umfuli* saw a sea creature off the Cape in 1893. They described it as a 'giant eel, 80 ft long, with 7-ft jaws'.

ORKNEYS, Scotland: A father and son out sailing encountered a creature 'with giraffe-like neck which rose 18 ft out of the water'.

SANTA CRUZ, California: An enormous carcass was washed up on the beach in 1925. A zoologist who examined it described it as '37 ft long, with a long, thin neck, distended head and a mouth like the bill of a duck'. He expressed himself totally baffled.

PRAH SANDS, Cornwall: A headless corpse was washed up in 1928. It was

30 ft long, with four small flippers and a tapering tail. Species unknown.

CADBURY BAY, Chatham Islands, British Columbia: Canada's best-known sea serpent, nick-named Caddy, was seen by an archivist on holiday in 1932. He said 'fold after fold of its body came to the surface', and he reckoned its total length to be 80 ft. More than 100 other people claimed to have seen Caddy in the same area.

LAKE OKANAGAN, British Columbia: Since the 1950s, there have been frequent sightings in the lake of a huge creature, 70 ft long, with four or more humps. The serpent has been nicknamed the Ogopogo. Its original title was Naitaka ('monster spirit of the lake'), the local Indians' name for it long ago. The most dramatic claim about the Ogopogo is that in 1854 it ate a team of horses belonging to a settler that were swimming across the lake.

GORVAN, Ayrshire, Scotland: A 35-ft-long creature, again described as having a giraffe-like neck, was washed up on the beach in 1953. Locals burnt the carcass.

FLORIDA COAST: Five miles offshore, five US Air Force divers floated on a raft in a thick fog late in 1962. Suddenly they detected a sickening smell and, moments afterwards, 'an enormous head and neck' towered over them. The divers fell into the sea in panic. Only one survived to tell this tale. According to him, the other four were dragged under, screaming in terror.

SIBERIA: A Moscow University team reported seeing an animal looking like a dinosaur in remote Lake Khaiyr in 1964.

GREAT BARRIER REEF, Australia: Diver Robert Le Serer found on the sandy sea bed 'a gigantic beast, 70 ft long, with jaws 4 ft wide'.

CONNEMARA, Ireland: An amateur zoologist set off an explosion in Lough Fadda in 1965 after studying reports of monster sightings there. He was rewarded with the sight of a huge creature threshing around 50 yards offshore.

NORTH ATLANTIC: Captain John Ridgway and Sergeant Chay Blyth were rowing across the Atlantic in their tiny craft in 1966. On one particularly calm night, Ridgway was suddenly awakened by the sound of a mysterious creature 'writhing and twisting' through the ocean. He estimated it as being between 30 and 40 ft long and said it gave off a phosphorescent glow.

LOCH MORAR, West Scotland: In 1969, two fishermen reported seeing a basking monster with a gaping mouth and ribbed back.

Since then, there have been several other reports of monsters in lochs and bays along Scotland's rugged west coast. All, however, pale into insignificance beside the most mysterious monster that ever surfaced from the deep – the creature whose exploits are told in the following story.

In the steps of Bigfoot

What is the monstrous creature that stalks the world's snowy wastes?

When the first gorilla was seen by a white man in the early part of the last century, the reaction to the news was one of natural astonishment. Native stories about such creatures were well known but had been largely written off as mythology. The actual discovery of these enormous, intelligent and sensitive animals was a fresh reminder that the wilder regions of the earth could still hold surprises for man.

The amazing coelacanth, fished out of the Indian Ocean in 1952, caused just as much of a shock, for it was believed to have become extinct 100 million years before. The pigmy hippopotamus, the white rhinoceros, the giant panda and the Komodo dragon are other recent discoveries of hitherto unknown wildlife. Yet these creatures have been no secret to the natives of the regions they inhabit. The tough, abrasive skin of the coelacanth, for instance, was used by the natives of Madagascar in place of sandpaper for mending punctures in bicycle tyres.

So how many more creatures may yet turn out not to be legendary, as always supposed, but real? Are there other living fossils – even missing links in the story of evolution – still hiding away in the remotest regions of the globe? There is certainly a wealth of folklore to suggest so. . .

From the still-mysterious mountains of the west coast of North America to the snowy slopes of the mighty Himalayas, there exist stories, and evidence, of the most intriguing creature that walks this earth. It is called variously Bigfoot, Sasquatch, Shookpa, Alma, Meti, Kang-mi, Migo and dozens of other names. It has also achieved international fame as the yeti, or Abominable Snowman.

The existence of the yeti was first reported to the West in 1832 by an adventurous Briton, B. H. Hodson, who went to live among the Nepalese high in the Himalayas. Hodson wrote about a tall, erect, ape-like creature covered in thick hair. But those who read his reports believed his sightings were simply of the large langur monkey or the Himalayan red bear. It was not until 1887 that an outsider first saw direct evidence of the existence of the yeti. Another Briton, Major Lawrence Waddell, of the Indian Army Medical Corps, told of remarkable footprints he had seen in Sikkim – 'said to be the trail of one of the hairy wild men who live in the eternal snows'.

When an international mania for mountaineering broke out in the 1920s and 30s, more details of the remarkable yeti were brought back by expeditions

Everest hidden in cloud.

seeking to conquer the unknown peaks of the Himalayas. It was at this time that a journalist coined the name 'Abominable Snowman'.

According to the stories of Nepalese villagers, Tibetan lamas and hardy Sherpas, yetis had always lived along the snow line that separates the thickly wooded lower slopes of the Himalayas from the desolate icy wastes above. Their terrain was between 12,000 and 20,000 ft and they were assumed to live in caves and to emerge mainly at night. The animals were said to be anything up to 12 ft high, yet extremely agile. They walked erect with a loping gait, their long arms swinging by their sides. Their heads were slightly conical and their pale, virtually hairless features were half ape-like, half human. Their bodies were covered in thick, coarse hair, the colour of the red fox. They were said to be shy and to approach human habitation only when driven by hunger. Their diet was mainly lichen and rodents, and they disembowelled their prey before eating it – a peculiarly human trait. They made a loud yelping sound when alarmed.

This then was the Abominable Snowman, as represented by local inhabitants. But where was the proof of its existence? Tibetan lama monasteries were said to contain scalps, skins and even mummified bodies of the creatures, but no Westerner had been able to remove one of these relics for analysis. The only evidence was the reports of the natives – until, in 1921, Colonel C. K. Howard-Bury became the first European to see the yeti. . .

Colonel Howard-Bury was leading a British expedition attempting to scale Mount Everest, when he and his men spotted a strange group of creatures at about 17,000 ft on the Lhapka-la Pass. When they reached the spot they found footprints in the snow – 'each of them about three times the size of a human print'. Colonel Howard-Bury was told by his Sherpas that the tracks were those of the yeti. But, despite his own description of the prints, the sceptical Englishman could not bring himself to believe they were caused by a yeti and instead attributed them to a wolf.

Further sightings followed. One scientific expedition reported seeing an ape-man pulling roots out of the ground. There was a report of a 13-year-old girl being kidnapped by a yeti, and of a yeti being sighted carrying a crude bow and arrows. In 1936, the expedition of Ronald Kaulback confirmed the widespread existence of mysterious footprints. And a year later, the first photograph allegedly showing a yeti's footprint was taken by Frank Smythe and published around the world.

During World War Two, five Polish prisoners being held in a Siberian labour camp escaped from their Soviet captors and made an incredible march across Mongolia and Tibet to Bhutan, where, in 1942, they crossed the Himalayas to India and safety. There, they recounted a strange episode which had occurred in the mountains.

They said they had looked down from a ledge and had seen two burly ape-men only a few feet below them. The creatures were aware that they were observed but showed no emotions whatever and, seemingly ignoring the strangers, continued to shuffle through the snow. The Poles watched the creatures for fully two hours, and their description fits those of most previous witnesses.

A pair of less friendly ape creatures were encountered by two Norwegian prospectors in Zemu Gap, Sikkim, India, in 1948. One of the men, Jah Frostis, said he was badly mauled about the shoulder by the larger of the beasts. But the Norwegians were armed, and when they opened fire the creatures fled. It was yet another story to intrigue the world, coming as it did from a largely unexplored region of the globe. But it was, after all, just a story. Apart from the inconclusive 1937 photograph, there was still no documentary evidence about the Abominable Snowman's existence.

All that changed in 1951. On 8 November of that year, veteran mountaineer Eric Shipton was climbing in the Gauri Sankar range with fellow Briton Michael Ward and Sherpa Sen Tensing when they came across a series of clear footprints on the Men-lung Glacier at an altitude of 18,000 ft. They were made by a creature with a flat foot and five toes, one much enlarged. The prints were 13 in. long and 8 in. wide, and indicated a creature about 8 ft tall. (A further run of prints was also photographed, but these were less conclusive: it was later suggested that they were made by a running mountain goat and were later grotesquely enlarged by the action of the sun.) The photographs and Shipton's impeccable credentials convinced many. New interest was aroused.

Scientists examined a mummified finger and thumb found at Pangboch, Nepal, and declared it to be from a Neanderthal man. Then, in 1952, Everest was finally conquered by Sir Edmund Hillary and Sherpa Tensing. But although Hillary found prints, he always denied the existence of an Abominable Snowman.

Two years later, the London *Daily Mail* sent an expedition to the Himalayas to try to prove or disprove the existence of the yeti once and for all. Sadly, it did neither. The team did, however, discover several 'yeti' scalps covered in coarse red hair. The lamas who were custodians of these relics allowed the expedition to remove a few hairs. These were later analyzed, and scientists were unable to identify the creature to which they had belonged. The *Daily Mail* expedition also found several footprints and droppings containing part-animal, part-vegetable material.

A further expedition, sponsored by Texas oilman Thomas Slick, took up the trail in 1957. They too found tracks and were told by Nepalese villagers that yetis had recently killed five people in the area. But of the creatures themselves they saw no sign.

In 1970 British mountaineer Don Whillans spent a day photographing mysterious but inconclusive tracks at a height of 13,000 ft in the mountains of Nepal. That night he saw by clear moonlight an ape-like creature bounding along a nearby ridge on all fours.

And in 1973 a young Sherpa girl was attacked by a yeti. She had been tending a small herd of yaks in the Koner area when the creature pounced from some undergrowth and knocked her unconscious. When she came round, five of the yaks were dead.

Further clues to the Abominable Snowman certainly exist in the remote monasteries of Tibet. If they were allowed to examine these relics, scientists could hope to identify them. But since the Communist takeover, Tibet has been out of bounds for Westerners. The mystery of the Abominable Snowman looks like remaining precisely that for some time to come.

More readily accessible – although in many ways even more mysterious – are the mountains and forests that make up the spectacular wilderness that runs along the entire west coast of the USA and Canada, from California in the south to Alaska in the north. In that wilderness lurks Bigfoot – an ape-like creature of no known species.

Bigfoot and his Canadian cousin, the Sasquatch, have been around for a long time. Early settlers in the West were told by local tribes about the wild, hairy creatures of the forests. They were described as being about 8 ft tall, walking stooped but on two legs, with a broad chest and shoulders but with virtually no neck, and covered with auburn hair. In the early 19th century, explorer David Thomas became the first European to discover evidence of this strange animal, in the shape of 14-in-long footprints near Jasper, Alberta. Since then, many giant prints have been found, and casts taken of them, to substantiate the Indian legends.

Nowadays, those who believe in the existence of Bigfoot are no longer regarded as cranks. And there is sufficient evidence to brush aside suggestions that it is all an elaborate hoax.

One of the earliest Bigfoot sightings was recounted by President Theodore Roosevelt – a keen hunter – in the story he told of two trappers in the Salmon River district of Idaho who were attacked by the mysterious creature. And the *Seattle Times* of 16 July 1918 published an account of an attack by 'mountain devils' on a prospector at Mount St Helens, Washington.

In 1924 came the remarkable case of a 'kidnapping' by one of the creatures. Lumberman Albert Ostman, of Langley, British Columbia, said he had been camping opposite Vancouver Island when he was snatched by a Sasquatch. He was carried away, still in his sleeping bag, to the animal's lair, where he was held for a week. The Sasquatch's family, which fed him and treated him well, consisted of an 8-ft male, a 6-ft female and two children. Believing himself to have been abducted as a suitable 'husband' for one of the Sasquatch children, the apprehensive Ostman escaped while the head of the household was examining the woodman's snuff box.

Another encounter was reported in 1924, from the area now known as Ape Canyon in Washington, close to the Oregon border. Over the years, dozens of Bigfoot creatures have been seen in that remote, mountainous region. But the first, and possibly the most dramatic, encounter was when prospectors shot one of a group of hairy 'ape-men'. The other creatures attacked the prospectors' cabin and caused considerable damage but no loss of life. Reporters who later visited the site saw hundreds of giant footprints.

In 1933, two men at Pitt Lake, northern British Columbia, saw a creature

President Theodore
Roosevelt.

leisurely eating berries in a clearing. They described it as having a 'human-like face on a fur-clad body'.

The Chapman family, of Ruby Creek, British Columbia, fled their lonely farmhouse in 1940 when a Sasquatch approached menacingly. It overturned a barrel of salted fish but then lost interest and meandered away.

An insight into the feeding habits of the Sasquatch was obtained in 1955 by a man travelling near Mica Mountain, in the east of British Columbia. He watched, hidden from sight, as a female Sasquatch only 50 ft away from him placed branches of bushes in its mouth and stripped the leaves.

In 1958, a road construction worker near Bluff Creek, in Humboldt County, northern California, encountered a Bigfoot which, he said, he could get rid of only by offering it a candy bar. Suddenly Bluff Creek – more easily accessible than most previous Bigfoot haunts – became a popular hunting ground for Bigfoot-searchers.

Early one morning, after a night of weird noises, construction site workers sleeping in cabins at Bluff Creek emerged to find 16-in. footprints in the snow, made by a creature which took strides of up to 5 ft. Even more disconcerting was the discovery that a 50-gallon fuel drum had been manhandled across the camp. A party set out to track the creature, and eventually they picked it up in their truck headlights. They gave chase on foot but had to abandon the hunt in dense woodland. Their dogs continued the chase, however. Their

---

WHAT WAS *HOMO POINGODES*?
A considerable scientific argument blew up in 1969 over the authenticity of a creature encased in a block of ice and sent on a tour of fairgrounds in the United States. No one took claims about the beast's past too seriously - until two respected zoologists, Anglo-American Ivan Sanderson and Belgian Dr Bernard Heuvelmans, appeared to give it serious credence. Heuvelmans even described the creature as 'a previously unknown form of living hominid' and named it *Homo Poingodes*.

The creature was tall, half-man, half-ape, with enormous hands and feet. It was said to belong to an eccentric Californian millionaire, who eventually reclaimed it when the publicity became too hot. It was variously described as having been found floating in a solid block of ice in the Bering Sea and having been shot by a girl it attacked in the woods of Minnesota.

But despite the claims of the showmen and the probings of scientists, it is now thought most likely that *Homo Poingodes* **was an extremely cleverly constructed foam rubber model.**

shattered bodies were said to have been discovered some time later.

Oilman Slick, whose passion until then had been the Abominable Snowman, also launched a hunt for Bigfoot, but again without success. In 1963, however, the creature returned to the Bluff Creek area and attacked another construction site. According to newspaper reports at the time, it was even credited with sufficient strength to have overturned a truck.

The big breakthrough, however, came in 1967. On 20 October, Roger Patterson, an ex-rodeo cowboy and rancher who had decided to devote his life to Bigfoot-hunting, was tracking through forests near Bluff Creek with a part-Indian friend, Bob Gimlin. They emerged into a clearing by a creek – and saw, less than 400 ft away, a female Bigfoot loping along the bank. The creature glanced towards them, then strode off into the dense forest. But before it vanished from sight, Patterson aimed his movie camera and shot 29 ft of film – the first photographic evidence of the creature's existence. The film was later examined by experts and certified genuine. Patterson and Gimlin also took several footprint casts. The film, shown world-wide, renewed interest in the mysterious creatures, and Bigfoot-hunting became a national pastime.

In Oregon, in 1967, a family of 'ape-men' was reported to have been seen picking through a rock pile for hibernating rodents, then eating them 'like bananas'.

For the next few years there was a number of poorly documented sightings. But in 1969 more than 1,000 giant footprints were counted at a garbage dump near Bossburg, Washington. The following year, hunters chased a Bigfoot in Skamania County and discovered the half-eaten carcass of an elk, surrounded by footprints. Further authenticated sightings were made in 1972 and 1974 near Mount Jefferson and on the Hood River, Oregon. In both cases, the animals were described as timid, graceful creatures.

Despite Patterson's film and the hundreds of sightings by responsible and sincere witnesses, there is still no concrete evidence of Bigfoot's existence. No corpses or bones have ever been found.

A Canadian publishing group offered $100,000 to anyone who could capture a Sasquatch alive. That was in 1973, and no one has yet claimed the reward. Yet, precisely the conclusive evidence which sceptics have long been waiting for may have been produced a century ago. . . .

In 1884, the driver of a train travelling down the Fraser River valley in British Columbia spotted a hairy creature sleeping beside the track. He jammed on the brakes, waking the animal, which ran off. The driver and the rest of the train's crew gave chase and finally cornered the creature, knocking it out with a rock. They named their prisoner Jacko and took it to the next town down the line; Yale. There it was examined and described in the newspaper *Victoria Colonist* as being of human form but covered in inch-long hair except for its hands and feet. It was 4 ft 7 in tall – presumably a young Sasquatch – and weighed 127 pounds. Its diet was berries and milk.

So what happened to Jacko? The story is that he died while being crated for another rail journey – this time as an exhibit in a travelling sideshow. And where he is buried, no one now knows.

THE RUSSIANS HAVE THEIR BIGFOOT, TOO
Experts of the Soviet Academy of Sciences formed themselves in 1957 into four expeditions to areas where, for years, mysterious 'ape-men' had been reported. They journeyed to Mongolia, the Pamir Mountains, the Caucasus and the Himalayas. All four teams reported back that there was strong evidence that an early form of man still existed in remote areas of the globe.

The expeditions' findings were enthusiastically received by Professor Boris Porshnev, eminent director of the academy's modern history department, and his successor Dr Jeanne Korfman. In 1964, Dr Korfman set up a permanent study centre in the Caucasus to sift local reports of a race of wild men called Almas. She claimed to have discovered two lairs of the creatures, stocked with larders of berries and vegetables.

But the most remarkable evidence of the existence of Almas was produced back in 1925 by Major-General Mikhail Topilsky, who was pursuing a band of defeated White Army troops through the Pamir Mountains, near the Afghanistan border. They followed footsteps in the snow to the mouth of a cave, and after a warning they fired into the opening. A creature staggered out and fell at their feet.

An army doctor examined the body and pronounced it 'not human'. Yet it was the size and shape of a man, although entirely covered in hair. The forehead receded, the nose was flat and the jaws large and protruding - a perfect description of Neanderthal Man. The puzzled soldiers buried the creature and moved on.

Lasseter's lost reef

Somewhere in the hostile, scorching desert of central Australia may lie a fortune in gold. It is the gold reef of Harold Lasseter, somewhere beyond the Petermann Mountains.

Lasseter, a tough, down-to-earth prospector, stumbled on the reef in 1897.

But it was another 14 years before he could raise enough money to launch an expedition. Tragically, it was doomed to failure because of the dreadful desert conditions the men encountered. Lasseter and his group battled on gamely for as long as they could, but they eventually had to abandon the bid and were lucky to save their lives.

Lasseter still clung to his dream and immediately set about organizing a second expedition. It took him until 1930 to finance it, and once again it was defeated by the desert. Every one of Lasseter's companions died, leaving him to struggle on alone with two camels. Then he fell victim to sand blindness and eventually starved to death.

Years later, his body was found in a cave where he had sought shelter. But none of the prospectors and fortune-hunters who have since tried have ever been able to find the fortune that lured him to his death.

The lost gold of Arizona

Hunters for Lost Dutchman's Mine find only death

America's history is littered with stories of fabulous gold strikes, but there are none more intriguing than the tale of the Lost Dutchman's Mine in Arizona's unwelcoming Superstition Mountains. Nobody has successfully traced the location of Lost Dutchman's Mine since 1890. Yet adventurers still search for it in the hope of finding a fortune just waiting to be dug from the ground. About 20 men have died in this search.

Apache Indians were almost certainly the first to discover the mine. In the days before they feared the white man and became aware of his insatiable lust for gold, they showed the mine to Spanish monks from Mexico. Inevitably, stories of the rich ore which could be dug out by the sackful soon leaked out and set men talking and dreaming.

Many people made successful expeditions to the mine, until years later it passed into the ownership of a Spaniard, Don Miguel Peralta. In 1871, his grandson, also called Don Miguel, shared his secret with two German immigrants, Jacob Waltz and Jacob Weiser, when they rescued him from a fight in the town of Arizpe in the Sonora district of Mexico. Don Miguel told them that previous generations of his family had obtained fortunes in gold from the mine by taking with them a private army of guards and labourers so strong that the Apaches dared not attack, but that in 1864 his father and his work party had been overwhelmed by the Apaches in a bloody battle lasting three days. There were few survivors to return to Mexico, but one who did return carried a map which pinpointed the position of the mine.

Don Miguel himself had no money to finance a large guard of men for a full-scale march on the mine. So he asked Waltz and Weiser to go with him and a handful of men on a surprise raid to a spot where gold dug from the mine by the Apaches was hidden awaiting collection. The two Germans agreed and they and Don Miguel soon returned with their share of the gold, worth about $60,000.

Before setting off, Don Miguel had made it a condition that he was to receive a half share of what they brought back. When they returned to Mexico, Don Miguel changed his mind. He struck a deal with Waltz and Weiser whereby they gave up their share for ownership of the mine.

Before Waltz and Weiser could return to the area, however, the mine's existence was revealed to another man, Dr Abraham Thorne. The doctor had cared for some Apaches and, to repay his kindness, they said they would reward him with a gift of gold. If he was prepared to ride 20 miles, he could carry away as much gold as he could manage. Dr Thorne agreed and was led, blindfolded, to a canyon which contained a pile of rich ore. He was not shown the mine, but while he was loading up the gold into his saddle-bags he made a note of two distinguishing landmarks – the remains of a ruined rock fort and a sharp towering rock called Weaver's Needle – about a mile to the south.

As Dr Thorne came away with $6,000 worth of gold, he determined to find the spot again. So, a year later, he took some friends in search of the canyon – only to be driven away by a fearsome attack from the Apaches.

When Waltz and Weiser eventually returned to the area, they were alone. Using Don Miguel's map to guide them, they found the mine and started working the gold seams. But one day Weiser was left alone for a while, and when Waltz returned, his partner had disappeared. Only his blood-soaked shirt and tools, surrounded by Apache arrows, lay on the ground where he had been working. Waltz quickly packed all the gold he could into his bags and rode away from Superstition Mountains as fast as his horse would travel. He eventually settled in Phoenix, and lived there until 1891.

But, miraculously, his partner Weiser had not been killed in the Indian attack. Although he was gravely wounded, he escaped and reached the nearby home of a doctor, John Walker. He told Dr Walker all about the gold mine in the mountains, and gave him Don Miguel's map. But Walker did not make use of it, and when he died in 1890 it could not be found.

The last time Waltz visited the mine was in the winter of 1890. He travelled alone and returned to Phoenix two days later with a small sack of gold. He was almost certainly the last person to visit the mine, and when he died shortly afterwards the secret of its location died with him. Because people in the town thought from his accent that Waltz was from Holland, they called the mine the Lost Dutchman's Mine.

Before he died, Waltz told a friend that the mine was situated in country so wild that a man could be right in the centre of it and yet still be unaware of it. He said the ore was superbly rich and easy to dig from the rock. He and Weiser, he said, hit the rock with their heavy hammers, and nuggets of the precious metal simply fell into their hands. The mine was shaped like a funnel, but someone had cut a tunnel through the hillside and into the bottom of the mine to make it easier to drag the gold out.

Waltz also confessed that once, when he and Weiser went alone to the mine, they found two Mexican labourers from one of their expeditions helping themselves to the gold. They shot them dead.

Two young soldiers who stumbled on the mine by chance in 1880 suffered a similar fate. They arrived in the town of Pinal with their saddle bags full of fabulous gold nuggets and told their story of finding a funnel-shaped mine in the Superstition Mountains. They agreed to take a local man back to the mine, using their army training to retrace their steps. Some time later, their naked bodies were found. At first, it appeared they had fallen victim to the Apaches. But the bullets taken from their corpses were identified as the type used by the US Army.

Years later, an Indian called Apache Jack told the story of the way his people did their best to hide the mine. In this way, they hoped to stem the flood of unwelcome white men who invaded their territory in search of riches. In 1882, Apache Jack said, the squaws were given the task of filling in the mine with rocks. Then the entrance was covered over. There was also an earthquake in that area, and it may well have destroyed the landmarks.

In the years since then, many people have trekked to the area in search of the gold. None have found it, but at least 20 have lost their lives. In 1931, Adolph Ruth went off into the mountains after telling relatives and friends that he had bought a map of the route to the Lot Dutchman's Mine from a member of Don Miguel Peralta's family. When he failed to return, a rescue party went out to look for him – and were confronted by a macabre sight. Ruth had been shot twice in the head and then beheaded.

In a coat pocket was a slip of paper on which were written some directions, the words 'about 200 feet across from the cave', and then the Latin inscription *Veni, Vidi, Vici* ('I came, I saw, I conquered'). There was no trace of Ruth's map.

In 1947, another gold-hunter was found murdered in the area, but there was no sign of any gold and his killer was never traced.

Perhaps one day a prospector will succeed where so many others have failed. For there are plenty of clues in the countless stories of the mine and its massive gold seams. In 1912, two adventurers discovered gold nuggets in the tall grass at the very spot where Don Miguel Peralta's father and his men had been slaughtered in 1864. Not far from Weaver's Needle, a landmark that constantly cropped up in tales of the mine, there were indications that many men had once worked. There were deeply worn trails and a large pile of Mexican sandals hidden in a cave.

But despite all the clues, all the stories, to this day the vast store of riches under the ground lives up to its name . . . the Lost Dutchman's Mine.

The Bermuda Triangle

Despite the sceptics, losses of boats and planes defy explanation

At 2 pm on 5 December 1945, a flight of five Grumman US Navy bombers took off from Fort Lauderdale for a training flight in perfect weather. Shortly afterwards, the pilots radioed that their flight instruments were all malfunctioning. Their gyro-compasses were 'going crazy'. Two hours after take-off, all contact with the aircraft was lost.

A Martin bomber was immediately dispatched to search for the missing planes. Within 20 minutes, radio contact with it had also been lost. No trace of any of the aircraft was ever found. In all, six planes and 27 men had vanished into thin air.

The disaster introduced a new phrase to the English language – the Bermuda Triangle. For that was the area of the Atlantic where the long-held fears of airmen and sailors were at last proved well founded.

The disappearance of the six planes was far from being the first mysterious incident in the area – for years, navigational problems and strange magnetic forces had been reported. The disappearance was not even the greatest disaster within the triangle. That befell the 19,000-ton US Navy supply vessel *Cyclops*.

The *Cyclops* was sailing from Barbados to Norfolk, Virginia, in March 1918, when it vanished with its crew of 309 from the surface of the ocean without making a distress call and without the slightest scrap of wreckage ever being found.

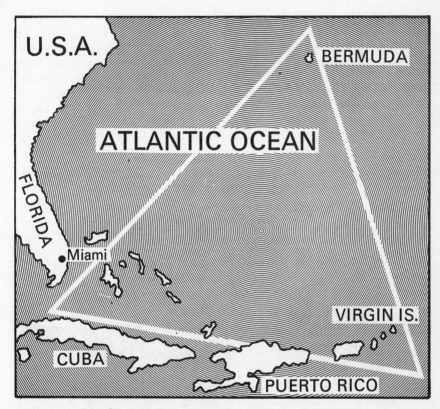

The Bermuda Triangle.

It is since 1945, however, that the Bermuda Triangle has entered legend. It has been variously labelled the Devil's Triangle, the Triangle of Death, the Hoodoo Sea and the Graveyard of the Atlantic. And it is reputed to have swallowed up 140 ships and planes and more than 1,000 people. These are some of them:

1947: Army C-45 Superfort vanishes 100 miles off Bermuda.

1948: Four-engined Tudor IV lost with 31 lives.

1948: DC-3 lost with 32 passengers and crew.

1949: Second Tudor IV vanishes.

1950: Giant US Air Force Globemaster lost.

1950: American freighter, SS *Sandra*, 350 ft long, sinks without trace.

1952: British York transport plane lost with 33 aboard.

1954: US Navy Lockheed Constellation vanishes with 42 aboard.

1956: US Navy seaplane, Martin P5M, disappears with crew of ten.
1962: US Air Force KB-50 tanker plane lost.
1963: *Marine Sulphur Queen*, 425-ft-long American freighter, vanishes with entire crew. No Mayday signals and no wreckage ever found. Two US Air Force giant stratotankers disappear on simple exercise. C-132 Cargomaster also vanishes.
1967: Military YC-122, converted to cargo plane, lost.
1970: French freighter *Milton Iatrides* disappears.
1973: German freighter *Anita*, 20,000 tons, lost with crew of 32.

US Navy seaplane, Martin P5M.

Those are just some of the major disappearing acts that have taken place within the Triangle. But in more recent years, a healthy scepticism has grown up around some of the more outlandish claims made for the area's mysterious powers.

Writing about the Bermuda Triangle became a virtual industry in the 1960s and early 1970s, and some of the theories put forward by authors have been far-fetched, to say the least. Time warps, water spouts, subterranean volcanoes, reverse gravity and black holes have all been blamed for the rash of disappearances. It has been suggested that UFOs have been collecting earthling specimens in the area, and that the people of the lost civilization of Atlantis are still exerting their powers somewhere in the deep.

One best-selling book propounded the theory that navigational instruments are thrown into confusion by a vast solar crystal that once provided the energy for Atlantis and now lies on the seabed.

Such ideas may easily be discounted. But that still leaves the mystery of those hundreds of lost lives.

The search for El Dorado

It may not have been a place after all - but a person

Adventurers have fought, killed and plundered in their search for the fabled treasure-houses of El Dorado. Often, they have given their own lives, too – chasing what may have been just a greedy dream.

It all began when the Spaniards invaded the Inca empire of Peru in 1532 and discovered incredible hoards of gold, including many beautiful works of art. They captured the city of Cuzco and could hardly believe their eyes when they saw the plunder that was there for the taking. There was gold-plating on the walls of the emperor's temple, and even the palace waterpipes were fashioned of gold.

The Spaniards overran the Inca empire and captured its emperor, Atahuallpa. Then they held him to ransom, demanding that a huge room 22 ft by 17 ft square should be filled with gold to a height of more than 8 ft. The Incas paid this enormous ransom, but then the treacherous invaders, led by the notorious Francisco Pizarro, cold-bloodedly killed their hostage. Not content with the incredible riches they had already acquired, the ruthless conquerors set about stripping the Inca empire of more of its wealth.

Their greed knew no bounds when they heard stories of even greater treasures in the north, beyond the Inca frontiers – at a place some people called El Dorado. The stories and myths surrounding El Dorado were many and varied. Some said it was a lost city, others a treasure-filled temple hidden deep in the jungle. Some even claimed it to be a mountain of solid gold.

The most widely accepted theory, however, is that El Dorado, which is Spanish for the Gilded One, was a person – probably the chief of the Muisca people, who lived in the extreme north of the Andes, somewhere in the region which is now the Colombian city of Bogota.

El Dorado took his exotic name from a tribal ritual that marked his installation. His people would gather on the shores of the circular Lake Guatavita – which is completely ringed by high mountains – for several days of celebration. At the height of the festivities, the chief and his priests boarded a raft made of rushes and were rowed out to the centre of the lake. Incense was burned and flutes wafted their music eerily across the waters. When the raft reached the centre of the lake, the new chief was stripped naked and then his entire body was coated with gold dust. With the sun glinting on his body, he then took gold treasures and dropped them into the waters as an offering to the gods. This was the signal for the chief's people assembled on the shores of the lake to add their tribute by also throwing objects of gold into the water. In this way, the lake eventually held one of the richest collections of gold in the New World.

Strangely, El Dorado's people had no source of gold of their own. They gathered it by a combination of war and trading. They possessed the only emerald mine in the whole continent and they also had vast deposits of salt. So they traded these two valuable commodities for gold.

In June 1535, Georg Hohermuth, the German governor of Venezuela, set out to find El Dorado, having learned from the natives that 'where the salt comes from, comes gold'.

He set out with an expeditionary force of 400 men and searched for three years, encountering the most appalling conditions. When he returned, 300 of his men had perished, and, ironically, they had passed within 60 miles of the lake of gold.

The following year, Sebastian de Belelcazar, the formidable conquistador, also set out to find the lake, and a few months later a German adventurer, Nicholaus Federmann, embarked on the same mission.

At the same time, Spanish lawyer Gonzalo Jimenez de Quesada organized an expedition into the Andes. He led his men to an area rich in salt, and they captured a succession of villages. They tortured the inhabitants until they revealed the source of their emeralds. One Indian told Quesada that the village of Hunsa was the 'place of gold'. Quesada conquered it and found many

Francesco Pizarro.

gold plates in the wooden and wicker houses. He also discovered large collections of emeralds and bags of gold dust. Quesada's men took the gold rings from the ears and noses of the Indians they slaughtered. They pillaged the village chief's house – which was lined with massive sheets of gold and contained a beautiful throne of gold and emeralds.

Quesada continued in his search for El Dorado, and eventually met up with Belelcazar and Federmann in central Colombia. There they founded the city of Santa Fé de Bogota.

Ironically, even if the fortune-hunters had found the lake of gold, they would not have found El Dorado. For he no longer existed. The dynasty of Muisca chiefs who held the ceremony of the golden raft had been deposed in a power struggle a few years earlier.

In 1545, a determined attempt to rob the lake of its treasures was made by Quesada's brother, Herman. He enslaved a large number of Indians of the Muisca tribe and forced them to form a human chain from the edge of the lake to the top of the mountains. They took water from the lake in buckets and passed it along the line to be tipped away. This operation went on for three months and the level of the lake was lowered by about 9 ft. Several hundred gold objects were recovered from the receding waters on the rim of the lake before the attempt was abandoned.

A more ambitious attempt was made 40 years later. A Spanish merchant recruited 8,000 natives and attempted to cut a deep channel to drain off the water. This was more successful and the level fell by 60 ft. Many gold objects and valuable emeralds were found, but landslips eventually blocked the drainage channel and this scheme was also abandoned.

Early this century, a British company tried to drain the lake. They succeeded in drilling a tunnel which lowered the water level, but the mud on the lake was too soft and too deep to walk on. Then the fierce sun baked the mud rock-hard. By the time the company transported drilling equipment into the area it was too late to use it. The baked mud had blocked the original drainage tunnel and the rains had filled the lake again.

The Colombian government has since introduced legislation protecting the entire site from treasure-hunters. But the fabled wealth of El Dorado continues to intrigue adventurers. Modern travellers who have visited the land of the Incas say that some Indians descended from the tribes who took part in the gold ceremonies still hold secret rituals away from the prying eyes of outsiders. They journey to a secret valley high in the mountains and hold their ancient ceremonies, with the priests dancing before their people, all wearing golden masks, just as their ancestors did. So the spirit of El Dorado lives on – as well as the mystery of his treasure.

Pizarro seizing Atahuallpa (Millais).

How did Glenn Miller really die?

Ever since band leader Glenn Miller's military aircraft disappeared on a flight from England to France on 15 December 1944, theories about his fate have abounded. It is a mystery which today still intrigues millions of music lovers all over the world.

Miller was 40 and at the peak of his career when he vanished. His unique big-band sound had made huge hits of numbers like 'In the Mood', 'Moonlight Serenade', 'American Patrol' and 'String of Pearls'. Their popularity swept the world, and the band was soon earning more than £1 million a year.

America's entry into the war led to Miller's enlistment as a captain and then his promotion to major, leading the United States Air Force Band in Europe. It was in this role that he was to visit Paris to prepare a Christmas broadcast – although such an arrangement would normally have been taken care of by the band's manager.

Despite fog warnings, Miller took off in a single-engined Norseman D-64 aircraft from Twinwoods airfield, Bedfordshire. With him were the pilot and another American officer. The aircraft and its occupants were never seen again. Despite repeated searches, no bodies or wreckage were found.

The most widely accepted theory at the time was that the light aircraft iced up and dived into the English Channel, drowning those trapped inside. Many people, however, refuse to accept this official and seemingly logical conclusion, and as the name and music of Glenn Miller has continued to live on in the world, his disappearance has become the subject of various strange theories.

One of the more recent and most startling claims has come from the most dedicated Miller fan of all time. English businessman and former RAF pilot John Edwards has devoted more than 12 years and about £10,000 in attempts to solve the Miller mystery. One of his claims is that Miller was not aboard the Norseman aircraft when it crashed. He says he has evidence that the band leader was murdered in Paris three days after the plane disappeared. He believes that Miller, known to be a womanizer, died of a fractured skull in the Pigalle, then the haunt of Paris prostitutes and criminals. Authorities covered up this scandal by claiming that Miller was on board the lost aircraft.

Edwards has spoken to a man who claims he saw Miller land safely in the ill-fated Norseman after making only a short flight to an airfield at Bovingdon, Hertfordshire. The band leader then switched to a Dakota and took off again.

The Dakota reached Paris safely.

Edwards also supports his theory of an official cover-up by pointing to the lack of a full inquiry. He said: 'I have met great difficulty in trying to solve this mystery. Records have been reported burned. Other information, like the aircrew report, is unaccountably vague. Even the weather conditions were listed as unknown.

'But pieces of information I collected over the years eventually all fell into place. I have evidence that an American military doctor in Paris signed Miller's death certificate. A retired US Air Force lieutenant-colonel recalls being told by the provost marshal's police office in Paris that Miller had been

Major Glenn Miller giving a US private some tips.

murdered. And I know a man in Miller's band who stated that it was common knowledge to those close to him that his boss was murdered in Paris.'

In an eerie seance session at the now-derelict Twinwoods airfield, an English medium, Carmen Rogers, claimed that she was able to look into the past and see what happened to Miller.

'I could see him walking to the aircraft with two other men,' she said. 'Miller was disturbed and worried about his domestic and other affairs. He did not want to make the trip to Paris. He felt sick and afraid. After they took off, Miller asked the pilot to land. The pilot put down as soon as possible, and let Miller get out. The aircraft touched down on the Essex side of the Thames estuary. Then Miller got out and made a phone call to London and arranged his own disappearance.'

Countless other theories about Miller's fate have been put forward over the years. He was a spy on a top-secret mission which went wrong. He was so terribly mutilated in the aircraft crash that he preferred to live in secret. He was an amnesia victim. He was mistakenly shot down by a British fighter over the Channel . . . and so on.

Various wrecked wartime aircraft have been discovered in the Channel, each prompting the hope that here, at last, was the Norseman that could provide the answers to the Miller mystery. But the plane has never been discovered.

So the death of the man who set the world humming to his big-band hits remains shrouded in controversy. But for some people the attempt to solve the riddle has a special incentive. It is thought that when the band leader left England he took with him a briefcase containing the original scores of Glenn Miller music that had never been played. Anyone finding them intact would certainly strike it rich.

How do birds migrate?

The world's cleverest navigators leave man in the dark

It is one of the oldest unsolved mysteries. It has baffled man since the dawn of civilization. How does a fragile bird with a tiny brain find its way twice a year from one side of the world to the other?

Every spring and autumn millions upon millions of birds are on the move. Some fly as far as 12,000 miles and as high as 30,000 ft. Where they go and where they come from was a mystery for centuries. It was only in our own age

MORE MIGRANTS

It is not only birds that migrate vast distances with
unfailing accuracy. Fish, insects, reptiles and mammals all
have strong homing instincts which appear to be lacking
only in man.

Green turtles leave the beaches of South America every
year to swim 1,500 miles to tiny Ascension Island in the
Atlantic. Somehow they manage to make the necessary
allowance for changing tides and sudden storms to reach
their target, which is only five miles wide.

Eels from both Europe and North America head annually
for the drifting weed masses of the Sargasso Sea. There, they
breed before returning up to 2,000 miles to their familiar
river-beds. The navigation of the eels - and of salmon,
which perform a similar remarkable feat - has been partly
explained by their acute sense of smell.

Butterflies, notably the Monarch and the Painted Lady,
fly annually between Canada and the Mexican border,
always returning to the same nesting sites.

The lemmings of Scandinavia, which breed at an
incredible rate, have their own method of population
control. As if at a single command, they migrate from the
hills in a vast living unstoppable river, passing through
homes and across streams. Eventually they tumble into the
sea. One theory is that their mass movement is prompted
by an instinct to migrate from Scandinavia to Britain - an
instinct implanted in their senses before the Ice Age
bridge between the two land masses melted.

Even domestic pets retain an inexplicable homing
instinct, as is evidenced by the numerous stories of dogs
and cats returning to their owners after long journeys. A
hardy fox terrier made its way through the burning heart
of Australia from Darwin to Adelaide, and a pining cat
pursued its owners from New York to California. These are
just two of the feats by man's best friends that even man
cannot comprehend.

that their journeys were charted by attaching rings to the legs of the birds and
recording the point and date of their departure and arrival.

The results of such experiments astounded ornithologists. They discovered,
for example, that geese migrate regularly between Siberia and India, flying
over the Himalayas at heights of up to 30,000 ft – higher than Mount Everest.
An Arctic tern was ringed in Greenland and recaptured in South Africa – a
journey of almost 10,000 miles in less than three months.

In fact, Arctic terns are the migratory record holders. They fly from their

An arctic tern and its migratory path.

Arctic breeding grounds in Canada, Siberia and northern Europe across the globe to their winter haunts in Antarctica – and then they fly back again. Their life is almost perpetual motion. They are on the wing, 24 hours a day, for eight months of the year, and each bird covers up to 24,000 miles.

Why do they do it? They are not following any particular climatic or feeding pattern. On the appointed day for migration they all set out, even if feeding conditions remain excellent. Equally, if the time for migration has not arrived, they will stay put, even in the most appalling conditions.

How do they do it? An airline pilot takes years of training and a fortune in equipment before he can find his way from one vast airport to another. A bird can make a journey of the same length, without altering its course for a moment, until it arrives at the very same nest that it left the previous year.

Great shearwaters, for instance, gather four million strong every year to fly from Newfoundland, Greenland and northern Europe to lay their eggs in their traditional and only nesting grounds 6,000 miles away. They make their way unerringly to the tiny island of Tristan da Cunha, a mere dot in the vast southern Atlantic, almost 2,000 miles from the nearest land.

Ornithologists captured a Manx shearwater on the coast of Wales. They placed it in a darkened box and airfreighted it across the Atlantic to Boston, Massachusetts, where it was released. It found its way back to its nest on a Welsh cliff 12 days later. How could it have plotted its course so precisely without ever having made the journey before?

Birds rarely begin their long migratory journeys in overcast conditions. So perhaps they are guided by the sun or by the shadows that it makes on the ground. Yet ornithologists have discovered that during the seasons of migration, more birds are in flight at night than during the day. The sun could not be helping them then. So are birds also able to 'read' the map of the stars?

Such feats would require amazing ingenuity – for the sun's height and angles change by the minute, and the stars alter their pattern in the skies nightly. The information that a bird would need to contain in its tiny brain would be literally astronomical. So, in this respect, do birds know more than man? If so, the term 'bird brain' is a slur on some of the cleverest little creatures in the world.

The Siberian fireball disaster

How a 40-mile-wide track of the earth was utterly devastated

Even in northern Siberia, with its freezing winters and scorching summers, the early hours of a June morning are a time to be enjoyed. And farmer Sergei Semenov had taken a break from his wheat fields to snatch a few moments' rest in the sunshine on the porch of his farmhouse.

It was just after 7 am on 30 June 1908 and to Semenov, miles away from the revolutionary fever that was beginning to sweep parts of the country, it seemed a good time to be alive.

At precisely 7.17 am his reveries were brought to an abrupt halt. An enormous explosion rent the horizon with a blinding light.

He said later: 'There appeared a great flash. There was so much heat, my shirt was almost burnt off my back. I saw a huge ball of fire that covered an enormous part of the sky. Afterwards it became very dark.'

It was then that the enormous force of the blast threw the farmer from his porch and knocked him unconscious. When he regained his senses, a mighty, thundering noise swept across the tundra. 'It shook the whole house and nearly moved it from its foundations,' he said.

Farmer Semenov was lucky. If he had been nearer the centre of the holocaust he would not have lived to tell his strange and frightening tale. And but for the fact that the disaster occurred in the remote Tunguska River valley, the devastation would have been even more appalling than it was.

The inferno laid waste an area the size of Leningrad. Herds of reindeer were incinerated. Virtually all the trees in an area more than 40 miles across were ripped from the earth and thrown from the centre of the blast to lie like the spokes of a giant wheel. Nomad tribesmen 45 miles away were hurled to the ground, their tents ripped away by a searing wind.

What was the cause of this awesome devastation? And could something like it happen again?

It was not until 22 years after the explosion that anyone got close to finding out the answers. In 1930, Professor L. A. Kulik, of the Soviet Academy of Science, spent almost a year in the area with a small team of investigators. It was his third attempt to reach the scene of the blast. His two previous expeditions had been abandoned because the marshy forests were impenetrable.

Professor Kulik eventually found a landscape pock-marked with craters. He found nearly 2,000 square miles of uprooted, rotting tree trunks. And, most important of all, he found eyewitnesses of the blast. They told of a vivid ball of fire sweeping across the sky – 'so bright that it made even the light from the sun seem dark'.

People who had been more than 50 miles away from the centre of the explosion spoke of 'violent vibrations' followed by 'a fiery body trailing a wide band of light across the sky'. One said: 'I was washing wool in the River Kan when I heard a noise like the whirr of the wings of frightened birds. The water in the river began to form waves. Then there was a jolt so violent that one of my friends fell into the river.'

Some 250 miles away in the town of Kirensk, people had seen a pillar of fire followed by 'several thunderclaps and a crashing sound'. And even 600 miles away at Turukhansk, a witness reported 'three or four dull thuds, like distant artillery'. Many of the witnesses could have been describing a nuclear explosion. Several observers described a fireball followed by a mushroom-shaped pillar of smoke many miles high. But could an atomic blast have occurred nearly 40 years before the devastation of Hiroshima and Nagasaki?

Some scientists have indeed suggested that the explosion could have been nuclear. They put forward the startling theory that a spaceship of visitors from another planet became damaged on entering the earth's atmosphere. The nuclear fuel became critically overheated and set off an explosion equivalent to that of a 30-megaton nuclear bomb.

Australian journalist John Baxter and American scientist Thomas Atkins followed up the work of Russian scientists and supported the exploding-spaceship theory with the following evidence:

- In a nuclear explosion, the earth's magnetic field is disturbed. After the Siberian blast, it was.
- Nuclear blasts leave a particular pattern of destruction. The Russian explosion did just that.

Atomic fungus over Hiroshima after the explosion.

- The atomic bombs dropped on Japan in 1945 caused weird plant mutations. The Siberian disaster caused similar mutations.
- Nuclear explosions leave behind tiny green globules of melted dust called trinitites. These were found after the Russian blast. And, according to Russian experts, these trinitites contained traces of metal not normally found in the Tunguska region, and not usually part of the make-up of meteorites.
- Finally, the two refer to eyewitness evidence from people who saw a large bluish, cylindrical object racing through the sky with a roaring sound, leaving a vapour trail behind it, just before the blast.

Other, less extraordinary, solutions put forward by scientists include:

The comet theory. Comets are thought to be giant balls of frozen gases and debris. One could have entered the earth's atmosphere – although there were no reported sightings – and generated such heat that it exploded in mid-air.

The anti-matter theory. Some scientists think that a mass of anti-matter – material that corresponds to that found on earth but made up of positive particles (positrons) instead of negative particles (electrons) – could have plunged into the earth's atmosphere. As soon as it came into contact with atoms of ordinary matter there would be an enormous explosion.

The black hole theory. Black holes are thought to be stars which have collapsed to a tiny size. Because of their immense mass – the weight of the earth could be contained in a black hole the size of a tennis ball – their gravitational pull is strong enough to prevent light escaping, so the objects cannot be seen – there is only a black hole in space where they exist. It has been suggested that a black hole hit Siberia.

The meteorite theory. One of the most popular theories, although it was at first discounted, is that a giant meteorite fell to the earth. Meteorites are entering the earth's atmosphere at the rate of 200 million every day, although most burn up before reaching the planet's surface. A meteorite that fell on Arizona in prehistoric times left a crater three-quarters of a mile across. Scientists at one time claimed that, as there was no crater in Siberia, the explosion could not have been caused by a meteorite. But it has since been discovered that a meteorite made of rock, rather than metal – which is more common – could explode just before hitting the ground, so causing extensive damage but no crater.

Whatever caused the Siberian blast, one thing is certain. The fact that it happened in a virtually uninhabited area was a stroke of good fortune. If the object from space had plummeted on to a major city the result would have been the greatest disaster in the history of mankind.

Comet Kohoutek, 4 January 1974.

The black holes phenomenon

Even giant suns are sucked into these vast whirlpools in space

Beyond the earth's atmosphere lies an infinity of space that man has only just begun to explore. Its secrets are being tapped, one by one. Yet with every discovery made comes a new and often greater mystery.

One of the most baffling that scientists have ever faced is the phenomenon known as black holes. They cannot be seen, and the only evidence that they exist is the effect that they have on other objects. They are like whirlpools in space. Any debris plunging its way through space that may stray too near a black hole is sucked into its dark maw. Where it goes, scientists can only guess. What happens to it no one knows. Atomic particles, galactic dust, even giant suns can disappear without trace. Do they cease to exist? Or do they travel in some strange fashion through time and space to another dimension?

Scientists do not have the answers. American physicist John Wheeler calls black holes 'the greatest crisis ever faced by physics'.

Black holes are giant stars which have suddenly collapsed inwards. According to one theory, the process is infinite. It goes on and on, with the star getting smaller and smaller and more and more dense. A star ten times bigger than the sun would end up as a black hole only 40 miles across. A spoonful of this matter would weigh millions of tons. Because the gravitational pull of this relatively small, dense object is so great, nothing, not even light, can escape from it. And all the normal scientific laws no longer apply.

The first black hole was identified on 16 May 1973. Scientists were already investigating 'dead' stars. These include the so-called white dwarfs – which our own sun will become when it cools down in about 8,000 million years. Larger stars die in a different way and become what are known as neutron stars. Others are called pulsars because of the regular signals they emit. But, scientists asked, what happens to the biggest stars of all?

The key to the mystery came from the constellation Cygnus, The Swan. A super-giant star in this constellation was behaving in an odd way. Further investigation showed that the star was being affected by the gravitational pull of an invisible neighbour. Although it could not be seen, all the evidence pointed to its powerful existence. Then some intense study by three English scientists – Peter Sanford, Fred Hawkins and Keith Mason – provided proof that this invisible force was what was termed a black hole. Similar investigations were launched to prove the existence of another black hole in the Speilon Aurigae star system.

Study of the super-giant in The Swan constellation has shown that great clouds of gas are being drawn from the star into the black hole. As the star approaches the 'event horizon' – the point of no return after which it cannot be seen – the gravitational pulls of the star and the black hole conflict. Light emitted from this region travels so slowly that it seems almost to stand still.

In theory, if a man entered a black hole he would be stretched out, the part nearest the hole being attracted more quickly than the part furthest away. His image would linger for millions of years, even though his fall into the black hole would take only a fraction of a second. The tremendous force of gravity would finally break him down into atoms. But, by this point, time and space would have lost their conventional meanings. He would have entered what scientists call a singularity – the point where an infinitely small object has infinite density and gravity.

Some scientists have asked what would happen if a man could avoid destruction on entering a black hole. One answer they have come up with is that, because black holes defy all normal physical laws, when he emerged on the other side, he could find himself in a different universe – or even travelling backwards through time.

Another theory holds that man could eventually tap unlimited sources of energy from black holes by dumping rubbish into them and trapping and storing the gravitational energy that would be produced. There is one snag to this, though. If the greatest care were not taken, the black hole could grow large enough to suck the earth – and eventually the whole universe – into oblivion.

Black holes may help solve another great mystery – what holds the universe together? According to the 'big bang' theory, the universe was created by a gigantic explosion and is constantly expanding. But in that case, what is stopping the universe from flying apart indefinitely? The great scientist Albert Einstein suggested that there must be enough mass in the universe to hold it together. This mass could be black holes, counteracting the effects of the 'big bang' and drawing other stars and their planets towards them. If this is so, then the process would over millions of years speed up, the black holes eventually consuming every heavenly body. And, instead of ending with either a bang or a whimper, the universe would simply be swallowed up.

Still no one knows why the 'Hindenburg' crashed

The cool, calm words of radio reporter Herbert Morrison were recording the arrival of the giant Zeppelin airship, the *Hindenburg*, as it nosed its way to the mooring tower at Lakehurst naval station, New Jersey. It was unlikely that his commentary would even be broadcast. After all, it was just a routine flight and there was nobody famous on board.

'The ropes have been dropped and they have been taken hold of by a number of men on the field,' Morrison said. 'The back motors of the ship are holding it just enough to keep it . . .'

Then suddenly his gentle voice broke into a scream: 'It's burst into flame!'

With a popping noise, a tiny flicker of flame had appeared at the rear of the *Hindenburg*'s giant gas balloon, then burst into a sheet of incandescence that swept along the airship. Morrison's words became an almost incoherent babble as he sat helplessly watching the catastrophe unfold before his eyes: 'This is terrible . . . the flames are 500 feet in the sky . . . it is in smoke and flames now . . . those passengers.'

Tiny figures tumbled from the holocaust, and Morrison sobbed: 'I'm going to step inside where I can't see it. I . . . I . . . folks, I'm going to have to stop for a while. This is the worst thing I've ever witnessed. It is one of the worst catastrophes in the world.'

When Morrison resumed his recording only seconds later, the disaster was virtually over. The airship – the pride of Hitler's Germany – was a mass of incandescent rubble.

It was 6 May 1937. And until then the *Hindenburg* had been known not only as the world's biggest-ever airship but as the safest. With unfailing regularity it had ploughed its way through rain, storms and fog across the Atlantic. It was 830 ft long, 125 ft high, and under its belly – beneath nearly 7 million cubic ft of highly inflammable hydrogen – it carried 35 passengers in luxurious comfort.

The *Hindenburg* had finally convinced the world, after earlier American and British airship disasters, that the age of airship travel had come to stay. German ingenuity and efficiency had overcome the dangers.

Ernst Lehmann, the first commander, who was travelling as observer for the captain, Max Pruss, had told a passenger: 'Don't worry, my friend. Zeppelins never have accidents.' And Chief Steward Howard Kubis told another passenger: 'We Germans don't fool with hydrogen.'

Safety precautions were stringent. All matches and lighters were taken from

The smoking wreckage of the *Hindenburg* after the explosion.

passengers when they came aboard, catwalks were covered with rubber to prevent sparks, crewmen working in possibly hazardous areas wore felt boots and asbestos suits devoid of metal fastening. And the air pressure inside the travelling quarters was sufficient to expel any leaking hydrogen.

The *Hindenburg* first approached Lakehurst at around 4 pm, but Pruss did not like the look of some dark storm clouds and, true to the Zeppelin tradition of never taking a chance, he decided to delay landing. Two hours later the storm clouds had disappeared and preparations were made for what looked like being a routine arrival. The passengers were even handed back their lighters and matches. Radio officer Willy Speck was telling the *Hindenburg*'s sister ship, the *Graf Zeppelin*, that there had been a safe landing.

Then disaster struck.

Pruss stayed at his controls until his cabin hit the ground. He was badly hurt, but not so terribly as Lehmann, who was found slouched in the rubble murmuring over and over again: 'I can't understand it.' He clung on to life for another two days, and just before he died he was asked: 'What caused it?' His last word was: 'Lightning.' But a puzzled frown crossed his face, as if he doubted his own words.

Altogether 20 crewmen, 15 passengers and one member of the ground staff died, and a dozen more people were badly injured. But, miraculously, the rest of the 97 people on board escaped unharmed.

The inquiry officials seemed as puzzled as everyone else about what had caused the disaster, but finally blamed a freak electrical charge in the atmosphere.

Thirty-five years later, author Michael Macdonald Mooney, in his book

Hindenburg, placed the blame on crew member Eric Spehl, a young rigger. Mooney said that Spehl, encouraged by an anti-Nazi mistress, placed an incendiary bomb aboard the *Hindenburg*. It was due to go off after the Zeppelin had landed, but Spehl had been unable to foresee the delay caused by the weather. . .

Several other crew members certainly believed that the inferno was caused by sabotage, motivated by a desire to dent the prestige of Hitler's Germany.

There had been hints of the impending disaster: the German ambassador in Washington had received a letter warning him that a bomb had been planted aboard the airship; before the *Hindenburg*'s departure from Frankfurt, one of its officers had suddenly begged to be allowed to say farewell to his wife 'for the last time'; and another officer had been told by a clairvoyant that he would die in a burning airship.

But whether the disaster was caused by sabotage or misfortune, one thing is certain – the *Hindenburg*'s demise also spelled the end of the most magnificent form of air travel the world had ever seen.

They Came from the Sky!

I n July 1982, a Winnipeg man heard an almighty crash at his home. It was as if the roof had exploded. Hurrying into his hallway, he saw a sinister black disc amid the chaos of dust and splintered wood.

It was a wheel from a Canadian DC-4 freighter, which landed safely at Winnipeg Airport a few minutes later. Investigators said the accident was very rare.

All kinds of bizarre objects have been reported to drop from the skies – from

---

The Finger of Fate

In the summer of 1982, a dream came true for Mr Howard Hewitt of Lyndhurst, Hampshire. A golfer of 12 years standing, Mr Hewitt holed in one on his home course in the New Forest.

On the following day at the nearby Bramshaw Club, Mr Hewitt holed in one again.

As he stood on the green with his colleagues, discussing the extraordinary double phenomenon, a third event occurred. A ball from an adjoining fairway struck him on the back of the head and laid him out cold.

Wanted
Extraterrestrials. Researcher wants to meet people from other
planets or space-time continuums. Please write with details.
Confidentiality guaranteed.
The *Guardian*

monster hailstones to blocks of frozen urine. But the most remarkable falls have concerned living creatures – fish, frogs, and even worms. They have been so commonly reported, in fact, that they have scarcely been deemed worthy of more than a snippet in the newspapers. The *Scientific American* of 12 July 1873, for example, noted: 'A shower of frogs which darkened the air and covered the ground for a long distance is the reported result of a recent rainstorm in Kansas City, Mo.' A North African event drew an even terser statement from the *Sunday Times* of 18 December 1977: 'It was raining frogs in the Moroccan Sahara last week. Freak whirlwinds are blamed.'

Those 'freak whirlwinds' have commonly been blamed for fishfalls too. Slithering cascades were reported in Singapore in 1861, following an earthquake: torrents of fish fell in the streets and were collected by the bucketful. Sceptics believed that the fish had in fact issued from the flood waters of swollen rivers, but one reporter found fish in his own walled courtyard which the flood waters could not penetrate. And the incident is not unique. In July 1959, a rain of fish was reported at Townsville airport in Australia.

Wormfalls are scarcely less remarkable. The authoritative journal, *Nature*, recorded on 2 March 1876:

'The *Morgenblad* of Christiania states that a singular phenomenon was observed there after a recent violent storm. A number of worms were found crawling on the snow, and it was impossible to find the places from which they had issued, everything being frozen in the vicinity. Similar circumstances were reported from several places in Norway.'

An almost identical phenomenon was noted in Virginia by the *Scientific American* of 21 February 1891. It is possible, of course, that the worms had not fallen with the snow, but emerged from dormancy in the earth with the sudden change in climate. This theory has often been used by sceptical scientists to explain frogfalls – though it can scarcely satisfy the Birmingham case of June 1954, when witnesses saw hundreds of little frogs bouncing off people's heads.

American journalist Charles Fort rejected both freak whirlwind and dormancy theories. An obsessive collector of newspaper snippets concerning strange events, Fort believed in a multi-dimensional universe and detected the dark laughter of the gods in such occurrences. In *The Book of the Damned*, published in 1919, he attempted a reasoned statement of his beliefs. Falling objects, he suggested, might come from 'a region somewhere above the earth's surface in which gravitation is inoperative'. Into this mysterious zone, objects were sucked from the ground, to be shaken down later by storms.

Certainly, some falls have appeared to deny orthodox analysis. What to make, for example, of the rains of blood occasionally reported in mediaeval Europe? Precisely such an event occurred in Britain on the night of 30 June

1968. The bloody deluge, however, proved capable of scientific explanation. The red rain was found to be composed of fine sand picked up by dust storms in the Sahara and carried northward in the upper air to fall over Britain during a thunderstorm.

The Minnesota Iceman

Dr Bernard Heuvelmans, the eminent Belgian zoologist, had researched and written about many rare creatures during his long and distinguished career. He had studied reports on the Himalayan yeti, publishing his conclusions in *On the Track of Unknown Animals*; he had made it a rule never to reject out-of-hand even the wildest rumours concerning strange animals. For Heuvelmans had found that even the most improbable tales might have some foundation in truth.

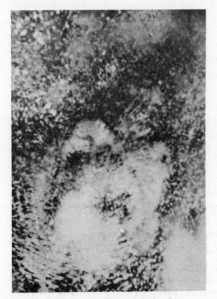

Face of the Iceman

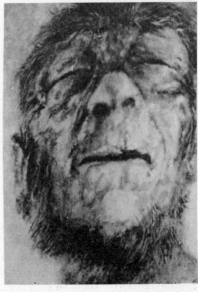

Artist's reconstruction of the face

The case of the Minnesota Iceman, however, beat them all.

'Is it a Fake? Is it an Ape? or is it . . . Neanderthal Man?' asked the headline of an extended feature in the *Sunday Times* of 23 March 1969 from which much of the following information is drawn:

'A strange ape-like creature frozen in a block of ice is providing American anthropologists with one of the most intriguing questions they have faced in recent years. Is it a fraud, a freak, or is it a form of human being believed to have been extinct since prehistoric times? One thing is certain; it has two large bullet-holes in it. Just as a precaution, the FBI have been called in.'

Heuvelmans had been invited to view the creature in New Jersey by science writer Ivan Sanderson. Imprisoned in its frozen coffin, the iceman was in the custody of a Minnesotan showman called Frank Hansen. Hansen said that it had been found floating in a block of ice in the Baring Straits, and had been purchased in Hong Kong.

Hansen believed that the creature had existed for centuries in the ice block. This was unlikely. Heuvelmans knew that even if a living creature is frozen in natural ice at death it will start decaying very rapidly: Siberia's frozen mammoths were preserved in bog ice which has antiseptic properties. But as the expert examined the showman's exhibit in an ill-lit trailer, he grew more and more excited. Using a torch to illuminate the creature, he listed its salient features.

The Iceman was six foot tall and covered all over with brown hair. The skin appeared white and wax-like. The neck was short and the torso barrel-shaped. Long arms terminated at huge hands.

One arm was bent at a peculiar angle, apparently broken. There was a gaping hole in the left eye. Examining the creature through the clouded ice, Heuvelmans concluded that it had been shot fairly recently with a high-calibre rifle. One bullet had passed through the arm which it may have raised to protect itself; the other had penetrated the eye. The expert was unable to examine the back of the head, but Hansen stated that it had been shattered.

The feet were not those of ape or man. The big toe was unable to move freely

---

Hole Swallows House and Car
Winter Park, Florida, May 10. – A giant hole in the ground slowly expanded and filled with water today after a house had fallen into it with six cars and part of several buildings and a swimming pool yesterday. No one was hurt.

Officials estimated the hole, which opened suddenly on Friday night, was more than 1,000 ft across and 170 ft deep.
The Times

> **A Living Toy**
> An 18-inch Shetland pony has been bred by Mr Ray Allman, a
> farmer of Madley Heath, North Staffordshire.
> *Daily Telegraph*

like a thumb and this suggested an ape. But the soles of the feet were too
wrinkled. The soles, moreover, were more markedly padded than those of a
human being.

Systematically, Heuvelmans drew up a list of possibilities: Was it a
manufactured fake? This seemed improbable. A hoaxer would have had to
reproduce the hair in incredibly minute detail. The ice, moreover, had been
scraped away in parts to give people a closer look. In one place it had been
pared off so much that the expert could smell decaying flesh. Heuvelmans
dismissed the possibility of the thing being fashioned from plastic or wax.

Was it a composite creature, stitched together out of the limbs of different
animals? Certainly there were precedents for such an exhibit. In the 19th
century, for example, fake mermaids were commonly created by fitting
together the top halves of monkeys and the bottom halves of fish – the objects
were known as 'Jenny Hannivers'. But to create the Iceman, the faker would
have needed a hairy human head and the body and limbs of a gigantic ape –
and where might the extraordinary feet be obtained?

Was it the corpse of some freakish human being? This theory stretched the
bounds of credulity. Even the most bizarre fairground curiosities could not
compete with the Iceman for deformity.

Was it then some unknown species of Homo Sapiens – even a surviving
Neanderthaler? Neanderthal Man was a species of early man which existed
before Homo Sapiens evolved. The Iceman had the long arms, short neck,
barrel chest, and large hands and feet associated with early hominids. The feet,
with their long second and third digits, were especially reminiscent of what was
known of Neanderthalers.

Incredible as the proposition appeared, Dr Heuvelmans found himself
tormented. For many nights after he viewed the exhibit he could not sleep.
Since the creature had clearly been shot in recent years, it seemed to reinforce
theories that a race of unknown hominids existed in the remoter parts of Asia.

The expert was anxious to buy the Iceman, but Hansen was reluctant to part
with it. Heuvelmans turned to the Smithsonian Institute in Washington, who
took an immediate interest and an investigating team was set up. Heuvelmans,
meanwhile, published his findings in Belgium, provoking intense enthusiasm
among his colleagues. Also interested were the FBI – for if something like a

human being had been shot and killed, a capital crime might have been committed.

It seemed that the anthropological world was on the verge of one of the most exciting discoveries ever made in the study of man. And then, a veil of mystery descended over the affair.

Frank Hansen claimed that the Iceman was the property of a wealthy, unidentified man. The owner took possession of it, and only allowed a replica to be exhibited in future. The Smithsonian Institute were allowed to see the model – but not the original. They concluded that a hoax was being perpetrated while the FBI declared that there was not enough evidence for them to proceed either.

Hansen, meanwhile, took an exhibit (it was not clear whether it was the original or the replica) to Canada to show at provincial fairs. On the way back to the United States, customs officials seized it. They stated that Hansen did not have the proper documentation to return a 'hominid' to the country. The showman described it as a 'fabricated illusion', the customs officials asked to see core samples.

Hansen refused, on the grounds that removing samples would ruin his exhibit. Eventually, after telephoning his senator and a lawyer, he managed to get the creature back to the United States without an investigation, and continued to show the Iceman at carnivals for some months. But the showman alleged that his contract to display the object ran out in the spring of 1970. Thereafter, the owner took possession, and the exhibit was withdrawn from public view.

The lack of positive evidence has made most zoologists conclude that the Iceman must have been a clever fake. Heuvelmans, however, remains convinced that there was something more to the frozen creature he examined in the torch-lit trailer. An aura of mystery still lingers about the whole affair.

Chapter two

SCIENCE AND DISCOVERY

Science boasts an ever-increasing fund of knowledge, but for every breakthrough, there remains a blank page. Exactly how was the great pyramid of Giza built? Is the image on a shroud truly that of Christ? Until these and many other questions can be answered, science can only stand humble in the face of so much that remains beyond explanation.

The riddle of human spontaneous combustion

Victims who have for no apparent reason suddenly burst into flames

Widow Mary Reeser was a plump woman of 67 who lived quietly in a modest but pleasant apartment in St Petersburg, Florida. On the morning of 2 July 1951, a telegram arrived for her. The landlady, who lived in the same building, tried to deliver it but could get no reply from Mrs Reeser. She tried the doorknob. It was so hot to the touch that she cried out in pain.

Two painters were working nearby, so the landlady called them over and asked them to break in. They put their shoulders to the door and, with a splintering of woodwork, it swung open. The landlady and the workmen reeled back under a blast of furnace-hot air. But when shortly after they crept inside the apartment there was no sign of the conflagration they had expected. All they could see was a feeble flame flickering on the partition wall which separated them from the apartment's small kitchen. They easily put it out, and peered round the partition into the kitchen.

The landlady expected to see Mrs Reeser, perhaps sleeping in her armchair. But all she saw of the armchair were a few springs – and all she saw of Mrs Reeser were a few unrecognizably charred bones, a skull shrunken to half-size by intense heat, and a single satin carpet slipper containing a left foot burnt off at the ankle. . .

Plastic utensils in the kitchen had been melted and a mirror had been shattered by the heat. But the only other sign that there had been a fire was a small area of scorched floor. A newspaper lying near by was quite untouched.

At an inquest held into Mrs Reeser's death, experts professed themselves utterly baffled. The blaze which had consumed her body had been more intense than the $2,500°$ Fahrenheit needed to dispose of the corpses in the city's crematorium. Yet the fire had not spread by more than inches from the old woman's body. No cause could be found for the blaze, and a police suggestion that Mrs Reeser had fallen asleep while smoking and had set fire to her clothing was laughed out of court by the pathologist.

The experts admitted defeat. Their only other course would have been to admit the possibility of one of the strangest and most argued-about scientific phenomena of all time – spontaneous combustion, the sudden bursting into

Spontaneous combustion in Dickens's *Bleak House*.

flames of a human body, during which the clothing is sometimes not even scorched.

The unfathomable case of Mrs Reeser is only one of the more recent cases of spontaneous combustion. Such 'human torch' blazes have been discussed for centuries. (Charles Dickens referred to one in *Bleak House*.) But because 20th-century scientists are highly sceptical about the phenomenon, cases of it are seldom well documented and rarely studied. Even so, apart from the death of Mrs Reeser, there are some other well-substantiated cases.

In 1880, an eminent physician, Dr B. H. Hartwell, was among several witnesses to the death of a woman at Ayer, Massachusetts. Flames suddenly burst from the woman's torso and legs, and she sank to the ground and died in a horrifying blaze.

In England, in 1919, a well-known author of the day, J. Temple Thurston, died at his Kent home, his body horribly burned from the waist down. The inquest verdict was that he had died from heart·failure. But no one could explain how he came to be burned over half his body when there was no sign of fire in his room and when the rest of his body was untouched, and how his body had blazed away beneath his clothes without even singeing them.

In 1922, Mrs Euphemia Johnson, a 68-year-old widow, was burned to a pile of blackened bones at her home in Sydenham, London. The fire that consumed her body must have been as intense as that of a furnace – yet her clothes were untouched.

Two similar, horrifying cases of spontaneous combustion occurred in England in the 1930s. The first involved a 19-year-old secretary, Maybelle Andrews, who was dancing with her boyfriend at a club in London's Soho. Flames suddenly shot from her chest and back, consuming her within minutes and resisting all attempts by other dancers to beat them out. At the inquest no solution was offered to the mystery of her death. Her numbed boyfriend, William Clifford, said: 'The flames seemed to come from within her body.' The inquest verdict: death by misadventure, caused by a fire of unknown origin.

The second case was reported in 1938. Phyllis Newcombe, 22, was leaving a dance hall at Chelmsford, Essex, when blue flames suddenly engulfed her body. She was reduced to a pile of ashes within minutes. The coroner who investigated her death said: 'In all my experience I have never come across anything as remarkable as this.'

Another case in England that same year was investigated by biologist Ivan Sanderson, who founded the Society for the Investigation of the Unexplained, in New Jersey. This was the case of Mrs Mary Carpenter, who was with her family aboard a boat on the Norfolk Broads on a hot summer's day. Suddenly, as her husband and children watched in horror, she burst into flames and was reduced to ashes.

Two of the best-authenticated cases of spontaneous human combustion in recent years have occurred in the United States. The first involved Billy Peterson, who was sitting in his parked car in Detroit when flames apparently burst from his body. When rescuers pulled out his charred corpse they found that the heat inside the car had been so intense that part of the dashboard had melted. Yet Billy Peterson's clothes had not even been singed.

The second and equally remarkable phenomenon occurred on 5 December

1966. Early that morning Don Gosnell started his working day reading gas meters in Coudersport, Pennsylvania. One of the first houses he called at was the home of Dr John Bentley, a 92-year-old retired family physician. Knowing that the old man could move around only with the help of a walking frame, Gosnell was not particularly surprised when no one answered the front door. He let himself in and walked downstairs to the basement to read the meter. There he found a neat little heap of ashes on the floor. Gosnell wondered how it had got there but did not think to look up at the ceiling, where a charred hole gave a clear view into the bathroom. The ashes had fallen like powder through the hole.

Gosnell read the meter and walked back upstairs, calling out for Dr Bentley. Traces of smoke hung in the air and as Gosnell walked down the hallway to investigate he sniffed 'a strange, sweetish smell'. He opened the bathroom door and fell back in horror.

The doctor's soot-blackened walking frame lay on the floor, overhanging a gaping hole, its edges scorched by fire. Also on the floor lay all that remained of Dr Bentley – a right foot, still in its carpet slipper and burnt off at the calf.

At the inquest which followed, the coroner recorded a verdict of 'death by asphyxiation and 90 per cent burning of the body'. All the comment he would make later was: 'It was the oddest thing you ever saw.'

The curse of Tutankhamun
Death struck down those who disturbed the sleep of the Pharaohs

In an English country house in the middle of the night a dog suddenly started howling. The constant, pitiful noise awoke the sleeping household. The wretched animal would not be comforted, and the howling continued until, breathless at last, the dog lay down and died.

This strange occurrence took place at the Hampshire home of a titled amateur archaeologist, 57-year-old Lord Carnarvon. At the moment the dog started howling, Carnarvon was himself drifting towards death, thousands of miles away in a room at the Hotel Continental, Cairo. The curse of the Pharaoh boy king Tutankhamun had claimed its first two victims. Many more were to follow.

The curse of the Pharaohs had been well known to Carnarvon, a fanatical Egyptologist. He had been reminded of it while still in England planning his latest and biggest expedition to Egypt to seek the fabled, treasure-packed tomb of Tutankhamun. He had received a cryptic warning from a famous mystic of the day, Count Hamon. The message read: 'Lord Carnarvon not to enter tomb. Disobey at peril. If ignored will suffer sickness. Not recover. Death will claim him in Egypt.' Carnarvon was so concerned about the warning that he twice consulted a fortune-teller, who each time forecast his impending death in mysterious circumstances.

Nevertheless, Carnarvon went ahead with the expedition, which was the culmination of a dream that had inspired him for years. When he arrived in Egypt he even affected a jaunty bravado and made light of the curse that was having such a profound influence on the frightened native diggers at the excavation site at Luxor. One of his close associates on the expedition, Arthur Weigall, was driven to remark: 'If Carnarvon goes down into the tomb in that spirit, I don't give him long to live.'

On 17 February 1923, Carnarvon and his team broke through into the funerary chamber of the boy king. Inside, Carnarvon and his American partner, Howard Carter, found treasures even they had never dreamed existed – gold, precious stones and gems as well as the solid-gold coffin containing the mummified body of Tutankhamun. Above the tomb was an inscription, which they translated. It read: 'Death will come to those who disturb the sleep of the Pharaohs.'

Two months later, the now-famous Lord Carnarvon awoke in his room at the Hotel Continental and said: 'I feel like hell.' By the time his son arrived, Carnarvon was unconscious. That night he died. Carnarvon's son was resting in an adjoining room at the moment of his father's death. He later recalled that 'the lights went out all over Cairo – we lit candles and prayed'.

Carnarvon's death was attributed to an infected mosquito bite, which debilitated him and caused the onset of pneumonia. Strangely, the mummified body of King Tutankhamun was said to have had a blemish on the left cheek in exactly the same spot as Carnarvon's mosquito bite.

Shortly afterwards there was another death at the Hotel Continental. American archaeologist Arthur Mace, one of the leading members of the expedition, complained of tiredness and suddenly sank into a coma. He died before his doctors could decide what was wrong with him.

The deaths of other Egyptologists followed one upon another. A close friend of Carnarvon, George Gould, rushed to Egypt as soon as he heard of the earl's death. Gould visited the Pharaoh's tomb. The next day he collapsed with a high fever. He died 12 hours later.

Radiologist Archibald Reid, who X-rayed Tutankhamun's body, was sent home to England after complaining of exhaustion. He died shortly afterwards.

Carnarvon's personal secretary on the expedition, Richard Bethell, was found dead in bed from heart failure.

British industrialist Joel Wool was one of the first visitors invited to view the

Lord Carnarvon and Howard Carter on the site of the excavation.

tomb. He died soon afterwards from a mysterious fever.

Within six years of the excavation of Tutankhamun's tomb, 12 of those present at the discovery had died. And within seven years only two of the original team of excavators were still alive. No fewer than 22 others connected with the expedition had died prematurely, including Lady Carnarvon and the earl's half-brother. He apparently committed suicide while temporarily insane.

One of the lucky survivors was the expedition's co-leader, Howard Carter. He continued to scoff at the legendary curse, and died of natural causes in 1939.

But the curse of the Pharaohs was still taking its toll years later. In 1966, Egypt's director of antiquities, Mohammed Ibraham, was asked by his government to arrange an exhibition of the Tutankhamun treasures in Paris. He argued against the decision and had a dream that he would face personal danger if the Pharaoh's treasures were to leave Egypt. As he left a final, unsuccessful meeting with government officials in Cairo, Mohammed Ibraham was knocked down by a car and killed.

Three years later, the sole survivor of the Tutankhamun expedition, 70-year-old Richard Adamson, gave an interview on British television to 'explode the myth of the curse'. Adamson, who had been a security guard with Lord Carnarvon, told viewers: 'I don't believe in the myth for one moment.' Later, as he left the television studios, his taxi crashed, throwing him out on to the road. A swerving lorry missed his head by inches. It was the third time that Adamson had tried to put paid to the legend. The first time he spoke out, his wife died within 24 hours. The second time, his son broke his back in a plane crash.

After his road accident, Adamson, recovering in hospital from head injuries, said: 'Until now I refused to believe that my family's misfortunes had anything to do with the curse. But now I am not so sure.'

Fear of the Pharaohs' curse was revived in 1972 when the golden mask of Tutankhamun was crated in Cairo for an exhibition at London's British Museum. In charge of the Cairo end of the operation was Dr Gamal Mehrez, who, as director of antiquities, was a successor to the ill-fated Mohammed Ibraham.

Dr Mehrez did not believe in the curse. He said: 'I, more than anyone else in the world, have been involved with the tombs and mummies of the Pharaohs, yet I am still alive. I am the living proof that all the tragedies associated with the Pharaohs have been pure coincidence. I don't believe in the curse for one moment.'

The doctor was at the Cairo Museum to organize the removal of the treasures on the day the shippers arrived to load the priceless cargo on to

The mask of Tutankhamun.

lorries. That evening, after watching the operation, Dr Mehrez died. He was 52. The cause of death was recorded as circulatory collapse.

Unperturbed, the organizers of the exhibition continued with the arrangements. A Royal Air Force Transport Command aircraft was loaned for the job of conveying the relics to Britain. Within five years of the flight, six members of the plane's crew had been struck by death or ill fortune.

Flight-Lieutenant Rick Laurie, chief pilot aboard the Britannia aircraft, and Flight-Engineer Ken Parkinson were perfectly fit men. But both were soon to die. Parkinson's wife said that her husband suffered a heart attack every year after the flight, each one at the same time of year. The last one, in 1978, killed him at the age of only 45. Chief pilot Laurie had died two years before him, also of a heart attack. At the time his wife said: 'It's the curse of Tutankhamun – the curse has killed him.' Laurie was just 40.

During the flight, Chief Technical Officer Ian Lansdowne had jokingly kicked a box containing Tutankhamun's death mask, saying: 'I've just kicked the most expensive thing in the world.' That leg was later in plaster for five months, badly broken after a ladder inexplicably collapsed under Lansdowne. The aircraft's navigator, Flight Lieutenant Jim Webb, lost all his possessions after his home was destroyed by fire. A girl aboard the plane had to quit the RAF after a serious operation.

A steward, Sergeant Brian Rounsfall, disclosed, 'On the flight back we played cards on the coffin case. Then we all took it in turns to sit on the case containing the death mask and we laughed and joked about it. We were not being disrespectful – it was just a bit of fun.' Rounsfall was 35 at the time. In the following four years he suffered two heart attacks.

Is there any logical explanation for the mysterious deaths and misfortunes of so many people connected with the Tutankhamun relics? Journalist Phillip Vandenburg studied the legend of the Pharaohs' curse for years. He came up with two remarkable suggestions. In his book, *The Curse of the Pharaohs*, he says that the tombs within the pyramids were perfect breeding grounds for bacteria which might have developed new and unknown strains over the centuries and might have maintained their potency until the present day.

He also points out that the ancient Egyptians were experts in the use of poison. Some poisons do not have to be swallowed to kill – they can be lethal by penetrating the skin. Poisonous substances were used in wall paintings within the tombs, which were then sealed and made airtight. For this reason, those who raided tombs in ancient days first bored a small hole through the chamber wall to allow fresh air to circulate before they broke in.

The most extraordinary explanation of all for the curse of the Pharaohs was put forward in 1949. It came from the atomic scientist Professor Louis

Bulgarini. He said: 'It is definitely possible that the ancient Egyptians used atomic radiation to protect their holy places. The floors of the tombs could have been covered with uranium. Or the graves could have been finished with radio-active rock. Rock containing both gold and uranium was mined in Egypt 3,000 years ago. Such radiation could kill a man today.'

A FATEFUL CARGO

In 1912, a liner was crossing the Atlantic with a valuable cargo - an Egyptian mummy. It was the body of a prophetess who lived during the reign of Tutankhamun's father-in-law, Amenhotep IV. An ornament found with the mummy bore the spell: 'Awake from the dream in which you sleep and you will triumph over all that is done against you.'

Because of its value, the mummy was not carried in the liner's hold, but in a compartment behind the bridge, on which the captain stood. The captain's name was Ernest Smith, Commodore of the White Star fleet. And it was partly because of his errors of judgment that the liner he commanded rammed an iceberg and sank with the loss of 1,513 lives.

The liner was the *Titanic*.

The great pyramid of Giza

A building whose construction would have daunted modern engineers

The Great Pyramid at Giza, in Egypt, was designed to be a lasting and fitting memorial to King Khufu, better known by his Greek name of Cheops – one of the most powerful rulers the ancient world had known. About 40 pyramids stand along the banks of the Nile, but none can compare with the Great Pyramid. It stands more than 450 ft high and covers an area of 13 acres – enough space in which to cluster together Westminster Abbey, St Paul's Cathedral and the great cathedrals of Milan and Florence.

The accurately cut blocks of stone used to build it – 2,300,000, each weighing from two to 15 tons – would provide more than enough material to construct all the cathedrals, churches and chapels built in England since the coming of Christianity. Napoleon's surveyors calculated that it contained enough stone to build a wall three yards high and a yard thick around the whole of France.

Its base is a perfect square, the four sides accurately facing the four points of the compass. The corners are almost perfect right angles.

Even today, it is difficult to imagine how awesome it is without standing in its huge shadow. But 5,000 years ago it was even more magnificent, when it was faced with gleaming white limestone – long since plundered for building material elsewhere – and topped by a 30 ft capstone of beaten gold.

But is the Great Pyramid merely a technological marvel, or something that has a much deeper, mystical significance?

As more and more is discovered about the ancient past, irrefutable evidence comes to light that ancient civilizations often reached astonishing levels of scientific expertise. Some seem even to have possessed knowledge that we lack today. How, for example, did the ancient Egyptians, who had not yet even discovered the wheel, raise the Great Pyramid with the aid only of levers and rollers? How did they carve their giant blocks of granite with such amazing precision? How did they harden their bronze tools to a strength that cannot be duplicated today? And how did they acquire the confidence to launch a project whose scale would daunt even the most adventurous of modern architects and engineers?

The Great Pyramid stands on a rocky plateau ten miles west of Cairo. It is thought that a perfectly level foundation was made for it by building a mud wall around the plateau and flooding the area. As the water was gradually drained, bumps were revealed and were cut away until a flat surface was left. On to this foundation, even more level than that beneath a 20th-century skyscraper, gangs of labourers hauled giant blocks of sandstone from nearby quarries. The facing surface of gleaming limestone had to be brought further, from quarries on the far bank of the Nile. The stones were drawn on sledges up gentle ramps. Once in position, teams of stonemasons took over, cutting them to perfection.

In case King Khufu should die before the work was completed, a tomb was tunnelled deep into the solid rock foundations beneath the pyramid, and later another was created within the pyramid itself but at a lower level than the planned burial chamber. This was placed in the heart of the pyramid, 138 ft above ground level. It was reached by a tiny passageway which opened out into a majestic 25-ft-high gallery. Huge granite 'plugs' were placed within the passageway so that it could be blocked forever once the priests had completed the rites inside the funerary chamber.

But despite all these elaborate arrangements, it seems that a body was never placed in the Great Pyramid.

Egyptologists who have studied the pyramids closely are basically divided into two groups – those who think the pyramids have some deep and mysterious significance and those who think they are merely tombs. But if the Great Pyramid is merely a tomb, why the absence of a body, and why the mathematical accuracy of every wall, slope, corridor and cavity?

As is shown by the tombs in the Valley of the Kings – where Tutankhamun's grave was found – bodies were normally buried surrounded by artefacts and valuables. Thieves, when they raided the tombs, would steal what was valuable and very rarely carry away the bodies. Yet, when the Great Pyramid was first breached in about AD 800 – by a young caliph of Baghdad, Al Mamun – nothing was found in it.

Al Mamun was, in fact, after knowledge, not plunder. He had heard legends that the Great Pyramid contained astronomical charts and maps, unbreakable glass and purest metals. After a hazardous and difficult assault on the tomb, which entailed his men carving out passages around the giant granite plugs, he finally reached the King's Chamber. All it contained was a lidless and empty sarcophagus, or stone coffin.

It seemed impossible to the caliph, after he had seen the undisturbed granite plugs, that anyone could have been there before. He searched for evidence of forced entry or plundering – but in vain. Finally, he left, disappointed – and baffled as to why the vast monument had been built.

The Great Pyramid was then left virtually undisturbed for centuries until British and French scientists and mathematicians started to take an interest in it during the 17th and 18th centuries. In 1638, the Oxford scholar John Greaves explored the King's Chamber and marvelled at its accuracy 'even to a 1,000th part of a foot'. His findings attracted the attention of his fellows, including Sir Isaac Newton, and they laboured – unsuccessfully – to discover the secrets of the Great Pyramid.

In the 1830s an English adventurer, Colonel Richard Howard-Vyse, led a team which stumbled across two 9-in. conduits leading from the north and south walls into the King's Chamber. When these passages were cleared it was found that the temperature inside the chamber, regardless of the climate

THE 'POWER' OF THE PYRAMIDS

It has long been claimed that the pyramids contain mysterious forces that cannot be explained. There have been tests attempting to prove that the structures are magnets for cosmic rays, or that they are power-houses of static electricity. There are also many stories of visitors to the pyramids being able to foresee their own fates. Tourists sometimes go into shock or faint.

On 12 August 1799, Napoleon visited the King's Chamber inside the Great Pyramid. After some time, he asked his guide to leave him. When he finally emerged, Napoleon, the conqueror of Europe, was white and shaken. Asked what had happened, he said brusquely: 'I do not want this matter referred to ever again.' Later in his life, he hinted that he had foreseen the future while in the Great Pyramid. Shortly before his death on St Helena, he seemed about to reveal his secret to an aide. Then he said: 'No. What's the use? You'd never believe me.'

But the most extraordinary cases of pyramid power have been experienced by ordinary people with non-scientific minds who have never been anywhere in Egypt. They are the folk who claim remarkable successes by using cardboard, metal or plastic models built to the precise scale of the Great Pyramid. These models are said to keep razor blades sharp for great lengths of time, keep food fresh, promote feelings of peace and contentment, and even help shape the future.

During the 1850s, a Frenchman named Bovis visited the

outside, remained a steady 68° Fahrenheit – ideal for storing the scientific weights and measures that featured in the legendary tales about the tomb.

Another Englishman, John Taylor, the son of the editor and publisher of *The Observer* newspaper, made further discoveries 30 years later without even straying from his own study. He made a thorough examination of all that was then known about the Great Pyramid and, in his book *The Great Pyramid : Why Was It Built and Who Built It?* he reached the conclusion that the Egyptians 'knew the earth was a sphere and, by observing the motion of heavenly bodies over the earth's surface, had ascertained its circumference, and were desirous of leaving behind them a record of the circumference as correct and imperishable as it was possible for them to construct'.

His studies revealed that the height of the pyramid bore the same relationship to its perimeter as the radius of a circle does to its circumference. This seemed to show that the Egyptians knew of the value of pi, the invaluable mathematical principle that was not thought to have been discovered until

---

Great Pyramid. Inside, among the usual debris left behind by tourists, he found the body of a dead cat - a remarkably well-preserved mummified body. When he returned home, Bovis experimented with model pyramids, built to scale, and found they helped to keep food fresh.

A hundred years later, Czech engineer Karel Drbal read of Bovis's experiments. There was a shortage of razor blades behind the Iron Curtain, and Drbal wondered whether the pyramid power would extend to metal. He built a model pyramid and found that the razor blades he placed in it never became blunt. When he went to the patent office in Prague in 1959 he was not believed. But, after the chief scientist there tested the idea, Drbal was granted patent No. 91304.

Why the technique should work nobody knows. The only clue is the old World War One legend that razor blades left out in the moonlight go blunt. The edge of a razor blade is composed of minute crystals. If the energy generated by the rays of the moon can blunt a blade, could the energy said to be generated by a pyramid help keep it sharp?

There are certain rules to be followed for the pyramid to work. It must be built on a base-to-side ratio of 15.7 to 14.94 and its sides must be aligned with the four points of the compass. The razor blade must rest 3.33 units high, and the sharp edges must face east and west.

Nobody can explain the secret power of the pyramid, but there are thousands of people around the world who swear that it works.

3,500 years later. His findings were confirmed by the brilliant mathematician, Charles Piazzi Smyth, who became astronomer royal for Scotland.

Other theories then followed thick and fast. Some were inspired, some eccentric, some religious and deeply mystical, others practical and scientific. One idea put forward was that the Great Pyramid had been built as a giant clock. In 1853, the French physicist Jean Baptiste Biot deduced that the wide, level pavements adjoining the northern and southern faces were graduated shadow floors. In the winter, the pyramid would cast its shadow on the northern pavement, and in the summer, the polished limestone face would reflect the sun on to the southern floor. In this way the time of day and the day of the year could be seen. David Davidson, a British structural engineer from Leeds, and fellow-Yorkshireman Moses B. Cotsworth followed up Biot's idea and claimed that it was correct and that the Egyptians could measure the length of the year to within three decimal places.

Another idea was that the Great Pyramid is, in fact, a huge observatory. The 19th-century British astronomer Richard Proctor pointed out that the corridor known as the Descending Passage was precisely aligned with the Pole Star. The Pole Star in those days, because of the earth's slight shift on its axis over the centuries, was Alpha Draconis. But as the Great Pyramid has moved along with the earth, the Descending Passage is now aligned with Polaris, the present Pole Star. Proctor pointed out that the various slots and notches to be found in the Grand Gallery of the Great Pyramid could have been used to support movable benches and platforms for observers to study with their instruments the passage of the stars across the entrance opening of the Grand Gallery.

Members of the Institute of Pyramidology, in London, believe that the Great Pyramid accurately prophesies the future of humanity. They claim that it can be shown, through a complicated system of measurements and mathematics, that the Great Pyramid predicted the exodus of the Jews from Egypt, the Crucifixion of Christ, the outbreak of World War One – which, they say, was the beginning of the breakdown of the Old Order as foretold by both Daniel and Jesus – and the beginning of the Millennium in the autumn of 1979. This, the group says, marks the beginning of Christ's 1,000-year rule on earth which will end with Armageddon and the Day Of Judgment in 2979.

Author Peter Tompkins, who made an exhaustive study of the mysteries of Giza, wrote a book in 1971 which attempted to solve the enigma of the Great Pyramid. Tompkins claimed that the priests of Egypt promised Khufu a mighty tomb. But once the king had sanctioned and financed the building, they set about constructing not a tomb, but a monument to their scientific knowledge. And when he died, the deluded Khufu was not buried there.

With Dr Livio Strecchini, professor of ancient history at New Jersey's

Oxen threshing wheat at the foot of the Great Pyramid.

William Paterson College, Tompkins studied the scientific achievements of the pyramid builders and came up with the following conclusions:
- The Great Pyramid is a carefully located landmark from which the geography of the ancient world was worked out.
- It served as an observatory from which maps and tables of the stars were drawn with remarkable accuracy.
- Its sides and angles were the basis of all ancient map-making.
- Its structure incorporated a value for pi.
- It may have been a practical library of the ancients' system of weights and measures.
- Builders knew the precise circumference of the earth, and the length of its year, including its 'left-over' .2422 of a day. They may also have known the length of the earth's orbit around the sun, the specific density of the earth, the 26,000-year cycle of the equinoxes, the acceleration of gravity and the speed of light.

Could the ancient Egyptians, 3,000 years before the birth of Christ, have known all this? And if they did, how did they gain this knowledge, and why was it forgotten for centuries?

It is obvious to everyone who sees the Great Pyramid that an advanced civilization was responsible for building it. Did this civilization also possess powers that today we can only wonder at?

The secret of Stonehenge

Was it a massive Stone Age observatory?

Gaunt and hauntingly remote, the megaliths of Europe – massive, monumental stones – rear up in a giant's chain. From Sweden and the Shetland Isles in the north to Spain and Malta in the south, they stand as mysterious monuments to the imagination, ingenuity and skills of our distant ancestors – people once dismissed as ignorant savages.

There are at least 50,000 sites, where great stones form rows, circles, ovals, crosses or horseshoes, sometimes amazingly precise in their geometry. Some stones still stand, but many more have toppled over. Countless others have been destroyed by man or nature.

None could have been more imposing than the Grand Menhir Brise at Lochmariaquer, in Brittany, which once stood 150 metres high and weighed between 300 and 400 tons. Now it lies split into four pieces. At nearby Carnac, uniform rows of stones, more than 3,000 of them, stretch away beyond the horizon.

Early European man's obsession with raising these giant pillars of stone

The megaliths of Stonehenge.

spanned a period of more than 2,000 years, coming to an end around 1500 BC. But the questions they arouse have never been satisfactorily answered. Who were the people who spent so much time and effort on hewing the great rocks and dragging them to selected sites? And why did they do it?

In earlier times the stones were thought to have been raised by legendary creatures – giants, wizards, demons, even the Devil. More recently, a popular myth linked the megaliths with the Celtic priests called Druids and their pagan rites – although it is now certain that they were built centuries before the time of the Druids. Yet another theory suggests that survivors from the lost city of Atlantis inspired this curious and widespread surge of building.

Another widely held belief was that ancient cultures of the eastern Mediterranean – advanced civilizations like those of the Greeks and Egyptians – had spread their influence westward by means of voyaging merchants or missionaries. But modern scientific techniques have cast serious doubts on this theory, and it is now known that stone monuments were being set up in Brittany possibly 1,000 years before the Egyptians built the Pyramids.

To underline the point, scientific dating methods show that the earliest megaliths are those on the fringe of the Atlantic seaboard and that the stone monuments become younger as they move eastward inland.

Experts who have studied the way primitive peoples live today think that the megaliths may have been used for a number of social and religious purposes: as rallying points, markets, temples, or a combination of all three. Certainly many of the stones marked Stone Age burial sites, and investigation of bones that have been preserved indicates that the sites were used as family vaults. Ancient tribes may have started the process by building stone cairns over their dead. And it is not difficult to imagine how different communities would want to erect bigger and better monuments as each tried to enhance its prestige over its neighbours.

But could the mystery of the megaliths have a more profound explanation?

Recent thinking has focussed on the astonishing connections between many of these stones and the heavenly bodies. Some scientists claim that the sites were astronomical observatories, used to provide information of practical value to farming and seafaring peoples. If this is the case, then our 'primitive' ancestors must have been men of remarkable knowledge and intellect.

At the heart of the observatory theory stands the vast, brooding enigma of Stonehenge, not the largest but easily the best known and most impressive of 900 or so sites scattered across the British Isles. This great stone circle, rising from the bleak expanse of Salisbury Plain, holds a special place among prehistoric sites because it is the only one where the blocks have been cleverly shaped and fitted together to form a carefully planned whole.

In the early 1960s, an American astronomer, Professor Gerald Hawkins, claimed to have solved the Stonehenge riddle. He made a close study of the numerous sight lines between the sun and moon and various points in the stone circles. When he fed his information into a computer the startling results showed that the site was indeed a huge observatory and could be used for extremely complex calculations and predictions. Stonehenge, in fact, was itself a kind of giant Stone Age computer.

These exciting ideas are by no means universally accepted among scientists and astronomers. But there is no doubt at all about the incredible feats of engineering design and technology that went into the building of Stonehenge.

There were three distinct stages in the development of the site, covering more than 1,000 years. And none of the three groups of builders quite managed to complete its task – leaving yet another mystery.

The first builders were Neolithic people who worked on the site around 2700 BC. They set out the encircling ditch and bank and the famous Heelstone, which lines up with the Midsummer's Day sunrise from the central point of the circles. These Stonehenge pioneers also dug the curious Aubrey Holes, named after the 17th-century writer who discovered them. The 56 shallow pits, which form a ring just inside the bank, contain cremated bones and were apparently filled in soon after being dug. Their purpose is still a matter of guesswork.

Stonehenge II was built some 800 years later by the Beaker People, so called because they buried pottery with their dead. Their almost incredible achievement was to bring to Stonehenge by sea and river 60 to 80 giant bluestones, each weighing more than four tons, from the Prescelly Hills in South Wales – a journey of 200–250 miles. In a further tremendous feat of strength

---

IS THERE A STONEHENGE 'LIFE FORCE'?
Could all the stone circle sites of Europe be linked together by a strong but indefinable 'life force'? Many of the circles are undoubtedly designed to line up with particular points on the horizon, and in some cases with each other.

This has led some investigators to put forward the theory of ley lines, lines of force that sent a powerful, beneficial energy across the countryside - energy which could be felt by people who were more in tune with the rhythms of nature than is modern man.

Supporters of this theory believe that although the system is no longer active, the ancient stones have not completely lost their 'magical' properties. Some photographs seem to show light radiating from the stones, and, in other experiments, people claim to have received electric shocks from the stones.

and skill, the Beaker People went on to set up the bluestones to form a double circle inside the earlier enclosure.

Still more breathtaking was the building of Stonehenge III, probably around 1500 BC, when the gigantic sarsen stones, nowadays the most familiar feature of the site, were placed in position. These huge standstone boulders, each weighing up to 50 tons, were transported more than 20 miles from the Marlborough Downs to the north.

All this was taking place at a time when there were no wheeled vehicles. Everything had to be moved either by water, where possible, or even more laboriously by primitive sledges hauled overland by large teams of men.

The builders of Stonehenge II (whose work was later to be uprooted by the third group) must have been possessed of a rare determination even to contemplate shifting their bluestones from the south-west corner of Wales all the way to the heart of southern England. It involved a journey of daunting complexity. First they probably had to drag the great stones from the mountains down to the coast, then manhandle them on to rafts to carry them up what is now the Bristol Channel. For the remainder of the journey they would have had to transfer the massive loads to canoes, lashed together for two separate river passages and further hauls by sledges.

Although the sarsen stones used in Stonehenge III had to be moved only 20 miles or so, this was an even more formidable problem. For these 50-ton monsters would have needed as many as 1,000 men at a time to heave them by rope across country on sledges and rollers.

Even when the last generation of Stonehenge builders had managed to bring their raw materials to the site, their task was far from complete. They then had to chip and pound the colossal blocks into shape, using chunks of the same stone – and sarsen is the toughest of all British stones to work.

Next came the positioning of the pillars, possibly achieved by raising the stones bit by bit on timber ramps or scaffolding until they could be tipped into their prepared holes. Finally, the great stone lintels would have been lifted on to the tops of the towering 21-ft uprights, again by means of a gradually raised timber square.

While we marvel at the brute strength expended on this massive project, we must also admire the expertise of craftsmen who fashioned accurate peg-and-socket joints to fit the slabs together, who had the geometric and architectural vision to cut the horizontal blocks with gentle curves that joined to form one continuous curve, and who balanced them with delicate precision on a sloping hill site.

How did 'primitive' man learn such skills? And how can it be explained that Stonehenge shares with scores of other sites throughout Europe a standard unit of measurement – the 'megalithic yard' of 2·72 ft? How, too, was the impetus to build maintained over so many years? No one can be sure how long the builders of Stonehenge laboured on their vast undertaking, but one estimate is $1\frac{1}{2}$ million man-days.

What compelling force drove men to spend hundreds of years virtually moving mountains? And why did they suddenly abandon their project?

Finally, perhaps a still more intriguing puzzle: if Stonehenge was planned and built by men of such skill and learning – pioneering engineers, architects, mathematicians and astronomers – why did they never create anything else (the wheel, for instance) to further man's development?

Is this the face of Christ?

The image on the Turin Shroud has staggered the Christian world

Photography was a hobby only for the dedicated in 1898. Secundo Pia, an Italian archaeologist, was a mere amateur. But the photograph he took in the Chapel of the Dukes of Savoy at Turin Cathedral was of profound significance to Christianity. For the negative that Pia produced appeared to show the face of Christ.

The young archaeologist was the first person to be allowed to photograph the cathedral's most famous relic, the Turin Shroud, in which Christ is reputed to have been wrapped after the Crucifixion. The shroud had always been said to bear the faint outlines of Christ's body – although the same claim had been made for 40 or more other pieces of linen preserved in various churches around Europe. But when Pia took his photograph, the result was a clear negative picture of a crucified man.

Because scientific photography was a relatively untried medium, Pia's remarkable picture was not at first universally accepted as genuine. It was not until 1931 that the shroud was again properly photographed, this time by a professional cameraman, Guiseppe Enri. And it was his remarkable picture which converted many of the sceptics, as well as prompting world-wide interest in the relic.

Nowadays, following years of scientific investigation, the Holy Shroud of Turin can be 'read' almost like a book. It tells a story that spans almost 2,000 years.

The shroud is 14 ft long and $3\frac{1}{2}$ ft wide. It is made of a mixture of cotton and linen, woven into a regular herringbone pattern in the style common in

Palestine during the 1st century AD. Swiss scientists have even analyzed pollen in the cloth and dated it to the same period. The cream-coloured material is marked by a faint brown outline of a man's body, with darker, rust-coloured stains of blood. The marks indicate that the man was naked, 5 ft 11 in tall and had shoulder-length hair and a beard. It is also clear that he had been tortured and crucified. The hands had been nailed through the palms and the feet had been fastened together by a single nail. The stains indicate that the body had received more than 100 lash marks, many inflicted with a scourge – a flail with heavy metal balls attached – and that the man's side had been pierced by a spear.

It is easy to accept that blood would have stained the shroud, but it is not so simple to understand how the outline of the body could have been dyed into the fabric and remained for so many centuries. One popular explanation is that the resurrection caused a supernatural release of energy which scorched the linen. More scientific is the theory that the stains were caused by gas from the skin (probably ammonia) or sweat, mixed with ritual Jewish burial spices.

The most recent and most startling theory, however, is that put forward by US Air Force scientists who believe that the image on the shroud was caused by a micro-second burst of intense radiation.

Much research was carried out to trace the journey of the shroud back to its origins. The first reference to the Crucifixion shroud comes in St Mark's Gospel, which states that the cloth in which Christ was wrapped was found in his empty tomb. Three hundred years elapsed before the shroud was next mentioned in the reports of pilgrims to Jerusalem. The cloth then found its way from Palestine to Constantinople, and from there to France, where it arrived in the 13th century.

In the late 15th century it was given for safe keeping to Louis I, who built a chapel at Chambéry to house it. But in 1532 fire swept the chapel and damaged the silver casket in which the relic was kept. It is assumed that this was when the folded shroud acquired the symmetrical burn marks which disfigure it. The fabric was carefully mended by nuns and was eventually moved to Turin Cathedral in 1572.

If the history of the shroud is so uncertain, why are so many Christians convinced that it represents the only true picture of Christ? Thousands of people were crucified by the Romans. Why single out this burial cloth as being that of Christ?

The answer has been provided by the scientists. They say that the imprint on the shroud indicates that the victim's hair was matted with blood and that blood had coagulated in scratches across his forehead. It is evidence that tallies with Biblical stories of the crown of thorns thrust mockingly on to the head of the 'King of the Jews'.

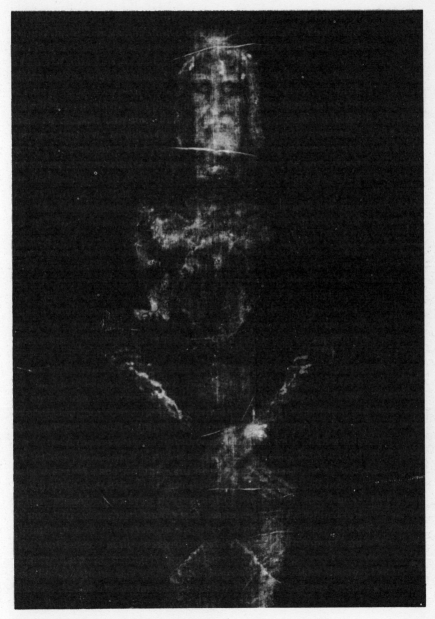

The image on the Turin shroud.

Was Columbus the true discoverer of America?

Many nations claim they were the first to set foot on the continent

Christopher Columbus is famed as the man who opened up the New World when he sailed from Spain to the West Indies in 1492. But his voyage was far from being the first to the Americas. It is likely that before he set foot on the great land to the west, the Chinese, Vikings, Irish and even the Phoenicians had visited its shores. So who really discovered America?

Carbon-dating has established that man lived in America at least 12,000 years ago. And it is now thought that the first 'outsiders' to reach the vast continent were the Mongoloid people of eastern Russia, who crossed into Alaska some 40,000 years ago by way of a land bridge – long since vanished – across the Bering Strait. They then travelled down the Pacific coast into Central and South America.

A remarkable discovery, which dates man alongside the long-extinct giant mammoth on the American continent, was made on a farm at Tepexpan, 20 miles north-east of Mexico City, in 1950. Farmer José Cortes was digging a drainage ditch when he struck something hard. Scooping away the earth, he found the fossilized remains of a mammoth. When the fossil was examined by Mexican palaeontologists, the tip of a weapon was found in the animal's rib cage. Apparently the mammoth had become bogged in mud, making it easy prey for a band of hunters armed with spears and stone implements.

Simple tools made of stone and animal bones, seemingly belonging to the same culture, have been found in Siberia, Alaska, the Yukon and Mexico, thus adding weight to the theory that man spread down through America from Asia.

A claim that the Chinese discovered America as early as AD 458 was made recently by a Peking University professor, Chu Shien-chi. He says that a Buddhist priest, Hoei Shin, sailed across the north Pacific with four other monks and landed somewhere on the Central American coast, perhaps Mexico. Hoei Shin named the country Fusang, after a Chinese plant which he likened to vegetation growing there.

Austrian ethnologist Robert von Heine-Geldern goes further. He is convinced that the Chinese influenced the development of civilization in America around 2000 BC. Certainly, sculptures found in the ruins of some Central

American cities are similar to those used in the Buddhist religion. And China's oldest manuscript, the *Shan Hai King* of 2250 BC, contains what appears to be a description of the Grand Canyon.

A Pacific crossing even earlier than 2000 BC is suggested by pottery found on the Valdivian coast of Ecuador and dated at around 3000 BC. It is almost certainly of Japanese origin, being decorated in the same manner as pottery from the Jomon region of Japan.

On the Atlantic side, Irish monks are said to have visited North America

Columbus's first mass in America.

around the 6th century. A 10th-century Latin manuscript, the *Navigatio Sancti Brendani*, tells of the voyages of a Saint Brendan and how he set out around 540 with a party of 14 monks to find the 'Land Promised to the Saints'. The manuscript is so full of marvellous achievements and devout thinking that for years it was considered to be just a collection of tales. Brendan is said to have been helped on his way by a whale and guided from time to time by angels disguised as birds. But modern scholars think the voyages actually did take place, although they may not all have been led by Brendan.

According to the *Navigatio*, Brendan, an experienced seaman and navigator, is supposed to have set sail for the Promised Land from Kerry in a 36-ft wooden-framed boat covered with oxhide and greased with butter to make it waterproof. The party took a northerly course and eventually came across a floating tower of crystal, which suggests that they had encountered a giant iceberg and had passed around Greenland and into Davis Strait, well known

INDIANS WITH BLOND HAIR

American Indians with blond hair and blue eyes, and others who become white-haired in old age - are they mistakes of nature or the descendants of white people who landed in America centuries ago, perhaps even before Christopher Columbus set foot in the New World?

According to a plaque set up in 1953 at Fort Morgan, Alabama, by the Daughters of the American Revolution, a group of Welsh explorers led by the great Prince Madog ap Owain Gwynedd allegedly 'landed on the shores of Mobile Bay in 1170 and left behind, with the Indians, the Welsh language'. The party - accounts of the numbers vary from 50 to 300 - is said to have sailed from North Wales across the Atlantic in the sweep of the North Equatorial Current and through the narrow gap separating Florida and Cuba.

Anthropologists have found striking similarities between the Welsh and the now virtually extinct Mandan Indians, who lived along the upper reaches of the Missouri River. The Mandans used boats very much like Welsh coracles, responded immediately when they heard the Welsh language, and became white-haired with age, a characteristic not shown by other Indians. An 18th-century French traveller to the area described the Mandans as 'white men with forts and permanent villages laid out in streets'. The ruins of three Welsh-style fortresses have been found near Chattanooga, in Tennessee.

The Mandans were wiped out by men who may have had the same ethnic origins as themselves - white fur traders

for its floating ice. They passed through an area of dense mist, which could be the Newfoundland Banks, where the warm Gulf Stream meets the Arctic current. The party encountered whales and 'an animal with big eyes, tusks, a spotted belly and a bearded jaw' – a walrus? – before landing in a country of autumn sunshine, possibly Labrador.

Later Brendan and his men landed on a flat, tropical island covered with exotic vegetation, surrounded by crystal clear water and inhabited by beautiful birds and naked dark-skinned pygmies. Perhaps Brendan had sailed down the coast of North America out of sight of land and arrived at an island in the Bahamas. The pygmy people could have been the Arawaks, the original inhabitants of the islands. Brendan and his party went on to discover another land – 'odorous, flower-smooth and blest' – which is now thought to have been Florida.

The whole story is hard to believe. And not having been written down until

who started a smallpox epidemic among the Mandans in the mid-19th century.

Eighteenth-century explorers along the Lumber River of North Carolina found a tribe of grey-eyed Indians who spoke a kind of English and claimed that their ancestors could 'talk in a book' - which was taken to mean that they could read. Their descendants, the Lumbee Indians, still live in Robeson County - and blond hair and blue eyes are not uncommon features among them.

It is thought that the Lumbee Indians could be the remnants of Sir Walter Raleigh's lost colony of English settlers who disappeared from Roanoke Island, on the coast of North Carolina, around 1590. The colony was established in 1587 under Governor John White, who then returned to England for supplies. War between England and Spain prevented him from revisiting the colony for three years. When he returned, White found the fort dismantled. The 117 settlers, including 11 children, were missing. The only clue to their fate was the word 'Croatoan' carved on a post. White took it to mean that the settlers had moved south to the island of Croatoan, known to be inhabited by the friendly Hatteras tribe. He made no attempt to find them.

If White was right and the settlers did move to Croatoan and interbred with the natives, their descendants could be the Lumbee Indians. However some historians believe that the word 'Croatoan' refers to the name of a tribe that attacked and massacred the settlers. It is a mystery that is unlikely ever to be solved.

A Viking ship.
Opposite Columbus's *Santa Maria*.

several centuries after the events it described, it is possible that it was con-siderably embellished. However, the ancient sagas of the Norsemen admit that the Irish were there first.

The Viking voyages to North America are now established as historical fact. The intrepid Norsemen land-hopped via Iceland and Greenland and, under Leif Ericson, reached the coast of North America in the year 1000. The stories of their heroic voyages to this land beyond the sea – referred to as Markland, Helluland and Vinland – are told in the Norse sagas, written in Iceland between 1320 and 1350. Not much attention was paid to these sagas until as recently as 1837, when they were re-examined and it was found that their descriptions of Vinland's climate, geography and native life fitted that of the coast of New England.

The recent discovery of the stone foundations of eight houses, four boat sheds, a smithy, cooking pits and implements at L'Anse aux Meadows, on the northern tip of Newfoundland – all carbon-dated to the Viking era – lends credence to the story that Leif Ericson established a settlement on his arrival in North America. 'The find,' says Norwegian Dr Helge Ingstad, who helped make the discovery, 'furnishes the first incontrovertible archaeological proof that Europeans set foot in America centuries before Columbus's voyage of 1492.' But there is still controversy over whether the Vikings penetrated in-land or confined their exploration to the coast.

A startling find was made in 1898 by a farmer clearing land at Kensington, Minnesota. Digging out the roots of a tree, he came across a square slab of rock, $2\frac{1}{2}$ ft high and 6 in. thick. An inscription of 220 characters had been chiselled on its face and along one side. It allegedly relates to a 30-strong party of Norwegians and Goths on a 'journey of discovery' west from Vinland in 1362 and tells of a massacre in which ten of the party were killed. Many experts have condemned the so-called Kensington Stone as a 19th-century fake. Others say that it is genuine and that a forger would have needed an outstanding knowledge of history, geology and Norse dialect.

Some scholars have suggested that the Newport Tower, a stone structure in the centre of Newport, Rhode Island, was built by Vikings. The tower, circular and about 24 ft high, is said to have been a church. Others differ, and say that it is the work of 16th- or 17th-century settlers.

The *Vinland Map*, a map of the world said to have been drawn in 1440 by a Swiss monk, has been fiercely argued about over the years. The map, acquired in 1965 by Yale University, clearly depicts the location of Vinland as North America. Experts on both sides of the Atlantic have carbon-dated the map and pronounced it genuine. But recently, a group of American ink analysts studying particles of the map announced that they were convinced it is a 20th-century fake.

Meanwhile, a collection of megalithic ruins in New Hampshire has raised recent speculation among American archaeologists as to whether they are of British – or at least Celtic – origin. The ruins – at a place appropriately named Mystery Hill – consist of 22 stone huts, walls, passages and what appears to be a sacrificial table with a speaking tube arrangement through which voices can be projected. Huge blocks of local granite are held in position by their own weight and by corbelled vaulting – horizontally laid stones that each project a little beyond another. Thousands of artefacts from many periods and different cultures have been found at the site, including a number of stones bearing chiselled inscriptions in what is thought to be Ogham, the ancient language of the Irish and Picts. Dr Barry Fell, of Harvard University, has been studying the stones for several years and dates them tentatively from about 800 BC to the 3rd century AD.

English historian Geoffrey Ashe visited the site in 1960 and declared that it may date back to the banishment of Cronus and the adventures of Odysseus. According to Homer, Cronus was banished to a land where the sun never set, north-west of the Mediterranean. In Homer's *Odyssey*, Odysseus sails to the far frontiers of the world, to the land of the Cimmerians, an area of fog and darkness which has been taken by some to be Newfoundland.

In a serious study, science fiction writer André Norton speculated that Mystery Hill may have been a Phoenician-Carthaginian settlement: 'In 335

Newport Tower.

THE PLATE OF BRASS

Few discoveries in America have aroused more interest than the finding of an old brass plate on the north shore of San Francisco Bay in 1936. Beryle Shinn, a shop assistant, found the plate under a rock while picnicking with his companions. He put it in his car and took it home. It lay forgotten until early in 1937, when he came across it again. He cleaned the plate with soap and water and discovered some writing on it. Shinn could just decipher the word 'Drake'.

He telephoned Dr Herbert Bolton, the professor of history at the University of California, who could hardly believe his ears. Shinn's description of the plate, especially that of a hole in it, suggested that it could be the famous Plate of Brass on which Sir Francis Drake is said to have recorded the formal annexation of California - which he called New Albion - to England in 1579. According to narratives of Drake's round-the-world voyage, the plate, which was fixed to a great post, had a hole cut in it for the insertion of a sixpence, showing the image and arms of Queen Elizabeth.

Shinn sent the plate to Bolton, who cleaned and deciphered the engravings:

BEE IT KNOWNE VNTO ALL MEN BY THESE PRESENTS

JVNE 17 1579

BY THE GRACE OF GOD AND IN THE NAME OF
HERR MAJESTY QVEEN ELIZABETH OF ENGLAND
AND HERR SVCCESSORS FOREVER I TAKE POSSESSION
OF THIS KINGDOME WHOSE KING AND PEOPLE FREELY
RESIGNE THEIR RIGHT AND TITLE IN THE WHOLE
LAND VNTO HERR MAJESTIES KEEPEING NOW NAMED BY
ME AND TO BE KNOWNE VNTO ALL MEN AS NOVA ALBION.

FRANCIS DRAKE

It was found that an Elizabethan sixpence fitted perfectly in the jagged hole beneath the inscription and that the wording tallied with accounts of the setting up of the plate. Dr Bolton was convinced of its authenticity and a few weeks later announced to a stunned meeting of the California Historical Society: 'Here it is, recovered at last after a lapse of 357 years. Behold, Drake's Plate - the Plate of Brass. California's choicest archaeological treasure.'

Sceptics were quick to challenge the authenticity of the plate and pointed out that almost anyone could have studied accounts of the voyage and engraved an inscription on an ancient piece of brass.

Chemists of the University of California, which acquired the plate, subjected it to exhaustive tests for seven months and reported: 'It is our opinion that the brass plate examined by us is the genuine Drake plate referred to in the book *The World Encompassed*, by Sir Francis Drake, published in 1628.'

No one can be absolutely certain that the plate is the one set up by Drake. But it has been pointed out that no more than ten people in the world would have been expert enough in Elizabethan English to have executed such an inscription on the plate without flaws.

BC, Aristotle, in his list of 178 marvels, names as item 84 a mysterious over-seas land which the Phoenicians kept a strict secret because of trade.' The Phoenicians were, without doubt, the finest sailors in the ancient world. They circumnavigated Africa and established a trading network covering such far-flung places as Africa, India, Cyprus and Spain. And, according to inter-pretations of texts by Plato and Diodorus, they also traded with America around 1000 BC. From measurements made at the Mystery Hill site, it is believed that the structure was not built in yards, feet and inches, but in the ancient cubit unit of measurement used by the Egyptians and the Phoenicians. Mystery Hill indeed seems destined to remain a mystery.

Scottish claims to settlement in America before the arrival of Columbus hinge on a stone known as the Sinclair Rock, at Westford, Massachusetts, which is claimed to mark a landing point by Prince Henry Sinclair, of the Orkneys. The prince is said to have sailed with a small band from his island kingdom in 1395 and to have made several distant landfalls. The rock bears the heraldic markings of the Sinclair clan.

The mystery of which race was first to 'discover' America may never be solved. It could have been just about anyone from the Orient or the Old World. Yet Christopher Columbus remains in most history books the man who opened up the New World to the Old.

The money pit
A fabulous treasure or an unfathomable mystery?

On a lonely island off the east coast of Canada, a fortune in pirate's gold lies buried. So, at least, goes the legend. The access to this fabled treasure is a seemingly bottomless pit which fortune-hunters have sought to plumb for almost 200 years. All have failed.

The hunt was launched in 1795 when 16-year-old Daniel McGinnis, of Chester, Nova Scotia, went exploring in the canoe his parents allowed him to use on nearby Mahone Bay. But on this occasion Daniel paddled further than usual – across the bay to lonely Oak Island. Few people had ever visited the island, and, as young Daniel ventured to the heart of it, he may have thought he was walking where no man had trod before.

Suddenly he stopped in his tracks, pulled up by a most unexpected find. Hanging from a large oak at the centre of a clearing was an old ship's tackle block. Daniel walked over to take a closer look. He noted that the main branch of the oak had been cut off about four feet from the trunk. He also realized that he was standing in a depression where the ground had sunk by a couple of feet. Someone, he conjectured, must have been digging there, searching for something – or burying something.

McGinnis paddled home and returned the next day with two friends, 20-year-old John Smith and 13-year-old Anthony Vaughan. Together they began to dig. It did not take them long to clear the carefully laid topsoil and uncover a shaft, perfectly rounded and 13 ft in diameter. They immediately thought of buried treasure.

The young men went off to get picks, shovels, ladders and ropes. They virtually made their home on the island, and they spent from dawn to dusk digging for the treasure.

Their first major find was at 10 ft down. They came upon a sturdy platform of oak logs, carefully embedded into the side of the pit. Certain that treasure lay beneath, they levered the logs out, only to find new depths of firmly impacted earth below. The soil was clay with flint embedded in it, and the work of digging was back-breaking. But the three laboured on until, at a depth of 20 ft, they encountered a similar platform – and more impacted earth. The same thing happened again at 30 ft.

The three abandoned their excavation while they sought backing for their venture. They realized that they would need cash and machinery if they were to dig deeper. But no one in the little town of Chester was interested in such a hare-brained scheme – particularly as Oak Island was reputed to be haunted. It was not until 1804 that the young men raised the interest of a doctor, Simeon Lynd, who managed to persuade local business folk to back the project. The great dig continued. But after their nine-year wait the hopes of the three adventurers were quickly dashed once again. At every 10-ft interval they found yet another oak platform – even more firmly cemented in place with putty and fibre.

At a depth of 90 ft the explorers became almost feverish with excitement. They broke through the most strongly constructed platform they had yet encountered. It was bonded by charcoal, ship's putty and coconut fibre. Once they had hacked their way through this barrier, they discovered a flat stone on which were undecipherable markings. The stone was sent to the mainland for expert examination, and although it was later mysteriously lost, the Oak Island treasure-hunters were told that the message on it meant: 'Ten (or possibly 40) feet below, two million pounds are buried.'

Daniel McGinnis and his partners felt sure they were near to final success, fame and fortune. They gouged out another 10 ft of soft earth and struck something solid. It sounded like metal. But it was now long past dusk on a Saturday night and the men decided to rest until Monday.

Early on Monday the expectant partners returned to their diggings, by now labelled the Money Pit. They peered over the rim, and found the pit two-thirds filled with water . . .

Bitterly disappointed, they tried to bale out the pit, but made little headway. For several months, they abandoned their efforts. But in 1805, they returned for a brave new attempt.

They dug a fresh pit nearby to an incredible depth of 110 ft, then ran a shaft at right-angles to join the Money Pit at the point they believed the treasure to be. But they were lucky to escape with their lives when an underground channel suddenly flooded their workings. Penniless, they gave up their ten-year dream.

The next attempt at unplugging the Money Pit was in 1849. McGinnis had died a bitterly disappointed man. Of Smith there is no record. But Vaughan was still alive, and he was recruited by a newly formed syndicate to help them dig out the old workings.

The team, led by James Pittbaldo, of Truro, Nova Scotia, found it impossible to drain the old pit, so they decided to drill it instead. The drill churned easily through the first 98 ft, the depth reached by the original miners. But the new excavators found no sign of metal at that level – only a further oak platform. They pushed their way through it. By raising and examining the drill-bit at short intervals, they deduced that the drill next passed through the top of an oak chest, through some loose metal, through the bottom of the chest and then through a second similar chest. Two metal-filled chests. . . . It just had to be the treasure.

There were reports, but no confirmation, that tiny links of gold were brought to the surface on the drill-bit. What is known is that Pittbaldo removed an object from the bit – then removed himself from the mine camp. His workers believed that he had found a precious stone. It is not too unlikely a theory, because a few days later he returned to the camp with a wealthy backer and tried to buy sole rights to the venture. But by now, no one was in a selling mood. The treasure-seekers scented success at last.

It was not to be, however. The over-eager miners drilled still deeper, probing for further signs of the elusive fortune. They pushed through another wooden platform – of spruce, not oak, this time – and caused the base of the pit to collapse into what seemed to be a muddy cavern. Down into the depths, along with the wreckage of the final platform, went the 'treasure chests'.

But the excavation had not been completely futile. For the first time, it was realized that the water filling the pit was sea water, which rose and fell with the tides. The ground being of clay, the only explanation for the movement of the water was that the shaft was linked by a further channel to the open sea. A search of the shoreline soon revealed at Smith's Cove, almost 500 ft away, an elaborate, concealed system which flooded and drained the Money Pit.

The syndicate built a dam across the cove, then began to pump the water from the pit. Before they had completed their task, however, a high tide swept away the dam wall, and all work stopped. The syndicate were bankrupt.

Twenty years later another syndicate took up the search. With the optimistic title of The Oak Island Eldorado Company, they built another dam, which kept out the sea for a short time. They then pumped out the Money Pit and uncovered the flood and drainage system. It was at a depth of 110 ft and formed of stone. But before further work could be carried out the Eldorado Company's dam was breached and the pit filled yet again.

In 1894, a local businessman, Frederick Blair, formed the Oak Island Treasure Company and set about the most extensive search attempt so far to solve the exasperating mystery. Blair drilled down to the subterranean flood tunnel and dynamited it. The outlet to Smith's Cove was sealed for ever. But, amazingly, the water in the pit still rose and fell with the tide.

Blair poured dye into the pit and watched for its reappearance. It emerged not at Smith's Cove, but on South Shore – the opposite coastline. The members of the Oak Island Treasure Company were utterly baffled. They were not to know the secret that would be revealed only after many more excavations: below the level of the Smith's Cove inlet were two further channels, one, man-made, at a depth of 160 ft, also leading to Smith's Cove, and the other, at about 180 ft, seemingly a natural watercourse leading to South Shore. It was through this lower channel that the dye had run.

Frederick Blair made dozens of exploratory drillings to determine what lay beneath the original stone drainage systems 110 ft down. For a further 40 ft below this mark he encountered little but soft clay, presumably the clay into which the 'treasure chests' had sunk and broken up. But at a depth approaching 150 ft, Blair's drill hit some material which he sent for chemical analysis. The astonishing answer came back: 'man-made cement.'

Immediately beneath this thin layer was some rotten wood. Then came what Blair could only describe from the reaction of the drill as soft metal objects in the form of bars. Below this was a layer of small pieces of metal, then further bars, then a solid iron obstruction.

To the treasure-seekers, the soft metal bars could mean only one thing – gold bars. And small pieces of metal just had to be coins. This interpretation must have been an irresistible lure to Blair, who remained in the area for many years, every now and again making new tests at the site. But there was insufficient backing to launch a new and concerted attempt to recover any treasure.

In 1935, a wealthy mining expert, Gilbert Heddon, went into partnership with Blair and his son. Electric pumps were set up, powered by cable from the mainland five miles away, but the sea water continued to flow in. Three years later, Edwin Hamilton, a New York professor of mechanical engineering, launched the first scientifically based investigation of the site. Over the next four years he sank several shafts and uncovered the two lower channels which had caused Blair such trouble. But of treasure, there was no sign.

So far, the Money Pit had claimed more cash than was ever likely to be recovered from it. But in 1965, it also claimed human lives. Four men who were excavating for the Smith's Cove tunnels were poisoned by carbon-monoxide fumes from their water-pump.

But even they may not have been the first lives claimed by the Money Pit. For, five years later, a Montreal consortium calling itself the Triton Alliance lowered a television camera with powerful lighting about 200 ft into the labyrinth of pits and shafts . . . and picked up the faint outline of a human hand. Other shadowy shapes appeared to be three chests and an axe. But the team was unable to recover anything of value.

The Money Pit continues to be a magic lure to treasure-seekers. But the area has now been so heavily mined, and so many shafts have collapsed upon one another, that the precise location of the pit found by Daniel McGinnis is uncertain. Perhaps it will never be accurately located again and the questions that surround it will remain unanswered forever: who built the Money Pit, how – and why?

There are several theories, most of them put forward and investigated by author Rupert Furneaux, whose book *The Money Pit Mystery* is the classic work on this intriguing mystery. The first clue is that at the time young McGinnis first visited Oak Island in 1795 the place was thought to be haunted. Locals on the mainland spoke of midnight fires on the tiny island and the disappearance of some of the menfolk of Chester who went to investigate. No one has been able to put an accurate date to these events, but the likelihood is that the stories originated around 1700.

A rather better-known event occurred at around that time 3,000 miles away in England, where Captain William Kidd was hanged for piracy in 1701. As he went to the gallows in Wapping, London, he mouthed a curse on anyone who sought his 'treasure', the legend of which grew after his death. Could Kidd and his men have dug the Money Pit?

In the 1930s, a retired English lawyer, Hubert Palmer, found three charts hidden in a secret drawer of a desk at his home in Eastbourne, Sussex. The desk had once belonged to Captain Kidd, and, having heard of the Oak Island search, Palmer compared the charts with a map of the island. There were strong similarities but no proof of treasure – and no indication where it might have been buried.

At about the same time, Blair's partner Heddon also came across a map, this one in a book about Captain Kidd. The map was of an island resembling

Oak Island. Heddon travelled to England to trace the author, who told him that he had copied the map from one shown him by a Dutchman. Where had the Dutchman obtained it? As far as the author could remember, it had come from under a cairn of stones on an island off Nova Scotia.

Heddon examined directions marked on the map: 18 W by 7 E Rock 30 SW 14 N Tree 7 by 8 by 4. Back on Oak Island, he found two granite boulders with drill holes in them, and plotted his course from them, using the old English measure of rods. The directions led him to an overgrown thicket. On clearing the undergrowth, Heddon found a triangle of half-buried stones – pointing directly to the Money Pit. Add to this remarkable discovery the scientific reports of the Triton Alliance – that relics found in the pit were wood and iron from British ships – and the case for accepting the Captain Kidd theory becomes even more convincing.

Yet there is a flaw. The block and tackle which McGinnis found hanging from the sawn-off branch of the oak tree in 1795 could not have survived for nearly 100 years. Even the tree itself may not have existed at the time of Kidd's death. And how could a ship's crew carry out such a remarkable feat of engineering unseen and unaided on an inhospitable island?

For, whatever the purpose of the Money Pit, it was, if nothing else, a miracle of mining. From the evidence, it appears that, in total secrecy, a skilled team of engineers and a small army of labourers dug a perfectly formed pit 180 ft into the ground. On a platform at the bottom, directly over a subterranean stream, they placed their treasure – which, to have warranted so much effort, must have been of great value.

These engineers then ran a 4-ft-high shaft a distance of 500 ft to a point below high tide in Smith's Cove – without, at that stage, allowing any water to enter. They then cemented over the top of the treasure chamber, covered it with 50 ft of clay, and topped it with a platform of spruce. The next step in this remarkable enterprise was to tunnel yet another shaft to Smith's Cove, running directly above the first. To enable them to dig like moles along this narrow shaft, a further pit was sunk to act as an air vent half-way between the Money Pit and the sea. We know of this vent because in 1878 a farmer's wife was ploughing with two oxen when the ground collapsed and she fell into it.

Again somehow managing to keep the sea out of the tunnel, the miners stacked two or three 'treasure chests' on the spruce platform. They topped this with an oak platform and the mysterious cipher stone. Then came more platforms at 10-ft intervals. Finally, the ground was covered with topsoil and all evidence removed, except, strangely, for the block and tackle.

No pirate could have managed such a feat. It would have taken the resources of an army. And that conclusion led author Rupert Furneaux to his own remarkable theory . . .

In 1778 the American War of Independence was being fought. The British garrison in New York felt threatened by Washington and British commander Sir Henry Clinton feared that the army's pay-chest might fall into enemy hands. Did he then order the Royal Engineers to conceal the money – perhaps somewhere near their outpost in Halifax, Nova Scotia?

It is an ingenious theory and, if true, raises another question. Since no great sum of money was ever reported lost by the British, did the Royal Engineers later return to Oak Island and recover the treasure through one of the side-shafts? Has the Money Pit been empty for more than 200 years?

A Cabinet of Medical Curiosities

According to the *Charlotte Observer* of 1926, the Reverend Mr Taylor and the Reverend Mr Dick conducted a learned public debate at Edenton on the question: 'Will the Negro retain his present colour in heaven?' Mr Taylor contended that the Negro's colour will change.

It is not clear what scientific evidence Mr Taylor marshalled to support his argument; the report merely illustrates how weirdly racial prejudice may affect otherwise intelligent people. But cases of individuals' skin changing colour have occurred; and in places where racial laws operate, the results can be disquieting.

In January 1970 Mr Alphons du Toit, for example, a South African White, was stung from head to toe when he walked into a swarm of bees in the middle of Johannesburg. He turned black. A housewife was shopping nearby when the incident occurred, and declared: 'He was unrecognizable.' Another passer-by telephoned for an ambulance. The official at the other end of the line asked: 'European or non-European?' The passer-by replied; 'Non-European – I think.'

Accordingly, Mr du Toit was put into an ambulance for non-Whites and driven to the non-White section of Johannesburg General Hospital for treatment. While the patient was being given emergency treatment, however, the nurses discovered that he was white. Should they carry on regardless, or interrupt treatment to have Mr du Toit moved to the White section? Prejudice won; and in a desperate state, the unfortunate patient was wheeled out of the non-White area and into the White. His condition was critical.

The vagaries of apartheid were further exposed by the case of Mrs Rita Hoefling, a white South African woman who had an operation to remove her adrenal glands in 1969. After the operation her skin turned progressively darker and darker, discoloured by pituitary secretions. A Cape Town hospital worker, Mrs Hoefling found herself being treated as a black maid, ordered off Whites Only buses, subjected to countless slights and humiliations. In January 1978 she wrote a formal letter to protest to the South African Premier, John Vorster, to tell him 'what apartheid is doing to my life and those of others'.

Skin changes may, of course, work in reverse through a pigmentation disorder, Eddie Mae Kearney of New York changed from black to white in 1959. In 1981, she turned black again – spot by spot.

Skin change cases may still provoke strange news stories where racialism persists; sex-change cases, however, have become so routine in recent years that only the most bizarre are likely to feature in the press. The tale of Marion Yerrill in 1977 belonged to the latter category. The lady in question was born and brought up as a girl, and married in 1967. While living with her husband, however, she started posing as a man, wearing men's clothes and using a man's name – usually Paul Jennings. In 1975 she met a 19-year-old girl, through a dating agency. They began to go out together and eventually got married at Hertford Register Office.

Marion Yerrill lived for two and a half months with her 'wife' after their honeymoon. Then Mrs Yerrill suddenly left. She reappeared three days later and explained that she could not live the lie any longer. Mrs Yerrill had been having hormone treatment for some time, and when the case came up for trial she appeared in dock wearing a grey checked suit, collar and tie with short dark hair and a beard.

The workings of the human body are strange indeed. Dora Watkinson trod on a darning needle one day, and part of it broke off and entered her foot. The foot was X-rayed, and a fragment of the needle removed. She appeared to feel no ill effects. About a year later, however, her tongue started to scratch on something in her jaw – and she removed from between two of her lower teeth half an inch of the broken needle trodden on 12 months earlier. It had toured her body through the bloodstream.

Readers of *The Times* in November 1974 blenched at the headline: 'Kilted Soldiers Sought for Virility Tests'. The article described how scientists at the Western General Hospital in Edinburgh were to examine a theory that tight underwear was making man less fertile than animals. The experts had shown that men produce only 60 per cent 'good sperm' whereas animals can produce

Eddie Mae Kearney turns black – spot by spot

98 per cent. 'We think this might be because animals wear no clothes,' a specialist declared. In consequence, soldiers who wore the kilt in the traditional manner, without underclothes, were required for samples.

Kilted or otherwise clad, people have proved themselves fertile for quite a long time now; and the natural consequence, of course, is childbirth. Babies have been born under every imaginable circumstance: underwater, in helicopters, in lift shafts and motorcycle sidecars. It is not uncommon for a mother, especially one slightly overweight, to be pregnant and not know it until the joyful day. In a recent case, one such unwitting mother-to-be gave birth at her daughter's wedding. A haunting fear common to practically all prospective parents is that something will 'not be quite right' with the baby. It would be distasteful to catalogue the variety of malformations which have attracted the interest of the press. Two cases will suffice, both with happy endings.

In 1977 a four-legged boy was born at a Lincolnshire hospital, and moved to Sheffield Children's Hospital. After six weeks, doctors prepared to carry out the rare and delicate operation of removing the handicap. According to a newspaper report of 22 March, the operation was a success and the child doing well.

In 1982, a child was born in the United States with a bullet in his brain. His 17-year-old mother gave birth to the boy more than two months prematurely after she was shot in a love-triangle quarrel. The bullet passed through her lower back and through her kidney before lodging in the brain of the unborn child. The boy, Daniel, was delivered by Caesarian section several hours later. He was put on a life support system and it was two months before the operating team at Broward General Hospital in Florida felt able to remove the bullet. Dr Greg Melnick, who supervised the operation, announced: 'He was born in a bad condition and I felt pretty certain he would die. His recovery and survival instinct have been quite remarkable.' The *Daily Mirror*, which carried the story, stated that Daniel was now growing up into a perfectly normal toddler.

A much less chilling case, though distressing no doubt, was that of Tricia Reay, aged 12, appropriately enough from Sutton Coldfield. Tricia could not stop sneezing. On 19 March 1980, the newspapers announced that she had scored a world record for Britain by sneezing non-stop for 156 days; and still she kept on sneezing, on average, once every 20 seconds. Relief was to come eventually when she was taken from her home to a clinic in the Pyrenees where doctors managed to cure the condition. From October 1979, when she caught a cold, to 29 April 1980, Tricia had sneezed for over 200 days.

While various nations around the world sought a cure for the common cold, South Africa devoted its attention to developing a device which would cause people to sneeze. The Sneeze Machine was developed as an aid to riot control, and sprayed crowds with a mixture of talcum powder and tear-gas. It made its first appearance in June 1977. Opponents of South Africa's apartheid regime derived some comfort only two weeks later when newspapers reported that the police officer who operated the device was himself in hospital in Johannesburg suffering from tear-gas poisoning. He had been over exposed to the talc and tears mixture while using the machine on black students in Soweto.

Home cures for commonplace ailments have been colourfully reported over the years. One of the most persistent pieces of advice is to get stung by a bee as a cure for rheumatism; if it really works, it is because the formic acid present in bee venom acts as a counter-irritant. Of less certain efficiency are such remedies as boiled cockroaches stuffed into a bad ear and infusions of mice applied to a bad back. During a whooping cough epidemic of 1982, *The Times* recalled that Charlotte M. Yonge, the Victorian novelist, had the following suggestions for ague: 'to be taken to the top of a steep place, then violently pushed down', and 'to have gunpowder in bags round the wrists set on fire'.

The recent developments in transplants and spare part surgery have created some very weird news stories, particularly those exposing illicit trade in organs. In 1978, three mortuary technicians at North Staffordshire Royal Infirmary were sacked after allegations that they had been holding gland sales. The technicians were paid 20p expenses for removing pituitary glands from post mortem cases, and were alleged to have made handsome profits by retailing them to a Swedish company.

For sheer Gothic horror, however, the following snippet surely surpasses all. It has caused at least one researcher (the author) to shriek aloud in the silence of the Bodleian Library in Oxford. You have been warned:

'Paris – The former director of the French eye bank, has been charged with manslaughter after the death of a man who was given the cornea of a rabies victim during an eye operation. The eye bank was later closed.'
The Times, 10 October 1981

How sick can you get? Very sick indeed, if the *St Petersburg Gazette* of 1914 is to be believed. The newspaper recorded the case of a girl so ill with typhoid that she was practically burning alive. Her temperature reached such abnormal heights that it burst one thermometer capable of registering 113°F – the mercury column simply shot up to the full limit and the glass was shattered. Doctors then took her temperature again and registered 132°F.

The case of the St Petersburg girl is especially interesting in that *The Guinness Book of Records* cites a modest 112°F as the highest body temperature endured. (Readers who find such statistics dull may like to know that the same volume asserts that a 15-year-old girl once yawned non-stop for a period of five weeks, and that human snoring can attain a loudness of 69 decibels, approximating the noise of a pneumatic drill.)

Strange Nature

Breakfast was a colourful occasion for pensioners Jim and Lillian Barbery. Their hen Goldie laid blue eggs.

'When she laid her first blue egg I didn't really think a great deal about it,' Mrs Barbery told reporters at her home in Cornwall. 'But when she laid six in a row it shook me a bit.'

Stranger still was the case of a hen belonging to Yorkshireman Jack Pelter. His hen laid perfectly normal eggs for two years – and then turned into a cockerel.

From the earliest days of the press, newspapers have delighted in reporting curious natural phenomena, be they sex-change hens or six-legged calves. Among such freaks of nature, the following item is hard to beat for silent menace: 'Salta, Argentina, May 13 – An 18-inch snake, with two heads and two tails, was captured in the town of Saladillo today. One head eats voraciously, but the other does not function at all.' (*The Times*, 14 May 1975)

For sheer weirdness, however, the widely reported Cat with Wings, found in an Oxford garden in 1933, surpasses all. 'I have just seen a cat that has on its back fully-developed fur-covered wings, with which, it is stated, it can fly,' announced an incredulous reporter. The bizarre creature had been found by an Oxford housewife. With black and white markings, the feline freak was prowling around her back garden; later it found its way into her stables. 'I saw it move from the ground to a beam – a considerable distance, which I do not think it could have leaped – using its wings in a manner similar to that of a bird,' she said.

Two officials arrived from the Oxford Zoo and captured the animal, which was placed on display in the zoo. 'I carefully examined the cat tonight,' a reporter declared, 'and there is no doubt about the wings. They grow just in front of its hindquarters.'

Some creatures are born strange; others acquire strangeness through circumstances. 'Mice Grow Fur Wraps in Freezer' announced the *Daily Telegraph* of 15 July 1982, and it had a curious tale to tell. In Norwich, a family of mice had found their way into a refrigerated room stocked with frozen meat carcasses. The conditions were Arctic, with temperatures maintained at between minus 26° and minus 28° centigrade. The mice survived by growing extra thick woolly fur coats. A health official said: 'They were just like little balls of fluff and looked quite different from ordinary mice. It must have taken them several months to adapt to the conditions but it shows how quickly they can change to suit their environment.'

The cat with wings found in Oxford, 1933

The super mice lived on rock-hard frozen meat carcasses in the refrigerated room until they were rounded up by astonished pest control experts. The official continued: 'Half a dozen of these fluffy mice were caught and I was amazed when I saw them. It certainly is the most unusual case of survivors that I have ever come across. They were completely immune to commonly used rat poison. When they were fed with it they thrived.' How they got in remained somewhat mysterious, but it was pointed out that it was almost impossible to make anywhere totally mouseproof: 'They can squeeze through a gap only an eighth of an inch wide by flattening their skulls.'

The flexible cranium of the mouse, however, pales to insignificance beside the discovery made by biologists at Michigan State University in 1977. Their research showed that headless cockroaches learn quicker than their intact counterparts. The *Sunday Times*, reporting this curious phenomenon, announced that 'headless cockroaches can live for seven days after beheadings because of nerve cell clusters elsewhere in their bodies. The Michigan researchers report that the roaches learn to avoid painful electric shocks more quickly than normal ones with heads.'

Freak phenomena in nature are not, of course, confined to the animal world. Giant carrots, monstrous marrows and other vegetable wonders are commonly reported. More discreetly enigmatic, however, is this little snippet from the *Daily Mirror*: 'A tomato grown by miner Ben Croft of Eckington, near Sheffield, had a ripe strawberry inside.'

No less appetizing than Mr Croft's tasty crop were the onions which grew in the allotment of Bradford horticulturalist Stanley Blazevics. His onions grew ready cooked. Mr Blazevics uprooted an onion one Sunday morning, and, when he peeled back the browned skin and cut it in two with his penknife, the layers fell away as if the onion had been cooked in boiling water. Others in the same patch of allotment were also 'done to a turn'. Reporters were invited to come and examine Mr Blazevics's ready-cooked onions. 'I sampled a slice,' commented a *Sunday Express* man. 'It tasted like any other cooked onion.'

Blazevics discovered that a particular patch of earth in the allotment was hot to the touch – a thermometer from his tropical fish tank registered temperatures as high as 100°F. 'I've thought maybe I dug through an electric cable by accident, causing a short circuit through the soil. But that is ruled out because I have dug deep around the hot spot and found nothing,' said the puzzled gardener.

Scientists were fascinated and took soil samples, testing the earth with a geiger counter for signs of radioactivity. The newspapers followed the story with equal interest. Finally, *The Times* announced: 'Ready Cooked Onion Mystery may be Solved'. A lecturer in earth sciences at Bradford University had concluded that the cause of the phenomenon was a layer of compost, about half a spade deep, beneath the surface. The compost, dug in during the autumn, had not broken down because of a severe winter. The reaction of bacteria with fertilizer had caused intense heat; the Victorians, it seemed, had used a similar method to heat greenhouses.

The private life of plants is imbued with mystery. Experiments conducted with polygraphs (lie detectors) suggest that vegetation responds to threat or caress much as plant-lovers have asserted for generations. The case of Norfolk's Weeping Tree, however, took plant sensitivity beyond the bounds of normal expectation. The tree, at Stonehouse Farm, West Harling, began crying in 1939. Tears trickled incessantly down trunk and branches in perfectly dry weather. When puzzled villagers cut away a branch, tears positively gushed from the wound. Examined by experts, the phenomena finally submitted to an orthodox explanation; an underground spring had forced its way up through the trunk.

Much more deeply mysterious is the case of the suicidal trees reported by the University of Sussex in November 1977. Research carried out there suggested that Dutch elms, ravaged throughout Europe by a mystery disease, had not as reported been killed by the fungus *Ceratostomella ulmi*; they had sealed off their own sap-carrying vessels as a pre-emptive suicidal measure.

Chapter three

UFO's

The daunting dossier of UFO data over the years means that we can no longer shrug aside these tales as mere pie in the sky. There has been too much substantiated evidence for sceptics to ignore such outlandish mysteries. Each year brings forth more evidence from reliable witnesses of the highest calibre. We cannot now ignore the facts put before us – UFO's are being watched the world over.

Year of the UFOs

Animals give the warning signals

Gary Flatter could not believe his eyes as he jammed on the brakes of his truck. Crossing the road in front of him was a curious menagerie of animals – seven rabbits, a raccoon, a possum and several cats. At the same time he was aware of a weird, high-pitched noise. The animals had emerged from a nearby field, and when Flatter glanced over the hedge, he soon found out why. Two silver-suited figures were staring at him.

It was October 22, 1973, and America was in the middle of a wave of UFO sightings. Flatter had accompanied his friend, Deputy Sheriff Ed Townsend, to State Road 26 near Hartford City, Indiana, where a car driver had reported two strange creatures standing on the highway. When they arrived, the highway was empty, and the sheriff decided to get back to town. But Flatter opted to stay on and look around.

When he turned a spotlight on the creatures, he saw that they were about four feet tall with egg-like heads that seemed to be covered by gas masks. Far from seeming upset by the light, they began putting on a show, jumping high into the air and floating down again. Then they flew off into the darkness, leaving a faint red trail.

Five days earlier, Paul Brown had seen two beings matching Flatter's description as he drove near Danielsville, Georgia. He told police that a bright light passed over his car with a swishing sound, and he saw a cone-shaped object land in the road some 300 feet ahead of him. He skidded to a halt, and as tiny figures emerged from the object, he grabbed his gun from the glove compartment, crouching behind the open driver's door ready to challenge them. They advanced no further, returned to their craft and quickly took off. Brown claimed he fired some shots at the disappearing UFO, but did not hit it.

Rex Snow ordered his dog to attack two silver-suited figures cavorting in his brightly-lit backyard at Goffstown, New Hampshire shortly after midnight on November 4 of that same year. The dog, a German shepherd trained to obey commands, bounded towards the intruders. But when she got within 30 feet of them, they curtailed their antics and just stared at her. She stopped in her tracks, growled at them, then slunk back past her surprised owner and lay down inside the house, whining and clearly frightened. Snow said later that he too was overcome by a sudden sense of fear. He had his 38-calibre pistol with him, but was shaking too much to hold it properly.

He quickly followed his dog inside the house, and watched the weird beings through the window. They seemed to be luminous, with over-sized pointed ears, dark egg-shaped recesses for eyes, and large pointed noses. Their heads were covered in Ku Klux Klan type hoods of the same colour as their suits.

The figures seemed to be picking things from the ground and putting them in a silver bag with slow, deliberate movements. After a time, they walked off towards some nearby woods. Snow rang the police, but before they arrived he saw the woods light up eerily, then become dark again.

Police were convinced that Snow had seen something odd and frightening. They said he was shaking like a leaf and still pale when he told them his story.

Three months earlier, on August 30, reliable witnesses in 22 towns in Georgia claimed they had seen strange craft in the sky. And on October 3, a deputy sheriff and four park rangers watched a saucer-shaped object 'the size of a two-bedroom house' manoeuvre over Tupelo, Mississippi, the birthplace of Elvis Presley. They described it as having red, green and yellow lights.

Dr J. Allen Hynek, who established a Centre for UFO Studies at Granston, Illinois, collected 1,474 authenticated reports of UFOs during that year. Major-General John Samford, a former director of intelligence at the Pentagon, admitted: 'Reports have come in from credible observers of relatively incredible things.'

And Senator Barry Goldwater, formerly a major-general in the US Air Force Reserve, said: 'I've never seen a UFO, but when air force pilots, navy pilots and airline pilots tell me they see something come up on their wing that wasn't a plane, I have to believe them.'

A Gallup Poll at the end of 1973 showed that 15 million Americans believed they had seen a UFO – and 51 per cent of the adult population believed that UFOs were 'real'.

Water diviners from space

Farmer Pat McGuire claims that 5,000 acres of his ranch near Laramie, Wyoming, were turned from dry sagebrush desert into fertile grassland because aliens on a UFO gave him a piece of good advice.

McGuire, his wife, eight children and a couple who live on his farm all say that unidentified flying objects of various shapes and sizes have hovered over their land almost every night for seven years.

'They are mostly about 300 feet wide and 60 feet high, and there seems no limit to how fast they can go,' McGuire told reporters. 'At first we were frightened by them, especially after we found mutilated cattle on the spread. One evening in 1976, my brother-in-law and I saw a craft hovering over a young calf. We heard the beast bawling for quite a while, then, when the UFO flew away, it took the calf with it.'

The visits continued, but the herds were left untouched. McGuire and his family gradually lost their fear. Then, one night, the aliens made contact with the farmer, and took him aboard their craft.

He recalled the event under hypnosis administered by Dr Leo Sprinkle, a para-psychologist with the University of Wyoming, and watched by an assistant psychiatrist.

In his trance, McGuire described the aliens as around six feet tall, with large eyes, thin lips and bald heads. They told him to drill a well in high plains country, near his ranch.

McGuire consulted geologists and drilling experts a few days later. They told him the land was 7,000 feet above sea level, and he had no hope of finding water there. But McGuire went ahead regardless, even though neighbours called him crazy. He bought the land, bored his way through the upper crust – and struck a massive underground stream just 350 feet down. Soon 8,000 gallons of pure soft water were gushing from the desert every minute.

In 1980, after studying McGuire's claims both while he was conscious and under hypnosis, Dr Sprinkle said: 'I believe the craft appearing over his farm could be goodwill ambassadors of an alien civilization. I believe people like Pat McGuire are being chosen to spread the word that they are among us. And I believe we will see full-scale contact over the next decade or so.'

The first flying saucer

Though unidentified flying objects have been reported above Earth for centuries, the first time they were described as flying saucers was on June 24, 1947. That was the day Kenneth Arnold, a fire-appliance salesman and an experienced pilot, took off from Chehalis Airport, Washington State, to help search for a C-46 Marine Transport plane that had crashed in the Cascade Mountains.

As he circled the area, looking for wreckage, a flash of light caught his eye. 'I observed, far to my left and to the north, a formation of nine very bright objects coming from the vicinity of Mount Baker, flying very close to the mountain tops and travelling with tremendous speed,' he said. 'I could see no tails on them, and they flew like no aircraft I had ever seen before ... like a saucer would if you skipped it across the water.' Next morning, a newspaper coined the expression 'flying saucer', and the Idaho businessman had his place in UFO history.

Visitors to the archery club

When two UFOs arrowed in on the Augusta Country Archery Club, Virginia, William Blackburn got the shock of his life.

Blackburn, who lived in nearby Waynesboro, was working alone at the club when he spotted two objects in the sky. He watched as the smaller of the two circled down to the ground, landing only 18 yards from where he was standing, open-mouthed with amazement.

Three extraordinary beings emerged from it, each three feet high, and wearing shiny suits the same colour as their craft. One had an extremely long finger, and all possessed piercing eyes which 'seemed to look through you'.

The aliens advanced a few paces towards Blackburn. Although he had a double-edged axe in his hands, he was frozen with fright, unable to move. 'They uttered some unintelligible sounds, then turned and went back to the ship, going in through a door which seemed to mould itself into the ship's shape,' Blackburn said. 'Then the ship flew up and disappeared.'

Blackburn told UFO investigators that he had reported the incident to a government agency – he refused to say which one – and had been interrogated, then warned not to mention what he had seen to anyone.

Not in the curriculum

UFOs hover over school grounds

Brenda Maria's encounter with a UFO was almost too close for comfort. It happened in the grounds of the local high school in Beverly, Massachusetts.

At 9 pm on Friday, April 22, 1966, her neighbour's daughter, 11-year-old Nancy Modugno, burst into the room where her father was watching television, claiming that an oval, football-shaped object, the size of a big car, had just flown past her bedroom window, flashing green, blue, white and red lights.

When Brenda and another neighbour, Barbara Smith, arrived, Nancy was almost hysterical. Lights could still be seen flashing from the direction of

A US coast-guard photographer at Salem, Massachusetts air station noticed from the station photo-laboratory several brilliant lights in the sky. He grabbed a camera and recorded this sighting.

the nearby school fields, but the two women, now joined by the girls' mother. Claire, suggested walking down there to put the child's mind at rest and prove that what she had seen was an aircraft.

On reaching the fields, however, they saw three brilliantly lit, oval, plate-like objects flying in circles around the sky. One hovered over the school building, the others were farther away. Suddenly, the nearest UFO began to move towards them. Claire and Barbara turned tail and ran, failing at first to realize that Brenda was not with them. Eventually, at the top of a rise, they turned to witness a terrifying sight. Brenda was screaming and covering her head with her hands, and the object was hovering only 20 feet above her.

'All I could see was a blurry atmosphere and bright lights flashing slowly round above my head,' she recalled later. 'I was very, very excited – not scared – very curious. But I was afraid it might crash on my head.'

When the UFO soared back towards the school, the three women raced back to their homes to alert neighbours, several of whom also saw the objects. One called the police. Two officers arrived in a patrol car, and drove into the school grounds while HQ alerted the Air Force.

At the sound of two approaching planes and a helicopter, the three UFOs flew away. The neighbours were certain, from the lights and engine noises of the investigating planes, that the objects they had seen were no ordinary aircraft. For they had been completely silent – even when hovering right above Brenda Maria's head.

Communicating by numbers

Gary Storey's flashlight conversation

U FO enthusiast Gary Storey claims he exchanged messages with an unidentified object that flew past his brother-in-law's house in Newton, New Hampshire early on Thursday, July 27, 1967.

Storey had set up a telescope to observe the Moon when a bright glow had attracted his attention. Changing lenses, he focussed on it, and saw a series of lights flashing in sequence along the side of what seemed to be a large disc.

On impulse, Storey's brother-in-law flashed a torch three times. The object suddenly went into reverse without turning round. Then it dimmed its lights three times in answer to the torch.

The two men, both former radar operators in the armed services, could not believe their eyes. They flashed again, four times, then five. Each time the number was repeated by the disc, which was moving back and forth.

Suddenly they heard a jet approaching. 'The object extingished all its lights until the jet passed,' Storey said. 'We thought it had left. Then it reappeared, an oval-shaped white object, at least ten times brighter than it had been before.'

The two-way flashlight conversation began again. The strange craft responded to one long and one short signal, repeating exactly the number and duration of every flashed message during nine or ten passes. Then it flashed all its lights once more, and vanished behind a line of trees.

Several scientists and UFO organizations investigated the claims of the two men, but none could find a conventional answer to the sighting. The local minister vouched for Storey's brother-in-law and his sister, saying both were God-fearing folk who would not lie or seek publicity. Their evidence was added to the dossier of sightings that suggest UFOs may be manned by intelligent beings keen to make contact with humans.

'Boomerang' swoops on factory

A friendly inspection from above

Workers on a repair gang at the Morenci copper-smelting plant in Arizona claim a massive spacecraft swooped on the factory in January 1981. It seemed to be examining one of the two 650-foot smokestacks by beaming a light ray down it.

The four men who were repairing the other stack said the UFO was shaped like a boomerang, and as big as four football fields. It had 12 small red lights on its surface, in addition to a large white searchlight beam underneath.

'It just sort of stopped in mid-air above the smokestack and shone the big light right into it,' said workman Randel Rogers, 20. His colleague Larry Mortensen added: 'I have never seen an airplane hover like that. I got the feeling that it wasn't aggressive. Certainly it did nothing to frighten us. Whoever was in it was friendly.'

A third member of the gang, Kent Davis, said that during examination of the stack, one of the red lights at the edge of the 'boomerang' suddenly darted away from the craft at fantastic speed, returning after a few moments. The whole object then turned, without warning, and shot off like a rocket.

The UFO was also seen by 100 members of a high school marching band holding a practice session on the football field of Morenci High School, just over a mile away. Director Bruce Smith said: 'I looked up and saw all these lights in the shape of a V. There was no sound. It hovered for a few minutes, then disappeared high into the sky.'

Alarm on the farm

A shiny silver saucer paid three visits to a farm at Cherry Creek, New York, on August 19, 1965. The four young farmhands who watched it turn clouds green and leave a red and yellow trail as it descended were not too perturbed, but the farm animals were clearly alarmed. A bull bent the iron bar to which he was tethered – and the milk yield of one cow slumped from two-and-a-half cans to just one.

Halos over the mission

The Papua sightings

Anglican priest Father William Melchior Gill finished dinner at his Boianai mission in Papua, New Guinea, and decided to take a stroll in the compound. He looked up to see Venus shining brightly. But what was that new light just above the planet?

As he stared upwards, he noticed more brilliantly-lit objects rising and falling through the increasing cloud cover, casting halos of light on the clouds in passing. Then he spotted something even more fascinating. Figures resembling humans emerged from one object and began moving about on it. There were two of them, then three, then four. They were doing something on the deck. Teachers, medical assistants and children came out to watch the strange activities several hundred feet above the ground. A total of 38 people spotted the figures over a three-hour spell before darkness fell.

Father Gill was a calm, painstaking and methodical man. He took careful notes of what had happened, and obtained signatures from 25 adult witnesses for his report. He dated it June 26, 1959.

The following night, the strange shapes returned. A native girl alerted Father Gill at 6.02, just as the sun was setting. There were still 15 minutes of good light left to observe four creatures moving around the deck of what seemed to be a 'mother ship', while two smaller UFOs hovered, one overhead, the other in the distance beyond some hills.

'Two of the figures seemed to be doing something,' Father Gill noted. 'They were occasionally bending over and raising their arms as though adjusting or setting up something.'

When one of the figures looked down, the priest stretched his arm to wave. He was astonished when it waved back. Another of the watchers waved both arms over his head. The two figures still on deck did likewise. Soon all four were on top of their craft, waving energetically.

One of the mission boys ran to collect a torch as darkness fell, and directed a series of Morse dashes towards the object. The figures could be seen waving back, 'making motions like a pendulum, in a sideways direction'. The UFO advanced for perhaps half a minute, and the group of witnesses – now about 12 strong – began shouting and beckoning for their visitors to land. There was no response. 'After a further two or three minutes, the figures apparently lost interest in us for they disappeared below deck,' Father Gill said later.

The UFO stayed hovering over the mission for at least an hour, but later in

A hoax in the House

There was laughter in the British House of Commons when a Conservative MP quizzed the Air Ministry over a 'flying saucer' which alarmed villagers in Lancashire in March, 1957. Mr J. A. Leavey, who represented Heywood and Royton, demanded to know whether the Minister knew about 'The Thing'.

Parliamentary Under-Secretary Charles Orr-Ewing rose from the Government Front Bench and turned towards the Speaker. 'This object did not emanate from outer space,' he assured the House, 'but from a laundry in Rochdale ...'

When the guffaws had died down, he added: 'It consisted of two small hydrogen balloons illuminated by a flashlight bulb and devised by a laundry mechanic.' The man responsible for starting the scare in Wardle, a village near Rochdale, was Neil Robinson, 35. He said later: 'I bought the balloons for fivepence each and sent them up as an experiment in tracing air currents. I never thought my little tests would be raised in Parliament.'

the evening visibility became poor as low cloud moved in. Then, at 10.40, a tremendous explosion woke those at Boianai who had gone to bed. They rushed outside, but could see nothing in the sky.

Father Gill reported what he had seen to the Australian Air Attaché, who later contacted the US Air Force. The priest admitted that at one stage he thought the shapes 'might just be a new device of the Americans'. But the air force had no craft that could hover close enough for men to be seen on it, or could hover in silence. They had their own explanation – the sighting, they said, was 'stars and planets'. But as astronomer Dr J. Allen Hynek wrote 15 years later after visiting the mission site, 'I have yet to observe stars or planets appearing to descend through clouds to a height of 2,000 feet, illuminating the clouds as they did so.'

Father Gill himself wrote to a friend: 'Last night we at Boianai experienced about four hours of UFO activity. There is no doubt whatever that they are handled by beings of some kind. At times it was absolutely breathtaking ...'

There were nearly 60 separate sightings of UFOs over Papua that June. Trader Ernie Evernett gave what was probably the most vivid description. He saw a greenish object with a trail of white flame. 'It hovered about 500 feet above me,' he reported. 'The light faded apart from four or five portholes below a band or ring round the middle of the craft, which were brightly illuminated. The object had the silhouette of a rugby ball.'

Panic in the jungle

'All generators stopped ...'

Battle-hardened American GIs in Vietnam grew used to the unexpected during the long years of jungle war. But on June 19, 1966, men at the 40,000-strong Nha Trang camp got the shock of their lives – and it came from the skies.

Hundreds of them were out of doors, watching movies on a newly-arrived projector, when suddenly a bright light appeared from nowhere. Sergeant Wayne Dalrymple described what happened next in a letter to his parents.

'At first we thought it was a flare, which are going off all the time, and then we found out that it wasn't. It was moving from real slow to real fast speeds. Some of the jet fighter pilots here said it looked to be about 25,000 feet up.

'Then the panic broke loose. It dropped right towards us and stopped dead still about 300 to 500 feet up. It made this little valley and the mountains around look like it was the middle of the day. It lit everything up.

'Then it went up – and I mean up. It went straight up and completely out of sight in two to three seconds. What really shook everyone was that it stopped, or maybe it didn't, but anyway our generator stopped and everything was black, and at the air base about half a mile from here all generators stopped and two planes that were ready to take off, their engines stopped.

'There wasn't a car, truck, plane or anything that ran for about four minutes. There are eight big bulldozers cutting roads over the mountain and they stopped and their lights went out, too. A whole plane load of big shots from Washington got here next afternoon to investigate.'

Dalrymple checked out all six of the affected diesel-powered and independently operated generators for faults, but found none. Later it was discovered that a Shell oil tanker anchored offshore had also lost power at around the same time, for no apparent reason.

Please, Sir ...

Twenty children aged six and seven dashed to the study of headmaster Michael Yates at Wawne Primary School, Humberside, and told him they had seen a strange object in the sky. The children had never heard of flying saucers, but they described a classic UFO – 'like a dish upside down and with a hump on the top.'

Captured on camera

Japanese photographers go into action

UFOs have been reported all over the Far East, and some have even been photographed. On October 10, 1975, Osamu Tsugaane snapped a picture of a golden shape that looked like a deep inverted pudding bowl over an air base at Hya Kuri. On March 7, 1973, Akiteru Takao spotted a silver globe over a suburb of Bangkok, Thailand, while on holiday there, and captured it with his camera. And on July 9 of the same year, police sergeant Yoshiyuki Matsuda took photographs of a traffic-accident scene on a corner in Nagai City – and revealed an oblong, egg-like glowing object in the sky which defied explanation by experts who studied it.

Hideichi Amano had no chance to take a picture of the frightening alien he met near Sayama City on October 3, 1978. Amano, a radio ham, had driven to a hilltop near the city to transmit messages without interference, leaving his two-year-old son asleep in the back seat. But when he returned to the vehicle, he found the boy bathed in an eerie light and foaming at the mouth.

He tried to start the car, but nothing happened. Then he felt a metallic object being pressed against his forehead, and looked round to see a creature with a round face, large pointed ears, big, round blue eyes and no neck. The object touching Amano's head was some kind of tube from the being's mouth.

For five minutes, strange space messages were passed telepathically through the tube into the man's mind; later he repeated them under hypnosis. Then the alien simply vanished, and everything Amano had switched on in his panic – car ignition, lights, radio – burst into life.

The UFO below was photographed over the Iki Isles, Japan.

The China syndrome

Sightings—ancient and modern

Chinese airmen and scientists have also spotted strange craft in the sky. Though the government imposes a news blackout on such incidents, reports of two sightings in recent years have reached the West.

In July 1977, astronomer Zhang Zhousheng and several colleagues at the Yunnan Observatory watched a glowing object pass overhead, from north to west. 'It was yellow at the core with a giant spiral extension,' Zhang was reported as saying. 'It was very bright even in the moonlight, and its colour was greenish-blue.'

Ten months later, Air Force pilot Zhou Quington and other pilots were watching films outside their barracks in north-west China when a huge glowing object crossed the sky.

'It passed over our heads at 21,000 feet and disappeared behind some houses,' Zhou said. 'It seemed to have two large searching lights at the front and a bright tail-light. The lengths of the columns of light kept changing, creating a misty haze around the object.'

Flight of the bubble bees

Three girl scouts from Malden, Massachusetts, saw a whole flight of UFOs in broad daylight on a camping holiday in August, 1965.

It happened as they were hurrying from their log cabin at East Derry, New Hampshire, to fetch water from a well after sighting storm clouds on the horizon. Dorothy Doone, 13, was the first to spot what she thought was an approaching group of low-flying aircraft, and pointed them out to her friend, Patricia Walton, 12, and her younger sister Shirley.

As they watched the 'jets' get closer, their fascination turned to fright. There were nine objects, but none of them had wings, propellors or insignia.

'They looked like big, black overgrown bubbles with silver tails,' the girls recalled. 'Before we could run they passed right over the field next to us. They sounded like a swarm of bees. Then a big spark jumped between the last three objects.'

Questioned first by their Scout leader – Dorothy's mother – and later by UFO investigators, the girls convincingly proved that they had not seen aircraft or helicopters.

Chinese history also records curious sightings. Shen Kua was a famous scientist and scholar who lived at Yangzhou, beside the Yangtze river, more than 900 years ago. He wrote of 'a big pearl' that rose from marshes near the town, and hovered over a nearby lake. It had a round double shell and several people had seen it open. Inside was a bright, silvery light, the size of a fist, which dazzled anyone who looked at it. 'All the trees around had their shadows cast to the ground,' the scientist wrote. 'The shell would leave suddenly, as though flying through the waves. It seemed to be surrounded by flame.'

A cure for paralysis

AFrench doctor claims a UFO light beam cured a paralysis that human specialists had been unable to treat. The doctor had been partly immobilized by a wound received in Algeria in 1958, and was also nursing a leg injured while gardening.

On November 2, 1968, he was wakened by the crying of his baby son, and hobbled to the kitchen to get him a drink of water. He saw lights flashing outside, and walked out on to the terrace to investigate. He saw two objects which merged into one before descending towards the house. A beam of light shone on him, then the UFO vanished as abruptly as the image on a television set that has just been turned off.

As he rushed to tell his wife what he had seen, he realized he was running – his wound, which had shown no improvement during months in hospital, had suddenly healed.

Death of the lavender plants

AFrench farmer said he was immobilized by two figures he disturbed beside a UFO in his lavender fields. It was July 1, 1965, when Monsieur M. Masse spotted a craft shaped like an egg and about the size of a car on his farm at Valensole, in the Basses Alpes region. As he approached stealthily through his vineyard, he saw two 'boys' bending over lavender plants, and stepped forward to reprimand them.

He looked into the startled faces of two creatures unlike any he had ever seen. Both of the small 'men' had a large head, long, slanting eyes, high puffy cheeks, a slit-like mouth and a long, jutting chin. One of the creatures pointed a stick at him, and he was unable to move. They watched him for a while, then floated up a beam of light into their craft. Its six legs turned, a central pivot began to throb, and the object floated upwards before vanishing.

It left a muddy hole in the bone-dry earth, and within days all the lavender plants close to the site had withered and died. New plants would not grow there for years.

Diplomatic incident

Portugal was plagued by a mysterious invasion of inexplicable flying objects during August and September, 1977. A senior British diplomat was one of many who reported sightings.

The alarms started when dozens of residents in the town of Viano do Castelo claimed they had seen a strange craft in the night sky. Then fishermen at the port of Portimao, familiar with the layout of stars, began to notice a curious intense light in a spot where no star usually shone. Finally, 12 firemen in the city of Guarda, returning from a call-out, reported a mysterious shining object circling in the sky.

In September, the British official for the Algarve region, Mr D. M. Armstrong, was alerted. An Englishwoman from the town of Alvor phoned to say that both she and her husband had heard a humming sound and seen an object hovering over their home.

The pro-consul fetched his binoculars and scanned the sky over Alvor, four miles away. He clearly saw an object flashing red, white and green lights, and estimated it was 25–30 degrees above the horizon.

In January, Mr Armstrong wrote to Lord Clancarty, a UFO enthusiast in London, who had tried to instigate an official investigation into flying objects.

He reported his initial contact with the UFO, and added: 'Subsequently I was able to see at least one – and sometimes four – every night until mid-November, when we had bad weather, and have had almost continual cloud cover since.

'On one occasion I was watching two over the sea. I could see both in my field of vision when one moved suddenly and rapidly higher in the sky. I followed it and was interested to see, a few minutes later, that the second one had followed it.

'The effect is always the same, a rapid red-green-white flashing around what would appear to be a circular base. I have seen nothing by day, only in the evening.'

The diplomat added: 'As you may imagine, I received derision from my acquaintances, but when people came to dinner I would mention the fact and then take them into the garden with my glasses. Everyone had to admit there was "something unusual" there. The derision ceased at once.'

The Portuguese Embassy in London was unable to throw any light on the sightings. But it then admitted to an 'incident' involving a Portuguese airliner. The pilot had radioed that he was being buzzed by a circling object that was nothing like any aircraft he had ever seen.

A UFO photographed at 4,000 feet by Shinichi Takeda of Fujisaw, Japan.

'Cigar' over the Seine

Unidentified Flying Objects of different sizes operating together were reported from the small French town of Vernon in the early hours of August 23, 1954. Businessman Bernard Miserey had just parked his car in his garage at 1 am when he spotted a huge, long, silent, luminous cigar-shaped object suspended over the river Seine, 300 yards from where he stood. It cast an eerie glow over the dark houses of the town.

M. Miserey watched for several minutes. 'Suddenly from the bottom of the cigar came an object like a horizontal disc,' he recalled. 'It dropped in free fall, then slowed, swayed, and dived horizontally across the river towards me, becoming much brighter, surrounded by a halo. A few minutes after it disappeared behind me, going southwest at a prodigious speed, a similar object came from the cigar and went through the same manoeuvres.'

Five discs in all fell from the cigar, and shot off in different directions. After the last emerged, the cigar faded into darkness. M. Miserey went next morning to tell the police what he had seen – and was informed that two policemen and an army engineer had seen exactly the same thing, at the same time.

Out among the berries

Two Norwegian sisters told police they spoke to a man from a flying saucer in August 1954. The women, aged 32 and 24, said they were picking berries in the hills near Mosjöen, in central Norway, when a dark, long-haired man in a buttonless khaki outfit motioned them into a hollow. In it they saw a saucer-shaped craft about 16 feet wide.

The man tried to communicate with words, gestures and drawings. But the sisters could not understand him, and he showed no signs of comprehension when they spoke to him in French, German and English.

Finally the stranger climbed back into the saucer, which rose fast into the air with a humming sound, like a swarm of bees.

Army manoeuvres

Two British soldiers say they saw a UFO while on exercises with the Royal Armoured Corps in 1978. Mike Perrin and Titch Carvell were driving their Land-Rover on the Yorkshire moors when they saw a dome-shaped silvery object hovering 50 yards away, making a strange buzzing sound.

'It was about the size of five Land-Rovers and had portholes,' said Perrin, 27. 'Lights inside were flashing red and white. I tried to start our vehicle, but the engine was totally dead. We watched the UFO for five minutes, then it shot off and all the power returned to our engine.'

He added: 'It's army policy to dismiss UFO reports, but when we went back to the area next morning with a sergeant, we found a large circle of burnt grass where the object had hovered.'

'Draw what you saw ...'

When netball teacher Bronwen Williams spotted a strange object in the sky during a game she was supervising in February 1977, she knew exactly what to do. She ushered her nine pupils inside Rhos-y-Bol county primary school at Anglesey, gave them pencils and paper, and told them to draw, without conferring, what they had seen. The pictures tallied remarkably – a cigar-shape with a black dome.

That same night policeman's wife Hilda Owen was looking out of her kitchen window when she too noticed a shape gliding silently in and out of the clouds. She drew it in lipstick on the window glass, and her husband made a copy on paper when he returned from duty. It might have been drawn by one of the schoolgirls.

Mrs Owen said the UFO appeared from a 'tongue of flame' over Aberffraw Common. 'At first I thought an aircraft was on fire, but within seconds the flame appeared to form a circle and a domed figure appeared,' she said. 'There was no mistaking the shape. I could see portholes quite clearly.'

The shape was still in the sky when her husband arrived home just after midnight. 'It was the colour of the setting sun and about twice the size of the sun as we see it,' he said. 'By the time I got my binoculars out, it had vanished.'

This UFO was photographed over Lago Maggiore near the little town of Arona,
Italy at 10.30 pm on March 3, 1979. The event was witnessed by many and the

photograph was published in local newspapers.

The hole in the hedge

'I was cold and terrified ...'

Nine-year-old Gaynor Sunderland dashed home breathless and too scared to speak one day in July 1976. Her mother Marion calmed and comforted her, then listened to her description of what was later described as 'probably the best UFO encounter ever documented in Britain'.

Gaynor had seen a strange, silver, saucer-shaped object land in a field a mile from her home in Oakenholt, near Flint, North Wales. She lay quietly, terrified but fascinated, peering through a gap in a hedge. Two silver-suited people emerged from the craft and probed the ground with equipment. They were short and angular with large pink eyes, and seemed to be a man and a woman.

The craft they came from was around 35 feet long and nine feet high. It had a band of yellow windows along the side, and a flashing box on the top. There was a loud humming noise when it took off again after about half-an-hour.

Gaynor told her mum: 'I was cold and terrified – I was sure both of them had seen me.' But for 18 months, her story remained a family affair. Mrs Sunderland explained: 'Gaynor was frightened of ridicule.' At last the child plucked up the courage to tell others. She was twice questioned under hypnosis, and produced drawings of what she had seen.

UFO watcher Jenny Randles, of *Flying Saucer Review*, said: 'Gaynor's description is among the most detailed ever recorded.'

The clicking 'dolls'

Three women in northern England claim to have seen white, doll-like aliens emerge from UFOs. All reported their experience to researchers, but insisted on remaining anonymous.

The first encounter came in September 1976. Two women, aged 63 and 18, were walking near their homes at Fencehouses, Tyne and Wear, when they saw a small, oval object, and found themselves hypnotically attracted by it. As they approached, two beings, 'the size of large dolls', appeared. They had large round eyes and white hair. They seemed startled, and retreated quickly.

Exactly three years later, a 23-year-old woman was in her bedroom at Felling, Tyne and Wear, at 4 am when a glowing, glittering bell-like disc actually entered the room. 'There was a buzzing noise everywhere and I felt paralyzed,' the woman told investigators. 'Then 12 white creatures appeared, small, like dolls. They were making clicking noises and seemed to be watching me. One even touched me. Then they disappeared.'

UFO researcher and author Jenny Randles said: 'I am convinced the women are telling the truth about genuine experiences. In one way the reluctance of the witnesses to get involved lends credence to their stories. At least we know they are not after cheap publicity.'

At nearby Killingworth, a 21-year-old nurse who would agree only to be identified as Linda, reported a UFO flying between two houses in February 1978. There was a deafening build-up of sound, and her mother hid under the bedclothes, convinced a plane was about to crash. But Linda looked out of the window, and saw, only feet away, a silvery object with a string of coloured lights. She said it looked 'like a tin containing expensive cigars'.

Weird happenings in the South West

A courting couple, a builder's wife and a deck-chair attendant all saw something strange in the sky on the night of Saturday, May 21, 1977. All the sightings were near Poole, Dorset.

Pretty 18-year-old tax officer Karen Iveson and her boyfriend, apprentice technician Cliff Rowe, 19, had just parked their car on a lonely road near Parley Cross when a beam of light struck the back of it.

'We couldn't see what was causing it, but it scared us a little, so we decided to move on,' said Cliff. Back on the road, they saw what had disturbed them.

Karen said: 'A large, silvery disc-shaped object hovered over a field, and a silver-green, cone-like beam of light shone down from the centre of it. We stopped to watch, and it seemed to stay there for ages. Then it suddenly veered off fast and dropped behind some trees, much lower than any plane could go. We both panicked afterwards. It was not like anything I'd ever seen before.'

Builder's wife Pauline Fall, 31, saw the same thing only miles away as she drove down a dark country lane near the village of Longham. A beam of light fell across the car bonnet four or five times, 'as if something was tracking us', but at first Pauline could not see where it came from.

'One minute there was nothing in the sky, the next there it was, looking like the underside of a big dinner plate,' she recalled. 'Out of the centre came a silvery white light, narrow at the top and widening into a cone. It was solid light, as if a line had been drawn round it.

'I'm not normally one to panic, but the pit of my stomach went ice-cold. A friend with me was unnerved, too.'

Pauline kept driving for home, even though the beam seemed to be getting shorter as the object descended. 'Then it just disappeared as if it had been swallowed up by the ground.'

When Pauline got home to Wimborne, husband John thought from the look of terror on her face that she must have had an accident. Her hands were as cold as ice, and it was an hour before warmth began to creep back into them.

Odd things happened to Pauline's car after that night. Petrol consumption shot up, and the engine, perfectly all right when John was at the wheel, inexplicably cut out when Pauline was driving. She refused to take it out alone at night for four months.

'I've done a lot of soul-searching, but I haven't found a logical explanation for what I saw,' Pauline said. 'I just wish someone could tell me what it was, where it came from, and what it wants from us.'

The third person to see the craft was deck-chair attendant Richard Morse, 27, who spotted a flickering light behind clouds as he hurried to a bus in Poole. 'I thought it was the Moon, then I saw the Moon in another part of the sky.

'Just looking at it made me feel weird. It was a flying saucer shape with another shape on top and a beam of white light from its centre to the ground. Time seemed to stand still as I watched, then the thing started to move off, banking very fast, before it disappeared. It wasn't like anything from this planet ... I was really glad to hear others had had similar experiences that night, because my friends were starting to think I was mad!'

Along the coast at Parkstone, Dorset, Mrs Ethel Field had a strange encounter in March, 1978, when she left her husband and daughter watching television to bring in washing from her back garden.

'Suddenly I saw this object in the distance, rising from the sea,' she said. 'It ascended and came closer. It was circular with a dome on the top. Beneath it were several lights, shielded by hoods that looked like eyelids. When the lids slid back, there were spotlights lighting the ground.

'I was frightened and stunned. It hovered directly above me. The lights were so strong that I put my hands up to screen my eyes.

'Then I saw two figures standing in front of an oblong window. They had longish faces and were wearing silver suits and what looked like skull caps. They seemed to be standing at some controls.

STRANGE OBJECTS HAVE BEEN SIGHTED IN THE SHEFFIELD SKIES

- The Air Ministry cannot explain them

- This picture has been analysed by experts. It is genuine, they say

- **WE SAY:** How much longer dare we pooh-pooh stories such as these?

These UFOs were sighted and photographed over Conisbrough, South Yorkshire, England on March 28, 1966.

'I felt that some power was holding me where I stood. I waited, shielding my eyes. Then one of the figures turned away from me to look at his companion. The minute he did that, I felt a release and ran petrified to call my husband and daughter. They laughed at me and wouldn't leave the TV.'

Mrs Field spent several sleepless nights worrying about what she had seen. Then red blotches appeared on the hands that the light had hit. Soon her hands were raw, with skin flaking and scaling all over them. 'I went to several doctors about it, but only one listened seriously to what I told him,' she said.

A Scottish saucer

Two ten-year-old girls at Elgin, north-east Scotland, described 'a silver-coloured saucer with a bump on the top' which they had seen hovering in a wood. The craft glowed with a red light and a silver-suited man stood beside it. Mrs Caroline McLennan, mother of one of the girls, said: 'When my daughter told me about it, I remembered having heard a strange whirring noise and saying to my neighbour, "Sounds like a flying saucer." The girls led us back to the wood and we found a big patch of flattened grass. The leaves on the trees nearby were scorched.'

Backwards in time

Salesman Alan Cave, 45, of Taunton, Somerset, remembers the precise moment he became a 'time traveller'. As he was driving, one October morning in 1981, from Bath to Stroud, his car passed directly beneath a strange, orange, cloud-like object in the sky.

'I know it was exactly 11 o'clock,' said Alan, 'because a newsreader announced the headlines on the car radio. But then I glanced at my watch and it said 8 o'clock. My digital pen said 9. Both were right when I set out.

'Then the speedo started going back – it was weird. It lost 300 miles, though a mechanic has since told me it was impossible.'

Alan doesn't believe in flying saucers, 'but something very odd occurred in those few seconds and I wouldn't like it to happen again.'

The British Flying Saucer Research Bureau later said they investigated several reports of a UFO in the same area. They added that checks on aircraft movements had not provided an explanation.

Scary New Year

Weird sightings were reported throughout Britain on New Year's Eve, 1978. Schoolboy Andrew McDonald, 13, claimed he was buzzed by a UFO as he rode his bike home through Runcorn, Cheshire.

'I heard a hum like a high-pitched engine' said Andrew. 'I looked up and there was a big white light with a very bright trail above me. It stayed with me for about ten seconds, then soared up into the sky. I could feel it trying to lift me off the ground.' Andrew was so unnerved that he could not cycle any farther.

In London, night club waitress Patricia White saw a blazing white shape as a taxi drove her home through Wembley. 'It shone like a big, bright star, but it was following the cab,' said Mrs White, 34, of Harrow. 'I was petrified, and so was the cab-driver.'

Scared witnesses also reported seeing unexpected lights and shapes above Newcastle upon Tyne, Sheffield, Manchester, Norwich, and places in Scotland. But the Ministry of Defence said: 'We are not being invaded. We think it is just some space debris burning up.'

Marooned on the moors

A Good turn proved a nightmare for Lillian Middleton. She drove out onto the lonely Northumberland moors to rescue a friend who was stranded – and ended up being chased for miles by a terrifying UFO.

The ordeal began at 2.30 am on August 21, 1980, when the bedside phone rang at Mrs Middleton's home in Seaton Delaval, Whitley Bay. The 33-year-old woman agreed to drive out to her friend, whose car had run out of petrol. But as she reached the moors, she saw a bright flash of light.

'I thought a plane had caught fire or exploded in mid-air,' she said later. 'I slowed down and peered out of the window. I was shocked to see a huge rugby ball shape giving off a brilliant light and hovering in the sky. It suddenly zoomed down towards me. I was terrified.

'It seemed about the size of two big cars. I put my foot down and was soon doing 70 mph in an effort to get away, but the thing kept with me, hovering just above the roof. It moved to the side from time to time, as if it was trying to see who was inside. After what seemed an eternity, I saw my friend beside his car. He too had seen the shape.'

The UFO followed them all the way to the petrol station, a few miles away. A taxi driver and a couple in another car had also watched it approaching. Armed with a can of petrol, Mrs Middleton set out again for the stranded car.

'This time the UFO zoomed right down low to car rooftop height,' she recalled. 'My friend became as scared as I was, and we turned round and went back to the service station. I wasn't going down that lonely road again. I cried with relief that someone else had seen what had happened. The other couple were still at the garage, and we all watched the thing for some time until it suddenly shot off at speed and disappeared.'

Mrs Middleton rang the police, who were sympathetic. Indeed, their own chief inspector had also reported seeing the UFO. But the experience left its mark. 'I was in a state of shock for several weeks,' Mrs Middleton said. 'Now I won't go out driving after dark, and for a long while I couldn't bring myself to look into the night sky.'

Aliens over Russia

For years, the Kremlin authorities mirrored the attitude of air chiefs in America – UFOs did not exist. Sightings were dismissed as cloud formations, planets and the like, or fobbed off with some other logical explanation; and people who reported strange craft were considered idiots who also believed in goblins and fairies.

But in the late 1970s, *Pravda* began publishing accounts of mysterious visitors all over the country. And they were every bit as astonishing as those reported in the West.

Dr V. G. Paltsev, a veterinary surgeon, was making his country rounds, 500 miles from Moscow, when he came across a grounded craft. Three small humanoids with egg-shaped heads and long fingers were standing beside it, but as he approached them, he was knocked out by a strange force.

He came round to find his watch had stopped. Above him, a glowing saucer shape was disappearing. Dr Paltsev went home, and carried on working as if nothing had happened. But at night, he repeatedly dreamed that he had been carried onto the craft while unconscious.

A doctor interrogated him under hypnosis – and decided that the vet probably had been taken for a ride on the saucer.

Dr A. I. Nikolaev, a respected historical sciences professor, spent three months in hospital recovering from his close encounter. He and three academic colleagues were on a camping holiday in southern Russia when they came across a metallic, saucer-shaped craft partly hidden in long grass. One of them threw some stones, which seemed to disappear inside the object.

All four men then felt a strange force. Dr Nikolaev was knocked out. The others, though drowsy, dragged him away. Two stayed with him while the third went for help: but both sentries soon fell asleep.

When they woke, two three-foot figures in space suits and helmets were staring at them. At the first signs of life, the small humanoids scurried back to their craft, vanishing from sight through the hull. The object glowed, then disappeared.

Professor F. Zigel, who led the official team of investigators into the case, said: 'There is no doubt that a spaceship landed – possibly because of illness among the crew.'

Only days later, three other scientists saw an alien craft just 67 miles from Moscow. They too were camping, and that night in their tents they heard a babble of loud voices. None of them recognized the language, but all felt a sense of unaccountable fear.

It was half-an-hour before they dared look outside – and there stood a shining violet-coloured object, about 80 feet high, looking 'something like a giant electric light bulb'. It rose, swayed slightly, then soared upwards into a fluorescent cloud.

Next morning, the campers found a circle of flattened grass 500 feet from their tents ... and called in the investigators.

The Russians showed unexpected interest in an English UFO sighting. Hope and Ruby Alexander spotted a bright, triangular light hovering over Hayes Road, Bromley, Kent, as they drove home one evening in 1978 after a concert. Their sighting was reported in the local newspaper, which noted that there seemed no explanation for it. The two women preferred to let the subject drop.

But two years later, the paper received a postcard from the Soviet science city of Novosibirsk. Someone signing himself V. I. Sanarov asked for a copy of the article, and any further information available. Hope said: 'We were astonished at the interest after all this time.'

Charles Bowen, editor of the British magazine *Flying Saucer Review*, said: 'Soviet scientists have a great interest in UFOs. For several years the Soviet Academy of Science has been ordering three copies of every issue of the *Review*, and last year I had half a dozen letters from people in the Soviet Union asking for information on the subject.'

The Bermuda riddle

The US Navy supplyship *Cyclops* vanished with 309 on board on March 4, 1918. The speed of its disappearance is witnessed by the fact that the ship's officers had no time to wireless a distress signal.

Dozens of ships have disappeared in the Bermuda Triangle since the US Navy craft *Cyclops* sank with 300 men in 1918. Aircraft, too, have vanished without trace, including five Avenger bombers from Fort Lauderdale that reported having lost their bearings on a routine flight in 1945, and were never seen again. But in 1978 it was a mystery arrival which baffled the experts who keep watch on the area of sea between Florida, Puerto Rico and Bermuda.

Radar crews at the Pinecastle Electronic Warfare Range near Astor, Florida, suddenly found a zig-zagging shape on their screens at a time when no military or civilian planes were expected. And it quickly became clear that this was no ordinary plane. The object was moving in a very erratic way, changing direction at incredible speed, suddenly stopping, then accelerating, within seconds, to 500 mph. Officers scanned the skyline with binoculars, and saw a circular craft emitting curious red, green and white lights. Nobody knew what it could be.

'It manoeuvred in such a way and at such speeds that it could not have been an airplane or helicopter,' said one technician. 'I've never seen anything like it – and I don't want to see anything like it again.'

At 5.30 am on September 27, 1979, two children on the island of Bermuda claimed they were immobilized by strange noises from a UFO. Laquita Dyer,

13, and her brother Melvin, 11, were sleeping in separate rooms when both heard a loud, rasping, buzzing sound coming from above their roof.

'When I tried to get up, I couldn't move at all, I was paralyzed,' said Melvin. His sister said: 'I tried to get to the window, but couldn't.' After about ten minutes, the noise switched to a softer tone, then stopped. Only when it died away could the children move their limbs again.

The children's ordeal came only hours after many other people reported a UFO streaking across the sky to the south of the island. Jeffry Schutz, a consultant with the US Department of Energy, was one of them. He was with his mother and sister on the patio of his home. 'At about 9.45 pm we saw an object travelling from west to east, climbing at an angle of 45 degrees,' he said. His sister Betsy, 23, said: 'It was a yellowish, whitish ball, faster than a satellite but slower than a shooting star. It was climbing in a clear sky, with a white vapour trail. We watched it for 20 seconds, then it vanished with a greenish glow.'

English teacher Nigel Kermode and his wife Julie also saw the UFO from their porch. He said: 'It was much too bright and big to be an airplane.' She said: 'It seemed to lose momentum and then speed up again. Then it just disappeared.'

Local tracking stations had no explanation for the sightings.

The green-suited Superman

Astrange flying humanoid dropped in on a family in Puerto Rico on July 12, 1977, according to a man who lived in the town of Quebradillas. He said he and his daughter were at home that day when a small figure ducked under their fence and approached the house. He presumed it was a child, and asked his daughter to switch on the lights.

This seemed to alarm the visitor, who immediately doubled back. The couple saw that he was about $3\frac{1}{2}$ feet tall, in a green suit with padded feet, and a green helmet with a transparent face-plate. Affixed to this was an antenna, and on his back was a box, attached to his belt. The figure also had a tail.

To the amazement of the watchers, the alien ducked under the fence again, pressed the front of his belt, and took off, zooming Superman-fashion, towards some flashing lights in the distance.

Mr Jimmy Carter

Grenada's Mr Eric Gairy

Actress Elke Sommer

Boxer Muhammad Ali

Celebrity sightings

One film star who has seen a UFO is German-born actress Elke
Sommer, who in 1978 was in the garden of her Los Angeles home
when a shiny orange ball, about 20 feet in diameter, appeared out
of the blue. 'It was glowing and floating about like a big moon,' she
said. 'It came towards me and I fled into the house. When I
reappeared, it had vanished.'

Boxer Muhammad Ali was on a training session in New York's
Central Park in 1972 when he encountered a UFO. He said: 'I was
out jogging just before sunrise when this bright light hovered over
me. It just seemed to be watching me. It was like a huge electric
light bulb in the sky.'

Statesmen and politicians who have seen UFOs include John
Gilligan, Governor of Ohio, who in 1973 reported seeing a UFO
near Ann Arbor, Michigan. He described it as 'a vertical shaft of
light which glowed amber'.

Sir Eric Gairey, Prime Minister of the Caribbean island of
Grenada, tried unsuccessfully in 1978 to have the United Nations
officially investigate UFOs. He said he himself had seen one – 'a
brilliant golden light travelling at tremendous speed'.

But the most famous UFO spotter of all is Jimmy Carter who,
while still Governor of Georgia, in 1973, was sitting out on a
verandah with 20 other people after an official dinner at
Thomastown when, in his words, they witnessed a UFO 'which
looked as big as the Moon and changed colour several times from
red to green'. He launched a $20 million study into UFOs after
becoming US President.

UFOs Down Under

Something strange was happening in the skies above Australia and New Zealand at the end of 1978. During one ten-day period, six pilots separately reported curious objects flying alongside their planes. Radar stations recorded inexplicable bleeps on their screens. Wellington air traffic controllers watched for three hours as objects darted erratically around at remarkable speeds. Above Cook Strait, ten shapes blipped across the screen, 'radically different in behaviour from normal aircraft'. Then, at midnight on December 30, a television crew aimed their camera at a blazing light approaching a plane. And experts who analyzed their amazing pictures said: 'It may be a spaceship.'

The TV crew were from Channel O in Melbourne, Australia. Anxious to check out the spate of strange sightings, they boarded an Argosy turbo-jet used to make newspaper deliveries between Wellington, Christchurch and Blenheim, New Zealand. Captain Bill Startup, an airline pilot for 23 years, had seen gleaming oval objects over the Cook Strait during his regular run a few days earlier. Now, as he flew over the same area with the TV team, they were there again. Reporter Quentin Fogarty, 32, said: 'We saw a blazing white fireball about 50 miles ahead. It was brilliantly lit at the bottom and seemed to have orange rings round it.' Cameraman David Crockett began shooting film as his wife Ngaire switched on the sound equipment. As the plane got closer, Crockett became convinced that the shape in his sights was not a natural one. Then he noticed smaller objects around it. They were moving in 'intelligent' fashion. They seemed 'in control of the situation, not of this world'.

Captain Startup said: 'One object resembed a large ball of light. No aircraft would have the kind of acceleration that this thing did. It came within 18 miles of us and we decided to go in closer. It went above us and then below, and shot away at tremendous speed.' Co-pilot Bob Guard added: 'We watched the objects for almost 20 minutes. It was almost like watching strobe lights.'

Next morning, the TV team examined the evidence. Leonard Lee, a 32-year-old documentary film producer and a senior member of the Channel 0 news staff, said: 'The film sent a shiver down my spine. Every time I looked at it, my whole body tingled. We realised we had obtained something absolutely phenomenal, but we decided to make no claims about it other than what our film crew had seen.'

The film was sold to countries all round the world, and screened on news bulletins. Interest in it was astonishing. For the first time, professional cameramen had captured evidence of what seemed to be a mechanical craft from somewhere other than Earth.

But there were plenty of doubters, even in Melbourne. Professor Ronald Brown, head of the city's Monash University chemistry department, said: 'All my training as a scientist tells me the spacecraft theory is extremely unlikely. Looking at the film, I think it is quite feasible that an unusual shower of meteors could have had a similar appearance.' The professor, one of the world's leading galacto-chemistry specialists, added: 'It is possible that life forms exist elsewhere in the universe, but I do not believe other creatures would be able to shift a solid object such as a spacecraft at such enormous speed. An incredible amount of energy would be required to propel such a craft, and science already knows that the universe contains only a limited amount.'

But TV man Lee brushed aside such sceptics. 'It seems a natural reaction from certain people,' he said. 'They dismiss something simply because they cannot explain it.' He decided to take the film to America for appraisal by UFO experts.

Navy physicist Dr Bruce Maccabee, also a senior official with the National Investigatons Committee on Aerial Phenomena agreed to study the film frame by frame. Lee arrived in America in January 1979 with his evidence in a suitcase, sealed with a secret combination, and handcuffed to his right wrist. 'The very existence of this film makes it extremely important,' Dr Maccabee explained. 'It has a whole lot of organisations jumping, wanting to get a look at it. So much of our work ends up in shooting down turkeys. This is one turkey that deserves the closest possible research.'

Pot shots

For six years defence chiefs were baffled by the UFOs that periodically rained down on the Arizona plains. They showed up on radar at a Colorado tracking station, but when the apparent landing sites were checked, there was no sign of them.

Then, in July 1979, federal narcotics agents were told by an informer that Mexican drug smugglers were using home-made rockets to shoot marijuana across the border into America. When dates were checked, at least one drug consignment coincided with the UFO sightings.

Major Jerry Hix said at the tracking station: 'It wasn't strong enough to spark off a nuclear alert, but it did have us a bit puzzled.' A narcotics agent said: 'It sure as hells adds a new meaning to the old saying about taking pot shots ...'

Lord Dowding's admission

The Royal Air Force's late Air Chief Marshal, Lord Dowding, was a staunch believer in UFOs. As early as 1954, he said: 'I have never seen a flying saucer, yet I believe they exist. Cumulative evidence has been assembled in such quantity that, for me at any rate, it brings complete conviction.

'There is no alternative to accepting the theory that they come from an extra-terrestrial source. For the first time in recorded history, intelligible communication may become possible between the Earth and other planets.'

Although Dowding admitted never having seen a flying saucer, he would have received numerous reports of UFO sightings by the fliers under his command during World War Two.

He spent weeks poring over the film, examining some frames with digital computer enhancement processes. He saw a perfectly-formed glowing triangle, which he estimated to be the size of a house. Another frame showed an oval with a slight dome protruding. A third section of the film captured a circular object travelling at immense speed. Dr Maccabee said: 'The computer study unarguably shows that the images could not have come from stars or planets, or from the ground or sea surface.'

The physicist also flew secretly to New Zealand to interview the eye-witnesses. 'I didn't want anyone to know about the project,' he explained. 'It had been given a lot of publicity earlier in the year, and I wanted to do my inquiries with a minimum of fuss.' He taped statements from Captain Startup and his co-pilot, from cameraman Crockett and his wife, and from reporter Fogarty, who had been admitted to hospital after being emotionally drained by the entire episode.

Dr Maccabee also listened to tapes of conversations between Captain Startup and air traffic controllers, who had spotted inexplicable objects on their radar screens on the evening in question. 'All the witnesses agreed to submit to lie detector tests if their veracity was questioned,' he said.

Finally, the Navy expert concluded that the film and the interviews were a significant advance in UFO research. Stanton Friedman, a nuclear physicist and another of America's foremost aerial phenomena experts, added: 'We are definitely dealing with a genuine unidentified flying object. What makes this sighting so important is not just the film, but the wealth of additional evidence. Few reported sightings have ever had so much attention focussed on them, and the quality and quantity of the research has been impressive.'

The Channel O film was not the only pictorial evidence of UFOs during the spate of sightings early in 1979. A New Zealand camera team took to the air, and filmed 'an illuminated ping-pong ball, rotating, pulsating and darting around' over South Island. And private detective José Duran filmed what he described as 'a man from outer space' from the garden of his home near Adelaide, Australia.

UFO experts who examined Duran's cine-pictures agreed that they seemed to show a 'human embryo-like' object disembarking from a flying saucer and hovering between two 'spacecraft'. Duran said he first saw a red and amber light, moving slowly from the north-west towards the south-east.

'I watched through binoculars for a little while, then the light seemed to approach me,' he added. 'I filmed it from the garden. There was a strange kind of flashing, and although it was travelling very slowly with no sound, I thought at first it might be a plane.

'To my surprise, when I developed the film, I saw something I hadn't actually noticed when I was taking it. There was a white object travelling from an angle. It stopped for a couple of seconds above what I thought was a plane. It made a jerking movement above the flashing light, then moved off in a different direction. The whole movement on film looks like a large V-sign. Moving between the spacecraft was a humanoid, flesh-coloured at one end, but the rest of its body covered in a blue shroud. Microscopic examination of the film has shown two more humanoids in and around the spacecraft.'

Experts from Contact Internatonal, the British UFO research body, spent months analysing the film, and decided that the balls of light were probably alien craft. Research officer Derek Mansell said: 'The lights cannot be those of aircraft, and space agencies have confirmed that there was no debris entering the Earth's atmosphere at that time and place.'

More sightings in 1979

UFO sightings in early 1979 were not confined to Australasia. From Israel came reports of a rash of red balls and flashing lights. In northern Italy, dozens of villages on the slopes of the Gran Sasso mountains were plunged into darkness after a UFO was seen hovering over a hydro-electric plant. Technicians said their equipment suddenly went haywire.

In America, TV reporter Jim Voutrot was amazed when he read about the New Zealand pictures. For he too had captured UFOs on film, at around the same time. And his shots were remarkably similar.

It happened as Voutrot cruised near Pease Air Force Base, a Strategic Air Command bomber post in New Hampshire, with Betty Hill, the woman who claimed she was abducted by aliens in 1961. 'She was telling local meetings on her lecture circuit that UFOs were being sighted over the air base,' Voutrot explained. 'Several reporters did stories with Betty, but I'm a sceptic, and wanted to do one when I was sure there was no chance of being set up.

'So I called Betty one day and we were out looking about five minutes later. Suddenly we saw a big, round white object in the sky. I was surprised and bolted out of the car to start filming. Then, all of a sudden, it was gone. I haven't the faintest idea what it was – quite honestly, I've never seen anything like it, before or since. But I know it wasn't the Moon or Venus, it wasn't aircraft landing lights, and it wasn't a balloon.'

Mrs Hill said: 'We were driving up a hill, just a hop and a skip from Pease, when Jim yelled, "There's one." He was out of the car before I could stop it, and was filming.' When the 15-second film was magnified and examined, investigators discovered an undetected second object in the sky, with a tail of light behind it, like a comet. Further magnification disclosed yet more similar tailed lights, just as on the New Zealand film. And the fast, erratic movements of the larger light defied explanation.

Voutrot checked with sources at the Pease base, and found that nothing had been reported, visually or from radar watches. Tower staff told him their air space often played host to unidentified pieces of 'junk'. Air Force spokesmen were also unable to help. But CIA documents have revealed unexplained objects sighted over air bases in Maine, Montana and Michigan in the past.

The most incredible report of a sighting from that period came from South Africa. In January 1979 Mrs Meagan Quezet, a former nurse, said a pink unidentified object landed near her home in Krugersdorp, west of Johannesburg – and a squad of dark-skinned little men emerged from it.

Mrs Quezet said she saw them just after midnight, as she took her son André, 12, for a walk because he could not get to sleep. 'As we walked down the road, we both saw a pink light come over the rise,' she said. 'Suddenly we came across this thing standing in the road about 20 yards away. In front of it were five or six small beings. These people were dark-skinned, as far as I could tell. One of the men had a beard and seemed to be the leader.

'I said hello to one of them, but I couldn't understand what he was saying. I told André to run off and bring his father, and as he did so the creatures jumped about 5 feet into the air and vanished through a door into their craft. The door slid closed and the long, steel-type legs began to stretch out. Then it disappeared into the sky with a humming noise.'

Both Mrs Quezet and her son said the craft had bright pink lights on either side of the door. The humanoids appeared to be wearing white or light pink suits and white helmets.

Many scientists and astronomers around the world poured scorn on this flurry of UFO sightings. They dismissed them as an unusual concentration of meteors, or space debris burning up on entering the Earth's atmosphere. Sir Bernard Lovell, director of Britain's Jodrell Bank radio astronomy station, said the reports were 'pure science fiction'. But, as we shall see, the facts about UFOs were often even stranger than fiction.

Clear for landing

The town of Arès, in the French Bordeaux region, has made UFOs an offer it hopes they will not refuse – a safe spot to land. Engineer Robert Cotton, who works at Bordeaux Airport, came up with the idea for the Ovniport. He believed UFO pilots were reluctant to land because ordinary airports get too crowded. He persuaded officials at Arès to set aside land on the town borders for a landing strip. 'We have installed a number of landing lights and markings so we believe it can easily be spotted by UFO pilots,' said the mayor of Arès, Christian Raymond. So far, none have arrived to to entertain the tourists who regularly turn up to watch and hope.

The Warminster visitations

The Thing that terrorised the Salisbury Plain

Warminster was for centuries just a quiet, unremarkable country town on the edge of Salisbury Plain. Little happened to disturb the day-to-day routine of its 14,000 inhabitants. Then, early on Christmas Day, 1964, a strange drone jolted postmaster Roger Rump from his sleep at his home in Hillwood Lane. He heard a violent rattle, like tiles being ripped off his roof. The Thing had arrived.

Two weeks later, his neighbours, Mr and Mrs Bill Marson, were woken three times in one night by the sound of 'coal being tipped down our outside wall'. Then Mrs Rachel Attwell, wife of an RAF pilot, was roused by a curious noise at 4 am. She looked out of her bedroom window in Beacon View and saw a cigar-shaped, glowing object hovering in the sky, bigger and brighter than any star. Another housewife who spotted it, Mrs Kathleen Penton, described the craft as 'something like a railway carriage flying upside down, with all the windows lit up'.

Soon more and more people were scanning the heavens above Wiltshire. On June 2, a total of 17 people – including Mrs Patricia Phillips, wife of the vicar of Heytesbury, and three of her children – watched the cigar-shaped Thing for 20 minutes in the late evening. By the end of 1965, three people had even taken pictures of it. And strange things were starting to happen.

A flock of pigeons mysteriously fell from the sky. Naturalist David Holton examined the bodies, and declared that the birds had been killed by soundwaves not known on Earth. Then a farmer found that several acres he had left fallow were now a mass of weeds – silvery thistles of a type considered virtually extinct in England since 1918. And in Warminster itself, the East Street garden of Harold and Dora Horlock became another horticultural attraction when ordinary thistles that normally grew to only 5 ft 6 in soared to nearly 12 ft tall.

The curious freaks of nature brought newspaper reporters and television teams flocking to the town. And as news of the UFO sightings spread, observers from all over Britain turned Warminster into a Mecca. They were not disappointed. Few months went by without a sighting. The months turned to years, and the area of activity was pinpointed as a triangle roughly bordered by Warminster, Winchester in Hampshire, and Glastonbury in Somerset. Local folk became used to their curious visitors. Mysterious lights in the sky, agitated animals, stalling cars and electrical equipment going haywire became almost commonplace. Then, in November 1976, the Thing made contact with the humans.

Mrs Joyce Bowles, 42, was out driving in the countryside near her Winchester home with a family friend, retired farm manager Ted Pratt, 58. Suddenly she felt the car 'seem to take to the air' before it stopped completely. The two stared into the inky darkness of the lonely lane. Then Mrs Bowles began screaming in terror. A huge pink-eyed creature was peering at them through the windscreen.

'Those eyes were horrible, as bright as the sun,' she recalled. 'They belonged to a figure who looked like a well-built man in a silvery boiler-suit. There was a sound like a kettle whistling just before we saw him. After examining us, he returned to a glowing, cigar-shaped craft which was hovering in a field only yards from us. We could see three people inside it. When the figure got back in, the craft swiftly disappeared.'

Mr Pratt, who lived at Nether Wallop, Stockbridge, Hants, said: 'I was frightened when the car began to shudder, but when the creature looked at me I suddenly felt very calm. I suppose he must have given me some power to look after Mrs Bowles, because she was in a dreadful state. It was an unnerving experience.'

It was only the first of four close encounters of the third kind for Mrs Bowles. Weeks later, she was again driving in the country with Mr Pratt when they heard the same shrill whistling, and the car began to rock.

'Suddenly we were both inside this machine,' Mrs Bowles recalled. 'One of the spacemen standing a few feet from me was the same man I saw the first time. Lights were blinking and flashing everywhere. The man told us this was his field, whatever that meant. One of his colleagues pulled out a paper which had all sorts of lines on it. In the middle was a circle with rings round it.

'The men all had high jackboots with pointed toes. The boots were luminous, like their silvery suits. In the middle of their belts was something like a glittering stone, and the man next to me kept pressing his stone or touching it. Ted believed it was something to do with receiving messages.

'It all ended quite suddenly. We just seemed to come round, and found ourselves back in the car, stationary. By a river, completely lost. A powerful beam of light filled the car, then gradually seemed to shrink away into the sky.'

A month later, on March 7, Mrs Bowles could guess what was coming next when her car again faltered in a dark country lane. But this time she was with Ann Strickland, an old friend who had been very dubious about her earlier stories of meeting spacemen.

'We both got out of the car, then we saw this oval shape, glowing luminously, making a humming sound,' Mrs Bowles said. 'A man got out and walked towards me, holding out his hands. He came right up to me and took my hand. He eyed Ann up and down. She was terrified. So was I, but I didn't show it.

'The man started to speak in a foreign language. Then he switched to broken English. I said 'Yes', but I wasn't sure what he'd said. Then he said something to me which I understood. But I can't tell anyone what it was. I wouldn't dare.

'The man looked like a spaceman I had seen in the area before, but his hair was rather longer. It fell in front of his shoulders like a woman's. I could see what looked like buckles on the bottom of his legs, and he was wearing something like gaiters. His touch was warm, like a human being.

'Once he had told me what he had to say, he turned round and walked back to the Thing. We watched it rise in the air and slip away into the sky with a high-pitched hum. Ann and I had been on our way to visit friends, but we went straight back to my home in Winchester.'

Mrs Strickland, 65, said: 'I didn't hear what the man said to Joyce and she refuses point-blank to tell me because of a promise she made to him. My mind went blank. I was so surprised and shocked to see him there, and frightened. I've never had such an experience before. At my age I'm a bit too old to have shocks like that.'

Mrs Bowles's health suffered after this encounter. She had a chest infection, then her hands swelled and she had to remove her wedding ring because the area around it was raw.

There was still one more meeting to come, this time in broad daylight. In June 1977 Ted Pratt was again the passenger when the car was seized, as if by a mysterious force, and deposited in a lane off the Petersfield Road out of Winchester. Two men got out of a silver machine hovering 70 feet away and walked towards them. They were different from the figures Mr Pratt had encountered before.

'These had sandy hair and were wearing dull metallic suits,' he said. 'They said something that sounded like trying to help mankind – something about war. They held out their hands and took our hands. I was very frightened. They were making signals with their hands that I could not understand. They said they were scared man would destroy himself, and pollute the atmosphere.

'Then they just said goodbye and returned to their spacecraft. It soared away into the sky and disappeared out of sight. We stood there totally shaken. I suppose we had been with those people for about ten minutes.'

Mrs Bowles said: 'Something like a silver disc was pressed in my right hand. Later a peculiar white mark appeared on my palm. They said they would be back, but I don't want any more. I feel like a marked person. It's no good talking to anyone about it. People don't believe me.'

But many people did believe Mrs Bowles – people who had met what they, too, believed to be beings from outer space.

Tough German parachutist Willy Gehlen had seen many years service with the French Foreign Legion. He liked to keep in practice, and in mid-September 1976 he was on his way from home at Bishops Castle, Shropshire, to the Army Parachute Centre at Netheravon, near Salisbury, when he decided to stop for the night and sleep in his estate car. After searching in vain for a camping site, he pulled in beside a farm gate near Upton Scudamore, a village two miles from Warminster on the Westbury road.

He fell asleep after locking all the doors, but woke shivering in the early hours to find the hatch-door at the back of the vehicle wide open. He slammed it shut, turned the key, and curled up again in his blankets. The same thing happened.

'Normally I sleep very lightly and hear the slightest sound,' he said. 'But I had heard no one open that door. Feeling uneasy and a little unsettled, I decided against more sleep and started to prepare a cup of coffee on my camping stove. It was 3 am.'

Then, above the sound of a distant train, Gehlen heard a strange humming sound, 'like a swarm of bees in flight', and became aware of a figure standing behind the farm gate 10 yards away. 'The sheer size of this person made me wonder – he was almost 7 feet tall – but I was not frightened. I assumed it was the farmer guarding his animals against rustlers, and explained that I was only camping there for one night. There was no answer. Instead he shone a sort of square-shaped torch at me from his chest. The light was dark orange, and I thought he needed some new batteries.

'I got on with making my coffee, and when I looked up a minute or so later, he had gone. Then I heard the humming noise again, and saw a large shape lift off the ground. There was a pink, pulsating glow underneath it, and I watched it disappear across the field. It lifted to about 45 degrees above the ground, but I assumed the farmer was towing something up a hill. It was only after it became light that I realized there was no hill.'

The baffled ex-airman discussed the incident with pals in his local pub when he got home. When he took their advice, and consulted a UFOlogist, he realised that he might have met an alien.

Londoners Steve Evans and Roy Fisher have made frequent special trips to the Warminster area since 1971 to try to spot UFOs. They claim to have seen at least 30, and to have had two even closer encounters.

The first happened as they gazed at the sky from the top of Cradle Hill, one of several vantage points around the town. 'A forcefield seemed to move through the grass like a snake, crackling furiously like static electricity,' Evans said. 'It came straight for Roy's feet, then veered suddenly to the right. Sheep in the field were going frantic. When daylight came, we found flattened grass, as though something had landed.'

That same weekend, the two friends had an unnerving experience at the top of nearby Starr Hill. Evans said: 'We got the distinct feeling we were being watched. I glanced over my shoulder and saw a figure in a sort of white boiler suit, with a white hat, running towards a clump of bushes. I started to chase him. I was making a row myself, crashing through the bracken, but I swear he wasn't making any noise at all. After a while he slowed down, looked back for a second, then disappeared into the bushes.'

Fisher added: 'When Steve ran, I followed instinctively, even though I didn't know what he was after. I reached the bushes after he did, then someone brushed up against me and ran away. I didn't see or hear anything, but it wasn't imagination. He felt as solid as a man of average size and weight.'

Sally Pike and her husband Neil also saw something strange on Starr Hill. They were among a group of eight UFO watchers, and had spotted two unidentified, high-flying objects when they all felt the air grow suddenly warmer.

Sally went on: 'These two figures appeared. They were about 7 feet tall, and it was as if they were made out of smoke. We could see their outlines down to their waists, then they gradually started to fade away.

'When Neil approached them, he just seemed to blend in with them. He couldn't see them when he got close, but we watched him walk straight through the figures and out the other side. The figures remained in the same place for about half-an-hour, then disappeared.'

Ken Rogers was so intrigued by the mystery of the Warminster Thing that he moved to the town from London to study the evidence at first hand. One night he came across an enormous white object blocking a track down Cradle Hill.

'It was a classic saucer design, perfectly outlined,' he recalled. 'As I got closer, I got very hot and my hands started perspiring heavily. I walked on right through it, whatever it was. It seemed like fog, only you could see every detail absolutely clearly.'

Rogers, a director of the British UFO Society, added: 'I think UFOs are extra-terrestrial forces. It is the most likely explanation for them. Remember, 50 years ago people were laughing hysterically at the notion of man going to the Moon. I believe it would only take a race maybe 50 years more advanced than us to make visits of this kind feasible. I don't think the UFOs mean us any harm, so I'm not frightened at all. I believe they are studying our progress.'

Glastonbury Tor, Somerset, south-west England.

Tapping the energy

Why did the Thing choose Warminster? That is the question that has baffled UFO experts. The town is close to a large army base, and large areas of nearby Salisbury Plain are used by the armed forces for exercises. Many so-called UFO sightings over the years have been traced to flares or equipment used by the Services. But many remain inexplicable. And a Territorial Army commander is among those who have reported the enigmatic cigar-shaped flying saucer. It stalled his car in January 1979.

UFOs have, in fact, often been spotted near military bases all over the world. The US Defense Department admitted in secret papers that unexplained aerial activity over missile sites and nuclear silos gave cause for concern during 1975. But the number of separate sightings at Warminster, over so many years, is unique. And if UFOs, as many people believe, are manned by intelligent beings, they would know that there are far more important military targets on Earth than Salisbury Plain.

Two other theories for the sightings, which have averaged two a week since 1964, have been put forward. Just outside the Warminster Triangle lies Stonehenge, thought by many to be an ancient 'computer' for astronomers. And the town of Warminster itself lies at the crossroads of 13 ley lines, the mysterious straight lines formed by monuments, graves, burial grounds, stone crosses and other ancient holy places.

Several scientists and historians believe the ley line network had strange powers that tapped the energy of the Earth centuries ago, and that Stonehenge was a powerhouse for this energy. Man has lost the ability to use it, though some people claim to receive electric shocks from some of the ancient stones. Could it be that aliens can tap the energy, or are attracted to Earth because of it? Could it even be that they guided the early Britons to create the lines during earlier visits to Earth?

Other UFOlogists look to the West Country to account for the concentration of activity over southern England. The historic town of Glastonbury forms one outer limit of the Warminster Triangle. Legend says that the Holy Grail – the cup from which Jesus Christ drank at the Last Supper – was brought to Britain by Joseph of Arimethea, and buried at Glastonbury Tor in about AD 60. Many people who have spotted the bright lights in the sky over Warminster sincerely believe that they herald the Second Coming.

Brazilian balls of fire

For some unknown reason, Brazil seems to get more than its fair share of UFOs. They are seen frequently, coming from both the sea and the sky.

On June 27, 1970, Mrs Maria Machado looked from the window of her Rio de Janeiro home as she prepared lunch, and saw a metallic grey disc with a transparent dome apparently sailing on the ocean. Two figures in shiny clothes were moving around on the deck. Her husband, four daughters and a policeman also saw the strange craft. After 40 minutes, it skimmed along the surface and took off, leaving behind a white hoop-like object which floated out to sea.

On September 12, 1971, typewriter mechanic Paulo Silveira claimed that two figures in one-piece blue suits dragged him inside a shining disc. He told the authorities he was driving home at Itaperuna, north of Rio, when the disc blocked the road. A luminous beam shot out and his car engine died, then his own energy drained away. He heard an engine start as the two aliens, about the size of ten-year-old children, carried him aboard; then he went into a coma. He came round to find them carrying him out again. They laid him beside his car, returned to their craft, and took off. Another motorist found him dazed, blinded and disoriented, and drove him to hospital. He had lost three hours of his life.

In January 1981, farmer Domingos Monteiro Brito claimed that he met two strange beings when a grey, glowing flying saucer landed at dawn on his land at Camaracu Island. The aliens, who resembled humans, asked him a string of questions in his own language – how many people lived in his village, were there any large uninhabited areas nearby – but he was too paralysed with fear to remember if he answered. The craft took off again, but the beings told him they would be back.

Early in 1980, the 30,000 residents of Tres Coroas, south of Rio, experienced one of the strangest concentrations of UFOs ever recorded. Over 20 days, balls of fire chased cars, flames erupted without burning anything, and scores of strange shapes zoomed through or over the city.

Bicycle-shop owner Joao Jose de Nascimento was driving home late at night when a fire-like object appeared beside his car, apparently following him. He said: 'It was strange and I was afraid. I felt it was trying to capture me.' When he got home, his son Vicente told him he had seen another UFO – an onion shape revolving in the sky, with lights which switched from green to orange to blue. Estate agent Roberto Francisco Santana said he saw the shadow of a saucer travelling very fast as he drove through town with his wife and children. Then he spotted two more saucers flying over city buildings. 'While I was looking up, I smashed into a car in front of me,' he said. 'The things we saw were very frightening.'

Military police commander Antonio das Gacas Santos said he raced to a neighbour's home when he noted that the back garden was curiously illuminated. 'I saw very clearly a creature about the height of a human being with its arms extended. I couldn't see any physical details, but I heard a low whining noise, like a puppy. My neighbour touched the creature, then fell back shocked. I was afraid, but it wasn't a normal fear. I still get goose-bumps thinking about it.'

Rio psychiatrist Dr Gloria Machado was astonished by what she saw when she and her husband Mario, president of the Brazilian Association of Parapsychology, arrived in the city. 'There was a fire which didn't burn anything, and flashes of light which exploded in the tree tops,' she said. 'Indoors I saw a box of matches floating in mid-air, bottles breaking for no reason, chairs flying around ...'

Her husband persuaded people watching a brightly-lit UFO to try to communicate with it. He said: 'We began uttering the letters of the alphabet, and heard sounds from behind the lights. The letter D came back long and hard. Lights started flashing everywhere, and we heard something that sounded like a beating rhythm. Then suddenly everything went dark.' Lawyer Josefino de Carvalho, who watched the experiment, said: 'I'm sure that we are dealing with intelligent beings.' And police chief Santos said: 'I now believe that on other planets in other solar systems there exist forces which can manifest themselves here.'

Through Earth's windows

Aerial researchers in America think they have located two UFO windows on this world – the sleepy New England town of Winsted, Connecticut, and the Michigan Rectangle of the mid-West.

The people of Winsted have grown used to strange shapes in the sky over the last 20 years. In February 1967, a businessman was one of three witnesses who reported an object that hovered over the town for 15 minutes before disappearing with red and green flashes. Only a few nights later two girls heard lawnmower-like sounds from a barn, and saw three humanoid creatures approaching their house. A passing car frightened them off, and minutes later the girls – and their neighbour – saw a UFO rising from a nearby hill.

Later that year, a cone-shaped object with red lights was spotted on two consecutive nights, and a month later a shape flashing red and green lights was observed hovering noiselessly over trees before zooming off at high speed.

In 1968, the sightings included a very bright globe, a balloon near the Moon, and an orange moon-like shape on a night when the Moon itself could not be seen.

In 1976, 13 girl campers and their leader heard a high-pitched whine as they climbed Blueberry Mountain, just outside the town. They looked up to see a silver, flat-bottomed saucer, about 25 feet wide. It was surrounded by a purple mist and had a red dome on top. It hovered for 30 seconds before vanishing. In 1977, a policeman and three other people saw a red-topped object hovering soundlessly near the town's sewer treatment plant, and examining the ground with two yellowish-white beams of light. The same year, people saw UFOs apparently diving into the local reservoir, and splashing upwards again.

Connecticut UFO investigator Ted Thoben is one of those who believe Winsted is a window through which UFOs arrive on Earth. He says: 'Windows are a magnetic deviation in the terrain, where these things slip through. But I don't believe they come from another planet. I think they exist at a different vibratory or frequency rate so that we cannot see them most of the time. They inhabit the same space that we do, and places like Winsted are the exchange point between different dimensions.

'That theory is far more logical than saying that UFOs are from outer space. For one thing, the Earth is in the boondocks of the Milky Way galaxy. I can't see that after 2,000 years, some distant planet still finds us so intriguing they could allot so much effort to come here when there are so many other planets out there.'

The term Michigan Rectangle was coined by David Fideler, head of the local Anomaly Research organization. After studying reports of strange happenings from north of Kalamazoo to the Indiana state-line in the south, he said: 'The rectangle may be a centre of window phenomena – in other words a gateway from the ordinary world to the supernatural, where unreality leaks into the reality of the everyday.'

Fideler has chronicled strange shapes and lights in the sky as far back as 1897. There have also been many reports in the area of phantom panther-like creatures and of Bigfoot – a human-shaped creature covered in hair, with brilliant, gleaming red eyes. And Fideler says that before the white man arrived at Lake Michigan, the Indians called it Magician Lake. He believes geophysical and electromagnetic disturbances could account for the region's bizarre events.

The 1897 sightings included a brilliant white light, a huge ball of fire and a mysterious airship. A woman also reported hearing voices from the sky. In April that year, at least a dozen people watched an unexplained light fly over the centre of Kalamazoo.

In 1950, a DC-4 crashed with 58 people aboard – and Fideler says a curious ball of light was seen in the sky at the time.   In 1966, a policeman was among those who saw a UFO 'so bright you couldn't look straight at it'. Then a UFO nearly 40 feet long was spotted cruising above a highway, blinking its lights at drivers. In 1970 there was a mysterious explosion, heard four miles away, and a gaping 40-foot hole was ripped in the ice of Upper Scott Lake. Chunks of ice flew more than 100 feet from the lake.

In 1974, police cars chased a UFO for 45 minutes. It flashed white and coloured lights, moved at 35–40 mph, and kept a height of around 600 feet before vanishing. Two years later a misty, glowing figure was reported floating a few feet above the ground, and in 1978 an unusual shape shot beams of light down on to Cook nuclear power station.

Fideler says: 'There are too many bewildering reports from a small area over a long period of time for them to be simply dismissed as unrelated incidents, or the ravings of crackpots.'

UFOs – all in a row

The year 1954 saw an unprecedented wave of UFO sightings over central Europe – and French parapsychologist and science writer Aimé Michel found a fascinating link as he studied some of the most reliable reports. When he plotted them on a map of his country, they formed a straight line running between and beyond the towns of Bayonne and Vichy.

All they need is love

The people of a tiny town in the Arizona desert claim UFOs have been visiting them for more than 30 years. And they say they bring only one message for the human race: 'We love you.' The town is Childs, an isolated settlement on the East Verde River between Flagstaff and Phoenix. Clarence Hale, 64, said: 'We've seen hundreds of UFOs – I first saw one 1947. We see so many of them we don't pay them any attention any more.'

His wife Mamie Ruth, 62, added: 'We can tell when the starships are around. We don't even have to go outside and see them any more. It's a feeling we get, a really warm and kindly feeling. It's a sort of love-thy-neighbour feeling deep inside, a feeling of humanity.

'We truly believe that aliens from outer space are trying to talk with the people of Earth. The strong feeling of love and compassion we get is their way of contacting us. They are trying to make Earth and the universe a better place to live – there is absolutely no reason to fear them.'

The good neighbours claim to have provided the authorities with evidence of UFO landings – powder and strands of silvery 'angel hair'. Power-plant manager Cliff Johnson found five circles of the powder on his new-mown lawn one morning, each about 12 feet in diameter.

'The powder was greyish-white until I touched it,' he said. 'Then it turned black, like soot. There was no other evidence that anything had touched down, just those big circles of powder. Some of them had spots of ash in the middle of them.'

Clarence Hale also found powder circles after watching a 'starship' land outside his home. 'It was about 8 am and I saw it coming in over the ridge line at about 30 mph, a big saucer-shaped ship, about 200 yards long. I could see windows and portholes with lights shining through. The ship was a silver colour, like metal. It landed and took off. When it left I found the powdery ash.

'I also found the angel hair. It looks like fine cobweb, but it feels synthetic. It sits on the trees and bushes after take-off. I gathered up about 30 feet of it one night, but when I wadded it up in my hand, it just vanished.'

University and government laboratories which tested the powder were unable to pinpoint its chemical make-up or origin. A top research scientist for the US Geological Survey admitted: 'It has got us baffled. We could not match it with anything we know on Earth.'

The people of Childs believe the 'angel hair' may be a device to protect humans from damage during take-offs. Kathy Soulages said: 'I think it's a flame retardant. Whenever a starship comes anywhere near where it might harm someone, it ejects the material to protect us from the heat.'

Terror in the outback

Eerie objects in the sky have worried the people of a small town in Australia for more than 12 years. Trucks and cars have been chased and threatened, and one man even took a shot at a UFO with his rifle.

The town is St George, 300 miles west of Brisbane. Max Pringle, editor of the local paper which serves the 2,500 residents and the outlying farms, said: 'There have been several hundred sightings since 1967, most of them by upright citizens, not the sort to look for publicity. Nobody knows why these things are scaring the wits out of the people here. God only knows what's behind it.'

Pringle says he saw his first UFO in 1977. 'It was orange, shaped like a football, and soaring silently about 500 feet off the ground,' he recalled. 'It had green flashing lights on top, and red underneath. I was stunned – I'd never seen anything like it.' By 1980, he had seen at least two dozen more.

Lorry fleet boss Jack Dyball claims he was buzzed by a silver-grey craft in 1975 as he drove near the town in a truck. 'It headed straight for me, then suddenly pulled up and flew out of sight,' he said. 'I tell you, it really frightened me. It wasn't a plane, it had no wings. I really thought it was going to crash into me. When it lifted off, I saw big blue flames coming out of five burners in the back.'

Rancher's son Murray Beardmore took a pot shot at an orange UFO in September 1978. It flashed red and green lights as it flew in front of a truck he and two friends were driving. Beardmore says he stopped the truck, grabbed his rifle, and fired one shot. Then, scared, they drove very fast to his home with the UFO trailing them. At one stage, their engine inexplicably cut out. The boy's father, John Beardmore, said: 'He was really shaken when he got here. All three of them were pretty ashen-faced. My sister, my wife and I all saw the thing, and got in the car to chase it, but it disappeared.'

The Broadhaven triangle

Fifty sightings in a single year

Who or what haunts the Broadhaven Triangle? It is a mystery that has baffled scientists, military investigators and UFOlogists.

The triangle lies between Swansea, mid-Wales and Broadhaven. And it has been the subject of more UFO visitations than almost anywhere else in the world. In one year alone, more than 50 positive sightings were made.

At first it was thought the rash of reports from the triangle was connected with the intense defence activity in the area. Within a tight radius there are: the Royal Aircraft Establishment Missile Range; RAF Brawdy, an operational station; The Army's Pendine Ranges; a missile testing ground; supersonic low-flying corridors, and an American submarine tracking station. Spokesmen for the establishments are non-plussed by the flood of sightings. And very few can be explained away by defence operations.

Certainly the sight that terrified Billy and Pauline Coombs in their farm cottage has baffled the experts. They were sitting in their front room at 1 am when Pauline suddenly turned to look at the window. Blocking it was a towering, eerie figure wearing a silver suit.

Too terrified to scream, Pauline stared, transfixed, at the 7-foot figure. Sensing her fear, Billy turned in his seat and saw the monstrous outline. 'Good God! What the hell's that?' he yelled.

'It was wearing a helmet with some sort of shiny visor,' Pauline recalled. 'A pipe went from the mouth to the back of the head. I was petrified. We were rooted to the spot with terror.

'It radiated a sort of luminous light and when it touched the window, the pane started to rattle like all hell had broken loose – yet there was no wind.

'When I got my wits together, I raced upstairs to see if the children were all

Broadhaven Primary School, showing the area beyond the school where a landed UFO was seen.

right. Billy put our labrador Blackie outside, but he went mad with fear. He had to be destroyed six months later.'

The Coombs telephoned for help, but by the time police arrived at their home, Ripperton Farm, near the village of Dale, Dyfed, the eerie visitor had disappeared. The couple also telephoned neighbours to report what they had seen. Billy's boss, farmer Richard Hewison, drove over as soon as he got their call. 'They were genuinely terrified,' he said. 'They were frightened out of their wits.'

The family had two souvenirs of the incident – a burned out TV set, and a rose bush near the window, which was badly scorched.

The ordeal in the early hours of April 24, 1977, was not Mrs Coombs's first brush with the unknown. Two months earlier, on February 24, she had been driving three of her five children home from nearby St Ishmael's shortly after 8 pm when one of the boys saw a light which seemed to be coming towards them at great speed.

As the children started crying with fear, Mrs Coombs, 33 and said to be a down-to-earth type by those who knew her, put her foot on the accelerator. 'I thought the thing would come through the windscreen,' she recalled. 'In the end it went just over us and did a tight U-turn.'

The craft now flew alongside them, skimming over the tops of the hedges at 80 mph as Mrs Coombs kept her foot down. For 10 minutes, the bizarre chase continued through deserted country lanes. The object was no bigger than a football, but glowed yellow and had a beam of light underneath.

Finally, the car came in sight of the farmhouse ... and the engine cut out. Hysterical, Mrs Coombs grabbed her children from the back seat and rushed into the house. As she gabbled her amazing story, her eldest son saw the object disappearing.

For a year after that, inexplicable happenings made the family's life a misery. The children frequently saw bright lights landing in the fields, and found scorch marks next morning. On a trip to the coast at nearby St Bride's Bay, they saw two silvery-suited figures, and a flying disc which seemed to disappear into rocks. Two of the children received strange burns. Five television sets and eight cars mysteriously burned out. Then, as suddenly as the incidents had begun, they stopped.

The Coombs's neighbours also reported curious happenings. Mr Hewison's wife Josephine looked out of the bedroom window one morning to see a 50-foot silver spacecraft standing beside her greenhouse.

She said: 'It was as high as a double decker bus, there were no visible windows or openings. It stood there for about 10 minutes then took off. It left no mark. Not even a broken twig.'

Teenaged shop assistant Stephen Taylor, of Haverfordwest, may have come the closest to an extra-terrestrial encounter – when a figure similar to the one that terrified the Coombs suddenly appeared by his side. He was walking home late one night when he saw a black shape in front of him.

He said: 'It looked about 40 or 50 feet across. I noticed a dim glow around what seemed to be the underside. Suddenly this figure popped up, right next to me. I was terrified. It was dressed in silver. It seemed to have high cheekbones.

'Its eyes were like fish eyes – completely round. I took a swing at it and ran. I don't know whether I hit it. I ran the three miles home. When I got there, my pet dog started snarling at me. It wouldn't let me near it.'

Louise Bassett, wife of a restaurant owner from Ferryside, Carmarthen, said: 'I was driving home one night when my radio went dead. At the same time, I saw flashing lights in the sky. I took a detour to avoid them but they appeared again three miles further on.' When Mrs Bassett's radio cut out, so did dozens of other people's radios and televisions in the area. Mrs Bassett's dog was in the car with her at the time. 'It has never been the same since that night,' she said.

Artist John Petts, 62, was working in his studio near Carmarthen when he saw a brilliant light in the sky. 'It was a cigar-shaped object. One minute it was there, the next it was gone,' he said.

Perhaps the best witnesses of all are the children of Broadhaven Primary School. Fifteen of them – 14 boys and a girl – were playing football when they rushed inside to tell their headmaster that they had seen a spaceship in the sky. The head, Mr Ralph Llewellyn, split them up and asked them to draw pictures of what they had seen. He compared the finished results and was astounded by their similarity. It was no prank. Mr Llewellyn said: 'I do not believe that children of this age could sustain a hoax of this nature.'

The sighting that excited investigators from the British UFO Research Association and which is regarded as the most authentic so far was by two company directors as they drove in bright daylight from Carmarthen to Newcastle Emlyn – straight through the centre of the triangle.

One of the men, Elvet Dyer, described their experience: 'A huge cigar-shaped machine, at least 20 feet long, crossed our path 100 yards ahead. It was flying so low it would have taken the top off a double-decker bus. It made no sound and we thought it was going to crash.

'We braced ourselves for an explosion as it passed out of sight into a field, but when we looked into the field there was nothing there at all.'

The two men, non-believers in UFOs, were badly shaken and unnerved.

Mr Randall Pugh, regional investigator for the UFO association, said: 'We know there is something very strange going on in this area. Many of the reports have been from intelligent, educated people who are not disposed to exaggerate or misconstrue what they have seen.'

Dozens more reports of unexplained sights have flooded into the UFO association. Randall Pugh has noticed one common link in the sightings. 'People who encounter these phenomena suffer severe headaches, trembling and sleeplessness,' he said.

It is no wonder the people living in the Broadhaven Triangle are getting jittery. They believe that they have been singled out for surveillance by interplanetary beings.

A local police inspector said: 'After what I've seen round here in the last few years, nothing would surprise me now.'

Air mysteries

Dead pilots and vanished planes

The best planes and pilots Earth can muster have taken off to challenge UFOs in the sky – and all have been found wanting. In the late 1940s and early 1950s, when US Air Force aces were under orders to shoot down aerial intruders, not one victim was claimed. But the interceptors suffered casualties.

On January 7, 1948, USAF Captain Thomas Mantell led three F51 Mustang fighters into action after Kentucky police were inundated with reports of a hovering 'giant air machine', in the form of a glowing disc 300 feet across. The control tower staff at Godman Field air base had seen it as well.

Mantell was an experienced pilot, a veteran of World War Two air battles. He closed in on the silvery shape over Fort Knox. 'It's a disc,' he radioed to Godman. 'It looks metallic and is tremendous in size ... it has a ring and a dome, and I can see rows of windows ... the thing is gigantic, it's flying unbelievably fast. It's going up ... I'll climb to 20,000 feet ...'

Then the voice cut out and the radio went dead. Two hours later the wreckage of the plane was found scattered over an area a mile wide. Mantell's body lay nearby. The authorities refused to let anybody see it.

Top-level inquiries were held; but the findings, announced 18 months later, were unbelievable. The Air Force announced that Captain Mantell had probably fainted from lack of oxygen as he climbed to 20,000 feet – and what he had seen was probably the planet Venus. A planet with windows? A planet chased by an experienced pilot? Later statements changed the story. The object was simply a naval research balloon.

In June 1953, an F-94C jet fighter-interceptor took off from Otis Air Force base on Cape Cod after a UFO had been reported. At 1,500 feet the engine cut out and the entire electrical system failed. As the aircraft's nose dipped towards the ground, pilot Captain Suggs yelled at his radar officer, Lieutenant Robert Barkoff, to bale out.

Normal procedure was for the radar officer to pull a lever which triggered explosive bolts to jettison the canopy. He then pulled a second lever, which ejected him and his seat from the plane, and when the pilot heard the second explosion, he pulled his own ejection lever. Captain Suggs baled out before he heard the second explosion, because the jet was already down to 600 feet and only seconds away from crashing.

Suggs landed just after his parachute opened in the back yard of a house. The owner, sitting near an open window, was astonished. Suggs was equally amazed. Why had the man not heard the plane crash? And where was the radar officer?

A full-scale search was launched. Cape Cod was combed on foot and from the air, and divers scoured nearby Buzzard's Bay. When the hunt was called off three months later, not a trace of the jet or of Lieutenant Barkoff had been found. They had seemingly disappeared.

On November 23, 1953, Lieutenant Felix Moncla and radar officer Lieutenant R. R. Wilson took off from Kinross Air Force Base to chase a UFO spotted over Lake Superior by Air Defence Command radar operators. The F-89C jet was guided towards the object from the ground, and controllers saw the plane close in on the UFO blip. Then, 160 miles from the base, at 8,000 feet and 73 miles off Keeweenaw Point, Michigan, the two blips merged and faded from the screen. The jet and its occupants were never seen again.

At first the Air Force said the F-89C had identified the UFO as a C47 of the Royal Canadian Air Force. But the RCAF denied that any of its planes was in the area. The official line was 'that the pilot probably suffered from vertigo and crashed into the lake'.

Pilot and co-pilot both survived the next disastrous attempt to intercept a UFO, but four civilians were not so lucky. On July 2, 1954, an F-94C was diverted from a routine training flight by Rome Air Force base after reports of a balloon-like object over the village of Walesville, New York. Radar scanners had shown two unidentified tracks. The first turned out to be a Canadian C47, but the second could not be identified.

What happened next was contained in an official report of the incident by Air Force investigators. 'As the pilot started a descent,' it said, 'he noted that the cockpit temperature increased abruptly. The increase in temperature caused the pilot to scan the instruments. The fire warning light was on ... the engine was shut down and both crew members ejected successfully.'

The plane crashed in Walesville, hitting two buildings and a car. Four

Double saucer over the Thames

The British Air Ministry was forced to take an interest in UFOs in 1955 when Flight Lieutenant James Salandin filed a report of a strange encounter over the Thames Estuary. He was flying his Meteor jet fighter at 16,000 feet in a cloudless sky when he spotted a metallic silver object approaching him. He described it as two saucers joined together, with a dome or bubble on top. He saw no visible portholes or jet pipes, and estimated that the craft, about 40 feet wide, was travelling at twice his 600 mph.

A Venusian spacecraft photographed in the summer of 1956.

A UFO from the constellation of Coma Berenices containing nine people who talked with the photographer for 90 minutes.

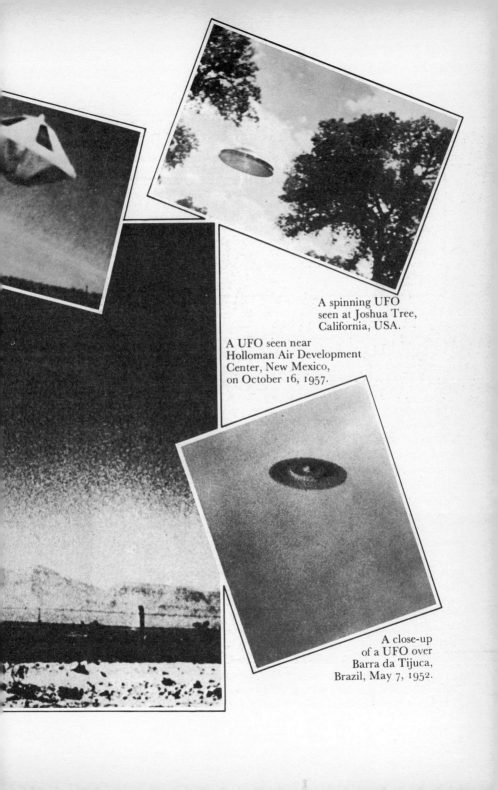

A spinning UFO
seen at Joshua Tree,
California, USA.

A UFO seen near
Holloman Air Development
Center, New Mexico,
on October 16, 1957.

A close-up
of a UFO over
Barra da Tijuca,
Brazil, May 7, 1952.

Scientists who knew too much?

Suicide verdicts were recorded on two top US scientists who died after studying UFOs, having decided that they were extra-terrestrial spaceships investigating life on Earth. Atmospheric physician Professor James McDonald, of the University of Arizona, was found with a bullet in his head in 1971, and astronomer Professor Robert Jessup was discovered in his gas-filled car in 1959. A friend of Jessup claimed: 'He knew too much, they wanted him out of the way.' But fellow scientists felt both men had suffered depression after battling for years against a brick wall of governmental UFO denials and evasions, and the scorn of sceptical colleagues.

people were killed, two of them children. The Air Force dismissed the second object seen by radar operators as 'probably a balloon'.

Why did the Air Force cover up what really happened in all four incidents? Documents released since 1954 reveal that, contrary to statements at the time, there was a genuine belief that the objects chased by the jet were craft manned by intelligent beings.

As early as September 23, 1947, Lieutenant General N. F. Twining of Air Materiel Command had sent a memorandum to Brigadier-General George Schulgen, Commanding General of the Army Air Forces, saying: 'It is the opinion (of this Command) that the so-called flying discs phenomenon is something real and not visionary or fictitious ... The reported operating characteristics, such as extreme rates of climb, manoeuverability and evasive action when sighted or contacted by friendly aircraft and radar lend belief to the possibility that some of the objects are controlled either manually, automatically or remotely.'

The immediate suspicion of the Americans was that the discs might be some spectacular advanced technology that the Russians had captured from the Nazis during World War Two. After the Mantell crash, an urgent investigation of possible threats to national security was launched. In August 1948, the Air Technical Intelligence Centre drew up a top-secret report concluding that UFOs were not of Russian origin, but were interplanetary craft. Air Force Chief of Staff General Hoyt S. Vandenburg ordered: 'Burn it.' And on December 27, 1948, the ATIC study on UFOs, code-named Project Sign, was wound up. The public were told: 'Reports of flying saucers are the result of misinterpretation of various conventional objects, a mild form of mass hysteria, and hoaxes. Continuance of the project is unwarranted.'

But the project was not closed down. In February 1949, it resumed inquiries under a new code-name – Project Grudge. UFO sightings continued, and in 1952 a new upsurge of reports forced the government to act again.

On July 26 of that year, three F-94 jet fighters scrambled to investigate a cluster of curious lights which appeared above the White House in Washington. The lights had also been spotted a week earlier, but this time there were more of them, nearly a dozen, zigzagging erratically at high speed.

Two of the intercepting pilots found no trace of them. But the third said he flew straight into a group of the whitish-blue lights, which travelled alongside him for 15 seconds before dispersing. All three planes returned safely, and the lights – labelled the 'Washington Invasion' by the Press – were never seen again.

That month, the UFO investigating team – now working under the diplomatically more acceptable title of Project Bluebook – were receiving between 20 and 30 sightings every day, 20 per cent of them objects that no one could identify or explain away. Embarrassingly for touchy Air Force chiefs, one of the witnesses was Dan Kimball, the Secretary of State for the American Navy. He said two disc-shaped UFOs buzzed the plane in which he was flying to Hawaii, circling it twice before shooting off at more than 1,500 mph, then repeating the exercise round a Navy plane 50 miles away.

When Kimball later inquired what progress Bluebook was making on his report, he was told that no action had been taken and that officers were forbidden to discuss case analysis with anyone. Furthermore, no copies of reports could be returned.

By 1953, public pressure for information about UFOs forced the Central Intelligence Agency (CIA) to make some sort of gesture. It convened the Robertson Panel, under a respected Californian scientist, H. P. Robertson, and asked it to evaluate UFOs. There were three possible findings, that UFOs were explainable objects and natural phenomena, that there was insufficient data in reports to make a conclusion, or that UFOs were interplanetary spacecraft.

According to Edward Ruppelt, former chief of the Air Force UFO Project, the panel opted for the second possibility, and urged that Bluebook manpower be quadrupled, bringing in skilled scientists and observers to try to solve the problem of what UFOs really were. It also recommended that the public be told 'every detail of every phase' of UFO investigations. Privately, said Ruppelt, almost every member of the panel was convinced that UFOs were extra-terrestrial.

The CIA suppressed the report, finally releasing a censored version of it in 1966. And they ignored its recommendations, instigating instead a 'debunking' programme. A secret document released years later read: 'The debunking aim would result in reduction of public interest in flying saucers which today evokes a strong psychological reaction. This education could be accomplished by mass media such as television, motion pictures and popular articles. Basis of such education would be actual case histories which had been puzzling at first but later explained. As in the case of conjuring tricks, there is much less stimulation if the secret is known.'

While the public was told that UFOs did not exist, servicemen were ordered to shoot them down. People who reported seeing flying saucers were ridiculed. Forces personnel were threatened with jail or fines if they broadcast what they had seen. 'Only false statements and fictitious reports may be published,' read one Air Force order. 'All real reports must be treated as secret and forwarded to the appropriate authorities.'

Once the Americans realized that UFOs were not a Soviet secret weapon, the race was on to capture one before the Russians did. Insight into such advanced technology would be of incalculable value to either power. Meanwhile, public debunking of UFOs might make the Russians less interested in trying to bring one down.

The ploy did not work. Moscow had come to the same conclusions as Washington. In 1957, anti-aircraft batteries around the Soviet capital opened up on an object in the sky – until the guns' electrical systems mysteriously went dead.

In 1967, American Air Force agents monitored a broadcast from one of two Cuban jet fighters sent up to intercept a curious UFO. The pilot said he had just seen his partner's plane disintegrate without smoke or flames as he tried to shoot the object down. Stanton Friedman, who revealed the story after leaving his job as a space-related nuclear technician for the US government, claimed that tapes of the conversation were sent to the National Security Agency, which ordered the loss to be listed as equipment malfunction.

Not all UFOs proved so lethal. One spotted above the English counties of Norfolk, Suffolk and Cambridgeshire in 1956 seemed almost playful when a plane came close. The excitement started at 9.30 pm on August 13 when radar operators at USAF Bentwaters spotted an object which zoomed off the screen at what seemed to be 5,000 mph. Then a group of slow-moving shapes were tracked out to sea. They seemed to link up into one object before disappearing with a stop-go-stop motion. More sightings were reported at 10 pm and again at 10.55 pm when observers saw a blurred white light pass overhead. A C-47 aircraft radioed that it had passed below them at extraordinary speed.

Bentwaters alerted radar crews farther north at Lakenheath, and they too saw the object, on screen and visually. Its antics were baffling, changing direction crazily, shooting off at right angles without stopping, and scorching to enormous speeds from a standing start.

Two jet fighters diverted to intercept could find no trace of the object. Then a Venom single-seat fighter, equipped with nose radar, took off from Waterbeach, and was guided from the ground towards the UFO, at that stage motionless and clearly visible, between 15,000 and 29,000 feet, over Lakenheath.

The pilot radioed that he had radar contact and 'gunlock' – then he lost sight of his quarry. 'Where did he go?' he asked ground control. 'Roger, it

The foo fighters of World War Two

A secret new German weapon was revealed to the world on December 13, 1944. An Associated Press report filed from Paris said 'mysterious silvery balls which float in the air' had been seen on the Western Front, and added: 'It is possible that they represent a new anti-aircraft defence instrument.'

Only after the war was it revealed that the balls were not sent up by the Germans. Their forces had seen them too – and thought they were a British or American device. Pilots from either side in both Europe and the Pacific war zone had seen similar shapes flying alongside them on bombing raids, sometimes in formation. The Allies had christened them 'foo fighters', a word derived from a popular comic-strip catchphrase, 'Where there's foo, there's fire.' The official verdict was that the balls were electrical phenomena called St Elmo's fire, but many of the pilots thought they knew better.

appears he got behind you and he's still there,' came the reply. The UFO had zipped into position in an incredible right-angled flight too fast for most of the radar watchers to follow. Once behind the Venom, it had split into two separate units, one behind the other, and locked on to the fighter.

A bizarre game of hide and seek began. For ten minutes, the Venom pilot dived, climbed and circled, trying to shake off his pursuer. But the UFO stuck to his tail, always 100–200 yards behind. Finally the Venom headed for home, its fuel running low. The UFO followed it down, then stopped, hovered in triumph for a while, and vanished.

Cynics pointed out that the East Anglian terrain is notorious for generating false radar traces, known as 'angels', and that the incident occurred at the climax of the Perseid meteor shower, which passes Earth each year and appears as a series of luminous white blobs.

But the official report on the incident, filed on August 31 by Captain Edward Holt of the 81st Fighter-Bomber Wing, Bentwaters, said: 'The object . . . followed all manoeuvres of the jet fighter aircraft.'

Nearly a year later, the six-man crew of a US Air Force RB-47 jet reported another playful UFO. It chased them for more than 1½ hours in a 1,000-mile flight across Mississippi, Louisiana, Texas and Oklahoma early on the morning of June 17, 1957. Curiously, they added, the object occasionally vanished from sight momentarily – and when it did so, it also disappeared from their radar screen, only to reappear within seconds in the same place.

The debunking of UFOs worked quite well for a while. Project Bluebook successfully managed to 'investigate' sightings, and to produce unsatisfactory answers. Then, in 1964 and again in 1967, came fresh waves of UFO activity. In response to renewed public pressure, the Air Force announced that renowned physicist Dr Edward Condon would lead a University of Colorado inquiry into the sightings, to run parallel with the Bluebook investigations.

In January 1969, Condon's report said: 'Careful consideration of the record as it is available to us leads us to conclude that further extensive study of the UFOs probably cannot be justified in the expectation that science will be advanced thereby.' It admitted, however, that 30 per cent of cases it investigated remained unexplained.

The 1,000-page report was condemned as a whitewash – and worse. One UFO research group pulled out of the investigations because of Condon's negative and subjective comments; and two of the inquiry team, Dr Norman LeVine and Dr David Saunders, were fired for leaking a memorandum that read: 'The trick would be, I think, to describe the project so that, to the public, it would appear a totally objective study but, to the scientific community, would present the image of a group of non-believers trying their best to be objective but having an almost zero expectation of finding a saucer.'

The memo was written by assistant project director Dr Robert Low, whose job was to coordinate the inquiry. The two doctors were not alone in having no confidence in him. Condon's administrative assistant quit, saying: 'Bob's attitude from the beginning has been one of negativism.'

Criticism of the Condon Report was loud and long. Congressman J. Edward Roush told the House of Representatives that he had 'grave doubts as to the scientific profundity and objectivity of the project'. He added: 'We are $500,000 poorer and not richer in information about UFOs ... I am not satisfied and the American public will not be satisfied.' Aviation pioneer John Northrop, the 80-year-old founder of Northrop Aircraft Company and co-founder of Lockheed, said: 'The 21st century will die laughing at the Condon Report.'

The Condon inquiry did one service for the subject of UFOs. The fact that such a distinguished scientist was prepared to study them allowed other top boffins to take UFOs seriously as well. Even after he debunked them, others felt free to continue their studies without fear of ridicule. And though the Air Force announced, on December 17, 1969, that it was closing down Project Bluebook because UFOs 'didn't exist', it too continued to monitor and analyse reports through the Aerospace Defence Command.

In the 1970s, laws concerning freedom of information, and the more enlightened attitudes of other governments, notably France and Italy, and even Russia, allowed greater access to UFO reports, and there were more frequent reports of confrontations between unidentified objects and Earth aircraft.

A squadron of F-106 jet fighters scrambled in 1975 when a fleet of mysterious shapes appeared at 15,000 feet over Montana. As they approached the shining lights, the objects simply vanished.

An even stranger encounter emerged only a few years after it happened. Captain Lawrence Coyne and three crewmen took off in a US Air Force helicopter from Columbus, Ohio, at 10.30 pm on October 18, 1973, heading for Cleveland. Forty minutes later, they were 2,500 feet up over Mansfield when one of the men noticed a red light approaching from the east at high speed. Coyne dived to 1,700 feet but a collision seemed inevitable. He braced himself for the impact. It never came.

About 500 feet away from the helicopter, the UFO stopped abruptly. Coyne noticed a huge grey metallic hull, about 60 feet long and shaped like a streamlined fat cigar. The front edge glowed red, green lights flickered at the back, and there was a dome in the centre. A green light suddenly swivelled and flooded the helicopter cockpit. Coyne tried to radio an SOS, but his set would not transmit or receive. Then he looked at his instrument panel and gasped.

The helicopter was being lifted into the air.

'I could hardly believe it,' he said. 'The altimeter was reading 3,500 feet, climbing to 3,800. I had made no attempt to pull up. All the controls were still set for a 20-degree dive. Yet we had climbed from 1,700 feet to 3,500 with no power in a couple of seconds, with no G-forces or other noticeable strains. There was no noise or turbulence either.'

Finally the crew felt a slight bounce, and the UFO zipped away towards the north-west. Seven minutes later, the helicopter radio started working normally again, and Coyne reported the incident to incredulous ground controllers.

Phantoms versus UFOs

One early morning in September 1976, an F-4 Phantom jet fighter streaked into the skies of Iran from Shahrokhi Air Force base. It had been ordered to investigate a dazzling bright light spotted by hundreds of people south of Tehran. The fighter closed on the object, but when it was 30 miles away, all radio contact was lost.

As the pilot broke off and headed back to Shahrokhi, his radio crackled back to life, and he reported that all communications and instrumentation systems in the plane had suddenly and inexplicably cut out.

A second Phantom was already in the air and in pursuit of the UFO at a speed much greater than the speed of sound; but the craft was still accelerating away from it. The pilot, Lieutenant Fafari, radioed that it seemed about the size of a 707 passenger aircraft. Suddenly the UFO released a smaller, disc-shaped object which also glowed brilliantly. It hurtled straight for the jet.

Fafari reached for his weapon control panel and pressed a button to release an AIM-9 air-to-air missile. Nothing happened. All his electrical systems had blacked out. He swung his defenceless plane into a dive to avoid the approaching disc, which changed course to follow him for four miles. Then it zoomed back to the larger UFO.

As Fafari's instruments started working again, he again went after the 'mother ship', which was moving away rapidly. Then it shed another disc, which fell at great speed towards the Earth. Fafari watched it go down, expecting an explosion, but it stopped just above some hills, casting an eerie glow over a two-mile area. Fafari looked up again, and realised that the larger

UFO had used the disc the distract him while it vanished. He returned safely to base. The Iranian government later filed reports of the incident to the Pentagon in Washington. A year later the Italian government revealed that its jets had also encountered UFOs. It listed six separate encounters during 1977 and 1978, two of which involved air force personnel, and one a civilian airliner. On February 23, 1977, a fighter pilot spotted an intense ball of light over Milan. 'When radar gave me authorization to intercept, the object went up to 12,000 feet and kept its distance,' he said. 'It was in my sight for 23 minutes.'

On October 27 of the same year, a football-shaped UFO buzzed a helicopter during NATO exercises at Elmas Air Force base, near Cagliari, Sardinia. The Defense Ministry quoted an air controller as saying: 'I saw a UFO that flew at the speed of a jet, around 565 mph. It was behind a helicopter that was participating in military manoeuvres.' Three other helicopter pilots and jet fighter crews also reported seeing the UFO, which flew alongside some of them. Later a jet was sent up to intercept a separate cigar-shaped object, but it proved too fast.

Three other sightings in the Italian report were by air traffic controllers using binoculars. At Naples on August 4, 1977, officials watched a pulsating star-shaped object for 90 minutes. At Elmas on November 5, a UFO was observed for eight minutes, during which it rose from 5,000 feet to 30,000 in 30 seconds. And at Pisa on November 23, staff saw a strange glowing shape change colour from red to violet to green for two hours at 15,000 feet.

The last of the objects, all listed as 'genuine UFOs', was seen on March 9, 1978. The pilot of International Airlines flight 1H-662 radioed Milan control tower to report 'a green rocket moving above and below us about a mile away'. He asked if it could be another aircraft, and was told none were in the area.

'I thought I was going mad,' the pilot later told officials who interviewed him. 'I only reported the sighting for information. When other pilots said they had seen it too, I knew I wasn't seeing things.'

Three Austrian air force jets took to the sky on May 7, 1980, after a KLM liner pilot told Vienna air controllers that a grey spherical object was flying above him over the Dachstein mountains. Two of the fighters were ordered to intercept, while the third filmed the confrontation. But both missions proved impossible. All three made visual contact with the object, but could not get close because of its unpredictable, erratic behaviour. It soon vanished completely.

Action over the Arctic

Russian pilots have also reported seeing UFOs, and one even had a 'dogfight' with one. Professor Felix Zigel, of Moscow's Aviation Institute, said: 'His name was Arkady Apraksin. He was flying a jet fighter when he encountered a cigar-shaped UFO. Radar had also spotted it, and he was ordered to force it to land, or open fire.

'Apraksin began his approach, but the mystery craft fired a fan-shaped beam which momentarily blinded him and killed his controls and the engine. He had to glide into a landing.'

On June 14, 1980, another Soviet flier reported a UFO above Moscow that played cat-and-mouse with him. 'Its manoeuvres were too bizarre for our jet to duplicate,' said Professor Zigel. 'Suddenly it took off at incredible speed.' The pilot said the craft seemed almost 900 feet wide, and was circular.

Four months later, on October 22, Captain Vladimir Dubstov spotted a similar-size saucer hovering below him as he flew his patrol bomber over the Arctic Ocean. He changed course to circle it.

'He told me it was truly immense,' said Professor Zigel. 'A cone of light protruding down from it gave it an eerie appearance, but it showed no sign of life. Then Dubstov's instruments went haywire, and he lost altitude. The UFO took off vertically and soared past him, leaving behind a greenish-blue cloud. Dubstov nursed his crippled jet home and reported the incident.'

Phantoms fight 'cover up'

American airline pilots were furious in 1954 when the CIA and USAF imposed military-style curbs on them reporting UFOs. The clamp-down followed a conference in February when Military Air Transport Service Intelligence officers met the heads of major airlines to try to speed up the process of reporting UFOs spotted during civilian flights.

Until then, pilots had reported strange objects after they landed. Now the Air Force instructed them to radio the news to MATS HQ in Washington, or the nearest air base, while in flight. And it asked them not to discuss sightings, or give information to newspapers.

A month later, regulations threatening Air Force pilots with ten years jail and a fine of $10,000 for 'failing to maintain absolute secrecy' were extended to cover civilian air crews. Understandably, the airline veterans reacted angrily. A protest petition was signed by 450 men, 50 of whom, all with at least 15 years service, said at a meeting that the censorship bid 'bordered on the ridiculous'. It was, they said, 'a lesson in lying, intrigue, and the Big Brother attitude carried to the ultimate extreme'.

The pilots knew that the curbs were part of a cover-up, for all had seen a UFO with their own eyes. Many had seen several. They revealed that five or ten sightings were reported every night by commercial pilots in America alone, and said that it was almost routine to warn passengers to put on seat belts when UFOs were near.

Some of the civilian sightings over the last 40 years have been every bit as spectacular as those reported by the air forces.

Early on July 23, 1948, Captain Clarence Chiles and his co-pilot John Whitted saw a craft from their Eastern Airlines DC-3 over Montgomery, Alabama. A cigar-like projectile was heading for the Dakota from the northeast.

Chiles swung his plane to the left, and as the UFO passed it 200 yards away, he noted two rows of portholes emitting an uncanny light along the side of the metallic, wingless shape. 'There was a deep blue glow on the underside of the craft, and a 15-yard trail of orange-red flame,' the pilot reported. The object stopped when it drew level with the plane, then shot upwards at great speed. The Dakota wobbled, as if caught in the blast. Chiles later found one passenger who had not been sleeping, and had seen the 'great streak of light'.

Six years later, the crew and passengers of the BOAC stratocruiser *Centaurius* watched an even better in-flight show. As the plane approached Goose Bay, Labrador, on June 29, 1954, en route from New York to Shannon and London, Captain James Howard noticed a large dark object emerge from clouds four miles to his left, apparently flying parallel with him. It was surrounded by six smaller blobs.

Howard radioed ahead to Goose Bay, and two US F80 Sabre jets scrambled. What happened next was seen by the 11 crew and 19 passengers of the stratocruiser, and described later by investigator John Carnell.

He wrote: 'When 15 miles away, one of the fighter pilots radioed that he had the unknown objects and the airliner on his radar scope. At that instant the six smaller objects, which seemed like discs, moved into single file and appeared to enter the larger object, which then began to fade, disappearing as the fighter appeared overhead.'

Carnell, who described the mother ship as 'a large, shape-changing object, rather like a swarm of bees, but solid,' said the same formation was seen several times that year, over both America and Europe.

Keeping tabs on Concorde

People living near London's Heathrow Airport claim to have seen UFOs keeping watch on the Anglo-French supersonic jet Concorde. Mrs Dee Godden, 65, of Chiswick, West London, said she first saw one in August 1979.

'A huge reddish ball of light appeared in the sky right in Concorde's flightpath,' she said. 'I thought there was going to be an almighty crash, but when Concorde reached the spot, it just flew straight through it. The shape looked as if it was keeping watch on the plane.'

Her husband Ernest, 64, also saw the light. 'I was sceptical when my wife told me what she had seen,' he recalled. 'I looked out of the window of our flat, and saw a shimmering object. It stayed in the sky for about 17 minutes.'

At Heathrow, officials said: 'Nothing was picked up on radar, so we cannot explain the sighting.' But UFO researcher Barry Gooding said: 'It is quite possible that UFOs from another planet are keeping watch on technological advances such as Concorde.'

Unchartered activities

Adream trip to a sunshine island turned into a nightmare flight for 109 German and Austrian tourists when UFOs took too close an interest in their charter jet in November 1979. Captain Javier Lerdo-Tejeda, 34, a pilot with 15 years flying experience, was at the controls as the Caravelle took off at 9.30 am from the Mediterranean isle of Majorca, bound for the Canary Islands. But soon after levelling out, he noticed two very bright red lights in the sky.

'I was intrigued because they seemed to be flying in formation,' said Captain Lerdo-Tejeda. 'They were moving abreast at a slight angle to me, but getting closer all the time. They were about 15 miles away when we were at 23,000 feet, but only half a mile off when we reached 28,000 feet. Soon I realised they were almost on a collision course – they were virtually on top of me.'

The pilot ordered his passengers and six crew to put their seat belts back on, and radioed ahead to Barcelona control tower. He was told there were no aircraft in his flight path, and nothing on the radar screens.

'I decided to call in help from the Spanish air force and the Madrid radar station,' said Captain Lerdo-Tejeda. 'The equipment there is more sensitive than that used for civilian traffic, and they had picked up two objects which seemed to be very close to my plane.

'I swung my aircraft away sharply from the red lights and began descending at 5,000 feet a minute to 15,000 feet – an extremely steep dive for the passengers. Madrid was still monitoring the UFOs, and said the objects suddenly dropped 12,000 feet in just 30 seconds, following me. I know of no aircraft capable of doing that.'

He continued to take evasive action, trying in vain to shake off the two shadows. Then, 30 miles out to sea off Valencia on Spain's south-west coast, an air force Mirage fighter arrived. The pilot instantly spotted the two glowing red shapes, apparently chasing the airliner. But seconds after the fighter jet zoomed into sight, the lights suddenly vanished.

A shaken Captain Lerdo-Tejeda swung back to Valencia for an unscheduled stop, and filed a full report of his dramatic encounter. 'I have never known such danger, and I have been flying for nearly half my life,' he told stunned officials. His crew backed his account in separate interviews.

Spain's Transport and Communications Minister, Sanchez Teran, was in Valencia at the time, and spoke to Captain Lerdo-Tejeda. He said later: 'I am now prepared to believe that unidentified flying objects do exist.'

Chichester and the UFO

**Probably the first air-to-air sighting of a UFO was by Francis
Chichester, later to earn fame as a round-the-world yachtsman. In
1931, he was piloting a tiny plane from Australia to New Zealand
when a strange airship appeared, a dull grey-white colour with
brightly flashing lights. The disc followed him for some miles
across the Tasman Sea, occasionally vanishing behind clouds,
before accelerating out of sight.**

They never returned

Have UFOs caused civilian planes to crash? In 1953, the pilot of a
DC-6 airliner flying from Wake Island in the Pacific to Los Angeles
reported UFOs approaching before his radio went dead. Searchers
later found wreckage and 20 bodies. And over Michigan, as reported
elsewhere in this book, witnesses saw a curious ball of light in the sky on the

night a DC-4 crashed, killing 58 people.

On a Saturday evening in late October, 1978, Frederick Valentich vanished while flying his single-engined Cessna 182 from Melbourne, Australia, to King Island. He was near Cape Otway, 35 miles south of Melbourne over the Bass Strait, when he told air controllers he was being followed by an aircraft with four bright lights.

When officials asked if he could identify the plane, he radioed: 'It's not an aircraft, it's ...' The set went dead. Two minutes later it came alive briefly again, and Valentich said: 'I'm orbiting and the thing is orbiting on top of me also ... it has a green light and sort of metallic light on the offside.' He added that his engine was choking and rough-idling, then all contact was lost.

Rescue planes and ships scoured the area but found nothing except an oil slick, thought to be too large to be caused by a light aircraft. Valentich's girlfriend, Rhonda Rushton, 16, said: 'I know he is alive, and we will see him soon.' She added that she had given government officials 'top secret' information. A spokesman said: 'We promised to keep details of the interview confidential.'

Authors Kevin Killey and Gary Lester used the disappearance as evidence of their claim, in 1981, that the Bass Strait was another Bermuda Triangle. They said a new four-engine plane carrying a crew of two and ten passengers had vanished there in 1932, and in 1979 a racing sloop and her crew of five disappeared without trace. They renamed the waters between Melbourne and Tasmania the Devil's Meridian.

'Flying saucers, the size of battleships ...'

Three UFOs were also spotted over the Iberian peninsula by the crew and 100 passengers of a British Airways Trident. Captain Denis Wood saw them as he flew to Faro, Portugal – and again as he made the return flight to London later the same day.

It happened over the Portuguese west coast on July 30, 1976. Captain Wood, 42, from Haslemere, Surrey, was told by air traffic controllers that an unidentified flying object had been reported in the area. He scanned the skies, and saw a bright object like nothing he had seen before in 20 years of flying. 'It was not a satellite, weather balloon or a star,' he said later.

As he invited the passengers to look at the UFO, two more objects appeared in the night sky. 'They were cigar-shaped, and appeared to come from nowhere,' said First Officer Colin Thomas, 38, from Camberley, Surrey. 'They took up positions to the right and below the first object. It was just after 8 pm, and I could see them clearly for eight minutes. They did not move.' Thomas had served 12 years as an RAF fighter pilot, and had flown with British Airways for seven years, but he too had never seen anything like the UFOs.

After dropping the 100 holiday-makers at Faro, Captain Wood, Flight Officer Thomas and the third crewman, Stephen Sowerby, of Richmond on Thames, set out at once for home. As they flew through the area where they had seen the UFOs, Captain Wood switched on his radar scanner and tilted it towards the spot where the shapes had been. They were still there.

'The two cigar-shaped objects were exactly where they had been,' said Captain Wood. 'We got to within seven miles of them, then they just disappeared off the side of the screen.'

The crew described the UFOs later as 'flying saucers, the size of battleships'. But it was ten months before they told the world about them. 'We were afraid people would ridicule us,' said one of them.

Some people did just that after they announced their sighting. The Science Research Council, in London, said the main 'UFO' was probably a giant research balloon, on its way from Sicily to America. Rays of the setting sun would have caught the plastic fabric, making it appear brilliantly lit. And the secondary UFOs were probably either ballast being thrown overboard as the gas of the balloon cooled, or clouds of fine steel shot used to measure the wind.

Watchers on the Moon?

Atop American space consultant claims that two UFOs were watching when Neil Armstrong took his 'one small step for a man, one giant leap for mankind' by walking on the Moon's surface on July 20, 1969.

The astronaut spotted them on the rim of a nearby crater as he stepped out of his Apollo 11 spacecraft, according to Maurice Chatelain, who had left the National Aeronautics and Space Administration team by the time he made the claim in September, 1979.

While Armstrong was reporting his sighting to Houston control, Chatelain said, co-pilot Buzz Aldrin filmed the alien craft from inside Apollo.

But, alleged Chatelain, NASA ordered a cover-up of the incident. Mission

controllers blacked out Armstrong's radio report from worldwide broadcasts of the historic event 'for security reasons'.

NASA dismissed the story as 'absolutely ridiculous'. Chief spokesman John McLeaish said: 'The only breaks in transmission from Apollo 11 occurred when it was on the other side of the Moon. The only conversations we have never made public were private talks between the astronauts and doctors.'

Chatelain's story received unexpected backing – from Moscow. Physicist Dr Vladimir Azhazha said: 'We heard about this episode two years ago. I am certain it took place, but it was censored by NASA.'

Soviet space expert Professor Sergei Boshich added: 'It is my opinion that beings from another civilization picked up radio signals from Earth and spied on the Apollo landing to learn the extent of our knowledge. Then they took off without making contact.'

Other American astronauts have had close encounters with strange craft. In 1953, Gordon Cooper, later to join the NASA programme, saw a UFO while piloting a plane over Germany. He said: 'I now firmly believe in extra-terrestrial craft.'

In 1965, James McDivitt and Ed White were orbiting Earth 100 miles up in Gemini 4 when they spotted a silver cyinder with protruding antennae. McDivitt started taking pictures of it, but then the two men had to prepare for evasive action as the UFO moved closer. Just when a collision seemed inevitable, the curious craft vanished.

Mission control at Houston dismissed the shape as one of Gemini's booster rockets, in orbit alongside the ship. But McDivitt said: 'It was in the wrong place at the wrong time for that.'

Eight years later, astronauts Jack Lousma, Owen Garriot and Alan Bean saw a rotating red shape from Skylab 2. They spent ten minutes photograph-ing it, 270 miles above Earth. Again NASA denied that the shining capsule was another spacecraft.

Gordon Cooper said: 'NASA and the Government know very well that intelligent beings from other planets regularly visit our world to enter into discreet contact and observe us.

'They have an enormous amount of evidence, but have kept quiet in order not to alarm people.'

Buzz Aldrin standing on the Moon, with Neil Armstrong and the Eagle landing craft reflected in his visor.

Grilling the police

Patrolman Gene Bertrand did what any good cop would in an emergency when faced with a hostile intruder – he dropped to one knee and drew his revolver. But he was faced with no ordinary intruder. The object hurtling towards him really was out of this world.

Bertrand had been called into headquarters at Exeter, New Hampshire, to investigate the story of a kid who had come in 'all shook up about some object that had chased him'. Norman Muscarello had been hitch-hiking home from Amesbury along Route 150 in the early hours of September 3, 1965, when a glowing red object had appeared in a field beside the road, and moved towards him.

Bertrand knew the boy. He said: 'He's real tough, but something must have really scared him. He could hardly hold his cigarette and was as pale as a sheet.' They drove out in the squad car to the field. They parked and sat in the car for several minutes. Nothing happened.

'I radioed the station and told them there was nothing out here,' Bertrand recalled. 'They asked me to take a quick walk in the field before coming back in. I must admit I felt kind of foolish walking out on private property after midnight, looking for a flying saucer.

'We walked out, me waving my flashlight back and forth, then Norman shouted, "Look out, here it comes!" I swung round and could hardly believe what I was seeing. There was this huge dark object, as big as a barn, with red flashing lights on it. It barely cleared the trees, and it was swaying from side to side.

'Then it seemed to tilt and come right at us. I automatically dropped to one knee and drew my service revolver, but I didn't shoot. I remember suddenly thinking that that would be unwise, so I yelled at Norman to run for the cruiser. He just froze in his tracks. I had to almost drag him back.

'The thing seemed to be about 100 feet up. It was bright red with a sort of halo effect. I thought we'd be burned alive, but it gave off no heat and I didn't hear any noise from it. I did hear the horses in a nearby barn neighing and kicking in their stalls, though. Even the dogs around the area started to howl. My brain kept telling me that this doesn't happen – but it was right in front of my eyes.'

Bertrand's partner, patrolman Dave Hunt, arrived while the UFO was still in sight. The three stood watching in amazement for ten more minutes. 'It floated, wobbled, and did things that no plane could do,' Bertrand said. 'Then it just darted away over the trees towards Hampton.'

As the policemen went back to their office to write their reports, Bertrand's mind went back to the woman he had met an hour earlier on Route 101. She was sitting in her parked car, 'real upset' about a red glowing object that had chased her. He had sent her home without thinking much about it. Now he knew what she had seen.

Others had seen it, too. The men had not long been back in the station when a telephone operator from Hampton called. A man from a public call box claimed he had been chased by a flying saucer ... and it was still out there. The line went dead before he could say more, and though the officers tried to locate him, they could not do so.

Air Force investigators who interrogated Bertrand and Hunt told them to keep quiet about what they had seen, so that it would not get into the newspapers. But a local newspaper reporter had already got the story.

Unable to keep it quiet, the authorities began issuing a string of curious denials. The Pentagon at first blamed the sighting on a temperature inversion that had caused 'stars and planets to dance and twinkle'. Officers Bertrand and Hunt protested that such a statement put their reputations as responsible policemen at risk.

Then the Pentagon claimed that Big Blast Coco, a high-altitude Strategic Air Command exercise, was responsible. The town of Exeter was within the traffic pattern used, said the war chiefs, adding: 'During their approach the aircraft would have been displaying standard position lights, anti-collision lights and possibly over-wing and landing lights.'

But Bertrand had an answer to that one, too. He wrote another protest letter, saying: 'Since I was in the Air Force for four years engaged in refuelling operations with all kinds of military aircraft, it was impossible to mistake what we saw for any kind of military operation ... Immediately after the object disappeared we did see what probably was a B-47 at high altitude, but it bore no relation at all to the object we saw.'

The two officers also pointed out that they saw the UFO at 3 am, nearly an hour after the exercise ended.

Grudgingly, the Air Force gave way – but only a little. 'The early sightings ... are attributed to aircraft from Operation Big Blast Coco,' their final statement said. 'The subsequent observations by officers Bertrand and Hunt occurring after 2 am are regarded as unidentified.'

Even such a small admission was a huge advance for UFO believers frustrated by years of officialdom's stubborn refusal to acknowledge that there could be such things.

The following March, Exeter was again visited by a UFO. One Sunday night, a police sergeant checking doors in the town around 10 pm saw a fast-moving white light falling to the west. He climbed a hill to get a better view, and saw what looked like a lighted egg with rotating red, white, blue and green lights underneath it, moving slowly back and forward. Then it plunged quickly down to hover over power lines.

The sergeant radioed headquarters, and a lieutenant arrived, carrying binoculars. He had always been sceptical about UFOs, despite the sightings the previous September by his own men. Now, as he peered at the egg-shaped object with a bright white dome on top, he was converted. Officer Bertrand and a newspaperman also saw the UFO. But this time nobody made a fuss about it. The town was clearly determined to live down the notoriety aroused by the earlier sightings.

No pictures please

Police chief Jeff Greenhaw lost both his wife and his job because of what he claims he saw on the night of October 17, 1963. But he stuck to his story.

It was just after 10 pm when he took the call at his home in Falkville, Alabama. A woman said she had seen a UFO with flashing lights land in a field west of town. Greenhaw, 26, was off duty at the time, but decided to investigate anyway. He took his camera.

As he drove up a gravel road towards the remote landing site, he saw a figure in the middle of the track. It was about the size of a large human, but was clad in a silvery suit that looked like tin foil. Antennae seemed to sprout from its head. As it moved towards him, he shot four flash pictures, then turned on the revolving light on top of his car. The figure turned and ran, 'faster than any human I ever saw'.

Greenhaw agreed to publish his pictures, which showed the blurred shape of an astronaut-type figure. But within four weeks, he was to regret it. His wife left, unable to cope with the publicity and 'side effects'. Greenhaw's car engine blew up, then a caravan he owned went up in flames. Finally, on November 15, he was asked to quit his job.

Whether he saw an alien or a hoax invented by someone with a grudge was never established. Many other people reported odd lights that night, but despite their evidence, Greenhaw's superiors felt that his credibility had diminished.

This UFO entity was photographed by Police Chief Jeff Greenhaw at Falkville, Alabama on October 17, 1973.

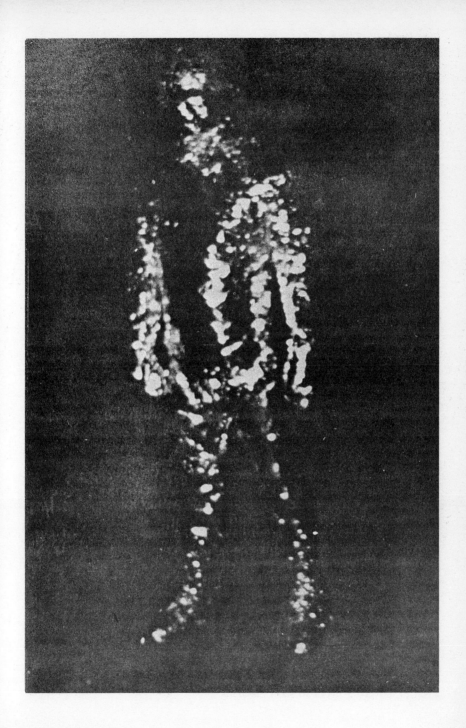

In pursuit of the unknown

The black Chevrolet shot past the courthouse at Socorro, New Mexico, far faster than it should have done. Patrolman Lonnie Zamora gunned the engine of his patrol car into action, and swung out into Old Rodeo Street in pursuit. He noted the time for his report – it was 5.45 pm on April 24, 1964. Zamora would never catch the speeder, but he would remember that day for the rest of his life.

As he accelerated out of town, he noticed a flame in the sky, a mile or so to the south-west. He also heard a roar. The noise came from the direction of a dynamite storage shack. Had it blown up? He decided to abandon the chase and investigate.

He swerved off the road and on to a rough gravel track. The tapered blue and orange flame seemed to be descending against the setting sun. He lost sight of it as he struggled to steer the car up a small hill. Three times he had to reverse and try another route as gravel and rock spun the wheels.

At the top of the hill, Zamora looked round for the shack. Then a shiny object 150 yards away caught his eye. 'It looked at first like a car turned upside down,' he recalled. 'I thought some kids might have turned it over. I saw two people in white coveralls very close to the object. One seemed to turn and look straight at my car. He seemed startled, to quickly jump somewhat.'

The officer began manoeuvring his car closer, with the idea of giving help. When he next looked at the object, the two figures – small adults or children – had vanished. The oval shape was whitish, like aluminium. He stopped the car, and radioed to HQ that he was leaving to investigate a possible accident.

As he put down his microphone, Zamora heard two or three loud thumps, 'like someone hammering or shutting a door hard'. Then the roar began, growing louder and increasing in frequency. 'It was nothing like a jet,' the policeman told investigators. 'I know what jets sound like.'

Now he saw the blue and orange flame again, and the object was going straight up into the air. He noted that it was oval and smooth, and saw no doors or windows, only a red insignia drawing, about 30 inches wide. As the roar increased, Zamora turned and ran – 'I thought the thing was going to blow up.'

He ran past his own car, stumbling as his leg struck the back bumper, and kept going, glancing over his shoulder a couple of times to see what was happening. The craft was still rising slowly from the deserted gully where it had landed. The officer dived over the top of a ridge and spread himself on the ground, covering his head with his arms.

As the roar stopped, he gingerly peeped over the hilltop. The object was speeding away towards the south-west, about 10 to 15 feet above the ground. Then it suddenly lifted higher into the sky and flew off rapidly, without sound or smoke, finally disappearing behind nearby mountains. Zamora radioed his story in to the duty desk sergeant, and a second squad car sped to the scene. The reinforcements noted 'landing marks' about 2 to 3 inches deep in the hard-packed, sandy surface. Greasewood bushes and grass around them were scorched and smouldering.

Air Force investigators arrived a few days later, intent on finding some natural explanation for what patrolman Zamora had seen. They tried hard to establish that some man-made craft had been in the area, but without success. Colleagues described Zamora as a solid, well-liked citizen, a down-to-earth character of integrity. Cynics said that residents living near the site had seen and heard nothing; that the scorch marks could have been caused by a cigarette lighter; that the 'landing marks' could have been created with a small shovel, or by moving boulders; that the land was owned by the town's mayor, who would welcome the publicity and tourists attracted by a UFO report.

Other investigators, however, were forced to admit that Zamora had probably seen some real phenomenon of undetermined origin. One of them was Dr J. Allen Hynek, who, talking later of the scorn some critics poured on UFO reports, said: 'It is paradoxical that the testimony of policemen, which in some cases might be sufficient to send a man to the electric chair, is in instances like this often totally disregarded.'

Similar sightings, of a white, aluminium-like oval shape, were reported right across the United States that spring. It was seen at La Madera, New Mexico, Helena, Montana, and Newark, New Jersey. The last witness also reported seeing curious child-size creatures beside the grounded craft.

The acrobatic disc

Detective Sergeant Norman Collinson watched a disc-like object perform 90-degree turns at incredible speed above the town of Bury, Lancashire, in April 1976. The officer, who later became an inspector, said: 'After a while it streaked away at an even higher speed, reaching the horizon in around two seconds.'

Column of light

Inspector Desmond Condon was among the many people who reported a column of light, stretching almost 3,000 feet, above Earlsfield, south-west London, in November 1977. 'It was a perfect pillar,' he said. 'It glowed with a bluish haze and stayed motionless for about 30 minutes. I've never seen anything like it.'

Cops in confusion

A woman police officer and a male colleague spotted a long, cigar-shaped object hovering 500 feet above the select residential district of Rickmansworth, Hertfordshire, at 3.25 am on November 29, 1979. It was brilliantly lit along its entire length, and had red lights above and below it. It made no sound. WPC Anne Louise Brown, 21, admitted later: 'I was scared stiff when it was above our car. I don't know what it was, but it was definitely too big and too bright to be a plane or a star. I told my colleague he must be crackers to report it back. I was sure people would think we were potty.'

Minutes later, two other officers, both men, saw the same shape above nearby Chorley Wood, and gave chase in their Panda car after alerting HQ. It flew quietly out of sight, but two hours later they spotted it again.

Hertfordshire police checked with West Drayton air traffic control, and confirmed that no planes were in the area. Inspector George Freakes said: 'This is being treated seriously. We are convinced the officers saw something – they are very genuine types – but as yet no one can explain exactly what it was.'

Patrolmen from several forces gave chase when a UFO was spotted over Will County, Illinois, south of Chicago, in the pre-dawn darkness of November 25, 1980. And the mysterious shape led them a merry dance.

Sheriff's deputies Lieutenant Karl Sicinski and Sergeant Jay Mau were first to see the UFO, about 1,500 feet up and two miles away. It drifted south, shot off east, then turned north, and finally ended up to the south-east of them.

'It was faster than any plane I ever saw,' said Sicinski, who flew fighter jets during his days in the US Navy. 'I've never seen any aircraft that can manoeuvre as tightly as this object did. It was huge and very bright. It was shaped like a teardrop lying on its side and had a pinkish-whitish cast to it.'

Policemen in neighbouring towns Frankfort, New Lenox and Mokena overheard Sicinski radio his report to HQ, and saw the shape he mentioned. Frankfort patrolman Sam Cucci was driving west towards the UFO when he spotted it rising, getting brighter, then dimming its lights.

'Suddenly I lost sight of it,' he recalled. 'I asked two other squad cars where it was and they said, "It's behind you." So I whipped the squad car round to the east and, with the two other units, gave chase at about 60 mph. I put on my spotlight, but the UFO veered away and then just dissipated, like it was a light and someone shut it off.'

In New Lenox, officers Carl Bachman and Charles Proper watched the UFO zigzag across the sky for 20 minutes. 'I won't forget that night,' said Bachman. 'There is something out there we don't know about.' Proper said: 'It was a bright light, and all of a sudden it just went straight up and disappeared. In a matter of just one or two seconds it was out of sight.'

Mokena patrolman Tom Donegan, who also saw the UFO, said: 'It makes you wonder who's out there watching us.'

In March 1981 came news of a bizarre encounter involving a chief of police. Miguel Costa, in charge of the force at Melo, Uruguay, was driving with his wife Carmen and friends Armando and Maria Pcna along a gravel road near Tacuarembo when a huge shape, gleaming with orange and yellow lights, loomed out of the early morning darkness in front of them.

Costa stopped the car, and, on impulse, flashed the headlights. 'All of a sudden the UFO hesitated, then zigzagged up and back as if answering our call,' the police chief reported.

'As soon as we started out again, it was there following us. I again stopped the car and flashed my lights. Again the UFO wavered in reply. We drove on once more on the twisting road and the UFO stayed with us, always about half-a-mile away. This went on for almost 30 miles. That's when the strangest thing of all occurred.

'We were all glued to the windows watching as the disc suddenly shot towards the ground as if it was going to crash. It stopped 50 to 100 yards from the earth, and we could clearly see its round, dome-like shape with a large flat plate underneath. There was a slight ring of cloud around the dome. The top was reddish but the bottom was a brilliant glowing white.'

Feeling somehow menaced by the craft's new, lower flight path, Costa turned the car round and headed back towards Tacuarembo, the nearest town. The blazing light of the UFO remained constant in the rear window. Costa pulled over and parked under some trees.

'We walked over to a little clearing and looked up,' the policeman said. 'A second disc was moving some distance behind the first. They never touched, but they seemed to be travelling together. They moved up and down and clouds started to form.

'They passed over the top of the clouds and lit them up like a halo. Then they faded, getting smaller and smaller until finally they had gone. It was dawn. They had been over us for 90 minutes. We looked at each other without speaking. We still couldn't believe what we had seen.'

Chief Costa paused, then added: 'I never believed in UFOs before, but I realise now that I have seen something special and unreal.'

Follow that UFO!

Five policemen saw a multicoloured flying object hovering above the town of Dumfries, Scotland, late in 1979. Two of them later described the sighting at a press conference.

The officers were called in after a flood of calls from people going home after the pubs shut. They saw the huge shape for about 20 minutes before it streaked away over nearby hills.

Sergeant Bill McDavid, 39, said he drove to within a mile of the thing. It was larger than any aircraft and seemed to be 500 feet up. Its shape was like that of an airship, with five or six white lights shining from separate compartments.

PC James Smith said: 'I never believed in UFOs up to now. It was raining at the time and the cloud base was very low. The shape remained stationary for 20 minutes then vanished over the hills to the west.'

Mary Blyth, 22, and her sister Vicky, 19, were just two of the people who rang the police after they spotted the UFO. 'The lights appeared from nowhere,' said Mary. 'We just stood there and stared at it in amazement.'

Glasgow weather centre said it was not unknown for low clouds to reflect bright lights from Earth, but a spokesman added: 'If light from the ground is reflected, it is usually just a yellowish glare. I have never heard of a cluster of coloured lights in the way that has been described. I have no explanation as to what these people really saw.'

Two patrolmen in Minnesota spotted a glowing white ball after being called out by Farmington housewife and computer programmer Karen Anondson in September, 1979. 'It was definitely a UFO,' said patrolman Dan Siebenaler, of the Farmington Force. 'I am familiar with what is in the night sky, and that thing did not belong there.' Steve Kurtz, an officer from neighbouring Apple Valley police, said: 'It was something unexplainable, I've never seen anything like it before.' Mrs Anondson, 32, said she had seen the ball at least nine times as she drove home from work. 'It's become a normal thing,' she said. 'I look for it when I come out of the office.'

A few months earlier, a Minnesota deputy sheriff reported a frightening encounter with a UFO. Val Johnson was driving his patrol car on a lonely road near Warren when he saw a bright light about $2\frac{1}{2}$ miles away. 'I drove towards it to find out what it was,' he recalled. 'After I'd gone about a mile, the light rushed towards me. It was a brilliant light, so brilliant it was almost painful.

'I remember the brakes locking when I applied them, and I remember the sound of breaking glass. Then I lost consciousness for about 30 minutes. When I came too, I radioed for help.'

Officers who examined the car found that both the windshield and a headlight had been broken, and the top of the hood was dented. Even more curious was the fact that the two spring-loaded whip antennae on the roof had been bent at an angle of 90 degrees. 'The damage to the hood, windshield and headlight might have been caused by stones or rocks,' said UFO researcher Allen Hendry. 'But there's no explaining how the antennae, which are extremely flexible, got to be bent that way.'

Doctors who checked the deputy sheriff after his ordeal had to treat burns round his eyes. They were of the kind welders suffer when they fail to use protective masks.

A dozen policemen in Tennessee watched a UFO for two hours in February 1980. It amazed the people of three towns in two counties with its aerial antics, hovering, then shooting off at impossible speeds and incredible angles.

Deputy sheriff Franklin Morris, from Winchester, first heard about the strange sight over his radio, and raced to a hill to get a good view of it. 'At first I thought it might be a plane, but there was no noise at all, no engine, no rocket. It hovered a while, three or four minutes. Then it decided to take off, and moved so fast you could hardly watch it. I've seen some pretty fast jets in my time, but never anything like this.'

Forest phantom

Two policemen responded to a 999 call at Hainault Forest, Essex, early one May morning in 1977, and spotted a tent-like object glowing red through the trees. They watched it 'pulsing' for three minutes, then it dissolved into the darkness.

Arrest that saucer!

PC Chris Bazire and WPC Vivienne White spotted a flying saucer 500 to 700 feet above Salisbury Plain, Wiltshire, in November 1977. 'It was oblong with a domed top and flat bottom,' they reported. 'It was travelling very slowly at first, then shot off at tremendous speed, leaving a vapour trail.'

Winchester patrolmen Milton Yates and Gerald Glasner saw bright red and white lights coming towards them as they drove on the east side of town. 'It was coming towards us and it stopped, sat two or three minutes, then shot off at 500 or 600 mph,' said Sergeant Yates. 'The way it took off it couldn't have been an aircraft. It had no moving lights, no noise, just those flashing lights, and it went round in circles. I feel real sure it was a UFO.'

Officer Glasner added: 'It was not like anything we've got here on Earth. The speed, manoeuverability, those flashing lights, the silence.' Officers from nearby Monteagle and Cowan also watched the UFO in amazement. When they checked with the National Weather Service station at Nashville, officials could offer no alternative natural explanation.

Two Michigan policemen chased a multicoloured, shapeless craft for more than 26 miles in March 1980 after picking it up in the sky over Gladstone. 'It was glowing orange, with a green light in the rear, red lights top and bottom, and a blinking white light at the front,' said patrolman David Mariin, 26.

The men radioed for assistance as they followed the lights for nearly an hour through winding roads and dense forest. Two more police units joined the chase, and the four officers in the other cars all saw the object above the trees as it darted from side to side, leading them on, then vanishing at astonishing speed.

'I was rather sceptical about UFOs before this,' said Mariin's partner, Mark Hager, 22. 'But this made a believer out of me.' The men checked with nearby K. I. Sawyer Air Force base, but were told nothing unusual had been spotted on the radar. 'No one there seemed very interested,' Mariin said. 'It was almost as if they didn't want the public to know.'

Three policemen were among hundreds who saw a gigantic bullet-shaped object which cruised through the night sky above Kansas and northern Missouri for four hours on November 18, 1980. Adair County deputy sheriff Charles Cooper and Missouri highway patrolman Bob Lober were amazed when it flew backwards without turning round. And patrolman Mike Leavene said: 'I've never seen anything like it before.'

People in at least 22 towns reported seeing the UFO as it crisscrossed the two states. Don Leslie, a 42-year-old welder from Milan, Missouri, said: 'It was at least as big as a football field.' Roger Bennett, 40, of Huntsville, Missouri, said: 'It was so big it would make a B-52 bomber look like a Piper Cub.'

He added: 'It was like a big fat cigar, travelling very high from east to west. You could hear a faint rumbling when it was overhead. Just before it disappeared above some clouds it ejected about six smaller objects in a fan-shaped burst. They sped off in different directions.'

Truck driver Randy Hayes, 26, also saw the UFO drop its 'satellites'. He said: 'They were round and had a bluish glow. The mother ship was so big, it blocked out a lot of stars.'

In Trenton, Missouri, photographic student Rick Hull, 19, took a picture of a triangle of lights, which looked like a boomerang. He said the object seemed to make a banking movement, thus revealing lights from 'the windows of a cockpit'. Music teacher Buddy Hannaford and his wife Karla both saw lights 'as if from the cabin of a plane'. Karla, who watched through binoculars, said: 'The thing was delta- or triangle-shaped, with two white lights and a red beacon on the bottom. It passed right over our house.'

The object was picked up on radar at the Federal Aviation Administration station north of Kirksville, Missouri. Technician Franklin West said: 'It went through the area four or five times. I estimated the speed at about 45 mph. I'm not saying it was a flying saucer. I am saying it was an unidentified flying object, because I couldn't identify it.'

The burning cross

Two Devon policemen hit the headlines in 1967 when they chased bright lights in the shape of a pulsating cross. Constables Roger Willey and Clifford Waycott spotted the glowing UFO over Hatherleigh at 4 am on October 24 while on routine patrol in their car, and pursued it for some distance along narrow lanes before it shot off across fields. Critics said the shape could have been aircraft refuelling in mid-air from a tanker plane, which would explain the cross-like effect, and the British Defence Ministry confirmed that such exercises were going on in the area. But they had been completed by 9 pm the previous evening.

Encounters of the third kind

The case for UFOs is backed by astronauts – and the US President

When Barney and Betty Hill told their story, no one believed them. Barney, an American social worker, told how he had been driving with his wife along a lonely road in New Hampshire when a spaceship landed in front of their car and a strange figure got out. There followed a lost two hours which were totally erased from the Hills' memories. The next thing they recalled was looking at their watches and finding themselves on the same road but 30 miles further on.

The couple's story was intriguing but unbelievable – until they were put under hypnosis and questioned about their missing two hours. The stories they then told were identical. They said they had been taken aboard the spaceship and subjected to tests. They also drew pictures of the walls of the craft, which were covered in star maps.

The maps were shown to astronomers, who found them puzzling. For the charts included distant stars which were not known to astronomers at that time – but which have since been discovered.

The Hills are just two out of millions of people round the world who have seen what are now termed UFOs – Unidentified Flying Objects. And among those millions are the chosen few – the people who claim to have encountered the occupants of such spacecraft face to face. Such witnesses risk being labelled cranks, drunks or liars when they report their strange encounters. But nowadays scientists are loth to dismiss such evidence. After all, US President Jimmy Carter claims to have seen a UFO: 'an advancing and receding object which changed from blue to red, shining with a luminous glow'.

Astronaut Gordon Cooper says: 'Intelligent beings from other planets regularly visit our world. The US government and the space agency have a great deal of evidence of such visits, but they keep quiet so as not to alarm people.'

Ed Mitchell, who was the sixth man on the moon, says: 'I am completely convinced that some UFO sightings are real. The question is not whether there are UFOs, but *what* they are.'

The Royal Air Force's late Air Chief Marshal Lord Dowding was a staunch believer in 'flying saucers'. As early as 1954, he said: 'I have never seen a flying saucer, yet I believe they exist. Cumulative evidence has been assembled in such quantity that, for me at any rate, it brings complete conviction. There is no alternative to accepting the theory that they come from an extra-terrestial source. For the first time in recorded history, intelligible communication may become possible between the earth and other planets.'

Although Dowding admitted never having seen a flying saucer he would have received numerous reports of UFO sightings by the fliers under his command during World War Two. But UFO reports began a long time before our present airborne age. One of the firmest sightings of all time, for instance, was made more than 700 years ago. . . .

On New Year's Day 1254, a group of English monks at St Albans stared skywards in awe at 'a kind of large ship, elegantly shaped and of marvellous colour'. Thirty-six years later, monks at Byland Abbey, Yorkshire, recorded the sighting of 'a large, round silver disc' in the sky. And in 1566, one of the most spectacular UFO phenomena in history occurred when a host of glowing discs covered the sky over Basle, Switzerland.

But it is within the last century that the UFO mystery has really captured the imagination. The sightings seem to have run in phases.

A vintage year was 1897, when a rash of reports came out of the United States. A large 'space object' landed at Carlinville, Illinois, but took off at speed when curious townspeople approached. More than 10,000 people saw a mysterious 'airship with flashing lights' hover over Kansas City for ten

---

THE FIRST 'SAUCERS'

On 24 June 1947, a clear and sunny day, American civilian pilot Kenneth Arnold was flying over Mount Rainier in Washington State, when he saw in the distance a formation of nine glistening objects. At first he thought they were fighter planes, but as they darted towards him and skimmed the mountain tops at incredible speed, Arnold realized that they were 'like nothing I had ever seen before'. He watched them move erratically across the horizon and estimated their speed at 1,300 miles an hour. When he landed he sought words to describe the mystery objects . . . and came up with the phrase: 'like saucers skimming over water'. Thus was the term 'flying saucers' born.

minutes before shooting off into space. In the same year, a member of the House of Representatives, Alexander Hamilton, watched an enormous object land outside his home near Le Roy, Kansas. He described it as 'cigar-shaped, some 300 ft long, transparent and brilliantly lighted'. Six strange creatures were visible within the craft, but, when approached by members of Hamilton's staff, it took off and flew out of sight at amazing speed.

There was another spate of sightings in 1909, this time in Britain. Within two months, there were reports of spacecraft from 40 towns. The most dramatic was from Caerphilly, South Wales, where a large cylindrical object was seen to land. Two creatures got out, but, when approached, dashed back inside and took off. There was a similar spate of UFOs in New Zealand that same year, and in Ontario, Canada, four years later.

The advent of air travel led to a dramatic increase in the number of UFO reports. Perhaps the first air-to-air sighting was by pioneer aviator Francis Chichester, later to become famous as a round-the-world yachtsman. Chichester was flying his plane *Gipsy Moth* from Australia to New Zealand when a strange airship appeared alongside him. It was circular and glowed brightly. It followed him for some miles before accelerating into the distance.

There were many UFO sightings during World War Two – not surprisingly, considering the increased aerial activity – but a security veil was drawn over most of them. It was after the war that the dossiers on UFOs and flying saucers really began to bulge.

1947: American pilot Kenneth Arnold sights flying saucer formation (see panel).

1948: Hundreds see huge white object in the sky over Madisonville, Kentucky. Three P51 Mustangs are sent up to investigate. One of the pilots gives chase as the object speeds away. The wreckage of his plane is found later that day.

1952: Amateur astronomer George Adamski, of Palomar, California, produces the most famous (but nowadays generally disregarded) photographs of a UFO. Taken through his reflecting telescope, they purport to show a flying saucer hovering half-a-mile up.

1952: Mysterious glowing craft lands and then lifts off vertically from Marseilles airport, France.

1952: Mysterious lights over Washington DC, labelled by the press as the Washington Invasion (see panel).

1953: US Air Force F89 jet chases a UFO over Lake Superior. Trackers watch the pursuit on radar, see the plane catch up then disappear from the screen. UFO speeds north out of radar net. Searchers fail to find any trace of the jet.

1953: L. Gordon Cooper, later to become a US astronaut, sees a UFO while

A popular image of a UFO occupant.

piloting a jet over Germany. He says : 'I now firmly believe in extra-terrestial craft.'

1953 : Pilot of DC-6 airliner flying from Wake Island in the Pacific to Los Angeles radios to report UFOs approaching. Radio falls silent. Searchers later find wreckage and 20 bodies.

1954 : Crew and passengers of a Boeing Stratocruiser flying from New York to London watch a formation of seven craft travelling alongside the airliner for several minutes. The UFOs appear to be six flying saucers and a larger 'mother ship'.

1956 : Glowing UFOs are seen by dozens of eyewitnesses over eastern England. Confirmed by radar trackers at Lakenheath air base, Suffolk.

1958 : Two men in a car approach a 100-ft-long glowing, egg-shaped object hovering above a bridge near Baltimore, Maryland. It shoots skywards in a flash of light and heat. The men's faces later show signs of radiation burns.

From the early 1960s, a wholly inexplicable plethora of UFO reports began to be noted – all from rural areas of Britain. Over the years, a pattern developed and two of the areas have become famous for their space visitations. One is centred on Warminster, in Wiltshire, and the other is a part of Wales that has become known as the Broadhaven Triangle. The people who live in these and other UFO-prone areas of Britain have not always emerged unscathed from their encounters with the spacecraft.

It was one o'clock in the morning when Mrs Pauline Coombs had her close encounter in the Broadhaven Triangle. She was sitting with her husband in their lonely farm cottage when she glanced towards the window. Mrs Coombs stifled a shriek of terror when she saw framed in the window 'a towering 7-ft figure. . . . It was dressed entirely in silver and was surrounded by a luminous glow, but it had no face – no features at all, just an empty black hole'.

Terrified, the young wife was at first speechless. When she regained her voice, she screamed at her husband, Billy, who was sitting with his back to the window. He phoned neighbours for help but by the time they arrived the figure had vanished. Mrs Coombs said : 'We were sweating, trembling and crying with fear. Our dog, which normally barks at the slightest sound, just ran around in circles and later refused to leave the house.' A local farmer who was first on the scene said : 'The couple were terrified – scared out of their wits.'

They had reason to be. Only three days earlier the Coombs family had been out for a drive when their car was pursued by what they described as a glowing ball in the sky which chased them back to their cottage in Ripperton, Dyfed.

A year later the family had their most extraordinary encounter of all. They were out with two of their five children when a silver disc appeared in the sky. It circled them, then headed off towards the nearby coast and seemed to disappear into a large rock. The family followed the path the UFO had taken.

'When we got to the rock,' said Mrs Coombs, 'we saw two tall figures in glowing silver suits. They walked around for a while, then just vanished into the rock.'

UFOs have picked out the Broadhaven Triangle for no apparent reason. One of Mrs Coombs's neighbours, housewife Josephine Hewison, looked out of her bedroom window one morning and saw what she claims was a 50-ft silver spacecraft standing beside her greenhouse. After about ten minutes, it took off and flew away.

Louise Bassett, wife of a restaurant owner from Ferryside, Carmarthen, said: 'I was driving home one night when my radio went dead. At the same time I saw flashing lights in the sky. I took a detour to avoid them but they appeared again three miles further on.' When Mrs Bassett's radio cut out, so did dozens of other people's radios and televisions in the area. Mrs Bassett's

---

'THEY'RE TELLING THE TRUTH'
American medical experts have used hypnosis to test the truth of stories told by people claiming to have had personal encounters with alien beings. The results have often been startling.

A 16-year-old high school boy, who claimed to have seen a tall, green-eyed creature in his garden, agreed to tests at the South-west Montana Mental Health Centre, Anaconda. The youth had forgotten what happened after he encountered the creature, but under hypnosis he said that three aliens had dragged him into a spacecraft. They had examined him, then told him he would forget the entire incident.

Dr Kent Newman, who conducted the experiment, said: 'I believe that the boy honestly reported what he had experienced.'

A similar view is taken by Dr Leo Sprinkle, of the University of Wyoming, Laramie, whose tests revealed that most space encounters took place against the subjects' wills and that they were generally terrified and highly emotional. They often experienced physical effects and amnesia. Dr Sprinkle said: 'I don't know whether these people experienced physical or out-of-the-body encounters, but my personal and professional bias is to accept their claims as real.'

Dr Alvin Lawson, of California State University, Long Beach, is more cautious. After placing under hypnosis several witnesses who claimed to have been abducted, he said: 'Their stories are at least partially true. But that does not mean that their experiences are necessarily "real" physical events - any more than hallucinations are.'

dog was in the car with her at the time. 'He has never been the same since that night,' she said.

Shop assistant Stephen Taylor was out walking near his home ten miles from the Coombs's cottage late one night when he saw a glowing object in the sky. He said: 'It was 40 or 50 ft across and the light seemed to be coming from the underneath. Suddenly a dog shot out of some bushes ahead of me. Then a tall figure popped up right next to me. It was dressed in silver. I was terrified, so I took a swing at it, then fled. When I got home that night my pet dog started snarling at me. It wouldn't let me get near it.'

Perhaps the most convincing witnesses of all are the children of Broadhaven Primary School. Fifteen of them – 14 boys and a girl – were playing football when they rushed inside to tell their headmaster that they had seen a spaceship in the sky. The head, Ralph Llewellyn, split them into groups and asked them to draw pictures of what they had seen. He compared the finished results and was astounded by their similarity. Over years of questioning, the children stuck to their story.

A similar sighting was made at Wawne Primary School, 250 miles away in Humberside. Twenty children aged six and seven dashed to the study of headmaster Michael Yates and told him they had seen a strange object in the sky. The children described a classic UFO – 'like a dish upside down and with a hump on the top'.

At Elgin, in north-east Scotland, two ten-year-old girls described 'a silver-coloured saucer with a bump on the top' which they had seen hovering in a wood. The craft glowed with a red light, they said, and a silver-suited man stood beside it. Mrs Caroline McLennan, mother of one of the girls, said: 'When my daughter told me about it, I remembered having heard a strange whirring noise and saying to my neighbour: "Sounds like a flying saucer." The girls led us back to the wood and we found a big patch of flattened grass. The leaves on the trees nearby were scorched.' A saucer-shaped craft with a beam of light shining down from it was independently witnessed by several people in the same area on the same night.

Karen Iveson, a young tax officer, saw it while out with her boyfriend in Parley Cross, Dorset. She said: 'It was like nothing I had ever seen in my life before. It was a large silvery disc-shaped object with a conical silvery green light beam shining down from the centre of it. The ship hovered over a field for ages, then sped away at a fantastic speed just above tree level. We both panicked a bit.'

The same vision startled Mrs Pauline Fall and a friend. Mrs Fall said: 'It looked like the underneath of a dinner plate, and out of the centre of it came a cone of silver light. The light was shining straight on to my car, and the craft was getting lower and closer to us all the time. My stomach went ice cold.

Then the craft vanished. The car has never worked quite the same since that night.'

A little to the north of the Dorset sightings lies the UFO 'capital' of the world – Warminster, in Wiltshire – UFO-watchers in this small town started an information centre and newsletter to keep their members informed of the latest sightings. Dozens of reports have been registered of a glittering flying saucer known as the 'Warminster Thing'.

Neil Pike and his wife, Sally, are two of the Warminster UFO-watchers, and they claim twice to have seen spacecraft and spacemen. On one occasion the couple were with a party of sky-watchers on a hill near Warminster when they spotted what they thought were two UFOs. Mrs Pike said: 'Suddenly the air became warmer and two shadowy figures appeared. They were very tall and we could see their outlines – but they appeared to be made out of mist or smoke. They had no features.' Her husband, a bank security officer, walked towards the figures. They faded from his vision. But Mrs Pike said: 'The rest of us watched as he walked straight through the figures and out the other side.'

Though Warminster may be the 'UFO capital' it is the United States which claims to have recorded the biggest and the most startling appearances of alien spacecraft.

1964: Police patrolman Lonnie Zamora sees a UFO land near the town of Socorro, New Mexico. He races to the spot and encounters two strange figures, which he describes as 4 ft high, standing beside a glowing, oval spacecraft. They flee inside and take off. Indentations that could have been made by the UFO's landing gear are later discovered.

1965: James McDivitt, in orbit 100 miles above the earth in Gemini 4, sees cylindrical object with antennae protruding. Starts photographing it but McDivitt and fellow astronaut Ed White become alarmed that craft will collide with theirs and they prepare to take evasive action. Before they can do so the UFO disappears.

1965: William Howell and his family, of Foggy Hill, Texas, are out in their car when an amazingly bright blue light appears overhead and keeps pace with them. As Howell accelerates, so does the light. Eventually, the UFO shoots away at incredible speed.

1965: Farm workers at Kelly, Kentucky, report shooting at alien creatures 100 yards away. Whenever one of the creatures is hit by a rifle bullet it keels over – then floats upright again without making any sound.

1972: Muhammad Ali is on a training session in New York's Central Park when he encounters a UFO. He says: 'I was out jogging just before sunrise when this bright light hovered over me. It just seemed to be watching me. It was like a huge electric light bulb in the sky.'

1973: John Gilligan, governor of Ohio, reports seeing a UFO near Ann

Arbor, Michigan. He describes it as 'a vertical shaft of light which glowed amber'.

1973: Jimmy Carter, then governor of Georgia, is sitting on a verandah with 20 other people after an official dinner at Thomastown, Georgia, when, according to Carter, they witness a UFO 'which looked as big as the moon and changed colour several times from red to green'.

1973: Astronauts Jack Lousma, Owen Garriot and Alan Bean, 270 miles up in Skylab 2, photograph a rotating red UFO for ten minutes.

1973: Police chief Jeff Greenshaw, of Falkville, Alabama, drives up to a 6-ft-tall metallic figure on the road. The figure flees up the road, pursued by Greenshaw in his patrol car. The creature outpaces the car and vanishes into the distance.

1973: Off-duty shipyard workers Charles Hickson and Calvin Parker are fishing near Pascagoula, Mississippi, when, according to the two anglers, a 100-ft-long silvery craft hovers before them. A hatch opens and three grey-coloured aliens float out. They have wrinkled skin, claw-like hands and a single slit for an eye. The anglers are miraculously lifted off their riverbank and join the space creatures, who float back inside the craft. Once inside, the two men are laid on their backs on a table and a camera descends from the ceiling to examine them. After about 20 minutes the two friends are released by the aliens and then report their experience. They are hypnotized and given lie-detector tests but their stories remain the same.

1975: Forestry worker Travis Walton is a passenger in a truck with five friends near Snowflake, Arizona, when they see a bright light hovering above some trees. Driver Mike Rogers pulls up. Walton leaps out and runs towards the UFO, but before he gets far there is a bright flash and he falls to the ground. His friends drive on to get out of the firing line but return shortly afterwards to rescue Walton. He has disappeared. Five days later he reappears in the nearby town of Heber and claims to have spent the time with 'weird creatures like human foetuses'. Walton is given a lie-detector test which indicates that he is telling the truth.

1977: Two off-duty nurses are out walking on Staten Island, New York, when they see a cigar-shaped object land in a lightly wooded area. Thoroughly shaken, they stop a police patrol car which goes to the scene – just in time to see a UFO 'bigger than the Goodyear airship' shoot into the air and speed away. The police chase it across the state line into New Jersey, but it vanishes in a silver blur.

1978: Sir Eric Gairey, prime minister of Grenada, tries unsuccessfully to have the United Nations officially investigate UFOs. He says he has seen one – 'a brilliant golden light travelling at tremendous speed'.

1978: German-born movie actress Elke Sommer is in the garden of her Los

Angeles home when a shiny orange ball, about 20 ft in diameter, appears out of the blue 'glowing and floating about like a big moon'. It hovers towards her and she flees into the house. When she reappears it has vanished.

In that same year, 1978, two of the world's great mysteries merged into one for just two hours. That was the length of time that radar operators managed to keep track of a UFO as it zigzagged around the Bermuda Triangle, a mysterious offshore graveyard of ships and planes that have disappeared without trace.

The UFO was also seen by eye-witnesses. It was a circular craft emitting red, green and white light and travelling in an incredibly erratic manner. No civilian or military aircraft were in the vicinity at the time. Experts at the Pinecastle electronic warfare range, near Astor, Florida, struggled to track the strange craft as it kept abruptly changing direction. One moment it would be stationary, the next it would accelerate to 500 miles an hour.

One of the radar operators said: 'It manoeuvred in such a manner and at such speeds that it could not have been an airplane or a helicopter. I've never seen anything like it and I don't want to see anything like it again.'

The most remarkable spate of UFO sightings in recent years began in the closing days of 1978. An Australian television team were flying over the Kalkoura area of New Zealand's South Island on New Year's Eve following earlier UFO reports by airline pilots. The newsmen took the first worthwhile television film of a UFO – one of several round objects marked with bright orange rings which darted around their plane.

At the same time as the sighting, air traffic controllers at Wellington recorded a series of erratic blips on the control tower radar. They moved around the screen at remarkable speed for more than three hours. One of the operators said: 'Six pilots have seen UFOs in the past ten days, and there has been a host of radar sightings. There is obviously something strange out there.'

Not to be outdone by the Australians' TV scoop, a New Zealand camera team took to the skies in the same area of South Island early in January, 1979.

THE WASHINGTON INVASION
Flying saucers and UFOs normally seem to shun densely populated areas. But one of the most famous visitations of all time happened directly over the capital of the USA. The press labelled it the Washington Invasion.

On the evening of 19 July 1952, five strange, strong lights zigzagged across the sky, watched by thousands of people. A week later, on 26 July, they appeared again - with reinforcements. This time, they were between 6 and 12 of them, and their speedy, erratic movements ruled out the possibility that they were aircraft.

Three F94 jet fighters were sent up to buzz the mystery objects. Two of the interceptors could find no trace of the UFOs but the third pilot flew straight into a cluster of brilliant bluish-white lights. The lights, he said, travelled alongside him for 15 seconds before dispersing at remarkable speed.

The pilot returned safely to base, and the lights were never seen again.

They filmed an object which they described as 'an illuminated ping-pong ball, rotating, pulsating and darting around'.

While all this activity was going on in Australasia, similar sightings were being reported from all corners of the globe. In Britain, eyewitnesses from Scotland to the south coast were terrified by white balls in the sky. Some people claimed that they were 'buzzed' by the objects.

In Israel, a rash of close encounters with red balls and flashing lights was reported. In northern Italy, dozens of villages on the slopes of Gran Sasso Mountain were plunged into darkness after a UFO was seen hovering over a hydro-electric plant. Technicians said the instruments suddenly went haywire and machinery stopped. In South Africa, a young mother met 'six darkish skinned spacemen' on a country road near Johannesburg. They spoke in high-pitched voices but fled in a glowing spacecraft when she became excited.

Around the world, scientists and astronomers scorned suggestions of a space 'invasion'. They attributed the sightings to meteors or space debris burning up on entering the earth's atmosphere. Sir Bernard Lovell, director of Britain's Jodrell Bank radio astronomy station, dismissed the sightings as 'pure science fiction'.

Many people over the years have poured similar scorn on UFO sightings. Few have felt able to back the claims of the sincere and often frightened people who have had close encounters with objects from the skies. Yet the sightings continue, growing daily. The UFO riddle is a mystery that simply refuses to go away.

Puzzles of the past

Though reports of UFOs have increased dramatically in the last 40 years, they are by no means unique to the 20th century. Researchers have documented more than 300 sightings before 1900. Monks at St Albans in Hertfordshire saw 'a kind of ship, large, elegantly shaped and well-equipped, and of a marvellous colour' on the night of January 1, 1254. And in 1290, the abbot and monks of Byland Abbey, Yorkshire, noted 'a large round silver disc' flying over them.

Author W. Raymond Drake, of Sunderland, Tyne and Wear, who has written many books on UFOs, says: 'The belief in beings from the skies who surveyed our Earth persisted in human consciousness throughout the Middle Ages.' The most spectacular display from that time was probably the one recorded at Basle, Switzerland, on August 7, 1566. Giant glowing discs covered the sky, to the consternation and amazement of the locals.

In March 1716, Sir Edmund Halley, the British astronomer who gave his name to the world's most famous comet, reported seeing a brightly lit object over London for two hours.

On December 11, 1741, Lord Beauchamp claimed he watched a small oval ball of fire falling over London. About 750 yards up, it suddenly levelled off and zoomed eastwards, its long fiery tail trailing smoke as it rapidly disappeared.

And on March 19, 1748, Sir Hans Sloane, later president of the Royal Society, observed a dazzling blue-white light with a reddish-yellow tail dropping through the evening sky. It was, he said, 'moving more slowly than a falling star in a direct line.'

A stream of saucer-shaped objects were seen flying over the French town of Embrun on September 7, 1820. Witnesses reported that they too changed direction, performing a perfect 90 degree turn without breaking their strict formation. And in 1882, astronomer William Maunday saw a huge disc moving quickly as he studied the north-east horizon from London's Greenwich Royal Observatory. It passed the Moon, he said, then changed into a cigar shape.

In America, too, strange things happened in the sky during the 19th century. In 1878, Texas rancher John Martin was out hunting south of Denison on January 22 when he saw an object coming down from the sun, 'about the size of a large saucer'.

Nine years later, in April 1897, more than 10,000 people were said to have seen an airship over Kansas City, Missouri. Charles Fort, who had also

Spectacular black globes were seen over Basle, Switzerland on August 7, 1566.

reported a 'large, luminous craft' over Niagara Falls back in 1833, wrote of the Kansas sighting: 'Object appeared very swiftly then appeared to stop and hover over the city for ten minutes at a time. Then, after flashing green-blue and white lights, it shot upwards into space.' The same craft was reported over Iowa, Michigan, Nebraska, Wisconsin and Illinois. The *Chicago Record* newspaper reported that it actually landed in fields near Carlinville, Illinois, but took off when curious townsfolk approached.

Alexander Hamilton, a member of the House of Representatives, had an even more incredible story to tell. He made a sworn statement to the effect that on April 21, 1897, he was awakened by a strange noise outside his home in Le Roy, Kansas, and watched a 300-foot cigar-shaped craft, with a carriage underneath, land near his farm. 'The carriage,' he said, 'was made of glass or some other transparent substance alternating with a narrow strip of material. It was brilliantly lighted and everything within was clearly visible. It was occupied by six of the strangest beings I ever saw. They were jabbering together, but I could not understand a word they said.' Hamilton said he and two of his men tried to move even closer to the craft, but the beings turned on some strange power, and the UFO soared up into the sky.

Both Britain and New Zealand seemed besieged by UFOs in 1909. People in more than 40 towns across Britain reported strange shapes and lights in the sky, most of them during the third week in May. At Caerphilly in Wales, a man said he met two curious figures in fur coats as he walked near his home at 11 pm on May 18. 'They spoke in excited voices when they saw me, then rushed back to a large cylindrical object which lifted off the ground and disappeared.'

The New Zealand sightings were almost all of cigar-shaped objects. Hundreds of people reported them over both the North and South Islands, by day and at night, during the six weeks from the end of July to the start of September. In February 1913 it was Canada's turn, with groups of UFOs appearing over Ontario on six separate days.

In those days, with aeroplanes still in their infancy, space and space travel were mere dreams, fantasies to be indulged in the pages of novels by H. G. Wells. It would take two world wars to produce the hotbed of technological invention that began to make exploration of the universe a possibility. During the 1960s and 1970s, science learned about space at first hand. And what was learned cast new light on some puzzles of the past.

The Siberian space catastrophe

It was the greatest space disaster of all time. A stricken interstellar craft changed course towards the nearest planet, its nuclear engines overheating uncontrollably. The crew were racing against time, and they lost. Just a mile from the surface, there was a blinding flash, and both they and their ship were blasted to oblivion. And it happened on Earth . . . on June 30, 1908.

That is the latest startling theory from scientists trying to explain one of the most baffling mysteries of the 20th century, the Great Siberian Fireball. For years, investigating teams returned from the desolate and devastated explosion site around the Tunguska River, unable to attribute the amazing damage they found to anything but a gigantic meteorite plunging from the heavens. Then human achievements in the arms and space races threw new light on the affair.

It was just after dawn when the fireball was first spotted. Caravans winding their way across China's Gobi Desert stopped to watch it scorch across the skies. Soon people in southern Russia picked it up, a cylindrical tube shape, glowing bluish-white, leaving a multicoloured vapour trail. It was getting lower all the time. Then at 7.17 am came the explosion. To the peasants of the sparsely-populated area of swamps and forests, it seemed like the end of the world.

'There appeared a great flash of light,' said farmer Sergei Semenov, who was sitting on the porch of his home at Vanarva, 40 miles south of the centre of the blast. 'There was so much heat that I got up, unable to remain where I was. My shirt was almost burned off my back. A huge ball of fire covered an enormous part of the sky. Afterwards it became very dark.' At a nearby trading post, customers shielded their faces against the intense heat. Seconds later they were flung into the air as shock waves of enormous force reached the village. Farmer Semenov was also bowled over, and knocked unconscious. Ceilings cracked and crumbled, windows rattled and shattered. Soil was gouged out and flew through the air.

Closer to the Tunguska, the devastation was even worse. Tungus guide Ilya Potapovich had relatives who owned a herd of 1,500 reindeer. 'The fire came by and destroyed the forest, the reindeer and the storehouses,' he told investigators later. 'Afterwards, when the Tungus went in search of the herd, they found only charred reindeer carcasses. Nothing remained of the storehouses. Clothes, household goods, harnesses ... all had burned up and melted.'

The pillar of fire that followed the explosion was seen from the town of Kirensk, 250 miles away. So were the thick black clouds that rose 12 miles above the Tunguska as dirt and debris were sucked up by the blast. The accompanying thunderclaps were heard 50 miles away. A seismographic centre at Irkutsk, 550 miles south of the Tunguska, registered tremors of earthquake proportions. Hurricane-force gusts shook windows 375 miles from the explosion. Five hours later, British meteorological stations monitored violent air waves across the North Sea. When scientists all over the world later compared notes, they discovered that shock waves from the Siberian blast had twice circled the globe. And when exploration teams arrived at the spot where it had happened, they understood why.

Virtually all the trees in an area 40 miles wide had been blown over and scorched. Giant stands of larch had been uprooted and snapped as if they were twigs. The earth, too, looked unreal. Leonid Kulik, who led the early investigations for the Soviet Academy of Sciences, reported: 'The peat marshes of the region are deformed and the whole place bears evidence of an immense catastrophe. Miles of swamp have been blasted ... the solid ground heaved outwards from the spot in giant waves, like waves in water.' Kulik's researches revealed that the explosion had been seen or heard by people in an area four times the size of Britain. He revised his initial theory that the blast

Scenes like this at Hiroshima, Japan after an atomic bomb was dropped look similar to the devastation at Tunguska, Siberia. The clue led to the atomic bomb explanation of the mystery surrounding this site.

was caused by a single meteorite, concluding that an entire shower of meteorites was responsible.

Yet that hypothesis posed problems. Whenever meteorites had hit the Earth before, they had left craters. In Arizona, a hole 570 feet deep and nearly three-quarters-of-a-mile wide had been gouged by the largest one thus far known. There were other inconsistencies, too. Though trees for miles around had been blown over, some at what appeared to be the centre of the explosion were still standing, gaunt and eerie after losing their foliage and branches. In addition, some Tungus had reported finding unusual pieces of shiny metal, 'brighter than the blade of a knife and resembling the colour of a silver coin'. Others claimed that, since the blast, their reindeer had contracted a strange new disease which produced scabs on their skins.

For years scientists argued about the fireball. Was it a gaseous comet, which would not leave a crater on impact? Was it a meteorite that had exploded in mid-air? Then, in August 1945, America exploded an atomic bomb 1,800 feet above the Japanese city of Hiroshima. And when Soviet scientist Aleksander Kazantsev saw the blitzed area, he realized he had seen scenes of identical devastation – in Siberia. At Hiroshima, trees directly under the blast still stood, while those at an angle to it were flattened, along with buildings. The mushroom cloud, the blinding flash, the shock waves, the black rain of debris – all had been noted in 1908, nearly 40 years before the nuclear age. Kazantsev was convinced that he had the answer to the Tunguska riddle. But it was far from being proved scientifically. So he alerted his colleagues to the possibilities in a novel way. He wrote a science fiction story in a magazine that mingled fact and fiction, surmising that a nuclear-powered spaceship from Mars had exploded over Siberia.

Other scientists took up the nuclear theory, though keeping an open mind about the space suggestion. They compared the Tunguska evidence with what happened when both Russia and the United States held H-bomb tests. And in 1966, Soviet investigators V. K. Zhuravlev, D. V. Demin and L. N. Demina issued a definitive paper which declared that the Siberian fireball had been, without doubt, a nuclear explosion. Further studies, both in Russia and America, revealed that the energy yield of the blast was 30 megatons   1,500 times greater than at Hiroshima.

Soviet experts examined and dismissed suggestions that the blast was caused by anti-matter or a black hole from space. In both cases, they argued, a crater would have been caused on impact. Professor Felix Zigel, an aerodynamics teacher at Moscow's Institute of Aviation, and geophysicist A. V. Zolotov both re-examined the evidence and the site, and discovered that the area of destruction was not oval in shape, as had been thought, but roughly triangular. To Zolotov it seemed that the explosive material had been in 'a container' when it detonated, a shell of non-explosive material.

Professor Zigel went through eye-witness statements about the cylindrical shape, the trail of fire behind it, and the trajectory of its flight, and came to the conclusion that the object had 'carried out a manoeuvre' in the sky, changing direction through an arc of 375 miles, before it blew up. Soil samples from the blast site revealed tiny spherical globules of silicate and magnetite, a magnetized iron.

Dr Kazantsev, whose science fiction story had prompted the new direction in Soviet investigations, commented: 'We have to admit that the thing long known as the Tunguska Meteorite was in reality some very large artificial construction, weighing in excess of 50,000 tons. We believe it was being directed toward a landing when it exploded.' The Russians claim that no UFOs were sighted for decades after the crash. When they were again reported, the craft were smaller and seemingly more manoeuvrable.

The greatest space disaster of all time? If there was a crew on the UFO, they were not the only victims of the blast. Soviet doctors believe thousands of Siberian peasants died as a result. Residents of the scattered villages around the Tunguska river were renowned for their good health and long life. Many survived long past their 100th birthdays. But after 1908, local medical men reported a big increase in 'premature' deaths from 'strange maladies'. By the time teams investigating the nuclear explosion theory exhumed some of the long-dead bodies, science had found a name for such maladies. It was radiation sickness.

The undertaker's secret

For nearly 100 years, the secret of what undertaker William Robert Loosley saw in an English wood remained locked away in his desk drawer. But when his great, great grand-daughter, clearing out her attic, discovered his report, experts were forced to the startling conclusion that a flying saucer may have visited Buckinghamshire on an autumn night in 1871.

Loosely was a highly respected member of the community of High Wycombe, now a thriving town, but in those days a small village. The carpenter woke, hot and uncomfortable, at 3.15 on the morning of October 4, and decided to take a walk in his garden to cool off. What happened next was detailed in the manuscript he locked away.

A light like a star moved across the sky, 'brighter than the full moon'. Then came a clap of thunder – 'odd because the sky was clear'. The object flew lower, stopped, then carried on descending, moving from side to side. It seemed to touch down in nearby woods.

Next morning, Loosely walked to the landing site, and after a long search, struck something metallic as he poked his walking stick into a pile of leaves. Scrabbling with his hands, he uncovered a strange metal container, 18 inches high and covered with curious knobs.

'Almost at once the thing moved a trifle,' Loosley noted. 'With the sound of a well-oiled lock it opened what looked like an eye, covered with a glass lens and about an inch across. Seconds later another eye opened and sent out a beam of dazzling purple light.'

Then a third eye appeared, and shot out a thin rod, a little thicker than a pencil. Loosely decided to leave, but as he moved away, the machine started to follow, leaving a trail of three small ruts. The undertaker came to a clearing, and noticed that the whole surface was criss-crossed with similar ruts.

The metal box stopped briefly, and a claw shot out into the undergrowth. The purple light shone on the corpse of what seemed to be a dead rat. Then the rod sprayed liquid on the body and the rat was pushed inside a panel that opened on the side of the machine.

Loosely dropped his walking stick in his hurry to get away, and the object picked that up, too. Then it followed him into another clearing, and started herding him, 'like an errant sheep', towards another, bigger metal box.

The undertaker was now close to panic. He looked up and saw a strange moon-like globe in the sky, which seemed to be signalling with lights. But before he could work out the sequence, it vanished. He fled back to his home.

As he lay in bed that night, unable to sleep, Loosely saw, through the window, a light falling into the clearing he had visited during the day. Then it rose again, and disappeared into the clouds. Baffled as to the meaning of all this, the bemused man jotted his experience down on paper, and locked the manuscript in his desk.

After it was discovered, almost a century later, science fiction expert David Langford studied the document, and later wrote a book about it. He said: 'The manuscript has withstood every test of authenticity. It is clearly not a fabrication, because the man's death in 1893 absolutely rules out the possibility that he could describe the scientific concepts apparent in his tale'.

Village that disappeared

P olice are still trying to discover why an entire village of 1,200 people and even the dead from their graves vanished without trace into the dark of a northern winter. The mystery began in 1930, when trapper Armand Laurent and his two sons saw a strange gleam crossing Canada's northern sky. Laurent said the huge light changed shape from moment to moment so that it was now cylindrical, now like an enormous bullet.

A few days later a couple of Mounties stopped at Laurent's cabin to seek shelter on their way to Lake Anjikuni – where, one of them explained, there was 'a kind of problem'. The Mountie asked a puzzled Laurent if the light he'd sighted had been heading toward the lake. Laurent said it had.

The Mountie nodded without further comment, and in the years that followed the Laurents were not questioned again. It was an understandable oversight. The Royal Canadian Mounted Police were already busy at that time with the strangest case in their history . . .

Snowshoeing into the village of the Lake Anjikuni people, another trapper named Joe Labelle had been oppressed by an odd sense of dread. Normally it was a noisy settlement of 1,200 people and today he'd expected to hear the sled dogs baying their usual welcome.

But the snowbound shanties were locked in silence, and no smoke drifted from a single chimney.

Passing the banks of Lake Anjikuni, he found boats and kayaks still tied up at the shore. Yet when he went from one door to another, there was only the unearthly quiet. And still leaning in the doorways were the men's cherished rifles. No Eskimo traveller would ever leave his rifle at home.

Inside the huts, pots of stewed caribou had grown mouldy over long-dead fires. A half-mended parka lay on a bunk with two bone needles beside it.

But Labelle found no bodies living or dead, and no signs of violence.

At some point in a normal day – close to mealtime, it appeared – there had been a sudden interruption in the day's work, so that life and time seemed to have stopped dead.

Joe Labelle went to the telegraph office and his report chattered into the headquarters of the Royal Canadian Mounted Police. Every available officer was despatched to the Anjikuni area. After a few hours search, the Mounties located the missing sled dogs. They were tethered to trees near the village, their bodies under a massive snowdrift. They had died of cold and hunger.

And in what had been the Anjikuni burial ground, there was another chilling discovery. It was now a place of yawning open graves from which, in sub-zero temperatures, even the bodes of the dead had been removed.

There were no trails out of the village, and no possible means of transportation by which the people could have fled. Unable to believe that 1,200 people could vanish off the face of the earth, the RCMP widened its search. Eventually it would cover the whole of Canada and would continue for years. But more than half a century later, the case remains unsolved.

Could UFOs also be responsible for other vanishing acts over the years? In 1924 two experienced RAF pilots called Stewart and Day crashlanded in the Iraqi desert during a routine short flight. When they failed to arrive, rescue parties were sent out. They soon found the plane, and footsteps leading away from it showed that the two men had set off on foot in the direction of their destination. But after a short distance the footsteps stopped. There were no signs of a skirmish, no other footprints in the sand, no other marks at all. The men's track just stopped suddenly, one foot in front of the other, indicating that they had been walking normally when something happened. The two were never seen again.

In 1900 three tough fishermen set out from Lewis in the Outer Hebrides to relieve three lighthouse keepers at the Flannan Isles beacon. They found nothing wrong at the lighthouse. There were no hints of damage or accident, no disorder, no signs of panic, no missing boats, no loss of fuel, no messages ... and no men. The three keepers had simply vanished off the face of the Earth.

In 1909, Oliver Thomas, an 11-year-old boy, walked out of a Christmas Eve party at his home in Rhayader – and disappeared for ever. Merrymakers dashed outside when they heard a sudden cry that seemed to come from the sky above the house, but they saw nothing.

Life on other planets

Many scientists believe that human life itself came from space – developing from viruses and bacteria brought to Earth by giant comets. Sir Fred Hoyle, for 20 years professor of astronomy at Cambridge, was scoffed at when he first put forward the theory in 1940. But now scientists all over the world believe he was right.

Hoyle was one of the first to identify giant dust clouds that float silently through space, swarming with the ingredients of life. He claimed that a comet plunged through one of these clouds 4,000 million years ago, picking up viruses and bacteria that became locked in globules of frozen water in its tail.

When the comet – our first UFO – crashed into Earth's atmosphere, friction melted the globules, and the life-forming cells were showered into the mists of the cooling planet to produce plants, animals and humans.

Dr Chandra Wickramasinghe, of University College, Cardiff, believes that millions of comets, 'dirty snowballs' of frozen gases and dust, bombarded Earth, carrying randomly constructed genetic molecules that took root here.

He pointed out to an international conference in Maryland that the Greek philosopher Anaxagoras had similar ideas in 500 BC, arguing that the seeds of plants and animals swarmed in the universe, ready to sprout wherever they found a proper environment.

New scientific techniques have proved that the dust clouds of space contain such chemicals as methane, formic acid, formaldehyde and other substances crucial to forming simple life cells. One cloud showed traces of cellulose – the vital glue of molecular chains.

Could comets have created life on other planets, and in other forms? Dr

Sherwood Chang, of the Ames Research Centre in Mountain View, California, says that the millions of impact craters on Mars and Venus were formed mainly by comets. And in the words of Dr Wolfram Thiemann, of the University of Bremen, West Germany: 'Chemical evolution is definitely growing on other planets and in interstellar material. There is more and more evidence that there are other planets like Earth in outer space.

Sir Bernard Lovell, one of the world's leading radio astronomers, believes there are about 100 million stars in our galaxy, the Milky Way, that have the right chemistry and temperature to support organic evolution; and there are billions more galaxies in the observable universe. The odds against Earth being the only planet with life are therefore ... astronomical.

The planet Venus photographed from Mariner 10.

Space collisions and explosions

Other planets have played a crucial part in the development of life on Earth – and are even responsible for the shape of Earth as we know it. That was the controversial theory put forward in 1950 by Immanuel Velikovsky, a Russian-born doctor and psychoanalyst who settled in America, in his book entitled *Worlds in Collision*.

Velikovsky claimed that cataclysmic disasters recorded in the Bible and echoed in the ancient writings of the Mayas, Chinese, Mexicans and Egyptians were all due to convulsions in the universe, which sent Venus and then Mars into orbits too close to Earth.

Venus, according to Velikovsky, was part of Jupiter until an explosion sent it crashing into space more than 4,000 years ago. It hurtled towards the sun, blazing brightly, and trailing a slipstream of dust and gases. Earth moved into the outer edges of this slipstream in the middle of the 15th century BC, and a fine red dust coloured our rain. 'All the water that was in the Nile turned to blood,' stated the Biblical Book of Exodus. Then came showers of meteorites, and according to the Mexican Annals of Cuauhtitlan, the sky rained 'not water but fire and red-hot stones'.

When gases coalesced to form petroleum, 'people were drowned in a sticky substance raining from the sky', in the words of the Mayas' sacred book, Popol-Vuh. Elsewhere, the petroleum was ignited by oxygen in the Earth's atmosphere, and a terrible deluge of fire was recorded from Siberia to South America.

Finally, said Velikovsky, Earth was subjected to the full gravitational pull of the new planet and was tugged off its axis. Hurricanes and floods destroyed islands, levelled cities and altered the face of continents. 'Heaven and earth changed places,' wrote the Cashinaua of western Brazil. The Persians watched in awe as three days of light were followed by three days of darkness.

It was then, Velikovsky argued, that Moses led the Israelites across the Sea of Passage. Freak gravitational and electromagnetic forces, as well as the convulsions of the Earth's crust, piled up the waters on either side of the seabed. As the Egyptians pursued their former slaves, a powerful electric bolt passed between Earth and Venus, and the waters flooded back into place, drowning them.

The few survivors of the worldwide catastrophes faced starvation. But suddenly food fell from the skies – manna from heaven to the Israelites, ambrosia to the Greeks, honey-like madhu to the Hindus. Velikovsky believed it was created either by bacterial action or by electrical discharges in the Earth's atmosphere working on hydrocarbons in the trail of Venus.

Just as Earth was getting accustomed to its new seasonal timings, Venus swung past again, in about 1400 BC, with equally disastrous effects. Then it settled into an orbit that left our ancestors in peace. But in the 8th century BC, it passed too close to Mars, dislodging the smaller planet, and pushing it into an orbit which clashed with that of Earth. Again there were geophysical upheavals, recorded in the Bible by the prophets Isaiah, Hosea, Joel and Amos, and in the *Iliad* by Homer. Once more the calendar had to be revised, because a year of twelve 30-day months was no longer accurate.

Velikovsky said that Mars returned every 15 years until 687 BC, the last time it caused great disturbances, when, according to the Chinese Bamboo Books, 'Stars fell like rain and the Earth shook'. In some parts of the world, the rising sun dipped back below the horizon as Earth again tilted on its axis. Then both Venus and Mars settled into orbits that no longer influenced us.

The controversial theory explained many aspects of ancient myth, legend and history, not least why Mars replaced Venus as predominant god among the Greeks and Romans. But it outraged scientists in 1950. One curator of a platetarium who backed Velikovsky was sacked.

Velikovsky had flown in the face not only of accepted scientific principles but of Darwin's theory of an ordered evolution. Yet in the next 30 years, as space travel revealed many more facts about Venus and Mars, his theories were proved right time and time again. He was ridiculed for saying that Venus had a comet-like tail, that it was much hotter than Earth, and that its atmosphere was far heavier than that of Earth. American and Russian probes proved the truth of his claims. He was derided for saying that Mars had a surface of craters, and that its atmosphere contained the rare gases argon and neon. Again, space explorations found he was correct.

Neither Venus nor Mars were exactly unidentified flying objects, but the powers they unleashed terrified and puzzled our ancestors. And even today there are flying objects we can identify, but which are every bit as baffling as UFOs.

The day it rained animals

By the known laws of nature, frogs, fish, mice and periwinkles do not fly. Yet all have fallen from the skies for no apparent reason, and without explanation.

At Sutton Park, Birmingham, in June 1954, shoppers in a crowded street were astonished by a deluge of tiny, pale frogs. They bounced off umbrellas and hats, fell into shopping baskets, and hopped so profusely about the road and pavements that screaming women dashed into the stores to escape them. By the time the downpour stopped, as suddenly as it had begun, hundreds of the small creatures had been crushed or killed, and hundreds more had hopped away into sewers, alleys and gardens.

But that shower was nothing compared to what had happened centuries beforehand in Sardinia. According to ancient Egyptian books in the library at Alexandria, a frog-fall on the island lasted three days. Frogs clogged the roads and ponds, blocked doors and poured into houses. The people could do nothing to stop the invasion. A Greek scribe wrote: 'All vessels were filled with the frogs. They were found boiled and roasted with everything the Sardinians tried to eat. The people could make no use of water because it was all filled with frogs, and they could not put their feet on the ground for the heaps of frogs that were there. Those that died left a smell that drove the people out of the country.'

Flakes of meat up to three inches square showered down on the American state of Kentucky from a clear blue sky in March 1876. One astonished fieldworker boldly ate some, and said they tasted like mutton. In May 1890, a shower of bright red rain drenched Messignadi, Calabria, southern Italy. The Italian Meteorological Society identified it as birds' blood.

Fish up to five inches long fell on Aberdare, South Wales, in a dense downpour in February 1859. They covered the roofs of houses and children scooped them up in the streets. Specimens sent to the British Museum were identified as minnows, and put on show at the zoo in Regent's Park, London.

A terrible thunderstorm swept the English city of Worcester in May, 1881. A donkey pulling a cart was struck dead by lightning in Whitehall, and hailstones tore leaves from trees and battered crops to the ground. In Cromer Lane, gardener John Greenhall raced to shelter in a shed, and watched astonished as the hailstorm suddenly turned into a deluge of periwinkles. They bounced off the ground and shredded the leaves of his plants, covering some parts of the ground to a depth of several inches. When the storm had passed townsfolk flocked to the area and collected the molluscs for hours. One man filled two buckets. Another picked up a huge shell and found it occupied by a hermit crab.

A rain of sprats, smelts and whiting fell on the county of Kent at Easter 1666. Some traders cheekily picked them up and sold them in Maidstone and Dartford. Hordes of yellow mice tumbled from the sky over Bergen, Norway, in 1578. Thousands fell into the sea and swam ashore like a tide. Norwegian legend has it that such showers are nature's way of replacing lemmings lost in periodic mass suicides when they rush over cliff-tops into the ocean.

What can be the real reason for these amazing falls of live creatures? The most common explanation is that they have been sucked up by whirlwinds and waterspouts elsewhere on the Earth's surface, and carried by the wind to be dumped unexpectedly where least expected. But if that were so, why are frogs not accompanied by some evidence of their environment, such as pond-weed, mud or tadpoles? How can the wind select only sprats or whiting from an ocean full of different species of fish?

Charles Fort, a 19th-century American writer, believed that such living showers originated in some kind of immense Sargasso Sea, somewhere in the atmosphere. These periodic showers replenished stocks or spread species to new parts of the globe. Sadly, nobody has yet located Fort's aerial sea.

If comets were the vehicles that brought humans to Earth, could they still be raining life down on the planet?

Deities from space

Man has found no use for the eerie, empty spaces of Peru's southern coastal plain. Nothing lives in the dry-as-dust flatland which stretches from the Pacific Ocean to the snow-capped Andes. But in 1939, two men in a plane looked down on it, and discovered complex lines and geometric patterns of astonishing precision, stretching for miles across the arid wastes. And ever since, people have been asking: was this once a landing place for aliens? Could it have been an intergalactic spaceship terminal for giant UFOs, which may have brought to Earth, in prehistoric times, the real ancestors of man?

Archaeologists and scientists have never been able to explain the sudden, dramatic evolutionary and technological leap made by *Homo sapiens* 10,000 to 15,000 years ago. There are no genetic clues to the sudden doubling in size of the human brain. In the trail pursued by the experts, there seem to be more missing links than clues.

But some say the clues are there ... in the deserts of the world and the legends of early civilized man. They point to god-like visitors from space who passed on skills and technological knowledge to primitive man, and may even have inter-bred with him.

The amazing patterns in the Peruvian desert near the city of Nazca cover an area 37 miles long and one mile wide. The plain consists of yellow soil covered by a thin layer of stones. Each line was made by removing the surface layer of stones. The task was comparatively simple, but the undeviating accuracy of the lines is stunning, stretching dead straight for mile after mile, passing over the horizon, crossing gullies and climbing slopes. Their precision matches anything modern engineering can achieve. And they show up clearly only in very high-level aerial photographs.

Scientists who tracked them, with difficulty, on foot, could find no reason for them. They led nowhere and matched no astronomical pattern. But from far out in space, deserts would seem the most obvious place to land on a planet with as much surface water as ours. When America aimed astronauts at the Moon, it chose the lunar equivalent of our deserts. There are reasons for believing that UFOnauts may have done the same thing.

Drawn on the desert floor beside the Nazca lines and patterns are birds, spiders and fish. These too are virtually invisible at ground level. Scientists dismiss them as ancient worship objects. But that may be exactly what they were – invocations to the aerial gods to visit Earth again.

A bird was almost certainly the only other thing known to early Peruvians

The second pyramid of Khefren illustrates the majesty and the mystery surrounding the building of these mighty edifices.

that could defy gravity by flying; and their desert bird has a tail that fans out like the blast-off trail of a rocket. The spider looks like the object we now recognize as America's spindle-legged Moon-landing craft. And the fish? They might represent the gods themselves.

On the fringes of another desert, the Sahara, lives a primitive tribe discovered just over a century ago by explorers from the West. The Dogons of Mali still worship intelligent, fish-like amphibians who, they insist, came from the sky. They called themselves the Nommos, landed in a whirling, spinning ark, and had to live in water.

They told the Dogons that they came from a tiny but heavy star called Sirius, which followed an elliptical orbit round the brightest constellation in the sky. Early explorers who listened to the tribe's story nodded their heads with amused condescension.

Then, amazingly, in the 1950s, astronomers using the most modern radio

Two of the amazing patterns (top, monkey; below, hummingbird) to be seen in the Peruvian desert near the city of Nazca.

telescopes discovered the tiny, heavy, elliptical orbiting star, exactly as the Dogons had described it. So faint was it that no optical telescope had previously detected it. So how did this African tribe know of its existence?

The Dogons were not the only people visited from above during prehistory. The Sumerians called their gods the Oannes, and they, too, were amphibians. They brought the secrets of mathematics, writing and astronomy to the people of the Tigris and Euphrates valleys of Mesopotarria, long acknowledged as the birthplace of human civilization.

Berossus, a Babylonian priest, described the Oannes god as part man and part fish. He plunged into the sea 'to abide all night in the deep, for he was amphibious'. In Philistine legend, the God was born from an egg which dropped from heaven into the Euphrates. Like the deities of the Dogons', the Oannes had a connection with Sirius. Their worshippers venerated the figure 50 – the exact orbital period of the star, as mentioned by the Dogons.

The theory that spacemen visited our ancestors is reinforced by the art of many ancient peoples. In 1950, archaeologists uncovered the tomb of an ancient Mayan priest at Palanque, Mexico. Clearly visible on the drawings was the figure of a man in a capsule. He was surrounded by levers and machinery, and there was a fiery trail, like exhaust fumes, at the back of the craft.

In caves below the Sahara mountain range of Tassili N'Ajjer, on the present-day borders of Algeria and Libya, there is a lasting pictorial record of the daily life of a tribe forced to move on when their green oasis was drowned by the shifting sands. Drawings show water buffalo, birds and parties of armed hunters.

Among the groups are the clear figures of what we can now recognize as space travellers. They are no bigger than the hunters, but they wear space suits and helmets – round headgear with antennae.

Mysterious markings on the floor of the barren Gobi Desert in Outer Mongolia puzzled explorers and archeologists for centuries. They were not made by any known form of fire or gunpowder. Then scientists found identical marks in the sands of the Nevada Desert in America ... after the United States triggered its first atomic bomb test in 1944. Had a nuclear-powered UFO visited the Gobi in the long-distant past?

Across the Himalayas, Indian priests still chant the Ramayana in praise of gods who arrived on Earth in 'vimanas', strange flying machines propelled by quicksilver and fierce winds. The words of the hymn relate that, 'at the gods' bequest, the magnificent chariot rose up to a mountain of cloud on an enormous ray as brilliant as the sun and with a noise like a thunderstorm...'

Such discoveries have suggested to scientists that other marvels of ancient man may be associated with the knowledge and skills of extra-terrestrial visitors. How did the ancient Egyptians build the pyramids, and how did they discover the seemingly magical properties of the Pyramid shape? Who built the giant stone figures on lonely Easter Island, and why? What was the secret wisdom of the ancient Greek oracles?

Even some devout Christians are beginning to wonder whether their religion is based on the visits of a space race. In the Old Testament Book of Ezekiel, the Hebrew prophet records how, in the 6th century BC, he watched a weird cloud descend in the desert beside the River Chebar in Babylon. It was amber, the colour of glowing metal, and surrounded by 'fire infolding itself'. Four objects came out of it, each a wheel within a wheel with a ring of eyes; and out of them came man-like creatures in suits of burnished brass, with 'crystal firmaments' on their heads. He might have been describing a 20th-century astronaut.

American UFO researcher Raymond E. Fowler is not alone in using such descriptive passages to determine the realities of Biblical legends. A pillar of fire guided Moses through the wilderness, and the prophet Elijah was taken to heaven in a fiery chariot. Both were clearly seen later with Jesus on the Mount of Transfiguration, glowing in contact with the 'cloud' on which they stood.

In the New Testament, a pillar of fire and voices from 'the host of heaven' told the shepherds of Christ's birth at Bethlehem; and a bright 'star in the East' guided the wise men to the crib where lay the child born to a virgin. Jesus had magic, mystical powers, and ascended to heaven on a cloud. 'If I have told you of earthly things and ye believe not,' He told disciples, 'how shall ye believe if I tell you of heavenly things?'

The 'angels' of the Lord were messengers of God who came from the skies – Daniel called them 'watchers' – and were allowed to intermarry and eat human food. Were they really UFO aliens who came to educate or 'save' a primitive people? Was the blinding light that converted Paul on the road to Damascus a UFO bringing Jesus back to repeat His message? And will the Second Coming, with fearful sights and signs in the sky, a host of clouds and angels, really be an invasion fleet of spacemen in UFOs?

Space shrine

British housewife Phyllis Henderson believes Jesus Christ was a flying saucer pilot from Saturn. She turned the garage of her home at Warrington, Cheshire, into a church after joining the Aetherius Society, a movement begun by George King, who claimed he met Jesus when a UFO landed at Holdstone Down, Devon, during the early 1950s.

Phyllis, 59, and her husband Steuart, 62, received temporary planning permission to use their asbestos and brick garage as a shrine. Then neighbours complained that their services were too noisy. 'The complaints are nonsense,' Phyllis said. 'Our church has only got seven members and they do not make a lot of noise.'

First UFO on film

Two Swiss astronomers from Basle observed a spindle-like object, surrounded by a glowing outer ring, pass in front of the sun on August 9, 1762. The sighting corresponded with a shape seen over Mexico by hundreds of people in the 1880s. The photograph which Professor Bonilla took there through a telescope at Zacatecas observatory on August 12, 1883 is believed to be the first photograph ever taken of a UFO.

Mysterious wreckage in space

The wreck of a spaceship from another planet is in orbit round the Earth – and could contain the bodies of alien beings. That was the astonishing claim of Russian scientists that made front-page news in 1979.

Top Soviet astrophysicist Professor Sergei Boshich revealed that scientists first spotted wreckage floating 1,240 miles above Earth in the 1960s. They identified ten pieces of debris, two of them measuring 100 feet across, in slightly different orbits, and fed their findings into a sophisticated computer, to trace the age of the wreckage.

'We found they all originated in the same spot on the same day – December 18, 1955. Obviously there had been a powerful explosion.' Man's first space rocket went up in 1957.

Another top Russian astrophysics researcher, Professor Aleksandr Kazantsev, said the two large pieces of debris gave clues about the shape and size of the craft. 'We believe it was at least 200 feet long and 100 feet wide. It had small domes housing telescopes, saucer antennae for communications, and portholes.

'Its size would suggest several floors, possibly five. We believe alien bodies will still be on board.'

Moscow physicist Dr Vladimir Azhazha ruled out suggestions that the debris could be fragments of a meteor. 'Meteors do not have orbits,' he said. 'They plummet aimlessly, hurtling erratically through space. And they do not explode spontaneously.

'All the evidence we have gathered over the past decade points to one thing – a crippled alien craft. It must hold secrets we have not even dreamed of.'

Russian geologist Professor Aleksei Zolotov, a specialist in explosions, added: 'The wreckage cannot be from an Earth spaceship – the explosion happened two years before we launched the world's first satellite, Sputnik 1.

'A rescue mission should be launched. The vessel, or what is left of it, should be reassembled here on Earth. The benefits to mankind could be stupendous.'

Leading American scientists were at first stunned, then excited by the revelations. Dr Henry Monteith, a physicist working on top-secret nuclear research at the Sancia Laboratories in Albuquerque, New Mexico, said the evidence warranted further investigation.

'It certainly sounds like a solid study by the Russians,' he added. 'It's very exciting – we could even send up a space shuttle. If it is an alien spacecraft, it would be the find of the century. It would conclusively prove the existence of intelligent life elsewhere in the universe.'

Dr Myran Malkin, director of the NASA Space Shuttle office of space technology, said: 'We would consider a joint salvage attempt if the Russians approached us.'

And nuclear physicist Stanton Friedman said: 'If we retrieved the fragments, there's a chance we could put the pieces back together.'

The British reaction was more cautious. Dr Desmond King-Hele, a space researcher at the Royal Aircraft Establishment in Farnborough, Hants, said: 'There are more than 4,000 pieces of wreckage orbiting the Earth. Each has a catalogue number to identify it. We would like to know the catalogue number of this wreck. It is possible to date wreckage after a considerable number of observations.

'Like the Americans, we would be interested to look at this if the Russians make the information available.'

American physicist William Corliss recalled an article written by astronomer John Bagby in the US magazine *Icarus* in 1969 – a time when government agencies had just decreed that UFOs did not exist.

He wrote that ten moonlets were orbiting the Earth after breaking off from a larger parent body. And he traced the date of the disintegration ... December 18, 1955.

'Bagby could not explain the explosion,' Corliss said. 'He was only interested in proving that the objects were out there, and dismissed them as natural phenomena. It seemed the safest thing to do at that time ...'

Other UFOs have successfully negotiated Earth's atmosphere, only to crash on to the surface of the planet, according to several American researchers. But proving their claims is virtually impossible, they say, because governments have kept all the incidents secret.

Mystery of the Andes

No reason was ever given for the tight security net thrown round an area near Mendoza in western Argentina in January 1964. But rumours that a UFO had lost speed and crashed, with tiny aliens in luminous suits aboard, in the foothills of the Andes, circulated for some years, and a photograph smuggled to the *Flying Saucer Review* magazine showed a mysterious cigar-shaped object, about 13 feet long, lying in rough scrubland.

The secret of the dead aliens

It was the worst storm New Mexico had seen in years. The wind and rain raged all night, and in the middle of it all, rancher Bill Brazel heard a strange explosion. At first light he saddled his horse and rode out to make sure his sheep were all right. What he found that morning, July 3, 1947, was to make his farm world-famous – and spark off a UFO controversy that continues to this day.

His fields were covered by small beams of wood and thin sheets of metal. The wood looked like balsa and felt as light, but it was actually very hard, did not burn, and would not break. Some pieces carried strange hieroglyphics. The metal looked like tin foil, but could not be dented or bent. Then Brazel noticed a huge battered disc. As he rode closer, he saw something even more strange. There were beings, who were not human, lying beside the object. Some were alive, but they could not speak. Brazel raced back to the house and called the sheriff. He alerted nearby Roswell Army Air Field.

Intelligence chief Major Jesse Marcel led the investigating team. As ambulances carried off the burned bodies, and army trucks arrived to collect the wreckage, he threw an immediate security cordon round the fields, and told rancher Brazel not to talk about what he had seen.

New Mexico was then the hub of America's atomic, rocket, aircraft and radar research. Roswell was the home of the 509th US Air Force Bomb Group, the only combat-trained atom bombers in the world. Marcel had no idea what the crashed craft was, but he knew it should not have been over such a sensitive defence area.

On July 8, his attempts to keep the affair under wraps were jolted when the base's public information officer, Walter Haut, issued a press release without the authority of his commander, Colonel William Blanchard. It read: 'The many rumours of the flying disc became reality yesterday when the intelligence office of the 509th Bomb Group gained possession of a disc through the cooperation of some local ranchers.

'The object landed at a ranch near Roswell some time last week. It was picked up at the rancher's home, inspected at Roswell Army Air Field, and loaned by Major Marcel to higher headquarters.'

Wire services quickly passed the news on to papers all over the world, and the Army came under pressure to release more details. But reporters now found the story had changed. A rash of denials poured out of Roswell and

Washington. A senior Air Force officer assured the public, via a Texas radio station, that the wreckage was the remains of a Rawin balloon. Newspapers were issued with a picture of him and another officer examining a balloon.

The official line soon cooled curiosity about what had happened at Roswell. But some UFO researchers were unsatisfied. Eventually Charles Berlitz, author of books on the riddle of the Bermuda Triangle, took up the trail. And in 1980 he published a book, co-written by William Moore, which accused the government of covering up the real facts – that the Roswell craft was a spaceship containing six aliens.

He quoted Grady 'Barney' Barnett, a government engineer, who told friends he was one of the first to reach the site on the morning of July 3. 'I was out on assignment,' said Barnett, 'when light reflecting off some sort of large metallic object caught my eye. It was a disc-shaped object about 25 or 30 feet across.

'While I was looking at it, some other people came up from the other direction. They told me later they were part of an archaeological team. They were looking at some dead bodies that had fallen to the ground. I think there were others in the machine that had been split open by explosion or impact. I tried to get close to see what the bodies were like. They were like humans but they were not humans.

'The heads were round, the eyes were small and they had no hair. They were quite small by our standards, and their heads were larger in proportion to their bodies.

'Their clothing seemed to be one-piece and grey in colour. You couldn't see any zippers, belts or buttons. They seemed to be all males and there were a number of them. I was close enough to touch them. While we were looking at them, a military officer drove up in a truck and took control. He told everybody the Army was taking over and to get out of the way.

'Other military personnel came up and cordoned off the area. We were told to leave and not talk to anyone about what we had seen – that it was our patriotic duty to remain silent.'

Berlitz and Moore could not get the story from Barnett himself. He died in 1969. His version of the events was related by friends to whom he had talked in 1950. Rancher Brazel was also long dead, but his son Billy told how his father had found the debris.

'Father was very reluctant to talk about it,' Billy said. 'The military swore him to secrecy and he took that very seriously. I don't know what the craft was, but Dad once said the Army told him they had definitely established it was not anything made by us.

'He told me the occupants of the ship were still alive, but their throats had been badly burned from inhaling gases and they could not speak. They were taken to California and kept alive in respirators, but they died before anyone had worked out how to communicate with them.'

Berlitz and Moore also quoted a California university physics professor, Dr Weisberg, who said he examined the disc. 'It was shaped like a turtle's back, with a cabin space inside about 15 feet wide. The interior was badly damaged. There were six occupants, and an autopsy on one revealed they resembled humans except in size.

'One body was seated at what appeared to be a control desk on which hieroglyphics were written. They were peculiar symbols. It was definitely not a known language. There was no evidence of a propellor or a motor. No one could understand how it was driven.'

A Los Angeles photographer, Baron Nicholas Von Poppen, claimed he had taken pictures of the crash ship after being approached by two men from military intelligence. He said they offered him a top-secret assignment at an exceptionally high fee – but warned that if he revealed anything he saw or photographed, he would be deported.

Von Poppen, who had developed a system of photographic metallurgic analysis, said he was escorted to the Roswell air base and took hundreds of pictures, which he had to hand over at the end of each day. He described the craft as about 30 feet wide, and the cabin 20 feet across. Its floor was covered with plastic sheets on which there were symbols. There were four seats in front of a control board covered with push buttons and levers, 'and in each seat, still strapped in, was a thin body, varying in height from two to four feet'.

The Baron added: 'The faces of all four were very white. They wore shiny black attire without pockets, closely gathered at their feet and necks. Their shoes were made of the same material and appeared very soft. Their hands were human-like though soft, like those of children. They had five digits, normal-looking joints and neatly-trimmed nails.'

Berlitz and Moore said Von Poppen smuggled one negative from the craft, and locked it away in a safe place, to be opened only after his death. When he died, in 1974, aged 90, no trace of the negative was found.

The authors claim that Major Marcel was interviewed again about the Roswell incident in 1978, after he had retired to Houma, Louisiana. Asked whether the wreckage he had collected from the ranch was really a weather balloon, he said: 'It was not.'

He went on: 'I was pretty well acquainted with everything in the air at that time, both ours and foreign. I was also acquainted with virtually every type of weather-observation or radar-tracking device being used by the military and civilians. It was something I had not seen before, and it certainly wasn't anything built by us. It most certainly wasn't any weather balloon.'

In that case, why say it was? Marcel said Brigadier-General Ramey ordered the cover story 'to get the Press off the Army's back'. Berlitz alleged that the bodies and wreckage were secretly shipped around the country by truck and train for analysis at various scientific centres.

'We have been able to track down people who have a clear recollection of the crash, technicians who examined the alien machinery and clerks who checked the bodies into various establishments,' he said. 'Their stories tally too well for the whole story to be just a legend.'

Berlitz believed the facts were covered up to avoid causing public panic, and for military reasons. Any nation that could work out how the disc was powered would have a massive advantage over its rivals in the missiles and space races.

Only successive incoming presidents were allowed to share the military secret. 'Eisenhower, Kennedy and Johnson carried it to their graves, Nixon, Ford, Carter and Reagan have to live with it.' Berlitz recalled that Jimmy Carter had promised to make government information on UFOs available to the public if elected. When the author rang the White House, he was told that reopening of UFO investigations was not warranted.

Berlitz commented: 'His silence was undoubtedly prompted by the fact that he had learned something which convinced him to keep quiet about the whole issue.'

UFO crashes

Have other UFO crashes been covered up? The secretive attitude of the authorities makes it impossible to confirm reports that spacecraft have fallen into the hands of earthbound investigators.

There were strong rumours in the late 1940s that a flying saucer had come down just outside Mexico City, and that the wreckage – and the bodies of three silver-suited occupants, all only three feet tall – had been loaded onto trucks and taken to the United States for study.

Raymond E. Fowler, an authority on UFOs, particularly in New England, received what could be confirmation of the rumours when he gave a lecture on UFOs at Boston.

In his book, *UFOs: Interplanetary Visitors*, published in 1979, he said that an assistant minister at a Boston church told him he was working for the Pentagon in naval intelligence at the time.

A colleague in Mexico was assigned to help investigate an air crash. 'When he arrived, the area had been roped off and personnel were loading remains of an oval object and its occupants into trucks ... He was quickly ordered out of the area by a superior, who told him not to mention what he had seen.

Fowler traced the minister's former colleague to Belfast, Maine, where he was living in retirement. He denied all knowledge of the incident, and said his friend must have made some mistake. But the minister stood by his story. Fowler concluded that the man might be afraid to reveal his secret because he was living on a pension from the Navy.

In 1957, fishermen at Ubatuba Beach, Brazil, claimed they had seen a flying object explode and fall into the sea. They also produced fragments of ultra-pure magnesium which, they said, came from the debris. The authorities were sceptical, even though they could not explain how simple fishermen could have come by magnesium which, as later tests showed, was forged by a directional casting method not even invented by 1957.

Ten years later, Raymond Fowler came across what may have been another UFO crash. He met Mr and Mrs Bill Marsden, who recalled driving towards Mattydale, a suburb of Syracuse, New York, during the winter of 1953–4. It was 3 am on a Sunday when they came across the flashing lights of four or five police cars, and slowed, thinking there had been an accident. The road was clear, but something in a nearby field caught Mr Marsden's eye. He told Fowler:

'I saw an object which appeared to be 20 feet in diameter and possibly 15 feet high in the centre. It had phosphorescent lights of several colours spaced over the surface. These lights were strong enough to make clearly visible quite a few men walking around the object and examining it. Some were uniformed and some were not. One had what appeared to be a large press camera with a strap and was taking pictures.'

On the Monday morning, Mr Marsden called his local newspaper to ask why it had no story of the event, then phoned the sheriff's office. He claims he was told: 'Yes, we know about that, but it is a military secret and we can't discuss it.' But when the newspaper talked to the sheriff's office, and to the Air Force, reporters were told that no such incident had taken place. The sheriff also denied that anyone had told Mr Marsden about 'a military secret'. Mr Marsden let the matter drop, even though he had checked the field next morning, and found indentations and tyre tracks. He knew that UFO supporters faced ridicule.

When Fowler made inquiries with the sheriff's office in 1967, he was told that the only objects which had fallen to earth during the winter of 1953–4 were a weather balloon, a wing tank from a plane, an aircraft, and a sand-filled imitation bomb dropped by mistake from another plane. None of those objects tallied with what Mr Marsden had seen – and he stuck to his story.

Bizarre autopsies

America has recovered a total of more than 30 bodies from crashed alien craft, according to researcher Leonard Stringfield. Many have been given autopsy examinations, and all are preserved either at the Wright-Patterson Air Force base in Ohio, or at the underground Air Force complex near Colorado Springs.

Stringfield, who says that the aliens are between $3\frac{1}{2}$ feet and 5 feet tall and slender, with oversized hairless heads, made his astonishing claims after talking to two doctors and six Forces personnel involved in the recovery and analysis of bodies over the last 30 years. He added that a specially trained force called the Blue Berets is on constant standby, ready to move instantly should a UFO crash.

All Stringfield's sources asked to remain anonymous, and he refused to identify them, even when questioned about his book. This is what he says they told him:

A doctor who observed an autopsy in the early 1950s described the alien corpse as just over 4 feet tall. It had a large, pear-shaped head with Mongoloid eyes recessed in the face. There were no eyelids, ear lobes, teeth or hair.

A former major and pilot in the Air Force observed strange bodies in an underground preservation chamber at Wright-Patterson during 1952 after secret Air Force instructions were sent out ordering pilots on UFO missions to shoot down strange craft.

Another USAF pilot watched three crates being delivered to Wright-Patterson in 1953. He was told they contained bodies from a flying saucer crash in Arizona. An officer said the humanoids were still alive when rescuers arrived, but died despite receiving oxygen.

An army intelligence officer viewed nine alien bodies which had been frozen at Wright-Patterson in 1966, and was told that there were 30 in various government establishments. The same man learned later that five UFOs had crashed in the Ohio, Indiana and Kentucky region between 1966 and 1968.

An Air Force sergeant and air policeman, identified only as Carl, said he was blindfolded and driven to a secret location to guard a room. When he peeped inside, he saw three small bodies, around 3 feet tall, with abnormally large heads.

A doctor who was present at an autopsy said the bodies had no digestive tracts or sex organs. And their blood was colourless.

Stringfield, whose claims were published by Mutual UFO Network, of Seguin, Texas, also tells of some aliens who got away. A colonel told him that, in 1968, he confronted strange beings who emerged from a saucer at the Nellis Air Force Base in Nevada. A beam of light paralysed him, and he could only watch as the figures returned to their ship and took off.

Some aliens are not so expert in controlling the humans they meet. And even when their crafts land safely, they face new hazards on Earth.

Bullets that bounced off

Agroup of farmworkers and their wives astonished police at Hopkinsville, Kentucky, when they burst into the station at midnight. They said they had just fired shotguns and rifles at goblin-type aliens from a UFO – but that their bullets had bounced off the creatures.

The Sunday evening of August 21, 1965, turned into a nightmare for the family at Kelly, a sprawling cluster of houses seven miles from Hopkinsville. The Langfords of Sutton Farm, eight adults and three children, had returned after church services when one of the youngsters saw a brightly glowing object descend behind a barn. People on nearby farms saw it too, but the family dismissed it as a shooting star.

Then, at around 8 pm, the dogs in the yard began barking. Two of the men went to the door to investigate, and saw, 50 yards away, a creature in a glowing silver suit, about $3\frac{1}{2}$ feet tall, coming towards them. It had a huge head, long arms that nearly reached the ground, and large webbed hands with talons. The men grabbed a 12-gauge shotgun and a 22-calibre pistol, and fired at close range. The being was knocked over – but to the amazement of the watchers, it then jumped up again and scurried away.

The stunned family locked themselves inside, turned off all the inside lights, and put on the porch lamps. Then one of the women screamed. She looked out of the dining room window and saw a face peering in at her, with wide slit eyes behind a helmet visor. The men rushed into the room and fired, but again the creature, although hit, ran away.

A total of almost 50 rounds were blasted at the five aliens over the next 20 minutes, but none of the bullets stopped them. Radio newsman Bud Ledwith, who interviewed the family next morning, said: 'Whenever one of the creatures was hit, it would float or fall over or run for cover. All the shots that struck them sounded as though they were hitting a bucket.

'The objects made no sound. The undergrowth would rustle as they went through it, but there was no sound of walking. The objects were seemingly weightless as they would float down from trees more than fall from them.'

When caught by bullets or flashlights, the aliens, who seemed to approach with their hands in the air, would drop their arms and run. But they kept coming back, apparently making no attempt to enter the house, but just standing and staring at it. After 20 minutes, the creatures melted away into the night. But the scared family stayed alert for another two hours before daring to venture outside, and drive to the police. Officers who visited the farm could find no trace of the visitors.

It was an amazing story, but only Bud Ledwith seemed interested in investigating it seriously. An officer looked into it for the United States Air Force Bluebook file on UFOs, since he happened to be in the area and heard news of it on the radio. Several points of his report were later found to be erroneous. After interviewing Mrs Lenny Langford, one of the women involved, he declared that she, her sons, their wives and some friends had attended a service of the Holy Roller Church that evening, and were 'emotionally unbalanced' after working themselves into a frenzy. In fact, Mrs Langford belonged to the Trinity Pentecostal Church, whose services are perfectly traditional.

Other investigators tried to find out whether there were any travelling circuses in the area, apparently believing that the farmers had seen escaped monkeys. Monkeys that floated? Monkeys in bullet-proof vests?

Bud Ledwith firmly believed that his witnesses were telling the truth, that they were simple folk who had no motive for trying to perpetrate a hoax. And as Dr J. Allen Hynek, whose Centre for UFO Studies later probed the case, pointed out, they had nothing to gain from publicity, and later 'suffered horribly from curiosity seekers, reporters and sensation mongers.'

The case was later used as an example in the secret air force training manual on UFOs – to show that humans can be dangerous for aliens! The textbook added: 'At no time in the story did the supposed aliens shoot back, although one is left with the impression that the described creatures were having fun scaring humans.'

The family decided they could no longer live at the farm and sold it.

Demons and demon-ships

Aggression by man against UFOs is nothing new. According to the US Air Force Academy textbook, supposed airships were treated as demon-ships in Ireland in about 1000 AD, 'and in Lyons, France, "admitted" space travellers were killed in around 840 AD'.

Vigilantes on the alert

U FO fever in Virginia led to the formation of local vigilante groups in January 1965. The *Richmond Times-Despatch* quoted Sheriff John Kent of Augusta County as saying UFO reports had got 'completely out of hand' and had become 'dangerous to country residents'.

A posse from the Brands Flat area of the Shenandoah Valley armed itself to go looking for creatures said to have landed in a UFO. But the Sheriff said that even if little green men had arrived, residents 'had no right to mow them down'.

That was not a view shared by Attorney General Robert Button. When a Fredericksburg justice of the peace consulted him, he replied, somewhat tongue in cheek: 'There is apparently no state law making it unlawful to shoot little green men who might land in the state from outer space.'

In March 1966, a man driving near Bangor, Maine, did shoot at a UFO. He spotted the metallic, oval shape hovering over a field, and got out of his car to investigate, taking with him the ·22 pistol from his glove compartment. When the mysterious flying object swooped towards him, scraping the tops of the bushes, the man began firing and heard bullets ricochet off metal as the craft passed overhead, before climbing out of sight at tremendous speed.

Not everyone was so unwelcoming. After a spate of local sightings, the mayor of Brewer, Maine, had a giant billboard put up inviting UFO travellers to settle down in the town.

Bullet-proof

Police at Fort Beaufort, South Africa, fired shots from only eight yards when a glowing metallic object landed on June 26, 1972. But the bullets had no effect. The machine merely took off with a humming noise.

Chapter four

GHOSTS AND GHOULS

Those who believe they have seen a ghost are almost always upset or disturbed by their eerie experence, though most learn to come to terms with it. But some encounters are more than a mere fright in the night. What did they see? What are the forces behind such apparitions? Are they visitations from beyond the grave? Are they proof of an unknown dimension? Or are they simply tricks of the mind?

The mummy's hand

Count Louis Hamon was famed as an occultist and psychic healer. He was often given exotic presents by grateful clients he had cured. But the oddest gift of all brought him nothing but trouble.

On a visit to Luxor in 1890, Hamon cured a prominent sheik of malaria. The sheik insisted that the healer accept a gruesome gift, the mummified right hand of a long-dead Egyptian princess.

Count Hamon's wife disliked the dry, shrivelled hand from the first. But her dislike turned to horror and revulsion when she heard the story behind it. In the seventeenth and last year of his reign, King Akhnaton of Egypt – the heretical father-in-law of Tutankhamen – quarrelled over religious matters with his daughter. And the king's vengeance was ghastly.

In 1357BC, he had the girl raped and murdered by his priests. Afterwards they cut off her right hand and buried it secretly in the Valley of the Kings. The people of Egypt were appalled, for the girl would be barred from paradise because her body was not intact at burial.

Hamon would have turned the relic over to a museum, but could not find a curator willing to accept it. He locked it away in an empty safe in the wall of his London home.

In October 1922, he and his wife reopened the safe – and stood back in horror. The murdered girl's hand had changed. Shrivelled and mummified for 3,200 years, it had begun to soften with new flesh. The Countess screamed that it must be destroyed. Although he had never before been afraid of the unknown, Hamon agreed with her.

He insisted on only one thing; that the hand of the princess must have the best funeral they could give it. They were ready on the night of October 31, 1922. Halloween.

In a letter to his life-long friend, the archaeologist Lord Carnarvon, Hamon wrote that he laid the hand gently in the fireplace and read aloud a passage from the Egyptian Book of the Dead. As he closed the book there was a blast of thunder that rocked the house into total darkness. The door flew open with a sudden wind.

Hamon and his wife fell to the floor and lay there in the sudden glacial cold. Lifting their eyes, they saw the figure of a woman. In Hamon's account, "she wore the royal apparel of old Egypt, with the serpent of the House of Pharaohs glittering on her tall headdress". The woman's right arm ended in a raw stump.

The apparition bent over the fire and then was gone as suddenly as it had appeared. The severed hand had vanished with it, and was never seen again.

Four days later, Hamon read that the Carnarvon expedition had discovered Tutankhamen's tomb and that they would enter it in spite of the ancient warning emblazoned at the threshold.

From the room in the hospital where he and his wife were under treatment for severe shock, Hamon sent his old friend a letter begging him to reconsider.

He wrote, "I know now the ancient Egyptians had knowledge and power of which today we have no comprehension. In the name of God, I beg you to take care."

Carnarvon ignored the letter and soon afterwards he was dead from an infected mosquito bite. One by one, members of the expedition followed him to the grave in what became known as the Curse of the Pharaohs.

Phantoms of the stage

All the world's a stage for the haunting performances of ghosts, but they seem particularly fond of theatres. Often they are connected with real dramas as strange as any fictional play.

William Terriss was a colourful adventurer turned actor. In December, 1897, he was playing the lead in a thriller called *Secret Service* at the Adelphi Theatre in The Strand. One night, as he left the stage door, he was stabbed to death and ever since his restless spirit has been blamed for a series of inexplicable happenings.

Actors have heard curious tappings, and the sound of footsteps. Mechanical lifts have been moved by invisible forces, and lights mysteriously switched on and off. In 1928, a comedy actress felt the couch in her dressing room lurch under her, as if someone was trying to move it. Then her arm was seized, leaving a bruise. The startled woman had not heard of the ghost until her dresser arrived, and explained that she was using the dressing room which had belonged to Terriss.

The phantom star's strangest performance came in 1955. Jack Hayden, foreman ticket collector at Covent Garden Tube station, noticed a distinguished figure in a grey suit and white gloves who looked as if he was lost. But when Hayden asked if he could help, the man vanished into thin air.

Four days later, the same figure returned and put his hands on the head of 19-year-old porter Victor Locker.

Pictures of Terriss were shown to both men, and they instantly recognised him as their ghost. Both also asked to be transferred. Other London Transport staff on the Piccadilly Line have spoken of a strange presence at Covent Garden, and in 1972 a station-master, signalman and engineer all reported seeing the man in grey.

More than 50 cleaners at London's Drury Lane theatre claim to have seen a phantom wandering the dress circle in a long grey coat. The 18th century dandy in a powdered wig has also been spotted from the stage during rehearsals, and actors regard the sightings as a good omen – they usually herald a successful run for a play. The eerie visitor could be linked with a macabre discovery by workmen in 1860. Inside a hollow brick wall, they found a skeleton with a dagger between its ribs.

A publicity gimmick that backfired introduced actress Judy Carne to the ghost of the Theatre Royal, Bath. A mock seance was arranged to promote her appearance in a production of the Noel Coward play, *Blithe Spirit*. But the light-hearted stunt became serious when the medium hired to host the proceedings started to receive real messages.

Judy, the "sock-it-to-me" star of the TV *Laugh-In* show, said: "We were all absolutely spellbound, including two cynical newspaper reporters. The voice of a woman told us she had been an actress who had starred at the theatre. She had been married, but had fallen in love with someone else.

"Her husband and lover fought a duel, and her lover was killed. Heartbroken, she hanged herself in the dressing room. As I listened, I became very emotional and felt real pain. I tried to talk to her, and ask if she was still unhappy, but the table we were sitting round rattled, and I heard weeping. I often went back to the theatre to try to contact her again, but she never re-appeared."

Could the heartbroken 18th century actress be the phantom lady in grey who haunts the theatre and the buildings on either side of it? She has often been seen by actors, sitting alone in a box. She was there on August 23, 1975, when the curtain went up on a performance of *The Dame Of Sark*, starring Dame Anna Neagle. Theatre staff have also noted a strong smell of jasmine whenever she is near – a scent also familiar to a succession of landlords at the Garrick's Head public house next door.

Bill Loud, Peter Welch and Peter Smith all sniffed it in the cellars during their tenancies, and all also reported tricks by unseen hands – phantom tapping on doors, cuff-links and pound notes disappearing, only to turn up later in rooms where nobody had been for days, candles flying across the bar, cupboard doors rattling, and a fridge being mysteriously switched off.

On the other side of the Theatre Royal is the house once occupied by Regency buck Beau Nash and his last mistress, Juliana Popjoy. Today it is a restaurant called Popjoy's. One would-be diner got more than he bargained for when he called just before Christmas, 1975.

He ordered his meal, then went upstairs to the bar while the dishes were being prepared. As he sat on a green settee, enjoying an aperitif, a lady in old-fashioned clothes approached, sat down beside him, and vanished. The terrified man rushed downstairs, blurted his story to a waiter, and fled, still hungry, into the night.

The jasmine lady may have been responsible for an unexpected drama on the Theatre Royal stage in June, 1963. One of the props for the production was a clock. When its hands reached 12.30, it chimed loudly three times. But stagehands had removed the chime mechanism before the performance began.

A lady in grey also haunts the Theatre Royal in York. Actress Julie Dawn Cole, best known as a nurse in the long-running British TV series *Angels*, is one of many who claim to have seen her. Julie said, "We were rehearsing on stage one Christmas when I saw her wearing a cloak and a hood. Her outline was irridescent, like gossamer, but I was left with a warm, happy feeling. I consider myself lucky to have seen her."

British actress Thora Hird does not have such fond memories of her brush with the supernatural. The popular TV comedy star was appearing on stage in London in a play set in Victorian times. She found a bolero-type jacket in a trunk of theatrical jumble, and at first it seemed ideal for her role, fitting her perfectly, but at each subsequent performance, it grew tighter, until it had to be let out.

Thora said, "One day, my understudy had to wear the jacket. That night,

Ghostly barking

Norma Kresgal, of New York, was awakened by the barking of Corky, her collie dog. But Corky was dead. Mrs Kresgal got up to investigate – and found that the house was on fire.

In Wichita, Kansas, Mrs Lowanda Cady was woken by the barking of her dead dog and drove off a thief who had been raiding her kitchen.

Walter Manuel awoke in terror the night he dreamed about his pet dog Lady which had died three weeks earlier. In his dream, Manuel heard the dead pet barking frantically. He awoke and rushed to the bedroom window of his home in a Los Angeles suburb. Outside he saw his two-year-old son, clad in pyjamas, topple into the garden pool. He rushed to the rescue and dragged the child from the water.

at home after the show, she saw the ghost of a young Victorian woman wearing the same jacket. Later, the wife of the director of the play tried the jacket on, and felt nothing. But when she took it off, there were red weals on her throat as if someone had tried to strangle her. We decided to get rid of the jacket.

"A few days after we did, three mediums held a seance on the stage of the theatre. One had a vision of a girl struggling violently with a man who was tearing at her clothes."

The site of a former theatre in Yorkshire is haunted by a woman who did not really exist. Old Mother Riley was a comedy favourite with British film, radio and music hall fans in the Forties and Fifties. She was the creation of comedian Arthur Lucan, who died in his dressing room at the old Tivoli Theatre, Hull, in 1966, a week before he was due to attend a meeting with local tax inspectors.

Ironically, when the theatre was demolished, a tax office was built in its place, and Lucan may be having the last laugh on the staff.

An Inland Revenue official said, "We do not like to say too much about what Old Mother Riley is up to in Hull, but people do stay away from a storeroom on the second floor. There is a strange atmosphere and it is said that the ghost of Mother Riley has been seen."

Stroll to oblivion

David Lang vanished from the face of the earth on September 23, 1880, and, has never been heard of since – apart from his ghostly voice. His disappearance, on a sunny afternoon and in front of five witnesses, remains one of the most baffling mysteries of all time.

During his last moments, Lang, a prosperous farmer, was strolling across a field in front of his home near Gallatin, Tennessee. His children, George, eight, and Sarah, 11, were playing in the front of the house. His wife had just walked out of the house to greet an approaching buggy carrying Judge August Peck and his brother-in-law.

David smiled, waved at the visitors and started walking toward the group at the farmhouse. He took a dozen steps, then Mrs Lang's horrified scream shattered the afternoon. Judge Peck dropped the buggy reins. The two men sprinted across the field to join Mrs Lang and the children at the spot where

---

Ripper's legacy

Two victims of Jack the Ripper have returned to London's East End to remind the capital city of its most celebrated unsolved crimes.

Polly Nicholls, a 42-year-old prostitute, was the first of the cruel butcher's six victims, found with her throat and stomach cut on August 31, 1888. She had been seen since, a huddled, pathetic figure, glowing eerily in the gutter of Durward Street, Whitechapel, where her body was discovered.

Harrowing screams heard in Hansbury Street, in nearby Spitalfields, are said to be those of another of Jack's victims, 47-year-old Annie Chapman.

David Lang had last been seen.

There was no trace of the farmer. In full view of five witnesses, he had simply vanished.

His wife fell to her knees and began to beat frantically at the ground. Judge Peck lifted her to her feet and the five fanned out in a frantic search of the pasture. The search yielded no sign of the missing man.

The judge summoned help. Neighbours began to arrive and search parties were formed. Far into the night, lanterns were swinging across the farm and through the woods beyond.

The next morning the county surveyor arrived and inspected the area where Lang had vanished. He announced that it was firmly supported by thick strata of limestone. There were no potholes or caves into which a man could fall.

Mrs Lang was by now numb with shock and under her doctor's care. As the search continued through days, weeks and eventually months, she stoutly resisted any suggestion of a funeral or even a memorial service for David Lang. She asked only that all churches pray for his return.

The shock of the experience had deeply affected the two Lang children – particularly Sarah. She turned into a shy, withdrawn child who spent long hours day-dreaming. Finally there was an astounding incident that prompted Mrs Lang to take her children away from the farm.

On an April evening in 1881, Sarah ran sobbing into the house to report that there was a "ring" around the spot where her father had vanished. When Mrs Lang went to investigate, the child said she could clearly hear her father calling. He was begging for help in a tortured voice, but it faded away into silence.

Mrs Lang did not hear her husband's ghostly voice, but in the pasture she made a strange discovery. Where her husband had last been seen, there was a perfect circle of withered yellow grass some 20 feet in diameter.

The fiend in bandages
"Cannibal" victim had his revenge

Only four men escaped when the British square-rigged yacht *Pierrot* capsized in the Atlantic in July 1884. Huddled in a battered dinghy, they drifted for 25 days. Near death from starvation and exposure, Captain Edwin Rutt then made a last desperate suggestion.

Lots should be drawn to determine which of the four would be eaten.

Two of the sailors agreed with Rutt, but 18-year-old Dick Tomlin, the youngest crewman, protested that he would rather die than eat human flesh.

Tomlin's resistance sealed his fate. At the first opportunity Rutt crept toward the sleeping boy and drove a knife into his neck.

The mate Josh Dudley and seaman Will Hoon had no reservations about cannibalism. When they were rescued by the yacht *Gellert* four days later, it was the slain boy's flesh that had sustained them.

The horror-stricken master of the *Gellert* rejected the idea of burial at sea. Hidden away underneath a tarpaulin, the body of the victim accompanied the three survivors to the Cornish port of Falmouth.

All three were tried and condemned to death for murder on the high seas. But the Home Secretary decided that there had been horror enough and commuted the sentence to six months' imprisonment.

No one could have known that the horrors were only beginning.

When the three men were freed from jail, they found little future. To keep body and soul together, Josh Dudley found work as a drayman. Two weeks later his team of horses saw something that frightened them in the middle of a foggy London street. Bolting, they tossed Dudley to the cobblestones where his head shattered.

Witnesses said the thing in the fog had been a figure swathed from head to foot in bloodstained bandages. After Dudley's death, the figure mysteriously vanished.

With fear beginning to take root, Captain Rutt went to the Soho slums and sought out Will Hoon. He found the old seaman far gone in drink, a sodden derelict in desperately bad health.

Rutt told Hoon that some vengeance-crazed relative was masquerading as Dick Tomlin's ghost, and he urged Hoon to help him ferret out the plotter. But Hoon wanted only more gin, and in a last delirium, he was taken to the charity ward of a hospital where he died in a screaming fit.

Witnesses said later that another patient "dressed all in bandages" had been holding Hoon down, apparently trying to soothe him. Then the patient vanished.

Now in a state of abject terror, Rutt went to the police. They scoffed at his tales of a "figure in bandages". But in view of the captain's mental condition, they offered him one night of lodging in a cell.

Rutt went gratefully to the cell, checking twice to be sure he was locked in. It was a cell block for the disturbed of London, and screams in the night were not uncommon.

But when at 3 am the police heard the captain, some distinctive quality in his cries brought warders running. They unlocked the door and went to his bunk, where Rutt lay with his knees scissored upward and his dead eyes like marbles.

Clenched in his fingers the shocked bobbies saw shreds of cotton. And bloodstained gauze.

Good and evil spirits

Ghosts can save lives - or take them

The deadliest spectral killer of all time was the 19th-century phantom of 50 Berkeley Square, London. No one knows what it was, because few who saw it lived to tell the tale. And those who did survive were generally reduced to incoherence by fright.

Sir Robert Warboys was one of its earliest victims. Challenged by friends to spend a night in the notorious house, he readily agreed. But the nervous landlord insisted on precautions. Sir Robert must take a gun. And if anything unusual happened, he must pull the cord which rang a bell in the room below.

At midnight, 45 minutes after Sir Robert had retired, the landlord and Sir Robert's friends heard the bell jangle violently. As they raced upstairs, they heard a shot. Sir Robert was dead when they burst into the room – but not from a bullet wound. His eyes stared out in terror, his lips curled away from clenched teeth. He had died of fright.

Years later, two sailors from Portsmouth wandered into Berkeley Square

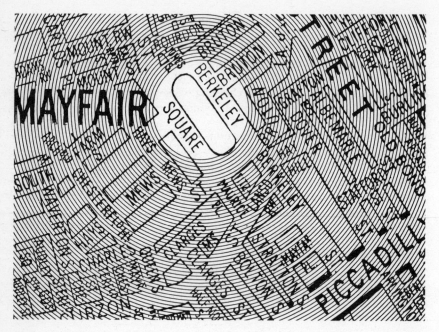

Berkeley Square in the heart of Mayfair.

and noticed a house hung with To Let signs. Edward Blunden and Robert Martin were not to know that the house contained a dreadful secret. To them it offered free lodgings for the night. They wandered through the disordered, neglected rooms and came at last to a relatively tidy top-floor bedroom. Martin soon fell asleep but Blunden was nervous. As he lay restlessly awake, he heard strange footsteps scratching their way towards the door. He woke Martin and the two men watched fearfully as the door slowly opened and something large, dark and shapeless entered.

The thing went for Blunden, trapping him near the window. Martin seized his chance to crash through the door and race downstairs into the street to obtain help. He blurted out his story to a policeman and they hurried back to the house. But they were too late. The shattered body of Blunden, his neck broken and his face fixed in a terrified grimace, lay on the basement stairs.

Other victims of the ghoul of 50 Berkeley Square included a girl guest at the house who went mad with terror, a man who slept there one night and was found dead the next morning, and the maid of a family renting the house who died in hospital after being found crumpled on the floor, whimpering: 'Don't let it touch me.'

Intrigued by these and other stories about the haunted house, a courageous 19th-century peer resolved to get to the bottom of the mystery. He was ghost-hunter Lord Lyttleton – a descendant of the man whose dead mistress told him he was doomed to die in three days' time (see page 170). Lyttleton resolved to spend a night in the haunted room. He took with him two guns, one filled with shot and the other with silver sixpenny pieces – charms to ward off evil spirits. During the night he fired a barrel of the silver coins at a shape which leapt at him. Perhaps the charms worked, for Lyttleton lived to tell the tale in his book *Notes and Queries*, published in 1879. In the volume he wrote that he had no doubt that the room was 'supernaturally fatal to body and mind'.

Today, however, the ghost seems to have given up its deathly vigil. Number 50 Berkeley Square is a bookshop, and the square itself has become better known as the haunt of a singing nightingale.

Breckles Hall, in Norfolk, is haunted by a strange scream for mercy. In addition, doors bang, mysterious footsteps are heard, and sometimes spectral dancers stage a ghostly ball.

Early this century, a body was found outside the front door of the hall. It was that of local poacher Jim Mace. He and another man had got drunk in a local public house and decided to bag a few partridges in the hall grounds. They knew the hall was empty and had been told that some nights the windows lit up to reveal a ghostly ballroom full of dancers. Their birds bagged, the two men went hunting for ghosts. They saw nothing and were turning for home when a coach and four horses swept silently into view at the bottom of the drive. Rooted to the spot, they watched the phantom coach come to a halt and a beautiful woman step out, decked in jewels. As she stared into Mace's eyes, he slumped to the ground with a piercing scream.

His friend raced to the nearest houses to get help, but no one would venture to the hall that night once he had told his story. It was the next morning before the vicar led villagers to the spot – and found the poacher, his face paralyzed with fear, his body stiff and cold.

Residents of Norfolk Island, in the Pacific Ocean 900 miles off the east coast of Australia, claim to have seen ghosts of shipwreck survivors, who lived for a while on the island, as well as the spectres of Irish convicts, hanged when the island was a British penal colony. The islanders also tell the story of Barney Duffy's curse. The giant Irishman had escaped from the colony's jail, but was found hiding in a hollow tree by two soldiers. 'If you take me back,' Duffy threatened, 'you'll die violently within a week of my hanging.' The soldiers ignored his warning. Two days after the execution, they went fishing near the hollow tree. Their beaten bodies were washed up next day on the tide. No one ever found out how they had died.

In 1804, a white phantom brought terror to Hammersmith, London, and cost two lives. It first appeared to a woman crossing a local churchyard. She fled but it followed her and seized her arms. She fainted and, though she was brought round, she never got over the shock and died at home a few days later. After 16 people travelling in a cart all fled from the ghost, local vigilante groups kept watch on the churchyard. And on the fourth night, Francis Smith, a customs officer, spotted a figure in white coming down a nearby lane. Smith shot at it and the figure fell. But it was not the ghost. It was bricklayer Thomas Milwood, coming home late from work in white overalls. Smith was sentenced to death for manslaughter but, on appeal, the sentence was commuted to a year in jail.

A spectre that killed was the phantom No. 7 bus seen racing around the

A London Transport bus of the Thirties.

Ladbroke Grove area of London in the early hours of one morning in 1936. The story was told at a West London coroner's court to explain why a car had swerved into a wall, killing the driver. A witness said the bus was ablaze with lights and it had vanished when the car hit the wall. Other drivers said they too had seen the bus. And a bus inspector swore he had seen it pull silently into his depot, then disappear. The bus has not been seen since.

Among the good spirits is one recorded by ghost-hunter Lord Halifax. A sailor, whose ship was ploughing through the North Atlantic somewhere off the Canadian coast, saw a strange man writing in the captain's cabin. When the log-book was checked, an unknown hand was seen to have written: 'Steer to the north-east.' The captain did so, and after some hours he came across a ship in trouble. As the survivors came aboard, the sailor recognized the man he had seen writing in the log. When this man rewrote the words that had appeared mysteriously in the log-book, the two specimens matched exactly.

During World War One, a driver of the 42nd Field Ambulance was taking a badly wounded soldier from Ypres to a casualty station at Poperinge. A flare lit the night sky, and the driver saw the silhouette of a sentry standing directly in front of him. He stopped. But when he looked again, the sentry had vanished. All the driver saw was a vast shell crater, only yards from his front wheels. The phantom sentry had saved two lives.

Dr S. Weir Mitchell, an eminent 19th-century nerve specialist of Philadelphia, USA, was dozing after a hard day's work when he heard a knock at his door. He opened it and saw a thin girl in a shawl who begged him to come and treat her desperately ill mother. Dr Mitchell followed the girl through a snow blizzard to the house where her mother lay. He soon saw that she had pneumonia. After he had sent for medicine and made her comfortable, he mentioned her daughter's mission. The woman looked surprised. 'My daughter died a month ago,' she said. The girl was now nowhere to be seen. Her shawl was hanging in a nearby cupboard, and there was no trace of snow on it.

In the 1880s, Britain's ambassador to Paris, Lord Dufferin, was staying with friends in Ireland. One night he awoke to see a hunched figure with an ugly, grizzled face carrying a coffin across the lawn. When he called to the man, the vision vanished. Dufferin's host was mystified when told the story at breakfast, and over the years the ambassador forgot the incident.

But years later, attending a diplomatic reception at the Grand Hotel, Paris, Dufferin walked towards the lifts and saw the ugly, grizzled man again – in servant's uniform. Dufferin refused to take the lift, and so missed death. When the lift reached the fifth floor its cable snapped and it plummeted to the bottom of the shaft. All those inside were killed.

The ghosts of an airline pilot and his flight engineer succeeded in grounding

A World War I soldier.

A Lockheed TriStar air-bus.

a plane belonging to one of the world's biggest airlines a few years ago. Pilots and cabin staff of Eastern Airlines in America said they had been warned not to fly the plane by the ghosts of Captain Bob Loft and Flight Engineer Don Repo, killed when their Lockheed TriStar crashed with the loss of 101 lives in Florida's Everglades in 1972.

After that crash, ground staff claimed that Repo's ghost helped them trace faults in other TriStars. Stewardesses reported sudden drops in temperature in some TriStars and a mysterious airline captain who vanished when spoken to. Repo was also said to have appeared on the flight deck of TriStar 318 to warn of a fire; hours later, the plane had to return to the airport with a blazing engine. In 1974, the warnings stopped as mysteriously as they had begun.

Good spirits can be more generous in death than they are in life. In 1780, a serving woman who went to Powys Castle, in Wales, to look for work was, as a joke, put in a haunted bedroom. But the woman had the last laugh. For she claimed that an elegantly dressed ghost led her to a locked iron box, showed her the key hidden in a nearby crevice and told her to send it to the owner of the castle in London. The owner returned to the castle and took the old woman into his care, offering her any money she wanted and letting her stay at his home. The secret of the box was never revealed.

A well-known miser called Mrs Webb died in the village of Barby, Northamptonshire, in March 1851. Few mourned her passing. But a month later, strange knocking sounds were heard from her house, along with the sound of furniture being moved. They continued even after a family rented the cottage from the nephew to whom she had left it. Then one of the tenant's children saw a tall woman standing over a bed. When neighbours heard the story, they agreed to keep watch with the tenant's wife, Mrs Accleton. Three of them were with her when a ball of light suddenly leapt into the air towards a trap-door in the ceiling. They told the nephew, who agreed to search the loft. There he found two bags, one holding a bundle of property deeds, the other full of coins and notes.

But Mrs Webb had not finished her business. As the knockings, moanings and strange noises went on, unpaid bills were discovered. And only when the nephew had paid the last creditor were the Accletons left in peace.

Pleas from the afterlife

Ghosts who bring messages to the living

Why do phantoms appear to the living? The vast majority seem to be 'ghosts of conscience', often victims of injustice appealing to the living for a decent burial, or for their wishes to be kept, or just for sympathy. Some seek peace. Others protest that their peace has been disturbed.

Raynham Hall, a magnificent stately home near Fakenham, Norfolk, has been haunted for nearly 300 years by a woman dressed in brown. She is believed to be Dorothy Walpole, sister of Sir Robert Walpole, who became Britain's prime minister in 1721.

Dorothy's father, also called Robert and also a member of parliament, was made guardian of a 13-year-old viscount, Charles Townshend. And as Dorothy and Charles grew up together they fell in love. But when they wanted to get married, Dorothy's father refused. He feared people would think the Walpoles were after the Townshend fortunes and estates.

Charles resigned himself to his fate and soon married a baron's daughter. But Dorothy could not shake off her feelings so easily, despite a wild whirl of parties. She went to London, then Paris, scandalizing the social set by setting up house with a rakish lord.

In 1711, when Dorothy heard that Charles's wife had died, she hurried home to Raynham, and within a year they were married. For a while they were blissfully happy. Then gossip about Dorothy's escapade in Paris reached Charles. He was furious and confined her to her rooms. She was not allowed out and no one was allowed in. Ten years later she died. The records said it was smallpox, but local rumour blamed her death on a push from behind at

King George III.

the top of the hall's grand oak staircase. Her ghost was soon seen by servants, family and guests alike.

In 1786, King George III was staying at the hall. He awoke in the middle of the night to see a brown-clad woman, her hair dishevelled, her face ashen, beside his bed. He fled the room in his nightgown and nightcap and stormed round the house, rousing everyone with his wrath. He vowed not to stay an hour longer.

Alarmed at upsetting so honoured a guest, the Townshends ordered a nightly watch by gamekeepers. And a few nights later, they too saw the woman in brown, walking down a corridor. One man moved out to challenge her – and she walked right through him. He felt an icy cloud pass into his bones and out again.

In 1835 she appeared again. Colonel Loftus, brother of the then Lady Townshend, saw her on consecutive nights at Christmas – always a popular time with ghosts – and described her as a stately woman in rich brown brocade with a cap-like head-dress. Her face was clearly defined. But where her eyes should have been, there were only black hollows. The woman appeared to several other guests in the days that followed, and cut short the Christmas merrymaking.

A few years later, Dorothy startled another distinguished guest. He was Captain Frederick Marryat, author of *Mr Midshipman Easy* and *The Children of the New Forest*, a tough seagoing man who scoffed at the story of the hauntings. Invited to see Dorothy's ghost for himself, Marryat stayed at the hall in a room where a portrait of the formidable woman was hanging. Late that night, he and two other guests saw the ghostly shape of Dorothy walking a corridor. They scuttled into a side room as the phantom approached. It stopped outside the open door and grinned wickedly. Marryat was unnerved enough to grab his pistol and fire a shot. It went straight through the still-smiling spectre and crashed into the door opposite.

Dorothy was seen infrequently after that. But in 1936 she returned in dramatic manner. Two professional photographers, commissioned to take pictures of the hall for Lady Townshend, were setting up their camera to take shots of the oak staircase. Suddenly one saw a vapid form take shape, and urged his colleague to expose the photographic plate. This he did, without knowing why. The flash made the shape vanish – but when the plate was developed, there on the stairs was the outline of a woman in flowing veil and white bridal gown. Experts who examined the plate were convinced it was not a fake. Had Dorothy decided to let the world see what she had looked like on that fateful wedding day 224 years earlier?

The ghost of Chambercombe Manor, near Ilfracombe, Devon – a tall, smiling woman dressed in grey – is less malevolent. She has even been known to join tourist parties looking over her former home. But she has every reason to be as bitter as Dorothy.

Her story began with her grandfather, Alexander Oatway, of Chambercombe, one of the notorious West Country shipwreckers of 400 years ago. During storms he used to wave lanterns on the shore, to lure ships on to the rocks. Then he plundered them. One day his son William followed him and rescued a Spanish girl who had survived the wreck. Later they married and had a daughter, Kate. The family had left Chambercombe Manor by then, shamed by Alexander's wrecking activities, and William and his family lived on Lundy Island in the Bristol Channel. But when they heard that the manor was vacant again they moved back and rented it.

Shortly afterwards, Kate married an Irish sea captain called Wallace, and moved with him to Dublin. Years passed. Then one night a vicious storm blew up and William hurried down to the shore in case a ship was in trouble. He found a woman lying on the rocks. She had been hideously battered and disfigured by the sea. He carried her back to the manor house, where she died that night.

At this stage, temptation got the better of honest William. He realized that with the jewels and money from the belt the woman was carrying, he could buy the manor house outright. So when an admiralty man called two days later, making inquiries about a missing passenger from the wrecked ship, William said he knew nothing about the matter. But when the visitor mentioned the name – Mrs Katherine Wallace – William realized what he had done. Filled with remorse, he walled up her body in a secret room and moved from the manor.

His secret was discovered only 150 years ago, when a farmer living in the house found Kate's skeleton while rethatching the roof. Her bones were buried in a pauper's grave at Ilfracombe. But her spirit still wanders – her ghost has been seen as recently as 1976.

Spirit manifestations at the home of the Ewing family in Lynton, Devon, led to a much belated burial. In the 1930s guests staying in a room above the scullery were disturbed at night by the eerie crying of a child and the ghost of an old woman. Then Mrs Ewing's brother-in-law noticed that the guest room was much smaller than the scullery beneath. A walled-up cupboard was discovered, and in it were a quantity of bones and a child's box. Once the bones left for the mortuary, the haunting ceased.

At Bisham Abbey, in Marlow, Buckinghamshire, an old woman in black has been seen wandering round the Thames-side grounds, washing her hands in a bowl that moves before her. She is believed to be Dame Elizabeth Hoby, who died in 1609 in great distress. Her son was a slow learner and one day was locked in a small room to finish his studies. A message from the Queen called Dame

Elizabeth away. When she returned, so one story goes, the boy was slumped dead over his desk. Another version of the story is that Dame Elizabeth beat the boy to death because he blotted his books. In 1840, workmen altering the abbey found children's books between some floor joists. One book was blotted with long-dried tears.

When the body of schoolboy John Daniel was found 200 yards from his home at Beaminster, Dorset, in 1728, death was assumed to have been from natural causes. His mother swore he suffered from fits. But seven weeks later, 12 fellow pupils saw his ghost sitting at a desk in their classroom, his coffin nearby. After local magistrate Colonel Broadrep had closely questioned each boy and found that their stories tallied, he ordered the body to be exhumed. An inquest revealed that John had been strangled. The murderer was never caught. John's pathetic figure has since been seen in nearby St Mary's Church.

A ghost in Australia helped to solve a disappearance riddle in 1826. Frederick Fisher, a farmer, was jailed for debt. To stop creditors seizing his land at Campbelltown, New South Wales, he transferred his assets to ex-convict George Worrall. Six months later Fisher was freed. One night he left a local inn after a heavy drinking session and was never seen again. Police investigated, but could find no evidence of foul play, though they suspected Worrall had killed his one-time friend.

Then one dark night Fisher's neighbour James Farley saw an eerie figure sitting on a fence and pointing to a spot in Fisher's paddock. Farley fled in fear but next day returned with a constable. When they dug up the spot indicated by the ghost, they found the badly beaten body of the farmer. Worrall was arrested, confessed and was hanged.

Burton Agnes Hall is not the name of a woman, but of a beautiful Jacobean house in a village between Bridlington and Driffield, Yorkshire. It was built by three spinster sisters with money left them by their father, Sir Henry Griffith, early in the 17th century. Soon after the hall was completed, the youngest sister, Anne, was waylaid by robbers at nearby Harpham. Her screams brought villagers to the rescue, but she had been badly beaten and, although she was carried home and cared for, it was obvious she would not recover.

Just before she died, she made the extraordinary demand that her sisters cut off her head before burying her body and preserve it in the walls of the home she loved. She warned vaguely of dire consequences if her wishes were disobeyed. Horrified at the idea, the sisters reluctantly promised they would do as she bid, although they had no intention of doing so. When Anne died, she was buried intact.

A week later the trouble started. First there was a crash in one of the upstairs rooms. Seven days later the household was awakened by doors slamming in every part of the building. On the third week after Anne's death, the house shook with the clatter of people running along corridors and up and down the stairs. Then came an awful groan. The sounds continued all night, and next morning the servants packed and left. The two sisters called in the vicar. When they mentioned Anne's dying wish, he agreed to open her grave. A shock awaited them. Anne's head had been cut from her body, and the flesh on it had shrivelled away to leave a bare skull.

The sisters took the head to the Hall, and the haunting ceased. Over the years, several subsequent owners of the hall have removed the skull, known as Awd Nance. Each time, mysterious shufflings and clatterings in the corridors, accompanied by slamming doors and terrifying groans, have forced them to restore the gruesome relic to its rightful place.

Disturbed bones gave an American family a harrowing time. The incidents were described by the *San Francisco Examiner* in 1891. A Mr Walsingham, a farmer, discovered the bones shortly after moving into his new house at Oakville, Georgia. He threw them into a lime kiln. He was not a superstitious man, and when curious things started happening in the middle of the night (doors banged, bells rang and chairs were overturned), he put it down to mischief by the family or neighbours. But he began to worry when his dog began barking furiously at a wall, lunged forward, then fell back yelping, its neck broken.

Hideous laughter, shouts and wails began to come from all over the house. A daughter saw a disembodied hand grip her shoulder. And Walsingham saw the prints of a man's naked feet form beside his as he walked in the rain.

But what finally persuaded the family to leave was a horrific dinner party. During the party, guests bravely shrugged off the strange groans coming from upstairs, but then a deep red stain started forming on the white tablecloth – what looked like blood was dripping from above . . . The men in the party raced upstairs and ripped up the floorboards. But all they found was dry dust – and the red liquid continued to drip below. Chemists who later examined the tablecloth confirmed that the stain was human blood. But by that time the Walsinghams had moved out.

Ghosts are often claimed to have avenged wrongs done to innocent people. In the 16th century, Kraster and Dorothy Cook owned a small farm overlooking Lake Windermere, in Westmorland. Wealthy Myles Phillipson, who owned the land around it, wanted the Cooks' site in order to build a magnificent new house. When the farmer refused to sell, Phillipson resorted to trickery. He invited the Cooks to share his Christmas dinner, and impressed them with a beautiful golden bowl. Next day, soldiers arrested the couple. For a week they were held in separate cells without explanation. Then they arrived in court to find that Phillipson had accused them of stealing the bowl. The outcome of the trial was never in doubt, for it was heard by the local magistrate – Phillipson. When he pronounced sentence of death, Dorothy Cook cried out: 'Look out for yourself. You will never prosper. The time will come when you own no land.'

Phillipson built his magnificent home, called Calgarth Hall, and held a Christmas feast to celebrate. But when Mrs Phillipson went upstairs to fetch something, she screamed in terror – for there on the banister were two grinning skulls. Her screams brought the rest of the party racing upstairs, swords drawn. The sight sobered the merrymakers, and though the skulls were thrown into the courtyard and denounced as a tasteless practical joke, the guests were uneasy when they went early to bed.

At 2 am more screams brought them running from their rooms. The skulls were back, grinning from a step on the staircase. Over the next few days, the Phillipsons tried every way they could think of to get rid of the skulls. But every day they returned. And gradually Dorothy Cook's curse came true. Phillipson's business declined, his wealth dwindled, and when he died the skulls screamed all night.

His heirs also suffered from the skulls, which took to appearing each Christmas Day and on the anniversary of the Cooks' hanging. Only when the family became too poor to keep the hall, and were forced to sell it, did the skulls disappear.

The three lives of Glenn Ford

Hollywood star joins the ranks of those who claim to have lived before

In 1978 Hollywood film star Glenn Ford got the shock of his life – his third life, that is. For when a doctor hypnotized him, he spoke emotionally of a previous existence as a Colorado cowboy. Later, at another session, he recalled being a piano teacher in Elgin, Scotland.

Listening to tapes of both sessions was a surprise in itself for Ford. But he was amazed when researchers discovered evidence that both his previous 'incarnations' had actually existed – and at about the times the actor had indicated. 'I'm very confused about it all,' Ford said. 'It conflicts with all my religious beliefs. I'm a God-fearing man and proud of it, but this has gotten me mixed up.'

Ford is not the first person to produce evidence of reincarnation. Indeed, Buddhists believe that man goes through a series of lives, both human and animal, before reaching the bliss of nirvana – the extinction of individuality and absorption into the supreme spirit. But Ford's is one of the best-documented cases on record of life after death.

The actor's first hypnosis session was at his home in Beverley Hills, California. Then aged 61, he spoke vividly about working as a cowboy, Charlie Bill, for a rancher called Charlie Goodnight, and of being ambushed and shot. Researchers from the University of California in Los Angeles went to Colorado and uncovered evidence of both Bill and Goodnight.

The second session, again tape-recorded, took place at the university. This time, equally vividly, Ford spoke of life as Charles Stuart, and said: 'I teach the piano to young flibbertigibbets,' a dated term for frivolous children. Ford also played the piano under hypnosis, though as he admitted later: 'I can't play a note.'

When University of California researchers visited Elgin, they found the grave of a Charles Stuart, who died in 1840. They showed a photograph of the grave to Ford. 'That shook me up really bad,' he said. 'I felt immediately that it was the place I was buried.'

Ex-British Army Captain Arthur Flowerdew retired to a cottage in the Norfolk village of Bramerton. Born and brought up in rural England, he had led a quiet life and had never travelled further than Europe. Yet this contented grandfather was convinced that he, too, had lived before – as a soldier in the rock-hewn Jordanian city of Petra, 2,200 years earlier.

Flowerdew told researcher Joan Forman, who was writing a book on the subject, that since childhood strange unexplained visions had invaded his mind. As a boy at the seaside, he had picked up red and amber stones, thinking: 'This is the colour of the rock of that city.' Later came mental pictures of a city cut out of the cliffs, men in long Biblical robes, golden treasure hidden in a temple, tombs carved in pink and amber rock, a narrow gorge running down to a desert, a battle as he and ten other men defended the gorge against a horde of invaders, and, finally, the pain as a spear thrown by a giant Syrian crashed into his chest.

Miss Forman checked what he told her against the known facts on Petra, and found that much of it tallied. She was further amazed when she introduced him to a local schoolteacher who had taken colour slides of the ruined

Glenn Ford.

city during a holiday in 1964. The teacher said: 'He could tell me more than what could be seen. He was able to describe what was next to certain pillars, off the edge of the photograph.'

Flowerdew said: 'I'm not the sort of chap to day-dream, and I have never understood how I received these pictures of my city. If pushed, I think I would come down on the side of reincarnation, but I can't see how it could happen.'

Dorothy Eady was born into a wealthy South London family in 1903.

When she was three, she tumbled down stairs and was declared dead by the family doctor. But when he and a nurse returned to lay out the body, they found the little girl alive. All was not well, however. Dorothy took to hiding under tables and behind furniture, demanding to be taken 'home'.

When the family visited the Egyptian rooms at the British Museum, she ran wild, kissing the feet of statues, hugging mummy cases, and screaming that she wanted to be left with 'my people'. When she was later shown a photograph of the temple to the god Osiris, built beside the Nile by Pharaoh Seti I, she told her father that the temple was her real home, that she had known Seti and that he was a kind man.

In 1930, Dorothy married an Egyptian and went to live in his country. When they had a son, she called him Seti, and herself Um Seti, 'mother of Seti'. It was 22 years before she visited Abydos, site of the ancient temple to Osiris, and when the train stopped near a range of limestone hills she said that she was 'home'. In 1954 she returned to live at Abydos, helping to look after the temple, praying daily to Osiris, and persuading the temple curators to let her be buried in the grounds when she died.

Flowerdew and Dorothy Eady are both unusual in that their visions of previous lives did not rely on hypnosis.

Many hypnotherapists and psychiatrists have cases on their files similar to the two recorded by Welsh hypnotist Arnall Bloxham, of Cardiff, in 1956. One was of a teenager who, under hypnosis, spoke vividly of a previous existence as a man in a land where people were decorated with scars and teeth. The other was a woman who claimed to be the daughter of Charles I and Queen Henrietta Maria. She knew little of history, but could describe accurately the court of King Louis XIV of France, where she and her 'brother', the future Charles II, stayed during the royal family's exile after the English Civil War.

American amateur hypnotist Morey Bernstein described the curious claim of a Colorado housewife in his book *The Search for Bridey Murphy*, published in 1956. Bernstein was taking Mrs Ruth Simmons, born in the mid-west in 1923, back to her childhood under hypnosis when she started talking as Bridey Murphy. She said she had been born in Cork, Ireland, on 20 December 1798, had married a lawyer called Sean McCarthy when she was 17, and had moved to Belfast. She had died after a fall in 1864 and could describe her own funeral and tombstone.

Researchers in Ireland found much of her story difficult to corroborate, but her descriptions of the Antrim coastline and a journey from Belfast to Cork were accurate, and records were found of a grocer called Farr, at whose store Bridey claimed to have shopped. Mrs Simmons had never been to Ireland, and her normal voice had no trace of an Irish accent.

The spinster's grave

How Hannah returned to guard her gold

Spinster Hannah Beswick died more than 200 years ago. Her body was embalmed, but her restless spirit still haunts a factory built on the land where her home once stood.

Hannah was a wealthy Lancashire landowner whose house, Birchen Bower, dominated acres of fertile land at Hollinwood, on the outskirts of Manchester. She was not normally fearful, but when in 1745 Bonnie Prince Charlie crossed the border into England and advanced south, she became so obsessed with the thought of the invading Scots that she hid all her money and valuables. They remained hidden for the rest of her life.

Apart from the Scots, her only real terror was that of being buried alive – a fear quite understandable in the light of what had happened in her own family. One of her brothers had fallen ill and, while unconscious, had been pronounced dead by a local doctor. Preparations were made for his funeral and he was laid in an open coffin so that friends and relatives could pay their last respects. While lying in his shroud surrounded by flowers he began to show signs of life. The unfortunate man was hastily removed to his bed.

Hannah died in 1768 without divulging where she had hidden her fortune. Because of what had happened to her brother, she took steps to ensure that her corpse was not buried.

She left Birchen Bower to young Doctor Charles White with the stipulation that he must have her embalmed and kept in a safe and respectable place above ground.

For some strange reason, she also insisted that every 21 years her body

---

A professor's warning

Night classes for ghost-hunters proved so popular at Glasgow University that four times the expected number of people enrolled. Students on the 10-week course included clergymen, accountants and senior citizens.

Professor Archie Roy, the university's head of astronomy, a keen amateur ghost detective, told his students: "My aim is to open minds to great mysteries. But I also warn of the dangers."

The scientist, a leading authority on ghosts, is often called in to investigate weird happenings, and spends his holidays seeking out old haunts.

should be taken back to the house and allowed to lie in the granary for seven days.

Old Hannah was duly mummified, her body coated with tar and wrapped in heavy linen bandages. In accordance with her wishes, the face was left uncovered.

For many years Dr White faithfully kept the body at his own home, Sale Priory, but when he died it was moved to Manchester Natural History Society's museum where it became a major attraction.

A century after Hannah Beswick was embalmed, the commissioners of the society, finding the museum over-filled with relics and needing room for new acquisitions, decided it was time she was given a proper burial. She was finally interred at Harpurhey Cemetery on July 22, 1868.

Some people had already claimed to have seen her ghost wandering through the rooms of Birchen Bower, dressed in her usual black silk gown and white lace cap. After burial the ghost became more agitated. Hannah was seen hurrying between the old barn and the pond as though deeply troubled. Sometimes, it was said, the old barn glowed as if on fire.

The house remained empty for some years, inhabited only by the spirit of Hannah Beswick. Then it was bought by a developer, renovated and converted into small dwellings to be rented out to cotton workers and labourers. The new tenants were often to see her drifting by, head bent as though in deep thought.

One particular aspect of her behaviour was puzzling. Sometimes she would disappear at a particular spot – a corner flagstone in the parlour of a house occupied by a handloom weaver. Hannah seemed to hover about this room as though reluctant to leave it.

The weaver decided to pull up part of the flagstone floor to make a place where he could install a new loom. To his amazement he found hidden underneath a hoard of gold. He had found part of Hannah Beswick's fortune.

After this, Hannah was seen frequently ... no longer thoughtful but angry and menacing. People spoke of a brilliant blue light darting from her eyes. Sometimes at night she was seen near the pond and at other times strange unearthly noises were heard in the barn. No one would venture there after dark unless they had urgent business.

It gave rise to the speculation that perhaps the rest of her valuables were hidden nearby and she was determined to protect them.

The hauntings continued until Birchen Bower was demolished. A factory was built on the spot and that was thought to be the end of the affair.

Then, people who knew nothing of her story began saying that they had caught a glimpse of a strange old world figure in a black silk gown and white lace cap ...

Legend of the hairy hands

Holidaymaker Florence Warwick had never heard of the ghostly hands that are supposed to terrify victims on Dartmoor in Devon, but she discovered all she would ever want to know when her car broke down on the moor one evening.

Florence, aged 28, was driving along the lonely road from Postbridge to Two Bridges after a sightseeing tour. When the car started to judder she pulled over to the side of the road to look at the handbook.

She recalled: "As I was reading in the failing light, a cold feeling suddenly came over me. I felt as if I was being watched. I looked up and saw a pair of huge, hairy hands pressed against the windscreen. I tried to scream, but couldn't. I was frozen with fear."

She watched wide-eyed as the disembodied hands that are said to have haunted this desolate place for 60 years began to crawl across the windscreen. "It was horrible, they were just inches away," she said. "After what seemed a lifetime, I heard myself cry out and the hands seemed to vanish."

Florence was so shaken she hardly noticed that her car started first time. By the time she had driven the 20 miles back to Torbay, where she was staying with friends, she began to think she had imagined the whole incident. But then her friends told her the legend of the hands.

The "curse" on the road began to be felt in the early 1920s. Pony traps were overturned, a cyclist felt his handlebars wrenched from his grasp and ran full tilt into a stone wall, horses shied and bolted. A doctor travelling on a motor-cycle with two children in the sidecar was nearly killed when the engine literally detached itself from the machine. An Army officer reported an enormous pair of hands covered in long dark hairs taking charge of his steering wheel, covering his own.

Things reached a head in 1921 when a newspaper sent investigators to the spot and the local authority had the camber of the road altered. But the hands refused to be deterred.

Not long after the road improvement a young couple were visiting the area with their caravan. As is common on Dartmoor, a heavy fog suddenly fell one evening as they were driving towards Plymouth. Rather than drive on and risk losing their way, the couple decided to park in a lay-by along the Postbridge road. They cooked themselves a snack and settled down to sleep.

The woman had only been asleep for a short time when she was awakened by a strange scratching noise which seemed to be coming from outside the caravan. Thinking it might be a dog wandering lost on the moors, she got out of bed to take a look. Suddenly a strange chill came over her and she turned to look at the window above her husband's bunk.

There, slowly crawling across glass right above her sleeping husband, was an enormous pair of hairy hands. The woman was too stunned even to cry out, but for some inexplicable reason, as she sat rigid with fear staring at the gruesome apparition, she made the sign of the cross and the hands vanished.

The incident was the talk of the county, and it gave rise to the inevitable jokes and hoaxes. Soon enough the local police began to ignore reports that came in, attributing many of the sightings to an over-indulgence in the local cider. But in 1960 a fatal accident on the lonely stretch of road raised again the spectre of the hands.

A motorist driving from Plymouth to Chagford was found dead beneath the wreckage of his overturned car. No other car was involved and there seemed to be no reason, other than a fault in the car itself, that could have caused the vehicle to career off the road. But when police experts examined the wreckage they could find no mechanical fault in the car. It is a mystery which has never been solved.

Motorists are not the only ones to have suffered the attentions of this unusual manifestation. Walkers making their way along the stretch of road have reported strange experiences and sensations even though they have never heard of the legend of the hands.

One hiker enjoying the rugged beauty of the scenery got carried away during his walk and found himself making his way along the road at dusk. Suddenly he was overcome by an inexplicable feeling of panic, he was rooted to the spot, yet he could see no reason for his sense of fear. Minutes later the feeling passed and he carried on his way puzzling over his strange experience. Only later did he hear the story of the hauntings.

Nobody has been able to explain the strange happenings on this lonely stretch of highway. The only clue to the appearance of the hairy disembodied hands is that in the far distant past a Bronze Age village stood along the once-busy but now-sinister Dartmoor road.

Girl in a raincoat

A limping blonde girl in a pale raincoat has startled several motorists on the A23 road north of Brighton, Sussex. In 1964 one driver saw her dash to the central reservation and vanish. In 1972, several people said they saw her north of the village of Pyecombe. She may be the ghost of a young girl killed in a motor cycle accident in the area.

The bloodstone ring
Severed hand trapped a killer

Gale force winds lashed the tiny English village of Willisham, ripping slates from the roofs and tearing limbs from trees. A huge old oak shuddered before the onslaught and then, caught by one mighty gust, toppled, its roots tearing at the earth beneath.

Villagers who rushed to the spot to see if anyone was hurt stopped in horror as they gazed between the gnarled roots. There lay some human remains.

Police Constable Klug, the only bobby in the East Anglian community, was called and he ordered that the body be taken from its strange grave. One of the dismembered hands had a ring on one finger. Acting on a hunch, the grim-faced constable carried the hand to Ellen Grey, sister of a girl who had vanished mysteriously 18 years before, in 1873. Ellen screamed and then hugged the ghastly relic to her breast.

"It's Mary's," she sobbed. "The bloodstone ring was my wedding gift. She was born in March, and it was her birthstone."

Klug understood. Though the case was before his time, it was so well known in the area it had been the subject of a popular ballad.

On her 18th birthday, Mary Grey had married Basil Osborne. She had written a letter to John Bodneys, her sweetheart since childhood, asking for his forgiveness.

An hour before the groom was to take her away on the honeymoon, Mary told her sister she wanted to spend a little time alone in the upstairs room they had shared. When Osborne arrived with the carriage, she still hadn't come down. Frightened, they forced their way into the locked bedroom, but found no trace of the bride.

One window opened onto a balcony where a flight of steps led to an enclosed garden. But the garden, too, was empty.

The abandoned bridegroom died a month later. The villagers blamed a broken heart.

Now, 18 years later, the village knew what had become of Mary – for the skeleton had a broken neck! Ellen refused to give up her murdered sister's hand. It had been brought to her for a purpose, she said. That purpose must be fulfilled.

Dying, she left a bizarre provision in her will. Her housekeeper Maggie Williams was to have her estate, but must display the hand in some public place "where it may some day confront the murderer."

Maggie opened what became the finest pub in Willisham and gave the hand a place of honour on one wall. Enclosed in glass against a black velvet background, the bony ringed fingers claimed the attention of everyone.

After the shock of the exhibit had worn away, the tale of Mary's murder was a frequent topic of conversation. On a dismal March night in 1895, a stranger sat listening to scraps of the talk.

"Must have been just such a night as this that the wind ripped out that old oak tree," said the publican.

The stranger, a brooding man with a ravaged face, looked up from his glass. "I don't understand. What oak tree?" he asked.

"Have a look at the case on the wall and then we'll tell you the story," the barman told him.

Moments later, the stranger was screaming. He sagged against the wall, blood dripping from his fingers. An older man at the bar recognised him as Mary's missing former sweetheart John Bodneys.

When Constable Klug arrived, the bleeding man confessed to the murder of Mary Grey. In a frenzy of jealousy, he had found the bride alone in her room. Muffling her cries, he carried her from the house.

Bodneys insisted that he had not meant to kill her. But when they reached the big oak tree, she was struggling so hard he had broken her neck.

He left her in a shallow grave under the oak and tried to put Willisham behind him forever. But there had never been a moment of peace since the crime, and inevitably he had been compelled to return.

Committed to the local jail to await trial, he died "of no known disease" before his trial could be held. The authorities dismissed the old wives' tale that a murderer's hands sometimes drip blood when he faces the proof of his crime. But the people of the village knew what they had seen.

They buried Mary Grey's hand with the rest of her skeleton – and then ceremoniously burned the shirt smeared by John Bodneys' bloody fingers the day he came face to face with his guilt.

Bewildered butchers

Butchers at Britain's best-known meat market, London's Smithfield, complained in 1654 about weekly visits by a phantom mischief-maker. They said the ghost of a lawyer called Mallett glided between their stalls each Saturday evening, pulling joints of meat from the slabs. Traders who had hit out at him with cleavers and carving knives had merely sliced through thin air.

Princess of death

Egyptologist Douglas Murray neither liked nor trusted the dishevelled American who sought him out in Cairo in 1910. The man had a furtive manner and appeared to be in the final stages of disease. But Murray, a refined Briton, could not resist the blandishments of his disreputable visitor – for the American was offering him the most priceless find of his career.

It was the mummy-case of a high princess in the temple of Ammon-Ra, who was supposed to have lived in Thebes in 1600BC. The outside of the case bore the image of the princess, exquisitely worked in enamel and gold. The case was in an excellent state of preservation.

An avid collector, Murray couldn't resist. He drew a cheque on the Bank of England and took immediate steps to have the mummy-case shipped to his London home. The cheque was never cashed. The American died that evening. Murray learned from another Egyptologist in Cairo why the price had been so reasonable.

The princess from Ammon-Ra had held high office in the powerful Cult of the Dead, which had turned the fertile Valley of the Nile into a place only of death. Inscribed on the walls of her death chamber she had left a legacy of misfortune and terror for anybody who despoiled her resting place.

Murray scoffed at the superstition until three days later. That was when he went on a shooting expedition up the Nile and the gun he was carrying exploded mysteriously in his hand. After weeks of agony in hospital, his arm had to be amputated above the elbow.

On the return voyage to England, two of Murray's friends died "from unknown causes". Two Egyptian servants who had handled the mummy-case also died within a year.

Back in London, Murray found that the mummy-case had arrived. When he looked at it, the carved face of the princess "seemed to come alive with a stare that chilled the blood".

Although he had made up his mind to get rid of it, a woman friend convinced him that he should give it to her. Within weeks, the woman's mother died, her lover deserted her, and she was stricken with an undiagnosed "wasting disease". When she instructed her lawyer to make her will, he insisted on returning the mummy-case to Douglas Murray.

By now a broken wreck of a man, Murray wanted no part of it. He presented it to the British Museum, but even in that cold and scientific institution, the mummy-case was to become notorious. A photographer who

Racing driver's spirit

Vincent Herman was the first man to die in a crash at the old Brooklands race track, near Weybridge, Surrey. Locals say the motoring pioneer still haunts the Railway Straight where his car overturned in September 1907.

took pictures of it immediately dropped dead. An Egyptologist in charge of the exhibit was also found dead in his bed.

Disturbed by the newspaper stories, the board of the museum met in secret. There was a unanimous vote to ship the mummy-case to a New York museum, which had agreed to accept the gift provided it was handled without publicity and sent by the safest possible means.

The case must be shipped by the prestigious new vessel making her maiden voyage from Southampton to New York that month. All arrangements were successfully completed. But the mummy-case never reached New York. It was in the cargo hold of the "unsinkable" *Titanic* when she carried 1,498 people to their doom on April 15, 1912.

The Titanic Disaster, April 1912. The liner goes down after striking an iceberg.

The hell hounds

Dogs, cats and horses have always been associated with the spirit world. They are said to sense, even see, ghosts which are invisible to the human eye. But some animals exist as four-legged phantoms themselves. The most terrifying are the giant black hounds of hell.

Almost every part of Britain has such legends: fiendish harbingers of doom with blazing eyes and snarling teeth. The Yorkshire version, the Padfoot, is said to be as big as a donkey. The Welsh call theirs Gwyllgi, and the Lancashire dog is known as Trash or Shriker. On the Isle of Man, the Mauthe or Moddey Dhoo is said to haunt Peel Castle, and soldiers once refused to patrol the battlements there alone.

One sentry who dared to serve solo was found gibbering next morning, and died three days later.

The most frequently documented hell hound is Black Shuck, whose name is derived from Scucca, the Saxon word for the Devil. Hundreds of people claim to have seen him at night in the lonely fenlands of East Anglia, the one eye in the centre of his head blazing scarlet or yellow.

He has been reported on the coast near Cromer, loping along lanes near the Norfolk Broads at Neatishead, and at Wicken Fen, near Newmarket. In Suffolk, people living near the heathland of Walberswick and Dunwich call him the Galley Trot. And it was in this area, during World War Two, that he gave an American airman and his wife a night they would never forget.

The couple had rented a flat-topped hut on the edge of Walberswick Marsh while the husband served at a nearby air base. One stormy evening they were startled by a violent pounding on the door. The airman peeped through a window and saw a huge black beast battering their home.

The terrified couple piled what little furniture they had against the door, then cowered as the attacker hurled his body against first one wall, then another, then leapt on to the roof. The ordeal lasted several hours before the noise faded away. The couple waited anxiously for daylight, and at dawn crept outside to inspect the damage. There was no sign of the attack, and no paw or claw marks in the soft mud around the hut.

The West Country is said to have a pack of wild black dogs, whose blood-curdling howls have been heard several times across the vast wastes of Dartmoor.

But a different phantom beast worried hundreds of people in five Devon towns when they woke one winter's morning in February, 1855. Clearly visible in the heavy overnight snow were animal footprints four inches long and almost three inches wide – footprints which, it was later discovered, stretched in a zig-zag trail for nearly 100 miles from Totnes to Littleham. Dogs brought in to track the mystery creature through undergrowth at Dawlish backed off, howling dismally. Baffled investigators found that at one stage, the trail went into a shed through a six-inch hole. In another place, the prints indicated that the animal had squeezed through a long narrow drainpipe. Next night, local people bolted their doors and refused to venture outside. They were convinced the Devil himself had walked through Devon.

Journalist and ghost-collector W T Stead told of a letter sent to him in 1902 by an Englishman who went hunting in the South African Transvaal. The man claimed he was riding back to camp when an eerie white horse carrying an unearthly rider emerged from a thicket of trees, and pursued him. That night, one of the hunter's guides told him of an earlier safari, when an Englishman shot seven elephants in the thicket. He returned next morning to collect the ivory tusks – and was never seen again. His white horse returned to camp alone, but died 24 hours later. The guide added, "I would not go into that bush for all the ivory in the land."

Petrified poacher

Poacher Jim Mace never lived to tell the tale of his midnight meeting with a beautiful woman. But his voice is still heard, just one of the unearthly sounds that make Breckles Hall one of Norfolk's most mysterious stately homes.

Mace and another man decided to go shooting partridge in the hall grounds one night early this century after drinking in a local inn. They knew the legends about the place. Screams for mercy, banging doors and strange footsteps had been heard, and on rare occasions the ballroom shimmered with the glow of spectral dancers. After bagging their birds, the intrepid hunters crept up to the hall in search of ghosts.

At first they were disappointed, for the windows of the empty mansion stayed dark. Only the wind disturbed the still of the night. The two men turned for home, then stopped in their tracks. A coach pulled by four horses swept silently into sight at the bottom of the drive, heading for the house. Rooted to the ground by fear, the men gazed as it came to a halt in front of the main doors, and a beautiful, bejewelled woman stepped out. She stared straight into Mace's eyes – and he slumped to the ground with a piercing shriek.

The sound seemed to break the spell which held his friend motionless. He raced to the nearest house to get help. But he could find no one prepared to go near the hall until daylight.

Next morning the vicar led a posse of villagers to the spot. The body of the poacher lay stiff and cold, his face a mask of terror.

Beware of the bones

The dead keep a vengeful watch

People who tamper with the remains of the dead, or ignore the last wishes of the dying do so at their peril. It seems that the spirits of the departed keep a careful watch on their earthly relics, and are quick to intervene if anything untoward happens to them.

An American farmer called Walsingham was exploring his new home at Oakville, Georgia, when he came across an ancient skeleton and threw it into a lime kiln. Soon doors began to slam in the middle of the night, chairs were mysteriously overturned, and bells tolled through the rooms.

Walsingham was not a superstitious man. He put the curious sounds down to mischief by neighbours. Then a series of things happened which he could not ignore. They were described by the *San Francisco Examiner* in 1891.

First the man's dog began barking furiously at a wall. One day the animal lunged towards it and fell back yelping, its neck broken as if somebody had hurled its body backwards.

Hideous laughter, shouts and wails began coming from all over the house. One of Walsingham's daughters saw a disembodied hand grasp her shoulder. And the farmer watched aghast as the prints of a naked pair of feet formed beside him as he walked in the rain.

The last straw for the family came at a dinner party. Guests shrugged off strange groans from the room above. Then a red stain began to form on the white tablecloth, spreading as more scarlet drips fell from the ceiling.

The men in the party raced upstairs and began tearing up the floorboards. But they found only dry dust, even though the liquid – later identified by chemical tests as human blood – continued to spread on the table. The Walsinghams packed their belongings and moved out of the haunted home.

A skull called Awd Nance has caused headaches for successive occupants of Burton Agnes Hall, a beautiful English mansion in a village between Bridlington and Driffield in Yorkshire. For more than 300 years the gruesome relic has insisted on staying in the house. Those who have tried to get rid of it have been forced to think again.

The hall was built by three spinster sisters early in the 17th century, financed by a legacy from their father, Sir Henry Griffith. Soon after the building was completed, robbers ambushed the youngest sister, Anne, as she returned from visiting friends in nearby Harpham. Villagers gently carried her battered body home. She was well cared for, but her injuries were so severe that it was clear she would never recover.

Shortly before she died, Anne made an extraordinary request. She insisted that her sisters cut off her head before they buried her body, and preserve it in the walls of her beloved home. She threatened that if they did not do so, dire consequences would follow. The two sisters promised they would follow her wishes, but the idea horrified them. When Anne died, they buried her body intact.

Seven days later, an inexplicable crash in an upstairs room woke the whole household. After another week, the family were again roused from their sleep when doors slammed in every part of the building. Three weeks after the funeral, they lay terrified in their beds all night as the whole house shook with the clatter of crowds of invisible beings running along corridors and up and down stairs. Agonised groans echoed through the rooms.

Next morning the servants quit. The sisters called in the local vicar, and when they mentioned Anne's dying wish, he agreed to open the grave. The body was just as they had last seen it – except for the head. That had been cut off, and all the skin had shrivelled away, leaving the skull bare.

Reluctantly, the sisters carried the grim memento into the hall. The haunting ceased. The skull stayed with them for the rest of their lives.

Several subsequent owners of Burton Agnes have dared to throw out Awd Nance, but each time, mysterious shuffling and scratching sounds, slamming doors and terrifying groans have forced them to restore the relic to its rightful place.

Other ghosts have been responsible for the finding of human bones in places where they should not have been. Such spectres vanish only once the bones have been given a decent burial.

Guests at a house in Lynton, Devon, complained during the 1930s that

Vigilante tragedy

A white phantom caused a bizarre tragedy in Hammersmith, London, in 1804. Vigilante patrols were set up after the ghost chased and seized a woman as she walked through a graveyard. She died from shock a few days later. Sixteen people travelling past the church on a horse-drawn cart also fled the eerie shape.

On the fourth night of the vigil, one of the volunteers, customs officer Francis Smith, spotted a figure in white moving down a nearby lane. He shot at it, and the figure fell. But it was not a ghost. It was bricklayer Thomas Milwood, coming home late from work in his white overalls. Smith was tried for manslaughter, and sentenced to death but, on appeal, the sentence was reduced to a year in prison.

Voices from the grave

Friedrich Jurgenson's tape-recorder plays back voices of the dead.
Jurgenson, a Stockholm artist, says he has no idea how the voices get on his
tapes. Yet over several years his machine has picked up more than 140
voices, including those of Adolf Hitler and Death Row's Caryl Chessman.

Hitler's voice was the first to appear on Jurgenson's tape in 1960. He had
recorded a memorandum and, when playing back his notes, heard other
voices. He had the machine tested, but nothing was wrong with it. Yet when
he made a further tape and played it back, his voice was drowned out.

This time the sounds were voices saying: "We live, we live. We are not
dead." A German engineer listened to the tape and identified the voice as
Hitler's. The voice seemed to be apologising for concentration camp
atrocities. The voice was compared with recordings of Hitler and was again
identified as the voice of the Nazi leader.

they could never get a decent night's sleep in the room above the skullery.
They told their hosts, the Ewing family, that they saw the ghost of an old
woman, and heard the sobbing of a child.

Then Mrs Ewing's brother-in-law realised that the haunted bedroom was
much narrower than the skullery below it. The family discovered a cupboard
which had been walled up. Inside was a child's box, and a collection of
ancient human bones. Only when they were removed did peace reign in the
house.

Frederick Fisher was a poor Australian farmer whose profits from crops
never covered the cost of his living. Eventually he was taken to court, and
jailed for debt. To stop creditors seizing his farm at Cambelltown, New
South Wales, he transferred it to the name of an associate called George
Worrall.

Six months later, Fisher finished his sentence and returned to his home.
But one night in 1826 he left a nearby inn after a heavy drinking session –
and was never seen again. Police investigated the disappearance, but could
find no evidence of foul play.

Months went by. Then came the dark night that neighbour James Farley
got the shock of his life. A strange figure was sitting on one of his fences,
pointing to a spot in Fisher's paddock. Farley was too scared to do anything
until daylight. Next morning he guided a police constable to the site the
phantom had indicated, and in the shallow grave, discovered the badly
beaten body of farmer Fisher.

George Worrall was questioned, and found to be an ex-convict. He
confessed and was hanged. His victim's ghost was never seen again.

Horror on a
university curriculum

The favourite classes of the curriculum at Camerino University, Italy, were those on the occult, held by a genial professor of psychology, Dr Giuseppi Stoppolini. At one of these classes in September 1950, Stoppolini introduced Maria Bocca to his students. She went into a trance and astounded them all.

In the trance, Maria spoke in the recognisable voices of dead men and women known to those present. But near the end of the seance, came an unfamiliar voice begging them to have mercy and listen.

It said, "I was born Rosa Manichelli. When I died, I was Rosa Spadoni, but my husband has died since then, too. We are both in the cemetery at Castel-Raimondo a few miles from Camerino. I am asking only that you help others, because the same thing can happen to them. Two days after the death certificate was signed, I was taken to the cemetery in a deep coma and buried alive!"

As the students sat in a shocked silence, Maria toppled to the floor in a faint.

The following day, Dr Stoppolini found that there had been a Rosa Spadoni who died in the Civil Hospital in Camerino on September 4, 1939. She was buried two days later at Castel-Raimondo. There were no surviving relatives to protest against exhuming of the body and a small group gathered at Rosa's grave on September 13, 1950.

In addition to Dr Stoppolini and the workmen he had hired, there were pathologists from the Camerino board of health, three officials representing the Italian government and a photographer. An hour of digging uncovered the coffin, and Stoppolini himself stood in the grave to raise the coffin lid.

The skeleton within lay on its back, skull turned to the left. The left arm was bent upward, with the finger bones thrust into the mouth and throat cavity. The knees were bent as if in an effort to force open the lid.

Worse, there were parallel scratches where Rosa had tried to claw her way out of the casket.

The pathologists issued a public statement, which said, "How Dr Stoppolini came by his knowledge is irrelevant. We must agree with him that Rosa Spadoni was buried in a coma when vital signs were undetectable – and that she awakened in her coffin beyond human help."

The race to eternity

A never-ending marathon

The day "marathon man" James Worson accepted a sporting challenge was the day he disappeared from the face of the earth. The proud, athletic, English shoemaker screamed once, and vanished forever.

On September 3, 1873, Worson boasted of his athletic prowess to two fellow townsfolk of Leamington, Warwickshire. He said that on more than one occasion he had raced from one town to another in record time.

The people of Leamington knew Worson's talents as a footracer, but his friends were sceptical. He might be as good as he thought, they told him, but could he prove it? Worson happily accepted the challenge. He would show them, he said, with a 20-mile run from Leamington to Coventry.

They began the test in high spirits. Worson put on his running clothes and set out. His friends, Hammerson Burns and Barham Wise, trailed close behind him in a horse-drawn gig, Burns carrying a camera.

The mood of the three was still festive a quarter of the way to Coventry. Worson appeared as tireless as he had claimed, running with ease and turning occasionally to exchange words with his friends.

The runner was never out of their sight. Running in the middle of the dirt road, Worson suddenly appeared to stumble. He pitched forward in a headlong fall and had time for only one piercing scream. Wise said later, "It was the most ghastly sound either of us had ever heard."

That terrible cry was their last memory of him. Worson's body never struck the ground – he vanished in the middle of his fall without touching the earth.

The road itself provided tangible evidence of what they had witnessed. Burns' pictures of the long-distance runner's tracks – clear footprints in the soft dirt, faltering and ending as abruptly as if Worson had crashed into a stone wall.

When the men returned to Leamington a massive hunt began. Searchers combed every inch of the terrain between Leamington and Coventry without success. Bloodhounds were strangely reluctant to approach the spot where Worson's footprints ended. And for years after his disappearance there were reports of a ghostly green runner on the empty night road from Leamington to Coventry.

Plea from the deep

The sailor sent on an errand to his captain's cabin got a shock when he opened the door. A strange man was poised over the log book, holding a quill pen. As the sailor challenged him, the intruder simply vanished.

When the captain was told of the incident, he checked the book, and found a curious plea written in an unknown hand: "Steer to the north-east."

The ship, ploughing through the North Atlantic off the Canadian coast during the last century, changed course as instructed, and within hours came across a ship in danger of sinking.

As the crew helped survivors aboard, the sailor recognised one of them as the figure he had seen writing in the log book. He was asked to write the words again. The specimens matched exactly.

Fishermen's fear

For hundreds of years fishermen on the east and south-east coasts of England have kept a watchful eye for a phantom schooner, the *Lady Lovibond*. They wonder how many sailors who met their deaths on the notorious Goodwin Sands had first spied the ghost of the three-master.

The *Lady Lovibond* ran aground on the Goodwins and sank with all hands on February 13, 1748. Captain Simon Peel, his bride and some of their wedding guests were on board. Legend has it that the first mate, who was in love with the bride himself, killed Peel out of jealousy and steered the ship to its doom on the Goodwins.

Fifty years later to the day, a three-masted schooner identical to the *Lady Lovibond* was seen heading for the Goodwins. The crew of a fishing boat followed her and heard the sounds of a celebration and women's voices. The schooner hit the sands, broke up – and vanished.

The same apparition appeared to another ship's crew exactly 50 years later and was next seen by a group of watchers near Deal, Kent, on February 13, 1898.

Does the phantom appear every 50 years? Watchers were on the lookout on February 13, 1948, but visibility was poor and they saw nothing.

North America also has a famous phantom ship lurking off Rhode Island. The *Palatine* left Holland in 1752, packed with colonists bound for Philadelphia. A fierce winter storm blew her off course and, when the captain was lost overboard, the panicking crew mutinied.

The passengers spent Christmas Day in confusion and terror. Two days later, the *Palatine* ran aground on rocks off Block Island and began to break up. As the storm abated, the doomed ship began to slip back off the rocks, drawn out to sea again by the tide. But before she could do so, dozens of local fishermen descended on the *Palatine*, took off the passengers and looted the ship.

When their frenzied rampage had ended and they had stripped the *Palatine* of everything of value, the fishermen set it on fire and watched it drift, ablaze from bow to stern, out to the open sea.

They watched in horror when they saw a woman appear from her hiding place on the *Palatine* and stand on the deck screaming for help until the flames swallowed her.

There have been sightings of the ghostly vessel off the New England coast ever since, blood-red flames rising from a wrecked hulk.

The ghostly swimmers

Seamen James Courtney and Michael Meehan were buried at sea on the morning of December 2, 1929. They had died the previous day, asphyxiated by fumes while working below decks aboard the oil tanker *Waterton*, owned by the Cities Service Corporation, and bound from California to Panama.

When the weighted bodies of the two sailors dropped into the Pacific, their fellow crewmen mourned deeply, for Courtney and Meehan were two of the most popular men on the ship.

One friend said, "Somehow they made everyone feel good."

But the crew of the *Waterton* were not without their dead colleagues for long. The day after their burial, the officers and crew saw two men swimming in the open sea. Captain Tracy put his binoculars on them and whispered, "Oh, my God!"

But when the ship slowed to ten knots and drew up alongside the swimmers, they faded like morning mist – only to reappear just 40 feet from the ship. At that distance there were no longer any doubts. The men in the water were Courtney and Meehan.

For three days the swimmers kept pace with the *Waterton*. Now there was no terror aboard the ship, because everyone saw that the dead men intended no harm. At one point they swam ahead of the vessel and seemed to be trying to divert her from the path of an approaching squall.

Reporting later in the New Orleans office of the shipowners, Captain Tracy told his employers about the death and reappearance of Courtney and Meehan. Tracy was provided with a camera and film and asked to substantiate his tale on the return voyage.

It was a voyage without incident until they were in the Pacific again and the deckhands saw two pale figures bobbing in the wake of the *Waterton*. By dawn they were once more alongside the vessel, and with full light the captain snapped eight pictures at close range. Within a few hours the swimmers had vanished.

They were not seen again in the days that followed, and back in port the captain took the film to company headquarters. Still wet from processing in a photographic laboratory, the roll of film was closely examined in company offices. One by one the negatives were rejected.

Then one of the executives lifted the eighth frame to the light. "There they are!" he said.

When prints were made from the negative, the two pale faces emerging from the waves were positively identified by friends and relatives as those of James Courtney and Michael Meehan.

Terror aboard UB65

Doomed duty of a dead officer

Night was falling at the end of a bitterly cold day in January, 1918, as the German submarine UB65 slid into the English Channel looking for action. She was 15 miles off Portland Bill as the grey winter twilight deepened. The sea was rough and sheets of spray drenched the conning tower.

The U-boat's starboard lookout, screwing up his eyes as he peered over the bridge, was astonished to see an officer standing just below him on the heaving deck.

What in God's name was he doing there? He must be mad. Come to that, how on earth did he get there anyway? All the hatches save that on the conning tower had been firmly battened down.

He was about to hail the officer to warn him that he was in great danger when the figure on the deck turned and gazed up at the bridge. Even in the twilight, the lookout recognised the face, and his blood froze.

It was the ship's former second officer, killed in an explosion on the maiden voyage, his body buried in the military cemetery at Wilhelmshaven.

It seemed hours before he could move his lips. "It's the ghost," he yelled. The U-boat's captain rushed to his side, and he too saw the upturned face, before the figure melted into the gathering darkness.

This was not the first time that the phantom of UB65 had appeared to strike terror into the hearts of the men who sailed in her. They had begun to dread the ghost as a harbinger of doom.

Ever since her keel was laid, disaster had followed disaster until UB65 became known as a jinxed ship. The submarine had been built in 1916, one of a fleet designed to operate off the coast of Flanders and create havoc in the Channel. Her crew was made up of three officers and 31 ratings.

Only a week after work started on her, things began to go wrong. A girder being swung into position slipped from its chains and crashed down killing one workman outright and pinning another to the ground. He could not be released for an hour and then died in agony.

Before the submarine was finished there was another accident, this time in the engine room. Three men, overcome by fumes, died before they could be rescued.

On her trial run UB65 ran into a fierce storm and a man was washed overboard. While she was on diving tests, one of the tanks developed a leak and it was 12 hours before she could be brought to the surface. The atmosphere was thick with poisonous fumes and when at last the hatches were opened officers and men staggered out half dead with suffocation.

But it was on her return from her maiden voyage that the UB65 suffered her most violent shock. As she was taking in torpedoes a warhead exploded and in the terrible explosion that followed the second officer was killed and several men badly injured. The officer was buried with full naval honours and the submarine had to go into the dockyard for repairs.

Some weeks later, just before the vessel was due to sail, a member of the crew crashed unceremoniously into the wardroom. Chalk white with shock, he gasped out, "Herr Ober-Leutnant, the dead officer is on board." The captain accused him of being drunk, but he swore that not only he but another rating had seen the dead officer walk up the gangplank.

The captain and other officers ran to the deck where they found the second seaman crouching against the conning tower. He explained in a voice barely above a whisper that the dead officer had come on board, walked towards the bows and stood there with folded arms. After a few seconds, he vanished.

The captain, fully aware of the impact such an incident would have on his superstitious crew, circulated the rumour that the whole thing had been a practical joke. Nobody believed him. Everyone knew the ship was haunted.

On each tour of duty the U-boat carried its ghostly second officer. Men on watch jumped at every shadow. Word spread throughout the German navy that the UB65 was haunted and nobody was anxious to serve on her.

Eventually, the authorities felt it was time such nonsense was stopped and sent a commodore to investigate. The high-ranking officer questioned the entire company. At first he could hardly conceal his impatience with what he believed was superstitious fancy. After hearing all the evidence, he was so impressed that he admitted he could understand the request by almost every member of the crew to transfer to another ship. Officially, the requests were never granted, but one by one men were switched.

The UB65 was withdrawn from active service and, while in dock at the Belgian port of Bruges, a Lutheran pastor was quietly taken aboard to carry out the rite of exorcism. When she went to sea again the U-boat had a new captain and crew. This captain refused to tolerate what he called "damn nonsense" and threatened any man who spoke of ghosts with severe penalties. Strangely enough, the ship carried out two tours of duty without trouble, but when the unbeliever was replaced, the spirit reappeared. The next trip was worst of all.

During May of 1918, the UB65 cruised in the Channel and later off the coast of Spain. The ghost was seen three times. A young petty officer swore he saw an unfamiliar officer walk into the torpedo room. He never came out again. After two more sightings, the torpedo gunner went mad, screaming that the ghost would not leave him alone. He threw himself over the side and his body was never recovered.

In spite of her terrible history, the UB65 managed to escape the massive onslaught on the U-boats which came in the final months of war. On July 10, an American submarine patrolling at periscope depth spotted her on the surface. The Americans prepared to attack and were on the point of firing when the UB65 blew up. The explosion was "tremendous, almost unbelievable," said eye witnesses. When the smoke cleared all that was left was debris.

Many rational theories were put forward to explain what had happened. It was suggested that the submarine had been rammed by another German sub or perhaps the UB65 herself had fired a torpedo that ran wild. But spectators admitted that none of them quite accounted for the force of the explosion.

The nearest anyone could guess was that by some means the mouth of a torpedo tube had been damaged so that when one was fired it fouled and detonated the rest of the torpedoes in the craft.

The company of 34 men went down with the UB65 – or maybe it was 35, for the ghost of the second officer was never seen again.

Perhaps he had finished the terrible job he had stayed on earth to do.

The ghost ship Ourang Medan

A dozen ships picked up the SOS, which read, "Captain and all officers dead. Entire crew dead or dying." And later, "Now I am also near death." Then the airwaves went dead.

It was a perfect day in February 1948 and, of all the vessels that heard the strange message, only one was able to identify the ship in trouble and pinpoint her position. The ship was named as the Dutch freighter *Ourang Medan*, bound for Djakarta, Indonesia, through the Malacca Strait.

Within three hours, the first rescue vessel was alongside the *Ourang Medan*. A crewman said later, "Sharks were surging around the hull, and it looked like every shark in the Bay of Bengal had homed in on her knowing there was death aboard."

When there was no response to flag or radio signals, a boat was launched and the rescue party climbed aboard. They found all the ship's officers massed in the chartroom as if their skipper had called them to a council of war against some unknown disaster. All had died there.

They seemed to have died within seconds of each other; their eyes stared in horror and their bodies were already locked in rigor mortis, some with their arms pointed to the heavens.

The dead seamen littering the decks had died in the same way. A doctor who boarded with the party later reported no signs of poisoning, asphyxiation or disease, but all seemed to have known that death was coming – even the ship's dog. They found it below decks with paws in the air, fangs bared in a silent snarl. In the radio shack, the telegrapher had fallen over his silent key.

The rescue ship tried to take the Dutch ship in tow to the nearest port, but when tackle had been readied and a towline rigged, there was a gush of oily smoke from one of the holds. Knowing they could not contain the blaze without flushing pumps and steam for the fire, the salvage crew fled to their own ship. They had only time enough to cut the towline before the stricken freighter exploded.

The blast scattered wreckage for a quarter of a mile and even killed some of the hungry sharks. What was left of the *Ourang Medan* sank.

In the short inquiry that followed, the doctor reported that something unknown had killed the seamen. Although the official verdict was "death by misadventure", the mystery of the ghost ship *Ourang Medan* has never been solved.

Unexpected guest for tea

A tea party was taking place at the home of Vice-Admiral Sir George and Lady Tryon in London's fashionable Eaton Square. The mansion was crowded with the cream of the capital's society. Sir George, in full dress uniform, walked down the graceful curved staircase towards his guests. Lady Tryon dropped her teacup and screamed.

The guests watched aghast as the famous admiral reached the foot of the stairs, calmly and silently crossed the room, opened a door and was gone. It was June 22, 1893, and the guests knew that they had just seen a ghost. For that day Sir George was on the bridge of his flagship, *Victoria*, off Tripoli and, tragically, was guiding her into one of Britain's greatest naval disasters.

His squadron steamed along in two columns as part of a carefully planned fleet exercise. *Victoria* led one of the columns, with the *Camperdown* heading the other.

The naval squadron consisted of Britain's entire Mediterranean Fleet – eight ironclad battleships and five cruisers. Sir George's plan called for the two columns to move within six cable lengths of each other. Steaming ahead on parallel courses, they would turn inward on command and then reverse course. But were six cable lengths – about 4,500 feet – enough?

One officer meekly suggested that the two columns could come dangerously close to a collision.

The Vice-Admiral agreed that perhaps there should be eight cable lengths. However, within minutes he again mysteriously changed his mind, ordering the manoeuvre to go ahead as planned. There was later testimony that his eyes were strangely dull when he re-issued the order.

At a combined speed of 18 knots, the two lead ships were heading toward each other on a collision course – yet Sir George gave no signal for the turn. He stood like a statue on the charthouse deck, his eyes still vague. When other officers pleaded that they must do something, the admiral failed to answer.

At the last moment, he shook himself like a waking dreamer and whispered, "Yes, go astern." The order was given too late.

Even with the propellers in reverse, the *Victoria*'s momentum carried her like a juggernaut toward the *Camperdown*.

As buglers sounded the call summoning "All hands on deck," the ironclads met in a terrifying collision. *Camperdown* pierced the flagship some 65 feet aft of the bow, on the starboard side. A dreadful shudder racked the *Victoria*.

The ship's pumps might have coped with the torrents of water, but compounding his first ghastly mistake with another, the admiral shouted at *Camperdown*, "Go astern with both engines!"

As the great ship backed away, the fate of the *Victoria* was inevitable. The flagship was swamped by a wall of water that flooded everything in its way; men, machinery and bulkheads.

The ship's hydraulic system was submerged, and below decks hundreds of men were caught in the smothering assault of the seawater. When the order came to report topside, many were either dead or dying in flooded compartments.

Among the 600 who leaped from the ship many were ground to fragments in the propeller blades or trapped in the suction of the foundering *Victoria*. A total of only 25 officers and 259 men were picked up by the boats, with 22 officers and 336 seamen dead.

Among the dead was Sir George Tryon himself, who was still standing on the *Victoria*'s bridge when she slipped beneath the waves.

Spirit of the deep
Trailed by a ghostly galleon

If there are ghosts of people who die, can ships also become spirits too? Captain Dusty Miller came close to answering that question, but he took his knowledge to a watery grave when his yacht, the *Joyita*, sank in 1955. For in the months before his last voyage in the South Seas, something unknown had stalked him and his ship.

Passengers reported that another ship was following in their wake, moving along mysteriously through the darkness with no lights or sound. The ghostly ship had a high superstructure aft, they said, but otherwise could describe her only as looking like an ancient galleon, "from the time of Columbus."

When Captain Miller glimpsed her in his binoculars on a voyage to Pago Pago, his face turned deathly white.

He ordered the running lights turned off and took over the helm himself, heading the *Joyita* into a squall. When the weather cleared there was no sign of the ghostly galleon.

The *Joyita* had the reputation of being an unlucky yacht, and Dusty knew

Cross of mystery

Two boats went to the aid of a strange vessel which was obviously in distress in heavy seas off the coast of Devon in 1959. As they came close to the vessel, they were able to identify it as a World War Two landing craft.

The flag that it was flying was the Cross of Lorraine, the symbol of the Free French forces. As the two boats came still closer, the ship was obscured from view by a sudden giant wave. It never reappeared.

this when he bought her.

Roland West, a film producer with RKO studios, had built her in the first blaze of Hollywood's glory and named her *Joyita* – Spanish for little jewel – in honour of his actress sweetheart Jewel Carmen. The romance fizzled and bad luck began to haunt the yacht even before her launching in 1931.

Workmen fell from the rigging and died. The Portuguese widow of one victim publicly laid a curse on the yacht and its owner.

On her maiden voyage, to Catalina Island, the ship was towed back into port after a disastrous engine room fire.

The *Joyita* was sold and went into charter service. The great stars of the screen were among those who sailed in her. But when a passenger mysteriously vanished, nobody wanted to know the boat any more.

The United States Navy took her over in World War Two, but put her back in dry dock when she kept running aground. Even out of service, her record was grim; a caretaker died from battery acid fumes, there was a series of unexplained fires, and two men were killed in a fight aboard her.

Sold as war surplus, the now shabby yacht went from owner to owner. Dusty Miller bought her with his last few dollars.

On October 3, 1955, the *Joyita* put to sea for the last time from Apia Harbor in Western Samoa. Held in port by order of unhappy creditors, she had almost rusted away for months before Miller could persuade them to let him take her out.

The *Joyita* carried desperately needed food and medical supplies for the islanders of Fakaofo 200 miles north, and she was to bring back 70 tons of copra. Besides the crew of 16, there were nine passengers.

Samoans living on the waterfront later claimed that, minutes after her departure, they saw a huge, dark vessel gliding in the *Joyita*'s wake. She was enormously high aft, and unlike any ship seen in those waters. She was travelling without lights and with no sound of motors, but she moved at an incredible speed.

Nothing was heard of the *Joyita* until November 10, 1955, when another freighter found her lying abandoned 90 miles north of Fiji. She had a 55-degree list to port and one rail was awash. Radio gear was smashed, the logbook was missing and there was no recognisable message – but carefully-placed signal flags in the rigging spelled out the letters WNQV. To this day investigators have not been able to discover what this may have meant.

No bodies were found in the flooded compartments, and the fate of the 25 persons aboard is still unknown.

In Suva, where the wreck was pumped out, marine inspectors found no answers. The tale of the mysterious ship was put down to native superstition, although it had been government men aboard the *Joyita* who had first reported the ghostly vessel.

But the sailors of the South Sea ports still have no doubts. They still see a clear link between the doomed *Joyita* and the strange, dark galleon from another age.

The Devil's Triangle
Tormented souls may hold Bermuda key

A startling theory to explain the mysterious disappearance of ships and planes in the notorious Bermuda Triangle is that the strange happenings in that region are caused by tormented souls from the spirit world.

The claim is made by two leading exorcists who believe that the "spirits" in the area known as the Triangle of Death, the Devil's Triangle and the Hoodoo Sea are from ten million negroes who were dumped or thrown overboard during the slave trade period. Their troubled souls can "take over" the minds of pilots and sailors, just as people on land are said to be possessed by spirits.

In a unique experiment, special prayers were held in the Bermuda Triangle to lay at peace these tormented souls who supposedly haunt the

Atlantic graveyard of 140 ships and planes and more than 1,000 people who over the years have disappeared without trace.

Backing this extraordinary theory is British surgeon and psychiatrist Dr Kenneth McCall. He said, "We call it the Possession Syndrome in patients who are mentally disturbed.

"It may be multiple or single, in a family or haunted place. The spirits have got to express themselves, so they possess us and control our minds.

"Just as in our world here, one or two people can cause torment or haunting disturbances. This can happen with the crew of a ship or plane – and on a very large scale in the Bermuda Triangle. It seems the spirits are trying to draw attention to their state. They are not concerned with destroying the other people.

"There is no such thing as time and space to the spirits. They are wandering and lost and possess people to draw attention to their own plight, just as a lost child will do to an adult.

"These unhappy lost spirits are in purgatory. Because they did not die naturally and were not committed to God, they are causing disturbance."

Dr McCall, at the age of 67, wrote a special service to be said over the troubled waters and this included the Requiem Mass and the Anglican Eucharist of Remembrance.

He said, "I think this will lessen the number of planes and ships that disappear there."

Dr McCall carried out 600 cases of exorcism, or laying on of hands, in the United States, Canada, Holland, Germany and Switzerland. He was a member of a Church of England Commission on Exorcism in Britain. He made many visits to America and with 12 American professors wrote a book on the subject.

It was after working as a missionary in China, where he was imprisoned, that he found he could cure other prisoners through the power of prayer.

He said, "When I returned to Britain in 1946 and learnt all about psychiatry, I realised that the same results occurred in mental hospitals. The patients were disturbed because they were possessed by a spirit."

His theory that millions of disturbed spirits are in the Bermuda Triangle – the area bounded roughly by Bermuda in the north to Miami and beyond Puerto Rico – came to him when he was becalmed on a small banana boat in the Sargasso Sea.

He said, "I had been on a lecture tour in the States and visiting relatives. The ship's boiler burst and we were drifting. It was calm and peaceful and I heard singing. I thought it was the coloured crew, but I couldn't think why they were singing all the time."

Dr McCall checked and found that none of the crew was singing and there was not even a record player aboard. "Then I realised it was a negro dirge, like a moaning chant. It went on and on solidly for five days and nights before we got moving again. My wife Frances also heard it. What we heard fitted all my other theories."

He believes that during the slave trade years, about ten million slaves went overboard. "They used to push them over because they got more money from insurance that way. Those who were pregnant or diseased were thrown to the sharks. Others preferred to jump over the side rather than die in slavery."

Of the many mysteries of the Bermuda Triangle, the most famous is that of the missing warplanes. It is also the case that first aroused widespread public curiosity and gave the area its name.

On December 5, 1945, a flight of five Grumann United States Navy bombers took off from Fort Lauderdale, Florida, for a training flight in perfect weather. Shortly afterwards, the pilots radioed that they were on course, although they were actually flying in the opposite direction. Two hours after take-off, all contact with the aircraft was lost.

A Martin bomber was immediately sent to search for the missing planes. Within 20 minutes, radio contact with it had also been lost. No trace of any of the aircraft was ever found. In all, six planes and 27 men simply vanished into thin air.

In Dr McCall's view, the leader of the training flight believed to the last that he was heading in the right direction, but that his judgement was distorted by spirits.

The spirit theory had been current among seamen for many years before the world heard of the Triangle. The greatest disaster in the area had taken place 27 years earlier, in March 1918. That was the month in which the US supply vessel *Cyclops* vanished from the face of the earth without making a single distress call. No wreckage or any of the crew of 309 was ever found.

The service and prayers aimed at ending such disasters were carried out in

The ghost of Grace Darling

Two lighthouse-keepers told television viewers in 1976 that they had both seen the ghost of Grace Darling on separate occasions. The men worked at the Longstone Lighthouse on the Farne Islands, off the Northumberland Coast.

Grace was born there in 1815 and became a national hero 23 years later when she and her father rowed out to rescue nine survivors from the storm-wrecked steamer Forfarshire. Grace died of consumption four years later. The men said they had seen her ghost in the lighthouse engine room, walking round in clogs.

the Bermuda Triangle by exorcist Donald Omand, a 74-year-old retired Church of England vicar and expert on the occult, who described himself as a spiritual surgeon. In previous exorcisms, he had driven spirits from people, buildings and animals.

Dr McCall was unable to go with him to the Triangle, but Omand was accompanied by an English doctor and writer Marc Alexander, who said, "The Rev Omand often works with medical men and psychiatrists. Nearly all his cases are referred to him by doctors.

"This is a sensational subject and my eyes were opened by a lot of the things he did."

Omand's work of laying spirits at rest has been supported by Peter Mumford, the Bishop of Hertford, who said, "He was a member of a church commission which reported a few years ago on exorcism. He is a recognised exorcist and an expert in this field. He is very experienced and well regarded and has contributed to our understanding of this field."

But whether he has placated the "spirits" of the Bermuda Triangle, only time will reveal.

'Help me in the name of God'

Awoman's ghostly cries for help are the only clues to the disappearance of a Mississippi riverboat that vanished 106 years ago. The strange voice was first reported on the evening of May 28, 1875. Picnicking near the riverbank, more than 50 Vicksburgh high school students told police they had heard a woman screaming for help somewhere on the river.

The police decided it was a prank. They made a thorough search of the waters, but there was no such woman. There has been no such woman in 106 years, though hundreds of different people have reported the same eerie cries. The reports have come from Vicksburgh, Natchez, St Joseph and other points along the Mississippi.

In most documented cases, the chilling screams are followed by words in French, "*Aidez-moi au nom de Dieu, les hommes me blessent!*" ("Help me in the name of God, the men are hurting me!")

No one can explain the disembodied voice or its message, but there are fishermen and residents of the riverbank communities who believe it is linked to a darker mystery that still haunts the "father of waters".

On a clear blue day in June, 1874, the riverboat, *Iron Mountain* set out from Vicksburgh for New Orleans carrying 57 passengers and towing a string of barges. The big paddle-wheel steamer was famous in her time, plying the Ohio and Mississippi rivers to every port between New Orleans and Pittsburgh.

But on this voyage, she was sailing into history, for after rounding a bend in the river, she vanished.

Not long after her departure, the string of barges was found bobbing in the water. The towropes had been slashed in two – something that would be done only in an emergency. But no emergency had been reported, and rescue craft converging on the scene could find no evidence of one.

Hundreds of miles of river bottom were dragged, but the waters yielded no trace of wreckage or bodies.

Of the many explanations advanced at the time, one has often reappeared through the years. In that troubled period after the Civil War, riverboat pirates still operated on some parts of the Mississippi, and there was tempting cargo of wealth and beauty aboard the *Iron Mountain*.

On the passenger list were several Creole women who spoke French. Could the big steamboat have been sacked by pirates who dismantled her and concealed the sections after a ghastly carnival of rape and murder?

Voyage of the frozen dead

The Yankee whaling ship *Herald* was cruising off the west coast of Greenland, inside the Arctic Circle. From the bridge, Captain Warren peered ahead at a three-masted schooner drifting through the ice floes like a ghost ship. Warren took eight men in a longboat and rowed to the silent vessel. Through the encrusted ice, they could make out the schooner's name: *Octavius*.

Warren and four of the sailors boarded the schooner. They crossed the silent, moss-covered decks, opened a hatch and descended to the crew's quarters. There they found the bodies of 28 men, all lying on their bunks and wrapped in heavy blankets.

They fumbled their way aft to the captain's cabin, where the nightmare continued. The master of the *Octavius* slumped over the ship's log, a pen close to his right hand as if he had dozed at work. On a bed against one wall of the cabin, a blonde woman lay frozen to death under piles of blankets. And in a corner there were a sailor and a small boy whose bodies told a tragic story.

The sailor sat with his flint and steel clutched in frozen hands. In front of him was a tiny heap of shavings, silent evidence of a fire that had failed to ignite. The little boy crouched close to him, his face buried in the seaman's jacket as if he had huddled there in pathetic search for warmth.

The men from the *Herald* clambered back onto the deck, taking with them the schooner's log book as proof of what they had found. Back aboard the whaler, they could only watch helplessly while the derelict schooner drifted away from them among the icebergs, never to be seen again.

It was well they had taken the log book. The world would not be ready to accept their story, which remains one of the strangest tales of the sea.

The last log entry was dated November 11, 1762. The dying captain wrote that the *Octavius* had been frozen in for 17 days. The fire had gone out and they could not restart it. The location of the ship at this time, said the captain, was Longitude 160W, Latitude 75N.

Captain Warren looked at the charts in disbelief. In those last hours of human life, the ship had been locked in the Arctic Ocean north of Point Barrow, Alaska – thousands of miles from where the whaler had found her. Guided by some unknown force, year after year the battered schooner had crept steadily eastward through the vast ice fields until she entered the North Atlantic. In doing so she had then achieved the dream of all mariners.

For centuries men had sought the legendary Northwest Passage – a navigable route around the Arctic Ocean between the Atlantic and the Pacific. On that historic 13-year voyage, the ghost ship *Octavius* with her crew of frozen dead had been the first to find it.

Screams of a betrayer

Britain's coastline is rich in salty tales of smuggling exploits, and many towns with rocky caves nearby claim they are haunted by the ghosts of contraband runners.

One such story is told of Marsden Grotto, a series of caverns between South Shields and Sunderland, on England's north-eastern coast.

The gang using the Grotto to land their booty were betrayed by one of their colleagues, a man called John the Jibber. Coastguards were waiting when they rowed their loot ashore from a lugger anchored in Marsden Bay. A friend of the smugglers got wind of the plot, and fired a pistol, alerting those aboard the lugger that something had gone wrong.

John the Jibber lived to regret his treachery. He was trussed up in a barrel, hoisted to the roof of the cavern, and left to starve to death. The Grotto – now a restaurant – has echoed with his screams for more than 150 years.

The lonely lighthouse

On the night the Eilean Mor Lighthouse went dark, two sailors on the brigantine *Fairwind* saw a strange sight. Cutting diagonally across their bow a longboat with a huddle of men aboard was bearing toward the lighthouse on the rocky Flannan Islands off the west coast of Scotland.

The sailors called, but there was no answer. The boatmen wore foul weather gear and when moonlight slashed through a rift in the clouds, their faces shone like bone. One of the would-be rescuers testified later, "Our first thought was that they were floating dead from some shipwreck. But then we heard the oarlocks and saw the movement of their arms."

Later on that night of December 15, 1900, a squall broke. Without the guardian light ships were in dire peril. There was one angry question from the skippers: Why was the lighthouse dark?

On the day after Christmas, the supply vessel *Hesperus* hove to off the islands to investigate. When there was no answer to repeated signals, crewmen set out in a small boat to the landing dock. Tying up, they were chilled by the strange silence.

The lighthouse had been staffed by three men, but no one was there to welcome the *Hesperus*. There were no signs of violence and the larders were well stocked. Lamps were all trimmed and ready, the beds made, the dishes and kitchen utensils shining.

As the searchers climbed through the empty lighthouse, they found only two things that struck them as unusual. On the stairway and in a cubbyhole office where the log was kept, there were shreds of a seaweed unknown to them.

There were no oilskins or seaboots in the building, which seemed to imply that all three men had left the lighthouse together.

No lighthouse keeper had ever been known to abandon his post, even in the worst weather, and this was a point repeatedly made during the inquiry which followed – an inquiry which was hushed to silence by the reading of the log book kept by keeper Thomas Marshall:

"December 12: Gale north by northwest. Sea lashed to fury. Never seen such a storm. Waves very high. Tearing at lighthouse. Everything shipshape. James Ducat irritable." And later that day: "Storm still raging, wind steady. Stormbound. Cannot go out. Ship passing sounding foghorn. Could see lights of cabins. Ducat quiet. Donald McArthur crying.

"December 13: Storm continued through night. Wind shifted west by north. Ducat quiet. McArthur praying." And later: "Noon, grey daylight. Me, Ducat and McArthur prayed."

Inexplicably, there was no entry for December 14. The final line in the log read: "December 15, 1 pm. Storm ended, sea calm. God is over all."

No explanation could be offered but that the men had been seeing visions. While the log entries had reported gales lashing the Flannan Isles, there had been none at all 20 miles away on the island of Lewis.

Locals pointed to an even more mysterious cause of the disappearance of the lighthouse men. For centuries, the Flannan Isles had been haunted. Hebridean farmers might sail there during daylight to check on their sheep – but few except the "foolish sassenachs" at the lighthouse dared stay overnight.

Final "proof", if the locals needed any, was the evidence of the sailors of the *Fairwind* – of the longboat crowded with ghosts.

Ghost 'capital' of the world

Every city, town and hamlet in Britain has its spirit

Every country of the globe has its ghosts and haunted sites. But nowhere is the spirit population greater than in Britain. It seems that in this land steeped in history and mystery, every city, every town, every hamlet, every historic building has its spirit.

Recent surveys reveal that about one in seven people in Britain claims to have seen a ghost. And they are in distinguished company. Over the years, kings, hard-headed scientists and scholars, sceptical authors like Sir Arthur Conan Doyle and Captain Marryat, bishops, and leading churchmen such as John Wesley have all been convinced by the evidence they have seen.

Ghosts have been seen in all kinds of places, from palaces and castles to humble farming crofts. Workmen busy at No. 10 Downing Street in 1960 claimed that they saw a misty figure in the garden. It could have been the ghost of the Regency politician said to haunt the house at times of national crisis.

The Tower of London, scene of many bloody deeds down the ages, possesses a veritable crowd of ghosts. The most frequent 'visitor' is Anne Boleyn, second wife of Henry VIII, who was imprisoned in the Tower and executed there in May 1536. In the 19th century, a guard attracted by a strange light in the chapel of St Peter ad Vincular, where Anne was buried, climbed a ladder to peer through a window – and saw a procession in Elizabethan dress file slowly up the aisle, led by a woman who looked like Anne. Then the eerie crowd suddenly vanished, leaving the chapel in darkness again.

In 1864, a sentry at the Tower was court-martialled for being found asleep on watch. He claimed a strange white figure had ignored his challenge. It wore a curious bonnet, but there was no head inside. And when he ran his bayonet into the figure, a fiery flash ran up his rifle. He fainted. Other soldiers and an officer testified to seeing the headless woman walk straight through the bayonet and the sentry. The court found the man not guilty.

Anne's ghost is said to arrive headless in a phantom coach at Blickling Hall, Norfolk, her childhood home, on the anniversary of her death, 19 May. It was also said to appear at the Tower on the eve of an execution. In February 1915, at 2 am, Sergeant William Nicholls and his watch all saw a woman dressed in brown with a ruff round her neck. She walked quickly towards the Thames, then disappeared into a 9-ft-thick stone wall. Just five hours later, a spy was shot in the Tower moat, one of 11 executed there during World War One. Anne was last sighted in 1933, when a sentry fled in terror after challenging, then bayonetting, the headless apparition.

But the unfortunate Anne is not the only mysterious visitor to the Tower of London. Two little children have been seen wandering the Bloody Tower hand in hand. They are said to be Edward and Richard, the princes allegedly murdered in the Tower by their uncle, so that he could take the throne as Richard III.

In 1817, Edward Swifte, Keeper of the Crown Jewels, whose family lived with him in Martin Tower, saw an apparition like a glass tube as thick as a man's arm, filled with white and blue liquid, hovering above his supper table. A few days later, a sentry saw what he thought was a bear coming out under a door to the Jewel Room. But when the keeper lunged at it with his bayonet, he only struck the wood of the door. He passed out from shock, and died a few days later.

Other historic buildings connected with British royalty are said to be

Screaming skull

A skull is kept at Bettiscombe Manor, Dorset. Whenever it is taken out of doors it is said to scream. And when the outbreak of war is near, the skull is said to perspire blood.

haunted. In the 17th century, an apparition of the armour-clad Duke of Buckingham appeared at Windsor Castle three times before a terrified servant called Parker, and commanded him to tell the Duke's son that, unless he mended his callous ways, he had not long to live. The son, Sir George Villiers, took no notice and six months later was assassinated. Other apparitions said to have been seen at the castle include those of Elizabeth I, Charles I and George III.

Hampton Court is haunted by two of Henry VIII's unhappy wives, Jane Seymour and Catherine Howard. But the best-authenticated visitor is Mistress Sibell Penn, nurse to Edward VI. Sibell died of smallpox in 1562 and was buried in old Hampton Church. But in 1829, the church was pulled down and her remains scattered. Soon strange noises and mutterings were heard from the room in Hampton Court where the nurse had lived. Since then a tall, thin, grey-robed figure with a hood over her head has been seen several times, her arms outstretched in appeal. In 1881, a sentry saw her walk through a wall.

Glamis Castle, built on the site where Macbeth murdered King Duncan, is nowadays best known as the favourite Scottish residence of Queen Elizabeth, the Queen Mother, and the birthplace of Princess Margaret. But Glamis has for centuries been surrounded by legends of secret rooms and hideous monsters. Rumour has it that a workman who stumbled on a secret passage was paid a large sum to emigrate by the then Lord Strathmore. The present earl denies all knowledge of a ghoulish creature haunting the castle, but there have been many reports of guests being awakened in the night by the howling and snarling of an animal.

One guest told of seeing a pale face with large mournful eyes staring at her from a window across the courtyard. It disappeared. Then she heard appalling screams, and saw an old woman scurry across the yard carrying a large bundle. Another guest was awakened by the sound of hammering – and learned later that, since the hanging in 1537 of Janet Douglas, wrongly convicted of witchcraft and treason, ghostly hammering foretells the death of someone in the household.

In 1869, a Mr and Mrs Monro were guests in the castle. In the middle of the night, Mrs Monro awoke to feel a beard brush her face. Someone, or something, was standing over her. As she fumbled for a light, the figure moved into the adjacent dressing room, where their son was sleeping. His screams of terror sent both parents racing to his bedside, and the boy explained that he had seen a giant. Then they all heard a thunderous crash. At breakfast next morning, other guests said they had heard the crash. And one said her small dog had awakened her with mournful howls. But no one had any explanation for their troubled night.

London's historic St Paul's Cathedral has its own strange ghost story. A

The Tower of London.

wooden box containing jewels was unearthed by workmen digging the foundations for a new building alongside the cathedral. The jewels were deposited with the British Museum, and an expert took them home to clean, polish and value them. As he and his daughter worked away, they puzzled over why the room suddenly grew cold.

A psychic visitor found an answer. He saw a tall, thin man in Elizabethan clothes standing behind the couple, angry that his booty had been disturbed. When the jewels went on display at the museum there was another surprise. A woman inspecting them fainted. When she revived, she said she had seen blood on one gold necklace. Although attendants could see nothing, the woman remained adamant that the person who last wore the necklace had been murdered.

Theatres are traditional haunts of ghosts. More than 50 cleaners at the Theatre Royal, in London's Drury Lane, claim to have seen a man in a long grey coat and a powdered wig wandering round the dress circle, often on the eve of a successful run. Could this 18th-century dandy be connected with a skeleton found bricked up in a hollow wall in 1860? The skeleton, discovered by workmen, had a dagger in its ribs.

Strange happenings at the Adelphi Theatre, Covent Garden, are blamed on the ghost of William Terriss, an adventurer turned actor, who was stabbed to death outside the theatre in December 1897, after playing the lead in a thriller called *Secret Service*. Curious tappings, the sound of footsteps, the moving of mechanical lifts and the switching on and off of lights are all ascribed to his restless spirit. In 1928 a comedy actress using his old dressing room felt her couch lurching as though someone was trying to move it. Then her arm was seized, leaving a bruise. She knew nothing of the stories of a ghost until her dresser arrived.

Terriss's strangest appearance came in 1955, when Jack Hayden, a ticket collector at Covent Garden underground station, saw a tall, distinguished, grey-suited figure with white gloves at the station. When Hayden asked if he could help, the figure vanished. But four days later it returned and put its hands on the head of 19-year-old porter Victor Locker. He screamed and ran. Pictures of Terriss were shown to both men, and both recognized him instantly. Hayden and Locker later asked for transfers. But since then, other London Transport staff on the Piccadilly line have spoken of a strange presence at Covent Garden. And in 1972 a stationmaster, signalman and engineer there all claimed to have seen the man in grey.

Another London landmark that once had a ghost was Smithfield Market. In 1654 butchers complained that the ghost of a lawyer called Mallet glided through their stalls every Saturday evening, pulling joints of meat off their slabs. When they went for the mischievous spirit with cleavers and carving

Borley Rectory.

knives, they hit nothing but air.

Ghosts also haunt family homes, often forcing the occupants to move out. That happened in the 1970s in Nottingham, where a lorry driver and his daughter both reported seeing the figure of what looked like a foreign legionnaire in their modest house. Psychic researchers moved in, and during their midnight vigil noted a sharp drop in temperature, a loud scream, hysterical sobbing and footsteps. At a seance it was concluded that the ghost was that of a window-cleaner in white overalls who had committed suicide after falling from his ladder and becoming paralysed. He had been in love with the lorry driver's daughter.

Perhaps the world's most famous haunted house was Borley Rectory, a gloomy mansion on the Essex-Suffolk border which was burned down in 1939. Built in 1863 for the Reverend Henry Dawson Ellis Bull, the 23-room redbrick house became a centre of controversy for those who believed in ghosts and those who did not.

As soon as the Bull family moved in, strange things started happening. Footsteps and tappings were heard in the night. Bells rang and voices answered. Ghostly chanting came from nearby Borley Church. One of the family's 14 children was awakened by a slap in the face. Another saw a tall man in old-fashioned clothes standing beside her bed. Twenty people saw a nun on the

330 GHOSTS AND GHOULS

lawn. Servants saw a phantom coach and horses gallop through the grounds. A headless man and a woman in white were sighted.

In 1929, poltergeist activity began at the rectory. Pebbles, keys and medallions were tossed through the air for no apparent reason. A cook reported that a door locked the night before was found open every morning. Newspaper reporters kept vigil one night, and spotted an eerie light in a deserted wing of the building.

From 1930, the house was in the hands of the Reverend Lionel Algernon Foyster and his wife Marianne. But the strange happenings continued and messages began appearing on walls and on scraps of paper. One said: 'Marianne, get help.' Mrs Foyster also heard a phantom voice calling her name and, after she was attacked by an invisible assailant, the family moved out.

Ghost investigator Harry Price, founder of Britain's National Laboratory of Psychical Research, moved in with a team of volunteer helpers. They reported sudden, inexplicable drops of ten degrees in temperature, books moving, curious incense-like smells, and pebbles – and even cakes of soap – flying through the air. A Benedictine monk was hit by flying stones while trying to hold a service of exorcism.

First theories ascribed the hauntings to a monk and a nun from nearby Bures, who eloped, were caught and punished in the traditional manner – he beheaded, she entombed alive. But in 1937, London medium Helen Glanville was told 'by a voice from beyond' during a seance at her Streatham home that the rectory was haunted by Marie Lairre, a nun induced to leave her French convent at Le Havre and marry one of the Waldergraves of Borley Manor. Her husband strangled her in May 1667, on the site of the rectory.

In 1939, the rectory, now re-named Borley Priory by the new owner, Captain W. H. Gregson, was gutted by fire. Several people claimed that they saw a young girl at an upstairs window as the flames raged. And the village policeman declared that witnesses told him they had seen a grey-clad man slip away from the inferno.

Though in ruins, the building continued to be beset by curious happenings. Chauffeur Herbert Mayes heard the thunder of hooves as he drove past. And wartime air-raid wardens were called several times when lights were seen at the windows. In 1943, the site was excavated, and fragments of a woman's skull and skeleton were found four feet underground, together with religious pendants. Was this the unhappy Marie Lairre? Or were the remains, as sceptics suggested, those of a plague victim buried in 1665?

Whether or not the Marie Lairre theory is correct, the fact remains that things have happened at Borley which no one can explain. And still do happen . . . As late as 1961, car headlights, cameras and torches all failed during investigations at the site.

Mystery of the planter's tomb

The riddle of the Barbados coffins is one of the most baffling supernatural mysteries of all time. For 12 years, unseen forces repeatedly desecrated a sealed tomb on the Caribbean island. Eventually the family which owned the crypt was forced to abandon it. Only then did the bodies of their departed rest in peace.

The Chase family, slave-owning sugar planters, acquired the tomb in 1808. It was built of stone, recessed into the cliffs above Oistin's Bay, and sealed with a marble slab. When the family took it over, it already held one wooden coffin, that of a Mrs Thomasina Goddard.

Twice within a year, the slab guarding the only entrance was rolled aside as the family buried two of their children, Mary Ann and Dorcas. In 1812, their father Thomas also died. Eight men carried the lead coffin up to the headland, but when the tomb was opened, the mourners gasped in horror.

Mrs Goddard's body still lay in its proper place, but the caskets containing the children were standing on end against one of the walls. There was no sign of a break-in.

Pallbearers gently restored the two tiny coffins to their positions, then lugged in the box containing Mr Chase. It was laid beside the others. Stonemasons carefully cemented the marble slab securely across the entrance.

Four years later, they returned to bury a boy relative, and found the seals were intact. But again there was torment for the tragic family. The same sight of desecration met their grieving gaze when the slab was removed.

Order was restored, with eight men struggling to lift Mr Chase's coffin back to its place, but by now, the tomb was the talking point of the entire

Judge who hanged his daughter

A judge who sentenced his own daughter to death has haunted Kilworthy House, at Tavistock, Devon, for nearly 400 years.

Judge John Glanville broke the heart of his daughter, Elizabeth, when he forbade her to marry the man she loved, a naval lieutenant. Instead he forced her to become the bride of a man he considered more worthy of her, a Plymouth goldsmith.

Elizabeth, her maid and the sailor murdered the husband, but were arrested within days. Judge Glanville sent all three to the gallows – and his penitent ghost has been suffering for it ever since.

island. Two months later, new coffins were added – and the same chaos was discovered. And the same happened in 1819 when the next burial took place.

Each time, Mrs Goddard's casket was undisturbed, which seemed to rule out flooding or earth tremors. The stone walls and ceilings were checked, but no faults found. There was only one way in, and each time the cement seals around the slab were unbroken. Fear of sacred places ruled out interference by the islanders, even if it had been physically possible.

Lord Combermere, Governor of Barbados, was among the stunned funeral party in 1819. As the family wept, he personally supervised the orderly arrangement of the coffins, which now totalled six, and sprinkled fine sand around them. When the entrance slab was again cemented in place, he added his seal to the joint.

On April 18 the following year, he unexpectedly asked the rector of the nearby church to open the tomb. The six coffins which had been laid in a neat line, the three smaller ones resting on top of those containing adults. Now they were again scattered around the cave.

Mr Chase's casket was once more standing upright, with only Mrs Goddard lying where she had been left. There were no marks in the sand, and Lord Combermere's seal was intact.

The Chases could no longer stand the notoriety the tomb was bringing them. All their family coffins were carried to Christ Church graveyard, and buried in a joint funeral ceremony.

Sir Arthur Conan Doyle, creator of Sherlock Holmes and an avid investigator of the paranormal, took an interest in the story. He put forward the theory that supernatural forces played havoc with the coffins because they were made of lead, and so delayed the decomposition of the bodies. He also believed that Thomas Chase committed suicide.

But for all his theorising, the abandoned tomb has kept its secret and may do so forever.

Gisele's burning memories

From the moment he saw the old house, Paul Fortier knew it would be an appropriate setting for the good years ahead. That they were going to be good years, he had no doubt.

His first novel, *Fields of Amaranth*, was doing well, and he was at work on a second that promised to be even better. What was more, he had a beautiful

Brush with a ghost

Vicar's daughter Elsie Marshall was just 21 years old in 1893 when she was murdered by bandits in China where she worked as a missionary. She is believed to be the invisible being which brushes past staff of the library which now occupies her former home in Blackheath, London.

young wife and a five-year-old daughter who was the image of her mother.

Denise Fortier also liked the house in Montreal, Canada – but with reservations. After they bought it in 1905, she began to wish that Paul had looked into its history as carefully as he had checked the foundations.

From neighbours she was to learn that the house had been involved in some of Montreal's most blood-chilling crimes.

Built in 1805 as a detention home for "wayward children", it was wrecked by fire after two of the children had murdered the owner and his wife. In spite of their age, the children were hanged.

The house was rebuilt, but for more than a century was plagued by disasters. They included arson, murder, and inexplicable double suicides. And there were "cold spots" – pockets of numbingly cold air that seemed to move from room to room.

Denise became increasingly apprehensive about their new home, and Paul began to look at her with growing doubt and pity. In desperation, Denise went to her priest. Though the good man listened sympathetically as she urged him to exorcise the house, she thought that his face mirrored some of Paul's scepticism. Denise went home that evening with the certainty that something frightful was going to happen.

Looking at her husband that evening, she was sure that Paul had changed. He drank too much wine at the dinner table and became morose. Something in their mood seemed to communicate itself to five-year-old daughter Gisele. Sensing that the little girl was frightened, Denise carried her off to bed.

The child whispered, "Can we leave here sometime soon?"

"I don't know, dear. Why?"

"Those cold spots you tried to show daddy – I think there was one in my bed last night. I woke up with my teeth chattering even though the room was hot."

Trying to conceal her own fear, Denise bent and kissed her. "It was probably just a bad dream," she said.

They were the last words the little girl heard from her mother's lips.

That night the child again woke to a nightmare. It began with a suffocating odour of smoke in the house. Screaming, she ran to her parents' bedroom and flung open the door. The walls and ceiling of the room were ablaze, but there were infinitely worse horrors.

Her father's body lay close to the bed with a pair of scissors driven into his throat. And in the deep, soft bed her mother was struggling with two naked boys scarcely bigger than Gisele. Denise's lips yawned in a silent scream as the giggling children pummelled her body.

But when Gisele returned from next door with help, the room had changed so inexplicably that the little girl's story would always be doubted.

There was no fire in the room, and no evidence that there had been one. The vicious children had vanished. Beaten almost beyond recognition, there was only her mother's unconscious body and the corpse of Paul Fortier.

Police concluded that Gisele's story was pure fantasy subconsciously devised to conceal the facts. Obviously there had been a savage family quarrel in which she had seen her battered mother kill her father in self-defence.

It was a theory Denise herself could neither confirm nor deny. In a catatonic state, she was taken to a hospital where she died three months later. The orphaned child went to live with her grandparents in Seattle.

Because of fear of its ghostly inhabitants, the Fortier house was never again occupied. It burned to the ground in 1906.

Date with doom

Lord Thomas Lyttleton was in surprisingly jovial mood as he sat down to breakfast with close friends at his home in Epsom, Surrey, on November 24, 1779. But his guests choked on their kidneys and kedgeree as he joked that he had been visited during the night by the ghost of a girl who had killed herself after he seduced and deserted her.

She said that in exactly three days he would be dead.

Later that day, the peer made a magnificent speech in the House of Lords. He continued his roistering life as one of the great characters of London society. He assured friends he had never felt better, and arranged to stay the following weekend with Peter Andrews, a Member of Parliament who lived in Dartford, Kent.

But on the third night, as the clock struck the eleventh hour, Lyttleton suddenly clutched at his side, collapsed and died in the arms of his valet.

At exactly that moment, Andrews woke at Dartford to find the peer standing beside his bed, wearing the dressing gown the MP had left out for him.

"It's all over with me, Andrews," said the figure. Andrews followed his friend, but found Lyttleton's room empty, the dressing gown still hanging on its hook. Next morning he learned of his friends death.

A lingering loss

Peter Turner has had more than his fair share of encounters with the supernatural. Some people have seen the same ghost on more than one occasion; but Peter Turner's experiences were years apart and completely unconnected.

The first happened in 1945 when Peter and a group of young friends were playing in a row of derelict houses in the Camp Hill district of Leeds, Yorkshire. The houses were awaiting demolition and provided a natural if dangerous, playground for the local youngsters in austere, post-war Britain.

It was a cold November day and Peter and his friends were playing in a house which had recently had its floorboards removed, leaving only rafters and beams.

As Peter walked across one of the upper-floor rafters he glanced out of the shell of a window. There below him was a neat little garden with an old man tending rose bushes in full bloom.

There was no rubble, no bricks, no broken glass, just a well-kept garden with grass and flowers. The fact that it was impossible for such a garden to exist there at that time, still less contain flowers in full bloom in the middle of winter, didn't occur to young Peter. All he could think about was not getting caught. He and his friends knew what to expect if their parents found out they had been playing in the derelict buildings.

They rushed off, counting their luck at not being spotted by the old man. It was only later that it occurred to Peter how impossible it was for the garden to have been there. He returned to the house but where he had seen roses and flowers there was just brick and rubble.

Eleven years passed and Peter was still living in Leeds and preparing for his wedding, just six months away. Homes were not easy to come by, so Peter and his fiancée Pamela were delighted when they got the top-floor apartment in a Georgian house at 10 Woodhouse Square, previously used as a nursery. One evening Peter and two friends had been decorating the rooms. Feeling hungry, two of them nipped out to get a fish-and-chip supper. On their return they found the third friend outside the flat, too terrified to go back in after hearing strange noises and feeling eerie sensations.

With the excitement of the wedding, the incident was soon forgotten. But no sooner had the newly-married couple moved in, than more strange things began to happen. The door of a large cupboard would swing open, despite being securely fastened. Then footsteps would cross the room and the living room door would swing open.

When Mrs Turner was working in the kitchen, the cupboard door would swing ajar, there was the sound of shuffling feet and the feeling that someone was standing behind her.

One night, after the Turners had gone to bed, they heard the sound of their settee being dragged across the floor of the living room. When they went to investigate, nothing had been moved.

The sounds continued until one night there was a tremendous crash, just as if the old iron mangle they owned had been thrown on its side. They leapt out of bed and as usual found nothing amiss. But that didn't stop the neighbours in the flat below complaining about the noise the Turners had made "moving their furniture late at night".

The Turners found another home as soon as they could – but not before they discovered a possible cause of the mysterious noises in the night.

By chance, they met an elderly woman who had been brought up in number 10. She remembered, she said, that when she was little, the house was reputedly haunted by a Victorian lady who constantly searched the nursery for her two children who had died there.

Arresting sights

Trainees at the police college at Bramshill, Hampshire are always on the lookout for troublemakers – of the ghostly kind. A "white lady" haunts the galleries of the stately building which now houses the college. Those who have glimpsed her have also caught the definite smell of her lily of the valley perfume.

Another ghostly appearance was reported by a security guard who challenged an unauthorised tennis player. The player instantly vanished through a wall. This ghost is thought to be a nobleman's son who met a tragic end.

A third ghost is reputed to haunt the college. He is known as "the green man" and is said to be a previous occupant of the house who was drowned in the lake in the gardens.

Chapter five

FAVOURITE HAUNTS

People who have experienced the uneasiness of unexplained noises, the shock of inanimate objects flying through the air for no reason, the terror of unreal and unearthly sights, have probably stumbled upon the favourite haunt of a ghoul or ghost! Shiver and shake as you read the torment of Calvados, tremble as you meet with the terror of Amityville...these inexplicable apparitions can be truly terrifying!

The royal haunted house guests

The British Royal Family are well aware of the truth of the old saying, "Uneasy lies the head that wears the crown". For the troubled spirits of their predecessors still haunt the historic royal homes. The Queen, Princess Margaret and the Queen Mother have come face-to-face with ghosts.

Windsor Castle, the royal retreat in Berkshire, is said to have at least 25 different spectral skeletons in its cupboards, four of them former monarchs. It was there that Princess Margaret saw the figure of Queen Elizabeth I, the last Tudor monarch, who has wandered the 12th century building since her death in 1603. She is spotted most frequently in the castle library. An officer of the guard once followed her into the room, but when he reached the door, Good Queen Bess had vanished.

King Charles I, who lost his head in 1649 during the Civil War, has been reported many times standing by a table in the library, while George III, who died on January 29, 1820, and was confined to the castle during the last years of his lunacy, has been seen and heard in several rooms, often muttering one of his most-used phrases, "What, what?"

The bulky figure of Henry VIII is another nocturnal visitor. Two guards saw him fade into a wall on the battlements as recently as 1977. They later learned that there had been a door at that very spot during Henry's reign.

Soldiers on sentry duty at Windsor have often seen the ghost of a young guardsman who killed himself in 1927. Many who have spotted him in the Long Walk believe at first that he has come to relieve them.

A Coldstream Guardsman found·unconscious in the Great Park in 1976 had experienced a very different kind of ghost. He told those who found him that he had seen Herne the Hunter, a man clad in deer skins and a helmet with antlers jutting from the forehead.

Hundreds of other people claim to have seen the same apparition over the last 250 years, silently speeding through the castle grounds with his spooky pack of hounds. When the tree from which he allegedly hanged himself was cut down in 1863, Queen Victoria reserved the oak logs for her own fire, "to help kill the ghost". But the sightings of Richard II's forester have continued.

In the 17th century, a terrified servant called Parker approached one of the castle guests, Sir George Villiers, with an extraordinary story. He said he had had three visits from the armour-clad ghost of Sir George's father, the Duke of Buckingham, and had been told that unless Sir George mended his callous ways, he had not long to live. Sir George laughed off the warning. Six months later he was assassinated.

Hampton Court, the palace by the Thames presented to Henry VIII by his disgraced Chancellor, Cardinal Thomas Wolsey, is still haunted by the spirit of the King's fifth wife, Catherine Howard, who was beheaded in 1542. She has been seen so frequently, running screaming to the chapel door in search of sanctuary, that she is now mentioned in the official guide issued to the thousands of tourists who visit the palace.

The third of Henry's six wives, Jane Seymour, has also been seen at Hampton long after her death. She emerges from the Queen's apartments carrying a lighted taper, and walks around the Silver Stick Gallery on the anniversary of the birth of her son, later Edward VI, on October 12, 1537. Jane died one week later, and the weakling boy, crowned for a short reign when he was only ten years old, was fostered by a nurse, Mistress Sibell Penn, who also appears at Hampton.

Mistress Penn was buried at St Mary's Church after she died of smallpox in 1568, but the church had to be rebuilt in 1829 after being struck by lightning. The nurse's remains were disturbed as her tomb was moved, and soon strange whirring sounds and mutterings were heard coming from behind a wall at the palace where there was no known room.

When the wall was knocked down, a spinning wheel was uncovered along with other relics which indicated that the nurse had once lived on the site. Many witnesses have also seen Mistress Penn wandering the corridors of the palace's south-west wing, where her old room was. She is a tall, thin hooded figure in a grey robe, her arms outstretched as if in appeal. In 1881, a sentry watched her walk through a wall.

Two male figures once haunted Hampton's Fountain Court, making loud noises in the middle of the night. The ghosts were never seen or heard again after workmen uncovered two skeletons in Cavalier dress buried beneath the courtyard. The skeletons were given a Christian funeral.

Perhaps the most bizarre Hampton phantoms were those encountered by a police constable on duty at the palace one cold February night in 1917. The officer, identified only as PC 2657, who had 20 years service in the force, opened a gate in the grounds for two men and seven women wearing strange old-fashioned costumes. He swore that they then walked on for 30 yards, turned to one side of the path – and simply faded away.

Today the Queen and her immediate family have abandoned Hampton Court to the tourists, and divide their time in Britain, between Buckingham Palace, Windsor, Sandringham in Norfolk, and Balmoral in Scotland. All have their own curious ghosts.

Windsor Castle, Berkshire, England.

Clock Court, Hampton Court Palace.

Hampton Court Palace,
Hampton Court, London.

Glamis Castle, Scotland.

These are some of the historic homes owned by the British Royal Family and said to be haunted. Glamis Castle above is central to Shakespeare's *Macbeth*. Hampton Court is also famous for its maze. Queen Elizabeth II is frequently at home at Windor.

It was at Balmoral that the Queen is said to have seen the phantom figure of John Brown, confidant and some say lover of the widowed Queen Victoria. He has often been reported stalking the castle's corridors and entrance hall, a magnificent sight in his kilt.

Sandringham has for years played host to a mischievous yuletide poltergeist. It livens up Christmas Eve in the second floor servants' quarters by flinging greetings cards about, ripping sheets from newly-made beds, and breathing heavily in the ears of unsuspecting maids. Prince Philip's uncle, Prince Christopher of Greece, once saw a mysterious masked woman while staying in one of the Sandringham guest rooms. He glanced up from his book and saw her head and shoulders framed in the dressing table mirror. She had soft, curly brown hair, a dimpled chin, and a mask over the top of her face.

Next day, while visiting Lord Cholmondely at nearby Houghton Hall, the Prince found out who she was. He saw a portrait of the same woman, carrying a mask, and wearing the dress he had noted in his mirror. It was Dorothy Walpole, unhappily married in the 18th century, whose ghost was also seen by King George IV in 1786.

The ghost of Buckingham Palace is that of Major John Gwynne, a private secretary in the household of King Edward VII early this century. Fearing that mention of his name in a divorce case had brought dishonour on the Royal Family, he shot himself at the desk of his first-floor office. And it is there that his dim shape has been seen several times since.

Gatcombe, the Cotswolds mansion home of Princess Anne and Captain Mark Phillips, is said by locals to be haunted by a huge black dog. They call it the Hound of Odin, named after the God of the Vikings who pillaged Gloucestershire 1,000 years ago, and was always accompanied by a fierce four-legged fiend.

Kensington Palace has three ghosts. A man in white buckskin breeches strolls the arcaded courtyards, Queen Victoria's Aunt Sophia sits working a spinning wheel, and, on the roof, King George II has been seen staring at the weather vane, and asking, in his thick German accent, "Why don't they come?" The King died at the palace on October 25, 1760, waiting for messengers with news from his native Hanover.

No ghostly goings-on have yet been reported from the Gloucestershire home of Prince Charles and Princess Diana, but St Paul's Cathedral in London, where they were married in July, 1981, was once the scene of a strange incident. Workmen preparing foundations for a building beside it unearthed a wooden box containing jewels. The gems were taken to the British Museum, London, and an expert took them home to clean, polish and value.

As he and his daughter worked, the room suddenly grew cold. A psychic

---

Corpse in the bed

A gruesome ghost haunts St James's Palace in London – the figure of a man propped up in bed with his jaw hanging open over a gashed throat. It has been seen frequently since the night of May 31, 1810, when Sellis, the Italian-born valet of Ernest Augustus, Duke of Cumberland and fifth son of King George III, was discovered dead on his bed.

The Duke told the inquest that, when he returned from a night at the opera, Sellis had tried to kill him, failed, and committed suicide. He denied later gossip that he had murdered his valet because he was being blackmailed after seducing the man's daughter.

---

friend who called a few hours later found out why. He saw a tall thin man in Elizabethan dress standing behind the couple, clearly angry that his hidden treasures had been disturbed.

There was another surprise when the jewels were put on display at the museum. A woman looking at them suddenly fainted, and explained after attendants revived her, that she had seen blood on one of the necklaces. Staff could find no trace of stains on the gems, but the woman remained convinced that the person who last wore the necklace had been murdered.

Of all the hauntings connected with royal buildings, the most intriguing are those of Glamis Castle. The towered and turretted fortress beside Dean Water, near Forfar, Angus, is the Scottish family home of the Queen Mother's family, the Bowes Lyons. Princess Margaret was born there. But its 16-feet thick walls have been cloaked with mystery ever since Macbeth usurped the Scottish throne by murdering King Duncan in one of the rooms in the year 1040.

The Queen Mother delights in telling the younger members of her daughters' families the spine-chilling tales that have sprung up about Glamis. How Lord Beardie Crawford and fellow revellers diced with the devil in a tower room, and were condemned to stay there, drinking eternally until the Day of Judgement. Of how the Ogilvies, fleeing from the Lindsays during a clan war, were locked in a room and forgotten, starving to death.

The Queen Mother herself is one of many who have seen the sad Grey Lady of Glamis, who haunts the Clock Tower. She is believed to be the ghost of Janet Douglas, wife of the sixth Lord Glamis, who was burned to death on Castle Hill, Edinburgh, in 1537 after being falsely accused of witchcraft and of plotting to poison King James V.

There is one Glamis phantom that few in the family have ever been prepared to talk about. Victorian high society was alive with rumours that a hideously mishapen beast of a man had been born into the Strathmore clan, an immensely strong and hairy egg-shaped creature whose head ran straight into a hugh body which was supported by toy-like legs and arms.

Unable to reveal the monster's existence, yet unable to kill it, the family were said to have locked their odd offspring in one of the secret rooms built at Glamis in the last years of the 17th century. There it lived for years, known only to the Earl of Strathmore, his lawyer and land agent, and, when he reached 21, the Earl's heir.

Guests returned from Glamis with strange stories that fuelled the gossip. Many said they had been woken in the night by the howls and snarls of an animal. One woman claimed she saw a pale face with huge, mournful eyes staring at her from a window across a courtyard. When it disappeared, she heard appalling screams, and watched an old woman scurry across the yard carrying a large bundle.

In 1869, a Mrs Monro woke in her bedroom at the castle to feel a beard brush her face. As she fumbled for a light, the shape that had been standing over her shambled into the next room, where her son was sleeping. The boy's screams of terror brought Mrs Monro and her husband racing to his bedside. As he explained that he had just seen a giant, they all heard a crash.

At breakfast next morning, other guests said they too had heard the crash, and one said she had been woken by the mournful whines of her small dog. But their hosts could offer no explanation.

In 1865, a workman who found a secret passage, and claimed to have seen something alive in a room off it, was "subsidised and induced to emigrate".

In 1877, essayist Augustus Hare watched the Bishop of Brechin offer to share the burden that was making the then Earl of Strathmore morose at a house party. Hare reported, "Lord Strathmore said that in his most unfortunate position, no one could ever help him."

Andrew Ralston, land agent to the Strathmores from 1860 to 1912, was once asked for the full story by the Countess, grandmother of Queen Elizabeth II. He replied, "Lady Strathmore, it is fortunate you do not know it, for if you did you would never be happy."

Dowager Lady Granville, the Queen Mother's sister once admitted, "We were never allowed to talk about it when we were children. Our parents forbade us ever to discuss the matter or ask any questions about it. My father and grandfather refused absolutely to discuss it."

And the 12th Earl, the Queen's great-grandfather, was quoted as saying, "If you could only guess the nature of the secret, you would go down on your knees and thank God it was not yours."

His warning failed to deter historians and ghost-hunters. For years they tried to unravel the nature of the secret. Once, towels were flown from the window of every known room, to try to locate the possible hideaways. Experts combed the family tree for clues, and in the 1920s journalist Paul Bloomfield came up with what seemed a plausible explanation.

According to Burke's Peerage the "bible" of British nobility, Lord Glamis, heir to Thomas, the 11th Earl of Strathmore, married Charlotte Grimstead on December 21, 1820, and was presented with an heir, Thomas George, later the 12th Earl, on September 22, 1822. But when Bloomfield checked Douglas's Scots Peerage, he surmised that Lord Glamis and his wife also had a son "born and died on October 21, 1821." Another reference book gave the date as October 18.

Bloomfield guessed that the first-born son did not die, but was badly deformed. He could never inherit the title and estates. Expected to live only days, he was kept alive and well cared for, but he survived both his father and his younger brother. A third son, Claude, became the 13th Earl, and was succeeded in 1904 by his own boy, Claude George, born in 1855 and who became father of the Queen Mother.

It is believed that he was the last heir to be initiated into the grim family secret, when he reached the age of 21 on March 14, 1876. His son and successor, Timothy, was never told the story, although he once said, "I feel sure there is a corpse or a coffin bricked up in the castle walls somewhere, but they are so thick that you could search for a week without finding anything."

Today, the legend of the monster lives on only in the name of the rooftop lead path where he may have been exercised at night – the Mad Earl's Walk.

The Grey Lady still prays silently in the chapel. Spirits still haunt the room where the Strathmore's personal hangman used to sleep. And Earl Beardie is still seen, a huge old man with a flowing beard, sitting by a fire in one of the castle bedrooms.

Yet for all their ghosts, none of the royal palaces and castles rank as the most haunted place in Britain. That title rests with an ancient fortification that kings and queens of earlier ages used for less civilised purposes ...

Long live the dead King!

The ghost of King George IV stalks the underground passages of Brighton Pavilion, the place he loved most.

He built the Sussex landmark after secretly marrying Mrs Fitzherbert while he was Prince Regent. His spectre has been encountered both in the passage that leads to the stables – now the Dome – and in a tunnel which once linked the royal cellars with those of the Druid's Head Inn.

The Pavilion was sold to the town of Brighton by Queen Victoria, for £50,000.

The Bloody Tower

History of horror goes back 700 years

The Tower of London's ancient battlements, colourful Beefeaters and legendary ravens attract millions of tourists each year from all over the world. They stroll the picturesque buildings and courtyards, and listen enthralled as guides bring to life the spectacular and violent happenings that shaped Britain's past. For the Tower was once the most blood-drenched spot in England, and for more than 700 years it has had the ghosts to prove it.

The first, in 1241, was that of Saint Thomas Becket, who had been murdered at Canterbury Cathedral 71 years earlier. Becket was a Londoner, and had been Constable of the Tower before becoming Archbishop of Canterbury in 1162. His spirit was seen by "a certain priest, a wise and holy man". It was said to have returned to demolish extension walls which were upsetting people who lived near the Tower. The priest saw the apparition strike the walls with a cross, whereupon they fell as if hit by an earthquake.

Later Tower ghosts had more personal reasons for returning to the London landmark. Anne Boleyn, the second of Henry VIII's six wives, is the most frequently seen spirit. Several sentries have spotted her over the years, and one even faced a court-martial because of her.

He was found unconscious outside the King's House on a winter's night in 1864, and accused of falling asleep on watch. At the hearing, he told how a strange white figure had emerged from the dawn mist. It wore a curious bonnet which appeared to be empty. The private, who served with the King's Royal Rifle Corps, challenged the figure three times, but it continued to move towards him. When he ran the bayonet of his rifle through the body, a flash of fire ran up the barrel and he passed out.

Two other soldiers and an officer told the court-martial they had seen the apparition from a window of the nearby Bloody Tower. After hearing that the incident had taken place just below the room where Anne Boleyn spent the night before her execution for adultery on May 19, 1536, the court-martial cleared the unfortunate sentry.

Anne, Queen for 1,000 days, had a horror of English steel in English hands, and her husband agreed to import a French executioner with a French sword for the beheading. But after her death, there were no more niceties. Her headless body was bundled into an old arrow chest and buried in unseemly haste in the Tower chapel of St Peter ad Vincular.

The Traitor's Gate at the Tower of London.

Sentries have often seen her ghost pacing up and down outside the tiny church, and one night, one of the guards noted an eerie light shining from inside the chapel. He climbed a ladder to peer through a window, and saw a ghostly procession of knights and ladies in Tudor dress file slowly up the aisle, led by a woman who looked like Anne. When she reached the altar, they all vanished, leaving the chapel in darkness again.

Anne's restless spirit does not confine itself to the scene of her death. Her headless body is said to arrive in a phantom coach at her childhood home, Blickling Hall, Norfolk, on the anniversary of her execution, and she has also been reported wandering through the grounds and attics of Rochford Hall, Essex, during the 12 days after Christmas.

But it is at the Tower where most of her rambles have taken place, often near the time of other executions. At 2 am on February, 1915, Sergeant William Nicholls and his watch saw a woman in a brown dress with a neck ruff. She walked quickly towards the Thames, which runs past one side of the Tower, then disappeared into a stone wall. Five hours later, a German spy was shot in the moat, one of 11 executed there during World War One. Anne was last seen in February, 1933, when a guard reported a headless apparition floating towards him close to the Bloody Tower.

The ghosts of three other 16th century ladies who lost their heads have also been spotted in the Tower. Catherine Howard, the fifth of Henry VIII's wives, was beheaded there in 1542, and has been seen walking the walls at night. Margaret, Countess of Salisbury, re-enacts the horrors of her 1541 execution on its anniversary. She was dragged screaming to the block, and the axeman chased her round the scaffold, missing his target three times before finally severing her head. Lady Jane Grey, who reigned as Queen for only nine days, has been reported several times.

Two sentries recognised her when they saw the figure of a woman running along the battlements of the inner wall, near the Salt Tower, at 3 am on February 12, 1954 – the 400th anniversary of her beheading on Tower Green, less than 150 yards away. Exactly three years later, two Welsh Guardsmen spotted a white shapeless form on the Salt Tower, where Lady Jane was imprisoned before her execution, at the age of 17.

In 1970, a man from Grays, in Essex, wrote to a London evening newspaper, saying his girlfriend had seen what seemed to be a ghost during a visit to the Tower. He said the figure of a long-haired woman, wearing a long black velvet dress and white cap, was standing by an open window in the Bloody Tower. A large gold medallion hung round her neck. The girl was the only one in her party to see the figure, and she said that, when she went up to the window, both on the visit and on a later occasion, she found it difficult to breathe. Experts believe she is one of the very few people who have seen Lady

Jane Grey in daylight.

Phantom men and children also roam the Tower. In 1890, a sentry described an encounter so vivid that he "Nearly died of fright." He was on duty in the Beauchamp Tower when he heard someone call his name.

He said, "I turned and there, floating in mid-air, was a face, red and bloated, with a loose, dribbling mouth and heavy-lidded pale eyes. I had often seen it in the history books – it was Henry VIII, with all the devil showing in him.

"I was so scared I did not stop running until I came upon two of my comrades. They were beginning to clamour, when they suddenly broke off – the face had followed me.

"The affair was hushed up, and we were all told not to breathe a word that the Tower was haunted."

During World War One, another sentry reported seeing a ghostly procession pass him near Spur Tower. A party of men were carrying a stretcher bearing the headless corpse of a man, his head tucked in beside his arm. Historians said this was the practice in earlier centuries, when bodies were returned to the Tower for burial after executions on Tower Hill.

Boadicea's return

Some of the oldest names in Britain's history books have emerged from the mists of time to appear as ghosts more than 1,000 years after their deaths. The warrior queen Boadicea poisoned herself in AD 62 to avoid capture after her army was routed by the Romans.

But on some mornings earlier this century, she was seen at the small village of Cammeringham, north of Lincoln, with two phantom horses pulling the chariot from which her hair and gown billowed behind her. The village is close to the old Roman Road, Ermine Street.

When the Romans withdrew from East Anglia in AD 410, Ella was crowned the region's king. And the people of Horning, near Norfolk, say his ghostly coronation is re-enacted every five years on July 21 beside the river Bure.

The boy-king Edward was murdered by his stepmother, Queen Elfrida, in AD 979, and his body taken to Shaftesbury Abbey, in Dorset, for burial. So many miracles happened while it was being transported that the boy later became St Edward the Martyr. Several people claim to have seen him being carried up cobbled Gold Hill in Shaftesbury by two ghostly men leading phantom packhorses.

At Tamworth Castle, Staffordshire, the figure of Editha, grand-daughter of King Alfred the Great, has been sighted climbing the stairs to the Tower Room, wearing her black nun's habit. Her sighs and moans have been captured on a tape-recorder.

The ghost of a former Duke of Northumberland has been seen so often on the battlements between the Martin and Constable towers that sentries have nicknamed the pathway Northumberland's Walk. Sir Walter Raleigh, the favourite explorer of Elizabeth I, who was imprisoned in the Tower by her successor, James I, and executed in 1618, has also been reported by guards; and two little children seen walking the Bloody Tower hand-in-hand are believed to be Edward and Richard, the two princes allegedly murdered on the orders of their uncle in 1483, so he could claim the throne as King Richard III.

Some of the Tower's many ghosts are not recognisable as personalities. The Keeper of the Jewel House, Major-General HDW Sitwell, woke one morning in 1952 in his quarters in St Thomas's Tower, on the outer wall, to see a monk in a brown habit through the open door of his bedroom.

Some of the ghosts are not even human. In October 1817, Edmund Swifte, then Keeper of the Crown Jewels, was dining with his wife, son and sister-in-law in his parlour in Martin Tower. As he offered his wife a glass of wine, she exclaimed, "Good God, what's that?"

He followed her startled gaze, and saw a cylindrical glass tube, about as thick as a man's arm, and filled with white and blue liquid which seemed to be constantly churning. It hovered between the top of the table and the ceiling, moving slowly from one person to another until it passed behind Swifte's wife, pausing over her right shoulder. She crouched and clutched her shoulder, shouting, "Oh Christ, it has seized me." Swifte lashed out at the cylinder with a chair, then rushed upstairs to check that the couple's other children were all right. When he returned, the apparition had vanished.

Only days later, a sentry outside Martin Tower watched vapour pour through the narrow gap between the closed door and sill, and take the shape of a giant bear. The guard lunged at it with his bayonet, but the cold steel passed through the figure and stuck in the wooden door. The man collapsed from shock, and never recovered. When Swifte visited him the following day, he declared him "changed beyond recognition". Within days, the sentry was dead.

The Tower also has its share of mischievous spirits. Several Yeoman Warders have found themselves bundled out of bed in one particular small bedroom in the Well Tower. In the autumn of 1972, a photographer was sent tumbling from a ladder as he set up his camera to take pictures of a mural in the Beauchamp Tower room where Lord Lovat, the last Tower prisoner to lose his head, had been held.

Perhaps the most curious fact about the Tower of London hauntings is that none have ever been reported in the White Tower, the largest and oldest of all the buildings, and the heart of the entire complex. Guy Fawkes, the man who tried to blow up the Houses of Parliament in 1605, was just one of the celebrities incarcerated there in cruel conditions before his gruesome death – but none have ever returned to the scene of their ordeals.

Masons restoring one of the walls in the late 1850s may have uncovered a clue to the reason for that. In the 11th century, when work on the White Tower began, it was believed that buildings could be protected against malevolent spirits by sacrificing an animal in them. Eight centuries later, the repair men broke into one of the thickest stone walls ... and found the skeleton of an ancient cat.

The Renishaw coffin
Dark secret of the Sitwells

Dame Edith Sitwell

In the Sitwell family it was always known as The Renishaw Coffin. The famous literary trio – Osbert, Edith and Sacheverell – heard about it when they were children and the stories of it and its ghost became part of their upbringing.

Their famous Renishaw Hall, a gloomy Derbyshire mansion dating from 1625, was always thought to be haunted. But it was not until their eccentric father, Sir George Sitwell, decided to improve the house by altering and enlarging the central staircase that the coffin came to light.

In order to carry out the work, two small rooms had to be demolished, one on the ground floor, one a first-floor bedroom. Sir George, who was fanatically proud of his family history, asked the clerk of works to take note of anything interesting he came across, hoping that some traces of ancient building might be found.

The coffin was discovered between the joists of the bedroom floor. From its construction, and the fact that it had nails rather than screws, it was presumed that it dated from the 17th century. It was firmly attached to the joists with iron clamps. Because of lack of space, it had never been fitted with a lid, the floorboards above it serving the purpose. The coffin contained no skeleton, but certain marks proved that there had once been a body in it.

The discovery threw new light on the frightening experiences of two women who had slept in that bedroom when they were guests at Renishaw. The first was a Miss Tait, daughter of Archibald Campbell Tait, the Archbishop of Canterbury. She had been invited to Derbyshire in 1885 to join the house party celebrating Sir George's coming of age.

In the middle of the night she was awakened by someone kissing her three times. The kisses were ice cold. The room was empty.

She ran to the room where Sir George's sister was sleeping and told her what had happened. Miss Sitwell made up a bed for her friend on her sofa, explaining that nothing would induce her to sleep in that room as she had once had exactly the same experience.

After the party, Sir George's agent, Mr Turnbull, came to see him about some business and during the conversation Sir George jokingly told the story of Miss Tait's phantom kisses.

Far from being amused, the agent looked shocked. Apparently, when Sir George had generously lent him Renishaw for his honeymoon, a friend of the agent's bride had come to stay. She had slept in that same bedroom and had had the same experience. She left next morning, obviously frightened, but the Turnbulls had simply credited her with an over-active imagination.

One autumn evening, a few years after Miss Tait's haunting, Lady Sitwell was entertaining a few guests in the upstairs drawing room after dinner. The room was brightly lit and the door stood open onto a passage. She was chatting to a friend who sat on her left when she became conscious of a figure in the passage outside. Friends noticed that she seemed to be following something with her eyes. She wrote later, "I saw the figure with such distinctness that I had no doubt at all that I was looking at a real person."

The figure was that of a woman, apparently a servant, with grey hair done up in a bun under a white cap. Her dress was blue with a full dark skirt. She moved with a furtive, gliding motion as though wishing to escape notice, but her arms were stretched out in front of her and the hands clasped. She moved towards the head of the staircase on which Sir George had worked 20 years before – and disappeared.

Lady Sitwell called out: "Who's that?" When no one answered, she urged her friends to find her the mystery visitor, and everyone joined in the search.

They were on the point of giving up when a young woman, looking down into the well-lit hall below, suddenly cried out, "I do believe that's the ghost!"

Just where the door of the old room used to be, she saw a woman with dark hair and dress obviously distressed and in deep thought. Her figure, though opaque, cast no shadow. It moved in a gentle glide, full of sadness, and melted away. What happened in the two rooms that Sir George demolished has never been discovered and the empty coffin has kept its secret.

Lord Brougham's pact

Lord Brougham struck a macabre deal with a fellow student as they discussed life after death one night at Edinburgh University. Whoever died first would re-appear to the other to settle the argument.

The two friends drifted apart after graduating. Brougham's friend went to India, and for years the peer heard nothing from him. But the pact was not forgotten. One day, Brougham stepped from his bath, reached for a towel – and saw his college classmate sitting in a nearby chair.

The peer made a note of the date in his diary: December 19. And in his autobiography, published in 1871, he wrote that shortly afterwards a letter arrived from India. His friend had died.

On December 19.

House of evil

Amityville jinx hit actor

Actor James Brolin is certain there was an evil jinx on the film *The Amityville Horror*, in which he starred. He played surveyor George Lutz who, with his family, was driven from his home by a terrifying series of demonic happenings. The film was based on the best-selling book by Jay Anson, to whom the Lutz family told their nightmare story.

Brolin said: "On the first day of filming I stepped into the elevator in my apartment block and pressed the button for the lobby floor. Before we'd gone three floors it shuddered to a grinding, screeching halt, the lights flickered and I was plunged into frightening darkness. I screamed for help but nobody could hear me.

"It was an eerie, frightening experience. You imagine all sorts of hair-raising things in the silent darkness. My pleas bounced back like an echo. Those 30 minutes seemed an eternity."

The jinx hit again the next morning. "I'd been on the set less than one minute when I tripped over a cable and severely wrenched my ankle," said Brolin. "I hobbled around in pain for days."

The film recorded the horrifying events experienced by George and Kathleen Lutz and their three children after they moved to Long Island, New York, to a house which had been the scene of a multiple murder in 1974.

Ronald Defoe, 23-year-old son of a wealthy car dealer, had drugged his parents, brothers and sisters at supper and at 3.15 am, he stalked from room to room shooting each victim in the back with a rifle.

He claimed in court that "voices" had ordered him to commit the crime. Defoe was sentenced to six consecutive life sentences.

For the Lutzes, the house's macabre history gave them the chance to buy a dream home at the bargain price of $80,000. Seen in the bright light of day, it was a beautiful, three-storied colonial-style residence, set on a well-kept lawn which sloped gently down to the bay, and its own boathouse. In the small, middle-class community of Amityville it was a showplace.

Soon after the family moved in they asked the local priest, Father Mancuso (played in the film by Rod Steiger) to bless the house. Author Anson wrote: "The priest entered the house to begin his ritual. When he flicked the first holy water and uttered the words that accompany the gesture, Father Mancuso heard a masculine voice say with terrible clarity, 'Get out!'

"He looked up in shock, but he was alone in the room. Who or whatever

A still from the film *The Amityville Horror* showing the Lutz's house.

had spoken was nowhere to be seen."

For the first two nights in their new home, the Lutzes were awakened by strange noises at 3.15 am. But the real horror began on the third night.

As usual, George Lutz checked that all doors and windows were locked before going to bed. The noises roused him again at 3.15, and this time he went downstairs to investigate.

He could not believe what he saw. The heavy, solid-wood front door had been wrenched open and was hanging by one hinge. With mounting terror he realised it had been forced from inside the house. The thick steel doorknob spindle was twisted, and the surrounding metal plate had been forced outwards.

From then on, the house seemed to have an evil life of its own. Windows opened and closed at will and a bannister was wrenched from the staircase.

Two weeks after the front-door incident. George woke in the night to find his wife Kathleen floating above the bed. George pulled Kathleen down by her hair and switched on the light. He was looking not at his attractive young wife, but at a hideous vision.

Kathleen caught a glimpse of her reflection in a mirror and screamed:

"That's not me. It can't be me!" Her appearance changed slowly back to normal over the next six hours.

A few nights later Kathleen was in the sitting room with George when she looked up and saw two glowing red eyes at the darkened window. She and George hurried outside and found strange tracks in the snow. Kathleen told Anson: "The prints had been left by cloven hooves – like those of an enormous pig."

After only 28 days the Lutzes fled the dream house that had become a nightmare.

As they hurriedly gathered a few belongings, amid a series of unearthly noises, green slime oozed from the walls and ceiling and a sticky black substance dripped from the keyholes.

Because of the curse, the film men dared not use the actual house. They found an almost identical building in New Jersey. They knew only too well of the frightening things that had happened to people connected with the story.

A photographer went to take pictures of Anson immediately after photographing the Amityville house. While he was in the author's home, his car caught fire and billowed orange smoke as it stood empty with the engine switched off.

Anson himself told of terrifying events linked with his book. He said: "A woman to whom I loaned some early chapters took the manuscript home. She and two of her children were suffocated in a fire that night. The only item in the apartment that was not damaged by the fire was the manuscript.

"Another man put the manuscript in the trunk of his car and attempted to drive home. He drove through what he thought was a puddle. It turned out to be a 12-foot-deep hole into which his car slid. When the car was fished out the next day, the only dry object in it was the manuscript.

"And when my editor picked up the completed manuscript at my office his car caught fire and he discovered that all the bolts on his engine had been loosened."

Anson himself suffered a heart attack, and his son and friend were nearly killed in a car smash.

The Lutzes are today alive and well in California, and planning another book about their experiences. Their Long Island house of horrors is now owned by James and Barbara Cromarty.

They say the place is not haunted.

Whatever the truth, the movie *The Amityville Horror*, will remain a chillingly realistic record of paranormal events. Director Stuart Rosenberg says that he would not have taken on the project if it was just another horror film.

He insists, "My first reaction was that it wouldn't be my cup of tea. But I read Jay Anson's book – and it had the ring of truth about it."

Riddle of the Rectory

A dark gloomy mansion on the border between the English counties of Essex and Suffolk has been described as the world's most haunted house. And even though the building, Borley Rectory, burned down mysteriously in 1939, its legend lives on in strange happenings near the spot where it once stood.

The 23-room red-brick house was built in 1863 for the Reverend Henry Dawson Ellis Bull. As soon as he and his family moved in, they heard puzzling sounds at night. Footsteps and tappings were followed by bells ringing and voices answering. Ghostly chanting was heard from the nearby village church.

Soon the disturbances took on a more physical form. One of the 14 children in the family was awakened one day by a slap in the face. Another claimed to have seen a man in old-fashioned clothes standing by her bed. A nun, a phantom coach and horses, a headless man and a woman in white were all reported in the grounds by passers-by or servants.

In 1929 poltergeist activity began. Pebbles, keys and mementoes flew through the air for no apparent reason, and a cook told her master that a kitchen door locked each evening was inexplicably open when she arrived for work the following morning.

Just before the Bull family moved out, newspaper reporters kept vigil one night, and noted an eerie light in a deserted wing of the building.

The Reverend Lionel Algernon Foyster and his wife Marrianne moved into the Rectory in 1930, and the baffling incidents continued. Curious messages started appearing on walls or scraps of paper, urging: "Marrianne, get help."

Mrs Foyster also heard a disembodied voice call her name, and she was later attacked by an invisible assailant. Soon after that, the couple fled for a more peaceful home.

Ghost investigator Harry Price, founder of Britain's National Laboratory of Psychical Research, recruited a team of volunteers to document exactly what was happening at Borley. They reported sudden drops in temperature of up to ten degrees, curious incense-like smells, stones and cakes of soap thrown across rooms, and books moving as if of their own accord. A Benedictine monk trying to hold an exorcism in the Rectory was hit by flying pebbles.

When Captain W H Gregson bought the building, he re-named it Borley Priory. But the new name brought the jinxed home no better luck. In 1939 it

Excavations for the nun's skeleton or church plate said to be buried near Borley.

was wrecked by fire. Several people claimed that, as the flames raged, they saw a young girl at an upstairs window. Witnesses told the village policeman a grey-clad nun had been sighted slipping away from the inferno.

Even though the Rectory was destroyed, arguments about its ghosts raged on. Some said they were the spirits of a monk and a nun who had eloped from nearby Bures centuries before, but had suffered the traditional punishment when caught – decapitation for him, being buried alive for her.

But London medium Helen Glanville claimed that during a 1937 seance at her home in Streatham, she was told that the Borley ghost was that of Marie Lairre, a nun induced to leaver her convent at Le Havre, France, to marry one of the Waldergrave family from Borley Manor. She was strangled by him in May, 1667 – on the site where the Rectory was built.

In 1943, excavations of the ruins revealed fragments of a woman's skull and skeleton four feet below ground, together with a number of religious pendants. Were they the bones of unhappy Marie, or were they, as some suggested, the remains of a plague victim from even earlier times?

The Rectory may be long gone, but its supernatural residents outlasted it for many years. Chauffeur Herbert Mayes heard the thunder of invisible hooves as he drove past the shell of the building. During World War Two, air raid wardens were called to the ruins several times when lights were reported at windows. And as late as 1961, car headlights, cameras and torches all inexplicably failed to work during investigations at the site.

Only a few miles north of Borley lies the Suffolk village of Polstead. There, too, the Rectory is said to be haunted. And when a young Irish vicar moved out after only five nights in his new parish, the church put the 350-year-old building on the market claiming it was "much too large and expensive to maintain."

The Reverend Hayden Foster, 35, arrived in Polstead from Dublin with his wife Margo and son Gerard in April 1978, and for four nights they all slept soundly at their new 16-room home.

On the fifth, the couple moved to another bedroom to accommodate guests who had travelled for Mr Foster's induction ceremony next day. What happened that night was enough to make the family pack their bags in the morning, and move back to Ireland.

Mr Foster told a reporter from the local newspaper, "At about 3 am, we were lying half awake when Margo saw the walls of the room change from being freshly-painted to peeling, damp old wallpaper – just as it might have looked 20 or 30 years ago.

"She heard screaming like a child's, but it wasn't Gerard. Then she felt as if she was being strangled or suffocated. She was trying to say the Lord's Prayer, but she couldn't get it out because of this overwhelming force. I felt too that there was real danger in that room. There is a definite feeling of evil in that place."

Villagers in Polstead were not surprised when the Fosters left. They knew the legends about the Rectory. Some said they had seen a procession of monks crossing the road outside its gates, their sandals six feet above the ground.

Others recalled that the Reverend John Whitmore, vicar from 1795 to 1840, had held an exorcism service in the house.

But the Diocese Bishop, Leslie Brown, had not been told the stories.

He said, "I knew nothing about the Rectory's reputation when the Fosters arrived. If I had, I certainly would never have moved them in.

"The previous vicar had said nothing to me at all, and when I asked his wife about it afterwards, she said, 'Oh well, we got quite used to hearing footsteps going upstairs.'"

Torment of Calvados
Diaries chart a castle nightmare

Diaries written by a French aristocrat who lived in a gloomy mediaeval castle set among the apple orchards of Normandy tell the story of one of the most violent hauntings ever recorded. Known simply as X, he recorded in vivid detail the extraordinary events that turned his historic home into a nightmare in the year 1875.

They began without warning. Everyone in Calvados Castle had settled down for the night when they were disturbed by ghostly wailing and weeping and rapping on the walls. The noises were heard by the entire household – X himself, his wife, his son, his son's tutor who was an abbé, Emile the coachman, and servants Auguste, Amelina and Celina.

After several nights of ever-increasing noise and disturbance, the aristocrat instructed that fine threads were to be strung across every entrance to the castle. He hoped, of course, that in the morning they would be broken, proving that someone had entered and was trying to terrorise them.

But the threads remained intact. There was no escaping the fact that the forces existed within the castle walls.

On Wednesday, October 13, 1875, X began keeping a diary. That night the abbé was alone in his room when he heard a series of sharp taps on the wall and a candlestick on the mantlepiece was lifted by an unseen hand.

The terror-stricken priest rang for X who found that not only had the candlestick been moved, but also an armchair which was normally fixed to the floor.

For the next two days, pounding on the walls, footsteps on the stairs and other un-nerving phenomena continued unabated. X and the abbé armed themselves with sticks and searched the castle from top to bottom. They could find no human explanation.

By October 31 the castle was hardly ever at peace. X recorded in his diary, "A very disturbed night. It sounded as if someone went up the stairs with superhuman speed from the ground floor, stamping his feet.

"Arriving on the landing, he gave five heavy blows so strong that objects rattled in their places. Then it seemed as if a heavy anvil or a big log had been thrown at the wall so as to shake the house.

"Nobody could say where the blows came from, but everyone got up and assembled in the hall. The house only settled down at about three in the morning ..."

The following night everyone was awakened by what sounded like a heavy body rolling downstairs followed by blows so ferocious they seemed to rock the castle. Over the next few days, the haunting had become so violent the family felt it could not possibly get any worse. But greater ordeals were to come.

On the night of November 10, X wrote in his diary, "Everyone heard a long shriek and then another as of a woman outside calling for help. At 1.45 we suddenly heard three or four loud cries in the hall and then on the staircase."

Cries, screams and moans which "sounded like the cries of the damned" seemed to fill the whole castle. Heavy furniture was moved, windows flung open and – more terrifying – Bibles were torn and desecrated. The family began to wonder if the powers of darkness had taken over.

X's wife suddenly became the focus of attention. Hearing a noise in the abbé's room, she crept up the stairs and put out a hand to press down the latch on the door. Before she could touch it she saw the key turn in the lock

---

Face in the floor

One of the world's most puzzling ghost stories began on an afternoon in August, 1971, in a cottage in the Spanish village of Belmez, near Cordoba, in Andalucia.

An old woman was busy in the kitchen, preparing the evening meal, when her grandchild started to scream. The grandmother turned from her oven – and saw a tormented face stare up at her from the faded pink tiles of the kitchen floor.

When she tried to rub the vision out with a rag, the eyes opened wider, making the expression of the face even more heart-rending.

The woman sent for the owner of the house. He ripped up the tiles and replaced them with concrete. But three weeks later another face began to form in the new surface, even more clearly defined than the first.

The owner called in the authorities, who excavated one section of the floor, and found what seemed to be the remains of a mediaeval burial ground.

The floor was repaired, but soon faces started appearing all over the carefully-laid concrete; first one, then another, then a whole group.

The kitchen was locked and sealed off, but faces began to appear in other parts of the house. Investigators moved in with ultra-sensitive microphones, and picked up agonised moans and voices speaking in a strange language, sounds undetectable to the human ear.

But before anyone could discover what they were, and why they were there, the faces and sounds just melted away, as suddenly and as mysteriously as they had arrived.

then remove itself, hitting her left hand with a sharp blow. The abbé, who had run up the stairs after her, saw it happen and afterwards testified that madame's hand was bruised for two days. That night something hammered on her door so furiously she thought it would break down.

The New Year brought only fresh terrors to the wretched family: louder knocking, more persistent voices. The worst day of all was January 26 when the noise was thunderous. "It sounded as if demons were driving herds of wild cattle through the rooms." Peals of demonic laughter rang through the ancient walls. The family had had enough.

Next day a priest was called in to exorcise the evil spirit and the family saw to it that every religious medallion and relic they possessed was placed in full view. The treatment was effective and at last the hideous uproar ceased.

To the family, who believed they would be forced to abandon their home, the peace that followed came as a blessed relief.

But the ghostly tormentors of Calvados had not quite finished. Shortly after the exorcism, all the religious relics disappeared and could not be found. Then, one morning, as the lady of the house sat writing at her desk an unseen hand dropped them one by one in front of her. There was one short burst of violent sound, then silence.

The haunting of Willington Mill

Phantoms in the Quakers' house

When Joseph Procter and his family moved into the mill house in 1835 they paid little attention to rumours that the place was haunted. The house was a pleasant, comparatively new building set by a tidal stream in the Northumberland village of Willington, in England's rugged north-east. The Procters were a highly-respected, devoutly Quaker family. Mr Procter was said to be a man of high intelligence and common sense, good and kind to his family and employees.

Yet after little more than a decade, the Procters were driven to leave in distress, unable to stand any more of the weird and ghostly happenings that plagued them from the day they first arrived at Willington Mill.

Invisible incline

James Herrmann could not believe his eyes as he brushed his teeth one night in February, 1958. A bottle of medicine slid 18 inches along a perfectly level shelf in front of him. Within days, bottles of shampoo and holy water were uncapping themselves and spilling their contents.

When porcelain figures and a glass bowl were smashed after flying through the air for no apparent reason, Mr Herrmann called the police to the house in Long Island, New York.

A baffled officer reported: "Something weird is happening there."

Only much later were they to learn that their house had been built on the site of an old cottage, that a terrible crime had been committed there years before ... and that a priest had refused to hear the confession of a woman who desperately wanted to unburden her conscience.

So prolific was the haunting of Willington Mill while the Procters lived there that when W T Stead, the writer and ghost hunter, first pieced together the story in the 1890s, there were still 40 people alive who had actually seen the ghosts.

The hauntings began one night in January 1835. A nursemaid was putting the children to bed in the second-floor nursery when she heard heavy footsteps coming from a room immediately above. It was an empty room, never used by the family. At first the girl took little notice, thinking it must be one of the handymen with a job to do. But they went on night after night, getting louder and louder.

Other servants and members of the family also heard them, but when they burst into the room to surprise the "intruder", no one was there. They sprinkled meal over the floor, but there were no footprints.

One morning, as Mr Procter was conducting family prayers, the heavy steps were heard coming down the stairs, past the parlour and along the hall to the front door. The family heard the bar removed, two bolts drawn back and the lock turned.

Mr Procter rushed into the hall to find the door open. The footsteps went on down the path.

Poor Mrs Procter fainted.

It became increasingly difficult to get servants to stay in the house. Only one girl, Mary Young, whom the family had brought with them from their previous home in North Shields, loyally refused to leave.

There was a period when it seemed as though the whole house had been taken over by unseen people. There were sounds of doors opening, people entering and leaving rooms, thumps and blows and laboured breathing, the steps of a child, chairs being moved and rustling sounds as if a woman in a silk dress was hurrying by.

Until a certain Whit Monday, the haunting remained entirely by sound. On that day, Mary Young was washing dishes in the kitchen when she heard footsteps in the passage. Looking up she saw a woman in a lavender silk dress go upstairs and enter one of the rooms. That night the noises in the house were worse than anybody had heard before.

Two of Mrs Procter's sisters arrived for a visit. The first night, sleeping together in the same four-poster bed, they felt it lift up. Their first thought was that a thief had hidden there, so they rang the alarm and the men of the house came running. No one was found.

On another night their bed was violently shaken and the curtains suddenly hoisted up then let down again several times.

They had the curtains removed, but the experience that followed was even more terrifying. They lay awake half-expecting something to happen when a misty, bluish figure of a woman drifted out of the wall and leaned over them in an almost horizontal position. Both women saw the figure quite clearly and lay there, speechless with terror, as it retreated and passed back into the wall.

Neither would sleep in the room another night and one of them even left the house to take lodgings with mill foreman Thomas Mann and his wife.

One dark, moonless night the Manns, their daughter and their visitor were walking past the mill house after paying a call on neighbours. All four saw the luminous figure of what appeared to be a priest in a surplice gliding back and forth at the height of the second floor. It seemed to go through the wall of the house and stand looking out of the window.

The focus of the hauntings seemed to be what the Procters called The Blue Room and in the summer of 1840 they agreed to allow Edward Drury, who specialised in supernatural investigation, to spend a night there. He took with him a friend who refused to get into bed, but dozed off in a chair.

Drury later wrote a letter describing what happened. "I took out my watch to ascertain the time and found that it wanted ten minutes to one," he said. "In taking my eyes off the watch they became riveted upon a closet door, which I distinctly saw open, and saw also the figure of a female attired in greyish garments, with the head inclining downwards and one hand pressed upon the chest as if in pain. It advanced with an apparently cautious step across the floor towards me. Immediately, it approached my friend, who was slumbering, its right hand extended towards him. I then rushed at it . . ."

It was three hours before Drury could recollect anything more. He had been carried downstairs in a state of terror by Mr Procter. Drury had shrieked, "There she is. Keep her off. For God's sake, keep her off!"

The grey lady was seen by others. So were unearthly animals and other startling apparitions. The Procters tried to shield their children from the worst of the haunting, but eventually they became involved. One day a daughter told Mary Young, "There's a lady sitting on the bed in mama's room. She has eyeholes, but no eyes, and she looked hard at me."

Then another daughter reported that in the night a lady had come out of the wall and looked into the mirror ... "She had eyeholes, but no eyes."

Another child saw the figure of a man enter his room, push up the sash window, lower it again, then leave.

In 1847 Joseph Procter decided his family could endure no more. They moved away to another part of Northumberland and were never again troubled by ghosts.

The house was later divided into two dwellings and eventually deteriorated into a slum. People continued to hear and see strange things from time to time. But Willington Mill House was never again to know the terrifying days and nights that afflicted the pious Quaker family.

Knock twice for terror

From the outside, it looked like any house. But the many people called in to investigate the strange happenings there knew differently. Journalists, psychic investigators, even the police, came to the same conclusion: the rented house in the North London suburb of Enfield, occupied by Mrs Peggy Hodgson and her four children, was haunted.

It all began in September 1977, when daughter Janet, then 11, heard a shuffling noise in her bedroom. It sounded like someone walking in loose-fitting slippers. Four loud knocks followed and Janet was horrified to see a heavy chest of drawers sliding away from the wall.

In the days that followed, other objects, including a heavy bed, began to move unaided. A hairbrush flew through the air hitting one of the sons on the head. A policewoman, who was called, saw a chair hurled across a room.

But fright turned to terror as the thing that haunted the house extended its powers and started to influence the children's behaviour. The girls, both in their early teens, spoke in coarse language with the voices of old men. But their lips did not move – the sounds just seemed to come from within them.

It also appeared that the children's lives could be in danger. Mrs

Hodgson's nine-year-old son Billy escaped narrowly when a heavy iron grate flew across his room as he lay in bed. As Janet lay asleep, she would suddenly find herself hurled into the air to wake screaming.

On one occasion the strange force nearly killed Janet. As she lay in bed, a nearby curtain wrapped itself tight around her neck. Hearing her daughter's choking scream. Mrs Hodgson rushed to the room and fought to pull the material from the girl's neck.

The family considered moving away from their home, but for a divorcée with four children such a step was not easy. And the family feared that "the thing" might follow them, for there had been strange voices and happenings when they were on holiday in a caravan at Clacton, Essex.

Many of those who heard of the family's plight were quick to dismiss it all as childish pranks, but not so the experts. Pye Electronics specialists who visited the house were baffled to find that video recording equipment which worked perfectly well outside would not function at all inside.

A policewoman who was called in admitted: "I saw a chair lift into the air. It moved sideways and then floated back to its original position. I have been called to the house several times, but there isn't much the police can do."

Psychical researcher Maurice Grosse tried communicating with "the thing" using a code of one knock for No, two knocks for Yes.

"Did you die in the house?"

Two knocks.

"How many years did you live here?"

Fifty-three knocks.

This was followed by a barrage of knocks. Bewildered, Grosse asked: "Are you having a game with me?"

In answer, a cardboard box filled with cushions leaped off the floor hitting him on the head.

It was Janet's sister Margaret who shed some light on what was happening. One night when she was asleep, she began to bounce up and down in bed and cried: "Go away, you ten little things."

Still asleep, she gave details about them. They included a baby, three girls, two boys and an elderly couple one of whom she identified as Frank Watson, "the man who died in the chair downstairs."

Then frightening, throaty growls began to come from Janet's direction, but investigators were convinced she could not have made the sounds herself.

One day the voice told researcher Grosse that its name was Joe, and on another day, Bill Hobbs. He said he came from Durant's Park graveyard.

Hobbs, whose voice was being taped, told them: "I am 72 years old and I have come here to see my family. But they are not here now."

The hauntings lasted three years, and then ended, never to resume.

The terrified Hodgson family, hosts to a poltergeist.

The smiling spectre

The ghost of a tall woman, dressed in grey, sometimes mingles with tourists looking over Chambercombe Manor, near the North Devon holiday resort of Ilfracombe. She was seen as recently as 1976, and is usually reported with a smile on her face.

Which is surprising, for the story of her life and death is far from happy.

Alexander Oatway was one of the notorious West Country ship wreckers of 400 years ago. On stormy nights, he would leave his fireside at Chambercombe and hurry to the shore carrying a powerful lantern, which he used as a beacon to lure trusting ships seeking safe harbour on to the rocks, where he and his friends plundered them.

One wild night his son William followed him to the beach. The lantern trick worked yet again, but a young Spanish girl survived the wreck. William rescued her, took her home and fell in love. The couple married, and settled on Lundy Island, in the Bristol Channel, leaving Alexander to his deadly hobby. They had a daughter, Kate.

Nearly 20 years later, William heard that his old home was vacant, and decided to move back to it. The rent was high, but he could afford it. The household bills were lightened when Kate fell in love with an Irish sea captain called Wallace. He took her home to Dublin as his bride.

Years passed. Then one winter's night a vicious storm blew up. William hurried down to the beach below Chambercombe Manor after spotting a ship in trouble. He found a woman lying on the rocks, disfigured after being battered by the sea. He carried her home, but she died during the night.

As he checked her belongings, William fell to temptation. The woman was carrying a belt with enough money and jewellery to enable him to buy his beloved manor house outright. Two days later, a man from the Admiralty called, making inquiries about a missing passenger from the wrecked ship. William said he knew nothing about it. Then the visitor mentioned the name of the missing woman – Mrs Katherine Wallace.

William and his wife were devastated. They had stolen from their own dead daughter, her face unrecognisable because of the impact of the rocks. Filled with remorse, they walled her body in a secret room and moved away.

Their guilty secret was revealed 150 years later. In 1865 a farmer living in the house was busy re-thatching the roof when he looked down, and saw a skeleton lying on a cramped bed in a room he never knew existed. The walls were taken down, and the bones buried in a pauper's grave at Ilfracombe. But Kate's ghost still haunts her former home.

Answer to an old man's prayer

The young family were happy moving into their new home until the night terror filled their lives. The family, known only as Smith, had started to renovate their 90-year-old wood-frame home in Rochester, New Hampshire. Work had gone well until Mr. Smith tore out an old cast-iron bathtub and put it in another room.

From then on, their lives became hell. That very night came strange sounds and moaning. Said Smith: "I heard footsteps on the stairs and shuffling in the hallway. There was a pounding on the walls and doors slammed shut by themselves." The next night Smith's two daughters were terrorised. The eldest, aged 14, woke up in the night to feel strong gripping hands pushing her by the shoulders into the bed.

She said: "I was terrified. I saw a big, grey-haired man standing in the bathroom doorway. He was wearing a full-length robe, but I couldn't see his features. He just stood there in the doorway – then vanished."

A few nights later, Smith's younger girl, aged two, ran screaming and trembling into her parents room. She huddled in her mother's arms shouting: "Go away, go away. Tell the man to go away."

At first the Smiths thought the girls were having nightmares but the terror returned night after night. They were so scared they slept together in the one room.

In desperation, the family turned to ghost hunter, Norman Gauthier. President of New Hampshire's Society for Psychic Research, Gauthier brought along a priest and a medium.

Both priest and medium agreed there was a ghost in the house, and its spirits came from the bathroom. There, the medium made contact.

"I could see him fully undressed in the tub. He was depressed and lonely. I felt he had a massive brain haemorrhage or a stroke. The old man wanted to know why the Smiths were living in his house and why his bathtub had been removed."

The medium spoke to the spirit and found out that the old man's wife, Althea, had died three years before him.

The medium told him "You are dead. It was a stroke ... calm down. You can see Althea, but you must realise you are dead. You must accept it."

The medium turned to Gauthier and the priest and said: "The old man can't accept he is dead and that his wife has gone."

Then the medium turned to the shaken Smith family. "You won't have any more trouble. The old man has left. He has just walked through the door."

Chapter six

MYSTERIES OF THE MIND

The human mind is capable of many things, perhaps none more
peculiar than the ability to prophesy future events or to show how it
can be more powerful than everyday matter. Strange events take
place that provide no logical explanation for their occurrence.
Exactly how does Uri Geller bend spoons? How did Mother Shipton
predict, among other things, the execution of Charles I? These and
other mysterious moments are chronicled in the following pages.

Joan Grant

Historical novelist Joan Grant believes that she has been on this earth at least forty times and that her 'far memory' of past lives has provided her with material for her books.

A striking woman, beautiful in her youth, she says that in previous lives she has been an Italian minstrel, a French prostitute, a witch, a Red Indian and an Egyptian ruler-priest. She claims she can remember each one of her deaths, and the even more painful experience of being reborn. Her most distant memories are of cave paintings, taking her back in time thousands of years.

Joan Grant's most famous book, *Winged Pharaoh*, published in 1937, translated into fourteen languages and still in print, was written (as were her other seven historical novels) without research. She claims it is the story of her own past life as Sekeeta, a Pharaoh's daughter who became a ruler-priest.

Describing her technique for recalling past existences, she says she visualizes time as a vast wheel with herself at the centre. Gazing along the radius in any direction, towards the rim, she picks up the distant echo of what she once was. Sometimes the details come flooding back in dreams, at other times through psychometry, holding something of significance in her hand.

As far as this present life is concerned she came into the world on April 12, 1907, as the daughter of wealthy parents. Her father, Jack Marshall, was a brilliant scholar who became the world's greatest expert on British mosquitoes. He was an atheist, and she approved of him. Her mother, Blanche, she thought, was a mistake.

She was conceived in the Blue Grotto at Capri and remembers the resentment she felt at finding herself trapped in the body of a baby again. She had glimpses of her other lives as a small child and told stories about who she had been before she was Joan. Nobody believed her. Holidays on the long, flat beaches of Hayling Island stirred the first latent memories. Once she knew she had chased along 'a hotter, brighter shore'. She remembered herself as a Greek boy, training to be a runner, and knew the feel of his muscles and the ache in them when he had run too hard. Her family lived in a fine Edwardian house in Primrose Hill Road, London, and in her autobiography *Time out of Mind* she admits that as a schoolgirl she longed to be a unit in a crocodile, safe and ordinary, but she had war dreams that were so vivid, so real, that the stench and smell of death made her sick. For weeks she tried to keep herself from sleeping by sitting on the cold lino at the top of the stairs and pulling hairs out one by one.

Close to her scientist father, she almost convinced herself that peering through microscopes was her vocation in life. Then the famous writer H. G. Wells came to stay. He was the first, and for a long time the only, person in whom she confided. She told him about the three-dimensional, secret part of her life and he advised her, 'Keep it to yourself, Joan, until you are strong enough to bear being laughed at by fools. But never let yourself forget it, and when you are ready, write what you know about . . . it is important that you become a writer.'

Joan led the life of a gay young thing, going to hunt balls and winning cups at golf, but there was always the other self. The sight of a group of nuns in their flapping black habits would send her mind back to some terror that had happened in the sixteenth century. She would turn her eyes away and hurry in the opposite direction.

She fell in and out of love many times. Her first engagement was broken because her fiancé's parents thought she was talking rubbish when she told them about the past lives which often as she grew older came to her in the form of vivid dreams. She met her second fiancé, Esmond, on a ski-ing holiday. They felt they had met before and became engaged within twenty-four hours. They planned to marry after he had been on a business trip to France. He spent the last night before leaving for the Continent at her home, but as she saw him walk away from her down a long corridor to his bedroom she had a presentiment that she would never see him again. She was tragically right. Just before he was due to return to England, he died in a shooting accident.

Some time after, she had a dream in which she heard a voice say quite distinctly, 'Go to Leslie.' At the time she did not know what it meant, but eventually she met and married Leslie Grant, who understood and was sympathetic towards her psychic experiences. He undertook the task of writing down her far-memory dreams from dictation, so that they were recorded from the minute she woke up.

Once in the British Museum she stood looking at some ancient sculpture — a winged figure and a winged, human-headed bull from the palace of King Sargon II of Assyria, dated 721 B.C. Gradually a scene took shape before her eyes. She was a soldier, standing at the doorway of the palace at the head of a flight of steps. From the foot of the steps stretched an avenue of crouching winged bulls with a double row of palm trees behind them. Along the avenue came a procession of soldiers returning from war, bringing their prisoners and plunder with them. In one bullock cart she saw a captured sacred golden cow adorned with a jewelled necklace. Suddenly there were great cries of 'Hathor the Mighty! Hathor the Magnificent!' and the king was brought from within the cool interior of the palace on a golden litter. She saw that his black hair and beard were elaborately curled, his limbs cluttered with jewels, his nails painted scarlet. The cruelty of the soldiers towards their captives became almost too much for her to bear, when suddenly a guide came round the corner with a conducted party and broke into her dream. Joan Grant had, it seems, several lives in Egypt, not always as a woman. At one time she was a man called Ra-ab Hotep, whose story she used in two books, *Eye of Horus* and *Lord of the Horizon*. Later she was a male contemporary of Rameses II. Several of her other incarnations were equally colourful. In the middle ages she was a witch, burnt at the stake for heresy; in the sixteenth century she became a singer with a group of strolling players wandering through Italy; and in England she lived the life of a wealthy Victorian girl until she broke her back in a fall from a horse.

But it was in her life as Sekeeta, the priest-ruler of First Dynasty Egypt, about 3000 B.C., that she found the most vivid identification.

In September 1936 she was staying with an old lady called Daisy Sartorius, a friend of the family, when one night she was given a turquoise blue scarab. Holding it to her forehead, she declared it was 'warm and lively' though she herself was shivering with cold. For the next hour she slipped into another existence and described what she was seeing. 'How a girl called Sekeeta was taken from the temple of Atet to undergo the ordeal of initiation, during which she must leave her body for four days and four nights, returning at the end of the fourth day to dictate to a scribe what she had experienced.' The degree of identification deepened until she heard a faraway voice calling 'Joan, Joan' and opened her eyes to find her husband leaning over her, briskly rubbing the hand from which he had removed the scarab. Night after night she returned to her old life as Sekeeta, first as a child of three playing beside a blue pool with little scarlet fishes, later as a young girl in love, then as the priest-ruler, the 'winged pharaoh'. The most astonishing thing she discovered was that in that existence Daisy Sartorius had been her mother. That, she felt, accounted for the strong love that had grown up between them.

A similar connection was also found between a previous life and her third husband, physician and psychiatrist Denys Kelsey. They met in 1958 and found they had an immediate rapport. Joan was certain they had been together before, not once but twice. When she was a young Roman matron she took him into her house as a physician, fell in love with him and when he did not respond, ordered him to cut her wrists. Later, she says, they shared a life together in eighteenth-century England as man and wife.

After their present-day marriage they worked together as a team at their home in Pangbourne, Berkshire. Joan had gained a great deal of psychiatric experience during the war. Now, with Dr Kelsey, she offered help to many people with a unique form of psychotherapy which took into account past lives. Joan believed profoundly that events in previous existences could have an effect on the present. She found she herself, for example, was unable to summon up the courage to touch a slow worm, though she knew there was no danger. In two previous incarnations, she says, she had died from snake bite.

Asked in a BBC interview which period she would choose if she was given the option, she said immediately it would be the First Dynasty of ancient Egypt. And why? 'I think that the ethics of that benign civilization gave everyone a better chance of being happy than he is likely to be given today.

A. J. Stewart

Ever since she was a child Ada F. Kay, successful playwright and BBC scriptwriter, had been haunted by the feeling that she was somebody else. Eerie shifts of consciousness, glimpses in the mirror of another face, scenes that receded into another century before her eyes, tormented and bewitched her, brought her near to breakdown and convinced her she had lived once before.

Who that person was she had only fleeting intimations. But one night in August 1967, while staying at a house in Jedburgh, the ancient town on the borders of England and Scotland, she learned what she believed was the truth. Her other self was James IV, the Scottish king who was killed at the Battle of Flodden in 1513 when the English forces massacred the Scots.

That night in Jedburgh she had hardly shut her eyes when with an almost audible click of consciousness she found herself on what seemed to be a sixteenth-century battlefield. Just a few yards away was a cluster of horsemen she knew to be English. One was mounted on a white charger, bearing a battle standard. There was an explosion in her head. Next minute:

I seemed to be lying on my back staring up at a tunnel of staves and blades . . . beyond them hands and merciless faces of men intent on killing me. My left arm I raised to cover my head to ward off the blows. All the world of hate was concentrated on me at that moment, and nobody was stopping it. I howled a howl of pure animal terror as the blades thrust down upon me.

The howls she let out brought her host running from another room to find his guest alone but deeply shocked.

She told him everything about her childhood experiences, her strange, passionate love for Scotland and her gradual realization as she researched material for a play about James IV that he might be her other self.

Next day he took her to Flodden, only a few miles from Jedburgh, and she almost fainted as she stood on the hillock where James's blood had been spilled. Suddenly, she was sure. The traumatic experiences the night before and at Flodden convinced her that she had been James IV in a previous life.

Ada F. Kay had what she called 'an antique memory' from earliest childhood. She was born on March 5, 1929, at Tottington in Lancashire. Her father, Ernest Kay, was a schoolmaster with a special interest in history. One of her first recollections was of seeing herself as a young prince being hauled by the hand through many stone-floored chambers and then stood on a chair to be presented by the king to his lords in council. Later she saw herself as a boy of fifteen clad in scarlet with a gold shoulder chain and riding out through a gateway at the head of a small band of horsemen while the guard rang out a salute with pike butts on cobbles. Her parents did not understand the fantastic stories she tried to tell them.

The family moved to Thornton Cleveleys on the Lancashire coast in January 1932 and Ada's antique memories went with her. She always felt she was Scottish and had a great desire to return to the North. One day waiting for a train with her parents on a station platform she saw a poster with a picture of Stirling Castle. She felt sick with excitement, forgot the new doll she had been given and tried to wish herself inside the castle gates and into another world.

During her early teens she was comparatively free from what she wryly calls 'back head interference', for her energy was being channelled into what she had a great talent for — writing. Certain things brought tingling memories. The sight of hawks or falcons reminded her of wide blue skies and open fells, and the appearance of her mother in a striking black and white evening dress brought a pang of nostalgia — were they not her royal colours?

When she was eighteen instead of going to university she opted to join the ATS and found herself stationed at Queen's Camp, Guildford. There was a strong Scottish contingent there with which she identified completely. She felt their separateness, their foreign quality and when they trooped off back to Scotland singing, 'We're no awa' tae bide awa' she felt like going with them. Only a short time later, to her delight, she was posted to Edinburgh.

As the train crossed the Tweed and the border she felt herself jolted out of a deep sleep by the thought 'I am back in Scotland.' The first time she saw Edinburgh in mist and morning rain she laughed with joy. She had been waiting eighteen years for this.

She loved the Army and her posting seemed like a gift from the gods. Only three weeks after she had arrived her parents travelled from England to see her and she was persuaded into taking them to see some of the historic sights. Much against her will, she escorted them to Edinburgh Castle along with hundreds of other tourists. Suddenly she found herself crammed into the tower room which contained Scotland's royal regalia. Her link with the crown on its velvet cushion seemed to be so intensely personal and strong that she had to look away. She gazed instead at the royal sword until she saw it trickling with blood. Hoping frantically she would not fall, she pulled herself together and the red colour cleared from her eyes. Her mother's words 'Are you all right, Ada?' seemed to come from a great distance.

Her health began to deteriorate soon afterwards and she suffered deep depressions. She continually had glimpses of Edinburgh as it was in the sixteenth century; her boundary on the north side of Edinburgh was Princes Street, beyond that she knew it was a superb place to hunt wildfowl, a marshland alive with bittern and glinting with small lochs. She took walks through the narrow alleyways of old Edinburgh searching for her past. 'I was not seeking ghosts but my own reality,' she wrote in her autobiography. One evening, from the Lawnmarket, she saw an open door, a stone spiral stair dimly lit by the pool of light cast by a gas lamp on a wall bracket. She felt she was expected, that people were waiting to greet her for supper, her host appeared, bowed low in salute and started to lead her up the stairs — then it all disappeared. Next day she tried to find the house again. But it had vanished.

Her ghosts were beginning to intrude on her Army life. From her window she could see ships in the Forth heading for Rosyth Naval Dockyard, but they were huge, black-timbered sailing ships and she knew they belonged to another age. These fleeting impressions and haunting experiences became too much for her. She asked to see the Army psychiatrist. Deciding that the balance of her mind was disturbed and she was heading for a breakdown, the Medical Board decided she had better go home. Her discharge from the Army, and therefore from Scotland, was a shock so great it made her physically sick.

As the train taking her back to England sped through the night she saw her reflection in the window. Her face looked older, narrower and gaunt, like her own but more masculine. It seemed to have a small circlet above it which flashed with points of sapphire blue light. She took it to be an optical illusion.

When she got home she burst into tears, went straight to bed and slept for three days and three nights. Picking up the threads of life again was not easy. But she was only twenty, red-haired and attractive. She began to write plays. She was prolific and undaunted by criticism. Soon her work was good enough to take her into the world of professional theatre. Her first real success, *Cardboard Castle*, was written within a week.

Ada F. Kay went to London in 1954 with £10 in cash and two

suitcases, and set out to make herself into a first-class playwright. She was asked to join the BBC's script-writing team. Her play *The Man from Thermopylae*, which was first produced with Alec Clunes and Lionel Jeffries in the cast in 1956, was acclaimed a critical success.

She met and married Peter Stewart, an architect who was able to give her a priceless wedding present — a Scottish name. The marriage was made difficult by her frequent yearning for Scotland. They were happiest when both had plenty of work to do and Peter was at the drawing board while she was at the typewriter. He suggested they bought a house in Hampstead, hoping to give her roots in England.

In 1959, script-writing took her back to Glasgow, her first significant return since her discharge from the ATS. Suddenly realizing how little she knew of Scottish history, she had to take a crash course and in the pages of an old book discovered James IV with red hair like her own and a face strangely familiar. From then on the very name of Flodden sent a shiver down her spine.

Over the next few years she only visited England for necessary business arrangements, discussion of plays and BBC script conferences. Outwardly she was a successful woman who appeared at smart literary parties and wrote excellent plays. Inwardly she was full of doubts and fears as to who she really was. Once, coming out of the bathroom, she caught a glimpse in a mirror of a figure with red hair wearing a black and white surcoat over a suit of armour.

By 1963 she rarely left Edinburgh except to spend holidays on the Isle of Arran and hardly ever saw her parents. When she had been married for eight years she and Peter agreed on a divorce. For six of those years she had lived apart from him in Scotland.

Plays were still being demanded from her, and in January 1966 she decided to write one about James IV, hoping perhaps to lay a ghost. She felt the whole period covering the last three decades of the fifteenth century and the first decade of the sixteenth was her own, and by using it as a background she could express her feelings about Scotland's greatness.

The writing only emphasized the problem she was having in trying to disentangle James's personality from her own. She had begun to dress in a long black sweater and black tights with a gold belt round her waist. When she was given a bound copy of James IV's collected letters she seemed to be drawn even deeper into his personality. Then came the traumatic night in Jedburgh.

Preferring now to be known as A. J. Stewart, she has written a book about James which makes him come alive on the page. Though tending to have fits of depression each year when the anniversary of his death comes round, she leads a perfectly well-adjusted life, as writer Ian Wilson found when he visited her at her flat in Edinburgh in 1978.

Below natural red hair and striking features, A.J., as she likes to be known, was dressed in black, the costume plain except for a white collar and cuffs and at her throat a neat gold brooch emblazoned with a black falcon. Black shoes, black stockings . . . her flat lined with drawings and prints of James and personalities at his court.

He found her to be a forceful and engaging personality who demonstrates how like the James portraits she is.

Still, 'Of one thing I am certain,' wrote A. J. Stewart. 'Had I grown up in a culture which allowed the possibility that man has more lives than one, I should have been spared much suffering.'

Bridey Murphy

There was nothing about Mrs Virginia Tighe, a trim, smart young American housewife who lived in Pueblo, Colorado, to suggest she held a key to the past. She and her husband, Rex, were part of the bright, contemporary social scene and filled their lives with bridge parties, cocktails and club dances. Under hypnosis, however, Mrs Tighe became someone quite different — a little girl who lived in nineteenth-century Ireland and whose name was Bridey Murphy.

The story of Bridey Murphy is one of the most celebrated in the records of regression hypnosis, a technique which, it is claimed, can sometimes take the subject so far back in time that previous lives are revealed.

It all began on the night of November 29, 1952.

Colorado businessman and amateur hypnotist Morey Bernstein had discovered that Virginia Tighe was a remarkably good subject. She had the ability to slip easily into a very deep trance. He asked if she would co-operate in an experiment in which he would take her back to infancy, then perhaps beyond. He had not attempted this before.

There was a feeling of suppressed excitement when she arrived at his home that night. He made her comfortable in a reclining position on a couch, lit a candle and turned off all the lights, with the exception of one lamp.

She drifted easily back through the years, reliving the memory of childhood scenes, until she was only one year old. Bernstein told her that her mind could go even further back to different scenes, in some other time. 'What do you see?' he asked her gently.

He leaned forward, holding his breath, as a child's voice with a soft Irish accent said: 'I scratched the paint off all my bed. Jus' painted it, 'n' made it pretty. It was a metal bed, and I scratched the paint off it. Dug my nails on every post and just ruined it. Was jus' terrible.'

'Why did you do that?'

'Don't know. I was just mad. Got an awful spanking.'

Her name, she told him, was Bridget or Bridey Murphy and she was four years old, had red hair and lived in a house in Cork . . . she had a brother called Duncan . . . and her father's name was Duncan too. . . .

Bridey Murphy's story slowly came together in a number of sessions in which 29-year-old Virginia Tighe slipped back into a life and character so different from her own. She had been born, she said, in Cork on December 20, 1798. She was the daughter of Duncan and Kathleen Murphy, both Protestants. Her father was a barrister in Cork and they lived in a white wooden house called The Meadows on the outskirts of town. She had a brother, Duncan, who was two years older than herself.

When she was fifteen she went to a day school run by a lady called Mrs Strayne. Asked what she had been taught at school, Bridey answered, 'Oh, to be a lady . . . just house things . . . and proper things.' Her brother married Mrs Strayne's daughter, Aime. In 1818 Bridey met a lawyer from Belfast called Sean Brian MacCarthy. His father was also a barrister and the families appeared pleased with the match, though she did not like him when she accepted his proposal. 'I just went with him . . . 'twas taken for granted, I think.'

There were certain difficulties from the outset. 'Brian', as she preferred to call him, was a Catholic, so after being married in Cork (to please her family) she had to go through another ceremony in Belfast, to please her husband. They made the journey north in a horse and carriage, and Bridey described the places they passed through.

She did not enjoy living in Belfast as much as in Cork, but seemed happy enough with Brian, and proud of the fact that he taught at Queen's University. They attended St Theresa's Church, where the priest was Father John Gorman, but she was not allowed to take communion or confession. Bridey shopped for provisions with a grocer named Farr, bought fruit and vegetables at Carrington's and blouses and camisoles at Caden House. She never had children, though she enjoyed visits to friends' houses and occasional trips to the sea. She was interested in Irish mythology, knew some Irish songs and was a neat dancer of Irish jigs. At the end of one sitting Mrs Tighe, not quite fully conscious, danced round the room.

Towards the end of her life she had a fall. Her death came quietly and without pain while her husband was at church one Sunday. She remembered that they had played the uillean pipes at her funeral. She also told how she watched her burial, describing the state of being after death. Somehow she was reborn in America, but could not explain how that had happened.

Morey Bernstein finished his sessions with Bridey Murphy in October 1953 and three years later published his best-selling book of the case, *The Search for Bridey Murphy*. In it his subject was given the pseudonym Ruth Simmons.

From the moment Bridey's story appeared in print there was a scramble to see who could be first to check the facts. Investigators and reporters swarmed over to Ireland, burrowing through records, talking to aged inhabitants and checking maps.

Some facts could not be checked. There was no possibility, for instance, of confirming the dates of marriages and deaths in Cork, as no records were kept there until 1864. On the negative side, no information could be unearthed about the wooden house called The Meadows, St Theresa's Church or Father Gorman. On the positive side, she gave an accurate description of the Antrim coastline and of the journey from Cork to Belfast. It was discovered that the shops she mentioned had all existed and the coins she mentioned in her shopping transactions had all belonged to that period. Bridey had said that uillean pipes had been played at her funeral, and it was indeed found to have been the custom because of their soft tone.

Despite certain discrepancies there was no doubt that Bridey's story gave a remarkably detailed account of the life of a fairly privileged

Dorothy Eady

For many years tourists visiting the ancient temple at Abydos on the banks of the Nile would see an elderly English woman who looked as if she belonged there. Her name was Dorothy Eady, but she only answered to Um-Seti, convinced that she was really an Egyptian priestess. She was born in 1903 into a wealthy South London family and, as a child, fell down a flight of stairs. Although she was believed dead she made a dramatic recovery and was nursed back to health. Dorothy never seemed the same child again, frequently asking to be 'taken home'. A few years later while visiting the Egyptian galleries of a museum, she ran wild, believing these to be her people and went on to study the ancient Egyptians. She married an Egyptian and went to Egypt to make her home. Their only child was named Seti and from then she called herself Um-Seti – mother of Seti. Her first pilgrimage to Abydos, the site of Seti I's temple and the tomb of Osiris was in 1952. Two years later she returned there to live for the rest of her life as she felt an overwhelming sense of place. In 1973 she asked the temple curators if she could be buried in the grounds of the temple when she died. She had convinced even them that her claim was far from ordinary. They gave their permission.

member of the professional class in nineteenth-century Ireland. It was full of the sort of trivial, intimate information that is seldom recorded in books but has to be experienced.

Mrs Tighe emphatically denied that she had ever visited Ireland or had much to do with Irish people. But one interesting fact emerged after the publication of Bernstein's book. She had been born in Maddison, Wisconsin, where she lived with her mother and father until she was three years old — and both parents were part Irish. After that she was brought up in Chicago by a Norwegian uncle and his wife who claimed Irish blood somewhere in the family. Could she have stored knowledge she heard as such a small child? Even that does not seem enough to explain how she came to have been Bridey Murphy or how without any dramatic talent she could so enter her personality as to make her seem a real person.

Jane Evans

One of the most famous and most widely believed of all reincarnation claims is that concerning Cardiff housewife Jane Evans, who took part in an experiment in hypnosis only to find herself giving details of her past lives, including that as a twelfth-century Jewess in York.

Mrs Evans was taken back in time by a technique called 'regression' — in which the memory layers are peeled off like onion skins — by hypnotherapist Arnall Bloxham, and her story became one of the highlights of the recorded hypnosis sessions known as 'the Bloxham tapes'.

Millions saw her on television in a programme introduced by Magnus Magnusson in 1976. Bloxham had by then achieved 400 regressions with various subjects, but Jane Evans produced the most intensely dramatic results. Her scream of sheer terror as she met her death at the hands of the mob in an historic massacre seemed to most people to have come right from the heart.

Few details of Jane Evans' life were revealed apart from the fact that she was born in 1939, had received an ordinary high-school education, then went on to secretarial college. After her marriage she devoted her life to her family and was said at no time to have studied history in the depth that would have been needed for her to fake her regressions.

Under Arnall Bloxham's guidance she appeared to live again in six past existences. First she was a Roman matron called Livonia living in occupied Britain in the fourth century A.D. Her fate was entwined with that of the Roman legate (and later Emperor) Constantius, his wife Helena and their son Constantine, who would himself one day become Roman emperor. Livonia was married to Titus, Constantine's tutor, and they lived well until their conversion to Christianity. Under hypnosis she described her last hours as she ran through streets where Christian houses were burning until she and her husband seemed to come to a violent end. Experts on Roman Britain said that as Livonia she seemed to know facts that only Roman historians would have at their fingertips. They thought a great deal of research would have to be done by anyone inventing such a story.

In another life she was Alison, a beautiful young servant in the house of the fifteenth-century merchant prince Jacques Coeur. She described with great accuracy his great château in the Loire Valley with its magnificent courtyard and romantic architecture. She showed a detailed knowledge of the history of France and the life of the time. As far as the ordinary reader was concerned Jacques Coeur was, it had to be admitted, historically little known, but sceptics pointed out she could have got a great deal of her information from a work of fiction based on his life and used it unknowingly.

Briefly, it seemed, she was also Anna, maid of honour to the Spanish Infanta, Catherine of Aragon. She accompanied her to England in the year 1501 for her marriage to Prince Arthur, eldest son of Henry VII. Another life saw her as Anne Tasker, a London sewing maid in Queen Anne's time at the turn of the 17th and 18th centuries. Her last incarnation before her present life was as Sister Grace, a member of an enclosed order of nuns in Des Moines, Iowa. For all these lives she showed a knowledge of contemporary events that one would not expect a twentieth-century Welsh housewife to have.

Most intriguing of all was the second life in her cycle of reincarnation — the life she supposedly entered some centuries after she had lived as the Roman, Livonia. It was featured in Jeffrey Iverson's programme about the Bloxham tapes on British television, when hypnosis took her back to twelfth-century York and the Jewish massacre that took place in 1190.

She said her name was Rebecca and she was the wife of a wealthy Jewish merchant in the city. She lived a luxurious and comfortable life until a bitter wave of anti-Semitism engulfed and destroyed everything she had known. She described being pursued with other Jewish families through the narrow, winding streets of York, hiding with her children in the crypt of a church, then being discovered and put to death. Her terror when the murderers entered the crypt was so real that listeners felt they were there at her actual moment of death.

The massacre of the Jews in York, while a known historical fact, is not an episode given at great length in popular history books, but Professor Barrie Dobson of York University, a leading expert on

Jewish history, commented that Mrs Evans's story was true to what was known of the events.

On the tapes the Jewess, Rebecca, could not give the name of the church where she hid with her family but said it was outside the gates of the city, close to Coppergate and within sight and earshot of York Castle. After listening to her Professor Dobson felt sure this had to be St Mary's Church in Castlegate, though St Mary's did not, as far as he knew, have a crypt. Then in September 1975, after Jane Evans had put her chilling memories on tape but before the TV programme was relayed, workmen undertaking repairs at St Mary's made a discovery. Under the chancel they found what seemed to have been an ancient crypt, but thinking it of no importance they covered it over before it could be examined by archaeologists.

At the time she was working on the tapes with Bloxham, Jane Evans said she had been to Yorkshire but never to the city of York itself. Her knowledge of history, she said, was the same as any schoolgirl's. She enjoyed reading but had never read history books or even books of historical fiction that contained such information. She knew that Jews had been persecuted all over the world but had never heard of this particular massacre in York. 'The only explanation I can give is that I must have had previous lives,' said the Welsh housewife.

Geraldine Cummins

Geraldine Cummins, a tiny Irishwoman from County Cork, sat at her desk in the 1920s and wrote a vidid, compelling addition to the New Testament. Her words, biblical in style, continued the story of Paul, telling how slaves tried to murder Barnabas, his companion of the great missionary journeys, and giving an utterly convincing picture of the political and religious turmoil of the Middle East after the death of Christ.

She was not writing fiction. The book she published, *The Scripts of Cleophas*, had been dictated to her, she claimed, by someone who had lived in biblical times and knew the course of early Christian history. The communicator — said to be an agent or messenger from the long-dead Cleophas of the title — poured out detailed information about the period between the death of Jesus and Paul's departure for Athens, filling in periods that had always been considered a closed book by religious scholars.

The scripts aroused great curiosity among churchmen. Many had doubts about the origin of the material. Some considered she had been sacrilegious in daring to add to Holy Scripture. But others were impressed — especially when they found she had no knowledge of the Greek, Latin or Hebrew that would have been necessary had she obtained her material simply through research.

Geraldine Cummins was in fact considered by many in psychic circles to be the greatest automatic writer this century. She produced a staggering amount of work from 'the spirit world'. The words dictated by the messenger of Cleophas were taken down at the rate of 1,500 words an hour. She eventually had notes totalling over one million words from which she wrote her best-seller. A small audience of distinguished churchmen, scholars and psychical investigators gathered in the Bishop of Kensington's study. They clustered round watching with amazement as she took up a pencil and started to write at a tremendous speed. Pages of the Cleophas scripts were being taken down before their eyes.

Afterwards a statement was issued. Scholars and churchmen admitted there was a great deal in the scripts which 'considering the life and mentality of the intermediary, Miss Cummins, appears quite inexplicable on the supposition of human authority.' The Bishop of London's examining chaplain, Dr W. E. Oesterley, went even further. He described the scripts as being 'wonderfully evidential'.

Geraldine Cummins herself had quite different feelings about the book she produced. 'I am not proud of the Cleophas series,' she wrote. 'They are not of me. They are foreign in character to my Celtic, racial self.' She did not like St Paul anyway because of his reactionary attitude towards women. 'Why then was I compelled against my will and prejudice to write about him in such glowing terms?'

She was born in 1890 in the county of Cork, one of eleven children of the Professor of Medicine at Cork University. A precocious Spiritualist, she was introduced to the psychic world by her father's coachman at the age of five. She did nothing much about it. Her literary talent, which blossomed at an early age, took up most of her time. She was only twenty-two when one of the first plays she collaborated on was performed at Dublin's famous Abbey Theatre. She wrote short stories for London's *Pall Mall Gazette* and turned out two successful novels, all by perfectly normal means.

Her psychic development came later, after meeting Helen Dowden, a famous medium and automatic writer, in Paris in June 1914. The two women became close friends, and under Helen Dowden's guidance Geraldine began experimenting with spirit communications, then tried her hand at automatic writing. She had to work hard. At first she did not seem to have a great deal of psychic aptitude, and her attitude to her work was always that of a researcher, cool and appraising. By the mid-1920s, however, she was producing automatic scripts at an astonishing rate.

Sitting alone in a room with nothing more than a pad of notepaper and a pencil, over the years she wrote fifteen books transmitted from 'the other world'. She often produced private communications by the same method, and those they were intended for always expressed astonishment at the amount of significant and convincing detail. Some of her sitters were very famous. Canadian prime minister Mackenzie King usually tried to see her on his visits to London. She was living in a house in Chelsea, but she was often smuggled into the hotel where he was staying in order to avoid attention from the Press. Once she conducted a séance sitting on his bed while he sat propped up with pillows after a bout of 'flu. At another séance, in 1948, she acted as intermediary for the former American President Franklin D. Roosevelt, who had died in 1945. He warned the Canadian premier of a bloody and terrible war in Korea and told him of General de Gaulle's coming to power as President of France in 1958.

Geraldine Cummins was a close friend of Rosamund Lehmann, the novelist, and of the two Irish writers Violet Martin of Ross — whose pseudonym was Martin Ross — and Edith Somerville, who together wrote the immensely popular stories about the Irish R.M. Everyone thought their collaboration was at an end when Violet Martin died, but she continued to contribute, unknown to the world at large, through the hand of the medium. The publishers were forced to agree to her name appearing with Edith's on works written after her death.

But it was not until 1959, when Geraldine was sixty-nine, that she achieved the high point of her mediumship with what became known as the Cummins-Willett scripts. Eventually published in 1965 in her last book *Swan on a Black Sea* they proved to be an astonishing series of communications from a dead mother to her sceptical son.

Geraldine was on holiday in Bantry Bay in the summer of 1957 when she received a letter from W. H. Salter, honorary secretary of the Psychical Research Society. He said he thought he had a case that would interest her. A member of the SPR had lost his mother some months ago and wanted to give her the opportunity of sending him a message. Salter told Geraldine he proposed to restrict the information given to her in order to make any success she had the more striking. He only told her that the member of the SPR referred to was Major Henry Tennant. She did not know him. His mother, the late Mrs Charles Coombe Tennant, was a formidable, fascinating woman, Britain's first woman delegate to the League of Nations, a society hostess, art patron and magistrate. She had also been, unknown to most people, a skilled medium working under the name Winifred Willett.

The crucial question was, did Geraldine Cummins know her fellow-medium's true identity? She shut herself away in a quiet room and five days after being given Major Tennant's name received the first script from his mother: 'There comes to me from the earth such a feeling of depression, of worrying, of anxiety, of fear of death and all derived from non belief . . . if they could but realize half the glory, even a fragment of the peace of this life I now experience.'

She worked, alone, for two years until forty scripts had been completed by November 23, 1959. They were full of detail about names, people, places, experiences and events in the Tennant family. It emerged eventually that part of the material she had taken down was 'too correct about private affairs to be published'. Mrs Willett's sceptical son found only one incorrect name and wrote to the medium, 'The more I study these scripts, the more deeply I am impressed by them.'

As to whether Geraldine Cummins knew of the link between Mrs Willett and Mrs Coombe Tennant before she began — the question was dismissed as irrelevant in view of the mass of detail in the scripts. How could she, people asked, produce such intimate information without contact?

Geraldine Cummins regarded the scripts as the most important work of her life. According to an article in *Psychic News*, she felt she was at last provided with the irrefutable evidence she demanded to satisfy her of survival after death.

She went to find out the truth in September 1969, dying in her own County Cork. She was seventy-nine.

Rosemary Brown

One dull afternoon in 1964 Rosemary Brown, a middle-aged housewife living in a Victorian terraced house in Balham, South London, sat down at her piano to play a simple tune. She had bought the instrument second-hand, taken a few lessons and could just about manage a few hymns and popular ballads. Suddenly her hands were flying over the keys, music she had never heard before was filling the air. She had a feeling of elation, of intense pleasure in the beauty of the sound. Looking up, she saw a striking figure standing beside her. It was the virtuoso Hungarian pianist and composer Franz Liszt, who had died in 1886.

That afternoon Liszt did not say a word to her. But he returned. 'He took over my hands like a pair of gloves,' was how she described her experience. The first few visits were dream-like, though she was fully conscious. Then she began to realize she was expected to write down the music. She had had very little instruction and did not possess natural pitch, but slowly and laboriously, with the help of the composer, she conquered the technicalities. Soon her first 'master work' was on paper.

One by one, she said, they came to her — the spirits of Chopin, Beethoven, Debussy, Schumann, Bach, Rachmaninov and Brahms, Berlioz and Monteverdi — queuing up to use her as their amanuensis to communicate their unwritten works. In their own individual ways they taught her how to notate orchestral and piano works, part operas and songs. Beethoven dictated part of his tenth symphony, Chopin gave her piano sonatas and Igor Stravinsky put in an appearance fourteen months after his death in 1971 to dictate sixty lines of music.

Critics who examined the manuscripts varied in their opinions as to their artistic merit. But most agreed that in their style and content the transcriptions bore an uncanny resemblance to the composers' known works and that only an advanced musician could have written them.

That afternoon in 1964 was not the first time she saw the ghost of Franz Liszt. He first appeared to her when she was only seven years old, though she did not realize who he was until much later when she saw a photograph of him, taken in old age, in a music book. The visitation took place in an attic bedroom at the top of the big old house she lived in with her parents. She was not frightened. She was already used to seeing spirits. Snuggled down in her rickety bed, she peeped over the covers and solemnly gazed at the figure of the Abbé Liszt with his long, white hair and black cassock. He simply said, 'When you grow up I will come back and give you some music.'

During her schooldays Rosemary had flashes of telepathy and some-times visions of 'people on a different plane'. Once she saw the street she lived in as it was before any houses were built there. But otherwise she was a normal, healthy, outgoing schoolgirl. She took piano lessons for a short time, practising at home in a freezing cold 'parlour' on a piano with several dud keys, then had to give them up because her parents could not afford them. Later in her teens she managed two terms with a good music teacher by paying for lessons out of the money she earned by running errands, and there were a few other lessons. She learned the basics, but hardly attained the standard of a concert pianist.

After school she worked in the Civil Service, married and had two children, but in 1961 her husband died after a prolonged illness, leaving her penniless. Her life became a constant struggle to make ends meet, but she began to feel the comforting presence of a spirit she realized later was Liszt.

The one luxury she had allowed herself during those difficult years was an old second-hand piano. One afternoon in 1964, recuperating at home after an accident in the school kitchen where she worked, she decided to play a few pieces to pass the time. Liszt, this time in his

Rosemary Brown communicating unwritten works of great composers

dark, handsome prime, appeared vividly by her side. She found he was guiding her hands. On later visits he communicated verbally in heavily accented English. Gradually, she says, she began to look upon him as a friend. They would discuss the world and its problems and subjects like reincarnation. But his fiery temperament had obviously not been changed by his removal to another world. One day when he had made her correct a passage over and over again she became frustrated and tired and muttered that he was nothing more than an old fuss-pot. He went off in a huff and did not return for three weeks.

Liszt introduced her to Chopin. 'He looks so very young,' she wrote in her autobiography. 'He has a beautiful clear smile . . . and exquisite manners. He looks and moves like an aristocrat, but his manner seems very natural somehow, not a pose.' Chopin offered to help her with fingering. 'He tells me what the notes and chords are and then we try it out on the piano. If I'm attempting a chord and my fingers are on the wrong notes, there will be a very gentle pushing until they are correct.' Chopin, she said, had a rather husky voice, not deep, but with a strong Polish accent. He proved to be a perfect gentleman, sometimes accompanying her to concerts. One day when they were immersed in a piano sonata Chopin suddenly held up his hand to stop her and reminded her that she had left the bath-water running!

Rosemary liked Brahms. She found him both serene and strong. 'He has extraordinary patience and usually manages to communicate without difficulty, sustaining the link for long periods at a time'. She took down piano music and string quartets from him, one of which was played at the end of a BBC documentary programme. 'Because of the string quartets, I have to take much of his music down by hand,' she wrote. 'I remember the first time he arrived with the intention of giving me music. I was sitting at the piano. I played what he gave me as well as I could but it became difficult as he uses tenths a lot. My hands, unfortunately, are too small to stretch this far, though I can manage better than I used to. I think that Brahms must have had an extraordinary span between his fingers when he was alive. . . .'

Beethoven did not arrive until 1966. For a long time he remained an enigma. One of the first things she realized was that he was no longer deaf. Communication between them was slow because Rosemary was in such awe of him. 'He is an awe-inspiring person to look at and there is no doubt he was one of the greatest souls to live in this world.' At first he would impress the music upon her mind without saying a word. At those silent meetings she was overwhelmed by his greatness, but gradually began to realize that Beethoven had in fact a great simplicity, which was truly sublime. Gradually a bond of sympathy sprang up between them. She even saw something of his notorious bad temper. He cried out, 'Mein Gott!' when the doorbell rang one day when they were hard at work.

Debussy rushed in and out and sometimes disappeared for weeks, Rachmaninov was difficult at first but friendly later, Schubert tried to sing his compositions to her in a rather flat voice. She enjoyed working with Bach: 'He is able to get his ideas over to me very clearly. He must have a very methodical mind. He dislikes my working at the piano and prefers just to tell me the notes.'

In 1970 a long-playing record of some of the works was released to a mixed reception from the critics, some of them obviously extremely puzzled as to what to make of it. Hephzibah Menuhin, brilliant pianist sister of the great violinist, said, 'I look at these manuscripts with immense respect' and Leonard Bernstein, and his wife, who entertained Rosemary in their London hotel suite, were impressed both by her sincerity and by the music she showed them. Composer Richard Rodney Bennett said, 'You couldn't fake music like this without years of training. I couldn't have faked some of the Beethoven myself.'

Why the great composers should have chosen this modest, pleasant housewife to communicate their unwritten works remains a mystery. But Rosemary Brown felt the motivation was explained in a statement which 'came through' from distinguished musician Sir Donald Tovey: 'The musicians who have departed from your world are attempting to establish a precept for humanity, i.e. that physical death is a transition from one state of consciousness to another, wherein one retains one's individuality. . . .'

She had enough humour, however, to admit that she found it hard to sit and listen to some classical music. 'Poulenc visited me once or twice and tried to give me some pieces. I didn't really care for them!'

Pearl Curran

Pearl Curran was regarded as nothing more exciting than a quiet, plain-living housewife by her friends and neighbours in St Louis, Missouri. She baked well, kept a tidy home but never showed any interest in the world beyond the southern United States.

Then, one fateful evening in July 1913, she somewhat reluctantly went to a séance. What happened there turned her into a literary phenomenon, a prolific writer of novels, poetry and plays, a creator of stories told in perfect Elizabethan English and of manuscripts rich in detail of places entirely foreign to her experience. Her friends could not believe that the woman they had known for years could become the author of such a wealth of literature. And, according to her account of the extraordinary affair, they were right. She was merely passing on the work of someone long dead, and had discovered her gift as one of the world's greatest automatic writers.

That July evening at the séance she placed her hand on the ouija board and waited, hoping for a message from a relative who had recently died. She became excited when the pointer began to move, apparently struggling to spell out a name. Eventually a message became clear: 'Many moons ago I lived. Again I come . . .' and the name Patience Worth was spelled out.

Further séances produced the information that Patience Worth was a Quaker girl who had died in 1641. She had been born and raised in Dorset, in England, and had to work long, hard hours in the fields as well as helping her mother with domestic chores until her family emigrated to America as settlers. She was killed when a raiding party of Indians set fire to their homestead. She had not enjoyed her life on earth but felt unfulfilled, as though she had something more to give the world. She wanted Pearl Curran to write books for her.

At first the material came via the ouija board, letter by letter, but that soon proved too slow and clumsy. Mrs Curran then tried the usual method of automatic writing, simply holding her pen over a sheet of plain paper and letting it write of its own accord. But the speed of delivery was too fast. Finally she brought in a professional shorthand-taker so that she could simply dictate the words and sentences that went racing through her head.

The sum total of her work amounted to more than three million words of manuscript, thousands of poems and the material for six published books, a great deal of it rare and historical. It astounded academics and critics on both sides of the Atlantic.

The astounding fact about Pearl Curran is that her experience of life had been so narrow before the appearance of Patience Worth. She was not fond of reading. She had been sent to an elementary school and her education ended before she was fifteen. She admitted her knowledge of history was so sketchy that she was convinced for years that it was Henry VIII and not Charles I who had been executed by Cromwell. Poetry was not one of her favourite subjects either. She thought Tennyson's favourite poem was called *The Lady of Charlotte*. After her marriage she seldom left St Louis but concentrated her energies on being a housewife and singing in the church choir.

Mrs Curran was fascinated by what was happening to her but sometimes bewildered by Patience Worth's quaint manner of speaking and her use of old Quaker dialect. On one occasion she was advised: 'Thine own barley corn may weevil, but thee'lt crib thy neighbour's and sack his shelling.' After that Mrs Curran somewhat tartly asked Patience Worth to spare her the rustic speech. For a time she communicated in modern English but later slipped back into her old way of talking.

The speed at which the material came over was astounding — one night Mrs Curran took down twenty-two poems. The quality of the writing was high-flown, literary, some of it possessing a beauty, style and philosophical depth wholly beyond the reach of a Missouri house-wife, however intelligent.

Over a span of nearly three decades Mrs Curran published a number of Patience Worth's historical novels, each one totally different in style and content. Critics lavished praise on *The Sorry Tale*, a book of 350,000 words written in two-hourly sessions. The story was that of a boy born in Bethlehem on the same night as Jesus Christ, whose life ran parallel to his and who ended as one of the thieves crucified with him on Calvary. Mrs Curran did no research for the story. The only previous knowledge she had of biblical lands was that taught by her

Sunday School teachers. Yet the details of social, domestic and political life in ancient Palestine and Rome and the customs of Greeks, Arabians and Jews are presented in a vivid and convincing manner. Some specialists said they were sure the books had been written by a scholar who had considerable knowledge of the Middle East at the time of Christ.

Another novel, *Hope Trueblood*, was a highly dramatic tale set in Victorian England, telling with considerable emotional power the story of an illegitimate child and its fight to be accepted by society. It was published in England under the name Patience Worth with no explanation of the strange circumstances surrounding it. The book was well received by both critics and public.

Another great success was her epic poem *Telka*, an idyll of medieval England containing 60,000 words and a great deal of Middle English phraseology. She had never studied the period at school even.

Research proved that both the Elizabethan prose she used and the Middle English were accurate and genuine, and perfectly suited to the idiom of the day. But how a sixteenth-century Quaker girl came to have such a knowledge of Christ's Palestine and Victoria's England is a question that has not been fully answered. Spiritualists suggested that Patience Worth came to know about it after death, 'when all things are known'.

As was to be expected, Patience and Mrs Curran were thoroughly investigated by the psychic researchers. Members of Boston SPR searched her house thoroughly for books of an estoteric nature that could have given her background material. They did not find any. Apart from the Bible and a few books of poetry with the pages uncut, the Currans did not keep an extensive library.

Mrs Curran never lost her sense of surprise that this should have happened to her. She confessed that only a few years previously she would not have been able to read her own novels with any understanding at all. She was often invited to literary receptions and there were attempts to lionize her, but she always sent her regrets. She had a feeling that for many people the mystery of who had actually written the novels was the greatest attraction.

Perhaps the strangest aspect of the whole business was something that did not concern the literary world. Patience Worth had obviously been a spinster in her short, unhappy life on earth. She conveyed to Mrs Curran a sense of frustration that she had never married and had children. One day she instructed Mrs Curran to adopt a baby girl so that they could bring it up together. Patience said the baby must have red hair, blue eyes and be of Scottish descent. She was obviously describing herself.

The Currans found a child to adopt who fitted the description perfectly and she became known as Patience Worth Wee Curran. The child grew up under the ghostly eye of Patience, who insisted on her wearing Quaker-like dresses with white collar and cuffs which made her stand out from the other girls at school. When she grew up she moved to California, where she married twice.

Mrs Curran died in 1938 and Patience Worth was never heard of again. But five years later, when she was only twenty-seven, her adopted, 'shared' daughter had a premonition of approaching death. She began to lose weight rapidly and just before Christmas 1943 died in her sleep.

So who was Patience Worth? She dictated the following poem to Mrs Curran which is all we shall ever know, for records have shown no trace of her.

A phantom? Weel enough,
Prove thee thyself to me!
I say, behold here I be,
Buskins, kirtle, cap and petty skirts,
and much tongue!
Well, what has thou to prove thee?

Coral Polge

Coral Polge would probably be considered an excellent portrait artist by any standard. Her work has one difference that makes it remarkable. When she draws in the features, hair-line and fine character details that make a face instantly recognizable she is not working from a living model. She is a psychic artist who draws her inspiration from the spirit world.

Through her thousands of people have received sketches in pencil or pastels of faces they thought they would never see again.

She has demonstrated her extraordinary artistic talent in Europe, Scandinavia, Canada, the United States and Australia. Television crews have filmed her at work, and she has been seen by large audiences at public demonstrations, projecting her drawings as they 'come through' onto an overhead screen so that every stroke of her pencil can be followed. Yet she still thinks of what she does as an intensely personal thing. Some people burst into tears when they see the outlines of a much-loved face begin to appear on a sheet of drawing paper. Others are just overcome with joy. Others are sceptical and talk about telepathy.

Her first drawings were done in graveyards. She grew up in the East End of London, where her father was a cinema manager, and as a schoolgirl had a morbid interest in death. She took to haunting churchyards, and used her emerging artistic talent to draw weeping stone angels.

The family moved to Harrow, where she attended Harrow Art School and decided to specialize in textile design. She was, she once said, fine at drawing things she could actually see, but her teachers considered her to have little imagination. 'Obviously in psychic art, imagination is a hindrance and just gets in the way, so my lack of it has proved an advantage.' Her first job on leaving art school was painting lampshades for a shop in Regent Street, then she found work as a commercial artist, drawing the illustrations for advertisements. Later she moved to a firm which specialized in retouching copies of old photographs, a job which demanded both patience and skill in dealing with fine detail.

As an attractive young woman of twenty-three, she was introduced to Spiritualism. Both her parents had visited spiritual healers at one time or another, but neither of them claimed any psychic bent. She had an aunt who read tea cups and a grandmother who might have possessed second sight, but she thought of herself as perfectly ordinary. One night, however, she went to Harrow Spiritualist Church and was singled out by a medium who asked her if she knew she had the potential to be a psychic artist. On separate occasions several other mediums asked her precisely the same thing.

With some trepidation Coral Polge took her first psychic 'circle' in 1950, just a year after her first marriage. She had no idea what would happen. To start with she found she was able to take down messages 'from the spirit world' in automatic writing. Then she found herself drawing lines, circles and meaningless shapes. Gradually faces began to appear on the paper in front of her.

To start with she tended to draw only spirit guides — solemn Red Indians and wise-looking Chinese — but as no one knew who they were, she felt her work had no point. It was when she began to draw recognizable faces that people began to get excited. One sitter watched her solemnly as she drew the features of an old man with a drooping white moustache. Suddenly she jumped up and exclaimed, 'That's my father, the living image of him!' Coral knew then she was on the right wavelength.

In the early days of her career she would usually ask the man or woman who had consulted her to give her a letter or something that had belonged to the dead person, but in time she realized it was better for her just to sit and wait until the drawing came through.

She does not, she says, see the person she is about to draw, nor is her hand controlled by psychic forces. When 'linking up' she feels a complete change of personality taking place within her. 'Having become that person, I attempt to portray his or her personality'. She 'feels' the person coming through. What appears first on the paper is an expression — a laugh or a scowl, a look of gentleness or of strength. Actual features follow after she has caught the personality.

The sketches are produced in a matter of minutes because, as she told the *Psychic News*, 'I know exactly what to draw without thinking about it. It's involuntary, like breathing or walking.' Remarkable likenesses appear on the paper of people she has never seen or known. Not only are their features usually instantly recognizable to those who love them but the psychic often portrays them in the sort of clothes they favoured when they were alive.

She married Arthur Polge in 1949, but became so engrossed in her psychic work that the marriage broke up after eight years. Faced with the necessity of earning her own living, she turned to full-time mediumship. Her second marriage was to Tom Johansen, secretary of the Spiritualist Association of Great Britain.

At the last count in 1984 Coral Polge was estimated to have produced in the region of 90,000 spirit drawings, which must make her the most prolific portrait artist of modern times.

Uri Geller

The night Uri Geller went on British television and by sheer concentration quietly proceeded to bend a variety of metal objects including forks, spoons and keys, caused a rumpus in the scientific world and an excitement among the millions who watched that has never quite died down again.

Handsome, dark-haired and only 26 years old, the Israeli entertainer seemed to demonstrate remarkable power over material things. Unable to explain what happened, he suggested, 'Perhaps everybody has got this ability within them, but it requires a certain power to trigger it off. I am sure the power must come from an intelligent form of energy.'

That evening on television, November 23, 1973, was not an exceptional one as far as Geller was concerned. He had been doing this sort of thing on stage in Israel and had achieved a certain fame as a glamorous young magician. But he was nervously aware of the immense audience watching him.

Viewers stared with amazement as David Dimbleby held a fork in his hand and it bent like wilting rhubarb as Geller stroked it with his finger. Suddenly the whole studio seemed to go haywire. A fork lying on a table bent without him even touching it, another contorted till it broke in half. Broken watches scattered in front of him began to tick but the hands inside a perfectly good watch suddenly curled up against the glass face. At the end of the programme the switchboard was jammed with viewers reporting that their own cutlery had begun to curl up as they ate TV suppers in front of the screen!

The excitement in Britain was reported all round the world. Some people posed the question if he could do that to one piece of metal was it safe to let him travel in a complicated piece of machinery like a jumbo jet. Controversy arrived with his fame and from then on he was either being treated like a pop star or accused of being a fraud. Only when he was subjected to controlled tests did the attitude change towards him. Scientists at the Max Planck Institute in Germany described his powers as 'a phenomenon which in theoretical terms cannot be explained'.

Uri Geller was born in Tel Aviv in 1946 and remembers 'strange energy forces' going back to the age of three. His family on his father's side was very religious, his grandfather having been a Rabbi in Budapest. On his mother's side he was distantly related to Sigmund Freud. When he started going to school he was given a watch which always seemed to be going wrong. Sometimes as he looked at it the minute hand would spin four or five hours ahead. Finally, he left the watch at home. His mother checked it every day but nothing unusual happened. He decided to try wearing it again, but when he glanced down in the middle of a lesson he saw the hands whirring round. When he was eating soup in the kitchen at home one day his spoon bent until the bowl fell off, and he was left holding the handle. Another time, when he was in a restaurant with his parents, forks and spoons on a near-by table began to curl up. Bewildered at first by these phenomena, he soon began to suspect that something in himself was causing them. By the age of thirteen he had gained some control over his powers.

For a time, after his parents divorced, he went to live in a kibbutz and was so unhappy there that his curious ability disappeared. There was not much time to think of it either during the 1967 war, when he trained as a paratrooper in the Israeli army and was injured by an Arab sniper. While recuperating he took a job as instructor at a children's camp about an hour's drive out of Tel Aviv. Sometimes he amused them by showing a few of the experiments he now practised in telepathy and metal-bending. They were mesmerized.

Tales of his magic spread, and by 1968 he was in demand at schools and private parties all over Tel Aviv. By the summer of 1971 he had turned himself into a brilliant entertainer who bent cutlery, broke metal rings and mended broken watches in front of huge audiences. Teenagers went wild about him. Stories about him reached the famous psychical researcher Dr Andrija Puharich, who decided it was worth flying from New York to Israel to see him. As he watched Geller perform in a discothèque in Jaffa his first impression was that Uri was no more than a skilful magician, but when he snapped a woman's dress ring in two by simply placing his hand over it as it was gripped in her fist, he began to have second thoughts.

Puharich asked Geller if he would submit to scientific tests. As he watched the Israeli raised the temperature on a thermometer by staring at it, moved a compass needle by concentration and bent a jet of water streaming from a tap by simply moving his finger towards it. Puharich flew back to America convinced that Geller was a genuine psychic with a definite power of mind over matter. He had promised he would go to New York at the earliest opportunity to demonstrate under controlled conditions.

First, Uri went to Germany. Arriving in Munich in June 1972, he was met by a crowd of reporters who asked him to do something 'really astounding'. He asked them to suggest something. 'How about stopping a cable car in mid-air?' Geller hesitated, then agreed to try. Reporters took him to the Hochfelln Funicular Line outside Munich. After two or three abortive attempts the car stopped in mid-air over a 140-metre drop. The mechanic called the control centre and was told that the main switch had flicked off of its own accord!

In America the Israeli found tough audiences, traditionally sceptical about miracle workers, and he was both tense and miserable. Most of the time, however, he was surrounded by scientists who were eager to test him. He met Wernher von Braun, famous inventor of the V-2 rocket, and impressed the great man by two incidents that took place in his office. Taking a gold ring off his finger, von Braun placed it on the palm of his hand and watched it become quite flat as Geller passed his hand over it. The scientist then found that his calculator battery was flat though he had only put it in that morning. Geller held it between his hands then passed it back to him in working condition. The delighted von Braun concluded that Geller was capable of producing strange electric currents.

Scientists at the Stanford Research Institute in California which carries out important research work for the US Government, took a film of Geller performing his feats and tested his powers of extrasensory perception. He was asked to pick out from ten small metal cylinders the one that contained a metal ball. After a few seconds concentration he went straight to the right cylinder. He succeeded in a similar test involving a cylinder of water. Geller was not always satisfied with his performance in scientific laboratories and said he was at his best before 'sympathetic audiences, small friendly gatherings of interested people'. He felt he needed the energy of others to generate his mental forces.

Soon after his triumph on British television in 1973 he set off to demonstrate his powers in Paris, Scandinavia, Spain, Italy and Japan, receiving superstar attention all the way. He returned to America, where he came under terrific pressure from his detractors, then moved on to Mexico, where he was a frequent guest at the home of the President. At the height of his fame in 1974 he wrote his autobiography and planned to star in a film about his own life. He even tried dowsing for metals from an aeroplane, and had considerable success working for gold and copper mines.

Still stealing headlines in 1984, the *New York Times* printed a report that Uri Geller had had secret talks with the former US President, Jimmy Carter, who ordered the Central Intelligence Agency to conduct a high-level review of supernormal research behind the Iron Curtain. The metal-bender warned that the Russians were studying psychic phenomena much more seriously than the Western world.

Happily married, looking handsome and fit, Geller announced in 1985 that he was planning to settle in England but he also intended to build a health centre in Israel and a laboratory for psychic research —after having worked with scientists in nearly every major country in the world.

Uri Geller tries his blindfold driving experiment

Robert James Lees

Was Victorian psychic Robert James Lees responsible for tracking down Jack the Ripper? There are authorities who believe he was, and that the results of his investigations lie in a black japanned box somewhere in the archives of the British Home Office.

Robert Lees was a remarkable clairvoyant who enjoyed royal patronage and was received more than once both at Balmoral and Buckingham Palace by Queen Victoria herself. His powers developed when he was very young. He was only nineteen when the Queen summoned him for the first time and discussed psychic matters with him at great length.

During the late summer and autumn of 1888, when the monster known as Jack the Ripper killed and mutilated five prostitutes in such an appalling way that a wave of terror swept over the whole East End of London, Robert Lees began to have visions. The police, desperate for clues, suspecting they were up against a sadistic madman, listened to him at first with incredulity. When his psychic detection finally led them to the 'Ripper', the information he put at their disposal being investigated, confirmed and acted upon, he was sworn to secrecy. So too were all the doctors, police and detectives who had been involved.

'Speculation has always been rife as to Jack the Ripper's identity', wrote Edwin T. Woodhull, ex-Scotland Yard man, in his account of Robert Lee's involvement in the case.

'He was never brought to justice but it is a mistake to think that the police did not know who he was. It was proved beyond doubt that he was a physician of the highest standing who lived in a fine house in the West End of London. To most people he was the most refined and gentle of men, both courteous and kind. But he was also an ardent vivisectionist and a cruel sadist who took a fierce delight in inflicting pain on helpless creatures.'

How Robert Lees became involved in the Ripper case is recounted in an early published version of his life.

One day, sitting in his study, he found himself drifting into a sort of trance and a scene began to form itself in front of him. He saw two people, a man and a woman, walking down the length of 'a mean street'. He saw them enter a kind of courtyard. They passed a public house, and by the light of a big clock he could see the hands stood at 12.30 — the time, at this period, when public houses closed.

The woman appeared to be drunk as she bumped into the man from time to time in the gas-lit alley. Judging by his walk, her companion was perfectly sober. Presently they turned into a dark place with an open door, and Lees could read the name quite clearly. It was 'George

Yard Buildings'.

They leaned against the wall. Robert Lees could see that the man was dressed in a light tweed suit, and that a black felt hat was pulled well down over his eyes. Over his arm he carried a dark overcoat or mackintosh. Suddenly he put his hand over the woman's mouth, drew a knife from his pocket and slit her throat. Blood streamed over his clothes. As the woman sank to the ground he bent over her and proceeded to cut and mutilate her with the knife. This done he dragged her body into the darkness of an open doorway, slipped on the dark overcoat, fastening it up to the neck to hide any traces of blood, and slipped away.

The vision, which left Robert Lees considerably shaken, took place on the day following August Bank Holiday in 1888. The psychic was even more horrified when he realized he had witnessed the first of the 'Ripper' murders, for the papers carried a full account of what happened to Martha Turner, found with her throat cut, in the dark doorway of a common lodging house in George Yard Buildings, Commercial Street, Spitalfields.

At Scotland Yard the psychic was listened to politely but with obvious scepticism. It was only after the inquest that notice was taken of his psychic evidence and even then the police did not trouble to get in touch with him. Giving evidence, a woman friend of the dead Martha Turner said she saw her at about 12.20 am walking in the company of a 'toff' who wore a light suit and carried a coat on his arm.

Robert Lees could not sleep for nights after his vision of the murder. His nerves were so badly affected by what he had seen that his doctor ordered him to take a holiday abroad. The psychic took his advice and went with his family to the Continent.

By the time he returned, fully recovered, two more murders had been committed, obviously by the same hand. The psychic had not been troubled by further visions, and tried to keep himself from thinking about the grisly affair.

One day, soon after the third murder, he caught an omnibus in Shepherd's Bush with his wife and began to experience the strange sensations which had preceded his first disturbing experience. At Notting Hill a man got on the omnibus and Robert Lees felt a numb, powerless sensation overtake him. As he looked up and met the man's gaze, he went icy cold. The new passenger was wearing a light tweed suit, a dark felt hat and carried a dark overcoat. 'The omnibus jogged and rumbled along until it came to Lancaster Gate, while Mr Lees was subject to every unknown feeling ever experienced by mortal man.'

At Marble Arch the man got off and Robert Lees, leaving his wife with a hasty word that he would follow her home later, also got off and began to follow him across Hyde Park. He lost him when he hailed a cab outside Apsley House. His frantic efforts to try to get a policeman to arrest him were in vain, but a police sergeant made a note of the incident.

That night he had a premonition that the Ripper was about to commit another murder. The scene was not as distinct as in his first vision but he saw clearly the terrified face of the victim. This time the clairvoyant went straight to police headquarters and demanded to see the detective in charge of the Ripper investigations. His revelations were by now so startling that it was decided to ask him to help in tracking down the sadistic monster. Accompanied by the chief detective and a number of police officers, he went to the scene of the Ripper's last murder and suffered mental agony as he 'saw' the scene re-enacted. When his clairvoyant vision ended he turned away and started to walk swiftly in a westerly direction. He had picked up the psychic trail.

Mile after mile police and detectives followed him until he reached a street in the West End of London and stood before a magnificent house. There was a terrible feeling of disappointment. This was the home of an eminent physician whose life and talents had been dedicated to the relief of suffering. But Robert Lees insisted this was where Jack the Ripper lived. Only when the psychic proved his clairvoyant powers still further by describing to them exactly what the house looked like inside, were they prepared to take a chance.

Under the most delicate questioning, the doctor's wife broke down, told how she had discovered a short time after their marriage that he had a mania for inflicting pain, how he had once nearly killed their four-year-old child and how quickly he could revert to his other self. It was a true Jekyll and Hyde story.

According to Edwin Woodhull, the doctor was declared insane and placed in a private asylum. To account for his disappearance from society it was announced that he had died suddenly from heart failure, and funeral rites were actually conducted. For his work in tracking the Ripper, Robert Lees received a life pension from the Privy Purse and was sworn to secrecy.

Peter Hurkos

Dutch detective Peter Hurkos has been connected with some of the most famous murder and missing person cases to hit the world headlines in the last few decades. He is not attached to any police force.

Only a handful of police chiefs will even admit they have consulted him. He works alone with only one weapon — his gift of psychic sight.

Hurkos has been involved with cases as infamous as the Sharon Tate murders committed by the devilish Charles Manson 'family', the tracking down of the Boston Strangler and the mysterious disappearance of America's Judge Chillingworth. In England he put his psychic power at the disposal of Scotland Yard when the Stone of Scone disappeared from Westminster Abbey, and in Holland he helped police capture an arsonist who turned out to be the son of a rich and respected family.

Some people in the world of psychical research refuse to take the big dark-haired Dutchman seriously, perhaps because after settling in the United States in 1958 he was taken up by the smart Hollywood set, many stars going to him for paranormal readings. Marlon Brando was reported to be fascinated, and Glenn Ford expressed an ambition to play him on screen. Hurkos basked in the bright lights. After all, before he fell off a ladder and the psychic gift came to him, he was only a run-of-the-mill house painter!

As he writes in his autobiography *Psychic*, he was born Pieter van der Hurk on May 21, 1911, in the small industrial town of Dordrecht, not far from The Hague in Holland. He adopted the name Peter Hurkos when he was in the Dutch resistance during the war. His father, a house-painter, did not make a lot of money but his mother was a typical meticulous Dutch housewife and he had a normal and happy upbringing. His only regret was that he had to abandon a high school course in radio engineering for lack of funds. About one thing he is certain. 'There was absolutely no history of extra-sensory perception, telepathy or any other psychic awareness within my family.'

He went to sea, first as a ship's cook, then as a stoker, finally taking a job in Shanghai as a talleyman. When the outbreak of war put an end to the Shanghai trade he returned home, married and agreed to join his father in his small business as a painter and decorator.

On a gloomy, misty day in June 1941, he was painting a four-storey building in The Hague with his father. He had agreed to tackle the high places, and to save time placed his ladder between two windows, calculating that with a bit of stretching he could paint both at once without having to climb down. But reaching for a pot of paint he lost his balance and fell. He remembers still how long it seemed to take, and how his whole life spun before him.

When he woke up in hospital he could not at first remember names, faces or dates. For a while he could not recognize members of his family. He had been unconscious for four days, suffering from concussion and severe neurological damage. He would undoubtedly have been killed but for the fact that he hit the ground shoulder first.

Something else had happened. He told his biographer, Norma Lee

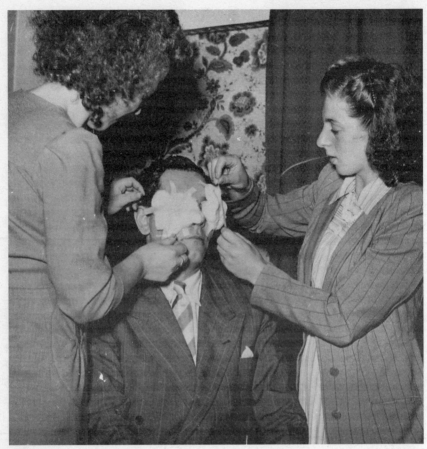

Peter Hurkos preparing to demonstrate his unique powers

Browning: 'When I woke up I had no mind of my own. I was in somebody else's mind and I was scared . . . my father and mother said it's not the same Peter any more . . . they said I had died and come back with two minds. It's God's truth, I came back with two minds.' He also came back with the gift of psychic sight.

One day a stranger stopped by his bed to wish him a speedy recovery. The instant they shook hands and said goodbye Peter knew he was a British agent and that he was going to be killed by the Germans a few days later. Shocked by what was going through his mind, Peter gripped the man's arm and tried to stop him. Nurses rushed in with sedatives to calm him down. Two days later the man's death was in the newspapers.

Before Peter was discharged from hospital the doctor told him there was a possibility that the fall had damaged certain functions of the brain and stimulated others. He soon found out what the doctor meant. As the days went by he began to have more and more flashing glimpses of the past and of the future. Sometimes he was able to describe places he had never been to.

Carrying forged papers with his new name, Hurkos, he worked for the resistance in Holland during the war. Captured and sent to Buchenwald concentration camp, he nearly died from starvation and beri-beri. On his release he was decorated by Queen Juliana.

He had lost his head for heights, so was not able to take up his old job as a house-painter. Somehow, he decided, he would use his new ability to earn money. He agreed to do a number of stage performances based on psychometry (asking a member of the audience for a personal possession, he would then attempt to 'read' their lives). He was a theatrical success but turned down an offer to tour Europe, feeling there was something more important he could do with his gift. Just one incident started his career as a psychic detective.

One morning, about 3 a.m., he was wakened by the ringing of the doorbell. He answered it to find a distraught woman on the doorstep. She begged him to help her. Her husband had disappeared. The police had not been able to find him but had told her not to worry, that he was probably out with some friends. She felt sure something was wrong, and offered Hurkos any amount of money if he could find him.

The psychic asked for some object that had belonged to her husband and immediately 'saw' a football and a uniform. The man, it turned out had been a famous footballer, but was now in the army. Hurkos found the words rushing out: 'I am sorry to tell you, madame, he has fallen into an ice trap . . . he decided to take a short cut through the woods . . . he fell into a ditch — no, it is a tank trap and it is filled with water . . . he struggles, but he is too weak . . . he has drunk bad booze . . . he freezes to death in the water . . . I am sorry, madame,' 'he told her gently. 'Your husband is dead. I am very sorry.'

Hurkos made a sketch for her to take to the police station showing where they would find the body, but the police laughed at her story. She insisted they took her to the place he had described. They found nothing. Furious by what they considered was a waste of time, they warned her not to listen to Hurkos. He was a fake. Next day the woman persuaded Peter to go with her to the police. After listening to him they agreed to return to Maljebaan in The Hague, where he had 'seen' the body. This time they found the missing man's cap in the bushes. After seven days of digging they brought up the body.

The story spread like wildfire. His reputation as a psychic detective was soon established as he worked on many cases of missing people and on murders. But he soon discovered something he had to learn to live with all his career: the police did not like to admit that a psychic had helped them in their investigations.

He left Holland to work in Belgium, where he set up his head-quarters at an Antwerp hotel, sometimes giving public readings but also working on cases. When the body of George Cornelis, a former hero of the Belgian underground, was found in the River Leie a verdict of 'death by misadventure—manner unknown' was brought in by the Ghent police. But when the Cornelis family asked Hurkos to investigate, he declared, after handling his picture, that he had been killed by a monkey wrench and thrown into the river. Working with the police, he eventually tracked down two men who had been Nazi collaborators during the war and were afterwards jailed as a result of the testimony of Cornelis. They confessed to beating him to death with a wrench and throwing his body into the river. The case brought him a considerable amount of publicity since the crime had not only been solved but actually discovered through the use of extrasensory perception.

Hurkos was spending Christmas 1950 with his family and his wife, Maria, at home in Holland when he heard that the legendary Stone of Scone had been stolen from Westminster Abbey in England. The Stone, upon which Scottish kings were once crowned, had been brought to England by Edward I. For 664 years it had been safely stowed away beneath the Coronation Chair in the Abbey. Now it had gone, and England was in an uproar.

Hurkos offered his services to Scotland Yard. While they met him in some style with a police escort at London Airport, and granted him access to the Abbey, he could see from the beginning that they were embarrassed about being helped by a clairvoyant.

Walking up to the Coronation Chair, he knelt down, touched it and felt its vibrations. Pictures began to flash through his mind. He 'saw' much of the history connected with the Stone but tried to concentrate upon the theft. After about thirty minutes of intense effort — during which he seemed to be in a semi-trance state and was perspiring heavily — he began to talk: 'I see five people were involved . . . three breaking in . . . two waiting outside in a truck . . . I see an old church by a river. . . .' On he went.

The next morning he was given a crowbar that had been used to break into the Abbey, a watch-strap found near the Chair and the plaque from the Stone. Standing in Tufton Street, where the plaque had been found, it was clear to him that it had been thrown from a vehicle and that the Stone had merely passed this site on its way to another destination. Exploring the Lower Thames Street area, he found the shop where the crowbar had been bought. By the end of the day he told the men from the Yard that the thieves were in Glasgow. They had taken the Stone there, and now it was hidden in an old church. He described the five men involved in the theft and said it was a student prank. He predicted the Stone would be back in the Abbey within four weeks.

Though he drove up to Scotland he did not find anything. He went home depressed by the 'cold and unbelieving attitude' of the police, and the ridicule of the British Press. But, just as he had predicted, the Stone was found in the ruins of an old church — Arbroath Abbey in Angus. It was returned four weeks later and the thieves were traced to Glasgow.

In the rest of Europe he was gaining recognition. He never claimed to be right every time, but the percentage of his correct predictions was incredibly high. After putting him through a gruelling test, the French police used his services for the next five years. He still gave private readings and used his gift for entertainment purposes in order to pay his bills. He seldom received a fee for police work.

Stories about him appeared in *Paris Match* magazine and were seen by Dr Andrija Puharich, who was working on psychical research at the Round Table Foundation Laboratories in Maine. He invited Hurkos to go to him for six months so that he could explore his psychic powers. The Dutchman was only too willing. He still did not understand quite what had happened to him when he fell off that ladder, and hoped to learn something about himself. He performed well in the laboratory under controlled conditions and the experiments went on for two and a half years. He soon became a regular crime consultant in America, and drifted towards the rich and famous in Hollywood.

One of the most sensational cases he worked on was that of the Boston Strangler early in 1964. He only carried on his investigations for six days but lost 15 lb in weight and took months to get over the experience. The mental punishment he suffered was largely because he steadfastly refused to believe that Albert DeSalvo was the Strangler. Norma Lee Browning, the *Chicago Tribune* columnist who wrote his biography after knowing him for years, devotes a large chunk of her book to his dilemma over the Strangler.

Hurkos was staying with Glenn Ford at his home in Beverly Hills when Assistant Attorney General John S. Bottomly — who was in charge of the whole operation — called and asked him to help. The Strangler had just finished with his eleventh victim, nineteen-year-old Mary Sullivan, and there had been a public outcry. 'I didn't want to take the case,' Peter Hurkos admitted. 'I didn't like the idea of going to Boston. I knew something was wrong on that case. I didn't want to go.' But Bottomly had set up a special Strangler Investigation Bureau and promised him every assistance.

On the first day Hurkos asked for a city map and requested that it should be laid upside down so that he could not see the streets. Then he asked for an object from one of the victims. Someone produced a small comb. With the teeth of the comb he began to trace the upside-down map of Boston. He moved the comb back and forth, up and down until it stopped in the Newton-Boston area. 'Here you will find the killer,' he said suddenly. 'He looks like a priest, dresses like a priest, but he is thrown out by the monks. He speaks French. He talks like a girl — like this' — and his voice rose to falsetto. 'He's a pervert.' Next day the detectives handed Hurkos a letter which had been sent to the nursing director at Boston College School of Nursing from an address in the area that Peter had indicated on the map. Instead of reading it he crumpled it in his hand, closed his eyes and concentrated. Suddenly he cried, 'This is the one . . . the murderer . . . son of a bitch, he do it.' The writer of the letter had asked to be put in touch with a good Catholic nurse. He had given his own doctor's name so that he could be checked up on. When the doctor was contacted he said the writer of the letter was a man in his fifties with a record of mental illness. He had a problem. His brother had tried once to get him committed.

Hurkos came up with a description of the man: 'He is not too big, high hairline with a mark or spot on his left arm, something wrong with his thumb. He has a French accent . . . he has to do with a hospital . . . he is a homo and a woman-hater . . . blue-grey eyes, a killer's eyes . . . his hair is thin, he has a sharp, pointed, spitzy nose and a big Adam's apple.'

Much of what Peter Hurkos revealed about the man burst out while he was in a restless sleep. Detectives kept watch by his bed as he tossed and turned, his voice alternating between his own heavy Dutch accent and a falsetto.

He said the man lived near a seminary where priests lived. He had once tried living in a monastic order, but he was a pervert and his religion had turned sour. He thought that by killing women he was offering to God clean, female sacrifice.

In his sleep Hurkos also saw that the man slept in a room 'like a junk pile' on a bed without a mattress, and the place was full of boxes of women's shoes that he sold from door to door.

Police investigated all he had told them about the writer of the letter and the details fell into place. He went with a group of detectives to call on the man. When the door opened and a high-pitched voice asked what they wanted, Peter Hurkos turned grey-white and started to perspire. He was looking at the face he had seen in his sleep.

They had every reason to think that they had at last got the Boston Strangler, but before any move could be made the doctor questioned him at length. He admitted he had once tried to get himself committed. The doctor signed committal papers and O'Brien was on his way to Massachusetts Mental Health Centre. There was no way he could be brought to trial.

Hurkos, worn out and swearing he would never work on another murder case, flew to New York.

DeSalvo was picked up a month after he left and while waiting trial on a charge of rape and breaking and entering suddenly confessed he was the Strangler. He was committed, and Hurkos believes the two men were in the same room together at the state mental institution, and that is how DeSalvo knew exactly what to confess. DeSalvo admitted he got a kick out of the publicity the Strangler received. Hurkos pointed out that while DeSalvo was an oversexed brute where women were concerned, his appetites were normal. The killer was a pervert who displayed his victims in gross and degrading positions, indicating a woman-hater. Four years later the Strangler case was reopened and just as suddenly closed again.

Another case that cost Hurkos a great deal emotionally was the terrible massacre of Sharon Tate and four other people by the Charles Manson 'hippy' family in the late sixties. He was brought into the case by a lawyer called Peter Knecht, who had been a personal friend of one of the victims, Hollywood hairdresser Jay Sebring. The beautiful, 26-year-old film actress Sharon Tate, eight months pregnant when she was butchered and mutilated, was the wife of brilliant film director Roman Polanski. Hurkos spent weeks telling the police what he 'saw', right down to describing 'a bearded guy named Charlie'. It was his first Hollywood case, and when it was all over he swore it would be his last.

Since then Hurkos has given a great deal of his time to being tested for telepathy, clairvoyance and extrasensory perception and established a foundation of his own to make systematic studies of psychic phenomena. For in spite of all he has witnessed as a psychic detective, he says, 'I believe the growing knowledge of psychic ability has given a glimpse into a new creative dimension of human nature, giving renewed hope and determination to mankind.'

Gerard Croiset

When Pat McAdam, a Scottish teenager, went missing after hitching a lift the day after a late-night party in Glasgow on February 19, 1967, Gerard Croiset, hundreds of miles away in Holland, had a clairvoyant vision of the place where she probably met her end.

The girl's body was never found, her fate never established, but so accurate was Croiset's description that investigators were able to go straight to the location he described. He was listened to with respect because for many years he had been regarded as one of the world's foremost psychic detectives.

Seventeen-year-old Pat and her friend, Hazel Campbell, were picked up on the London Road in the outskirts of Glasgow. The lorry driver told them he was going south to Hull and could drop them somewhere close to where they lived. Pat McAdam chatted to him while her friend dozed. They stopped for a meal in a transport café. They found him very friendly, and when he swung off the main road realized he was going to make a detour and take them all the way home. Hazel was dropped off in the centre of Annan. She waved goodbye, presuming Pat would be dropped in Dumfries. But the girl never reached home. She was never seen again.

The lorry driver was tracked down after a three-week search by police, and swore he had dropped Pat McAdam on the outskirts of Dumfries and that was the last he knew of her. An intensive police hunt was set up, but to no avail.

Three years later Frank Ryan, a Dumfries journalist who had been on the case from the beginning, happened to be in Holland and decided to contact Croiset. He showed the psychic a police poster with a picture of the missing girl. Croiset stared at it for a long time, then said he saw a place where there were fir trees and exposed tree roots on the banks of a river. Near there, he said, was a flat bridge over the river with grey tubular railings. It was at the foot of a hill in an area north of Annan. Across the bridge was a cottage with advertising signs on the side of it and a white paling fence. Croiset did a drawing on a large sheet of paper and handed it to Ryan. The journalist took it back to Scotland and with a colleague went out to look at the place.

Croiset seemed to have been describing the Williamnath Bridge near the village of Dalton, where the police search had been intense. Locals had reported seeing a huge articulated lorry near there, similar to the one that had picked up the girls. But the setting was nothing like that drawn by the Dutchman. They drove on, and coming to Middleshaw on the edge of the Birkshaw forest went cold with shock. There was the scene exactly as Croiset had seen it sitting at his desk in Utrecht.

The psychic asked for something that had belonged to the missing girl and Ryan borrowed her Bible. As Croiset took it in his hand he said sadly, 'She is dead,' and went on to insist that she was buried or concealed in the area he had 'seen', in a tangle of roots on the river bank. Asked if he could give more details, he concentrated on a detailed map, then talked of a building called 'Broom Cottage,' where he said they would find a wreck of a car with a wheelbarrow propped against it.

The bridge in Croiset's first vision crossed the river called the Water of Milk west of Middleshaw and the car in the second vision was, he said, just a little farther downstream. He mentioned it only to pinpoint the area more accurately. When Ryan and a small group of friends set out to find the cottage they had no difficulty. But how in heaven's name, they wondered, could Croiset have known there was an old, broken-down Ford with a wheelbarrow propped against its back end in this exact spot when he had never even been to Scotland!

The Dutchman said he had a mental image of Pat McAdam taking her last walk with a man by the side of the river, where some trees had been felled. Later he elaborated on this, saying she had been battered to death with a heavy spanner.

Croiset eventually flew to Scotland, visited the places he had previously seen only through clairvoyance and stated he was now thoroughly convinced that her body had been thrown into the Water of Milk, caught for a while in tangled tree-roots, then carried out to sea. The river, which ran into the Solway Firth, was prone to flash floods.

Pat McAdam's fate was never finally established, but ten years later the lorry driver, Thomas Young, was arrested on charges of murder and rape in quite another connection and sent to prison for life. He boasted of having had sex with more than two hundred women in the cab of his lorry.

Hundreds of cases were investigated by Croiset and kept on file at Utrecht University. In this country he was also involved in the hunt for Mrs Muriel McKay, wife of a top Fleet Street newspaperman, kidnapped in 1969. Relatives who had heard of his work called him in. Though he managed to tell them that she had been kept for a time somewhere in a hut on the Hackney Marshes, she was never found.

Croiset was a striking figure with craggy features and a wild mop of hair. Born in 1909, the son of an actor, he had a miserable childhood, mostly in the care of foster parents. His paranormal abilities began to emerge when he was only six. He told one of his teachers that he knew he had been away for the day in order to see a blonde girl who wore a red rose. The schoolmaster had, it was true, taken leave so that he could propose to his girlfriend. Croiset's adult life was just as restless as his childhood until he married at the age of twenty-five and set up a grocery store with money given to him by his in-laws. Unfortunately, like many sensitives, he was not a good businessman, and the failure of this enterprise led him to a nervous breakdown.

There were constant reminders of his psychic ability. Once when he was talking to a watchmaker he picked up a ruler the man had been measuring with, and images of his childhood came flooding into his mind. 'You are clairvoyant,' the watchmaker told him. Croiset had a clear presentiment of the Second World War years before it was declared. He was imprisoned by the Germans, first because his mother had been a Jewess, then because he was caught working for the Dutch resistance, like Peter Hurkos.

It was not until he was thirty-six that Gerard Croiset's extraordinary powers were used to give his life meaning and direction. One night he attended a lecture on parapsychology at an adult education class in his home town of Enschede. The lecturer, who impressed him deeply, was Professor Willem Tenhaeff of Utrecht University. Something impelled him to approach the Professor when he had finished speaking. Within minutes Dr Tenhaeff realized Croiset was someone out of the ordinary and asked that he visit him at his parapsychology laboratory at the University.

Croiset offered himself for investigation, and a collaboration began between the two men that made Croiset the most celebrated clairvoyant in Europe. Tanhaeff had forty-seven other psychics and sensitives with whom he carried out scientific experiments, but Croiset was undoubtedly the star turn.

He began to work with the police, for, as Colin Wilson points out in his book *The Psychic Detectives*, in Holland the attitude of the police towards psychics is altogether less prejudiced than in England or the United States. Dutch detectives often approached the Professor to see if any of his clairvoyants could provide clues in difficult cases. Since Croiset was his star subject, he was also looked upon as Holland's chief psychic detective.

By now the father of five, Croiset was especially sensitive when it came to cases of missing children. He was asked to help police in half a dozen countries in their search for both adults and children who had disappeared. He found that in cases of accidental disappearance, when no criminal was involved, he had an eighty per cent success rate. When it came to murder, however, he admitted he often could not pinpoint the killer, but he was able to give valuable clues through clairvoyance and, as in the case of Pat McAdam, set up the scene of the crime.

One instance which demonstrated how his psychic powers could work over immense distances was recorded in December 1959. Professor Walter E. Sandelius, head of the department of Political Sciences at Kansas University in the USA, was desperate with worry about his 24-year-old daughter, Carol. She had disappeared from a hospital in Kansas where she was receiving treatment, and had been missing for eight weeks. Dr Sandelius had read about Croiset, and telephoned Professor Tenhaeff in Utrecht. He was willing, he said, to do or pay anything to find her. Tenhaeff promised that Croiset would talk to him on the phone next day.

Sitting in an office at the University, Croiset told the Kansas professor, thousands of miles away, 'I see your daughter running over a large lawn and then crossing a viaduct. Now I see her at a place where there are stores and near them a large body of water with landing stages and many small boats. I see her riding there in a lorry and in a big red car. . . .' Sandelius interrupted, 'Yes, but is she alive?'

and Croiset replied, 'Yes, yes she is alive. Don't worry. You will hear something definite within six days.' On the sixth day, as arranged, Professor Sandelius went downstairs at eight o'clock in the morning to put a phone call through to Utrecht. He glanced towards the sitting room and was astounded to see his daughter, sitting on a sofa. Later she was able to confirm that the Dutch detective had seen her movements with astonishing accuracy.

Despite years of research, Croiset never really knew how his psychic power functioned. Once he described it as like seeing a fine powder which formed first into dots, then into lines. Out of these lines shapes and scenes would form, first in two dimensions, then three. Mostly he saw things in black and white, but curiously, if a corpse was involved, colour emerged.

Though his fame was established through his work as a psychic detective, the greater part of Croiset's life was taken up with healing. He declined payment for detection, saying that the only reward he wanted was for an account of each case to be kept in Professor Tenhaeff's records.

Croiset died on July 20, 1980, but the files at Utrecht University are a fitting memorial to a man who offered his psychic powers to help others.

Nostradamus

Reading the prophecies of Nostradamus is not a comfortable experience for twentieth-century man. The legendary French seer, who was proved time and time again to have an awesome gift for predicting the future, forecast that in 1999 our world would be shattered by global conflict in a war to end all wars. Four hundred years ago he wrote:

'In the year 1999 and seven months
From the sky will come the great king of terror . . .
Before and afterward war reigns happily.'

He seems to indicate, however, that the war, which will take place in the Northern Hemisphere, will involve two great powers in an alliance against the East:

'When those of the Northern Pole
are united together
In the East will be great fear and dread.
One day the two great leaders will be friends
The New Land [America] will be at the height of its powers
To the man of blood the number is repeated.'

'The man of blood' is identified elsewhere as being the world's third anti-Christ who will emerge in China. Thus, surprisingly, Nostradamus seems to be suggesting a war between that country and a Russian-American alliance. And after it is over?

'For forty years the rainbow shall not appear.

For forty years it shall be seen every day

The parched earth shall wax drier and drier,

And a great flood when it shall appear.'

This, he seems to forecast, would be the wasteland resulting from a nuclear war. He permits us one glimmer of hope. Before all hell breaks loose 'the Heavens shall show signs', perhaps giving mankind a chance to turn back from his folly.

Surveying our century from four hundred years ago, Nostradamus also predicted strife in the Middle East which would bring a Moslem rebellion against the Christian West; he wrote of the Iraq–Iran war and of how 'the city of Hashem' [Beirut] would be 'attacked by numerous armies and destroyed'. He is credited with having prophesied the atom bomb attacks on Hiroshima and Nagasaki in 1945.

Many of his predictions are stated in quite clear terms, even mentioning people by name, whereas others are phrased in such general terms that even the most devoted Nostradamus scholars sometimes disagree on their interpretation. But his reputation as Europe's greatest prophet rests on the number of times he was proved right, both in his own lifetime and beyond.

Nostradamus was born in Provence on December 14, 1503. His real name was Michel de Nostredame. He decided to change it to the Latin form when he was a student at university. His family was of Jewish descent, but their conversion to Christianity meant young Michel was brought up in the Catholic faith. His grandfathers undertook his education between them, teaching him classical languages, Hebrew and astrology. As an adolescent he studied philosophy at Avignon, then he went on to the University of Montpellier, where he took up medicine, proving himself a brilliant scholar. His fame as a doctor spread rapidly during an outbreak of plague, when he saved many patients who had been regarded by other doctors as incurable. Some of his success was undoubtedly due to his refusal to 'bleed' patients who were desperately ill — a revolutionary idea in the medical world of the early 16th century.

He had seen so much suffering during the plague that he began to search for a deeper insight into the meaning of life by reading every book he could lay hold of on alchemy, magic and the occult. Academic life proved too restricting, so he set out to travel throughout France in a quest for knowledge. He eventually settled in the town of Agen, where he married a young woman of aristocratic blood and went on to raise a family, but when the plague paid another visit to France it claimed his young wife and children as victims. With all his medical skills he had not been able to save them. Bowed with grief, his mind in a turmoil, he set out once again on his search for Truth.

After six years wandering in France, Corsica and Italy he returned to Provence in 1547 and settled down at Salon, where he married a rich widow. It was here his prophetic gift first came to light in written form.

In 1550 Nostradamus published an almanac containing predictions for the coming year, which proved to be so uncannily accurate that people begged him to produce another. He went on turning out almanacs year by year, but his prophetic vision had become so great that it could not be contained in annual predictions. He had in mind a far grander scheme: a complete series of prophecies dealing with events from his own time until the end of the world in the year 7,000. The prophecies were to be divided into ten books, all simply entitled *Centuries*, each volume containing one hundred predictions. They were to be written mostly in quatrains — that is, verses of four lines — their meaning obscured in order to prevent him being accused of witchcraft and brought before the Inquisition. He used a mixture of anagrams, symbols and Old French, as well as deliberately confusing the dated order of the prophecies, but scholars throughout the years have managed to decode his work. Only in the more obscure quatrains have they disagreed as to meaning. Nostradamus left posterity a picture of himself at work in one of his quatrains:

'Seated at night in my secret study
Alone, reposing over the brass tripod,
A slender flame leaps out of the solitude
Making me pronounce that which is not vain.'

Using an instrument similar to the forked rod still employed today for the purpose of divining, he would crouch over a bowl of water on a brass tripod and gaze into its depths as the rod dipped and swerved. From the movement of the rod around the bowl, which was divided into astrological segments, he would divine the future. The 'slender flame' he refers to is the moment of prophetic inspiration. Bowl and rod were used in much the same way that a fortune teller uses a crystal ball, merely to concentrate his powers.

His reputation was established in his own day by several incidents which demonstrated his remarkable mystic vision. While travelling through Italy, for instance, he fell on his knees before a young Franciscan monk called Felice Peretti and addressed him as 'Your Holiness.' Both the monk and those who witnessed this extraordinary behaviour were astounded. But in 1585 that same monk (who had become Cardinal Peretti) was elected Pope Sixtus V. Later, when Nostradamus lived in Salon, he was visited by Queen Catherine de Medici, one of his greatest admirers. The prophet was drawn towards a pale-faced boy in her entourage, singled him out and pronounced that one day he would be king. The boy was Henry of Navarre, who became Henry IV of France.

One of his most famous prophecies concerned Queen Catherine's husband, Henry II of France. Four years before his death he saw precisely how it would happen. Everyone at Court knew of the prediction but dare not speak of it aloud. Nostradamus wrote:

'The young lion shall overcome the old one
In martial field by a single duel,
In a golden cage shall be put out his eye
Two wounds from one, then shall he die a cruel death.'

The 'young lion' was an officer called Montgomery, captain of the French King's Scottish Guard who while jousting with Henry ('the old lion') in a tournament, accidentally pierced the monarch's golden helmet with his lance, putting out his eye and penetrating his brain. The King died after ten days of agony, thus fulfilling the 'cruel death'.

The death of another king, England's Charles I, was vividly described in several verses. Nostradamus spoke of how 'the fortress near the Thames' would fall, 'then the King that was kept within, shall be seen near the bridge in his shirt. . . .' In fact Charles was taken to Windsor Castle, overlooking the Thames, after his defeat by Parliamentary forces in December 1648. A few weeks later, wearing a white shirt, he was taken out and beheaded. In another verse Nostradamus wrote:

'The Parliament of London will put their King to death.
He will die because of the shaven heads in council. . . .'

Clearly the prophet was referring to the Roundheads whom he despised, saying that Cromwell was 'more like a butcher than an English king.' He was quite certain that the Great Plague of London in 1665 was divine punishment for the execution of Charles:

'The Great Plague of the maritime city
Shall not cease until the death be revenged
Of the just blood by price condemned without crime . . .'

He foresaw the Great Fire of London which swept through the capital the following year with such clarity that for once he gave a precise date, leaving out the first two digits as was his custom. 'The blood of the just shall be dry in London', he wrote. 'Burnt by the fire of three times twenty and six.'

Napoleon, the man whom Nostradamus considered the first anti-Christ (Hitler being the second and the third yet to appear on the world scene), is spoken of many times in the books as though Nostradamus could not rid his mind of the man who would bring France almost to her knees because of his ambition. In the first *Century* he refers to Napoleon's birth in Corsica, then an Italian possession:

'An Emperor shall be born in Italy
Who shall cost the Empire dear,

They shall say, with what peoples he keeps company!
He shall be found less a Prince than a butcher.'
Later the prophet saw with equal clarity the tragic fate of the little
Corsican whose meteoric rise to power changed the course of history:
'The Great Empire will soon be exchanged for a small place,
   which will soon begin to grow,
A small place of tiny area in the middle of which
He will come to lay down his sceptre.'
In fact Napoleon was stripped of his 'great Empire' and exiled to the
small island of Elba in 1814, but the following year he escaped and for
one hundred days sought to regain his power. His end came when he
was seized for a second time and sent to imprisonment and death on
the tiny island of St Helena in the South Atlantic.

Nostradamus actually named the second anti-Christ in his predictions, getting the name right except for one letter. He referred to him
as Hister instead of Hitler. The reference occurs in a verse thought to
describe the early years of the Second World War when German armies
swept across the Rhine into France:
'Beast wild with hunger will cross the rivers,
The great part of the battlefield [the Allies]
Will be against Hister.'
The prophet foresaw both the beginning and the end of Adolf Hitler
in this incredible verse:
'In the mountains of Austria near the Rhine
There will be born of simple parents
A man who will claim to defend Poland and Hungary
And whose fate will never be certain.'
He told of weapons the like of which the world had never seen before
and 'machines of flying fire', referring to bombers and the early V
weapons. He also foresaw Hitler's treatment of the Jews in concen-
tration camps and their death in the infamous ovens:
'The exiles that were carried into the Isles,
At the whim of a most cruel monarch [Hitler]
Shall be murdered, and put in the sparks of fire. . . .'
For once Nostradamus leaves the subject of man's infinite capacity for
self-destruction when he speaks of a romance which caused a king to
lose his throne — the abdication of Edward VIII, brought about
because of his love for the divorced American Mrs Wallis Simpson. In
one verse he says:
'For not wanting to consent to the divorce
Which afterwards will be recognized as unworthy,
the King of the islands will be forced to flee
And one put in his place who has no sign of kingship.'
The last line refers to the Duke of York, who, though he had no
training or experience, took over his brother's throne and became

George VI when Edward and Mrs Simpson slipped quietly into exile in France:

'A kingdom in dispute and divided between the brothers
To take the arms and the Britannic name,
And the English title. He shall advise himself late
Surprised in the night and carried into the French air.'

There seems to be no part of our history about which Nostradamus did not have some glimmer of knowledge. Returning to our own part of the 20th century, he foretold not only great conflict between Arabs and Jews but between Islam and the West. Some interpreters believe he referred to the conflict in Northern Ireland in a verse which begins 'Before the coming of the ruin of the Celts', and that he foresaw the Falklands War in a prophecy which reads:

'After a naval combat, England will know her greatest alarm.
Then the Soviet adversary will pale with fear
Having sown terror in the Atlantic (or the Atlantic Alliance)'

Nostradamus predicted great social upheaval before the end of our century in which all the old orders would be changed. He prophesied that the reappearance of Halley's Comet in 1985 would bring profound changes in human destiny. But for those of us who survive into the twenty-first century there is, he promises, a thousand years of peace, a Utopian world in which man will forsake aggression and war.

The prophet predicted his own death in 1566, and before it happened he went to an engraver in Salon asking him to engrave a date on a small metal plate, and instructing him that it should be placed in his coffin. In 1700 it was decided to move the coffin from the grave where it had laid for 134 years and move it to a more prominent site. Before it was lowered into the earth for the rest of eternity, those present decided to open the coffin. All that was left of Nostradamus was his skeleton, but on his chest lay the metal plate. The date engraved was 1700.

Jeane Dixon

The violence that cut down three brothers of the Kennedy family was foreseen by Jeane Dixon, America's famous modern seer. The beautiful, dark-haired prophetess predicted the assassination of two of them and the tragic accident that nearly killed the third.

Eleven years before his death she had a psychic vision of John F. Kennedy as she knelt in church one day. She saw an outline of the

White House, a tall, blue-eyed young man with a thick shock of brown hair standing in front of it and the numerals 1–9–6–0. A voice told her that a Democrat who would be inaugurated as President in 1960 would be assassinated while in office.

When John Kennedy was duly elected and became, many felt, a new symbol of hope Jeane Dixon prayed that her prophecy would prove to be wrong. But whenever she looked into the crystal ball which she used to concentrate her power, she saw a huge, black cloud over the White House. In the summer of 1963, when the Kennedys' infant son, Patrick, lost his brief struggle for survival, people asked her if that was the reason for the cloud. She said it was not.

As the year drew on towards November the dark cloud in her vision began to descend on the White House. There was talk of Kennedy going to Dallas. She felt compelled to speak out, to warn someone. She knew that Kay Halle, daughter of Cleveland philanthropist Samuel Halle, was a close friend of the Kennedy family. One day she made an appointment to see her.

'The President has just made a decision to go to some place in the South — you must get word to him not to take the trip,' Mrs Dixon said urgently. 'I know he will be killed. You must warn him.' Kay Halle was embarrassed. She knew Mrs Dixon was highly regarded as a seer, but she also knew that the Kennedy family had no time for psychics. She could not bring herself to deliver the message.

On November 22, 1963, the President and his wife flew to Dallas, Texas, and Jeane Dixon arranged to meet a friend for lunch in Washington. Somehow she had lost her appetite. She could not eat a thing. When, amidst great uproar, news went round the restaurant that someone had shot Kennedy she covered her face with her hands and said to her friend, 'He is dead.' When people protested he was only wounded she repeated 'No, he is dead.' After it was all over she admitted, 'I have never had anything overpower me like this vision.'

Within three months of the assassination of President Kennedy by Lee Harvey Oswald, she knew another blow was coming for the stricken family. She begged someone to warn the handsome young Senator Edward Kennedy to stay away from private aeroplanes for at least two weeks. But the morning after her prophecy news was announced that 'Teddy' had been gravely injured in a chartered plane crash. His back was broken.

Forewarning of the death of Robert Kennedy, who had been so close to the President, came to her in a startling way. She was addressing a convention at the Ambassador Hotel in Los Angeles when a questioner from the floor asked if she thought Robert Kennedy would become President himself one day. Suddenly she saw a black curtain fall between her and the audience. Shaken, she answered, 'No, he will not. He will never be President because of a tragedy that will take place right here in this hotel.' A week later, Robert Kennedy was gunned down at the Ambassador.

Jeane Dixon must be the most glamorous seer in the history of prophecy. Small, slim, with dark hair and blue-green eyes, at one time she used to carry her crystal ball to appointments tucked under her ranch mink coat. She is married to wealthy businessman James Dixon, and she lives in an impressive house with marble floors and antique French furniture, sleeping in a canopied bed once owned by the Empress Eugénie. Strictly vegetarian, she neither smokes nor drinks and attends church every morning. Many great seers have had the same abstemious pattern of life.

She was born Jeane Pinckert in a Wisconsin lumbering village in 1918, but moved to California early in her childhood. She was told by a gypsy that she had the gift of prophecy. When she was only nine she met a lady called Marie Dressler who was thinking of opening a boarding house because she was having no luck as an actress. The little girl looked into the crystal ball she had been given as a plaything and saw sparkling lights and dollar bills. She told her parents. They urged Marie Dressler to go on with her stage career. When she became one of the great names of cinema between the wars the actress remembered the nine-year-old's prediction and said she might never have had a career but for her.

When Jeane left school she went to work in a real estate office, proving herself a first-class business-woman. Stories of her psychic ability spread quickly. During the Second World War she was having her hair set in Westmore's Beauty Salon in Los Angeles when Carole Lombard, the beautiful blonde actress wife of Clark Gable, strolled in. As they were introduced she felt a warning vibration and begged her not to go anywhere by plane for six weeks. The actress replied that she had to leave almost immediately on a tour to promote the sale of war bonds. She laughingly tossed a coin to see whether or not to fly. The coin came down heads, she took her plane to the Mid-west and was killed when it crashed without ever reaching its destination.

After her marriage Jeane Dixon moved to Washington, where she established herself as a prophet on world affairs to whom some of the most powerful men in the world were prepared to listen. America's wartime President, Franklin Delano Roosevelt, summoned her to the White House. He was not the first President to consult a psychic. Abraham Lincoln was persuaded by his wife to send for a young medium called Nettie Colburn when he was anxious about the state of the nation. Mrs Dixon and Roosevelt talked about many things, and when he asked her bluntly how long he had to live she answered with equal frankness but refused to give the date of his death. She correctly predicted that China would turn communist at a time when most people thought that ideology totally alien to the Chinese way of thought.

Jeane Dixon in her husband's real estate office

Roosevelt enjoyed their meetings. 'Take good care of the ball,' he would say with a twinkle when she left him.

She became deeply interested in politics, and with her husband frequently attended embassy parties and developed friendships with several ambassadors. One afternoon in 1945 at a reception given by the Agent General for India, she met a military attaché, Nawabjaba Sher Ali, who asked her for a private reading. She received the soldier at her office and after looking into her crystal ball told him that a partition of India would take place within two years. He protested that no such thing could ever happen but she forecast the date it was announced — February 20, 1947.

Several years later Earl Jellicoe, visiting the British Embassy in Washington, invited her for lunch and asked how she could possibly have foreseen the partition of India two years before it happened. She told him the date had appeared quite clearly in the crystal ball. The numerals were as distinct as the prices listed on their menu. She also added that people from the East were much easier to 'read' than westerners because they did not put up such strong mental barriers.

Ruth Montgomery in *A Gift of Prophecy*, her biography of Jeane Dixon, tells how she forecast her own mother's death. While on a business trip to New York with her husband she had a premonition that they were going to experience a tragedy in the family. At dinner she could hardly eat. 'Death is very near me,' she said. 'It is either my mother or my father.' When they returned to the hotel where they were staying there was a telegram informing them that her mother had died suddenly from a blood clot on the brain.

Over the next few decades her predictions were read nationwide, sometimes in a syndicated column seen by millions of people. Her prophecies continued to be quite remarkable. When she met Winston Churchill in Washington in 1945 she told him that he would be out of office after the war but back in power by 1952. The great man retorted, 'You're wrong. Britain will never let me down.' But she was proved right. She foresaw the assassination of Mahatma Gandhi by a Hindu fanatic in 1948 and the rise in Egypt years later of another great leader, President Sadat.

By the sixties she had become so well known that letters from Europe and Asia addressed simply 'Jeane Dixon, U.S.A.' reached her without any trouble. She made many startling predictions about that decade including the explosion of racial violence in the South, which she rightly warned would grow to such terrible proportions that there would be rioting in the streets. She accurately foretold the death of Dag Hammarskjöld, secretary-general of the United Nations, in a plane crash and also "saw" long before it happened the suicide of Marilyn Monroe. The death of that beautiful and tragic star came to her in a 'psychic flash'.

Jeane Dixon has always been extremely devout and believes that the gift of prophecy comes from God. Once she was asked whether the constant revelations of tragedy did not sometimes weigh heavily on her. She said she did not let them. The only time she was really upset for an extended period was when she knew that President Kennedy was going to be assassinated and could do nothing to stop it.

She has won fame as a crystal gazer but some of her most remarkable premonitions were revealed by unsought visions. . . . Four years before the great Ecumenical Council called by Pope John in 1962 she had a fantastic vision in church one day. Reaching into her purse for coins to buy candles, she found her hands entangled in a mass of purple and gold balls. They floated upward and merged into a massive purple disc edged with gold. The most glorious sunshine flooded the church, and suddenly it was overflowing with people of every nation. When it was over she felt a wonderful sense of peace and completeness.

From experience Jeane Dixon found that the early hours before daybreak provided the clearest channels for psychic meditation. She gets up sometimes at two or three in the morning and sits in the darkness waiting for the dawn, crystal ball ready in front of her.

For this present generation her prophecy is as chilling as that of Nostradamus four centuries earlier: a great war breaking out in the 1980s and a new era of peace starting in 1999. But it is a comfort to know a few of her predictions that have not turned out to be right so far. Russia did not invade Iran or Palestine; China has not used germ warfare against the USA and the Vietnamese war lasted longer than her predicted ninety days. Better to hope she is right when she speaks of a great new world leader rising up in the East towards the end of this millennium, 'a leader who will draw all nations together'.

Joanna Southcott

Devonshire farmer's daughter Joanna Southcott was an eccentric eighteenth-century prophet who formed her own religious sect and at the age of sixty-four announced she was about to give birth to the new Messiah. One of her most bizarre prophecies was that only 144,000 souls would be admitted to paradise when the day of judgment arrived, but she assured her followers they could be certain of gaining entry with the signed and sealed certificates she offered them.

Two hundred years after her death her name has still not been forgotten, largely because of the mysterious affair of what has become known as 'Joanna Southcott's Box'. It was first heard of when a group of her latter-day admirers formed the Panacea Society at the beginning of this century. They announced that the prophet had left a sealed and corded box of writings that could only be opened by a convocation of the twenty-four bishops of England and Wales. Once the seal was broken such things as 'crime, distress and banditry' would disappear from the land. But, warned Joanna, if the convocation never met and the box remained sealed, mankind was doomed.

There are still Southcottians in England today, the Panacea Society, which study her works. They assure the world there is a box in existence, that the one opened by psychical researcher Harry Price in 1927 was not the right one and that there will be no peace until the bishops agree to meet.

Joanna was born at Gittisham, Devonshire, in April 1750, and as a girl worked in the dairy of her father's farm. He thought her too religious, and when her mother died sent her out to service. She worked in various households before gaining a post in Exeter, where she attended both the cathedral and the Wesleyan chapel as often as possible each Sunday. She was pressed to join the Methodists, and did so at Christmas 1791, upsetting the congregation by claiming she had arrived in their midst 'by divine command'.

She was forty-two the following year when, at an Easter meeting, she stood up and made some startling claims for herself. Her fellow Methodists, thinking she had a fever, advised her to go home and rest. She went to stay with her married sister at Plymtree and it was there after ten days in which she experienced 'the powers of darkness' that she began to write her prophesies.

They were put down in a mixture of rambling prose, full of spelling mistakes and peculiar grammar. To give her writings importance she hit upon the idea of sealing them up and forbidding anyone to open them until the predicted events had taken place. She used a small oval seal which she had found among rubbish in a shop where she used to work. It carried the initials 'I C' with a star above and below.

She returned to Exeter, broke with the Methodists, and in 1793 when some of her prophecies were beginning to come true began to demand recognition. She pestered clergymen to examine her claims, but vicars and bishops alike were wary of her. Convinced now she could see into the future, she continued to write her predictions year by year and seal them up, to be read at the appropriate time.

It was not until January 1801, when she issued her first publication, *The Strange Effects of Faith*, that people outside Exeter began to take any notice of her. Colonel Basil Bruce, whose father was vicar of Inglesham in Wiltshire, became her first convert of importance. He introduced her writings to several clergymen and other earnest gentlemen, and they descended on Exeter and after a 'trial' of her writings became her ardent disciples.

She moved to London in May 1802, settled at High House, Paddington, and zealously began to gather followers and build up her ministry. As she had received 'knowledge' that only 144,000 souls were eligible for eternal salvation she decided to issue sealed certificates to her own faithful. These certificates — printed sheets, bearing her oval seal in red wax — proclaimed: 'The sealed of the Lord — the elect precious man's redemption — to inherit the tree of life — to be made heirs of God and joint heirs with Jesus Christ — Joanna Southcott.'

By 1805, when 10,000 of these certificates had been issued, rumours began to circulate that she had made money out of selling salvation. The accusation was probably false. However, the bottom certainly fell out of the market in 1809 when a particularly nasty murderess called Mary Bateman was hanged at York, pronouncing herself to be a certificate holder!

Joanna continued to hold 'trials' or public debates of her prophecies at her home in Paddington. Wealthy people were often invited and received personal messages for which they made handsome contributions to the cause. She began to set up chapels for her followers in which she used the Anglican prayer book and preached fairly orthodox theology. One Southcottian chapel opened in Bermondsey, East London. It was established after her meeting with Henry Prescott, an apprentice who was generally known as 'Joseph' because of his marvellous and prophetic dreams. She interpreted his dreams for him and had them depicted on the chapel walls.

Travelling north, she set up chapels in Salford, Leeds and Stockton-on-Tees. Some extremely odd people were attracted to her. One Southcottian leader, for instance, a man named Benjamin Smith, threw himself from Blackfriars Bridge in London, fully expecting that angels would catch him. He hit his head on a stone buttress and perished.

But the most bizarre part of her ministry was still to come. At the age of sixty-four she announced in her *Third Book of Wonders* that she was to become the mother of 'Shiloh', the new Messiah, and she intended to go into retreat and wait for the birth. From October 11, 1813, she shut herself away from society in the house she now owned in Manchester Street, London. She saw only the two faithful female friends who lived with her, Jane Townley and Ann Underwood. Every bishop, peer and member of parliament she could think of received a personal letter from her telling them the glad news. She also informed *The Times* and *Morning Herald*. She expected 'Shiloh' to be born, she said, some time in the following year.

Joanna became ill on March 17, 1814, but it was not until August 1 that Jane Townley thought it necessary to call in the doctors. Nine prominent medical men attended her and were baffled. Some of them admitted that had she been a younger woman they would have concluded from her symptoms that she was four months pregnant.

There was great rejoicing among Joanna's followers when the news leaked out. They ordered a crib from Seddons of Aldersgate Street, silver feeding spoons and a superbly bound Bible, hand-tooled and blocked in gold leaf. A 'great personage' offered the Temple of Peace in Green Park as a suitable place for the confinement. When Dr Richard Reece visited her on November 19, however, Joanna told him that she was gradually dying and directed him to open her body four days after death.

On her instructions all the gifts prepared for 'Shiloh' were returned, and though Dr Reece could find nothing wrong with her she grew weaker and weaker until on December 27, 1814, she died. An autopsy was performed as she had wished. There was no sign of a physical pregnancy, no functional disorder or disease. Joanna Southcott had obviously gone through what we now call an 'hysterical' or 'phantom' pregnancy brought on by her desire to be mother of the new Messiah.

She was buried in St John's Wood Cemetery with a tombstone bearing the line 'Thou'lt appear in greater power.' When the stone was shattered by a huge explosion in Regent's Park in 1874 her followers hoped that it was a sign she would return again. The mystery of Joanna Southcott's box remains to intrigue another generation. The one that Harry Price opened contained, he alleged, nothing more than an old nightcap, a pistol and various oddments, none of them belonging to Joanna. The whereabouts of the real one remains a secret.

Mother Shipton

One of the most famous tourist sights in Yorkshire lies in the ancient town of Knaresborough on the River Nidd. There, enfolded in magnificent scenery, is a well with petrifying waters and Mother Shipton's cave, once the haunt of a legendary prophetess.

Ursula Sontheil — or Mother Shipton, as she became better known — was a sibyl who could look so far into the future that in the mid-16th century she prophesied:

'Carriages without horses shall go
And accidents shall fill the world with woe.'

And, anticipating the first modern telegraph of 1837, she promised her contemporaries:

'Around the world thoughts shall fly
In the twinkling of an eye.'

She looked like a witch with her misshapen body, crooked legs, strange goggling eyes and crooked nose, but it was said that any person who met or talked with her came away with the greatest respect for the odd little creature.

According to local legend she inherited her powers of clairvoyance from her mother. Agatha Sontheil was a wild creature, left an orphan at an early age and forced to earn her living by begging. Wandering through the Knaresborough woods one day, she met a young man of aristocratic bearing. They became lovers. Not only did he provide her with more than enough money for her needs but, says the legend, he announced that he was no ordinary mortal and would give her extraordinary powers, including the gift of prophecy.

Whatever the truth, people flocked to see her whenever she returned from her wanderings with the young man. On one occasion, the story goes, she was so angered by their curiosity that she invoked the aid of the winds and they were blown back into their own homes. This, and similar incidents, led to her being brought before the local justices on a charge of witchcraft, but she was acquitted.

Agatha gave birth to her daughter Ursula in July 1488 — 'Near this petrifying well I first drew breath, as records tell.' She was an ugly, deformed infant, and after producing her Agatha retired to a convent, where she soon died.

Ursula Sontheil was put into the care of the parish nurse, who found the task of looking after her more than she could manage. Eventually it was decided to send her to school, where she would be submitted to harsh discipline. Her teachers were surprised to find that she learned to read and write more easily than any of the other children, and demonstrated a quick intelligence. She was subjected to cruel taunts in the playground because of her deformities. In return, it was claimed, she used witchcraft to punish her tormentors so that they felt themselves pulled, pinched and hauled about even when she stood apart from them. Ursula was sent away from school for this reason and never educated again.

Little is known of her youth and early married life except that she became the wife of Toby Shipton from Shipton, near York, when she was twenty-four. She set up home in a respectable way, but as soon as it became known that she could see into the future people from all around flocked to her doorstep. At first she devoted her gifts to purely local matters such as predicting births, marriages and deaths, but it soon became obvious that her range of prophecy was greater than that, and she began to turn her attention to affairs of the world.

Mother Shipton (as she was known from now on) always prophesied in symbolic language. Her first great prophecy of European significance was recorded in the following words:

'When the English Lion shall set his feet on Gallic shore
Then shall the lilies begin to droop for fear.
There shall be much weeping and wailing among the ladies of that country
Because the princely Eagle shall join with the Lion to tread all that shall oppose them.'

The English Lion was Henry VIII of England, who in 1513 landed on the Gallic shore with a total force of 50,000 men. Lilies are the national emblem of France, and Henry's invasion did indeed create great fear. The princely Eagle was Maximilian, the German emperor who joined forces with Henry to overcome the French.

After Henry's victory in France Mother Shipton turned her attention to the great Cardinal Wolsey, who she called 'The Mitred Peacock', and foretold exactly what would happen when the proud prelate's wealth and influence began to equal that of the king himself.

'The Mitred Peacock now shall begin to plume himself

And his train shall make a great show in the world.

He shall want to live at York, and shall see it, but shall never come thither

And finally, after great misfortunes he shall finish with Kingston.'

Mother Shipton's prophecy with regard to his never seeing York was fulfilled, for though he held that bishopric, in addition to several others, he was prevented from going there when his 'great train' was stopped and he was arrested for high treason. After much humiliation he came into the care of Sir William Kingston, Constable of the Tower of London.

She foresaw the dissolution of the monasteries years before Henry VIII issued his ruthless orders, and rightly predicted the suffering of the poor who would no longer be cared for by monks. Looking further into the future, she predicted, as several other prophets did also, that traumatic event in English history, the execution of Charles I.

'The Crown then fits the White King's head

Who with the lilies soon shall wed;

Then shall a peasant's bloody knife

Deprive a great man of his life.'

The White King was Charles I, robed in white for his coronation. The lilies are a symbol of his French bride, Henrietta Maria, daughter of Henry IV of France.

Mother Shipton's prophetic verse covered page after page in symbolic couplets as she caught glimpses of a future she would never see. 'Men shall walk over rivers and under rivers, Iron in the water shall float', she predicted.

She foretold the death of that pathetic little Queen, Jane Grey 'a virtuous lady then shall die, For being raised up too high' and the defeat of the Spanish Armada 'And the Western Monarch's wooden horses, Shall be destroyed by Drake's forces'. Sir Walter Raleigh's popularization of the tobacco plant and the potato was predicted in the following lines:

'Over a wild and stormy sea

Shall a noble sail

Who to find will not fail

A new and fair countree

From whence he shall bring

A herb and a root. . . .'

A long time before her death Mother Shipton told her friends the day and hour when she would take her departure. Exactly to time in the year 1561 she took solemn leave of all those near to her, lay down on her bed and died. She was seventy-three.

Her memory is still honoured today, especially in Yorkshire. A stone has been erected to her memory near Clifton about a mile from the City of York.

John Dee

John Dee was the sixteenth century's 007, a man shrewd and sophisticated enough to be secret agent, spy and 'noble intelligencer' to Queen Elizabeth I. Yet this same man also claimed that he had found a way to talk to the angels and knew what went on in heaven.

Dee was given the code number 007 — also chosen by Ian Fleming for his popular fictional spy, James Bond — when he was sent to the Continent to find out what was going on in foreign diplomatic circles. The Queen called him 'my ubiquitous eyes'. But at the same time Dee was immersed in occult activities which rendered him trance-like, and made pronouncements that made his enemies regard him as a credulous fool.

John Dee was a scholar, highly revered for his work on mathematics and navigation, but besides being a man of science he also accepted the existence of a sixth sense which could emerge spontaneously in dreams, visions or intuitions. Through this sixth sense he believed he had learned the secrets of the angels, and knew which of them controlled various parts of the world. He also believed he had caught a glimpse of future traumatic events when in a trance-like state.

He looks out at us from sixteenth-century portraits with brooding, smouldering eyes. His beard is long, white and pointed and he wears a deep white ruff and a black cap. He was born on July 13, 1527, at Mortlake, which was then a pleasant village on the outskirts of London. An intense young man with a passion for books, he became an undergraduate at Cambridge when he was only fifteen, and got into the habit of sleeping only four hours a night so that he might study more. His efforts were rewarded when, before the age of twenty, he was also made a Fellow of the newly founded Trinity College. Even at this early stage of his career it was rumoured that Dee dabbled in witchcraft and was somewhat eccentric.

For the next thirty years he travelled widely in Europe, lecturing at universities and building up his reputation as a mathematical scholar and astrologer. He was said to have been largely responsible for the revival of interest in mathematics in England in the sixteenth century, and his work on navigation has earned him a place in all the reference books. But John Dee was as deeply engrossed with the magic formula for invoking Venus as he was with mathematical equations, charts and maps. He became intensely interested in the 'angelic magic' introduced by a priest called Abbot Trithemius in a scholarly work entitled *Steganographia*. He also cast the horoscopes of the great men and women of his time, and was unwise enough in 1554 to forecast when the reign of

Mary Tudor, who was on the English throne, would come to an end.

At this time Mary's half-sister, the Princess Elizabeth, was under house arrest, suspected of plotting with Thomas Wyatt in a rebellion against the Catholic Queen's rule of terror. Through one of her ladies-in-waiting the young Princess, hungry for intellectual companionship, began a correspondence with Dee. One day he sent her his horoscope for Queen Mary. It was discovered by two informers in Elizabeth's household and the letters between the young Princess and the scholarly astrologer were reported to Mary's Council.

Dee was immediately arrested and, suspected of plotting Mary Tudor's death by black magic, thrown into prison. 'They believe me to be a companion of hellhounds and a caller and conjurer of wicked spirits', he wrote to a friend, deeply distressed. He insisted that his acceptance of the sixth sense and his attempts to tap the powers that existed had nothing to do with witchcraft. He told Lord Burghley — who was to become Elizabeth's great Principal Secretary of State — that 'some people, like himself, had supernormal powers not of a magician but of a peculiar and scientific quality.'

Dee was eventually cleared of high treason but on his release was immediately rearrested and clapped into prison again, this time on the charge of being a heretic. No one could prove heresy and he finally gained his freedom at the end of 1555.

For some years he contented himself with scientific research and experiment. His library was famous throughout England, being exceptionally large for the period and containing books and manuscripts on every subject under the sun.

When Mary Tudor died in 1558 and Elizabeth ascended to the throne, John Dee came into his own. Always loyal and generous to those she considered had served her well, Elizabeth rewarded Dee for his past services by making him her personal astrological adviser. It was Dee who selected a propitious date for her coronation; he who was called upon for advice when she suspected that sorcery was being used against her. At the same time, realizing his shrewd understanding of all that was going on in Europe, she created him her secret agent 007 and sent him off on spying missions to foreign Courts.

Because Dee was such a favourite with the Queen he was allowed to carry on with his occult experiments. He used techniques that sometimes demanded the use of a divining rod, at other times a pendulum. In 1580 he began to experiment with different occult methods. 'I had a sight offered me in a crystal this day,' he wrote in his diary. He became increasingly absorbed in the 'angelic magic' expounded by the Abbot Trithemius and in October 1581 began his attempts to communicate with the angels. Perhaps, it has been suggested, the spirits were trying to get in touch with him. His sleep had been increasingly disturbed, his dreams strange, and there were mysterious knockings and rappings going on in his house for which he could not account.

He worked through several mediums, including a Greek peasant woman, but eventually in March 1582 he found Edward Kelley. This strange young man, who was only twenty-seven when Dee met him, had packed his short life full of mystery and dubious adventures. He had started out as a notary but was accused of forgery. He had studied alchemy and had in his possession strange elixirs, powders and cipher manuscripts. It was even rumoured that he practised necromancy, the rite of raising the dead for the purpose of prediction and divination.

Through Kelley, Dee became convinced he was in touch with the heavenly host. The young man obviously had occult powers. But Dee did not trust him. He persuaded the angels to answer in a language called 'Enochian', and according to one of them it was the same that was used in the Garden of Eden. Records of these conversations, compiled by Dee, have survived to this day. The spirit utterances were not particularly illuminating, apart from one passage which apparently records a contact between Dee and the angel Uriel on May 5, 1583:

Dee: As concerning the vision which was presented yesternight (unlooked for) to the sight of Edward Kelley as he sat at supper with me in my hall, I mean the appearing of the very sea and many ships thereon, and the cutting of the head of a woman by a tall, black man, what are we to imagine thereof?

Uriel: The one did signify the provision of foreign powers against the welfare of this land; which they shall shortly put into practice.

The other, the death of the Queen of Scots: it is not long unto it.

The angel, speaking through Kelley (who did not understand the Enochian language), was obviously prophesying the attempted invasion of England by the Spanish Armada in 1588 and the execution of Mary, Queen of Scots in 1587.

At first sight John Dee's records seemed to have been written in gibberish, but fellow scholars admitted that 'Enochian' after careful study did show traces of syntax and grammar. To the modern reader they would be almost impossible to decipher as they contained long references to Elizabethan forms of magic and alchemy.

The strange association between the rogue and the scholar lasted for seven years. They held hundreds of séances and the angels who spoke through Kelley seemed determined to keep the men on the move. Acting according to angelic instructions, they wandered all over Europe. By the spring of 1587, however, Kelley was obviously beginning to get bored. After quarrelling with Dee he went off to try his hand at alchemy, hoping to be able to transmute base metals into gold.

John Dee, unable to find another medium who could work with him, returned to England, gave up all his occult practices and returned to mathematics. He seems to have lost touch with the angels. He died in 1608.

Chapter seven

MYSTICS AND MEDIUMS

From earliest times man has been fascinated by people who claim to have experience of the occult and paranormal. To many, the idea of communicating with the 'other side' can be dismissed as poppycock! Nevertheless, even taking the frauds and cheats into account, there remains an impressive body of men and women who have given convincing evidence of genuine paranormal powers.

Harry Edwards

Harry Edwards was considered by many to be the greatest spiritual healer this country has ever known. White-haired, stocky, dark-suited, he could have been taken for any city businessman except for one thing: his charisma was such that he drew thousands to watch him heal in public and thousands more were inspired to write letters to him.

He was, he claimed, guided by the spirits of Lord Lister, the founder of antiseptic surgery, and by Louis Pasteur, the great French scientist. His patients ranged from the very poor to members of the royal family, foreign rulers, cabinet ministers, army commanders, judges and bishops. Lady Baden-Powell, wife of the founder of the Boy Scout movement, was a regular visitor to his Spiritual Healing Sanctuary at Shere, deep in the Surrey countryside. So too was Princess Marie Louise, grand-daughter of Queen Victoria. Famous conductor Sir Adrian Boult received healing from him, and so did the ex-Queen of Spain.

With strong, workmanlike hands he seemed to achieve miracles by soothing away pain, remoulding twisted limbs, banishing disease and restoring sight and hearing. He did not always have to be in the same room. Sometimes he achieved what he called Absent Healing, when he was hundreds of miles away from his patient. Huge files exist bulging with letters confirming that his treatment had worked, yet he never had any medical or surgical training and was not instructed in any school of psychology.

His origins were quite ordinary. Harry Edwards was born in Crayford Street, Islington, in 1893, the eldest of nine children. His father was a compositor in the printing industry. His mother, the driving force of the family, who lived into her nineties to see him become famous, worked as a Court dressmaker for a firm which had premises at the back of Liberty's in Regent Street, London.

He was a young tearaway, a holy terror who was constantly being punished for some misdeed or other. The family moved house several times in South London, but his formative years were in Wood Green. He became a reformed character when he fell in love with a butcher's daughter at the age of twelve.

After leaving school at fourteen, he was apprenticed to a publishing house where his first job was as a floor sweeper at six shillings a week. He slowly climbed the ladder until he became a 'reader', checking printers' proofs for error. Discovering politics, he became an ardent Liberal, often standing on a soap box at Hyde Park Corner to support his cause. But he was not successful as a candidate and had to content himself with being an organizer.

During the First World War he served with the Royal Sussex Regiment. He started off in the ranks, but when his battalion embarked for service in India in 1915 he found himself promoted by degrees. After a crash course in engineering, including bridge-building (which he swore lasted no longer than sixty minutes), he was sent off to join the General Headquarters of the Mesopotamian Expeditionary Force in Baghdad.

One day he was sent for by General Marshall, who asked him if he would like a commission. Edwards thought this preferable to being a corporal and answered, 'Yes, sir'. After being 'commissioned in the field' he was sent to Tekrit, a walled Arab town not far from Baghdad. Here he found himself in charge of a wild bunch of nomadic Arabs with instructions to lay a railway track between Tekrit and Baghdad.

He was remarkably successful, and so impressed his superiors he was sent to the sun-baked hills of north-west Persia (now Iran) with the grand title 'Assistant Director of Labour, Persian Lines of Communication.' He ended up with the rank of Acting Major and the task of building roads and bridges strong enough to carry military equipment, in the most inhospitable terrain.

Strangely enough it was here, as a slender, fair-haired young officer, that Harry Edwards showed the first glimmer of his great gift for healing. Local labour was used, and that meant women and children as well as able-bodied men clamoured for jobs. Casualties were high, if not serious, among the unskilled workers, and the 'director', with little more than iodine, bandages and castor oil in his medical kit, found himself expected to cure everything. Strangely enough, he found even chronic conditions of illness among these rough hill people responded to his quiet touch. Soon everyone in the area had heard of the great 'Hakim'.

One day a local sheikh decided to bring his aged mother for treatment. The frail old lady had been placed in a sort of curtained box on the side of a horse and one look told Major Edwards that she was pitifully weak, in great pain and not far from death. He knew he could not ask the sheikh to take her away and let her die in peace — he would most likely have been killed for refusing his 'treatment'. On the other hand, he had not the remotest idea what was wrong with her, and had only the contents of his primitive medicine box to deal with the emergency. After examining her carefully, laying his hands on her body and praying for inspiration, he quickly prepared a potion from carbolic toothpowder. He gave it to her with trepidation and groaned inwardly as the satisfied sheikh took her away again with a large bottle of 'Hakim's' medicine. When the sheikh returned again a few days later accompanied by an escort of tribesmen yelling and firing off their rifles, Edwards thought he was about to meet his end. Instead the sheikh greeted him with joy, saying he had come to tell the great 'Hakim' that his mother was completely recovered, was free from pain and looking better than she had done for years. To show his gratitude he had brought gifts of carpets and gold pieces worth a fortune. Edwards had to refuse, but pressed to accept a gift of some kind mentioned he would like to have some fresh eggs for breakfast. Next day three hundred arrived!

Though the war ended in 1918 it was not until three years later that Acting Major Edwards arrived home. He married Phyllis White, a farmer's daughter from Long Bredy in Dorset, who had written to him all through the long years he had been abroad, and they moved into a house in Balham. Printing was the only trade he knew, so with high optimism he sank all his savings and his war gratuity into a print-works of his own. Everything went wrong. Though his married life was happy and he became the proud father of four children, his business lurched from one awful crisis to another. For the next twelve years he lived with the threat of closure and bailiffs at the door. He had, fortunately, the great gift of being able to lock up his troubles at the end of the day and lead a fulfilling life in other spheres.

He returned to politics, and gradually moved into public life. He was asked to stand for London County Council, worked for the League of Nations and after his printing business began at last to prosper, became chairman of Camberwell Peace Council.

His first contact with Spiritualism was at a church in Clements Road, Ilford, Essex. He was by no means an easy convert. One of his hobbies was conjuring; he had a number of friends in the Magic Circle and he attended the Spiritualist Church in the first place to see whether he could work out what trickery was used to produce phenomena. To his surprise, the clairvoyant made a deep and lasting impression on him. When he attended another church at Cloudsdale Road in South London some time in 1934, he was told there were spirit guides who wished to co-operate with him and that he had undoubted powers of healing. He decided to test his views by trying to develop any psychic powers he might possess.

Through 'home circles' held in his own front room and at the houses of friends, he began to heal. Results were so good that he soon began to set aside several evenings a week specifically for that purpose. His first experience of healing someone who was miles away from him came with dramatic suddenness. He had been told by a medium that the next time he heard of someone desperately ill he must concentrate all his mind upon them. The opportunity came a few days later. While attending a home circle, someone told him about a friend of hers who was dying in Brompton Hospital from advanced tuberculosis with pleurisy and haemorrhages. He suggested they might try a healing experiment. Harry Edwards told what happened next in his *Thirty*

Years a Spiritual Healer:

We sat quietly in meditation, employing our thoughts for his recovery. As I did this, with my eyes closed, I became aware that I was looking down a long, hospital ward with my attention focused on a man in the last bed but one. I was conscious of all the surrounding detail and of the man himself. So strong was this picture that even over thirty years later I can revive it at will in all its vivid detail. When I checked the description of what I had 'seen' with a relative of the patient, it was found to be correct in every detail. It proved to be my first experience of 'astral travelling'.

A week later he received news that within twenty-four hours of his intercession the haemorrhages had ceased, all pleuritic pain vanished and the patient's temperature came down to almost normal. At the next check it was found that the blood and sputum were free from infection. The doctors were amazed. Within three weeks he was well enough to be sent to a convalescent home prior to discharge. Within months he was able to resume full employment, and subsequent inquiries established that the recovery had been maintained.

Harry Edwards, still regarding his gift with an open mind, was prepared to accept that this man's recovery could have been a remarkable coincidence, but when other incidents of a similar nature occurred he was convinced of his psychic power. Before long his work was known throughout South London and he had to set aside more and more time for healing. His fame spread through the war years. He

Harry Edwards heals a crippled child

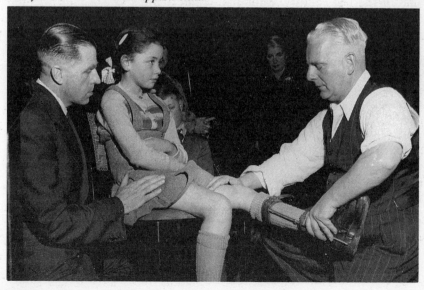

considered himself 'simply as an instrument or a channel for a higher power', though he received many letters from patients who had never been in his presence saying they had seen a man in a white coat bending over them at the time of healing.

When a bomb destroyed his London home Harry Edwards bought a typical suburban semi-detached house at Ewell in Surrey and turned the front room into his first Spiritual Healing Sanctuary. In the early days he was in the habit of using many techniques suggested by other spiritualists, including trying to link thoughts with his patient and seeking a trance-like state for himself. As the years went by he found all these things unnecessary. His methods became increasingly simple but increasingly effective. He would talk quietly with the sick person, lay hands upon the affected part of the body and in his quiet, authoritative voice tell the sufferer that his or her ailment was under control. Absent healing, too, became simpler when he found that his practice of asking a distant patient to concentrate on his illness at a specific time was not necessary. Once he had set his healing power to work it seemed to function regardless of time or space.

So many people were now writing to him and asking to see him that he had to employ a full-time secretary. He began to realize he was going to have to devote the whole of his life to healing.

The front room at Ewell became far too small for his ministry, so he began looking for something more spacious. In 1946 he was told of a house set in fourteen acres of woodland and gardens at Shere, deep in the Surrey countryside near Guildford. Burrows Lea, built at the end of the last century, rambling, comfortable and peaceful, was the perfect place for Harry Edwards. He took the plunge and bought it for £8,000, leaving himself with £18 in the bank.

After two years he began to get in the region of 3,500 letters a week, and as the number rose to over 9,000 he had to take on extra staff. Olive and George Burton joined him to help with the patients. Those who were able to travel to Burrows Lea were treated in a quiet, wood-panelled room like a chapel with a cross on the wall and masses of beautiful flowers from Harry Edwards's own garden. He loved flowers and grew and picked them in profusion. He usually performed his healing in a white coat. His hands were always left uncluttered, and he wore neither rings nor a watch. He believed the first task of a healer was to calm and steady the mind, and the first impression his patients got was of kindness, quiet strength and authority.

One of the most remarkable healing stories about him is told by Ramus Branch in his biography of the healer. (With his wife, Joan, Branch served with Harry Edwards for several years and took on the work of the Sanctuary after his death.) During harvest one August, Edward's young niece, Vivien, was critically injured in a farm accident. She was sitting on a tractor when a bale of hay slipped forward and knocked her under the heavy wheels. She suffered appalling injuries, her body being crushed and literally twisted into the ground. The tractor had to be jacked up to release her. After she had been carried gently to the farmhouse the local doctor arrived, examined her, then phoned the hospital. He was heard to say that she would probably be dead on arrival. Vivien's mother, Harry Edwards' sister, was informed of the accident and immediately phoned to ask him for absent healing. Vivien was still alive when she reached hospital but her family was warned that she would probably die during the night. Her injuries were too terrible for her to survive. Harry Edwards concentrated with all his power on trying to save his young niece. She did not die that night, or the day after. To the amazement of the whole medical staff she began to recover. Within five weeks she was well enough for them to consider her discharge; by Christmas, she was home.

Though reticent about naming VIPs and royal personages who went to him for help, Harry Edwards was openly delighted that he could do something for Lady Baden-Powell. He had, after all, been one of the first Boy Scouts to join the movement. She first contacted him when, due to keep an important appointment, she found her knee had become so swollen and painful that she could hardly walk. By telephone he told her to proceed with her plans and he would give her absent healing. Lady Baden-Powell had to be more or less carried to the train, but during the journey she began to feel better. By the time she reached her destination the pain had gone and so had the swelling. After that she often went to Shere to be 'pepped up', as she called it.

His public healing demonstrations, which started in a small way but ended with audiences of five or six thousand people at the Royal Albert Hall, became an important part of his work. He always conducted these sessions in his shirt-sleeves, and emphasized the 'spiritual' nature of any healing that people were about to witness. But his mischievous sense of humour sometimes broke through. When he had been accused by sections of the Church of conducting his meetings in an atmosphere of hysteria he turned to the audience, slowly rolled up his sleeves and said, 'I'm going to start now. By the way, don't let's have any hysteria. It'll be in the papers tomorrow!'

Advancing years seemed to make no difference to his power as a healer. Ramus Branch tells how one cold, foggy November night be and his wife — who had not yet joined Edwards at the Sanctuary — went over to Brentford, Middlesex, to see him conduct a demonstration. It took place in an unheated church, the yellow lighting casting an unreal glow over the packed audience. Harry Edwards asked if there was anyone present who was in constant pain. A hand shot up at the back of the church and he beckoned forward the sufferer.

Very slowly down the aisle came one of the most pathetic sights I have ever seen. It was a man of, I should think, about forty. He had tousled black hair and a beard and his clothes were like a bundle of rags around him for he seemed to be like a tramp . . . but it was the way he walked that stunned everyone to silence; he seemed to be half-crouching and was shuffling sideways, almost crab-like.

After a quick examination Harry Edwards declared that the major part of the man's internal pain arose as a result of severe restriction imposed upon the abdominal organs by the badly twisted and fixed state of the spine. All the time the healing was in progress the patient hardly said a word, but when it was over and he stood upright he seemed transformed into a new person. 'I can recall now the gasps of astonishment from the congregation as the man who had been barely able to walk before now literally marched back to his seat.'

But it was the sequel to this healing that Ramus Branch said he would never forget.

After the service my wife and I walked along to Kew Bridge to catch a bus home. The fog was even thicker than earlier and I asked her to wait for a moment or two whilst I went into a café to get a bar of chocolate. As I came out I was aware of a tall figure suddenly striding very rapidly through the swirling fog; so fast was he going that I had to step back quickly to avoid colliding with him. In that brief moment I could see it was the rough bearded man . . . as we both stood on the pavement gazing after him, we could hear him singing to himself as he vanished into the November fog.

In the last years of his life Harry Edwards visited South Africa and Southern Rhodesia (now Zimbabwe) and gave demonstrations of healing before vast audiences in both Johannesburg and Bulawayo. Back home at Burrows Lea he continued healing till the very end. On December 7, 1976, after a day on which he had signed batches of letters and made plans for the following day, he went to sleep in a chair, never to wake again.

Rose Gladden

Rose Gladden was only nineteen when she became fully aware that she was a psychic healer. She walked into a dry-cleaning shop in London and found the owner slumped over his counter. He was obviously in terrible pain. When she asked him what was wrong he managed to gasp out, 'I have an ulcer.' She felt a great desire to help him but did not know where to start. She has a clear memory of a voice saying 'Put your hand there.' But where? He had not even told her where the ulcer was. To her amazement she saw a tiny light, like a star, appear over his left shoulder. It floated down and came to rest on the right side of his stomach. She placed her hand there, and as she did so felt another hand cover hers and hold it steady. She seemed to be giving out tremendous heat and could not pull away. After a few seconds the man began to come round. Suddenly, he sat up. 'It's gone. The pain's gone,' he cried and rushed to tell the man next door about the incredible woman who had come to collect her cleaning.

Rose walked home knowing that it had been an important day in her life. She felt she knew now what she had come into the world to do. She had to become a healer.

Born in Edmonton, London, in 1919, she was only seven when she first realized she had a special gift of some kind. If she sat next to anyone at school suffering an ache or pain, she knew instinctively. Placing her hand on the cheek of a small friend with toothache, she would feel a warmth flow through her and into the hand she was using. The ache would, nine times out of ten, disappear.

This useful bit of schoolgirl one-upmanship did not make her life easy, far from it. She could not explain to people what happened, and also had to cope with occasions when she saw things other people did not see. During her twenties there was a difficult time when her experiences almost overwhelmed her. It was only when she met someone who recognized her as a natural psychic and taught her how to control and use her abilities that things fell into place.

Over the next forty-five years, until she slipped into semi-retirement to write her autobiography in 1985, Rose Gladden became one of the most dedicated and successful healers in Britain. An attractive woman she married twice, her second husband, Peter, playing an important part at the healing centre they set up at their home at Letchworth in Hertfordshire.

In the early days Rose Gladden saw everyone that turned up at her door. If one of her cases had attracted publicity and she had been featured in the morning papers, there would be a long queue before breakfast was over. After she had treated a ten-year-old Hitchin boy who had been confined to a wheelchair and considered inoperable by doctors, he appeared in a newspaper photograph playing football. For the next few days she was inundated with calls from anxious mothers all over the country asking if she could cure their children.

'It was like a conveyor belt,' her husband Peter said. 'Rose felt she could not do her best for people. We had to get organized, get things on a more professional footing. There are the occasional miracle-type cures which happen, but more often than not healing is a slow, gradual process.'

Mrs Gladden's home was overflowing with files of letters and reports on people who had found relief from their suffering and sometimes had experienced complete cures. Sometimes she received patients who were at the end of their tether, who had suffered so much for so long without getting relief from orthodox medicine that they were on the brink of suicide. She was often able to bring relief within minutes.

She is anxious to stress that by no means everyone experiences instant cure from healing of this kind. People should not expect miracles every time. 'The majority of those who experience improvement find that it is gradual, taking place over a period of weeks. It depends on the individual.' She believes that healing is done through the mind. 'Your hands guide the healing force and give comfort but it is the concentration of the mind that is doing the healing. You have to attune yourself to the patient and act as a channel for the healing energy.'

Rose Gladden has been a great success on both sides of the Atlantic. In America and Canada she has travelled thousands of miles, lecturing to medical specialists as well as to members of the public. At one meeting in Canada she discovered two women had travelled a thousand miles to see her.

She was asked by professors at several American universities to co-operate with them on tests. At the University of California she was wired up to a patient, a boy with a very serious nervous disorder, so that they could record what took place during the healing process. 'I am willing to submit to any test if it helps people to understand,' she says with deep sincerity.

Maxwell Cade, a psychologist who has carried out important pioneering work in meditation, relaxation and altered states of consciousness, also asked her to work with him. She helped him in the discovery of distinctive brainwave patterns in healers. The research demonstrated that on at least one level healers had a measurable effect on their patients, who after a few minutes picked up and imitated the same brainwave patterns. Rose Gladden was fascinated by this. It confirmed the theory she had had all along about the importance of being attuned to her patient.

As a natural psychic she claims to be able to see the 'aura', the protective circle of light and colour surrounding each human being. She reads the aura for ill health. One day she found she could also see silver spots and lines all over the surface of the body. It was not until some years later that she realized she was seeing the points and medians used in acupuncture. People would describe their symptoms to her but she often felt their trouble was not where they imagined it to be. She often saw the real trouble pinpointed by light. 'I'd put my hand in the light and the pain would go.'

Though she sees auras and things that other people do not — she once told a conference of nurses they must be sure to treat the dead with dignity for they often hung around their discarded frames for some time — Rose Gladden is a sensible, practical woman. Often after a healing session she will give the patient advice on how to avoid repetition of the trouble. 'But a lot of people expect you to do it all. You're the healer,' they'll say. 'You do it for me. But don't tell me to stop smoking or change my diet.'

She knows that many doctors simply shrug when her kind of healing is mentioned. But she does not see it as a substitute for medicine, only as an extension of orthodox treatment.

Matthew Manning

When sixth formers at Ashlyns School, Berkhamsted, in Hertfordshire, heard that they were to be lectured on the subject of healing by a well-known psychic they had no idea what kind of person to expect.

Probably the last thing they imagined was anyone like Matthew Manning. Young, slender, hair fashionably long, clothes fashionably casual, someone they could relate to without any difficulty.

He was breaking new ground when he accepted the invitation to speak from the headmaster of Ashlyns. As far as anyone knew it was the first time a psychic healer had ever taken a sixth-form class in a comprehensive school. He told them how by the age of eighteen he had experienced more psychic phenomena that most people hear about in a lifetime; how he had fled to the Himalayas to sort himself out after being treated as a psychic curiosity in the media; and how while he was there he realized he wanted to do something positive with his psychic power and returned to England to start work as a healer. His chief concern, he told them, was to try to convince people that unfaltering faith in the possibility of self-healing was one of the most exciting prospects for the future.

Matthew Manning's destiny was probably settled, according to some authorities, when he was still in the womb. His mother had an extremely severe electric shock three weeks before his birth. Many great psychics are thought to have been 'triggered off' by a traumatic physical experience.

He was born in August 17, 1955, and grew to be a normal, healthy, intelligent boy. The Manning family lived in an attractive modern house, open-plan, with floor-to-ceiling windows. There was nothing 'spooky' about it. On the morning of February 18, 1967, when Matthew was eleven years old, the poltergeist activity that came to be associated with him started. His father came downstairs early in the morning to find a favourite silver tankard lying on the carpet instead of being on the shelf where it was usually kept. No one in the house knew anything about it; Matthew, his sister Rosalind, eight, and his brother Andrew, six, all pleaded not guilty. It was treated as a joke until the following Wednesday when the same thing happened again. This time, it was noticed, other objects in the room had been moved. They began to suspect something freakish was happening.

The phenomena increased in power and activity. During one severe attack all the chairs in the dining and sitting rooms were jumbled together not once but twice. Suspicion that it was Matthew who was innocently responsible for the poltergeist activity increased when things started to move around him when he was in other houses.

In 1968 the Manning family moved into a beautiful old house in the village of Linton in Cambridgeshire which had been built in 1550 and extended some time between that date and 1730. There were a few 'odd happenings' they remembered later, but nothing too disturbing. Not at first. Suddenly in 1970 Matthew's bedroom became the focus of the most extraordinary activity. There were footsteps and raps, cupboard doors flew open, boots were hurled about, cushions took on a life of their own. By Easter 1971, all hell was let loose. The heavy cupboard in Matthew's room lurched away from the wall and moved towards him, his bed shook violently and started to rise from the floor. He spent the rest of the night in his parents' room on the floor in a sleeping bag and said he would not sleep in his own room again 'until something was done about it'. Next morning when the family went down to breakfast the house was in turmoil, as though a bomb had hit it. For the next few days they were subjected to the most violent poltergeist activity they had ever known, some of it purely mischievous, some quite frightening. One morning the bed in which Matthew's sister had slept was found with two of its feet hanging out of a first-floor window. On more than one occasion he saw the words 'Matthew beware' scribbled on the wall in child-like handwriting.

Now a boarder at a public school, Matthew began to feel he was only safe when he went back there after the holidays. But in the summer term of 1971 the disturbances finally followed him there. His father had already put the headmaster 'in the picture', but after what happened it was only with some difficulty that he was persuaded to keep Matthew at the school. There was genuine concern that the upheavals in the dormitory would endanger O-level studies. Heavy steel double-bunk beds moved of their own accord, glowing lights appeared on the walls, bookcases were upturned and broken glass, pebbles, cutlery and pieces of wood were hurled at windows. Fortunately for Matthew, the matron of his school possessed a certain amount of extrasensory perception and was sympathetic.

During a weekend at home Matthew had his first experience of 'hearing' a spirit voice, that of Henrietta Webbe, who had once lived in the house. Trying to project himself into the past, he fell into something like a trance and after a time heard a soft woman's voice near his head. He asked her questions he had prepared beforehand

and on waking recorded their conversation immediately. About this time he also found himself writing automatically in a handwriting different from his own. As these psychic abilities increased, the poltergeist disturbances began to wane.

The encounter with Henrietta Webbe had sparked off his interest in the history of his home, Queen's House, and in the people who had once lived there. He spent several mornings searching the Linton Parish Registers for clues, and believes that was the catalyst that sparked off the strange relationship that now began between him and a gentleman called Robert Webbe, who had died in 1733.

In June 1971 Webbe communicated with Matthew Manning through automatic writing and was to continue to do so for several years. It soon became obvious that he thought the house still belonged to him and he tried to assert his authority over the household. Robert Webbe introduced· himself in person one dark November night when Matthew's parents had briefly gone into the village and his sister was asleep in her bed. There were several raps on the door, but when Matthew opened it, no one was there. His heart began to beat heavily. He was, after all, only sixteen. Another tapping noise came from the top of the staircase. Matthew looked up and saw a figure standing there. At first he thought it was a burglar and wondered what he should do. Then he noticed the figure swaying slightly as if trying to support himself on the sticks he carried. A burglar with sticks? Suddenly, noticing his very odd clothes, Matthew realized he was looking at an apparition. 'Yet he appeared quite solid, solid enough for me to have mistaken him for a real human being had his clothes not given him away,' Matthew wrote of his encounter in his book *The Strangers*. This was Robert Webbe.

'I saw that he wore a green coloured frock coat which was embroidered around the edges with yellow thread. . . .' began Matthew's detailed description of the ghost.

'While I stood dumbfounded, he spoke in a perfectly ordinary human voice, without any trace of an accent. It sounded like the voice of a man tired after making an effort to walk with difficulty, almost as if he were out of breath. 'I must offer you my most humble apology for giving you so much fright, but I must walk for my blessed legs,' he said, apparently aware that he had frightened me.

Matthew politely asked him to wait while he fetched something, then tore into the kitchen to find pencil and paper. Then he stood on the bottom step and made a shaky sketch of his ghost. He noticed a very strong, spicy smell. Before the sketch was finished the apparition turned on his heels and disappeared somewhere between the landing and a bedroom.

When Matthew Manning was only seventeen he was approached by a publisher, and agreed to write an account of all his psychic experiences. *The Link* which dealt with the poltergeist manifestations, was eventually translated into fifteen languages. Later he wrote about the ghostly encounter with Robert Webbe in *The Strangers*.

His psychic powers became so strong that for two years he put himself at the disposal of various scientists in countries as far apart as Sweden and Japan, so that he could be tested under controlled conditions. He became very disillusioned about the science of parapsychology, and felt he was constantly being made to repeat experiments not because scientists did not believe him but because they did not believe the findings of their colleagues.

For a few years he was not very happy. He felt he had become a psychic curiosity exploited by the media. He felt he should be doing something more positive, that he should not be pushed around.

He left everything behind for a time, took a trip to India and made a pilgrimage to the Himalayas. Looking out over the great mountains as the sun rose, he said he felt a presence unlike anything he had known before. He had begun to realize that he had a capacity for healing, and decided when he went home he would devote his life to it. Since then he has treated hundreds of people from all walks of life and with a wide range of problems.

Daniel Dunglas-Home

One night in December 1868 three gentlemen of 'unimpeachable reputation' sat together in the dark in an apartment on the upper floor of Ashley House in London. One of them was Lord Lindsay, a notable scientist, the second was Lord Adare, and the third his cousin, Captain Charles Wynne. All three were silent, nervous and tense as though waiting for something extraordinary to happen. After a few minutes they heard the window in the next room being raised and almost immediately saw the figure of Daniel Dunglas Home floating in the air outside the window of the room in which they were sitting. He must have been at least eighty feet from the ground. Lord Lindsay wrote later: 'The moon was shining full into the room. . . . I saw Home's feet about six inches above the window sill. He remained in this position for a few seconds then raised the window, glided into the room feet foremost and sat down.' And Lord Adare gave his word: 'The fact of his having gone out of one window and in at the other, I can swear to.'

This astonishing feat of levitation, which is still the subject of controversy today, was performed by the Victorian psychic who is generally regarded as the most famous medium of all time. Not only did he rise into the air with aplomb but he extended his height to an extent not thought humanly possible, washed his hands in red-hot coals, produced spirit hands out of the air, talked with phantoms, created vapours and psychic breezes and moved furniture all over the place without touching it.

Although in his mature years Home could levitate at will and became best known to the general public for his spectacular drifting about in the air, he also levitated without seemingly being aware of it. On one occasion when his host drew his attention to the fact that he was hovering above the cushion in his armchair, Home seemed most surprised. To the end of his life he maintained that he could only fly through the air because he was lifted up by the spirits. 'Since the first time, I have never felt fear,' he wrote in his autobiography, 'Should I, however, have fallen from the ceiling of some rooms in which I have been raised, I could not have escaped serious injury. I am generally lifted up perpendicularly; my arms frequently become rigid and are drawn above my head as if I were grasping the unseen power which slowly raises me from the floor. . . .'

He continued to levitate and hold remarkable séances for forty years without anyone being able to accuse him of trickery. With his handsome features, cool grey eyes and curling red-brown hair, Home was unlike any other medium of his day. Women swooned over him, and he was welcomed into aristocratic drawing rooms and palaces all over Europe and America. He was lionized by society hostesses, admired by kings and princes. The Empress Eugénie threw a fit of temper when she thought he did not pay her enough attention. Tsar Alexander II, Napoleon III and Queen Sophia of Holland welcomed him to their courts. Intellectuals like Alexandre Dumas, Thackeray and John Ruskin were fascinated by him.

Most of his séances were given in houses he had never entered before, in rooms he had never seen, often in broad daylight. He scorned the use of a curtained alcove or 'cabinet' demanded by most mediums of the day. He would enter a room modestly, dressed in elegant clothes that fitted his slender body like a glove so that his audience could see that he had no gadgetry to assist him, no room for concealment. He never took payment in cash but stayed as a guest in great style at some of the most splendid houses and happily accepted rare and expensive gifts.

Daniel Dunglas Home was born in Currie, a village near Edinburgh, on March 20, 1833. His father, William, an engineer, claimed to be the illegitimate son of the tenth Earl of Home, so on the paternal side the medium was connected with one of the most ancient and noble Border houses. His mother, Elizabeth, was said to have second sight. One of eight children, Daniel was a nervous, delicate child, probably already prone to the tuberculosis that was to affect his health all through his life. He was adopted at an early stage by a childless aunt who took him to live with her and her husband in the state of Connecticut in the United States.

Visions and apparitions, mostly connected with the death of friends or relatives, were part of his adolescence. His aunt was not sympathetic when loud knocks and raps shook the family breakfast table as he took his seat. Nor was she very pleased when her best furniture began to move about mysteriously. He was just seventeen when an exceptionally distressing outbreak of poltergeist and telekinetic phenomena upset her so badly that she threw him out of the house. He took refuge with friends who were prepared to be more understanding.

In the early 1850s, when a tidal flood of spiritualism was sweeping through America, Home began to give his first séances. With his grey eyes, auburn hair and pale complexion, he was such an attractive figure that he was soon being accepted — usually through the influence of wives — into the homes of wealthy farmers, prosperous merchants, doctors, editors, and liberal clergyman. His conversation was amusing, his manners charming. He became a perpetual houseguest whose expenses were paid and whose needs were fully met by his sponsors. He made it clear, however, that he could only produce phenomena when the spirits moved him.

Home levitated for the first time in August 1852, when he was nineteen. It happened at the home of a wealthy silk merchant called Ward Cheney in South Manchester, Connecticut. Among the guests was a journalist called Frank Burr, editor of the *Hartford Times*, a fascinated observer but a sceptic. Afterwards he described what happened:

'Suddenly, without any expectation on the part of the company, Home was taken up into the air. At first his feet were only about a foot from the floor, but it happened twice more and the third time he was carried to the ceiling of the apartment with which his head and hands came in gentle contact. He was gasping and trembling as he rose.'

Home usually, though not invariably, went into a trance at his séances. It was in Boston that his powers suddenly developed to full fruition and people began travelling hundreds of miles to see him. Complete figures began to materialize, spirit hands which wrote messages and voices which could be recognized. People clamoured for more phenomena of this nature but Home's delicate constitution was beginning to feel the strain, and his doctors advised him to go to England, where the climate tended to less extremes than in America.

He sailed for England in March 1855, and within a few weeks had found supporters of the highest social standing. Without them he would have been penniless. Those who assembled to watch him were not all

Daniel Dunglas Home

devoted believers; the majority were men and women of the world, prepared to admit their profound scepticism when they first met him. They included monarchs, dukes, duchesses, society hostesses and scholarly men. Sir Edward Bulwer-Lytton, for instance, who was his host both at his Park Lane mansion and at his stately home at Knebworth, eventually acknowledged 'the extraordinary phenomena which are elicited by his powers'.

Among the most famous sitters at his séances were the poets Robert and Elizabeth Barrett Browning. Robert Browning loathed Home and gave vent to his feelings in a satirical pen portrait called *Mr Sludge the*

Medium. Could it nave been sheer jealousy? His wife, Elizabeth Barrett Browning, worshipped Home and remained his staunch ally to the end of her life. At one séance Home produced a garland of flowers from the atmosphere and laid it on the table, where a spirit hand took it up and placed it like a wreath of honour on Elizabeth's head. 'The hand was of the largest human size, white as snow and very beautiful,' she told a friend later. 'It was as near to me as this hand I write with, and I saw it distinctly . . . I was perfectly calm.'

Lionized in drawing room and royal court alike, Home continued to create extraordinary phenomena which even his worst enemies — Charles Dickens also detested him — failed to explain. His life was full of traumatic scenes as various jealous hostesses fought to keep the handsome medium to themselves. He had a triumphant progress through Europe, then suddenly in Italy, towards the end of 1857, announced dramatically that his mediumistic powers were about to leave him. He had been ill with tuberculosis, but on recovering went to recuperate at the home of an attractive Englishwoman who had separated from her husband. Though there was not the slightest hint of a sexual relationship, Home was riddled with guilt about the association and thought his spirit guides and controls had left him because he had behaved improperly. Fanny Trollope, the famous Victorian traveller who had been supporting Home over this period, demanded he leave the lady at once, and when he refused she withdrew her financial support.

Throughout the whole business in Italy Home felt that his invisible masters were trying to teach him a lesson. He was honest enough to acknowledge his own snobbery, love of finery and vanity. Remorseful, he joined the Roman Catholic Church and his confessor, Father Ravignon, became his close friend. Ravignon had secret hopes of persuading Home not to return to his activities as a medium, which the priest regarded as next door to witchcraft. But on the morning of February 11, 1857, the Emperor Napoleon III sent the Marquis de Belmont to ask whether M. Home had recovered his occult powers. Home sent back the answer 'Yes.'

No one was more delighted to see the medium return to his old form than the Empress Eugénie, who had complete belief in him. Home had predicted that his psychic power would leave him for a period of twelve months and he was right, to the very day. At the first séance he gave after his return there was almost a fight to get a seat. Home protested that the salon — at Count Alexander de Komar's house in the Tuileries — was far too crowded. He wanted only a small circle present. The Empress, quick to take offence, flew into a temper and swept out. Within less than an hour, however, the salon had been cleared and Eugénie returned to watch amazed as Home produced his repertoire of phenomena for the French audience as brilliantly as ever with spirit hands, vapours, tinkling chandeliers, moving furniture and levitation.

People usually arrived assuming that his séances would be, as most others were, conducted in near total darkness, as Brian Inglis points out in his *History of the Paranormal*. But Home's sittings were held in light good enough for his every action to be observed. Those who attended were usually sophisticated people, not easily duped. 'It was this combination — the calibre of the witnesses and the fact that they could see what was happening throughout the séances — that put Home in a different league from most mediums of the time.' Inglis felt that Home had somehow rediscovered the ancient abilities that shamans and witch doctors possessed, especially with regard to his capacity to levitate and withstand the effects of fire.

It was during a visit to Rome that Home met seventeen-year-old Sacha de Kroll, younger daughter of General Count de Kroll and a god-daughter of Tsar Nicholas. It was love at first sight. They sat next to each other at a supper party. 'Mr Home, you will be married before the year is ended,' she predicted to his amusement. She explained there was an old Russian superstition that this would happen if a man was seated, as Home was, between two sisters. Twelve days after their meeting, their engagement was announced. Four months later they were married in St Petersburg. Home's best man was French literary giant Alexandre Dumas. Tsar Alexander II gave them both his blessing and presented the bride with a magnificent diamond ring. When their son was born twelve months later, his birth was, said Home, accompanied by a number of signs and portents, including brilliant spirit lights and songs of invisible birds.

Home and his pretty little wife travelled continually, being received everywhere with flattering attention. They reached England in November 1859 after visiting France and Switzerland and séances were held at some of the grandest houses in the country, including those of the Duchess of Somerset and the Duchess of Sutherland. But Home's social status had undergone a subtle change. He no longer relied on patronage for his keep. His wife was wealthy. She was also the Tsar's god-daughter. He had, in other words, made a brilliant marriage.

The couple split their married life between Europe and Russia, where Home had made a friend of Count Alexis Tolstoy, who after watching a séance wrote, 'I would have gone a thousand leagues to see these things.' But fate demanded a cruel price from Home for his glittering success. After a pitifully few years of happiness Sacha became infected with tuberculosis and died in the South of France in February 1862. Home was overwhelmed with grief.

About this time, to make matters worse, he was coming under increasing attack by the sceptics. It seemed as though everyone had some idea as to how his phenomena were produced. Some of the most vitriolic remarks came from people who had never been present at a séance. Dickens, for instance, called Home an impostor but refused to watch him. Browning had become almost obsessed with depicting him as a slimy cheat.

To help himself get over the death of his wife, Home accepted every invitation offered. He held a series of séances with John Ruskin, returned to America for a spell, back to Europe then on to Russia, where the Tolstoys entertained him at their country home and he was the guest of the Tsar. He returned to England laden with emeralds and diamonds.

Exhausted by constant travel and Russian intensity, he laid low for a time, then there is a report of a remarkable séance at the North Hotel in Aberdeen. Among those who witnessed what happened was a General Boldero and his wife. Mrs Boldero reported 'The table quivered so violently and the plates rattled so much that General Boldero was obliged to stop eating.' A large armchair near the fireplace rushed across the room and up to the table, placing itself near one of the witnesses. Everyone thought this to be an astonishing manifestation, as Home had not been into the coffee room where they were at supper till they had all entered it together, and no thread or trickery of any kind could have moved the chair with the precision and velocity with which it left its place.

One of Home's firmest friends and supporters was Lord Adare, son of Lord Dunraven and one of those present on the night of Home's levitation at Ashley House. He was a Guardsman in his twenties when they met at the end of 1867. Adare, an honest English gentleman, recorded seventy-eight séances but at the end of his life said he was no nearer to understanding what happened than at the time of the recording.

In March 1871 Home submitted himself to a series of investigations by Sir William Crookes, an eminent Victorian scientist and psychic researcher. He began by showing how he could influence a spring balance from a distance, then went on to a dramatic demonstration of his control of fire. Crookes watched as he stirred up a pile of burning coals in a grate with his hand, then, taking up a red-hot lump, as big as an orange, he blew on it until it was white-hot, still cradling it in the palm of his hand.

Crookes both liked and trusted Home. In one celebrated experiment he tested the medium to see whether he could play an accordion through the power of psychokinesis. The accordion was placed in a copper cage and Home was allowed to rest his hand on the end farthest from the keys. The instrument soon began to play . . . and continued even when Home had removed his hand from it.

Everybody had expected Crookes to proclaim that Home was either a fraud or a failure. He was subjected to the most stringent test conditions. But Sir William wrote: 'The phenomena, I am prepared to attest, are so extraordinary and so directly oppose the most firmly rooted articles of scientific belief. . . .' In short, he went on to testify that in his opinion Home was what he claimed to be, a remarkable psychic medium. Crookes stuck to that opinion for the rest of his life, in spite of a great deal of derision being hurled at him. He went on to become the President of the British Association for the Advancement of Science.

On a visit to Russia Home met a beautiful dark-haired girl called Julie de Gloumeline, and after the experiments with Crookes he married her. After this second marriage, which made him financially independent, he decided to retire from the world gaze. His second marriage was as happy as his first, but from the age of thirty-eight until his death he only gave séances in small private circles.

Home was received into the Greek Orthodox Church and spent the last years of his life in Russia and the South of France. His old enemy, tuberculosis, caught up with him on June 21, 1886, at the age of fifty-three. He died at Auteuil and was buried in the Russian cemetery at Saint-Germain-en-Laye. A fine bronze bust of him is the first thing you see on entering the premises of the Society for Psychical Research in London.

Eileen Garrett

An attractive young Irish medium called Eileen Garrett leaped into the world headlines after a sensational séance at the National Laboratory of Psychical Research in London on October 7, 1930.

Two days before the séance took place the British airship R101 on its maiden passenger flight had crashed in flames at Beauvais, northern France, in the early hours of Sunday morning. Many passengers were killed in the horrific accident and the airship's captain, Flight Lieutenant Carmichael Irwin, also perished.

But the disaster was not uppermost in the minds of those who gathered in a small, darkened room at the National Laboratory as guests of its founder, Harry Price. Eileen Garrett herself did not know the purpose of the séance but had been prepared, as she always was, to offer herself for scientific research. Price was hoping that she would be able to contact his old adversary, Sir Arthur Conan Doyle, who had died a few months earlier. Australian journalist Ian Coster was there simply to observe.

Price felt that if anyone could reach Conan Doyle it would be Eileen Garrett. She had been a personal friend and knew of his desire to try to 'come through' after his death to prove what he had always believed in life — the reality of individual survival.

At three o'clock in the afternoon the séance started. After yawning deeply for several minutes, Mrs Garrett slipped into a deep trance. She spoke at first in the voice of her regular control, 'Uvani', an Indian, and conveyed various messages from the spirit world. But there was no sign of Conan Doyle.

All at once the medium became extremely agitated, tears rolled down her cheeks and Uvani's voice spelled out the name Irving or Irwin. Then a different voice came through, a breathless voice speaking in rapid, staccato outbursts and full of anguish: 'The whole bulk . . . too much for her engine capacity . . . engines too heavy . . . weather bad for long flight . . . fabric all waterlogged and ship's nose down . . . impossible to rise . . . cannot trim . . . almost scraped the roofs at Achy. . . .' On and on went the anguished voice, delivering highly technical information in a torrent of words almost too fast for Harry Price's secretary, a skilled shorthand writer who was sitting in to record the séance. 'Airscrews too small . . . fuel injection bad . . . gross lift computed badly . . . this exorbitant scheme of carbon and hydrogen entirely and absolutely wrong . . . never reached cruising altitude.' The voice at times almost reached hysteria. When it eventually faded away, everyone sat in a state of shock. There was no doubt in their minds that they had been listening to Captain Irwin of the dirigible R101.

Three weeks later Mrs Garrett reported that she had heard again from Irwin and from Sir Sefton Brancker, Director of Civil Aviation, who also died. They seemed above all anxious that people should know what had gone wrong. One thing was certain. Eileen Garrett did not know one end of an airship from the other. Experts at the Royal Airship Works at Cardington in Bedfordshire who later read the notes of the séance called it an 'astounding document' and admitted some of the details it included had been regarded as confidential.

Because Eileen Garrett appeared to know so much about the mechanics of dirigibles some people in England even suggested she should be arrested on a suspicion of espionage. But she was considered by all who knew her to be a woman of absolute integrity and an exceptional medium. Price chose her to contact Conan Doyle — which he said she eventually did — because 'she does not become emotional. She takes an academic interest in her powers, but has no explanation to offer concerning them.'

She has been described as the most thoroughly investigated medium of modern times. Most of her life was devoted to encouraging research into mediumship and its meaning, and she frequently offered herself as a guinea pig in new experiments, being as curious about the outcome as the researchers themselves.

Her personality and appearance surprised many people who had fixed ideas as to what a medium should look like. In her youth she was Eton cropped and elegant; later she attracted many by her vivacious and outgoing personality. She married three times and lost three sons, one at birth and two through illness, but she also had a daughter who shared her interests and carried on her work at the Parapsychology Foundation which she founded in New York in 1951.

Eileen Garrett was born in the historic town of Beauparc, County Meath (now in the Republic of Ireland) on March 17, 1893. One of the most familiar sights of her childhood was the Hill of Tara, ancient, mystic capital of Ireland. Her mother, Anne Brownell, who belonged to a stern Protestant family, had married a Catholic Basque named Vacho, and the religious strife that ensued led to tragedy. Eileen's mother drowned herself two weeks after her birth and her father committed suicide a few weeks later. She was brought up by an aunt and uncle, who had just returned to Ireland after service in India. The tragedy left its mark, however. In later years she rejected religion and often became impatient with the dogmatic pronouncements of some Spiritualists.

Like many sensitive children, Eileen had playmates who were invisible to others. She went to school in Meath before being sent to a boarding school in Merion Square, Dublin, where painful loneliness alternated with the joy of discovering Yeats, Synge and Joyce. When her uncle (who had been both kind and understanding) suddenly died she felt as though there was no one in the world she could turn to. Two weeks after his funeral she had her first major paranormal experience, and described it in her autobiography *Many Voices*. She wrote: 'One evening my dead uncle "appeared" to me in a vision, younger and more alert than I had known him; his Vandyke beard was well clipped and he stood strong and straight. He told me that in time I should leave my aunt and the farm and go to London. . . .' From that moment on she became interested in the whole question of life after death.

She went to London as her uncle had predicted, married an architect when she was little more than a schoolgirl and in the years that followed lost two of the sons she bore him in an epidemic of meningitis, the third at birth. The experience drained her spiritually. Left alone a great deal by her husband and perturbed by the new sensations she felt both waking and dreaming, she decided she must make a new, busy life for herself. She opened a tea room in Heath Street, Hampstead, which prospered and finally became a meeting place for some of the most famous literary men of the age. She came to know D. H. Lawrence well.

Eileen Garrett

With the outbreak of the First World War Eileen and her husband drifted apart and eventually divorced. She opened a hostel for wounded soldiers and on impulse married a sensitive artistic young soldier who was haunted by a premonition that he was going to be killed. Within a month he returned to the Front. Dining with friends at the Savoy Hotel in London one evening, she had a clairvoyant vision of her young husband being blown up with two or three of his comrades. As she sat at the dinner table she felt part of the action, and seemed to be enveloped in smoke and the stench of blood. Almost fainting, she begged to be excused. A few days later she was advised by the War Office that he was missing, believed killed. She never saw him again.

Her third marriage was to another wounded soldier, James William Garrett.

After the war she was introduced to Hewat McKenzie, director of the British College of Psychic Science, and under his guidance she began to discover the extent of her psychic powers. Sir Arthur Conan Doyle worked with her during the early days – 'He was a gentle soul and made a deep impression on me' — and Sir Oliver Lodge carried out a number of experiments with her. She was once invited to witness a Black Mass conducted by Aleister Crowley in a room in Fitzroy Square and came away unimpressed. 'If there was authority in Crowley's meetings with Lucifer I never knew it,' she wrote. 'I have really seen more uncanny things in the voodoo rites in Haiti.' She declined W. B. Yeats's invitation to collaborate with him in trying to contact the fairy people. Her scepticism was too strong.

She continued to work daily at the College, developing her faculties of telepathy, clairvoyance and clairaudience, but becoming principally known for her skill as a trance medium. Her two controls or intermediaries were 'Uvani', who claimed to have been a soldier in India centuries ago, and Abdul Latif, a twelfth-century physician from the Court of Saladin. In the early days she accepted them as helpers, but in time she began to doubt this and believed instead that they might be secondary personalities produced by her subconscious.

She worked on many poltergeist cases with McKenzie. Her role was to assume a trance state after she had entered the troubled house with the hope of contacting the cause of the disturbance. 'I often wondered if the whole matter was not a delusion until I saw for myself the breakages and, in some cases, wilful destruction. I was forced to the conclusion that these could well be some earthly beings with their own accounts to settle.' In the cool, detached way she had in dealing with the paranormal she decided that in the case of poltergeists the answer could often be found to stem from young children in the house with too much repressed nervous energy and a sense of discontentment. But often too she found 'an imprisoned ghost'. At one farmhouse where the father of two boys had taken a woman to live with him, she discovered the presence of the first wife, still hovering about, longing to tell her tale of their greed, injustice and intrigue. The boys, gentle children, were the unwitting channels of her poltergeist activity. The farmer, thoroughly frightened at what Eileen Garrett was discovering, ordered her out of the house and threw her umbrella after her. 'You've revealed a pretty kettle of fish,' chuckled Hewat McKenzie. She was called back, however, the farmer made a clean breast of his greed, settled his affairs decently and the poltergeist went away.

In 1931 the American Society for Psychical Research invited Mrs Garrett to New York. It was the start of years of important work in America. At Duke University she collaborated with Professor William McDougall and was invited to take part in the latest tests for extrasensory perception. She spent more than 500 hours submitting to tests by a famous New York psychologist, Dr Lawrence LeShan. One day he placed a square of material cut from a shirt in the palm of her hand. He did not tell her, but it belonged to a man who had vanished from a mid-Western city in the States and whose family were desperately trying to trace him. She not only gave a fairly accurate description of him but mentioned happenings only known within the family, and eventually stated that the man was now in La Jolla, California. He was located there and restored to his wife and children.

A spontaneous phenomenon of a physical kind occurred in 1931 when Mrs Garrett was lying on an operating table in hospital. Just after she succumbed to the anaesthetic the doctors and nurses around her heard a voice. The surgeon (who had been in India for some years) told her later that he recognized certain words of command in Hindustani. He knew it was not possible for his patient to utter a sound because of the way she had been prepared for the operation. He was so impressed by the experience that he made a special report for the records.

When she made her first visits to California in 1933 and 1935 Eileen Garrett was no different from any other tourist. She wanted to see the film studios. She did not realize, however, that what started as an amusing outing would end in an emotional confrontation with the great director Cecil B. De Mille.

On an exceedingly hot day she watched him direct a film with Elissa Landi in an Oriental setting. Soon she became aware of a little old lady standing by the side of De Mille and talking to him in a lively and vigorous manner. He did not seem to be aware of her presence, but just scratched his head and turned away. Eileen Garrett turned to her daughter, who was with her, and said, 'I think the heat must have affected my vision.'

A moment later she half turned to find the old lady standing behind her. 'She looked me straight in the face with the most vivid eyes. "I can't make him hear," she began. "I wish you would. Speak for me." '

'Who are you?' asked Eileen Garrett.

'I'm his mother. Few people know him . . . he's a lonely man.' The old lady then poured out a welter of motherly advice, encouragement, gentle criticism and loving words.

De Mille was not very pleased to see Mrs Garrett when she knocked on his door. He took her to be a hanger-on from a visiting party. But she caught his attention and passed on all the old lady had wanted to say to him. De Mille looked out of the window throughout. She was not even sure he was listening. But when he turned round tears were rolling down his cheeks. 'Where have you come from?' he asked. 'I loved my mother. It's true we didn't always understand each other but I had a great respect for her. I have waited for this for over twenty years.'

When she returned to her apartment it was filled with roses. The accompanying card from De Mille read: 'Do not come to California without first advising me.'

She was in the South of France when the Second World War broke out, and for a time ran a soup kitchen for children. She returned to New York when Paris fell and, demonstrating her wide range of interests, established a publishing firm which attracted authors of the calibre of Robert Graves and Aldous Huxley. She began to write prolifically, but after a break of ten years returned to psychical research full time, establishing the Parapsychology Foundation in New York which still supports important research.

Perhaps because of her lifelong tendency to bronchial trouble, she loved the South of France and set up the Foundation's regional head-quarters at Saint Paul-de-Vence. Towards the end she preferred to take a back seat and listen to scientists, philosophers and psychical researchers talk about the latest advances in knowledge and tech-niques. But when she could be persuaded to discuss mediumship she was listened to with the greatest respect. She died at Saint Paul in 1970, hoping that one day a real understanding of the nature of psychic phenomena would be found.

Doris Stokes

Doris Stokes, unquestionably the most famous medium of the present day, communicates with 'the other side' as though she was talking to someone in the next room. Faint-hearted spirits are quite likely to be told, 'Speak up, dear, I can't hear you', and the over-anxious are politely requested to wait their turn.

It is her natural, almost familiar, earthy approach to the spirit world that makes her so extraordinary. On May 4, 1984, she was appearing before a huge audience in Stoke-on-Trent when she heard a familiar voice among the spirits trying to 'get through'. She gasped with surprise and cried out 'Oh no, Diana, that can't be you.' Later that evening she checked with the local radio and they told her that actress Diana Dors had just died after her courageous fight against cancer.

Also typical of her approach is the way she made contact with the popular comedian Tommy Cooper, who collapsed and died in the middle of a performance being shown on TV. Doris said that as it happened she saw him get up and leave his body. Shortly after she happened to spend the night at a hotel in Leicester where Cooper had stayed just before his death. She said, 'There was a massive bed in the room and I was looking at it when I heard Tommy's voice say "I needed that" and there was a peel of his unmistakable wild laughter.' During the night she got up to make herself a cup of tea. As she climbed between the sheets again she heard him chuckle and say 'Enjoy the bed.'

Though she has in recent years built up a massive following all over the world, Doris Stokes admits that when she was young she did not welcome the realization that she had an extraordinary gift. 'I really didn't want to know. I wanted to be normal and ordinary.' She looks ordinary enough, pleasant, grey-haired and homely in spite of the expensive beaded gowns she wears for her public performances. But several photographs taken of her while she is listening to her spirit voices reveal a strength and force that is quite startling. Her smile is wide and friendly but her grey eyes have obviously seen things that others have not.

Doris Stokes was born in Grantham, Lincolnshire, just across the road from Margaret Thatcher. Her father, blacksmith Sam Sutton, was a sensitive man and probably a natural psychic. She was only a child when she first realized that she too had a psychic gift.

One night there was a terrible fire in the next street to where she lived. Her parents, hearing that the blaze had started at their friend Tom's house, rushed out to see if they could help. Excited and curious, Doris was not able to sleep. She slipped a coat over her nightie and followed them. Crowds were gathered in the street. She craned her neck just in time to see a terrible burned shape being carried out of the house on a stretcher — all that was left of Tom. She stared, horrified yet fascinated, then lifting her eyes from the stretcher she saw something else that made her freeze. Tom was walking beside his body, real and solid-looking, not a hair singed.

Sam Sutton suddenly saw his daughter, clipped her smartly round the ear and sent her home to bed. She was still sobbing with fright and incomprehension when he came home. She described what she had seen and he patted her hair gently. He realized that night she was going to be different from other girls.

Though there was never a great deal of money, Doris was part of a good family and had a happy enough childhood. She thought her life would fall to pieces, though, when her father died. They had been so close and he had taught her so much. But before he died he said to her, 'All you've got to do is put out your hand and I'll be there to take hold.'

She was twenty when war broke out and she joined the WRAF. Life was fun, with plenty of boy friends, dances and different experiences. Sometimes, though, she was disturbed when she saw the young pilots walking out to their planes. She almost knew the ones that would not come back. Sometimes she would tell fortunes, but her predictions began to get too close to the truth. When a giggling group of WRAFs went to see 'the spook show' at the local Spiritualist church one night, the medium told her, 'One day you'll be doing this.'

Soon after she married a handsome young airman called John Fisher he was reported missing in action, and a medium at a local Spiritualist church confirmed that he had been killed. It was the most traumatic experience of her life. She had become pregnant in the early days of their marriage, and now had a baby son. She returned home in a state of shock, and what happened next is described in her autobiography, *Voices in My Ear*:

The bedroom door flew open so sharply I thought it was my mother bursting in, and there stood my father. My mouth dropped open. He looked as real and solid as he did when he was alive. . . .
'Dad?' I whispered.
'I never lied to you, did I, Doll?' he asked.
'I don't think so,' I said.
'I'm not lying to you now. John is not with us and on Christmas Day you will have proof of this.' Then as I watched, he vanished.

Three days later the War Office informed her officially that John was dead, but to everyone's amazement she refused to believe it. They even began to think the shock had affected her mind as she clung to her hopes. Just as her father had predicted, news that John was, after all, still alive, though badly wounded, came through on Christmas Day.

She never trained as a medium but gradually became known in the Spiritualist church circuit, passing on messages from voices that became increasingly clear. Sometimes she earned a little money by giving private sittings. The death of her baby son when he was only five months old made her more conscious of her psychic gift. She was to lose three other children before she finally adopted her son Terry, and the sadness she experienced made her especially sensitive with regard to bereaved parents.

It is difficult to pinpoint exactly when she started to become a household name, but it was probably after her stunning success in America in 1978 when she went through a series of tests on television. Suddenly she was in demand everywhere. Her books became best-sellers, her public appearances great occasions. The waiting list for private sittings with her ran into thousands. She went on gruelling tours, and in Sydney the traditionally sceptical Aussies queued for hours just to get a ticket.

People were amazed at her down-to-earth attitude to the spirit world. It seemed to be as real to her as this one. Her utter belief in life after death communicated itself to her audience. Describing herself as being like a telephone exchange putting the spirits in touch with their loved ones, she performed as a clairaudient, hearing rather than seeing spirits. Sometimes she saw spirit children because she had a special empathy with them. She never promised to 'get through' to any particular person but would simply create a quiet, serene atmosphere and wait for things to happen.

The messages she gives are usually made up of trivial details, but the accuracy of these exchanges is usually enough to convince people that they are experiencing a paranormal event. Some people, trying to find a rational answer for what is going on, have suggested she is using extrasensory perception (ESP).

Those who attend her performance expecting a weird experience are disappointed. 'Hello, my loves' she greets those who have come to see her. She claims that she can see flickering blue lights above the heads of those she puts into contact. The longer a person has been dead, the stronger the voice. The newly dead tend to sound faint, sometimes fading away altogether. She has learned to cope with these awkward silences, though earlier in her life she was at times tempted to 'fill in'.

Doris Stokes recorded her contact with some very famous spirits in her book *A Host of Voices*. George Orwell, author of *Nineteen Eighty Four*, talked with her at some length. John Lennon and Marc Bolan, superstars of the pop world, came through, and so did the young actor Richard Beckinsale, who died from a heart attack when he was only thirty-two. He wanted her to tell his parents that he had taken up music, something he had always wanted to do on earth.

Doris Stokes

Perhaps the most poignant conversation she reported was with comedian Dick Emery. She has endured some traumatic physical illnesses in her life and was in hospital after her thirteenth operation for cancer when he came through. Trying to make her laugh, he joked that the spirit world wanted her so much they were taking her bit by bit.

Doris Stokes has always said there is no need to fear death. She has spent a lifetime trying to get that message over to as many people as possible.

Rudi Schneider

In the Austrian town of Braunau, where Adolf Hitler was born, two brothers, Willi and Rudi Schneider, made psychic history in the nineteen-twenties. Their father, Josef, was a typesetter with a local printing firm, a quiet, gentle man, respected in the community. Their mother, Elise, had given birth to twelve children, six of whom survived, all boys. Four of these boys were found to be mediumistic. Hans and Karl were only slightly so. The others became two of the most discussed mediums in the world.

Willi Schneider, a handsome youth with smooth, dark hair, began to show signs of psychic ability when he was fourteen; Rudi, five years his junior, demonstrated his powers when he was only eleven.

Their first experience of the supernatural was in their own home, a modest house in the main street of Braunau. His mother, fascinated by the current passion for spiritualism, decided to ask a few friends for supper so that they could experiment. Gathered round the parlour table, they used a planchette — a small board mounted on castors with a pencil attached, designed for taking spirit messages. They had little success until Willi strolled into the room and asked if he could try. When his hand rested on the planchette, it moved fluently. After a short time it began to move towards him before he even touched it.

Josef Schneider, in the meticulous account he kept of his son's career, said, 'The pencil began to write "Olga" in beautiful handwriting'. Willi had found his spirit guide. They were given to understand that Olga had once been Lola Montez, the tempestuous adventuress who was the King of Bavaria's mistress. When the family promised to say masses for her soul, she promised to make their name famous. Who or what was she? Some psychic observers believe a medium's control is his or her secondary personality dredged up from material deep in the unconscious, but this lady transferred her allegiance to Willi's brother at a later stage.

Whatever the explanation, from the moment she made herself known Willi Schneider became a subject of fascinating study for scientists all over Europe. His phenomena began in an unpretentious, domestic way. Olga apparently instructed the family to cover a kitchen stool with a large cloth and to place a handkerchief and a basin of water near it. Willi sat next to the stool, and within a short time strange things began to happen. The water began slopping about in the bowl quite violently, then two tiny hands materialized and a sound of clapping was heard. Objects placed near the stool appeared to move of their own accord. Throughout these activities Willi was fully conscious and seemed to enjoy the chaos going on around him.

Gradually news of what was happening in the Schneiders' parlour spread through the little town, causing great excitement. One of Herr Schneider's friends, Captain Fritz Kogelnik, was the first to realize the importance of what was going on. He was not a man naturally predisposed to believe in the occult, and was rather inclined to dismiss such affairs as 'antiquated medieval rubbish'. But his first encounter with Willi changed his whole attitude. 'Not even the slightest attempt was made by him to support the supernormal phenomena through normal means. He never fell into a trance at this stage in his life; he watched the manifestations with as much surprise and interest as anybody present.'

At a séance which Kogelnik attended in the early spring of 1919 when Willi was fourteen a tablecloth was slowly raised into the air, though no one was near it and the light was strong enough to see exactly what was going on. Willi was becoming, quite naturally, excited at being the centre of so much attention and Kogelnik suspected he might soon try to 'help' the phenomena in order to get more dramatic results. The Captain persuaded Herr Schneider to allow him to take Willi to his own house where he could see that his séances were rigidly controlled.

They did not have long to wait for dramatic effects. Willi began producing that strange substance known to mediums as ectoplasm. Kogelnik described it as being a cobweb-like material which first materialized at the shoulder, then wrapped itself round Willi's face. It seemed to disappear without trace. One day Kogelnik took a closer look. Standing barely a foot away from Willi's chair, he saw a faint, undulating, phosphorescent fog being emitted from the boy's head. It eventually settled on his hair like a cap before being withdrawn into the body through his nose.

Another time, Olga materialized and danced a tango in front of the astonished gathering. This was the first time that Willi had produced a full-form materialization. It did not happen often. 'The figure was about five feet tall covered with cobwebby veils,' Kogelnik recorded. 'I leaned back in my chair and they nearly touched me.' While this was going on Willi was in a deep trance, his head resting on Frau Kogelnik's shoulder as they sat comfortably on a sofa. At the end of the dance the phantom disappeared 'like lightning, just as she had come'. Those present found it very hard to convince anyone else of what they had seen.

Willi's phenomena began to attract international attention. Many scientists went to Braunau to investigate, among them Baron von Schrenck-Nötzing, one of the most important figures in psychical research in Europe. The Baron began systematic experiments with the boy in October 1919, and they were to continue for several years, during which time Willi left school and became apprenticed to a local dental technician. Schrenck-Nötzing eventually took him to Munich, where he became like an adopted son. He conducted 124 séances with the young medium and published his findings in 1924. Over ninety scientists, university teachers, doctors and other interested people had participated, and the results were claimed to be strongly positive.

The Baron found Willi Schneider to be soft-hearted, kind, obedient and modest, his actions more influenced by emotions than reasoning. He believed firmly in his mediumship. Willi was now producing the whole spectacular range of known phenomena, including sharp raps, cold winds, black shapes, the materialization of heads, hands and arms and the levitation of heavy objects. Sometimes, when they were particularly strong, he was frightened by them. Even while fully conscious he sometimes saw head-like formations and figures in white garments and veils similar to those observed during séances. The Baron was puzzled by them but came to the conclusion they were not caused by hallucination.

In May 1922 Dr E. J. Dingwall and Harry Price, the English psychical researchers, together visited Munich and after carefully checking the séance room for trap doors and false walls they watched Willi go into a trance. He was covered all over with luminous pins and there were luminous bracelets on his wrists so that they could see any movement he made in the dim light. When they returned to England Price was convinced that Willi was a remarkable medium.

He was, however, near the end of his career. His psychic talents were almost exhausted. When he visited London in 1924 his phenomena were disappointing and he decided from then on to concentrate on his dental studies. His mediumship became part-time. Waiting in the wings, however, was his younger brother, Rudi, who was to prove himself an equally remarkable medium.

At a séance one night Olga had insisted that she wanted Rudi to take part. The Schneider parents said they would not allow it because he was only eleven at the time and they thought he would be frightened. 'He will come,' said Olga through the entranced Willi. A few minutes later the young boy, apparently sleep-walking, appeared in the parlour and took his place at the table.

Rudi was a healthy, robust youngster more interested in cars and football than psychical research. On leaving school he became a motor mechanic and spent all his spare time with his pretty Austrian girl friend, Mitzi. But in a family so taken up with the supernatural he could not escape the fact that he was psychic. Olga shifted her allegiance as Willi Schneider's power waned and became Rudi's guide instead. He was to prove in some ways even more dramatic than his brother.

Herr Schneider, the boys' father, recorded in December 1925 that Rudi had been producing phenomena 'which few mortals ever got to see'. In his copious notebooks — in which details of every séance which took place in his home were carefully written down — he noted: 'At yesterday's sitting there were at least thirty appearances of an almost six-foot-high phantom. At one time there were two such phantoms. One of them touched a member of the circle.' Materialized hands were seen 'in profusion' and telekinetic phenomena were observed at a distance.

Schrenck-Nötzing more or less adopted Rudi, just as he had taken over Willi when he became his sponsor. The famous researcher conducted experiments with the younger brother first at home in Braunau, then in Munich. When the Baron died in 1929, Harry Price swiftly moved in to take his place, persuading Rudi to call him 'Uncle' and offering to become his mentor and guardian.

Things did not go too smoothly at first. The medium was not sure he wanted to continue working in the psychic field. He was more interested in trying to find a job in the motor industry in Munich, and did not particularly want to make the long journey to England which Price was suggesting. His employer in Germany, Karl Amereller, volunteered to go with him and he gave in.

Because of Price's well-known sense of showmanship and love of publicity, the new Schneider sensation was being talked about everywhere. On Rudi's first visit to England in the spring of 1929 he was scheduled to give a series of six séances. Price issued a £1,000 challenge to any conjurer or magician who could produce the simplest of the medium's phenomena under controlled conditions. No one offered to try.

By now everyone interested in psychical research was anxious to see this young Schneider. He would arrive for a séance in street clothes, then submit to being stripped, searched and dressed in a body-fitting black leotard over which he wore a black dressing gown with luminous stripes so that anyone in the room could see if he moved. He was checked for thermal rating, pulse rate and respiration — a startling

Harry Price reconstructing one of Rudi Schneider's séances

aspect of his mediumship was that his breathing was at a rate ten times or more faster than normal, yet he could keep it up for two hours at a time. He was fitted with electrical controls, and even his mouth was searched in case he had tucked away some small gadget that would help him.

The sittings in London all produced brilliant phenomena including levitation, but when he returned to Munich Frau Amereller, his employer's wife (who took a motherly interest in him), complained that Rudi had come back from England in a poor state of health. His nerves were on edge, he had little strength left and his blood pressure was much too high. He went back to work and played football for his local team before resuming séances on the Continent.

In October 1930 Rudi was invited by the distinguished Dr Eugène Osty, director of the Institut Metaphysique in Paris, to undergo a series of trials which lasted for fifteen months. With the help of his son, Marcel, the physicist had installed apparatus capable of photographing any telekinetic phenomena produced by mediums in total darkness. The photographs would give away a medium or any sitter who used physical force. Even more interesting, it was hoped that their infra-red equipment might give some clue as to *how* objects could be moved from a distance, and the identity of the force that was moving them.

The results of the trials were exciting, and impressed scientists more than anything that had gone before in the case of the Schneider brothers. The experiments pointed to the existence of a powerful force emanating from the medium which affected the infra-red rays used to test him.

There was no doubt the Osty experiments served to convince many researchers who had previously been sceptical. But once Rudi returned to Munich and took up with his old life again those closest to him began to feel his mediumship was coming to an end. His mind was not fully tuned to psychic affairs. He wanted to marry his delightful Mitzi, play football for the local team and work as a motor mechanic.

Séances trying to capture the last of his power were held at his home in Braunau under the most stringent conditions with every door and window sealed, every keyhole plastered over and with Herr Schneider locked in his bedroom. A large phantom was observed by those present, water splashed out of a basin, a handkerchief was tossed around and knotted. . . .

But blank sessions were becoming more frequent. Harry Price managed to persuade Rudi to travel to London for more experiments in which he produced faint materializations and moved objects. Photographs taken at the time show him slumped in a chair in a trance.

An automatic electric camera was used for the last séances. When the plates were being developed after the twenty-fifth session on April 28, 1932, Price saw that the camera had captured a shot of Rudi with his left arm sticking out behind his back, free from the grip of whoever should have been controlling him. Though Rudi had not produced any phenomena during that split second, Price believed that he had tried to cheat, and there was great bitterness over the incident. Others who had been present pointed out that Rudi had been startled in his trance state and could have jerked violently at the vivid photographic flash. Rudi said he could offer no explanation and remained silent about the whole business.

When Price published his report of the séance it led to such violent argument that for a time it proved a serious setback to psychical research. Many believed that Price had been jealous of the fact that Rudi Schneider had produced some of his best results under the eye of continental researchers. Strangely enough, some years later — long after the dispute had died down — Harry Price wrote, 'As far as psychical phenomena are concerned, the Schneider boys are the sheet anchor of psychical research.'

None of this mattered very much to Rudi. His powers almost gone, he married Mitzi, became a prosperous garage owner and settled in Braunau, quite happy for the rest of his life to let Olga and the phantoms sink back into the shadows from which they came.

Elliott O'D[

Doyen of ghost hunters Ellio[
quite possible that some of the[
human beings may not be of [
suggested with relish, the eart[
gentle spirits drawn back to th[

It was a very Irish thing to [
as though he was a magical m[
ancestry went back to Niall N[
fourth century, sometimes sty[
famous ghost in his own right)[   ], who wrote
the most chilling ghost stories in the world.

Peter Underwood, President of the Ghost Club, gives a splendid account of his friend in his book *The Ghost Hunters*, and tells how he saw ghostly things, including an extraordinary nude figure covered all over with yellow spots, from the age of five.

After leaving school he applied to join the Irish Royal Constabulary, but after studying for two years failed to pass the medical exam. He had no regrets. They were, he said afterwards, among the two happiest years of his life, with plenty of time to play football and cricket, which he loved.

A tussle with a highly unpleasant ghost which tried to strangle him at his student lodgings in Waterloo Road, Dublin, was the cause of his decision to adopt ghost hunting as a profession or life work. He did not enjoy the experience, but it interested him profoundly. That interest lasted unabated for fifty ghost-ridden years.

As Peter Underwood says, it was perhaps because he was always on the lookout for adventure that he found it. But he did not look for ghosts: they came to him. At twenty years old he decided to try his luck in the New World, and in 1882 headed for America and the great open plains. Later he visited the great cities, including New York, Chicago and San Francisco. He seemed to encounter paranormal activity wherever he went.

Back in England he tried his hand at teaching, usually as a games master at various private schools. He did not find it exciting enough, and for a time joined a drama school which taught him enough to become a touring player. This too palled and he eventually settled down to teaching again after getting married.

O'Donnell and his wife decided to run a small preparatory school together in Cornwall, where he looked forward to investigating some interesting cases of haunting. He did not have to look far. A new

...em close to a steep cliff, overlooking a path
...He moved in and prepared to open the school.
...was there alone with his housekeeper, a Mrs
...ng he began to hear strange noises at night, doors
...utting, footsteps ascending the stairs and walking up
...e passage outside his room. Not wishing to alarm the
...er he said nothing, but very soon she gave in her notice,
...he could no longer live in a house that was haunted. She
...ght the cause of the trouble was a set of antlers O'Donnell had
...erited and hung on the wall.

Other housekeepers arrived and left and when the school opened
several assistant masters complained about noises in the night. At last
O'Donnell could stand it no longer and decided to set up a ghost trap.
Once or twice loud knocks had shaken his bedroom door, but when
he opened it nothing was there. One night he sprinkled the passage
with flour and sand alternately, and fixed a line of cotton, breast high,
across it. The footsteps came again, and the bang on the door, but the
cotton was unbroken and the flour and sand undisturbed. Before long
he closed the school and sold the house. Local people told him that
before the house was built people passing the site late at night had
seen a very tall figure with a small round head suddenly rise from the
ground, cross the path in front of them with a swaying motion and
vanish over the cliff.

Another psychic experience that happened a few years later so
impressed him that he sent a report of it to the Society for Psychical
Research. This was odd in a way, says Peter Underwood, because
O'Donnell rather prided himself on *not* being a scientific psychical
researcher, and did not see what test tubes had to do with investigating
the other world or worlds.

He was standing one morning in August on the staircase of a house
where he and his family were staying in Newquay, chatting to his two
sisters and their old nurse who were in the hall only a few feet away
from him. Something made him look up. He saw Miss Dutton, a friend
who was also staying with them, come downstairs from the first landing.
As she approached O'Donnell moved to one side to allow her to pass.
He distinctly felt the swish of her dress against his trouser leg. She
went down the hall, passed his sisters and the nurse and went into the
front sitting room, slamming the door behind her.

Thinking it strange that she did not speak to them, O'Donnell and
his sisters followed her into the sitting room to see if anything was
wrong. There was no one there. The only exit was the door through
which they had just entered. Later that morning they met her on the
beach. She told them that at the moment the four people had seen her
on the staircase she was walking in town with a friend.

O'Donnell became a prolific writer on supernatural and occult subjects, crime and criminology. But he liked nothing better than to be told of a haunting he had not come across before, and to make plans to investigate. He would often spend the night alone in an empty house to make his own judgement. He would have only a candle for light and that would be extinguished when things began to happen.

One of the most spine-tingling cases he investigated was centred on the house in Somerset in which, and around which, Wilkie Collins wrote *The Woman in White*. Brockley Court was built on the site of a much older house, and several occupants declared they had seen two apparitions, one quite terrible, in the early hours of the morning. O'Donnell spent his first night there in the company of a Bristol journalist, and at 2 a.m. both men saw a pillar of light move across the room and vanish close to a window. On his second visit he took three friends, while a fourth (who had walked eight miles on a wet night in his enthusiasm) turned up at ten o'clock in the morning. This friend volunteered to position himself at the end of the corridor near the top of the stairs while the rest of the party settled down in the haunted bedroom. After two hours the silence was shattered by his piercing cries for help. He told them he had fallen asleep and dreamed that a tall figure with a terrible face had come leaping up the stairway, passed him and entered the 'haunted' room. The description fitted that of a ghost seen by the owner of the property.

The party returned to the haunted room and nothing further happened until four o'clock in the morning, when one of O'Donnell's friends was nearly scared out of his wits by an apparition with a long, swarthy, skull-like face. The others could see nothing, but O'Donnell noticed a red, rectangular light about six or seven feet from the ground that had not been there before. It began to move about and seemed to pass right through him. The atmosphere was so full of terror that O'Donnell decided enough was enough and suggested they all went home. Later he plucked up courage to visit the house again with a photographer. About two in the morning spherical lights floated round the room followed by trailing mist. The photographer took a flashlight picture which when developed showed quite clearly the face of a monk.

O'Donnell had no patience with people who scoffed at the idea of ghosts or said that no phantom would ever frighten them. He had had too much experience to accept that kind of talk. Had he ever been afraid? He freely admitted that on some occasions when he had been alone and had seen or felt that which reason and instinct had told him was something supernatural and not of this world, he had indeed been very much afraid.

He attended a meeting of the Ghost Club on May 6, 1965, and died not long afterwards.

Padre Pio Forgione

Padre Pio Forgione, a gentle Italian priest who died in 1968, was the most celebrated stigmatic since St Francis displayed the wounds of Christ in the thirteenth century. For fifty years he suffered agony from the terrible bleeding holes in his hands and in his left side. But he had no time for those who wanted to make him a saint.

For most of his life the humble Capuchin friar lived a life of strict devotion in the Italian monastery of San Giovanni Rotondo at Foggia. Far from exploiting his stigmata, he tried to avoid publicity and often covered his hands in public. But the world clamoured to see him.

With his grizzled beard and blunt features, Padre Pio looked like a peasant. He was born in the village of Pietrelcina near Benevento in 1889. His father was a poor farmer, and the Forgione family lived a frugal life, close to the soil. Padre Pio knew his vocation from an early age and at the age of seventeen entered a Capuchin monastery as a novice. During his youth and early priesthood he had a delicate constitution which was seriously affected by rigorous fasts and harsh discipline. He developed tuberculosis, began to see apparitions and was subject to 'diabolical attacks' which were similar to poltergeist outbreaks in which the sparse furniture in his cell moved of its own accord, his few possessions were scattered and his bedclothes thrown to the floor.

In 1915, when he was twenty-eight, he emerged from a long period of meditation with a queer stinging sensation in his hands. No one knew what to make of it, and it was soon forgotten. It was not until three years later that the significance of the sensation was realized.

On September 20, 1918, he was praying alone in the choir of the church at Foggia when, without warning of any onset of pain or illness, he gave a piercing cry and fell unconscious. His brother monks came running from other parts of the church to find him bleeding profusely from hands, feet and side. He showed, in other words, every sign of the stigmata, the five wounds suffered by Christ on the Cross.

Padre Pio begged those who had found him to keep his condition a secret, but word spread quickly of what had happened. From then on he was seldom free from pain and could move only with the greatest difficulty. The Provincial Superior who examined the wounds shortly after their appearance said that he would swear solemnly that he had seen clear through the holes well enough to have read print held on the other side. Sometimes as he lifted the Host during Mass he would pass into a state of ecstasy. A cupful of blood would flow from his wounds every day.

The faithful with Italy's semi-saint Padre Pio

It is interesting to note that genuine stigmata appear to have different characteristics from ordinary pathological wounds. The blood that flowed from Padre Pio's hands was clean, arterial blood, free from the discharges of disease, and there was no festering. Doctors of all denominations examined his stigmata many times over the years, but none could give a satisfactory explanation for his injuries. They dismissed the idea that the wounds could have arisen from any physical cause. Along with theologians they observed that most stigmatics are intensely devout people given to brooding deeply on the sufferings of Christ. The twentieth-century explanation is that an element of auto-suggestion is involved, but nothing has been proved.

Whatever the cause in Padre Pio's case, he carried on his duties with humility in spite of the open adulation of the peasants and the growing cult that surrounded him. Thousands began to descend on the church in Foggia, hoping to catch a glimpse of him. Money was sent to the monastery from people in all walks of life. The Vatican twice suspended him from his duties. The attitude of Rome from the beginning had been one of caution, and Padre Pio was aware that he was under constant surveillance by the religious authorities. When the money began to flow in his fame became something of an embarrassment, for he had taken a vow of poverty. Eventually he was absolved from his vows in this respect provided all the money sent to him was willed to the Church for charitable use.

In 1956 a hospital which cost in the region of £1 million was built at Foggia and completely paid for out of donations sent by people from all over the world who had come to see Padre Pio as a saintly figure. Even his home village of Pietrelcina began to prosper as crowds flocked to see the place where he had been born and brought up.

Apart from his fame as a stigmatic, Padre Pio had shown other signs that made him different from his fellow monks. He was credited with healing and other miracles and especially with clairvoyance.

Three men visiting the church on January 20 1936, were approached by Padre Pio, who asked them to pray with him for a soul about to meet his God. They knelt with him and were then told by the priest that they had been praying for George V of England. He had died while they were on their knees.

Perhaps the most extraordinary story concerning Padre Pio's faculty for the psychic is that concerning a certain Monsignor Damiani of Salto in Uruguay. The South American gentleman had met Padre Pio while on a visit to Italy, and was so impressed he declared he wanted to die in the priest's presence. Padre Pio said to him kindly, 'You will die in your own country — but you will have no need to fear.'

Damiani returned to Uruguay. Years passed and in the summer of 1942 he fell ill. The Archbishop of Montevideo was awakened in the early hours of the morning by a Capuchin monk who urged him to go immediately to Monsignor Damiani's bedside. When he arrived Damiani was already dead but on the bed was a slip of paper on which was written three words: 'Padre Pio Came.' Several years later the Archbishop met Padre Pio and recognized him as the Capuchin monk who had come to him.

Padre Pio died on September 28, 1968.

Theresa Neumann

Bavarian peasant girl Theresa Neumann was said to suffer Christ's Passion every Lent for the last thirty-two years of her life. Great weals appeared on her back from the scourging, bleeding punctures marked her forehead where it had been pierced by the crown of thorns and her hands, feet and side gushed blood as though they had been torn by nails and a sword.

Few people were allowed near her. She spent most of her life in bed wrapped in white linen and seldom gave any sign of curiosity about the outside world.

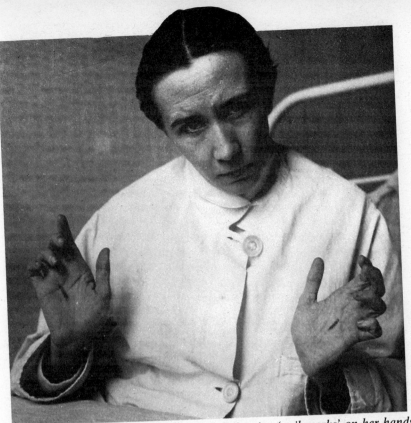

Theresa Neumann showing 'nail marks' on her hands

Born in 1898 in the village of Konnersreuth, Bavaria, she came from a very poor family but in her youth seemed no different from any other girl of her age. She went to work as a domestic on local farms, then suddenly succumbed to a series of mysterious illnesses which no doctor could explain.

During Lent 1926, when she was twenty-eight, she had an overwhelming vision of the Passion which cured her of her various afflictions but left her bearing the marks of the stigmata. Every Friday for the next thirty-two years she wept blood or bled from the wounds, but at Lent she went through the whole terrible ordeal of the Passion over again, writhing in agony, gushing blood from every wound. Sometimes she lost as much as a pint of blood and eight pounds in weight during her vision.

She was watched closely by the Bishop of Ratisbon, who wanted to protect her from the pilgrims, curiosity-seekers and miracle-hunters who poured into the village of Konnersreuth once her condition was known. Doctors were allowed to examine her thoroughly, taking advantage of her trances and periods of unconsciousness. Many said that her wounds bore a strong resemblance to those of St Francis,

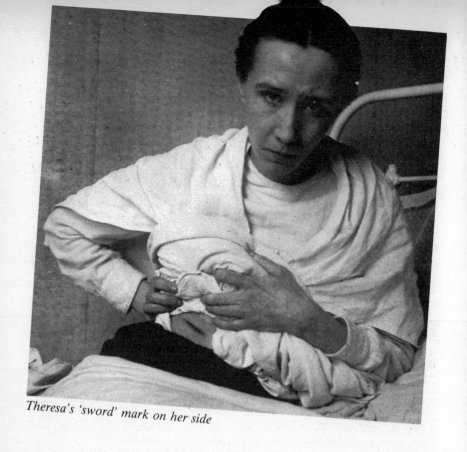

Theresa's 'sword' mark on her side

especially those on the hands which gave the impression of a forged iron nail piercing and protruding from them. The nail head was described as rectangular, admirably regular, its edges being delicately adorned with zigzag borders. The wounds remained dry until dawn broke each Friday, then the figure in white lying in bed would begin to stream with blood.

Theresa was said to be clairvoyant and to speak in Aramaic, Christ's own language, when in a trance. Another extraordinary aspect of her story is that no food or liquid, except the communion wafer and wine, had been seen to pass her lips for thirty-five years. Her total fast started in the twenties and she was subject to long periods of medical scrutiny. Doctors once kept her under strict surveillance for several weeks, night and day, but in the end testified that to the best of their knowledge nothing had passed her lips but the wafer and wine.

She was said to have remained in reasonable health, though photographs of her show a waxen, ghost-like image. Doctors noted that her excreta, which had progressively diminished since 1926, ceased altogether after 1930 and her intestinal tract simply withered away. She continued to have ecstasies and visions up to her death in 1962.

Versailles

Visiting the Palace of Versailles one August afternoon in 1901, two middle-aged English ladies walked down a grassy path in search of the Petit Trianon and found themselves in the eighteenth century. The account of their extraordinary adventure, which they recorded in meticulous detail, has become a classic of psychic literature.

Neither Miss Ann Moberly, daughter of the Bishop of Salisbury and head of an Oxford women's college, nor Miss Eleanor Jourdain, headmistress of a private school in Watford, were of a whimsical or over-imaginative nature. At the time of their visit they had not known each other long, having only recently been introduced, and their friendship was still at the slightly formal stage.

Miss Moberly had gone to Paris chiefly in order to be able to visit the great International Exhibition. Miss Jourdain had a small apartment in the French capital and was already on holiday there when her friend arrived. They agreed to explore the historical and architectural sites of interest in Paris together during the day and attend the Exhibition in the evenings.

Saturday August 10 turned out to be overcast and grey with a light summer breeze. After the great heat they had suffered all week they enjoyed the freshness and planned to spend the afternoon at Versailles visiting both the great Palace and its famous gardens.

By the time they had walked through the vast gilded salons and endless corridors it was almost time for tea. They made up their minds, however, before returning to the city, to visit the small, beautiful country house known as the Petit Trianon, built by Louis XV for his mistress, the Marquise de Pompadour, but for ever associated with a future Queen of France, the tragic Marie Antoinette. In its spacious grounds enhanced by decorative bridges, waterfalls, pavilions and scented groves, they also looked forward to seeing the 'toy village' where in simple farm cottages Marie Antoinette amused herself by pretending to be a milkmaid, shepherdess or peasant wife.

Setting out to walk, parasols and Baedeker in hand, they came to the head of a long lake and struck away down to the right through a woodland glade until they came to another stretch of water with an impressive building reflected in its surface, which they concluded rightly was the Grand Trianon, a château constructed for Louis XIV. They passed it on the left and came up to a broad green drive, perfectly deserted. If they had followed it, they would have reached the Petit Trianon directly, but instead they crossed it and went up the lane in front of them.

Miss Jourdain was a little way ahead when Miss Moberly caught sight of a woman shaking a white cloth out of the window of a cottage at the corner of the lane. She was surprised that her friend did not stop to ask the way. Only afterwards did she learn that Miss Jourdain had seen neither the woman nor the building.

At this point the two ladies were not aware of anything strange in their surroundings. They chatted about Oxford and mutual friends there, carrying on steadily up the lane then making a sharp turn right past a group of buildings. Now they had the choice of three grassy paths. They elected to follow the centre one, largely because they could see two men ahead and thought they would ask for directions. They presumed they were gardeners as they saw a wheelbarrow and a pointed spade close at hand, but they were dressed in long, greyish green coats with small, three-cornered hats and might easily have been officials of some kind. The men directed them straight ahead and they continued as before, deep in conversation.

At this point Miss Jourdain saw a detached, solidly built cottage with a woman and a girl standing in the doorway. She particularly noticed their unusual dress. Both wore white kerchiefs tucked into the bodice. The woman was passing a jug to the girl, who wore an ankle-length skirt and close white cap. Miss Moberly saw nothing.

From that moment both began to feel an odd sense of unreality, though not being on terms of intimate friendship as yet, neither liked to mention the fact to the other. Miss Moberly wrote later: 'We walked briskly forward, talking as before, but from the moment we left the lane an extraordinary depression came over me, which in spite of every effort to shake it off, steadily deepened until it became quite overpowering.' She did not know that Miss Jourdain was experiencing the same depression: 'I began to feel as if I were walking in my sleep; the heavy dreaminess was oppressive.'

They came to a grotto within which was a garden kiosk, like a small bandstand. Sitting by the side of it was a man wrapped in a heavy, dark cloak, a large hat shading his face. Suddenly he turned his head and looked at them. His face was pockmarked, repulsive, rough and dark, its expression odious. Miss Jourdain felt 'something uncanny and fear-inspiring'. The two ladies felt a moment of genuine alarm.

The place was so shut in that we could not see beyond it. Everything suddenly looked unnatural, therefore, unpleasant. Even the trees behind the kiosk seemed to have become flat and lifeless, *like a wood worked on tapestry*. There were no effects of light and shade, no wind stirred in the trees. It was all intensely still.

The sound of running footsteps on the path behind them came as a relief, but when they turned no one was there. Then they noticed another figure had appeared, this time a handsome fellow with black curly hair who was 'distinctly a gentleman'. He called out to them with great excitement, *'Mesdames, mesdames, il ne faut pas passer par là,'* then, waving his arms with animation, '*Par ici . . . cherchez la maison*', indicating that he wanted them to take the path to the right, not the left, for it would then bring them to the house. They went instantly to a little bridge on the right, then turned to thank him. To their amazement, he had disappeared. They heard running footsteps again, but saw no one.

Once over the bridge they were on high ground until they reached a meadow from which at last the front of the Petit Trianon itself could be seen. They walked towards a flight of steps leading up onto the terrace. At that moment Miss Moberly saw a lady sitting in the rough grass which grew right up to the house, apparently sketching. She turned and looked as they passed. Her face was not that of a young woman but it was strikingly pretty. Miss Moberly did not know why, but she did not find it attractive. She had puffed-out fair hair which fluffed around her forehead and supported a shady straw hat. Her dress, of a light summer material, was cut low in the bodice and trimmed with a fichu folded handkerchief-fashion across the shoulders. Miss Moberly felt as though she was walking in a dream and that the lady was part of it. She caught sight of her again as she stepped up onto the terrace. Miss Jourdain had not seen the figure at all.

They walked round to the west side of the terrace, looking for an entrance and feeling that the stillness and oppressiveness were becoming unbearable. Suddenly a door opened, a young man ran out, banging the door behind him, and ran rapidly towards the ladies, telling them they must not remain there. He offered to escort them towards the main entrance off the courtyard. His manner was jaunty, his smile slightly mocking and though he did not wear livery they gained the impression that he was a junior footman. He led them through a formal French garden, walled with trees, into the courtyard and they made their way to the entrance hall.

Suddenly everything seemed normal again. A guide arrived and they were invited to join a party of French tourists who also wanted to look over the house. Coming out they were able to hire a carriage to take them back to Versailles for tea. They noticed during the short drive that the wind was blowing and everything seemed natural again.

Neither Miss Moberly nor Miss Jourdain mentioned the Trianon visit again for a whole week, then as the former began to write a descriptive letter about her holiday in France the scenes of that day came back one by one. She dropped her pen and turned to her friend: 'Tell me, do you think the Petit Trianon is haunted?' Miss Jourdain answered without hesitation, 'Yes, I do.' It was only then they started to compare notes and realized they had not always seen the same things at the same time.

They returned to England and it was not until three months later, when Miss Jourdain paid a visit to her friend's college in Oxford, that they realized how important it was to record everything accurately as soon as possible. Already they had allowed too much time to elapse to satisfy those seriously interested in psychical research. They decided, very wisely, that each of them should set down her own experience independently of the other and sign it.

Miss Jourdain revisited the scene alone in the following January. She felt stunned as she discovered the whole place had changed, or seemed to have changed, and the route she and Miss Moberly had followed was almost untraceable. She asked friends in Paris whether they knew any story about the Petit Trianon being haunted. They told her there was a story that Marie Antoinette's ghost had been seen in the garden in a light summer hat and a pink dress. Some people from the village of Versailles had even gone so far as to say the whole ghostly court appeared on the anniversary of the sacking of the Tuileries on August 10, 1792, the day which led to Marie Antoinette's death on the guillotine.

The English schoolmistress hurried back to England to confer with her friend. For the first time they allowed themselves to ask the question that had haunted them for twelve whole months. Was it possible that on that August day in 1901 they had wandered into the past, seen the last day of the French Court, and that one of them had looked into the face of Marie Antoinette?

Both ladies returned to the Trianon in 1904. They retraced their steps with growing consternation. The gateway through which they had a glimpse of a broad green drive was derelict, the drive a tangle of weeds. There were no longer three clear paths for them to choose from; no cottage anywhere in the vicinity where Miss Jourdain had seen the woman and child with the jug. The little kiosk was not to be found, nor the bridge over the ravine which they had crossed when directed by their 'gentleman'. There were no steps leading to the front of the house, and the door through which the young man had rushed was invisible from where they stood because a wall intervened.

For the next ten years the two ladies devoted themselves to the task of trying to reconstruct the Petit Trianon as they saw it that day from documentary research. They delved into old records and documents, read contemporary accounts, tried to identify the people they had met.

So careful were they in checking and double-checking all the evidence that it was not until 1911 that anything was published, when the whole story appeared under the title *An Adventure*.

For a long time it was difficult to obtain detailed information of the arrangement of the Trianon gardens and outbuildings as they were in the 18th century. However, by sheer good fortune, in 1903 an old map was found hidden in the chimney of a house outside Paris. It had been drawn by Marie Antoinette's landscape gardener, Mique, about 1780. On examining the map closely it was possible to identify the vanished kiosk, the grotto and the cottage which Miss Jourdain saw but which had long disappeared.

Scrutiny of other original papers proved the existence of three distinct paths, a well-kept green drive and an artificial ravine which could only be crossed by a bridge.

Miss Moberly examined a portrait of Marie Antoinette by Wertmuller and came to the conclusion that it could have been her ghost she saw, though at the time she thought her to have been a tourist in extremely old-fashioned dress. Even the repulsive-looking man who sat by the kiosk was eventually identified. In 1789 there had been a Creole at the Court of Louis XVI, the Comte de Vaudreuil, who was feared because he looked so evil with his pock-marked dark complexion. He was in the habit of wearing a wide-brimmed hat to cover his face.

Miss Jourdain, who seemed to have the stronger psychic instinct, returned many times to Versailles during the years of research and sometimes felt there were people close to her she could not see.

The ladies remained friends for the rest of their lives. Miss Jourdain joined Miss Moberly at St Hugh's, Oxford, as her vice-principal and the two of them played a great part in pioneering, quietly and non-militantly, on behalf of women's emancipation. They were both loved and respected and considered to be of absolute integrity.

Their visions at Versailles have been taken up and dissected by many sceptics and critics, and dozens of explanations have been put forward. None of them hold water. Stories of death-bed confessions and the perpetration of a hoax have also been soundly disproved.

The two original accounts of 'The Adventure' were placed with the Bodleian Library in Oxford. The mystery of what happened on that August afternoon in 1901 remains to tantalize generations to come.

Joan Of Arc

Voices, visions and dreams led the simple country girl who was Joan of Arc to be the saviour of France, the tragic martyr of Rouen and the saint who is still revered to this day.

Born of poor parents at Domrémy on the borders of Lorraine and Champagne on January 6, 1412, Joan was not what one would think of as the usual type of visionary. She was a strong, healthy country girl, with no sign of hysteria, who went about her daily work of helping in the house, spinning, sewing and looking after domestic animals with vigour and cheerfulness.

The voices started when she was only thirteen. She told her cruel inquisitors at a much later date, when her glory was over and she was facing death at the stake, that they often came to her when she was alone in the woods or sitting quietly in church. Sometimes even the steeple bells seemed to speak to her. They had one message. Her destiny was to go to the aid of France's rightful king and save her country. God would help her.

France was at this time in great danger. The conquering English were running amok over the fields and vineyards of their old enemy, capturing cities and castles and putting villages to the sword. At the same time the nation was being torn by civil strife, with the Burgundians and the Armagnacs at each other's throats.

The first voice she heard was that of the archangel St Michael, who, she said, returned to her again and again when she was alone in the fields. She also heard the gentler voices of the two patron saints of Lorraine, St Catherine and St Margaret, telling her to have courage.

In 1428 news came that the English were beseiging Orleans and if the city was captured it was more than likely that the whole of southern France would fall into the hands of the enemy. Joan's voices, as she told her inquisitors, became more insistent. St Michael told her she must go to the Dauphin (the future King Charles VII), win back the kingdom and see him crowned and consecrated. Joan protested, saying she was only a poor peasant girl and not a leader of men, but she heard the voice tell her clearly, 'Go to Messire de Baudricourt, Captain of Vaucouleurs, and he will take you to the Dauphin.'

Vaucouleurs was about ten miles from Domremy and it was difficult for Joan to get there. She was afraid what her father would do if he found out. He would never understand the voices, but she dared not disobey them. She was, however, shrewd and devised a plan by which she could get to Vaucouleurs. A relative of her mother's, an uncle by marriage, called Durand Laxart lived with his wife in a village not far from there. Prompted by Joan, he asked her parents to allow her to nurse his sick wife. They agreed, and Durand went to fetch her.

On their journey Joan reminded Durand of an old prophecy that France would be made desolate by a woman and restored by a maid from Lorraine. No one had any doubt that the woman who had ruined France was Queen Isabella, who had allied herself with the English, and Joan had no doubt that she was the maid from Lorraine destined to restore France to her former glory.

She told Durand to take her to Robert de Baudricourt without delay. There must have been authority in her voice, for her uncle did not hesitate. Baudricourt heard her story and said, 'Box her ears and send her home to her mother.' However, in due course he changed his

Joan of Arc at the stake on May 30, 1431

mind. On February 12, 1429, she told him the French had been badly beaten by the English at the Battle of Herrings. They were hundreds of miles from the battlefield and the news was not received until two days later. Baudricourt took it as a sign that Joan was divinely inspired — some authorities believe she had a precognitive vision. He decided to send her to the Court at Chinon with two knights, Jean de Metz and Bertrand Poulengey, both of whom came to believe in her mission.

Joan got rid of her feminine clothes and dressed herself as a man with tunic, boots and leggings. She had her hair cut short and rode on an old horse bought for her by her uncle. Baudricourt gave her an old sword.

After reaching Chinon she had to wait for two days before being given permission to see the Dauphin. He received her at night in a hall lit by fifty torches. Three hundred nobles, magnificently dressed, watched as she entered. The Dauphin himself stood, in plain dress, apart from his throne, in order to test her. She knew him immediately and fell on her knees. He was so impressed that he took her aside and listened to what she had to say. Realizing he needed to be convinced that God had sent her to lead his armies, she demonstrated what could only have been a flash of psychic insight. She repeated to him his secret prayer that if indeed he was the rightful ruler of France, God would defend him, or at least allow him to escape in safety.

Though the Dauphin was completely won over, many of his council only half believed in her. But the situation was desperate, and, ready to try anything, they determined to send her with the troops about to be dispatched to the Duke of Orleans.

She now put on the accoutrements of a knight, being fitted out in a complete suit of white armour with a jerkin of scarlet and white. A great sword in a scabbard of red velvet hung at her side. The story of the sword became part of her legend.

It had once belonged to the great Charles Martel, who had stopped the Moslem invasion of France in the eighth century. For hundreds of years it had been hidden away, and few people knew where it was. Joan listened to her voices. They told her to ask for the ancient sword marked with five crosses which was buried in St Catherine's church at Fierbois. The clergy at Fierbois said they knew of no such sword. Joan told them that it was buried just behind the altar. Shovels were fetched, and the sword was found.

She rode from Chinon on a magnificent charger carrying a white banner fringed with silk and painted with fleurs-de-lys. At Blois she was given command of six thousand men collected for the battle to relieve Orleans. Appalled by the rabble she saw before her, she set to work to create a proper army. Camp followers and prostitutes fled, the foul oaths and blasphemies stopped. She ordered all soldiers to be regular in their attendance at Mass and to be clean and decent in their appearance. She filled them with the fire of patriotism, reminding them they were each and every one fighting, under God, for the glory of France.

Before setting out for Orleans she dictated (for she had never learned to write) a summons to the King of England, the Duke of Bedford, the Earl of Suffolk and two other English commanders, ordering them to surrender the keys of all the cities they had taken to the Maid who was sent by God to restore the royal blood of France.

Everywhere she rode, white banner streaming over her head, the French rallied to her and the English, suspecting she was of the devil, fled. After raising the seige of Orleans and gaining a great victory at Patay, Joan went to Rheims to see the Dauphin crowned in the Cathedral. Throughout the ceremony she stood by his side.

As soon as the coronation was over and Charles VII on the throne, Joan felt her mission was over. She asked permission to hang up her sword and return home. A foreboding of death came over her.

Many nobles were jealous of her success, the English wanted her dead at all costs. A treacherous and cowardly deal was arranged, and for a colossal sum the Burgundians handed her over to her enemies. The one man who could have saved her, the King of France, was too cowardly to come to her rescue. Brought before the Inquisition, mercilessly hounded by the brutal Bishop of Beauvais and abandoned by her voices, she was a tragic and pathetic figure. Initially she was indicted on seventy counts, many of them charges of witchcraft and sorcery, but by the time the trial was half over the count had been reduced to twelve and all references to witchcraft eliminated except one. After a trial that was both cruel and corrupt she was eventually condemned to death for her resistance to the Church. Almost her last words in prison to the Bishop of Beauvais were, 'Bishop, I die through you.' She realized that he, a Frenchman, was her worst enemy and had refused her every right.

Pronounced a relapsed heretic, Joan of Arc went to the stake at daybreak on May 30, 1431. An English soldier made a cross of two sticks and gave it to her as the fire was lit. A quarter of a century after her death, Joan was formerly exonerated and rehabilitated by the Church that had condemned her; in 1894 she was beatified and in 1920 declared a saint by the Pope. But from that day to this no one has been able to give an explanation for her voices and visions.

Bernadette

Bernadette Soubirous was a peasant girl of the greatest simplicity, belonging to a family that lived in abject poverty. She was poorly educated, asthmatic, hard-working and devout. Gathering firewood on the outskirts of the little town where she lived at the foot of the Pyrenees one cold February day in 1858, she looked up and saw the Virgin Mary.

Since then millions of people have made their pilgrimage to the place where she had her vision, and where the 'beautiful lady' appeared to her again and again. Lourdes has become a religious centre of the greatest importance to the Catholic faith, a focus of hopes and seemingly miraculous healing. Yet when Bernadette first spoke of what she had seen 130 years ago, she was beaten, accused of lying and regarded with suspicion by her parish priest.

No saint could have had a humbler beginning. Bernadette was born at Lourdes in 1844, the eldest child of an impoverished family. It was then a quiet place of mill streams, sheep and sun-baked rocks, the town itself a warren of narrow streets. Her father, François Soubirous, had been a miller but was sacked when he lost the sight of his right eye in an accident. By 1856 the family was in such dire straits they could not afford to pay rent and had to leave their simple house for a disused, vermin-ridden shack.

When cholera broke out in the Bigorre region of the Pyrenees where they lived, Bernadette was an early victim. Though she recovered she suffered from asthma for the rest of her life. For two years there was famine in Lourdes. Bernadette's father was arrested when he tried to steal for his family. It was decided that she should be sent away to stay with relatives in a mountain village where she would have food and a chance to regain her health tending sheep in the clear, pure air.

Above all things fourteen-year-old Bernadette wanted to learn her catechism and make her first communion. Her education had been neglected while she tried to earn money by working as a servant and as a waitress in a small café. She asked to be allowed to return to Lourdes and enrolled at the free school run by the Sisters of Charity.

Then came the February morning when she set out with her sisters to gather firewood. The girls crossed the River Gave by the old bridge leading out of the town, walked through an area of scrub, then came to the mill stream and a cliff face with a grotto. Two of the girls crossed the mill stream. Bernadette hesitated, then bent down to take off her stockings and shoes. She heard a noise like a gust of wind, looked up and saw a soft glow in the grotto. As her eyes became accustomed to the light a figure in white appeared with a soft, white veil falling each side of her face. Years later Bernadette wrote:

I put my hand in my pocket, and I found my rosary there, I wanted

Catholic pilgrims taking part in a candlelight procession at Lourdes

to make the sign of the cross . . . I couldn't raise my hand to my forehead . . . The vision made the sign of the cross. Then I tried a second time and I could. As soon as I made the sign of the cross, the fearful shock I felt disappeared. I knelt down and I said my rosary in the presence of the beautiful lady. The vision fingered the beads of her own rosary, but she did not move her lips. When I finished my rosary, she signed for me to approach but I did not dare. Then she disappeared.

On the way home Bernadette told her sisters what she had seen, referring to the figure as 'Aquero', which meant 'that one' in local dialect. They had seen nothing. When the story of the vision was repeated to their mother she became frightened, thinking that her eldest daughter was beginning to 'see things', to hallucinate. She thrashed all three girls and forbade Bernadette to go to the grotto again.

At confession that Sunday Bernadette told the priest what had happened but he merely thought her fanciful. Her parents, however, relented and allowed her to go back, this time with a bottle of holy water. For the second time the vision in white appeared, a blue sash round her waist, a yellow rosary round her neck. Nothing could distract the peasant girl from what she saw, and eventually, almost in a trance state, she had to be carried back to her home.

For the first time a whisper of interest ran through the town. Some thought the girl was trying to create a sensation, others were impressed by her sincerity. Her mother was angry and upset. The identity of the vision had still not been established. Bernadette still called the lady in white 'Aquero', but there was a theory among some of the devout people of Lourdes that it could be the soul of a pious girl who had died the year before. But when Bernadette summoned up courage to speak next time she knelt in the grotto she was told it was not necessary for her to know who 'Aquero' was. Speaking for the first time, the vision in white asked her to go to the grotto every day for fifteen days, telling her, 'I do not promise to make you happy in this world, but in the next.'

Between February 18 and March 2, Bernadette saw her white lady thirteen times. She discovered a spring in the grotto, and rumour went round that those who drank from it would be cured of their ills. The story spread to other towns and villages, and soon thousands of people congregated along the river bank trying to catch a glimpse of the miracle that was happening in their midst.

Not everyone was impressed. The parish priest treated her with the deepest suspicion; the police commissioner implied she was making a nuisance of herself, warned her not to go to the grotto again and admitted he did not know what to make of her. She was interviewed by the town's Imperial prosecutor, the examining magistrate and the regional commandant of constabulary, who was extremely perturbed about the ever-growing crowds. They all conceded that whatever the truth, Bernadette Soubirous appeared to be sincere, sane and modest.

The crowds became so pressing that eventually she had to be escorted to the grotto by armed soldiers and wore a hooded cloak to cover her face. A deep hush fell as she knelt and raised her eyes to gaze on the mysterious figure no one else could see. The Church kept silent until Bernadette told Father Payramale, the parish priest, that her white lady had instructed her that people were to be allowed to approach the grotto in procession and that a chapel must be built there. His reaction was one of perplexed anger, and he demanded a miraculous sign before he would believe her.

Bernadette returned to school, thinking her visions had come to an end, but on the morning of March 25, the Feast of the Annunciation, she woke up with a strong desire to revisit the grotto. This time the white lady revealed that she was 'The Immaculate Conception' (the complicated doctrine of the immaculate conception of the mother of Jesus had been proclaimed in 1854). This time the Church listened. Payramale was convinced at last that she had seen genuine apparitions of the Virgin Mary.

Two weeks later Bernadette went to the grotto before dawn. She knelt with a long candle in her hands but seemed to be in such a trance that she did not notice when the flame burned down through her fingers. A doctor in the crowd examined her hands afterwards. There was not a mark on them.

From then on Lourdes and its grotto became the destination of pilgrims from all over the world. Sick people were already arriving in their thousands. Bernadette, unable to return to the simple life she had led, found sanctuary in the local hospice of the Sisters of Nevers. In 1866 she asked to join the order, and went as a novice to the mother house. She remained a nun until she died in 1879 at the age of thirty-five. She suffered greatly through several long illnesses and became increasingly reluctant to talk about her visions.

Bernadette of Lourdes was beatified in 1925 and canonized in 1933. Today it is estimated more than three million pilgrims a year make their way to her grotto. She would hardly recognize it.

Harry Price

The name of Harry Price, probably the most famous psychical researcher and ghost hunter England has ever known, has come to be associated in the minds of most people with his most famous case: the haunting of Borley Rectory.

Price was involved with the weird goings on at that damp, rambling Victorian mansion — the most haunted house in Britain — for nineteen years, off and on. Because his investigations, as always, had a certain flamboyance about them he was bitterly criticized by fellow researchers who did not care for his flair for publicity. But the two books he wrote about his experiences at Borley became best-sellers and opened up the whole subject of psychical research to the ordinary man in the street.

Harry Price was different from most of the serious, academic-minded men who took part in psychical research in England in the first half of this century. He had something of the showman about him, a love of drama that made him a controversial figure from his earliest days. Physically he was small in stature, stocky and bald, but he gave out a quality of vital energy and had eyes that looked right through you. Even his most bitter critics had to accept that he probably knew more about ghosts, poltergeists and haunted houses than any alive. And, showman or not, he used the latest techniques and advanced scientific methods to carry out his investigations.

His association with Borley started one day in June 1929, when he was asked by a London editor if he would investigate the strange happenings that had been reported in a local paper. For years, it seemed, anyone who took up residence at Borley Rectory – which had been built in 1863 on the site of a medieval monastery near Sudbury in Suffolk — was pestered beyond endurance by what they could only describe as supernatural forces. On his first visit Price heard enough stories to capture his scientific interest for the rest of his life. Several ghosts, it seemed, haunted the place, including a grey nun who had been seen by literally dozens of people, a headless man, a tall, dark figure and a coachman driving his carriage at full gallop. People had heard bells ringing, footsteps, wailing, knocks, bumps, rattles coming from supposedly empty rooms, crashing crockery, breaking windows, ominous dragging noises, doors opening and shutting and, from the church, the sound of music and monastic singing.

Several incumbents had been frightened away when, in 1935, the Rev. L. A. Foyster and his wife decided they too had suffered enough and announced they were leaving. Mrs Foyster, whose Christian name was Marianne, had seen messages scribbled on the wall pleading with her to get help. One day a voice called out her name and she was attacked by an invisible assailant. After hearing their story, the administrators of Queen Anne's Bounty (owners of the house) decided it was not fit for a parson to live in. They put it up for sale.

Harry Price, by now completely enthralled by the goings on at Borley, decided after some hesitation not to buy it but to offer to rent it for twelve months. As no one else wanted to set foot inside the door, his offer was accepted.

On May 19, 1937, Price, by now well known as the founder of Britain's National Laboratory for Psychical Research and the veteran of a hundred ghost watches, advertised in *The Times* for 'people of leisure and intelligence, intrepid, critical and unbiased' to join a rota of observers at the rectory. From more than two hundred people who applied, he chose forty. These stalwarts, including doctors, architects, diplomats, scientists, soldiers — a cross-section of believers and non-believers — spent some uncomfortable nights in the cold, empty rectory where one room had been set up as a base. Price's friend and neighbour of many years, Sidney H. Glanville, was in charge of operations. That Glanville was a man of utter integrity my own family can testify, for he was my father-in-law's best friend.

Many of the volunteers drew a blank. They passed some eerie, uncomfortable nights but saw or heard nothing. Others, however, had very strange experiences, ranging from seeing objects move of their own volition to hearing strange noises in empty rooms. Dr. C. E. M. Joad, the philosopher, who formed part of the team, recorded a sudden and inexplicable drop of ten degrees in the temperature of the room he slept in. Price made a formidable list of what had actually been seen and experienced.

The grey nun was seen by many, including Price, who firmly believed in her. During a séance held by some of the investigators it was discovered that the nun's name was Marie Lairre, that she had been brought to England from France by one of the Waldegraves who inhabited the original Borley Manor and that when he wanted to contract a more 'suitable' marriage he strangled her and hid her body.

Confirmation of this came in an extraordinary manner. The rectory was burned to the ground in 1939, but the phenomena continued. Price received a letter from a clergyman, the Rev. W. J. Phythian Adams, Canon of Carlisle, who suggested that now the site could be excavated. Having read Price's first book on Borley and studied the plan of the rectory, he thought he knew exactly where they should dig. In August 1943 excavations began. On the exact spot the Canon had indicated — he had never visited the place — they found part of a woman's skull with the jawbone and teeth in good condition and pendants bearing religious symbols.

Some of Harry Price's fellow researchers went wild when his books on Borley Rectory were published. His findings and reports of his investigations were torn to shreds. He was even accused of having buried the nun's bones himself to make his story better. But as Paul Tabori noted in his biography of Harry Price, that took no account of his heart condition, which would have made heavy digging to a depth of three or four feet impossible.

Price was not unconscious of the antagonism he aroused among some psychical researchers. Everything he did seemed to attract attention, and he knew his love of publicity and desire to make what he did understandable to the man in the street jarred on the 'Establishment'. But his love of the unknown and the mysterious was utterly genuine.

Price was born in London in 1881 and his schooldays were coloured by his love of magicians and conjurors. As an incredulous eight-year-old he saw 'The Great Sequah' produce two pigeons out of an empty hat, and would not be content until he knew how he had done it. His father gave him a conjuring manual for his birthday. 'From that time,' he admits in his autobiography, 'I have never missed an opportunity of ascertaining, if possible, how the wonders I have witnessed were produced.'

As a boy he spent much of his spare time wandering round street markets and fairs looking at fortune tellers, hypnotists, quack doctors and conjurors and observing their methods. When he was fifteen he

Harry Price with American medium, Frank Decker

experienced his first haunting. He used to spend many of his school holidays in a little Shropshire village a few miles from Shrewsbury. In the village was an old manor house which had been leased to a retired Canon of the Church of England and his wife. Very soon after the old couple settled there strange happenings were reported. Stable doors would be found ajar in the morning, though fastened securely at night, animals were discovered untethered, pans of milk overturned, logs scattered. Servants kept watch, but saw no one. Suddenly manifestations outside ceased and terrifying activity began inside the house. The old couple left for the sake of their health and the house was empty when young Price talked the caretaker into letting him and his friend spend the night there.

There was a local story that a rich recluse who had lived at the manor many years before had strangled the young girl who kept house for him. The old man was said to have been found drowned next day in the river. Their restless spirits were thought to be responsible for the disturbances. Harry Price and his friend took up their vigil in the morning room of the manor with nothing but an old stable light to cut through the gloom and a couple of blankets to keep them warm. At about half past eleven his companion thought he heard a noise in the room above. Price heard it too, but thought it might have been rats. 'A few minutes later there was a thud overhead that left nothing to the imagination,' he wrote in his autobiography. 'It sounded as if someone had stumbled over a chair. The fact that we were not alone in the house almost paralysed us with fear.'

Just before midnight they again heard a noise in the room above, as if a heavy person was stamping about in clogs. Whatever 'it' was, it began descending the stairs. When it reached the hall, it paused before going back up again. The boys were too frightened to look out. When, about an hour after midnight, they heard footsteps on the stairs again, they decided to act. Young Price had rigged up photographic flash equipment in the hall. He pressed the switch to set it off in the room where they were hiding. There was an almighty flash and explosion and whatever was on the stairs *stumbled*. Gathering up whatever courage they had left, the boys rushed into the hall. No one was there.

The experience thrilled the young researcher and made him determined that if he ever got the opportunity he would investigate psychic phenomena on a more scientific basis. From that time on he attended every performance by a public medium he could find in the south-east of London (his home was in Brockley at this time); he went to spiritualist meetings and local séances and started to build his great library of magic and occult books.

His lively mind encompassed practical subjects as well, and he studied engineering, chemistry and photography at Goldsmiths' College in the City of London and elsewhere, and for a few years was interested in archaeology and the study of old coins. In 1908 he married a girl he had known since childhood. Though she had no interest in psychic affairs, they remained happily married for a lifetime. She had a small private income which helped to improve his financial status, and he was able to spend more time on psychical research.

During the First World War a heart ailment that troubled him all his life kept him out of active service. His knowledge of mechanical engineering, however, made him eligible to run a small munitions factory. He still found time to investigate twenty haunted houses.

By the time the war ended he had conceived a plan of great importance. He felt there should be in existence a laboratory where mediums and other psychics could be tested with the latest scientific equipment by people who had open minds on supernatural matters. He travelled all over Europe to find out what the great continental researchers were doing and in the mid-1920s opened his National Laboratory for Psychical Research in a blaze of publicity.

Price joined the Society for Psychical Research, an august body of men and women he was never really at home with, though their objects were the same: to weed out the fakes and frauds in the psychic world and concentrate on genuine phenomena. Within a very short time, he was involved in his first row. Price caused an uproar with his exposure of the revered 'spirit photographer', William Hope, whom he caught substituting a prepared plate for the marked one which had been given to him. Sir Arthur Conan Doyle, ardent spiritualist that he was, reared up in Hope's defence, and for a time his relationship with Price became very chilly indeed.

Soon after, however, Harry Price had a remarkable stroke of luck that brought him his first serious success and helped to establish his fame. In his autobiography he tells how one day he was travelling from London to his home at Pulborough in Sussex and found himself sitting opposite a young woman, a 'typical English girl with a charming personality and more than her share of good looks'. Having nothing to read on the journey she asked if she might have a look at his copy of *Light*, a psychic magazine among a pile of books and newspapers by his side. Price asked her whether she had an interest in psychic matters. She replied shyly that she had a purely objective, academic interest. Then something made her confide in him. For some years, she admitted, certain things had happened in her presence that greatly puzzled her. Perhaps two or three times a year she would find herself sitting in a perfectly quiet room with the windows closed when suddenly a strong breeze would whirl around her. Small objects moved of their own volition. There were raps and occasional flashes of light.

'Stella C.', as she was always known, turned out to be a gifted psychic who had never dreamed of becoming a medium. Harry Price persuaded her to take part in a series of séances and his detailed report on her was published internationally. She impressed some of the world's greatest scientists and researchers with her phenomena, and they believed her to be utterly genuine. Sir Julian Huxley, for instance, never forgot the curious sensations of cold he experienced in her presence. Price was impressed by her transparent honesty with regard to psychic matters, and remained grateful to her for the rest of his life.

Fake mediums had every reason to avoid him like the plague. Among those he investigated was the seventeen-stone materializing medium Helen Duncan, who produced spirit forms revealed by flashlight photographs to consist largely of cheesecloth. Observers of her in a trance state came to the conclusion that she swallowed, then regurgitated, her 'phantoms'. Price recorded that on being asked one night to agree to an X-ray examination at the National Laboratory, the large lady rushed off, opened the front door and fled screaming down the street hotly pursued by three professors, two doctors and various other sitters!

As a direct result of his report on 'Stella C.' in 1925 Harry Price was appointed as the London-based foreign research officer for the American SPR. For six years he travelled extensively, making contacts in Austria, France, Germany, Poland and Scandinavia. He worked with some of the most famous mediums of the time, probably the most famous of all being the brilliant young Austrian psychic Rudi Schneider. His association with Rudi lasted more than ten years and ended with a glorious row of the sort quite frequent in psychic circles. It blew up when Price more or less accused the Austrian boy of cheating by freeing one of his arms during a séance. There was a photograph which, he said, proved it. Everyone leaped to Schneider's defence, declaring that what had been captured by the camera could have been an involuntary trance movement. The Austrian had been regarded as one of the major discoveries of modern times, and Harry Price, accused of ulterior motives for his exposure, was out in the cold. The Schneider row rattled like a skeleton in his cupboard for years.

In 1933 he made an offer to found, equip and endow a department of psychical research at London University. Though the authorities agreed to it in principle, to his great disappointment nothing came of the idea. Late in 1936, however, he transferred to the University, on permanent loan, his magnificent collection of books on the occult and paranormal. The Harry Price Library is unique and still in constant use today. He also handed over his Laboratory. He always felt gratified that the University accepted his gifts, for it gave him a sense of public recognition. Just before the Second World War he revived the Ghost Club, which had twice faded out since it was founded in the nineteenth century. He was in his element, and at Ghost Club dinners, a dapper figure at the top table, he held its members spellbound.

His love of adventure and publicity sometimes landed him in ridiculous situations, none more so than the episode involving ancient magic on top of the Brocken in the German mountains. After it was over Professor Carl Jung, the great Swiss psychologist, wrote to him, 'For God's sake, tell me that it isn't true. How can you, a man of science, lend yourself to superstition?' His biographer, Paul Tabori, comments: 'Secretly, I think he enjoyed it all as a lark, and so did Dr Joad, his companion in this strange adventure.'

One Monday morning a person, who was never named, deposited an old manuscript entitled 'The Blocksburg Tryst', copied from the original High German 'Black Book' at the National Laboratory. Harry Price was fascinated, and announced his intention of carrying out the experiment in black magic on top of the Brocken in the Harz mountains. He arrived just in time for the Goethe centenary in 1932, accompanied by Dr Joad.

The ritual was supposed to turn a white billy goat into a handsome young man who would then be married to a 'spotless maiden'. The sight of Harry Price and Dr Joad in full evening dress on top of a

German mountain accompanied by a pretty young girl and a billy goat and bearing concoctions consisting of 'bats' blood, scraping of church bells, soot and honey' was manna for the world press, also gathered on the Brocken with cameras and notebooks.

On the ordained night the whole thing was supposed to be performed in full moonlight but there was a thick fog, and the goat remained a goat. One newspaper printed a picture of Price and Joad with the headline 'The *real* goats on the Brocken' and George Bernard Shaw laughed his head off and told Harry Price he would have liked to have been there.

The last ten years of Price's life were as full as the rest had been. He was deep into the Borley haunting, and every year answered thousands of letters from people who were interested in the occult and wanted to tell him their experiences. For years he had ignored the doctors' warnings about his heart. His work, especially at Borley, had involved long, tedious, and uncomfortable days. Haunted houses are not usually the healthiest places on earth. On Easter Monday, March 29, 1948, sitting in a chair in his study after lunch he had a major heart attack and died instantly. He was sixty-seven. Controversial to the last breath, he is still a dominating figure in psychical research.

Oliver Lodge

Few books can have been received with such a storm of protest, amazement and incredulity as that which greeted the publication of *Raymond* by Sir Oliver Lodge in November 1916.

Colleagues of the distinguished physicist were appalled by its contents; friends who did not share his beliefs worried about his mental health; and the general public began to regard him as a gullible crank.

The reason? The secondary title of his famous work was 'Evidence for Survival of Memory and Affection after Death', and it consisted mainly of conversations he claimed to have had with his much-loved youngest son, Second Lieutenant Raymond Lodge, who was killed by a shell in Flanders on September 14, 1915.

Lodge was a man of immense distinction, knighted for his contribution to science and the friend of literary giants like George Bernard Shaw, but he opposed materialists and declared that his psychic experiences had led him to a profound belief in man's survival after death.

'We do not know everything that is possible to a human organism and we are certainly not aware of all existences in the universe,' he told those who accused him of chasing after ghosts. 'That my occasional psychic utterances do harm to my scientific reputation — even so far as causing some of my fellows to think me more or less cracked — is manifest,' he admitted with his usual good-humoured tolerance. 'But I feel convinced that in due time science will take investigations of this nature under its wing and will bring them into more serious consideration. ... .'

Sir Oliver Lodge was one of the founder members of the Society for Psychical Research in England. He had a great and enduring friendship with another of the great pillars of that Society, F. W. H. Myers, and often visited him at his house in Cambridge, and they would walk and talk together in the Fellows' garden at Trinity College.

Myers died in 1901, and spasmodically began to 'come through' when Lodge visited certain mediums. Myers had, after all, devoted his life to proving survival after death, and Lodge had eagerly awaited the time when his friend would clinch that proof in an unmistakable manner. But it was not until fourteen years later, when young men were being slaughtered in the trenches of the First World War, that Myers came through with a vengeance.

On August 8, 1915, a well-known American medium called Mrs Piper told Lodge that she had a message for him from Myers in the form of automatic writing. She could not understand what she had written down but there seemed to be some urgency and she advised Lodge to act as soon as possible. The message, obscure to any but a classical scholar, read 'Myers says you take the part of the poet and he will act as Faunus', adding 'Ask Verrall.'

The name Verrall referred to Mrs A. W. Verrall of Newnham College, who was one of the Cambridge nucleus of the SPR. She explained that the reference was to a passage in the *Carmen Saeculare* in which Horace thanks Faunus for protecting him from serious injury when he was felled by a tree which had been struck by lightning. In other words, Myers was telling Lodge that he must prepare himself for a great blow but that he, Myers, would do everything he could to ease the pain.

On September 14, about five weeks after the message had been received, Second Lieutenant Raymond Lodge was struck by shell fragments as he led his company back from an expedition to one of the communication trenches in Flanders. He lived for barely three hours after being wounded, and was then buried in a garden adjoining a ruined farmhouse, under some tall trees. Wooden crosses were set at the head and foot of his grave.

Grief stricken at the loss of his 26-year-old son, a handsome, young Englishman full of ebullient humour and energy, Lodge realized that his old friend Myers had been trying to warn him of his death.

Many families in England were suffering the same kind of loss as the war went on. An old friend of the Lodge family, a French lady living in London, was in great distress because she had lost both her sons within a week of each other. She asked Lady Lodge if she would accompany her to a professional medium, Mrs Osborne Leonard. Though she had never heard of Mrs Leonard at that time, Lady Lodge agreed, hoping her friend would find some comfort.

Two sittings were held, at neither of which did the ladies reveal their identity. Lady Lodge reported later that on both occasions the two sons of her French friend communicated, but with difficulty. Another personality seemed to be trying to make contact at the same time. Suddenly the medium said she had a message from someone called Raymond: 'Tell Father I've met some friends of his.' When asked if he could name any of the friends Raymond replied, 'Yes, Myers.'

Sir Oliver Lodge himself went to London two days later and without announcing who he was had his first sitting with Mrs Leonard. In a short time after the medium had gone into a trance a youth was described in terms which fitted Raymond exactly. Stumbling sentences came through . . . 'I have met hundreds of friends . . . I don't know them all . . . I feel I have got two fathers now . . . I have you both. . . .' Later sittings indicated that the second father figure was Myers, who sent Lodge the message 'Your son shall be mine.' Lodge began to see that Myers had indeed kept his word and had lightened the blow by looking after and helping his son 'on the other side'.

Other mediums were also providing messages from Raymond, including a male Dutch clairvoyant called A. Vout Peters, who told Lady Lodge that before he died her son had posed with a group of officers for a photograph. In it he was sitting down on the front row, holding a walking stick. The Lodges had never been told of the existence of such a photograph, and being naturally very anxious to see it, made many inquiries to no avail. Two months later, however, the mother of a fellow officer wrote to say she had been sent a group photograph which included Raymond and would they like to see it?

Before the photograph arrived Lodge himself went for a sitting with Mrs Leonard and in his book described how he asked Raymond, through the medium, to tell him more about it. The information that came through was that Raymond was sitting on the ground while others were standing and sitting behind him. Somebody, he remembered, insisted on leaning on his shoulder, which did not please him. When the photograph arrived there was Raymond sitting on the ground exactly as he described with a fellow officer using him as a leaning post. His son, Lodge noticed, appeared rather annoyed!

As time went on the Lodge family found the accumulation of proof that their son still existed somewhere quite 'overwhelming'. But, as Brian Inglis points out in his *History of the Paranormal*, if Lodge had been unpopular with the predominantly materialistic science establishment before, he was now out in the cold. It also made him unpopular with the Church of England, which felt threatened by Spiritualism.

Sir Oliver Lodge was one of the first of the leading members of the SPR to come right out and say that the evidence for survival had totally convinced him. Scientists made it clear that in spite of his magnificent research into such things as wireless telegraphy, he had let the side down with his ghost hunting.

But Lodge had always had a natural feeling for what he called 'the imponderables', and as a physicist was drawn to things like electricity and magnetism — 'the things that worked secretly and had to be apprehended mentally'.

He was the eldest of seven sons born into a huge, prosperous Victorian family and grew up in the Potteries, where his father made a handsome living selling raw materials to the potters of the Five Towns. He married his childhood sweetheart, Mary Marshall, a student at the Slade School of Art, and himself proceeded to build a solid, happy family life with twelve children.

From an early age he felt he was a born physicist. In the eighties and nineties of the last century he held the Professorship of Physics at Liverpool University, where he carried out some of the most important experiments of his scientific life. His research into radiation and the relation between matter and ether was highly regarded and recognized as a brilliant achievement. Thousands read his books and attended his lectures. Most people felt he thoroughly deserved the knighthood that was conferred on him on the coronation of King Edward VII.

He was on the verge of fifty when he moved from Liverpool to Birmingham to become Principal of Birmingham University. He admitted that having so large a family was no joke, and that he had to work very hard to maintain his twelve children. But he knew how to enjoy himself, too, and led a 'full, hearty Edwardian life'. When he retired from Birmingham University in 1919 and moved to the south of England, he was held in such high regard by the citizens of Edgbaston that they collected enough money to present him with a motor car, together with 'a jewel for my wife'. He was quite overcome by the feeling shown towards him. 'The kindness of everyone was very great,' he wrote afterwards.

Threaded through his success as a scientist was his increasing fascination with psychic matters. As a young man, Lodge admitted, he considered ghost stories and the like a futile occupation for a cultivated man — baseless superstition. Then in the mid-1870s he met a young Cambridge classical scholar, Edmund Gurney, who was preparing a book called *Phantasms of the Living*. Lodge was impressed by his serious approach to the subject and became even more interested when Gurney introduced him to Frederick Myers, who was collaborating with him on psychic studies.

Lodge and Myers got on famously from the start. When Gurney, Myers and others formed the Society for Psychical Research in 1882 under the presidency of the formidable Professor Henry Sidgwick, Lodge soon became a regular attender at the early meetings.

He became involved in various experiments in thought transference or telepathy and felt convinced that this explained the appearance of phantasms of the living, cases in which ghostly figures were seen by relatives of those who had been involved in traumatic accidents or who were on the point of death.

In 1889 the Professor of Psychology at Harvard University wrote to members of the SPR about the strange powers of a medium he had found in Boston called Mrs Piper. She was invited to England. Lodge met her off the boat and took her to stay with Myers, where she was judged by everybody to be a 'perfectly genuine person'.

Lodge took the opportunity of having his first sitting with a trance medium. 'Her trance was a very thorough phenomenon', he decided. 'It took her some time to get into and some time to get out of and was unmistakably genuine while it lasted.' The result was quite astonishing. 'Messages were received from all kinds of people, but the special feature was that my Aunt Anne, who had played an important part in my young life and education, ostensibly took possession of the medium . . . she spoke a few sentences in her own well-remembered voice.'

He decided to invite her to his house in Liverpool for further experiments. The visit was most successful. 'I got in touch with old relatives of whose early youth I knew nothing whatsoever and was told of incidents in their lives that were subsequently verified by their surviving elderly contemporaries.'

Lodge gradually became convinced not only of human survival but of the power of the dead to communicate (under certain conditions) with those left behind on earth, and vice versa. His conviction was strengthened when Myers 'came through' after his death and when Gurney too made contact and conversed with him. 'The persistence of the mind and memory and character of the deceased individual was abundantly demonstrated,' he declared.

Then came the war and the loss of his son in action. There was a special affinity between Sir Oliver and his youngest boy. Lodge recognized himself in Raymond as a child and as a young man. Both of them hated parties and patronizing adults when they were small, and preferred a quiet corner with a book. Both had the same passionate love of engineering and machinery. Both of them were vitally individual. Lodge was absolutely certain that his son had returned to him.

He led a retired though active life until his wife's death in 1929. His immensely readable autobiography was published in 1931, and by the time he himself died in 1940 he had acquired the aura of a wise old sage.

Of the psychic world which had occupied so much of his life he wrote:

The subject still bristles with difficulties . . . the evolution of knowledge takes time; it is to be carried on at first by a few pioneers in the face of opposition . . . I do not think that physics and psychics are entirely detached. I think there is a link between them. All I plead for is study.

Conan Doyle

Sir Arthur Conan Doyle, creator of Sherlock Holmes, the immortal fictional detective who triumphed over his adversaries by the application of pure, cold logic, was himself a man who believed in ghosts and fairies. The very epitome of an English patriot, a trained doctor who never lost his interest in medical science and a hearty, all-round sportsman, he was also a dedicated ghost hunter and one of the pioneers of psychical research.

Those who judged him purely from the outside saw only a bluff, genial extrovert, a hale and robust countryman who stood over six feet tall and weighed seventeen stone. His reputation as a tough professional writer on the one hand, and as an amateur cricketer good enough to bowl W. G. Grace on the other, did not prepare anyone for the fervent spiritualist he became later in life. But the mystic touch had always been there. It was in his genes.

The Doyles were of Catholic Irish stock and fey with it. Conan Doyle, however, was born not in Ireland but in Edinburgh on May 22, 1859. His father, Charles Doyle, at one time assistant to the surveyor in the Scottish Office of Works, became epileptic and alcoholic, spending much of his time in nursing homes. In his autobiography Conan Doyle draws a picture of him as a dreamy, aesthetic figure who, while he was never unkind to his children, did not take much notice of them either. He kept an illustrated diary which showed a distinct leaning towards the occult and an interest in fairies.

Conan Doyle was brought up in an atmosphere of genteel poverty and sent to Stonyhurst to be educated by Jesuits. Medicine was chosen for him as a 'decent' career, but while he was studying at Edinburgh he suffered great hardship through poverty. Life was no easier as the impecunious junior partner to a doctor in Sheffield, so in his twenties he signed on as a surgeon on a whaling ship. The sea toughened him both physically and mentally.

Back on land he went into practice as a GP in Southsea, a suburb of Portsmouth, and after some difficult years when he hardly had enough to live on he became established and married a quiet, gentle girl called Louise, sister of a patient he treated for meningitis. His enthusiasm and energy extended to everything. Besides his medical duties, numerous public commitments, dedication to sport and family life he had found an increasing satisfaction in writing. He had also found spiritualism.

One night in Birmingham, out of curiosity, he went to hear an American medium, J. Horstead, who seemed to be in continual contact with the Methodist preacher John Wesley — 'though occasionally Lord John Russell came through and spoke in glowing terms of Gladstone'. He started to attend Spiritualist meetings in Southsea and took part in a series of experiments which convinced him that thought transference was possible through telepathic means.

Spiritualism had reached a feverish pitch in England in the 1880s. Conan Doyle was invited to join in private séances held in the front parlours of respectable Victorian villas in Southsea and he confessed later that he enjoyed the dramatic element in many of them, especially when one night a medium called Mrs Guppy managed to materialize a huge block of ice! He was, however, still cautious.

On the formation of the Society for Psychical Research in 1882, Conan Doyle was invited to join. Though he became a member, his life was too full already for him to become deeply involved in actual research. However, he wrote in his diary that man's aim should now be to 'break down the barrier of death; to found a grand religion of the future'.

One night, after he had seen the last of his patients, he jotted down some notes on a story he proposed to write called 'A Study in Scarlet' featuring an unusual detective called Sherrinford Holmes, a name he later changed to Sherlock Holmes. The story was published and followed in quick succession by another Holmes yarn, 'The Sign of Four'. Conan Doyle became immersed in his writing, though he tended to look upon his detective stories as light relief and spent a great deal of time researching and writing books on weightier subjects, most of them now forgotten. To his amazement stories about Holmes and his friend Dr Watson, snatched from him as soon as they were written by the editor of *The Strand* magazine, created a sensation. People began to regard Holmes as a real person. They went looking for his rooms in Baker Street, begged his creator to give them more of his adventures. Conan Doyle was overjoyed. He decided to 'cut the painter' and trust in his power of writing to earn money.

There is a touch of the occult in many of his stories. He was fascinated by death, ghosts, life after death and the unknown. His great Sherlock Holmes story 'The Hound of the Baskervilles' shows him to be a master at suggesting the supernatural. He claimed he did not know what fear was, and was prepared to look any phantom straight in the eye.

He fought in the Boer War — which he regarded as a great adventure — then entered politics for a time. His private life, however, was about to become extremely complicated and overshadow everything else. For the first time in his life, he fell passionately in love.

Conan Doyle had always felt tenderly protective towards his first wife, Louise, but strong emotion had never been part of their relationship. She was ill with tuberculosis when her husband met Jean Leckie on March 15, 1897. This poised, assured woman who rode to hounds, and had trained as a singer in Dresden, aroused in him feelings he had never known before. But Conan Doyle was above all a staunch Victorian moralist and he was determined to do the 'decent thing' and stay loyal to his ailing wife. He and Jean Leckie remained lovers in name only until Louise died in 1906. They married a year later.

By 1914 Conan Doyle was part of the Establishment: knighted in 1902, famous for his books, a great champion of the Empire, a truly upstanding, conventional Englishman. The First World War brought his life to a climax but by the end of it many people began to wonder if they had ever really known him.

To start with he regarded the war as one of the greatest challenges of his life. Though he was fifty-five when it started, he flung himself into it heart and soul. His principal occupation during those four dark years was to use his genius for propaganda. He wrote stirring recruitment pamphlets, visited the Front, rallied the faint-hearted. From his home at Crowborough in Sussex he marched, drilled and organized the Southern Home Defence.

At the end of it, however, he was left like millions of others with a burden of great grief. Kingsley, the only son of his first marriage, was badly wounded at the Somme and died from pneumonia in October 1918. Only a few months later his much-loved younger brother, Innes, died too. He became determined to seek for the truth about life and death in the supernatural world.

All the wartime deaths and the suffering, far from making him bitter, convinced him that those we love must continue to exist after death. He was immensely impressed by *Raymond*, the book by Sir Oliver Lodge about his psychic contact with his dead son. Soon he started on a campaign that was to dominate the rest of his life.

Throughout the twenties Conan Doyle was totally committed to spreading the word about Spiritualism. He regarded himself as a missionary for the movement and spent a quarter of a million pounds on his lecture tours and his psychic bookshop in London. On tour he visited nearly every town in Britain, finding critical but attentive audiences everywhere.

He was intent on getting his message over to the ordinary man in the street. After a triumphant tour of this country he went to Australia and New Zealand in 1920–1 and to the United States in 1922.

He had set out his beliefs in two books produced in rapid succession just after the war. Some spiritualists were alarmed by his robust, full-blooded approach, while others rejoiced in it. Basically he saw the spirit life as being predominantly of the mind with no food, money, sex or pain but with music, the arts, intellectual and spiritual knowledge being available to all. There would be beautiful gardens, green woods, pleasant lakes and even a reunion with one's domestic pets. All religions would be treated as valid and equal. And the spirit body? He believed it would be an exact counterpart to the one we had on earth save that all disease, weakness or deformity would have disappeared. Séances, he said, had given plenty of evidence that that would be so.

At the point of death, he said, the spirit body stood or floated beside the old body, aware of it and the surroundings. The dead person could not communicate with those left behind because living organs were only tuned in to coarse stimulus. He had a clear vision of what happened next. Arriving in the hereafter, he said, the spirit body would find itself among those who had gone before. It would be welcomed then allowed to sleep for anything from a few days to several months, depending on how much trouble had been experienced in life. When the spirit had refreshed itself, it would take its place in the sphere judged most suitable — a kind of probationary limbo for the less fortunate, a clinic for the weakly souls and glorious unlimited freedom for the higher spirits, those who had fulfilled their existence on earth.

Conan Doyle seldom questioned the information passed on to him by mediums. His mother had not approved of his involvement in the psychical world and his second wife, Jean, said she too felt the subject to be 'uncanny and dangerous'. The death of her own brother, Malcolm, during the war changed her feelings. Conan Doyle described how in 1921 she suddenly acquired 'a gift of inspired writing'. From that point on the family experienced direct spirit communication. The year after Jean Conan Doyle received her 'gift' an Arabian spirit guide came through for the first time and took control so that the writing changed to inspirational talking in a semi-trance. By this means it was found possible to communicate with Malcolm Leckie, Jean's brother, and later, to Conan Doyle's joy, with his own son, Kingsley, his brother, Innes, and his brother-in-law, E. W. Hornung. The level of communication, whether by automatic writing or through the Arab guide, was always very simple. John Delane, one of the great editors of *The Times*, seems to have come through one night to tell Conan Doyle that a pleasant home was being prepared for him.

His restless search for the truth led the old warrior into some

Sir Arthur Conan Doyle, 1927

extremes from which he did not emerge unscathed. There was, for instance, the famous case of the Cottingley Fairies. Like his father before him, Conan Doyle had always been interested in the little folk of myth and legend and, perhaps because of his Irish roots, believed it possible they did exist.

In November 1920 he published an article about fairies in *The Strand* magazine along with a series of pictures of what became known as 'The Cottingley Fairies.' For weeks people talked of nothing else. Here was the creator of Sherlock Holmes solemnly giving his word that the little folk were genuine and declaring that as far as he was concerned the photographs were among the most astounding ever published. His opinions were presented against the better judgement of many experienced psychical researchers who realized that the evidence for the pictures' authenticity had not been sufficiently explored. But Conan Doyle had the bit between his teeth, and in his passion for discovering ghosts and other psychic phenomena was led up the garden path and into a fairy ring.

The culprits were two pretty young girls. One hot day in July 1917 sixteen-year-old Elsie Wright borrowed her father's camera and took a picture of her ten-year-old cousin, Frances Griffiths, playing by the river close to their home at Cottingley in Yorkshire. They gave the film to Elsie's father to develop, and he was astonished to see that the little girl in her white summer dress was surrounded by dancing fairies. The five photographs showing the tiny spectral figures caused great excitement. Was this the proof the world had been waiting for? Conan

Doyle thought so. He was responsible for introducing the Cottingley Fairies. Besides *The Strand* magazine article, which proved something of a bombshell, he was in the middle of writing a book about fairies, and used the photographs to illustrate his belief that they were real.

Just as the whole thing was beginning to get out of hand the girls confessed it had been a prank. Tired of hearing their elders and betters scoff at little Frances when, her sensitive imagination taking flight, she talked about the fairy people they had met by the river, they decided to prove what she said was true. Taking a copy of *Princess Mary's Gift Book* and some illustrations by Arthur Shepperson, they got busy with scissors and paste. Next time they went to the river they fixed them to tree trunks and the river bank, using their mothers' hatpins. What started out as a simple prank grew into an enormous deception and Conan Doyle was by no means the only eminent figure to be engulfed in its whimsy. But his critics had a field day and Bernard Partridge drew a famous cartoon in which he is shown chained by public opinion to his great fictional character, Sherlock Holmes, while his head is wreathed in the clouds of Spiritualism.

During the last decade of his life Conan Doyle travelled all over the world expounding the gospel of Spiritualism. He paid two visits to the United States, the second time taking in Canada and addressing nearly a quarter of a million people. Some thought him just an elderly crank with a bee in his bonnet. But most people were fascinated and impressed, for he could hold an audience with skill.

Always on the alert for an unusual ghost story or a spectacular tale of psychic phenomena, he went out of his way to meet an ex-gangster named Morrell, who after some time in solitary confinement in a straitjacket in an American jail found he had the ability to leave his body and stand outside it as an extra-corporeal form. He also met Marconi, who told him that he had intercepted wireless waves at a length of 30,000 metres and had speculated whether they might be messages from another planet. Conan Doyle told him he thought it more likely that they were. attempts at contact from the dead.

He visited South Africa, Kenya and Rhodesia and in the late autumn of 1929 set out to take his message to Scandinavia and Holland. But his great constitution was beginning to flag. This great Victorian-Edwardian patriot did not like the modern world and felt deep depression when he realized that Spiritualism had failed to take it by storm. At the end of his Scandinavian tour he had a heart attack.

There was just one more book to write, and he worked on it during his convalescence. *The Edge of the Unknown* was a volume of essays on Spiritualistic themes. It was his farewell to a world that would remember him most of all for a character from his imagination, though to the end his adventures in the spirit world meant more to him than all his fame. He died on July 7, 1930.

The Fox Sisters

The Fox family, living in a small wood-frame house in Hydesville near Rochester in New York state, had not been sleeping at all well. During the last few nights of March 1848 their rest had been constantly disturbed by strange knocks and raps and sounds as though furniture was being moved about. Reluctantly the Fox parents, John and Margaret, came to the conclusion that they had moved into a haunted house.

Of their seven children only the two youngest daughters, Katherine, aged eleven, and Margaretta, thirteen, were still living with them. On the night of Friday, March 31, worn out with disturbed nights, they all retired to bed early.

For once the children were allowed to sleep in their parents' room, so, far from being frightened, when the noises started again the mischievous youngest child, Kate, began to imitate the raps. It became something of a game. Margaretta called out, 'Do just as I do. Count one, two, three, four.' Four raps came in answer. From this the game proceeded to a more advanced stage. The girls hit on the idea of calling out letters of the alphabet and asking the mysterious communicator to rap when a letter was appropriate. By this means simple 'yes' and 'no' were supplemented by whole sentences. After a time the rapper was revealed as the spirit of a 31-year-old peddler who had been murdered in that very house and whose remains were buried in the cellar.

What happened that night to a poor family living in rural America had astounding repercussions. It marked the beginning of the modern Spiritualist movement. The living, it appeared, had communicated with the dead and exchanged information. But, extraordinary as the Hydesville happenings were, they might well have remained a purely local sensation, as Ruth Brandon points out in her book *The Spiritualists*. After all, it was not the first time that spirits of the dead had communicated or purported to communicate with the living using very similar techniques. But America was caught up in the nineteenth-century passion for the occult. And the Fox girls had an older sister, Leah, who was ambitious and meant to make the most of their mysterious rappings.

The morning after Kate and Margaretta made contact with the spirit of the peddler, neighbours flocked to the house to listen and take part in the weird goings-on. They heard raps, put questions of their own and received answers. Some of the men decided to dig up the cellar floor to see if the story could be substantiated, but the ground was waterlogged and they had to abandon their attempts. Later, however, another digging party uncovered parts of a male body. Most people believed the peddler had been found.

Life in the Hydesville house became intolerable as far as the Fox parents were concerned. They were confused and upset by what was going on and seriously wondered at one point whether someone had put a curse on them. After a weekend in which three hundred people descended on Hydesville eager to hear the rapping, they moved out, taking Kate and Margaretta to stay with one of their sons, David.

To their dismay and astonishment, the raps moved with them. For the first time John and Margaret Fox realized that the strange noises were directly connected with their young daughters. The raps occurred only in their presence and wherever they went. Their lives were totally disrupted by the attention and publicity and eventually it was decided to separate the girls to see if the rappings would cease and leave them all in peace. Kate and Mrs Fox went to stay with Leah in Rochester, leaving Margaretta behind with her brother David, but it made no difference.

Leah Fox was a woman who knew how to get things done. Soon both girls were living with her and she hired the biggest hall in town so that they could give a demonstration of their powers. Both girls began to give séances and to produce new phenomena. People felt themselves being touched by spirit hands, objects moved of their own volition, musical instruments played though no one went near them. They attracted capacity audiences. Public opinion was sharply divided, however, and feelings ran high. The girls were ridiculed, physically attacked and even threatened with death by those who saw them as agents of the devil.

They were asked to submit to an investigation by a committee in Rochester, but when its members could find no evidence of trickery another was set up with instructions to make the tests more difficult. This second committee also failed to produce damning evidence so a third was appointed, this time made up entirely of women so that the sisters could be stripped and searched. But this committee too reported that the girls appeared to be totally genuine and that even when made to stand on pillows with their ankles tied together and their hands secured, the rapping came loud and clear from ceiling, walls and floor.

Two years had passed since the memorable night in Hydesville and it had now become almost impossible for the girls to lead a normal life. They were in constant demand. They left Rochester for the more sophisticated psychic circles of New York, where they gave public performances as professionals as well as private séances for wealthy clients. Many of their 'sitters' were sceptics who would have been only too delighted to reveal to the world how the Fox sisters operated. They emerged admitting that even if they were not convinced by the spirit messages they could not deny that the phenomena defied normal explanation. Horace Greeley, Editor of the *New York Herald-Tribune* and

The Fox Sisters

one of the most influential men in America, became their champion.

Then, out of the blue in 1851 came a shattering statement from a Mrs Norman Culver who was a relative by marriage to the Fox sisters. She claimed that Kate herself had confessed to her that both she and Margaretta had learned how to make rapping noises by clicking their toes. There was an uproar as the sceptics gleefully pointed out that they had been right all the time and that the girls were nothing more nor less than a clever vaudeville act. On the other side the girls' supporters were quick to unearth the fact that Mrs Culver had had a bitter quarrel with the girls' parents. Whatever she said was probably motivated by spite. They asked, too, how clicking toe joints could account for the other phenomena and the fact that at their séances and public performances all kinds of other noises were heard, ranging from hammer blows to the sawing of wood.

All through the fifties Leah, the girls' older sister, had been the organizing genius behind everything they did. She made a handsome profit out of them, and though Kate and Margaretta were responsible for the phenomena it was she who managed to gain a reputation as a great medium whose séances were a social event. By the end of the decade she had divorced her husband and married a wealthy New York banker. Her psychic establishment was closed down and she disowned the sisters who had been responsible for her success.

Both had tragic personal lives. Margaretta's marriage to Elisha Kent Kane, the famous Arctic explorer who had courted her, against his family's wishes, since she was thirteen was to end after only a few years when he died far away from her in Cuba. Kate, married to lawyer Henry Jencken in 1872, also lost her husband after a pathetically short marriage, though he left her two children to console her.

Margaretta was destroyed by the loss of her husband and though she half-heartedly gave spiritualist demonstrations in order to earn her living she also began to drink and take drugs. Leah did not want to know her. Kate Fox continued to make her mark as a medium. On a visit to England she was investigated by William (later Sir William) Crookes, the eminent scientist, who introduced her to the most famous medium in England, Daniel Dunglas Home. Usually Home steered clear of other psychics, especially when they insisted on operating in darkness, for he was proud of the fact that no one had ever been able to accuse him of trickery. But he allowed himself to be tested jointly with Kate Fox.

Crookes, who was not complimentary about Kate's intellectual capacity, nevertheless considered her a remarkable medium. He said it was only necessary for her to put her hand on any substance for loud thuds to be heard coming from it, like a triple pulsation sometimes loud enough to be heard several rooms away. 'In this manner I have heard them in a living tree, on a sheet of glass, on a stretched iron wire, on a tambourine on the roof of a cab and on the floor of a theatre.' At her wedding it was said loud raps were heard at the reception and the table on which the wedding cake stood was repeatedly raised from the floor! Kate had nine years of domesticity, then it was all over.

As the years passed both Margaretta and Kate, having lost their husbands, sank together into a life of drunken squalor. Leah was no longer available to organize things for them. Their psychic powers, if they ever had them, seemed to be coming to an end. Then, one momentous day in October 1888 the Fox sisters pulled the rug from under the spiritualist movement, and got their own back on Leah.

Standing up in front of a packed house at the New York Academy of Music, Margaretta confessed that as far as she was concerned spiritualism had been nothing but an imposture from the very beginning.

Barefooted, she demonstrated how she could produce raps and cracks with her big toe and the noise echoed loud and clear from the gallery, the back of the hall and the ceiling. Kate, sitting in a box overlooking the stage, said nothing, so it was presumed that she was in full agreement with her sister. A letter she wrote shortly afterwards explained why they had done such an extraordinary thing. They were penniless. The venture had earned them 1,500 dollars.

A few days after her appearance at the Academy Margaretta just as surprisingly retracted what she had said. Desperate for money, she had apparently agreed to collaborate with a journalist who wrote for the *New York World* in order to provide a story, and later a book, which could be headlined 'Death Blow to Spiritualism.' Quite a few people had felt all along that the affair was stage-managed. The sisters would only do themselves harm by such a confession. They felt justified in their suspicions when Margaretta said to another reporter, 'Would to God I could undo the injustice I did the cause of spiritualism. I was under the strong psychological influence of persons inimical to it.'

Sceptics felt sure the movement had been delivered a death blow, but after a sharp intake of breath it went on from strength to strength. The Fox sisters, however, never restored their standing as long as they lived. Their last years were a hopeless mess. Drunk, destitute, now hardly comprehending what they had started all those years ago, they died very soon after each other in 1895, Margaretta going first. They were buried in a pauper's grave.

Their old home in Hydesville started to collapse in 1904 but today a replica housing a museum stands in its place, and on a plaque erected outside marking 'The Birthplace and Shrine of Modern Spiritualism' their names are engraved in stone.

Madame Blavatsky

Search through the history of occult practice and you will find no more dramatic figure than the Russian mystic who was born Helena Petrova Hahn and became known to posterity as Madame Blavatsky. As a child she was constantly drenched with holy water by her Greek Orthodox nurses who thought she was possessed by the devil. As a young woman she stood out among the bizarre sights of Cairo as, dressed as an Arab and smoking hashish, she sat at the feet of occult gurus. In middle age she formed the Theosophical Society, dedicated to spiritual truth, with the help, she claimed, of long-dead Mahatmas (masters) with names like Koot Hoomi and Mahatma Morya. Towards the end of her life she came into a head-on collision with psychical researchers who said she was one of the most accomplished, ingenious and interesting impostors of history, yet at the same time her teachings were heavily influencing a young lawyer called Gandhi.

Helena Petrova Hahn came from a family which bristled with titles. On her mother's side were the blue bloods of generations of Russians, including her maternal grandmother the Princess Helene Dolgorouky. On her father's side she was descended from a noble German family, and her paternal grandfather rejoiced in the name of General Alexis von Rottenstern Hahn. She was born at Ekaterinoslav in the Ukraine on July 31, 1831. From the moment she arrived in the world cataclysmic things happened around her. She was conceived at the same time that cholera reached Russia and her birth took place as people in the same house were dying from the plague. Fire broke out at her baptism when a small cousin, bored with the ceremony and playing with a lighted taper, accidentally set fire to the priest's robe, nearly burning the man to death.

These incidents, taking place as they did in a society riddled with superstition, set her apart. Servants regarded her with awe and allowed her to do what she liked. From the earliest age she showed a terrifying will and strange excitability of temperament. She was liable to ungovernable fits of passion. Only the fact that she was gifted, daring and (when in a good mood) humorous made her bearable.

Her mother died when she was eleven and the young Helena was sent to Saratow, where her grandfather was civil governor, to be brought up by her grandparents. Still a difficult child, given to hypochondria and walking in her sleep, she began showing unmistakable signs of psychic 'peculiarities'. Her Greek Orthodox nurses considered her possessed by the devil, and had her exorcized. Her grandparents' great country house at Saratow was the perfect backcloth for her imagination. Vast, turreted, resembling a medieval castle, it was honeycombed with subterranean passages and long-abandoned galleries. She would sometimes be found walking through the long, dim corridors in deep conversation with someone invisible. Helena believed in spirits. In fact she seems to have had early in life all the characteristics of mediumship as well as the gifts of a clairvoyant.

Friends and relatives at Saratow were half-intrigued, half-frightened by this aspect of her nature. Visitors to the house would sometimes be shocked when after gazing at them intently she proceeded to tell them the date on which they would die or when some accident or misfortune would happen to them. Since her predictions often came true, she was regarded with considerable misgivings as the terror of the family.

Her life at Saratow is known in detail because of the vivid account of it written by her sister, Madame de Jelihowsky. 'She was a strange girl, full of uncontrollable mischief one minute . . . the next she would give it all up to devour books. Her grandparents' enormous library seemed hardly large enough to satisfy her cravings.' She loved to ride high-mettled horses, and by the age of fifteen could manage any Cossack horse on a man's saddle. She defied everyone.

Her defiance led to her first marriage. At seventeen she had plenty of suitors but turned them all down. Her governess, exasperated, said that if she carried on like this even old General Blavatsky, who frequently visited the family, would decline to have her for a wife. The challenge was too tempting for young Helena. She set her cap at the 'plumeless raven' as she secretly called Blavatsky, and though he was fifty years older than her, accepted his proposal.

The marriage lasted barely three months. After a brief, stormy relationship she took one of his horses and galloped off to Tiflis. Her family did not see her again for ten years. Bearing the name by which she would be known to posterity, Madame Blavatsky set out on her wanderings.

There is a story that for a time she worked as a bareback rider in a circus. She certainly contracted a bigamous marriage with the opera singer Metrovitch, and there is reason to believe she bore him a child. At one point she left him to become an assistant to Daniel Dunglas Home, the great spiritualist medium, but the affair was doomed anyway. In July 1851, they were passengers on board the steamship *Eumonia* when it sank after an explosion in the boiler room. Metrovitch was drowned but Madame Blavatsky was among the survivors picked up by a passing freighter.

The rescue ship put her ashore in Egypt and she made her way to Cairo and began her first serious study of the occult with an old Copt, a magician. From then on her thirst for knowledge was insatiable. Colonel Hahn, her father, who had kept in touch with her ever since her flight from Russia and who secretly admired her spirit, sent her money to continue her travels. She crossed the Atlantic to Canada to study the occult with Red Indians, went on to Mexico, then to New Orleans, where the chief interest of her visit was voodoo. Her American travels lasted for about a year, then she resolved to go to India and try to find a way through Nepal into the forbidden country of Tibet. Her first attempt was frustrated. She wandered on for two more years before making a second. This time with a Tartar 'shaman' or holy man as her guide she succeeded in penetrating a considerable way into the country which then held such mystery for outsiders. She had many strange experiences in the bleak lands of Tibet. On one occasion she said she saw the 'astral soul' of her guide separate from his body. It remained one of the high points of her occult experience, and she said she remembered it clearly to the end of her life. Madame Blavatsky and the shaman had to be rescued from the desert eventually by a party of horsemen from a lamasery, whom she believed had been directed to them by psychic powers. The incident in the desert put an end to her wanderings in Tibet. She was politely escorted back to the frontier.

She returned to India, but shortly before the Mutiny broke out in 1857 she was directed to leave the country by her 'spiritual protector'. After an absence of ten years she made a typically melodramatic return to Russia in the middle of a family wedding party at Pskoff, about 180 miles from St Petersburg. She proceeded to astonish everyone with demonstrations of her gathering psychic powers. Her sister, Madame de Jelihowsky, reported that as soon as she returned to live in the house they were aware of strange things happening in it. Raps and whispering sounds, mysterious and unexplained, were now being heard constantly wherever she went. 'Not only did they occur in her presence and near her but knocks were heard and movements of the furniture perceived in nearly every room of the house.' The house, it seems, was always full of visitors but Madame Blavatsky would sit quietly on a sofa, getting on with her embroidery while the rapping and banging went on around her.

Early in 1859 she went with her father and sister to stay in an old house in the village of Rougodero, near St Petersburg, where they remained for a whole year. During this time she often saw ghosts, which she described in detail. Once she encountered the phantom of an old lady, 'a fat old thing with a frilled white cap, white kerchief across her shoulders, a short, grey narrow dress and checked apron'. Servants identified her as a German who had been housekeeper there for twenty years. She also saw the apparition of an old man, very strange to look at, with a high black headdress and long grey coat. She particularly noticed his terribly long finger-nails. Two peasants identified him as their former master, Shousherin. His long nails, they explained, were the result of a rare disease. One of the effects of this illness is that the nails of the fingers and toes would not be cut without the sufferer bleeding to death.

While she was living quietly with her family she became very ill. Years before, travelling in Asia, she had somehow received a wound just under the heart which occasionally reopened and brought on high fever. The local doctor was sent for but emerged from her bedroom trembling with terror. He swore that as he bent over to examine her the shadow of a hand appeared and moved slowly up and down her body from head to waist, as though forbidding him to touch her. This, combined with the noises that were going on in the room, caused him to take to his heels.

Madame Blavatsky recovered and set out on a visit to her grandparents in the Caucasus. At Zadonsk, on the way, she and her sister were received by the Holy Metropolitan Isadore, an old friend of the family who had known them since childhood. He received them kindly, but, Madame Jelihowsky reported, they had hardly taken their seats in his drawing room when a terrible hubbub broke out: loud raps (which surprised even Madame Blavatsky) were followed by thumps and cracks all over the room. The chandelier overhead shook its crystal drops, then, on seeing a huge armchair sliding towards him, the Archbishop began to laugh outright. He told them he was very interested in these phenomena and had read a great deal about so-called spiritual manifestations. Before they left he blessed them and said to Madame Blavatsky: 'As for you, do not be troubled by the gift you are possessed of, do not let it become a source of misery . . . it was given to you for some purpose . . . use it with discrimination. . . .'

She knew she must return to the East. She went back to India and became a *chela*, a devout student sitting at the feet of gurus and mystics. She felt she was in spiritual touch with the great Mahatmas or masters of Eastern religion, and vowed to serve them for the rest of her life. For years she continued her wanderings, increasing still further her considerable store of occult knowledge.

By the time she decided to return to America in 1873 she was penniless. She hoped to gain patronage from wealthy families interested in psychic matters, but she spent months living in extreme poverty in a New York slum. Eventually she obtained work as a dressmaker and could at least buy food and cheap tobacco to make the cigarettes she smoked endlessly. Not even her desperate circumstances, however, interfered with her passion for the occult. The USA was, she said in a letter written home, 'a most prolific hotbed for mediums and sensitives of all kinds, both genuine and artificial'.

Madame Blavatsky was saved from poverty by the generosity of an American she had met on a previous visit. Soon she began to arrange meetings with other people who were interested in the psychic world. Aspiring to higher things, she also began to protest openly about being called a 'medium'. She did, she admitted, see ghosts when others did not — 'the shadows of terrestrial bodies from which in most cases the soul and spirit had fled long ago'. But she wanted above all to discover the soul, to communicate to the West the great philosophical truths of the East, to make the whole world more aware of spiritual truth.

It was at one of these meetings held at a farmhouse in Vermont owned by the Eddy brothers, two famous American mediums, that she met a man who was to be part of her life from now on — Colonel Henry S. Olcott. From the moment he was introduced to her she had a remarkable effect on him. He found her eccentric but utterly fascinating. The bespectacled, bearded American lawyer decided to throw up his professional career and devote his life to helping this extraordinary Russian present spiritual truth to the world.

Olcott was the one who suggested that she should form a society that could be devoted to studying these things. She agreed, and within a short time the Theosophical Society came into existence. Olcott became its chairman and missionary; Madame Blavatsky opted for the title 'founder' and stayed at headquarters doing secretarial work and writing.

Her relationship with the Colonel was not apparently romantic or sexual, but she could not do without him from now on. He was kind and generous to her, though she often treated him badly. Membership of the Society increased rapidly. Madame Blavatsky now lived in a more spacious apartment in New York, plainly furnished but littered with curios — huge palm leaves, tigers' heads, stuffed apes, oriental pipes and vases, manuscripts and cuckoo clocks. It always seemed to be teeming with people of all nationalities. Madame herself spoke Russian most of the time, shrewdly observing each visitor with what Olcott called her 'mystical blue eyes'. An American who became her friend found her 'from morning till night surrounded by people. Mysterious events, extraordinary sights and sounds continue to occur. I have been there many an evening and seen in broad gas light large luminous balls creeping over the furniture or playfully jumping from point to point while the most beautiful liquid bell sounds now and again burst out from the air of the room.' Madame Blavatsky seems never to have exhibited hysteria or the slightest appearance of trance. She was always in full possession of her faculties while the phenomena were taking place.

The hard life she had led had coarsened her complexion. She peppered her language with expletives, some witty and amusing, some violent. To be suspected as an impostor would bring forth a torrent of passionate abuse against some person or other who had misjudged her or her Society. Many outside her intimate circle found it difficult to believe in her as an exalted moralist trying to lead people to a better spiritual life. But she wrote to her sister: 'I am — heaven help us — becoming fashionable. I am writing articles on Esotericism and Nirvana and am paid for them more than I could ever have expected.'

In his book describing incidents in her life, her devoted disciple and friend, journalist A. P. Sinnett, quoted an article published in the *New York Times* in January 1885. It described her as a woman of remarkable characteristics. 'Those who only knew her slightly', said the writer, 'invariably described her as a charlatan; those who knew her better thought she was a learned but deluded enthusiast; those who knew her intimately were either carried away into a belief in her powers or were profoundly puzzled. . . .'

Her flat became a meeting place for the oddest group of individuals. She published a weighty tome called *Isis Unveiled*, which had a moderate success, and was in the process of becoming quite a cult figure. But it was in India, not the USA, that she felt her future lay and one February day in 1879 she collected a loyal band of disciples together and set off for the East.

The early Theosophists presented an eccentric picture. Their aggressive sympathy for the Hindu population and general contempt for the European set was rather overdone. Madame Blavatsky said she did not wish to be political in any way, but she did not really understand the social problems of the time. She lived almost entirely with the native society in Bombay, which brought her and her party under suspicion. They were put under police surveillance by the British authorities and were followed continuously, suspected of being agitators. It was not long, however, before they were accepted as harmless and left alone.

Madame had slipped into the habit of spending most of the day in an old red dressing gown or in voluminous kaftans to hide her bulk. After a time, however, she began to realize she had to learn to get on with the European community in India and she would dutifully slip into a black silk dress and sip sherry. Her effort brought dividends in the shape of A. P. Sinnett, then editor of *The Pioneer* in India. He and his wife were received into the Society, and they invited Madame Blavatsky and Colonel Olcott to stay with them at their house in Simla. Sinnett was fascinated by her. 'Personally her manners were rough,' he admitted, 'but she had a lively humour and bright intelligence . . . her rugged manners and disregard of all conventionalities were the result of a deliberate rebellion against refined society.'

The headquarters of the Theosophist Society in Bombay were established at a place called Breach Candy in a bungalow perched high above the road. Madame Blavatsky worked there from morning till night, smoking like a chimney and pouring out articles which brought in money to keep them afloat. Colonel Olcott travelled all over India forming new branches. The bungalow had been empty for some years because people said it was haunted, but Madame found the atmosphere sympathetic. Streams of visitors found their way there. She would greet them warmly, then hurry off to the seclusion of an inner room where, she explained, she could prepare herself in the silence to receive whatever messages or orders were coming through from her astral masters, the Mahatmas Koot Hoomi and Morya.

In 1882 she became seriously ill with a kidney disease and suspected that what she called the term of her physical life was over. She was completely restored to health by occult teachers and healers, including a Tibetan priest. Feeling her old energy return, she declared the bungalow was too small for the growing needs of the Society. A spacious house was found at Adyar on the outskirts of Madras, which stood in extensive grounds beside a broad, shallow estuary. She declared it perfect and moved there just before Christmas. The Europeans of Bombay did not pretend to be anything but relieved.

Theosophy prospered and soon there were seventy-seven branches of the Society in India alone. Sanskrit scholars and Buddhist priests became interested, and eventually eight more branches were established in Ceylon (now Sri Lanka). Madame Blavatsky felt she had at last found the tranquil retreat where she could spend the rest of her life. She had an 'occult room' where she retired to contact the Mahatmas and take down the teachings and advice they wished to be passed on to the faithful. What became known as The Mahatma Letters became the centre of a storm of controversy. It was blasphemously suggested by some that she had written the letters herself!

This was not the only storm brewing when Madame and the Colonel left India for a visit to Europe in February 1884. A married couple called Coulomb had for some years been working as housekeeper and gardener at the Society headquarters. The arrangement turned sour. Madame Coulomb began dropping hints that she had assisted Madame Blavatsky to produce some of her phenomena, and further suggested that the Society was under the patronage of the devil. The Coulombs sold to a Christian missionary magazine a bundle of letters which, they said, had been written by the Theosophists' founder to her housekeeper. They were, if genuine, painfully incriminating.

Madame Blavatsky furiously denied having written the letters. 'Sentences here and there I recognize. They were taken from old notes of mine. But there are so many mistakes. For instance, I am not so ignorant of Indian affairs that I would refer to the Maharajah of Lahore when every Indian schoolboy knows there is no such person. . . .' She also pointed out that she had been producing phenomena without the Coulombs' assistance for most of her life.

Nevertheless, the letters created something of a *cause célèbre* in the occult world. Finally the Society for Psychical Research sent Richard Hodgson to find out what was going on. His judgment was not favourable. Not only did he judge the Coulomb letters to be genuine but he also said that Madame Blavatsky was responsible for the Mahatma Letters. She accused Hodgson of examining only her sworn enemies, and protested that she had not been allowed to see one line of the controversial correspondence. Her only solace came from students of the Colleges in Madras, who joined together to welcome her back from Europe with a loyal address which began 'Dear and revered Madame . . . you have dedicated your life to the disinterested service of occult philosophy; you have thrown a flood of light on the sacred mysteries of our hoary religion and philosophies. . . .'

The scandal ended her life in India. Such was her burning sense of injustice that she would pace up and down her room in Adyar for hours, eyes blazing, raging and cursing in Russian. Eventually the doctors said she would drop dead if she did not have peace and quiet. Towards the end of March 1885 she left for good. Sick and totally demoralized by the accusations that had been made against her, she moved first to Italy, then to Germany, where she found quiet lodgings in the town of Würzburg. She began to write her magnum opus, *The Secret Doctrine*.

Countess Wachtmeister, a Theosophy student, heard that she was ill and lonely and offered to join her as nurse and companion. 'I had been told a great deal against her and can honestly say I was prejudiced in her disfavour,' she wrote in her reminiscences. 'It was only a sense of duty and gratitude which caused me to take on the task. I had gained a lot from Theosophy. After hearing the rumours circulating about her — that she was practising black magic, fraud and deception — I was on my guard. But after a few months I was ashamed of myself for having ever suspected her. . . . I believe her to be an honest and true woman, faithful to death to her Masters and to the cause for which she has sacrificed position, fortune, health.' The Countess stayed with her till the end.

Controversy was still rumbling round Madame Blavatsky's head when, in the spring of 1891, she suffered a severe attack of influenza. She was now living in England, lecturing to her still numerous followers and working on her enormous book. She did not recover and on May 8, 1891, died in the company of three of her Theosophists, who entwined her in their arms as she quietly passed away. The turbulent Russian spirit was still. Those present said a great sense of peace filled the room. Though she was cremated at Woking half her ashes were sent to her beloved Adyar, the rest to the American Theosophical Society, where it all began.

Chapter eight

MYSTERIES OF CRIME AND INTRIGUE

Mayhem, murder and mystery! These are the ingredients of the most intriguing crime stories of all – the crimes that go unsolved. In most major criminal cases, there is a neat ending. The misdeed is detected, the suspect arrested and the culprit punished. But not always, and documented in this chapter are some of the most fascinating crimes filed under the heading – UNSOLVED.

Mystery of the masked prisoner

On a freezing night in November 1703 a masked prisoner in the Bastille returned to his cell after attending Mass, complained of feeling unwell, took to his bed and died. It was all over so quickly he did not even have time to receive the sacrement.

Within hours, the most extraordinary steps had been taken to ensure that his identity, which had been kept secret from all but a handful of men for 30 years, should never be revealed. All the furniture and equipment he had used was burned or melted down. The walls of his cell were scraped and whitewashed. Every surface was scoured in case he had tried to leave a message for posterity. Even floor tiles were taken up and replaced and his clothes and personal possessions flung into a furnace.

By order of Louis XIV, the prisoner's face had been covered by a mask throughout his entire incarceration. He had been threatened with instant death should he try to remove it, to reveal anything about himself or to escape.

Legends about him spread all over France, then around the world. The solitary prisoner caught the public imagination. As one of the most enigmatic figures in history, he became known as 'The Man in the Iron Mask'.

Because so little was known of him or why he had been incarcerated in the top security prisons of France for so long, rumours spread like wildfire. Some claimed to have discovered that he was an illegitimate son of the Royal House, so closely resembling Louis that his face must never be seen. One astounding theory put forward was that Louis XIV himself was illegitimate and the prisoner was the rightful King. Other rumours named him as the twin brother of Louis, shut away to preserve the Sun King's glory.

Certainly, remarkable precautions were taken to ensure that no one ever saw the face behind the mask. He was always under the care of the same governor, M. de Saint Mars, who moved with him from prison to prison. He was forbidden to mix with other prisoners and his jailer had orders to kill him instantly if he tried to talk about anything other than his immediate neccessities. His name did not appear on the prison records and was never used in either direct address or correspondence. He was usually referred to as 'the prisoner you sent me' or in later days 'the ancient prisoner'.

Despite these harsh terms, he was treated in all other respects as an important person. The King and his ministers constantly inquired after his health and welfare. His food, clothes and furniture were of good quality, he

was allowed his rights as a devout Catholic and was always treated and referred to with courtesy.

The doctor who was allowed to treat him, but who had to examine his tongue and his body without removing the mask, said: 'He was admirably made. His skin was dark, his voice interesting.'

The only other reference to his physical appearance came at a time when the governor, M. de Saint Mars, was ordered to take the man from the island of St Marguerite, where he had been imprisoned, to the Bastille. On the way to Paris, the governor made a stop at his own chateau near Villeneuve, and local people caught glimpses of the masked prisoner. He was said to be tall, well made and white haired. When he dined with St Mars, servants noticed that the governor sat directly opposite his prisoner with two pistols by the side of his plate.

It is said that Louis XIV's great-grandson and successor, Louis XV, on being told the truth about the prisoner, exclaimed: 'If he were still alive I would give him his freedom.' But the secret was obviously not passed on. Louis XVI, in order to satisfy the curiosity of his wife Marie Antoinette, searched the royal archives in vain.

The first written references to the prisoner were available in 1761 when the journals of Etienne du Jonca, the King's Lieutenant in the Bastille, were published. He recorded for the year 1698: 'Thursday, 18 September at three o'clock in the afternoon, M. de Saint Mars, Governor of the Chateau of the Bastille, made his first appearance coming from his command of the Iles Sainte Marguerite, bringing with him in his litter a prisoner he had formerly at Pignerol, whom he caused to be always masked, whose name is not mentioned. . .'

Five years later du Jonca recorded the prisoner's death, stating that he was buried the following Tuesday, November 20 in the graveyard of St Paul under the false name of Marchioly.

It was du Jonca who referred to the fact that the prisoner was 'always masked, with a mask of black velvet'. Other sources described the mask as having been made of iron reinforced with steel, fitted with a chin piece of steel springs to allow the prisoner to eat. It was on the latter description that Alexandre Dumas based his novel *The Man in the Iron Mask* – but du Jonca was the only eye witness.

Until the French Revolution, little more was known about the mysterious prisoner. It was at one point widely believed that he was a man named Mattioli, an envoy of the Duke of Mantua who had double-crossed King Louis XIV and been imprisoned under the care of St Mars. The theory was given some credence as it was thought the name Marchioly was a French version of Mattioli. But this was later disproved.

With the Revolution came the first clues. When the archives of the Ministry of War came to be classified they were found to be in chaos. But many years of patient cataloguing and research produced a mass of letters which had passed between the Minister of War, the Marquis de Louvois and M. de Saint Mars.

Towards the end of July 1669, the year in which it is known the masked man was first imprisoned, St Mars received this message from Louvois: 'The King has commanded that I am to have the man named Eustache Dauger sent to Pignerol. It is of the utmost importance to his service that he should be most securely guarded and that he should in no way give information about himself nor send letters to anyone at all. You will yourself once a day have to take enough food for the day to this wretch and you must on no account listen for any reason to all to what he may want to say to you, always threatening to kill him if he opens his mouth to speak of anything but his neccessities.'

Letters from the King himself saying that he was dissatisfied with the behaviour of a man named Eustache Dauger were also found. The King wanted him kept 'in good and safe custody, preventing him communicating with anyone at all by word of mouth or writ of hand'.

Further letters giving details of his imprisonment as the years passed correspond exactly with what is known of the imprisonment of the masked man.

Who was Eustache Dauger? For a long time no trace of him could be found.

At last someone noticed that a lieutenant in the King's Guards had borne that name. It had been overlooked because his family was more commonly called Cavoye after a property they owned in Picardy. A record of his birth exists, but not of his death and references to him disappear after 1668. He was one of six brothers, four of whom were killed in battle. His fifth brother, Louis, became a close friend of the King and was eventually created a marquis. But Eustache was always in trouble and seems to have drifted towards the intriguers of the Court, even possibly being involved in the devil worship and Black Masses encouraged by the king's mistress, Madame de Montespan. But we can only guess.

No more is known and the mystery of the king's masked prisoner remains a mystery.

Exploits of Spring-heeled Jack

He had hands of ice, breath of fire and bounded on to rooftops

He came bounding out of the night, his eyes glowing like balls of fire, his hands icy claws and his mouth spitting flames. For more than 60 years this terrifying figure, reputedly able to leap over high walls or on to roofs with superhuman ease, held England in a grip of fear.

At first, in the 1830s, tales of a frightening devil-like figure bounding through the air were treated as hysterical nonsense. But reports, mainly from people crossing Barnes Common in south-west London, continued.

In January 1838, this strange creature received official recognition. At London's Mansion House the Lord Mayor, Sir John Cowan, read out a letter from a terrified citizen of Peckham. It described the phenomenal jumping feats of a demoniacal figure. There was an immediate uproar.

Other complaints flooded in from people who until then had been too afraid of ridicule to report their encounters with the creature who had become known as Spring-heeled Jack.

Polly Adams, a pretty farmer's daughter from Kent, who worked in South London pub, had been savagely attacked several months earlier while walking across Blackheath. The attacker fled, leaping great distances into the air.

A servant girl, Mary Stevens, was terrorized on Barnes Common. And by

Clapham churchyard a woman on her way home from a visit to friends was confronted by the same mysterious creature.

Across the Thames, 18-year-old Lucy Scales and her sister, daughters of a London butcher, were on their way home from a visit to a brother's house when they were attacked in Green Dragon Alley, Limehouse. A cloaked figure sprang from the darkness, spat flames at Lucy, temporarily blinding her, and then soared away.

The next victim was Jane Alsop, who shared a house in Bearhind Lane, Bow, with her two sisters and their father. One night in February there came a loud knocking on the front door. Jane hurried to answer it, and found a dark figure swathed in a long cloak standing in the shadows.

He swung round and said, 'I am a policeman. For God's sake bring me a light. We have caught Spring-heeled Jack here in the lane!'

Jane's heart skipped a beat. The news stunned and excited her. So the stories of the strange bogyman were true after all, she thought. She hurried back into the house to get a candle and handed it to the man. But, instead of hurrying away, the 'policeman' shrugged off the cloak – to reveal a terrifying figure clad in a horned, close-fitting helmet and a tight, white costume.

He grabbed hold of her by the neck, pinning her head under his arm. But, as he ripped at her dress and pawed her body, she tore herself away with a terrified scream. He gave chase and caught her again by her long hair, but Jane's sister, hearing her cries, raised the alarm. Help arrived, but before any of the startled rescuers could grab him, the figure bounded away into the darkness.

Jane later described her attacker to the authorities: 'His face was hideous, his eyes like balls of fire. His hands had icy-cold great claws, and he vomited blue and white flames.'

Her colourful description was to be echoed repeatedly by other terrified and presumably hysterical – victims. But it was a description that could hardly have helped the police in their search for the fantastic attacker. After all, where were they to start looking for such a creature?

Posses of vigilantes were organized, rewards were offered, the police strived in vain to track down the attacker. Even the Duke of Wellington, although nearly 60, armed himself and went out on horseback to hunt down the monster.

During the next few years, Spring-heeled Jack roamed the country. Sightings ranged from the back streets of London to remote villages.

In February 1855 the mystery spread to the West Country, where the folk of five South Devon towns awoke to find that there had been a heavy snowfall – and that mysterious footprints had appeared overnight. The footsteps ran along the tops of walls, over rooftops, and across enclosed courtyards. The frightened inhabitants labelled them the Devil's Footprints. Some attributed them to a ghostly animal (see p. 179) and others blamed Spring-heeled Jack.

Spring-heeled Jack was still bounding around the country in 1870. The army certainly took him seriously and organized a plan to trap him. The move was forced upon the authorities after sentries, many of them hardened veterans of the Crimean War, had been terrorized at their posts by a weird figure who sprang from the shadows to land on the roofs of their sentry boxes or to slap their faces with icy hands.

In Lincoln the townsfolk, wild with fear and anger, tried to hunt him down with guns. As always, he disappeared into the night with a maniacal laugh.

Jack's fiendish face was last seen in 1904 in Liverpool. He panicked people in the Everton area by leaping up and down the streets, 'bounding from pavement to rooftop and back again.' When a few bold souls tried to corner him, he melted back into the darkness.

Victorian Britain abounded in rich eccentrics, one of whom may have found it amusing to spend time and money in spreading terror through the country. Some people blamed the 'Mad Marquis' of Waterford. But, while he was wild and irresponsible, he was never vicious.

The mystery of Spring-heeled Jack remains unsolved. After his appearance in Liverpool, he disappeared – apparently for good.

_____

I was Napoleon's general . . .

On his death bed in Florence, South Carolina, in 1846, an obscure but popular French teacher weakly declared: 'I am France's Marshal Ney.' The final words of a frail old man might have been taken as the product of a wandering mind – except for some remarkable evidence that he was perhaps telling the truth.

Marshal Michel Ney was one of Napoleon Bonaparte's most able generals. But after his army was defeated at Waterloo, Napoleon was exiled to St Helena, and Ney, less lucky than his leader, was sentenced to death by firing squad.

Shortly after 9 o'clock on the morning of 7 December 1815, Ney was led by a contingent of the troops he had once commanded into the Luxembourg Gardens in Paris. He was placed against a wall where he addressed his men in the most emotional terms.

A British diplomat witnessed the execution. He said that Ney shouted to the firing squad: 'Comrades, when I place my hand upon my breast, fire at

A contemporary print of Marshal Ney giving the word of command for his own death.

my heart.' The soldiers levelled their rifles, Ney put his hand to his chest, a volley rang out and Ney fell, his coat stained with blood.

According to the observer, the body was then whisked away with suspicious haste. It lay in a hospital overnight and was buried in the cemetery of Pierre la Chaise early the following day. Madame Ney did not attend the funeral. Only one distant relative was there to see the famous general laid to rest.

Three years later in Florence, South Carolina, a middle-aged French teacher using the name of Peter Stuart Ney claimed that he and Marshal Ney were the same person. He said he had been saved from execution by a plot hatched by his old soldiers, with the aid of his former enemy, the Duke of Wellington, who had been horrified at the ignoble fate proposed for his fellow general.

The teacher explained that the Paris firing squad had aimed above his head. He said that he had held in his hand a container of blood, which he had released when he struck his chest. He had then been smuggled by ship to America.

No one believed Ney until a doctor examined him and agreed that scars on his body conformed to Marshal Ney's battle scars. The teacher also claimed that during the passage to America he had been recognized by a fellow passenger – a soldier who had once been in his command. The man was later traced and confirmed the story. The French teacher also boasted a remarkably intimate knowledge of Marshal Ney and his family and of military tactics.

The renowned New York handwriting expert, David Carvalho, examined letters written by the teacher and by the general. He had no hesitation in stating that they were produced by the same person.

Six years after the Paris 'execution', one of Ney's pupils brought him a newspaper reporting the death of Napoleon on St Helena. The teacher fainted before his class and was carried home. Later that day he tried to cut his throat, but the knife broke in the wound.

Peter Ney – or Marshal Michel Ney, if that is indeed who he was – died peacefully in 1846, maintaining to the last the strange story that no one has ever been able to prove or disprove.

The queen of crime's lost 11 days

The riddle of Agatha Christie's disappearance remains unsolved

Agatha Christie was the most successful crime writer of all time. Her tales of Hercule Poirot and Miss Marple have delighted millions for more than 50 years', and some of her intricate plots have puzzled even the most sharp-witted of fans. Yet, on her death in January 1976, she left behind her a real-life mystery as baffling as any she concocted herself.

In December 1926, when she was already celebrated as a mystery writer, Agatha Christie disappeared for nearly two weeks. The newspaper headlines screamed sensational theories to a breathless public. Suicide. Abduction. Murder. The police searched for some clue as to why she had disappeared – but in vain.

Agatha Christie was born in September 1890, the youngest daughter of a wealthy American who lived with his English wife in Torquay, Devon. The family lived a life of luxurious ease and Agatha received little formal education. But the house was full of books and her mother encouraged her to read.

In 1914 she married Colonel Archibald Christie, and while her husband was abroad with the army she served as a nurse. She qualified as a dispenser and it was during this time that she gained the detailed knowledge of medicine, drugs and poisons that were to stand her in such good stead as a mystery writer.

She wrote her first detective story while recovering from an illness, and by 1926 she was a literary success. Perhaps this irritated her husband – who turned to another woman and confessed the love affair to his wife.

This news, following on the death of her mother, drove her to despair. And on the bitterly cold night of Friday, 3 December, she dressed in a green knitted skirt, a grey cardigan and a velours hat, stuffed a few pounds into her purse, climbed into her two-seater Morris car and drove off into the night.

Early the following morning, the car was found empty at the bottom of a slope near Newlands Corner, barely half a mile from her 12-bedroomed Berkshire home. Its front wheels hung over the edge of a 120-ft chalk pit in a narrow, rutted lane. The brakes were off, the gear lever was in neutral and the ignition switched on. In the car was some clothing, including a fur coat.

The following Monday, the police released the news of her disappearance, and the newspapers headlined it. Hundreds of policemen and thousands of volunteers scoured the countryside. Deep-sea divers searched the Silent Pool, a so-called bottomless lake in the area.

The favourite theory was that the famous authoress had committed suicide. But where was the body?

While the hue and cry grew, an attractive redhead in her mid-thirties was making herself popular with her fellow guests at The Hydro Hotel, some 250 miles away at Harrogate, Yorkshire. Her name, she said, was Theresa Neele – the same surname as that of Colonel Christie's new love – and she was from South Africa. But the hotel's head waiter, who had been closely following the story of Agatha Christie's disappearance in the newspapers, thought the sociable guest looked suspiciously like the missing writer, and he contacted the police.

Eleven days after her disappearance, 'Mrs Neele' finished a game of billiards and went to change for dinner. When she approached the dining room, Colonel Christie lowered the newspaper he had been hiding behind and walked over to her.

The press immediately suspected an elaborate publicity stunt – even though Colonel Christie's claim that his wife had been suffering from loss of memory was confirmed by a doctor. The papers led a public outcry, demanding that the £3,000 that the search had cost the taxpayer should be repaid. But gradually the ill-feeling vanished and Mrs Christie regained her popularity. Two years later she and Colonel Christie were divorced, and he was free to marry Miss Neele.

In 1930, Agatha married archaeologist Sir Max Mallowan and travelled widely with him, using the exotic places she visited as settings for some of her novels.

With the passage of years, the memories of the novelist's disappearance faded. She would agree to interviews only on the understanding that the matter was not mentioned. Even her autobiography passes over the episode quickly; she merely hints at a nervous breakdown. But is this the real explanation of what happened all those years ago? If she had lost her memory, where did the clothes she wore at The Hydro and the money she spent there come from?

Did she, on that cold December night, intend to kill herself – and then, when fate took a hand and her car failed to plunge into the chalk pit, decide to get away for a rest while she thought things over? If so, why did she not let the police know the truth?

Was the episode a plot to gain the sympathy of her errant husband and win him back? Was it an involved way of bringing her husband's affair out into the open? Or perhaps, more sinisterly, was it all a scheme to punish her husband's infidelity? Suppose a suicide attempt had succeeded. The police would have investigated and discovered in Colonel Christie's affair with Miss Neele a likely motive for him to get rid of his wife. Far-fetched perhaps, but no more so than some of Mrs Christie's mystery plots.

Most of the people who could help reveal the truth of the matter are now dead. Miss Neele died in 1958 and Colonel Christie in 1962.

Agatha Christie's second husband, Sir Max, once admitted that *Unfinished Portrait*, a romantic novel which she wrote in 1934 under the name Mary Westmacott, was a thinly disguised autobiography. In it, the heroine is shattered when her husband tells her he is in love with another woman. She tries to commit suicide, but fails.

Over the years, Agatha Christie wrote more than 80 novels, was more widely translated than William Shakespeare and achieved sales of 300 million books. But despite this popularity, she remained a private, enigmatic person. And, right up to her death, she refused to provide the solution to her greatest mystery story – that of her own disappearance half a century before.

The Wreck of the Chantiloupe

When winter storms lash the sea to boiling and great waves pound across the bay, villagers snug in their cottages shudder at the memory of a hideous crime that taints them still. There are those who swear that, above the roar of the wind and breakers crashing on the shore, they have heard the screams of men and women who perished in a shipwreck more than 200 years ago.

But not all those who died were victims of the cruel elements. At least one, a wealthy woman passenger, was killed for her jewellery by heartless looters. Their names have remained a shameful secret ever since.

In summer, Thurlestone Sands, in south Devon, ring with the happy laughter of romping children, and the sunbathers soak up the warmth. But in winter, long after the last holidaymaker has gone home, as the gales howl in from the Atlantic, it is easy to picture the last moments of the Plymouth-bound brig *Chantiloupe* in 1772.

It had been a smooth voyage from the West Indies but, as she neared port, a south-westerly gale blew up so suddenly that there was no time to turn into it. The captain's only choice was to run before it, past Plymouth and up the Channel. Soon, with massive cliffs looming ahead, he was forced to strike sail and drop all anchors. But nothing could hold the *Chantiloupe* against the raging wind and sea, and the captain decided on a desperate gamble to save his passengers and crew.

Ordering full sail, he altered course by a few degrees and headed directly for the smooth, golden carpet of Thurlestone Sands. He told passengers and crew that he aimed to run his ship high up the beach, so they could all jump to safety.

The passengers hurried to their cabins to collect what valuables they could. One of them, Mrs James Burke, whose nephew was the famous Whig politician Edmund Burke, came on deck in her finest gown wearing all her jewellery.

The small ship raced for the shore as though on wings, carried on the shoulders of mighty waves, and it seemed the captain's daring bid would succeed. But one wave, higher than the rest, suddenly hoisted the stern. The keel beneath the bows struck bottom and the *Chantiloupe* swung broadside, almost capsizing under the next wave.

All on board were hurled into the raging sea, and most died within minutes. But Mrs Burke struck out for the shore and, miraculously, reached it alive. Gratefully she let strong hands grasp her and pull her from the water.

But these three men were not rescuers ... they were thieves and killers. Barely had her last scream been carried away by the wind before they were fighting over her jewels.

They ripped off her earrings and, finding her rings too tight to remove, hacked off her fingers. Then they buried her in the sand, and soon the raging sea had washed away any traces of the killing.

Perhaps it would never have come to light, if a man had not happened to walk his dog past the burial spot two weeks later. He was Daniel Whiddon, later to be immortalized in the folk song 'Uncle Tom Cobleigh'. His dog began scrabbling in the sand and unearthed Mrs Burke's body.

The secret was out, and the local paper reported the crime in these words:
> 'The savage people from the adjacent villages, who were anxiously waiting for the wreck, seized and stript her of her clothes, even cutting off some of her fingers and mangling her ears in their impatience to secure the jewels and left her miserable to perish.'

There was an autopsy, which showed that Mrs Burke was alive when she reached the shore. An inquest, before the jury of local men, returned the verdict: 'Murder by person or persons unknown.'

There can be no doubt that some people in the nearby villages of Thurlestone Sands, Galmpton, Hope and Bolberry, knew the identity of the killers. But lips were sealed. Edmund Burke himself visited the area to seek the truth, and learned nothing.

More than 100 years later, the Rev Frank Coope, Rector of Thurlestone from 1897 to 1921, probed the mystery. He wrote: 'It was well known in the neighbourhood who did it, and their surnames are remembered to this day. The three men who were "in it" all came, it is said, to a bad end within the year. One hanged himself in an outhouse, another went mad, ran into the sea and was drowned, and the third was killed in an accident.'

Was this the truth – or a tale to put the rector off the scent?

Today the neatly thatched villages around Thurlestone Sands are picturesque and welcoming. But behind the whitewashed walls and stout oak doors, there may still be families who know the names of those long-ago killers.

The Disappearing Parachutist

The skyjacker who commandeered the Northwest Airlines Boeing 727 flight from Portland, Oregon, to Seattle, Washington, was cold, calculating and ruthless. He terrified the cabin staff when he opened the canvas bag he was carrying in his lap and showed them a home-made bomb – tightly wrapped sticks of dynamite packed round a detonator.

As the jet cruised at 6,000 m (20,000 ft) above the Cascade Mountains, he threatened to blow apart the aircraft, killing himself and the 35 other passengers on board.

But the man who cruelly bargained with the lives of the passengers and the crew pulled off such a daring and lucrative coup that he is now fondly remembered as a folk hero, a swashbuckling pirate of the jet age. Songs have been written in his honour, fan clubs have been formed to cherish his memory and thousands of his admirers wear T-shirts emblazoned with his name. The souvenir industry and the posters in praise of D. B. Cooper would undoubtedly carry his photograph and glowing testimonials about his personal history – if anyone knew what he looked like or who he really was.

But the true identity of the man who literally vanished into thin air with his $200,000 booty still remains a mystery. No-one knows who he was, where he came from or where he went.

D. B. Cooper may be a frozen corpse, a broken body lying in a mouldering heap of banknotes in an impenetrable forest in the mountains of the northwestern United States. Or he may be sunning himself on a beach in Mexico and gloating over his perfect crime.

The last confirmed sighting of D. B. Cooper came from the pilot of the Boeing air liner from which the skyjacker leaped clutching a white cloth bag containing ten thousand $20 bank notes. Cooper vanished into thin air at 2,000 m (7,000 ft) as the air whistled past in a 90 metre per second (200 m.p.h) slipstream at a temperature of −23°C (−10°F).

That was the last time 'D. B. Cooper' was seen. The first time was in the departure lounge at Portland Airport, Oregon, when he bought his one-way ticket for the 400-mile journey to Seattle, Washington. It was 24 November 1971 – Thanksgiving Day – and the other travellers were all anxious to get home to their families for the annual holiday celebration.

The quiet middle-aged man with the canvas carrier bag and dark, tinted

glasses paid cash for his ticket and gave his name as 'D. B. Cooper'. After a
45-minute wait in the lounge, where no one looked at him twice, he filed
aboard when the flight was called and the jet roared off into the darkening
skies.

Halfway through the one-hour flight, Cooper pushed the button in the
overhead panel to summon one of the cabin crew to his seat. Stewardess Tina
Mucklow approached with a tray, ready to take his order for a drink.

Cooper simply thrust a crumpled note into her hand and then reached
under his seat to pull his canvas bag on to his lap. He waited a few seconds for
the stewardess to read the note. It warned: 'I have a bomb with me. If I don't
get $200,000 I will blow us all to bits.'

As the terrified stewardess tried to control her panic, Cooper calmly opened
the bag to let her glimpse the dynamite and detonator inside. While the girl
walked slowly up to the flight deck, Cooper settled back in his seat and peered
out at the storm clouds below.

Within seconds a special transmitter on the flight deck of the Boeing was
'squawking' its coded electronic message over the radio frequencies ...
'Hijack ... Hijack ... Hijack ...'

At Seattle Airport a team of FBI agents, local police sharpshooters, hostage
negotiation experts and airline officials were hastily gathered as the plane
prepared to land. The passengers were still unaware of the drama when the
jet came in for a perfect touchdown and rolled gently to a halt at the end of
the runway.

There was a groan of annoyance from the impatient travellers when the
captain made the terse announcement: 'Ladies and gentlemen, there will be a
slight delay in disembarking. Please remain in your seats until we are ready to
taxi to the terminal building.'

Only one passenger ignored the announcement. Cooper unbuckled his seat
belt and, clutching his bag, walked swiftly up to the flight deck and
positioned himself behind the crew. 'Now gentlemen,' he said softly, 'don't
bother to look round.'

In 20 minutes of unyielding demands over the ground control radio from
the flight deck of the airliner, Cooper stuck to his original threat and no one
dared to call his bluff.

As the passengers began to grow more and more restless, there was a hiss of
pneumatic power and the forward door of the Boeing slid open. The flight
engineers in overalls – undercover armed FBI men – came aboard with a
trolley of 'catering equipment'. They clearly saw the figure of the man with
the canvas bag watching them from the flight deck door, then, under
instructions by two-way radio from their superiors, they withdrew and the
door slid closed and locked again.

The trolley was wheeled up to the flight deck by a stewardess and Cooper studied its contents. It contained a tough white sack with $200,000 and two backpack and two chestpack parachutes.

Cooper complained that he wanted the money in a rucksack which he could have strapped on to his body. But he quickly relented and told the pilot: 'You can let the passengers go now.'

Loudly complaining, the unsuspecting travellers filed off the aircraft to a waiting bus and Seattle ground control breathed a sigh of relief. But they were still left with the problem of Cooper in charge of the aircraft and its three-man crew as the jet was refuelled to maximum capacity by two giant tankers.

Minutes before the Boeing took off again, three military pursuit fighters and a small fleet of helicopters were scrambled from Seattle Airport and a nearby us Air Force base with orders to try to keep the jet in sight.

'We are heading for Mexico now,' Cooper told the pilot, Captain W. Bill Scott. But 10 minutes after take-off he issued new instructions.

As the aircraft climbed away from Seattle and headed south, Cooper insisted with calm precision: 'Fly with the flaps lowered 15 per cent and the landing gear down, keep the speed below 90 metres per second (2000 m.p.h), don't climb above 2,000 m (7,000 ft) and open the rear door.'

'We'll burn up too much fuel,' Captain Scott protested. 'We'll have to put down for some more fuel if we fly like that.'

'OK,' Cooper snapped. 'Stop for refuelling in Reno, Nevada. I'll give you further orders there. Now just fly south and keep the door locked behind you.'

The hijacker paused only briefly on the flight deck to retrieve his ransom note from the captain's tunic pocket. He was determined not to leave any clues behind, not even a sample of his handwriting.

The whole aircraft filled with a deafening roar as the pilot throttled back and lowered the rear door ramp into the slipstream.

When the flight recorder 'black box' was checked later, the sensitive instrument measured a tiny change in the aircraft's altitude, equivalent to the loss of a weight of 73 kg (160 lb) in the tail section. The time was 20.13 hours, 32 minutes after leaving Seattle. That's when D. B. Cooper leaped out.

Four hours later, as the Boeing lost height and glided gently towards the twinkling lights of the airport at Reno in the Nevada Desert, the co-pilot unlocked the flight deck door to warn Cooper that the tail ramp would have to be closed for landing.

The cabin was deserted. Cooper and the money had gone.

Two parachutes had been left behind. A backpack chute was intact but a chestpack was ripped to shreds. Cooper had probably torn it apart to make a harness to strap his sack of money to his body.

The danger of mid-air death and destruction had passed. And the hunt to find D. B. Cooper was on. FBI and Federal Aviation Agency officials who plotted the flight path of the hijacked Boeing quickly realized that Cooper had bailed out over some of the most densely wooded, inhospitable mountains in the American West, where the chances of survival for an inexperienced woodsman were pretty slim. He had plummeted to earth clad only in a lightweight lounge suit, a raincoat and with a pair of flimsy moccasin shoes on his feet. In the thin atmosphere of the high altitude, the parachute would only have slowed him to a bone-crushing 18 metres per second (40 m.p.h.) before he hit the mountain peaks which tower up to the same height as the Boeing had flown.

Only a super-fit expert could have hoped to escape alive. Police began detailed and intensive scrutiny of the only group of men who would have the nerve or experience to attempt that kind of death-defying descent – the 'smoke jumpers' of the Forestry Service fire-fighting teams. But they drew a blank. Cooper was not a 'smoke jumper' and the professional experts who are trained to parachute into the high forests with full radio communication and ground support facilities agreed to a man that Cooper's leap from a speeding jet in a rain storm was suicidal.

Aerial searches covering thousands of square miles of the states of Oregon, Washington and Nevada failed to show any trace of a parachute canopy.

Then, three weeks after the hijack, came the first enigmatic clue. A typewritten note, posted in Seattle and signed by D. B. Cooper, arrived at a Los Angeles newspaper. The writer revealed:

'I am no modern-day Robin Hood, unfortunately I have only 14 months to live. The hijacking was the fastest and most profitable way to gain a few last grains of peace of mind. I didn't rob Northwest because I thought it would be romantic or heroic or any of the other euphemisms that seem to attach themselves to situations of high risk.

I don't blame people for hating me for what I've done nor do I blame anybody for wanting me caught or punished – though this can never happen. I knew from the start I would not be caught. I've come and gone on several airline flights since and I'm not holed up in some obscure backwoods town. Neither am I a psychopath, I've never even received a speeding ticket.'

The note sparked off a new hunt for Cooper and as the list of potential suspects dwindled, hundreds of troops from the Fort Lewis Army base in Portland, Oregon, were ordered to comb the mountains searching for clues. They were backed up by spotter planes and even satellite surveillance photographs from orbiting spacecraft.

There was still no sign of Cooper.

But FBI agents were confident that if Cooper had survived the jump, he would be nailed as soon as he tried to spend a penny of the ransom money. The serial numbers of every one of the bank notes in his haul had been noted and all US banks and major money clearing houses abroad had been alerted to raise the alarm as soon as they began to trickle into circulation.

In the meantime the airlines took the costly precaution of ensuring that no one would imitate Cooper's hijack and high level parachute escape ever again. All Boeing 727s were recalled to the manufacturers and their tail door ramps sealed so they could never be opened in flight.

And as the widely publicised FBI manhunt began to lose steam, the mystery hijacker began to gather a cult following from a fascinated public. Graffiti slogans appeared on public buildings and airline advertising hoardings over the Pacific north west – 'D. B. Cooper, where are you?' Disc jockeys dedicated records to Cooper.

A year after the hijack, when FBI officals adopted the official attitude that D. B. Cooper must have died in the parachute fall, they had to admit that there was no sign of the hijack money and that the $200,000 was probably still hidden with his body in the wooded mountains. Then the first groups of enthusiastic amateur explorers, calling themselves the 'Ransom Rangers', began scouring the woods in Oregon and Washington, searching for the ransom treasure.

Finally on 24 November 1976, the FBI officially closed the file on D. B. Cooper. Five years had elapsed since the crime, so under the Statute of Limitations if D. B. Cooper was alive, he was now a free man.

And not a single dollar of the ransom money had ever turned up. If Cooper was a corpse in the mountains, the money was there with him, just waiting to be found.

Most of the population of Portland and Seattle seemed to catch 'Cooper fever' and the hills were alive with the sound of marching feet. But they scoured the mountains in vain.

The fever subsided until 1979 when a solitary deer hunter in the dense forest above the village of Kelso, Washington, stumbled across a man-made intrusion in the virgin forest. It was a thick plastic warning sign from the tail door hatch of a Boeing 727. Its futile message read: 'This hatch must remain firmly locked in flight.'

Overnight the village became a boom town as thousands of amateur sleuths stormed the peaks trying to find Cooper's treasure one step ahead of the FBI teams who descended by helicopter. Astrologers, mapmakers and local tourist guides made almost as much money as Cooper's missing loot from the hopeful punters.

'The mountains were almost trampled flat by the crowds,' admitted State Police Inspector Walter Wagner. 'But none of us found a thing.'

Had Cooper got clean away with all the cash?

That riddle was partially solved seven and a half years after the hijacking.

Industrial painter Harold Ingram and his son Brian, eight, were wading along the sandy shore of the Columbia River just outside the Washington state border when they stirred up a bundle of weathered banknotes from the river bank.

The money amounted to about $3,000 of Cooper's cash, according to one of the 30 FBI men who cordoned off the Ingrams' family picnic site and fought off the new wave of treasure seekers.

Scientific tests on the bank notes and the mud caked around them showed that the money had probably been washed downstream six years before from an area 80 km (50 miles) upstream – on any one of hundreds of tributaries higher up the mountain range.

The hunters vanished over the rocky skyline, sawing and digging their way through the forests once more.

'That's the closest we ever came to him,' Special Agent John Pringle of the FBI reported. 'But we are still looking for an invisible needle in a mountain range of haystacks.'

If D. B. Cooper is still alive, he can freely identify himself to the FBI now. The legal time limit on his crime means he will never face a criminal prosecution for the Thanksgiving Day hijacking. But there is probably one big obstacle which could prevent the world's only successful skyjacker from coming forward ...

The FBI may have given up, but at the offices of the Internal Revenue in the nation's capital in Washington DC the file on D. B. Cooper remains open forever.

The skyjacker faces a bill for $300,000 – more than his ransom haul – and a 10-year jail sentence for failing to file income tax returns.

The taxman explained:

'We tax illegal money just as we tax legal money; it's all income as far as we are concerned.

D. B. Cooper became $200,000 dollars richer after the hijack and he never paid his tax on that money. Now he owes us interest on that sum and penalty payments. We have assessed his tax liability as a bachelor with no dependants and no additional source of income. If he wants to arrange an appointment with our auditors to claim some allowances and expenses we will be happy to meet him.

Until then we are still looking for Mr D. B. Cooper, and his assets. There is no Statute of Limitations for tax dodgers.'

The Canine Sherlock Holmes

It stands, just over 0.3 m (1 ft) high, as the ultimate, golden goal of some of the world's greatest sporting stars. Whether held high in triumph or simply coveted from afar, the Jules Rimet Trophy is the prize of prizes in the field of professional soccer.

It has embraced the dreams of hundreds of nations, of legendary players such as the great Pele and of literally millions of waving, cheering fanatics from all corners of the globe.

It is more commonly known as the World Cup – a once-in-a-lifetime reward every four years to one country and its eleven most gifted, idolized footballers.

Such is the occasion of its presentation that it is passed into the hands of the football players only from those of kings and queens, presidents and prime ministers.

When it was brought to England a few weeks before the start of the 1966 World Cup tournament it was promptly stolen. The cup over which rival countries had, through the years, fought so bitterly – even off the playing field and in the political arena – was pilfered from a stamp exhibition at London's Central Hall, Westminster, where it had been on display. It was considered an international scandal.

Scotland Yard was summoned immediately. Questions were asked in parliaments around the world. Huge rewards from all sorts of organizations were offered for the cup's safe return. Outside England the mood was hostile and angry, especially in those nations where soccer seems almost to vie with religion for the hearts and souls of the people. No cost or effort was to be spared to restore not only a football trophy, but also national pride, to its rightful place.

The police who had been ordered in hot pursuit of the World Cup thief or thieves found themselves on a cold trail. The trophy had, apparently, vanished into thin air and the hunt for clues or suspects was a bitterly frustrating one. It was unlikely that anyone would have stolen the cup simply to melt it down. The actual gold content was then worth only about £2,000 despite the fact that it was insured for £30,000. The real value, however, was priceless.

Private collectors, undaunted by dealing on the black market to procure their secret hoards of treasure, would have paid a fortune to have the legendary cup in a hidden vault. That was the only theory on which the beleaguered police could pin any hope.

For a fortnight in early March 1966, the world held its breath as the desperate search for the stolen cup continued in vain. It was a tragedy of enormous proportions to dedicated followers of football. But, more than that, it was an almighty embarrassment to England, which was playing host to the prestigious tournament for the first time in its sporting history.

It was vital that the cup was found immediately.

Screaming newspaper headlines posed all sorts of questions, some of them unthinkable to the hierarchy of FIFA, soccer's world governing body ... Was it in the hands of an unscrupulous millionaire? Was it stolen and then simply thrown away to be lost forever when the thief realized the enormity of his crime? Was it being held by a syndicate of villains, waiting to sell it off to the highest bidder?

Had it, been melted down or destroyed? The possibilities were endless.

The answer came, in the most unexpected – and rather unglamorous – way on the night of 19 March.

David Corbett, a 26-year-old Thames lighterman, was taking a family dog, Pickles, for a walk near his home in Beulah Hill, Norwood, South London, when, out of the corner of his eye, he spotted a glint, a reflection that lasted for just a split second.

It had come from what had appeared to be a bundle of dirty old newspapers under a laurel bush that Pickles, a cross-bred collie, had been sniffing and pawing at with great interest. Mr Corbett called to his dog. But Pickles would not come.

As David Corbett recalled later:

'I bent under the bush, lifted the top layer of newspapers, and there it was. I knew what it was at once. It was the World Cup.

I think that the first thing I actually saw was an inscription on the cup. The words 'Brazil 1962' were written near the base. I'm a keen football fan and I had been following all the reports in the newspapers. You can imagine how absolutely taken aback I was.

I took it back to our flat to show my wife Jeannie and then we phoned the police, who were as astounded as we were. Yet the truth is that I would not have given the old bundle of newspapers it was wrapped in a sideways glance or a second thought if it hadn't been for Pickles. He was the real hero of the hour.'

Indeed he was. Animal lovers from all over the world began to shower gifts on the canine sleuth. England's National Canine Defence League bestowed

Pickles and his owner at the *Café Royal* with Henry Cooper

on him its highest honour: a silver medal inscribed with the words 'To Pickles, for his part in the recovery of the World Cup, 1966.' At the ceremony at which it was presented, the league's secretary enthused: 'Pickles, by his action, has given prominence to the canine world and so helped us in our task.'

At the same ceremony – and there were many others for the 'furry Sherlock Holmes' as he was dubbed – a hotel pageboy stepped up with a silver salver of further gifts. There was a rubber bone, £53, collected among the hotel's staff – and the best steak for him to eat.

Pickles, oblivious to the importance of the occasion, simply lay down and yawned.

But the still unanswered question was: who actually stole the World Cup? It was a question, despite a number of suspicions, that the police were never to answer.

Yet, as in all unsolved crimes, when the finger of suspicion is pointed, however wrongly, there are people who are bound to suffer. That, amazingly, was the sad plight of none other than Pickles' owner, Mr Corbett. Less than two months after his alertness helped recover the prized trophy, Mr Corbett told a newspaper:

'I wish I'd never seen the damn thing. I was quite excited about it at the time but I seem to have had nothing but trouble since.

When I gave it to the police, they appeared at first not to believe my story about Pickles finding it under a laurel bush. They grilled me. They asked me where I was on the day the cup was stolen, whether I collected stamps, if I had ever been to Central Hall, Westminster, and so on.

Eventually, they believed me. But the trouble didn't end with the police. Ordinary people have been suspecting me of having had something to do with the theft of the cup. My wife and I were in Trafalgar Square and a group of boys saw us. They shouted at me: "He's the one who stole it. Let's drown the dog in the fountain." It was terrible.'

In the end, of course, Mr Corbett was completely vindicated – and received rewards totalling more than £6,000. He did not watch the World Cup itself, but he did join in the spirit of Pickles's success when he allowed the dog to be taken to meet each member of the West German final team – all of whom touched him for luck, hoping they would find the cup theirs at the end of the football match.

But it was not to be. England took the trophy and, thanks to Pickles, who sadly died only four years later, erased memories of the most embarrassing episode in soccer history.

Evita and the body-snatchers

The embalmed body of Eva Peron was missing for 16 years

Eva Peron died in 1952. Yet her hair is still blonde and beautiful, her face doll-like and delicate. She represents the perfection of the embalmer's art as she lies 15 feet underground in an armoured family vault in a Buenos Aires cemetery.

Eva, the most vibrant life-force South America has ever known, is resting at last. She was finally buried in her homeland after her frail body was returned from 16 years of secret, mysterious exile, 16 years during which the paint was never allowed to fade from the slogans that plastered the walls of Buenos Aires, the capital that adored her: 'Give back the body of Evita.'

Evita – 'little Eva' – was the pet name given to their heroine by the *descamisados*, the 'shirtless ones', the poor of Argentina. Their adulation made Eva Peron, for a while, the most powerful woman in the world.

Eva was born, the illegitimate child of a poor provincial woman, in 1919 – though she always claimed, with beguiling femininity, that the year of her birth was 1922. By the time she was 15 she had moved to Buenos Aires with her first lover and was trying to get jobs as an actress.

She was 24 when she met Colonel Juan Peron, who was twice her age. She was then a radio starlet earning $10 a week as a disc jockey and as heroine of the station's soap operas. Peron and the other leaders of Argentina's right-wing military junta arrived at the radio station to appeal for funds for the victims of an earthquake. The colonel – a young 48, straight-backed and athletic – was captivated by Eva's deep, seductive voice.

From that moment on, it was Eva who appealed for money on behalf of Peron's social services ministry. In doing so, she became his spokeswoman.

'He doesn't care a button for the glittering uniforms and the frock coats,' she purred. 'His only friends are you, the *descamisados*.'

When the too-powerful Peron was ousted by the rest of the junta in 1945, it was Eva who single-handedly organized the support of the young officers and the workers to reinstate him. Two months later, she married him. And the following year, with Eva at his side, Peron was swept into the presidential palace on the shoulders of the *descamisados* and with the backing of the powerful unions.

As the wife of the president, Eva was a woman of dramatic contrasts. She dripped with diamonds and wrapped herself in mink yet launched a social aid fund and organized the delivery of second-hand clothes to farms and shanty towns. With jewelled hands she threw the crowds toys for their children. The people were mesmerized. They worshipped her.

Then Eva fell ill with incurable cancer. She grew thin and shrunken. At the few political functions she attended she had to be physically supported by her husband. She complained: 'I am too little for so much pain.'

On 26 July 1952, at 8.25 pm, Eva died. She was 33. She had scarcely breathed her last when her body was rushed away to be embalmed by an eminent Spanish pathologist, Dr Pedro Ara, who had been standing by for weeks. He operated on her emaciated body, replacing her blood with alcohol, then glycerine, which kept the organs intact and made the skin almost translucent. The entire process of embalming took almost a year, and Dr Ara was paid $100,000 for his work.

All this time, the nation had been in mourning for Santa Evita – as she was now known – and when her body lay in state two million people filed past the coffin. Seven were killed in the crush.

Plans were made to build memorials to Eva throughout Argentina, but most of them got no further than the drawing board – for in July 1955 roaring inflation led to Peron's overthrow. The former president went into exile in Spain, from where he demanded that his successor, General Eduardo Lonardi, send him his wife's body. Lonardi refused, and instead he set about discrediting the Perons. He opened the former president's homes to the public and put on display Peron's 15 custom-built sports cars, 250 motor-scooters and safes containing $10,000,000 in 'ready cash'. Also revealed were his secret Buenos Aires love-nests – apartments lined with furs and mirrors where Peron had satisfied his appetite for teenaged girls, including his regular mistress, 16-year-old Nelly Rivas.

The new military rulers also displayed Eva's fabulous jewels. But this had no effect on her glittering reputation, for she had never hidden her personal wealth from the people. In fact, during the months following Peron's overthrow the Eva death cult grew. General Lonardi tried to summon up the courage to destroy the unflawed body, which still lay in Room 63 of the Confederation of Labour building in Buenos Aires. But before he could act, he himself was ousted from power, in November 1955, by General Pedro Aramburu. The new leader realized the danger of leaving Eva's body readily accessible in the capital – a rallying point for any future Peronist revival – and ordered it to be removed, secretly.

In December, Eva's corpse vanished. It was to remain missing for 16 years.

On the night that the body was stolen, Dr Ara was visiting Room 63 to make one of his regular inspections of the corpse. He heard the sound of heavy boots clumping up the main stairway. The door burst open and Colonel Carlos Mori-Koenig, head of the army's intelligence service, strode into the room, a platoon of soldiers at his heels.

'I have come for the body,' he said. And, ignoring Dr Ara's protests, he ordered his men to lift Eva from her flag-draped bier, place her in a plain wooden coffin and carry her out to a waiting army truck. The only explanation Dr Ara was given was that the body was to get 'a decent burial'. The truck started up and vanished into the night.

News of the body-snatching soon leaked out and the outlawed Peronists ran riot. Pictures of Eva and slogans demanding the return of the body appeared across the country. But General Aramburu remained silent. Rumours were spread that Juan Peron had arranged for the body to be stolen. But however much the military leaders of Argentina tried to repress the Peronists, their outcry over the missing Santa Evita grew even stronger.

To the *descamisados*, the theft was the crime of the century – a crime that could never be forgiven. It remained a source of grievance throughout the next 16 years, during which the body's whereabouts remained a mystery to the people of Argentina, and to Peron.

Much of the story is still a mystery today. What is known is that, after the army truck drove off from the Confederation of Labour building that night in December 1955, General Aramburu, concerned about public reaction, abandoned his plans to have the corpse destroyed.

Colonel Mori-Koenig ordered the truck to be driven to a quiet corner of a military barracks, where it remained throughout the rest of the night while he awaited further instructions. The colonel would have been happy to dispose of the body in any way his leaders demanded, for he had good reason to hate the Perons – as president, Peron had once demoted him after an argument. However, the order to destroy the body was never given. The colonel was simply told to hide it.

Eva's body was sealed in a packing case and moved to a warehouse close to military intelligence headquarters. It remained there for a month until, in January 1956, the crate was shuttled between half a dozen warehouses and

The remains of Eva Perón drawn through the streets on a gun carriage.

offices around Buenos Aires. It ended up at the smart apartment of Mori-Koenig's deputy, Major Antonio Arandia.

At this time, Peronist agents were still scouring the capital for Eva. Afraid that the trail might lead to him, Arandia took to sleeping with his revolver under his pillow.

One morning, just before dawn, Arandia awoke in a sweat. He listened terrified as footsteps approached his bedroom door. When it opened, he whipped his revolver from beneath the pillow and fired twice at the shadow framed in the doorway. His pregnant wife, who had just visited the bathroom, fell dead on the carpet.

Eva's body was then moved to the fourth floor of Mori-Koenig's intelligence headquarters. Her packing case was stamped 'radio sets' and stacked along with several others – all identical.

A few months later, the colonel was replaced as intelligence chief by the president's own head of secret service, Colonel Hector Cabanillas, who was horrified to discover the body still hidden in the HQ. He ordered it to be removed.

No one knows who personally organized the next moves in the macabre itinerary. But several identical coffins were made and weighted with ballast. The coffins, plus the packing case containing Eva, were transported to various parts of South America and further afield.

The coffins were all immediately buried, but Eva's packing case was shipped to Brussels, then taken by train to Bonn. There, unknown to the Argentinian Ambassador, it was stored in a cellar with his old files.

During September or October of 1956 the body was placed in a coffin and moved again, first to Rome and then to Milan. For the last stage of the journey it was accompanied by a lay sister of the Society of St Paul. She had been told that the body was that of an Italian widow, Maria Maggi de Magistris, who had died in Rosario, Argentina.

It was under this name that Eva was buried in Lot 86 of the Mussocco Cemetery, Milan. There she remained, her whereabouts known to only a handful of people, for 15 years.

During those years, a succession of military juntas in Argentina stumbled from one economic crisis to another. Eventually, the head of one junta, Lieutenant-General Alexjandro Lanusse, decided to invite the aging Juan Peron back to his homeland, despite the fact that Peron had personally ordered him sentenced to life imprisonment 20 years earlier. But first Lanusse arranged to return to Peron the body of his wife.

On 2 September 1971, a man who claimed to be Carlos Maggi watched as the coffin of his 'sister' was exhumed from its Milan grave and loaded on to a hearse for a 500-mile journey to Madrid. Carlos was in fact Hector Cabanillas, the now-retired intelligence chief.

The hearse spent one night in a garage at Perpignan, France, and arrived at Peron's home in Madrid the following day. Waiting there were Peron, now 74, his new 39-year-old wife, Isabel, whom he had met in a Panamanian night-club, and Dr Ara. The coffin of Eva was set down in the lounge and the lid prised open by Cabanillas.

Peron burst into tears as he saw the face of his long-dead wife, her blonde hair in disarray but otherwise seemingly as tranquil and beautiful as he remembered her two decades earlier. 'She is not dead,' he said. 'She is only sleeping.'

In 1972, Peron's long exile came to an end. He was allowed back home to Argentina. But he chose to leave the body of Eva behind in Madrid. The following year he was again elected president, with Isabel as vice-president. But his rule was short. On 1 July 1974, he died.

Isabel became president and ordered Eva's body to be flown home from Spain. Thousands of weeping Argentinians lined the route from the airport to throw flowers at the hearse containing their beloved Santa Evita. Her body was again laid in state, this time beside the coffin of Juan Peron, at the presidential palace at Olivos. Isabel mourned for both of them, trying to turn the reflected glory of Eva on to herself.

Isabel clung to power for two years before being ousted by yet another military junta. And the new leaders tried to erase the name of Peron from the history books.

Though Peron had been buried soon after his lying in state, Eva's body had been placed in storage again. The nation's leaders had been unable to agree on a final resting place for her. It was not until October 1976 that the new junta decided on a permanent burial place: Eva's still-beautiful body was placed in a tomb 15 feet underground in a private section of Recoleta Cemetery, Buenos Aires.

The tomb was built stronger than a bank vault – to discourage anyone from ever again trying to remove the body of Eva Peron.

Murder on Aconcagua

John Cooper and Jeanette Johnson tried to do the impossible – climb South America's highest mountain during the worst month of the year. But they never made it to the top of Mount Aconcagua, Argentina. Their adventure was cut short by murder, a brutal and vicious crime that has baffled authorities for almost ten years.

The macabre mystery began in the summer of 1972. It was then that eight climbers first got together to discuss scaling the 22,840-foot mountain. There was lawyer Carnie DeFoe, the group leader; John Shelton, a doctor; James Petroske, a psychologist; William Eubank, a geologist; William Zeller, a policeman; Arnold McMillen, a farmer; Jeanette Johnson, a teacher, and John Cooper, an engineer. They chose January 1973 as their starting date.

When the group arrived in the tiny town of Mendoza in the Andes, local experts and other mountaineers warned that January was a bad time of year to consider climbing Aconcagua. The expedition brushed their fears aside. But they agreed to hire local climber Miguel Angel Alfonso as a guide. Miguel told them to wait for better weather, but they were determined to begin as soon as possible, and on a freezing morning the party set out.

At first the climbing was easy but as the going became harder several of the group found they were not equal to the challenge. The first to drop out of the running were DeFoe and Shelton. They found that the combination of icy conditions coupled with a driving wind was too much. They urged the others to give up but to no avail.

Soon Eubank succumbed to the strain and dropped out. Alfonso takes up the story . . .

'From 5,700 metres there were only six of us left. By 6,300 metres Petroske was showing signs of mountain sickness. He was looking very weak and seemed to have lost control of his limbs. Whatever we did he did not seem to improve, and after a discussion, we agreed that he should be taken back to our base camp, several hundred metres below. They asked me to accompany him and in the end I agreed.'

Preparations were made and the guide left for the base camp – leaving behind Zeller, McMillen, Cooper and Johnson.

'That was the last time I saw Jeanette and Cooper alive,' Alfonso said. 'I went back to the camp with Petroske. The others told me they were going to carry on.

'Three days later I was in base camp, with a terrible storm blowing. I looked out of my cabin window and saw figures in the distance.

'I left the cabin intending to help the others. But the weather forced me back. The next day I went out again and managed to reach them. I was staggered to find only Zeller and McMillen. I had assumed the party had turned back and Johnson and Cooper should have been with them.

'Both men were in an awful state. Zeller had become blind because of frostbite, and McMillen was bleeding heavily around his face, also because of frostbite.

'Both were totally disoriented and incoherent. They were muttering and shouting: 'Cooper is sitting where the paved road gets near the trees.' 'Jeanette has been taken away by those women who came on mules'.

'I took them back to the camp, where Petroske questioned them in his tent. I don't know what was said. None of them would tell me.'

Later that year an Argentine expedition recovered the grisly remains of John Cooper. His face was pitted and scarred from the ravages of frostbite. His body was taken back to Mendoza and there doctors found a curious wound, probably caused by an ice pick, in his stomach. But they also found multiple fractures of the skull and it was those fractures that caused his death. An inquest called it murder.

Two years later another party of climbers came across Jeanette's corpse perfectly preserved by the ice. She had been brutally battered. Once again, the police decided it was murder.

No one has since been able to find the reason for the deaths. It seems the secret of the cruel killings will be kept by the massive mountain forever.

A Peer's Great Gamble

When Veronica, Lady Lucan, ran hysterical and bloodstained from her home in Lower Belgrave Street, Belgravia, London, on the night of 7 November 1974, her frantic cries for help sparked off one of the most baffling unsolved murder mysteries of the age.

Lying behind her in the elegant town house, just a stone's throw from Buckingham Palace, was the body of her children's nanny Sandra Rivett, aged 29, brutally battered to death, her body thrust into a canvas sack.

Lady Lucan reached the door of the crowded saloon bar of the nearby pub, The Plumbers Arms, and sobbed: 'Help me. Help me, I've just escaped from a murderer.'

Sandra Rivett

And the tale she told from her hospital bed to detectives a few hours later set them on the fruitless search to find her husband, John Bingham, the 7th Earl of Lucan. With bruising on her face and severe lacerations to her scalp, Lady Lucan, 26, told how she had tackled a tall, powerful maniac bent on murder.

She recalled how she had been spending a quiet evening at home with her two children – with the unexpected company of nanny Sandra who had originally been given the evening off to spend with her boyfriend. Sandra, who doted on Lady Lucan's children, had decided instead to stay in the house, in her own quarters.

Around 21.00 Sandra had popped her head round the door of Lady Lucan's lounge and offered to make a cup of tea for the family. Half an hour later when the nanny had not re-appeared, Lady Lucan walked down two floors to the kitchen, puzzled by the delay.

There she saw the shadowy figure of a man, crouched over the dead body of the nanny, bundling her lifeless form into a canvas sack.

As soon as Lady Lucan screamed, the man attacked her, beating her badly. She could not recognize the figure in the darkness, but as she struggled free and ran upstairs, she heard what she said was the unmistakable voice of her estranged husband call out after her.

Moments later, as she lay trembling on her bed, her husband was at her side, trying to comfort her. And when Lady Lucan ran from the house for help, her husband slipped away into the night.

A massive hunt immediately began for Lord Lucan. Police first checked his rented flat only a few streets away, where he had moved the previous year when he had separated from Lady Lucan and started divorce proceedings. But by that time, barely two hours after the murder, Lord Lucan had already turned up at a friend's house 72 km (45 miles) from the scene of the crime, driving a borrowed car.

There the socialite peer, a man-about-town and professional gambler, told one of his closest family friends his own version of the horror of the nanny's murder. He claimed he had been walking past his wife's home on his way to his own flat to change for dinner at one of his fashionable gambling clubs and saw through the venetian blinds of the basement kitchen what looked like a man attacking Lady Lucan.

'I let myself in with my own key and rushed down to protect her,' Lucan told his friend. 'I slipped on a pool of blood and the attacker ran off. My wife was hysterical and accusing me of being her attacker.'

Despite his denial, Lord Lucan never stayed around to confirm his version of events to the police – or to anyone else. The day after the murder, his car, which carried a portion of the same lead pipe which had been used to kill

Lord and Lady Lucan

Sandra Rivett, was found abandoned at Newhaven, Sussex, a port with a regular ferry service to France.

Police began a thorough check of Lucan's aristocratic friends in England, suspecting that wealthy socialites might be shielding him. But all lines of inquiry petered out.

A year later the coroner's inquest into the death of the nanny weighed up all the evidence and took the unusual step of officially recording her death as murder – and naming Lord Lucan as the man who had committed the murder. English law was changed shortly after that judgement to ensure that never again could anyone be named as a murderer until they were found, charged, tried and found guilty under normal criminal procedure.

Seven years after the murder, when Lucan had vanished without touching any of his bank accounts, without surrendering himself, and still undiscovered by any of the police searches which spread from Africa to America, the fugitive peer was declared legally dead.

The two policemen who led the search have both retired from Scotland Yard, still arguing about the unsolved crime. Superintendent Roy Ransom, who studied every single statement and grilled scores of witnesses, maintained: 'He killed the nanny by mistake, thinking he could dispose of his wife and get the custody of the children he loved. When he realized the error, he killed himself in some remote spot, like a lord and a gentleman.'

But Superintendent Dave Gerring, who supervised the same murder hunt, concluded: 'Lucan is still in hiding somewhere and he is the only man who knows the full story. He is a lord and a gentleman, but he is still a gambler. And he is still gambling on the odds that no one will ever find him.'

Suspect Deceased

The finger of suspicion pointed unwaveringly at Graham Sturley. He was the classic murder suspect. The 37-year-old former private detective had certainly studied case histories of people who had vanished and never been seen alive again. And when Linda, his own wife, went missing, Sturley had the know-how, the motive and the opportunity to have murdered her.

METROPOLITAN POLICE
Appeal for Assistance

AP/23A/82

MISSING

Mrs Linda Jacqueline STURLEY, 5'4" tall with shoulder length, fair hair and aged 29, left her home in Main Road, Biggin Hill, Kent, between 9pm on Friday 17 July and Saturday 18 July, 1981.

She was 6 months pregnant. She was last seen wearing a blue maternity dress.

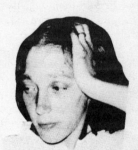

DO YOU KNOW HER?
HAVE YOU SEEN HER RECENTLY?
DO YOU HAVE ANY OTHER INFORMATION?

Please contact the Police at
CATFORD POLICE STATION
Tel: 01-697 9502

All information treated as strictly confidential

The detectives who first called at his home in Biggin Hill, Kent, were quickly convinced that Sturley, earning a living as a property developer, had killed his petite, unfaithful 29-year-old wife. He openly admitted to them his hatred for her flaunted love affairs with other men.

But the police began their investigation with one great disadvantage. Linda Sturley had been missing for 12 months by the time her worried mother, Mrs Ada Webb, walked into her local police station and reported her daughter's disappearance. She had been stalled long enough by assurances from son-in-law Sturley that, although Linda had left home, she had been in touch with him by telephone.

When the police arrived on the doorstep of Sturley's neat suburban bungalow he told them frankly: 'Yes, she's gone and I don't expect to see her again. I don't know where she is and I'm glad to get rid of her.'

Then the detectives began to piece together the facts.

Linda Sturley had last been seen at her home in July 1981, when her sister visited her. Tearfully Linda, who was six months pregnant, confessed that her husband had beaten her and punched her in the stomach during a violent argument the night before, when he raged that one of her lovers was the father of the child she was expecting.

The next day Linda, a pretty and vivacious sales representative for the Avon cosmetics company, vanished.

The Sturleys' home

Graham Sturley

With an air of finality, Sturley had told his two children, a six-year-old girl and a four-year-old boy, that their mother would never be returning. Neighbours noticed that Sturley had a garden bonfire, burning a complete wardrobe of his wife's clothes. And for the next year, until July 1982, Sturley lived as if Linda had simply gone away.

He even telephoned his wife's family to reassure them that Linda was still well, at the same time as someone with a detailed knowledge of the missing woman's bank passbooks had forged her signature to take everything out of her savings accounts and cash cheques for her maternity benefit payments.

Linda Sturley's family doctor revealed that the missing woman would need to give birth to her baby by Caesarian operation. Government health officials checked the records of every maternity hospital and clinic in Britain and no patient answering her description had been admitted.

And the police discovered that her jealous husband had even used the techniques of his former detective agency to tap his own telephone and record conversations between Linda and her lovers.

'We know your wife had a string of lovers and she was a bad wife,' one policeman told Sturley sympathetically. 'And we understand that sometimes pressure like that can drive a man to murder.'

But Sturley, who had a history of poor health and heart ailments, never faltered once during long sessions of police interrogation. 'You think I have buried her in the garden,' he accused bitterly. 'Well I wouldn't have been so silly, that would have poisoned the flowers.'

It was only a matter of time, police thought, before they found Linda Sturley's body and broke through her husband's brooding, angry defiance to gain a confession.

Sturley, unshakeably refusing to admit any part in his wife's disappearance, told them: 'She had walked out on me so many times in the past I didn't bother to report her as a missing person. I'm glad she's gone, I never want to see her again.'

When intense publicity in national newspapers and on TV and radio failed to bring any response from the missing woman, the search began in earnest for Linda Sturley's body.

The floorboards were ripped up in the living room of Sturley's house and the brickwork of walls probed for hidden cavities. Infra-red and heat-seeking detection equipment was used to scan the gardens around the house and tracker teams with dogs combed the surrounding woodland and parks. Police divers plunged into lakes, streams and ponds and forensic experts were sent to examine the bones of a woman's body unearthed in a forest 48 km (30 miles) away. But there was still no sign of Linda Sturley, dead or alive.

In a series of thorough interrogations Graham Sturley taunted the police, mocking their failure at every attempt to discover the fate of his wife. Detectives, aware of his history of heart trouble, handled him with kid gloves, probing and questioning as toughly as they dared.

After three months of intensive investigation, the head of the murder inquiry squad, Detective Chief Inspector George Cressy, examined all the circumstantial evidence and decided he had enough to recommend arresting Graham Sturley and charging him with the murder of his wife.

As police legal experts began preparing the case for his arrest, confident of their prosecution and eventual conviction, Graham Sturley died of a heart attack. The murder inquiry on Linda Sturley was closed, the case file marked 'Suspect deceased'.

Graham Sturley's lawyer revealed later: 'A will was left by Mr Sturley disposing of his assests, but there was nothing dramatic in it one way or another, no confessions, no admissions.'

The Kent detectives saw no useful purpose to be served by their presence a week later at Sturley's cremation after a ceremony in the quiet chapel in Honor Oak, London.

They never saw the strange final tribute that was laid on his coffin – a wreath with the message: 'Well you got that out of the way, Sturley. All my love...'

The Disappearance of Goodtime Joe

With a leggy showgirl on his arm, Judge Joseph Crater stepped out of a plush nightclub on New York's 45th Street and hailed a taxi. He gave his companion an affectionate squeeze and a kiss on the cheek. 'See you tomorrow, Ruby,' said the judge, whose unorthodox social life had earned him the nickname Goodtime Joe. But he didn't. A little later, he was seen buying a theatre ticket for the Broadway hit, *Dancing Partners*.

From that moment, on 6 August 1930, Judge Joseph Crater vanished, and it happened so mysteriously and in such politically-scandalous circumstances that in America 'pulling a Crater' is still used to describe a baffling disappearance. In New York, he is still officially listed as missing, although he would now be 93 years old, and the police department still checks regular reports of sightings.

Judge Crater was a sentimental family man – and a womanizer on a grand scale. He was a pillar of society, yet he enjoyed the company of rogues. He believed fervently in the sanctity of the law but became part of the most corrupt administration in New York's history. He had been a brilliant professor of law at New York University, but he wanted to be rich. As a lawyer with an obvious interest in making money, he was welcomed by the city's then-shady administration. In the summer of 1929 he acted as a receiver when the bankrupt Libby Hotel was sold to a finance company for $75,000. Six weeks later, the hotel was resold to the city of New York to be demolished in a road widening scheme. The price: $2,800,000. Many members of the administration, including Crater, made a lot of money from the deal.

By 1930, he had the life-style of a very rich man. More good fortune came his way when Franklin D. Roosevelt, then Governor of New York State, made him a justice of the city's Supreme Court. Crater had finally made it. He was rich and powerful. Then, on the evening of 2 August, something happened to threaten his cosy world.

He was on holiday with his wife at their summer cottage in Maine when he received a mysterious phone call. It was enough to send the judge hurrying back to New York. 'I've got to straighten some fellows out,' was all he told his wife, promising to return for her birthday a week later. She never saw him again.

In New York on 6 August he wrote two cheques for a total of $4,100 and sent his assistant, Joe Mara, to the bank to cash them. When Mara returned, Crater had stuffed papers from his office files into four large portfolios and two briefcases. He told Mara he was going 'up Westchester way for a few days'.

That evening, however, he turned up at his favourite nightclub on 45th Street, but after a few drinks with showgirl Ruby Ritz he left, saying he was going to the theatre.

Amazingly, it was four weeks and a day before the disappearance of one of the city's top judges finally leaked out. Friends and enemies alike, terrified at the idea of a scandal which might implicate them, were desperate to hush up the affair. Manhattan District Attorney, Thomas Crain, was anxious to question Mrs Crater. She refused to talk and the judge's politically-powerful friends kept Crain at bay.

Soon, reports of alleged sightings were coming in from around the world.

In 1955 a photograph of Crater was shown to the Dutch clairvoyant Gerard Croiset. He claimed that the judge had been murdered on the first floor of a farmhouse near the Bronx, New York, and his body buried in the garden.

Remarkably, there was just such a house in the area, which in Crater's day had been used by city officials for secret meetings with their girlfriends. Investigators discovered that the late owner, Henry Krauss, had once claimed that on the morning of 10 August 1930, he had found the kitchen covered with blood ... But of a body there was no sign.

Death at the Opera House

Snow swirled silently through the deserted streets and only the footprints of an occasional policeman or passer-by marred its crisp whiteness. It was Christmas in Toronto. But while most people were surrounded by joy, and laughter and goodwill, one woman remained alone, surrounded by silence and suspicion. Three weeks before Christmas Day 1919, Theresa Small's husband had mysteriously disappeared – and there were rumours of murder.

In a few years Ambrose Small, ruthless and mean, had made a fortune out of property. His most important possession was Toronto Grand Opera House. He had started there as an usher. Then he became treasurer. In the end he owned it. He was a millionaire before he was 40 and owned theatres throughout Canada.

At 56 he decided to sell his theatrical empire. A deal was fixed with a financier from Montreal and on 2 December 1919, Small and his wife met him at his lawyers in Toronto. The financier gave Small a cheque for $1,000,000 as down-payment and Small gave the cheque to his wife, who deposited it in his account. The Smalls then went to lunch with their solicitor.

Afterwards Mrs Small went home alone in her chauffeur-driven car while her husband went back to the opera house. He had arranged to meet his solicitor there at 16.00. He was seen entering the theatre. But nobody saw him leave.

His solicitor said later that he had stayed with Small and his secretary, John Doughty, for an hour and a half. Small, he said, was still at the opera house when he left at 17.30.

Doughty left the theatre to have supper with his sister. Later he said he had to go to Montreal and was driven to the station by his sister's husband. On the way they stopped at the opera house, where Doughty collected a small brown paper parcel. He gave this to a second sister in the car and asked her to look after it. Doughty caught the Montreal train – and it was to be two years before he would be back in Toronto.

Small failed to come home that night, so Theresa assumed he had gone to Montreal with Doughty. She waited and waited. But there was no sign of her husband.

It was the opera house manager, however, who raised the alarm. Police issued Small's description – and at once there was a sensational development. Found pinned to the door of a Toronto church was a card which read: 'Prayers for the soul of Ambrose Small.'

The search for a missing man had now become a hunt for a possible murderer. Suspicion fell first on Theresa Small. She was of German extraction, and Germans were far from popular just after World War 1.

Doughty, too, fell under suspicion. But where was he? The police announced rewards of $50,000 for the discovery of Small dead or alive and $15,000 for Doughty.

In the summer of 1920 police obtained a court order to open the strongbox at Small's bank. From their inquiries they expected to find a fortune inside. But bonds worth $105,000 were missing – and the last recorded visitor to Small's safety vaults had been John Doughty. Police investigations intensified. A boilerman at the opera house said that there had been a fight between Small and Doughty on the night Small was last seen alive. Officers raked out the boilers at the opera house looking for human remains.

Then a year later Doughty was discovered working in a lumber camp in Oregon. He was taken back to Toronto and the missing bonds were found in the attic of his sister's house. The police, convinced that they had a murder charge on their hands, confronted Doughty with the alleged fight in the opera house. He vehemently denied it and he was eventually charged with theft.

Doughty said he had taken the bonds from the bank on 2 December to use as a lever against Small who had promised him a share in the theatre deal. But he said he had panicked and fled across the border when he heard of Small's disappearance. Doughty was found guilty of theft and jailed for five years in March 1921.

Yet still there was no sign of Small. Police dug up the floors of his wife's house, but found nothing. Rumours persisted that he had been murdered by racketeers but again widespread searches revealed nothing.

Small was officially declared dead in 1924. Twenty years later the opera house was demolished and detectives made one last effort to solve the case. Again nothing.

To this day what happened to Ambrose Small remains as much a mystery as it was when he vanished off the face of the earth in 1919.

The Impossible *is* Possible

Neither the woman nor her 13-year-old daughter heard the alarm clock ring at 04.00 in the adjoining bedroom. Nor did they hear the soft 'phut' of the silenced gun. If they had, one of America's most baffling murder mysteries might have yielded a clue, however tiny.

Respectable family man Roy Orsini was dead, face-down in his pyjamas, shot in the back of the head by a .38 bullet fired at close range.

On the morning of 12 March 1981, veteran homicide detective Sergeant Tom Farley realized he had the 'impossible' crime on his hands. Orsini had been shot in his bedroom, with the door and windows locked from the inside. He could not possibly have committed suicide.

Orsini, a 38-year-old heating engineer, was a model husband and father. He lived with his wife, Lee, and schoolgirl daughter, Tiffany, in a pleasant suburb at North Little Rock, Arkansas. As far as anyone knew, he hadn't an enemy in the world.

Orsini went to bed early on 11 March to prepare for an early appointment with a client 96 km (60 miles) out of town. He set the alarm for 04.00 to beat the morning traffic jams.

Orsini always slept alone on such nights so that his early rising would not wake the household. The family would sleep in Tiffany's room, next to his own. Soon after 21.00 he kissed them both goodnight and went upstairs to the main bedroom. It was the last time they saw him alive.

Next morning Mrs Orsini rose at 07.00. She and Tiffany had breakfast and walked to the daughter's school nearby. Back home, she began her housework. When her downstairs work finished, she went upstairs to do the bedrooms, starting with her husband's. It was closed, not like Roy at all, she thought. Normally, when he was making an early start, he left the door wide open, and left the room in a bit of a mess.

She tried the handle. The door was locked from the inside. That door had never been locked since they moved in before Tiffany was born 13 years ago. Had he somehow slept in? Had he been taken ill? Again and again, she twisted the handle of the door, knocked and called: 'Roy, Roy, are you all right?'

There was no reply. Lee Orsini, by this time thoroughly alarmed, dashed out of the house and frantically called on next door neighbour Mrs Glenda

Bell. Together the two women managed to prise open the bedroom door. Lee Orsini uttered a piercing scream. Her husband still in his striped pyjamas, lay on the bed.

Sergeant Farley and his squad were on the scene within minutes of receiving Mrs Bell's telephone call. They quickly established that, like many Americans, Roy Orsini had a gun. But it was in a closed drawer several feet from the bed and, although it was a .38, the same calibre as the weapon which had been used to kill him, it was a Smith and Wesson. The fatal bullet had been fired from a Colt. It would anyway have been impossible for Orsini to shoot himself in the back of the head, replace the gun in the drawer and then go back to the bed.

Then there was the problem of the door and windows, all of which had been securely locked from the inside. The alarm clock had been set for 04.00 and had run down. Had the death shot been fired before or after this? There was no means of knowing.

Neither Mrs Orsini nor Tiffany had heard the shot, so the .38 must have been fitted with a silencer.

Farley ordered detailed inquiries into every known relative or business contact of Orsini. A similar discreet check was made on his wife. Both had led totally blameless lives and had been devoted to each other and their daughter. There was nobody who could have had a motive for murder.

Farley said: 'I've been involved with many homicides, but never anything like this. Any way you look at it, it belongs in a book, not in real life.'

A Riddle in Life and a Riddle in Death

One sweltering lunchtime in July, Jimmy Hoffa kissed his wife Josephine, promised to be home by four, and drove away in a bullet-proof limousine.

He was on his way to a lunch date. But how far he got towards keeping his appointment no one knows. For after leaving his luxury home on the outskirts of Detroit at 12.30 on 30 July 1975, Jimmy Hoffa, America's most notorious union boss, was never seen again.

A few hours later an anonymous gravel-voiced phone caller told the police where they could find Hoffa's abandoned car. It sounded more like an

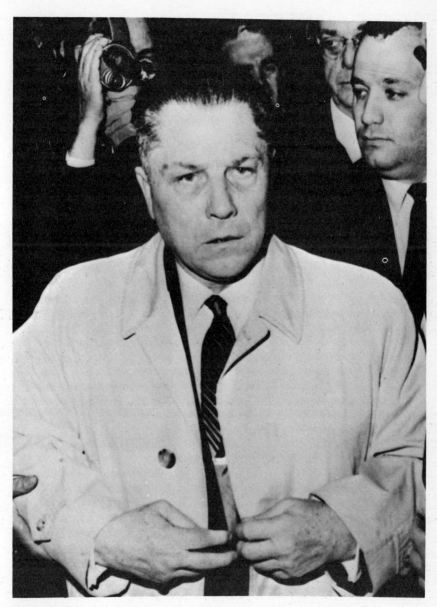

Frank Hoffa

epitaph than a tip-off. They found it shining in the sun, with no sign of a struggle and no body. Just a pair of white gloves neatly folded on the back seat.

There were three main theories about the disappearance of James – middle name Riddle – Hoffa, former president of the Teamsters Union.

The first suggestion was that he was eliminated by the Mafia who feared he would expose illegal 'loans' made by the Teamsters to underworld figures. The second theory was that he died because of a battle for power within the union. The third – and most intriguing – theory was that, knowing there was a contract on his life, he chose to disappear of his own free will. Just two days earlier he had withdrawn more than a million dollars from union funds. Like Hoffa, the money never came back to its rightful home.

His distraught family offered a $200,000 reward for information which might lead to the finding of his body, dead or alive. But there were no takers.

If there were violent and sinister overtones to the disappearance, no one should have been surprised. For this had been the pattern of Hoffa's life almost from the very beginning. As a teenager, he got a job loading trucks and, at 17, he organized his first strike. As a union leader, he favoured lieutenants who had criminal records. Many were chosen for their expertise in terror and extortion. Nevertheless, Hoffa became a hero to many of the Teamsters who had seen their wages virtually doubled in the space of a decade. He also poured millions of dollars into his own pockets and then bought a Miami bank to look after his wealth.

When the crusading Robert Kennedy was made chairman of the Senate Rackets Committee, Hoffa became his prime and very personal target. He described Hoffa's leadership of the Teamsters as a 'conspiracy of evil'. As a result of this probe initiated by Kennedy, Hoffa was eventually jailed in 1967, sentenced to serve 13 years for jury tampering and defrauding the union's pension fund to the tune of almost two million dollars.

Hoffa decreed that Frank Fitzsimmons, a long-time ally, should take his place as president on the strict understanding that he was simply holding down the job until Hoffa regained his freedom.

In 1971, Hoffa was pardoned by President Nixon on condition that he should hold no union office until 1980. But he still had a taste for power, and so began a campaign to persuade the appeal court to lift Nixon's ban.

Fitzsimmons, however, had no intention of relinquishing the reins. Detroit became a battleground as the Fitzsimmons and Hoffa factions fought for supremacy.

This, then, was the background against which Jimmy Hoffa disappeared. It seems probable that the lunch meeting never actually took place. A Hoffa aide received a phone call, supposedly from Hoffa, saying that his companions had not turned up.

But had someone set up the lunch with the intention of luring Hoffa into a trap and then abducting him at gunpoint? This was the theory the FBI favoured.

The FBI also investigated the story of Charles Allen, a former crook turned informer, who became friendly with Hoffa when they were in prison together. Allen claimed that Hoffa was beaten to death by a contract killer known as 'Monster Man' who was 2 m (6 ft 4 in) and weighed 108 kg (17 stone). The body, said Allen, was then taken to New Jersey, cut into small pieces, hidden in two oildrums, and flown to Florida.

The police, unable to verify the story, replaced the Hoffa file in the 'unsolved' category. James Riddle Hoffa was well named.

The Mysterious Mummy

A 'wax' mummy hung in an old amusement park funhouse for 50 years until a strange event revealed its horrible secret – that underneath the ghastly bandages was the embalmed body of an outlaw killed in a turn-of-the-century shootout.

The grim reality surfaced in December 1976, when a television production crew visited the old house to shoot an episode of the TV series *The Six-Million Dollar Man*. Filming was under way when one of the crew gave out a shrill scream ... One of the mummy's stick-like arms had snapped off and fallen. Where it had shattered were leathery shreds of skin and horrible clumps of human tissue clinging to the human bone.

The mummy was rushed to an autopsy room in the Los Angeles county morgue and history's strangest manhunt began. Under the many layers of wax, Los Angeles coroner Dr Thomas Noguchi found the withered body of a man. He had died long ago in his early 30s from a gunshot wound. The corpse had then been carefully embalmed with such heavy concentrations of arsenic that it had turned into a virtual mummy.

The thing had been on display in the Long Beach, California, funhouse since the 1920s, when it was brought from a bankrupt carnival operator. The time lapse meant that the police had little chance of solving the mystery. They feared that the mummy was the victim of a crime. But the only theory that anyone could come up with was stranger even than that. For it was suggested the mummy might have been a criminal himself!

The incredible story put forward by a former employee of the funhouse was that underneath the wax coating was the corpse of an Oklahoma outlaw named Elmer McCurdy.

Oklahoma authorities confirmed that there had been an Elmer McCurdy operating in the wild Oklahoma Territory in the early 1900s. He specialized in robbing trains and banks. After a Jesse James-type robbery in October 1911, McCurdy escaped to an outlaw hangout on the Big Caney River. When a posse from Pawhuska tracked him down, he died in the shootout.

But who would pick up the bill for embalming a footloose outlaw? The undertaker saw only one way to get his money: An embalmed Elmer stood in the corner of the funeral parlour where visitors could gape at him for a nickel apiece. He then fell into the hands of the travelling carnival man who sold him to the amusement park.

Fact or fiction? No one can be sure. The only question worrying Los Angeles county was what to do with the body. The answer was supplied by the Oklahoma Territorial Museum in Guthrie. The outlaw was returned to Oklahoma on 14 April 1977, and in an elegant old hearse pulled by a team of horses, Elmer was buried in the town's Boot Hill cemetery.

The Prairie's Murder Inn

One of the most notorious women in frontier America, bloody Kate Bender, operated a 'murder inn' on the Kansas prairie. Travellers who stopped there for a night were never seen again. For the few dollars in their carpetbags, Kate hid behind a curtain and split the lodger's skulls with a hatchet while they were enjoying one of her home-cooked meals.

Suspicious authorities finally raided the inn, but by that time Kate herself had grown wary. Officials found no trace of the woman, though evidence of her handiwork was plentiful. Digging behind the inn, they unearthed a human boneyard. Few of her victims were identified and the number of dead remains unknown. Even more grisly was the suspicion that Kate had fed some of her victims the flesh of earlier ones.

The riddle of Kate Bender's eerie disappearance intrigued mystery-lovers everywhere. In the hectic little mining camp of Silver City, Idaho, old-timers in the mercantile store pondered it as they sat around the pot-bellied stove.

Kate Bender's home

When Joe Monahan came in for his weekly supplies, they tested their theories on him. Not much of a talker, the young man was always a good listener. When they suggested Kate might have entered a convent or might even be running another murder inn, he simply nodded and went on his way.

To the rest of Silver City, Joe himself was a riddle. A frail little man, he shunned the camp's roaring saloons and girls of the line. Joe's home was a dugout cut into a cliff on Succor Creek near Silver City. To raise the few dollars he spent in the store he kept chickens, pigs and six scrawny cows.

In December 1903, Joe drove his cattle to winter pasture on the Boise River. But the hardships of the trail were too much. Soon after his return to Succor Creek he fell ill and died. When his body was prepared for burial, the barber-mortician ran out of the back room, stunned and sick ...

Unbelievably, little Joe Monahan had been a woman.

The dugout was ransacked for any clues to her identity. All they found was a yellowed clipping from the *Kansas City Star* about the unsuccessful hunt for Kate Bender. Inevitably, the camp drew its own conclusions: in spite of 'Little Joe's' mild personality, had she been the ruthless killer?

To the day of the funeral there were rumours that a group of 'public minded citizens' meant to dig up the body and send it to Kansas for identification. The minister had heard the rumours too. On that windswept afternoon, he murmured a brief prayer for the unknown woman, then raised his eyes to the graveyard which was jammed with miners. 'I don't believe that this poor woman was a killer,' the minister said. 'Whatever her secret may have been, she died trying to protect it – and, in simple mercy, I ask that you let it die with her.'

The miners drifted away. There was a public subscription that evening in Silver City saloons to cover the burial costs. No one disturbed the unmarked grave. So the mystery lived on.

Who Did She Bury?

In the little coal mining town of McVey, Washington State, Nels Stenstrom and his wife Anna were among the most industrious merchants. Working side by side, they spent twelve hours of almost every day of the week in the McVey Mercantile Store – 'Where Everybody Finds Everything'.

Then a mysterious tragedy entered their lives. On 5 June 1895, Nels Stenstrom vanished without a trace. There were those who said the big man had a roving eye and might possibly have left with a woman. But no one wanted to carry that rumour to the steely-eyed Anna, who was devoted to her husband.

But Anna kept on running the store as if Nels were at her side, and it expanded and grew more prosperous.

In the summer of 1902, Stenstrom was declared legally dead. And that same day Anna made the strange announcement that was to reach newspapers throughout the US: Although he might only be legally dead, she said, he would have a proper grave.

With or without a body, she wanted a casket, a burial plot and fitting church services for her husband.

It was an idea so unusual that crowds of reporters and curious spectators poured into the little town. There was standing room only in the church when the funeral began at 14.30 on 1 July 1902. Nels had been a war veteran, and the vacant coffin was prominently displayed under a US flag. After a few words from the minister, old friends appeared at the lectern to eulogize the departed.

Anna was the last to speak. But she had scarcely started when there was sudden confusion in the crowd. A grizzled derelict in shreds of clothing staggered into an aisle whimpering and clutching his breast. Some said he looked imploringly into Anna's face before he collapsed, unconsious, to the floor.

She was the first to reach him and grope for a pulse. The tears were running down her cheeks when she raised her eyes. All she could say was 'It's Nels.'

The town's one doctor signed the death certificate, marvelling that this alcoholic wreck could be the once powerful Nels. Hundreds watched as the remains of the vagrant were borne to the Stenstrom burial plot.

But the story had an incredible sequel.

While the nearby towns of Roslyn and Cle Elum prospered, the veins of coal ran thin in McVey. It became a shabby ghost town. After Anna died and was buried with her husband, a contractor bought the store for its old lumber.

When he was bulldozing the building down, shallow graves were found beneath the floorboards. Two skeletons lay side by side. Between them was the axe that had split their skulls.

One was the skeleton of a woman destined to remain as nameless as the vagrant buried with Anna. The man's body was equally unidentifiable ... Could it have been the body of the real Nels Stenstrom?

The Lady with Broadcaster's Teeth

Among all the bizarre maladies which may afflict a human being, the prize for weird comedy must surely be awarded to the broadcaster's teeth possessed by a housewife of Daytona Beach, Florida.

The lady in question agreed to talk to reporters only if her name was witheld; the phenomenon was an acute embarrassment. For the purposes of this piece we will call her Mrs X – but should incredulous readers doubt the account, they may confirm it by consulting the *Ottawa Journal* of 9 April 1970.

Mrs X began to receive musical radio signals through her teeth on the night of 16 March 1970. Whenever she opened her mouth, her teeth transmitted songs which included *A Long Way to Tipperary* and *Rambling Rose*.

Understandably distressed, Mrs X sought medical advice.

Electronics experts declared that the music was being played by someone using a wireless phonograph to send signals from one part of his house to another. A dentist explained why her teeth were picking up the signals. It appeared that two metals such as gold and amalgam fillings could combine with the acid in human saliva to set up a receiving system – Mrs X's mouth.

The housewife placed an advertisement in a local newspaper urging that whoever had been playing the songs should identify himself. A flood of calls ensued, 'but nothing concrete'.

Dolphins Equipped to seek Loch Ness Monster

In the summer of 1982, the *New Scientist* announced that Duane Marshall of the Academy of Applied Science, Boston, had taken out British patent application No 2 084 335 to further a remarkable project. The inventor planned to use trained dolphins to secure photographs of the Loch Ness Monster.

A camera was to be strapped to the side of the dolphin, which would then be sent off to seek out its target. An ultrasonic transmitter and receiver on the camera mount would be rigged up to trigger a motorized camera and flash unit when it approached something big underwater.

To prevent the camera wasting film as the dolphin passed its control ship, the camera would be equipped with a pressure sensitive switch. This would render the entire photo system inoperable until the dolphin had dived to the target depth.

The exhausted Mrs X then moved out of her neighbourhood and took to sleeping in a motel, out of range of the wireless enthusiast, to get some peace. But this offered no long-term solution. Finally, Mrs X became desperate. One Wednesday in April she had all her fillings but one replaced by plastic. The remaining metal filling was left because it involved a root and might have to be pulled.

The music stopped for three days. 'I thought I was free and was ready to throw a party,' she said.

And then her teeth tuned up again. *Rambling Rose, Rambling Rose* . . .

The music was much weaker than before, but still present, humming away in the last metallic molar.

The newspaper account ends there, with the reporter speculating that so far as the lone tooth was concerned, Mrs X 'might yet be driven to extraction'. I do not know whether the maverick filling was silenced once and for all, or whether the wireless enthusiast was ever located. In fairness, he was clearly an unwitting persecutor. If the couple did meet, we can only hope that Mrs X forgave him – and had no hard fillings.

Unquiet Graves

In August 1982, the newspapers carried a macabre report from San Salvador, where the body of a man had been illegally exhumed by his own relatives. It appeared that a lottery ticket seller had arrived at the dead man's house to ask why he had not claimed his prize of $40,000. Further comment is hardly necessary – it is not hard to picture the frenzied excavations, the desperate scouring of pockets; but the ticket was not found.

Graves have often been disturbed over the centuries by occult practitioners, and body-snatching cases have made regular appearances in the press since the celebrated affair of Burke and Hare in 1828. William Burke was tried for participating in the murder of 16 victims, whose corpses were destined for the anatomist's table of a certain Dr Knox, who needed subjects for dissection. William Hare, Burke's accomplice in crime, was granted legal immunity for testifying against his companion.

The trial was a sensation, perhaps the first of the great 19th century crime block-busters, and the public were as ghoulish in their interest as any modern crowd. 'No trial that has taken place for a number of years past has excited such an unusual and intense interest,' recorded *The Times*. 'All the doors and passages to the court were besieged at an early hour before daylight, and it was with the greatest difficulty and the utmost exertions of a large body of police that admission could be procured for those who were concerned with the proceedings.'

No details were spared to readers, of the lugging of corpses and the doings to death, though reports were couched in the cumbersome language of the early 19th century courtroom. Of the death of Mary Paterson, for example, *The Times* faithfully recorded that Burke allegedly 'murdered Mary Paterson or Mitchell by placing or laying his body or person, or part thereof, over or upon the breast or person and face of Mary Paterson, when she was lying in the said house in a state of intoxication'. The prosecution then went on to charge him that 'by the pressure thereof, and by covering her mouth and nose with his body or person, and forcibly compressing her throat with his hands, and keeping her down, notwithstanding her resistance, did suffocate or strangle her'. It was by much the same method that one James Wilson 'commonly called Daft Jamie' was done to death.

William Burke was hanged in 1829, in front of 25,000 people in Edinburgh, and his infamous name has survived in the verb to 'burke' – meaning to smother or suppress. Hare, his accomplice, got off scot free.

A more haunting fear even than that of body-snatching, however, is the prospect of premature burial. In earlier ages, with less scrupulous medical practices than we enjoy today, the hazard of revival in coffin or grave was very real. During mass epidemics, especially, the bodies of the dead and dying were examined only cursorily if at all. Where Victorian graveyards have been opened up, clear evidence of premature burials has been revealed on a disturbing scale.

To counter quite justifiable fears of being buried alive, our forebears devised a number of ingenious contraptions. At the mid-19th century cemetery of Frankfurt-am-Main, for example, a room was set aside for corpses; strings were attached to the fingers of the bodies and these were connected to warning bells. A certain Count Karnice-Karnicki devised a graveyard apparatus which consisted of a $3\frac{1}{2}$ in tube, a sealed box, and a ball which lay on the chest of the deceased. At the slightest movement, a signal was set off above the ground, a door in the coffin sprang open and light and air were admitted.

As late as 1926, the *American Mercury* recorded that 'a telephone and electric lights have been stored in the mausoleum in which the body of Martin A. Sheets, stockbroker, was entombed. Sheets asked before his death that his tomb be so equipped that he might have opportunity to talk with the outside world if he should awaken in it.'

William Burke, bodysnatcher

The Burial Reformer was issued in Britain from 1905–14, specifically to press for improvement in burial customs. Renamed *The Perils of Premature Burial* shortly after its inception, the magazine exposed such cases as the Accrington Sensation of January 1905, when a certain Mrs Holden, aged 29, was laid out as dead and prepared for entombment; the undertaker noticed a slight movement while completing his task, and revived the woman, who survived.

The magazine published a limerick popular at the time of the controversy:

> *There was a young man at Nunhead*
> *Who awoke in a coffin of lead;*
> *'It is cosy enough,'*
> *He remarked in a huff,*
> *'But I wasn't aware I was dead.'*

Despite all the advances of medical science, cases of corpses coming to life on morticians' slabs have persisted to the present day. Indeed, the practice of transplanting organs from the bodies of the newly dead has awakened the controversy afresh. *The Times* of 28 February 1976, for example, reported that a surgeon at a Birmingham hospital had described a 'dead' patient walking out of hospital having been rejected as a potential kidney donor. The patient was a middle-aged woman: 'Checks by experts showed no brain activity,' the surgeon said. Transplant surgeons had refused her body. She nevertheless recovered, and the surgeon had last seen her at an out-patient clinic.

The macabre experience of being buried alive was granted to Michael Baucom, aged 20, in 1982. Baucom was kidnapped, forced into a coffin and then buried under a Texas oilfield near Santa Fé. For four days he lay there in his underground tomb, with a little water, bread and a tube to breathe through. His parents tried to pay a $75,000 ransom, but the kidnappers failed to turn up to collect the money. The police, however, tracked them down and freed the kidnap victim, who survived.

Stranger still was the case of a 36-year-old Los Angeles man. As reported in the *Sun* of 14 September 1982, he managed to commit suicide by living burial in his own back garden. 'He even tried to pull a concrete slab over himself,' said police, who found hallucinatory drugs in a bedroom at his home.

Frozen Upright
A man was found in the Fleet Ditch standing upright and frozen to death. He appears to have been a barber at Bromley, Kent; had come to town to see his children, and had, unfortunately, mistaken his way in the night, and slipt into a ditch; and being in liquor could not disentangle himself.
The Gentleman's Magazine, 11 January 1763

Disappearing Dorothy

Judge Jules Forstein telephoned his wife one October evening in 1950 to let her know he'd be delayed at a political banquet. 'I don't expect to be too late,' he said. 'Is everything all right?'

There was a reason for the question. The judge seldom left his wife and children alone because of an incident at the house five years earlier. But on this occasion Dorothy was cheerful and she assured her husband that everything was fine. 'Be sure to miss me,' she said.

Mrs Forstein had lived in a state of panic for five years, dating from the evening of 25 January 1945. That day, after leaving her two children with neighbours she had shopped briefly in a supermarket and then walked home alone to the three-storey house in a Philadelphia suburb. As she entered the house, someone leaped out of the small alcove under the front stairs and attacked her in the darkness. She had time to scream only once.

The police crashed through the front door of the Forstein home to find her lying in a pool of blood. She had a broken jaw, a broken nose, a fractured shoulder and concussion.

There was money and jewellery in the house, but nothing had been taken. The motive was murder, said police. The attacker had entered the house without leaving fingerprints or disturbing the locks on doors and windows. And there was no clue as to how he had left the house, either.

Judge Forstein had an unimpeachable alibi for the time of the attack. And Mrs Forstein had no known enemies. The intruder could have been an enemy of her husband's but months of investigation turned up no suspect.

Though there was a slow physical recovery, Dorothy Forstein never recovered emotionally from the beating. She made a frequent ritual of checking and rechecking the extra locks that had been put on doors and windows. She constantly sought the companionship of relatives and neighbours sometimes during parties she would retreat into deep silence.

But she was getting better, Judge Forstein reassured himself when he returned late from the banquet that evening five years after the attack.

Inside the dimly lit house, the first thing he heard were the screams of his two small children, Edward and Marcy. He found them huddled together in a bedroom, crying convulsively. 'It's mamma,' they told him. 'Something was here and took mamma away.'

Sick with fright, Forstein searched every room of the house. There were her purse, money and keys, but Dorothy Forstein was gone.

Through bursts of tears, Marcy told him what had happened. She had been awakened by terrifying sounds in the night and had run to her mother's bedroom. Through a crack in the door, she saw her mother lying face down on the rug with a shadowy figure crouching over her. 'She looked sick,' the little girl wept.

The intruder had then picked up her mother and thrown her over his shoulder with her head hanging down his back. He saw the child watching and said, 'Go back to sleep. Your mother has been sick, but she'll be all right now.' He went down the stairway carrying Dorothy Forstein, who was dressed only in red silk pyjamas.

When the police arrived, they confessed themselves baffled. There were no fingerprints anywhere, and it seemed incredible to them that any man balancing a woman on his shoulder could have left the house without grasping something for support. Why had no one tried to stop him when he walked down a busy street carrying an unconscious woman in pyjamas? And how did he get into the Forstein home through the multiple locks on the doors and windows?

The police checked every hospital in Philadelphia, as well as rooming houses, rest homes, hotels and the morgue. The search yielded no information about Dorothy.

Whoever had abducted the judge's wife had taken her away for ever. Dorothy Forstein left behind her only the haunting memory of her last words: 'Be sure to miss me.'

Mystery at Wolf's Neck

It was a bitterly cold evening in January 1931 when bus driver Cecil Johnstone saw a fire on a desolate moor at Wolf's Neck between Newcastle upon Tyne and Otterburn in Northumberland. He stopped to investigate. What he saw was almost unbelievable. On fire was the car owned by his boss's daughter, Evelyn Foster. Beside it lay Evelyn, badly burned but still alive.

Johnstone drove her to her home at Otterburn, where she told her parents and the police that she had been attacked by a man who had set fire to her car. She died the following day and left behind her one of the strangest crime stories of the decade. If indeed it was a crime at all ...

Evelyn Foster was 28 and the daughter of Mr J. J. Foster, who owned a garage at Otterburn. She had her own car, which she ran as a one-cab taxi business.

At 19.00 on 6 January 1931, she arrived home and told her mother that a man who had got out of a car at nearby Elishaw wanted her to drive him to Ponteland, near Newcastle, to catch the bus home. She said the man had looked respectable and gentlemanly when she picked him up at the Percy Arms Hotel.

The next time her mother saw her was when she was brought home dying of burns later that night by her father's bus driver, Johnson. And this is the story she told her mother and a doctor, nurse and policeman who had been called to the house ...

After she had driven through the village of Belsay, about 8 km (5 miles) from Ponteland, her passenger suddenly asked her to turn back. She had turned round and was driving back when the man hit her in the eye and took over the wheel. He stopped the car at the top of the hill at Wolf's Neck and started 'knocking her about'. He then put her into the back of the car and raped her.

The man then took a bottle or tin out of his pocket and threw something over her. She just 'went up in a blaze'. She then felt a bump as the car was going over rough ground. Evelyn told her mother: 'I was all alight. I do not know how I got out of the car. I lay on the ground and sucked the grass. I was thirsty.'

Her last words were said to have been: 'I have been murdered.' And it really looked as though she had been murdered – until doubts began to surface at the inquest.

To begin with, nobody other than Evelyn saw a stranger in the village that evening. Her father admitted that he had not seen the man. And the owners of the Percy Arms pub, where Evelyn was said to have picked him up, said that no stranger had been in the bar and they had heard no talk about a taxi to Ponteland.

The pathologist who conducted the post mortem on Evelyn, Professor Stuart McDonald, said there were no external injuries on the body apart from the burns. There was no trace or evidence of bruising of the face to suggest that she had been knocked about and there was 'no sign at all' that she had been raped.

Doubts were also cast on Evelyn's suggestion that she and the car had been set on fire before it was driven off the road on to the moor. There were signs of burned heather where the car was found just off the road – but no sign of burned heather by the side of the road itself.

In his summing up the coroner, Mr P. M. Dobbs, told the jury they could rule out suicide. The only two points they had to consider were: Was Evelyn Foster murdered? Or did she set fire to the car to obtain insurance money and set light to herself accidentally?

It took two hours for the jury to reach a verdict. It was: wilful murder on the part of some person or persons unknown.

Later, the police took the unprecedented step of declaring that, in their view, the 'murderer' did not exist. The Chief Constable of Northumberland, Captain Fullarton James, declared in a newspaper interview that the verdict of the inquest was against the weight of evidence and Evelyn Foster had not been murdered.

Gradually, the mystery of Wolf's Neck dropped out of the news – until just over three years later. At the beginning of 1934, a Yorkshire groom, Ernest Brown, was sentenced to death at Leeds Assizes for the murder of his lover's husband. In a 'confession' on the scaffold he is reported to have said either 'ought to burn' or 'Otterburn'. But he died seconds later.

Did Brown murder Evelyn Foster? Or did he know something about her death? The answer is unlikely ever to be known.

Did Robin Hood really exist?

Deep in the heart of Sherwood Forest in the early 14th century roamed an outlaw whose escapades have established him as the most enduring folk hero of his time. His name is known today throughout the world – Robin Hood. Stories of his heroic deeds are legion. But are they true? And did Robin even exist?

Some historians believe that the stories of the sprite-like hero may be connected with a mythological pagan woodland spirit. Robin was a name often given to fairies, and green, which the outlaw was supposed to have worn, is the traditional colour of wood spirits. There is also a theory that

Robin Hood was simply one of the characters in the ancient May Day ceremonies who over the years became changed in legend into a historical character. Maid Marion may also have been Queen of the May in the same
celebrations.

However, records do show that in the 13th and 14th centuries a man
named Robin Hood lived in Wakefield, Yorkshire, and may have been the
outlaw of romantic legend. Robin (christened Robert) Hood was born in
about 1290. His father, Adam Hood, was a forester in the service of John,
Earl Warenne, lord of the manor of Wakefield. The surname in old court
documents is variously spelt Hod, Hode and Hood.

On 25 January 1316, Robin Hood's 'handmaid' is recorded as having been
brought before a court for taking dry wood and vert from the 'old oak'.
(Vert is the old English term for trees which provide shelter and food for
deer.) She was fined twopence. Other court records for the year 1316 show
that Robin Hood and his wife Matilda paid two shillings 'for leave to take
one piece of land of the lord's waste' to build a five-roomed house.

In 1322, Robin's landlord – at this time, Thomas, Earl of Lancaster –
called his tenants to arms in rebellion against King Edward II. A tenant had
no choice but to obey his lord implicitly, and Robin Hood followed the earl
into battle as an archer. The revolt was crushed. Lancaster was captured,
tried for treason, and beheaded. His estates were forfeited to the king and
his followers were outlawed.

Robin Hood fled into Barnsdale Forest, which at that time covered about
30 square miles of Yorkshire and was linked to Nottinghamshire's Sherwood
Forest, which covered 25 square miles. The forests were traversed by the
Roman-built Great North Road, which yielded rich pickings for robbers.
Here the legend of Robin Hood was born.

One of Robin's supposed escapades along the Great North Road concerned
the haughty Bishop of Hereford, who was travelling to York when he came
across the outlaw leader and some of his companions roasting venison. Taking
them for peasants, and infuriated by their flagrant breach of forest laws, the
bishop demanded an explanation. The outlaws calmly told him that they
were about to dine. The bishop ordered his attendants to seize them.

The outlaws prayed for mercy but the bishop swore that he would show
them none. So Robin blew on his horn, and the unhappy bishop found himself surrounded by archers in Lincoln green. They took him prisoner, with
all his company, and demanded a ransom. While the bishop was held captive,
he was made to dance a jig around a large oak tree. The tree is no longer
there, but the ground on which it stood is known as Bishop's Tree Root.

Several other oak trees in Barnsdale and Sherwood are associated with
Robin Hood and his band. Centre Tree, halfway between Thoresby and

Welbeck, is said to be the marker from which Robin Hood's network of secret routes stretched through the forest. But the most famous tree is Major Oak, at Birkland. It is reputedly 1,000 years old – predating the Norman Conquest of Britain – and has a girth of about 29 ft. Alfred, Lord Tennyson visited this oak in the last century and, in his poem 'The Foresters', has Little John referring to it as '. . . that oak where twelve men can stand inside nor touch each other'.

Among the stories passed down the centuries about Robin Hood's prowess is that of a visit he made with his closest friend, Little John, to Whitby Abbey. The abbot asked them to demonstrate their skill with the bow by shooting from the monastery roof. Both did so, and the arrows fell on either side of a lane at Whitby Lathes – more than a mile away. The abbot had two stone pillars erected on the spots where the arrows fell. The pillars survived until the end of the 18th century. The fields on either side were also named after the event: Robin Hood's Close and Little John's Close.

Little John, who was Robin's second-in-command, got his nickname because of his height. He was said to have died at Hathersage, in Derbyshire, and in 1784 his grave there was reopened. In it were found the bones of an exceptionally tall man.

Robin and his men have certainly been credited with far-flung activities. Robin Hood's Bay, many miles away on the Yorkshire coast, was named after the outlaw because it was here that he and his band were reputed to own several boats, for fishing and possible escape from the authorities.

On one of his journeys, Robin Hood visited St Mary's Church, Nottingham, where a monk in the congregation recognized him and alerted the sheriff. Robin drew his sword and slew 12 soldiers before being captured. But before he could be brought to trial, Little John led a band of the outlaws into Nottingham and rescued him. They also sought out the monk and murdered him.

But it was Robin Hood's championing of the underdog that made him a folk hero. His robbing of the rich to give to the poor, and his flouting of unpopular authority, became an inspiration to the oppressed peasantry.

One of the most famous stories to emanate from the oaks of Sherwood Forest is the tale of the meeting between Robin Hood and King Edward II. The story goes that the king, hearing that the royal deer in Sherwood were diminishing because of the appetites of Robin Hood and his band, determined to rid the forest of the outlaws. So he and his knights disguised themselves as monks and rode into the forest.

They were met by Robin Hood and some of his band, who demanded money. The king gave them £40, saying that was all he had. Robin took £20 for his men and gave the rest back to the king. Edward then produced the royal seal and told the outlaw leader that the king wished to see him in Nottingham. Robin summoned all his men to kneel before the seal and swear their love for the king. They then invited the 'monks' to eat with them – and fed them on the king's venison. Later Edward revealed his identity and pardoned all the outlaws – on condition that they would come to his court and serve him.

The story is told in *A Lytell Geste of Robyn Hood*, published in 1459. It may not be all fiction – the king was certainly in Nottingham in November 1323 and the story of his action fits what is known of his character. And a few months later, in 1324, the name of Robin Hood appears in the household accounts of Edward II. There is a record of wages paid to him until November of the same year. After that date, he vanishes into folklore again. Perhaps after enjoying the free life of an outlaw, he was unable to settle in service, even for his king.

Robin Hood's adventures in the forests continued until about 1346, when he is reputed to have died at Kirklees Priory. The prioress there is said to have hastened his death when he begged her help to relieve his pain during an illness. She is said to have bled him until he was too weak to recover.

Robin Hood, the story ends, managed to blow his famous hunting horn, which summoned his faithful companion Little John to his side. Robin then shot an arrow from the window of his room and asked to be buried wherever it might fall. The spot claimed to be his grave can still be seen to this day.

It is a romantic, ever-popular story which has been told and retold for 600 years. But whether it is myth or history, fiction or fact, remains a mystery.

Acrobats of Death

Ugo Pavesi stepped out onto the third-storey balcony of his home. An extortionist and general hoodlum, he liked to spend his evenings there while he plotted further criminal enterprises.

Usually, he would have been accompanied by his girlfriend but on this occasion 17-year-old Lorna Perricone was in hospital. As a disciplinary measure, he had put her there himself with a dozen savage blows to the face and stomach.

In the street below Pavesi's home, there were three witnesses who later reported seeing an impossible sight. They claimed to have seen a black giant 5.4 m (18 ft) tall emerge from the shadows and make his way towards the man on the balcony. The giant lifted him casually from the deck chair and let his squat body plunge to the pavement. Pavesi's severed head fell beside it, wrung from the body in an incredible display of strength.

In the deep, soft soil of the shrubbery surrounding Pavesi's home, police found the footprints of the killer. Displacement of the soil indicated that he had weighed no less than 410 kg (900 lb). But he had vanished completely in the confusion that followed the murder at Van Nuys, California, on the night of 13 November 1941, and no one knew where he would strike again.

A shrewd policeman who had been only a few blocks from the area was put on the case. Sergeant Lou Grandin toured the run-down area. One of his calls was on a psychic who called herself Madame Olga.

His visit was interrupted by the entrance of the old lady's three boarders, the powerful Perricone brothers Mario, Tony and Giorgio. Big, balding men with no-nonsense eyes, their timing and precision as an acrobatic team had won them high praise.

Mario, the spokesman, told Grandin that in 50 years of theatrical experience he had never known a giant like the alleged Van Nuys killer. Then he shocked the policeman by telling him: 'The girl Pavesi put in hospital was our sister, sergeant. And I'm using the past tense because she died a few minutes ago.'

'I'm sorry,' Grandin said humbly. 'I ask only that you stay in San Francisco until we get this thing cleaned up.'

But it was a warning that went unheeded. The date was 7 December, 1941 and something was to happen that day that changed the history of the world. The Perricone brothers were among the first to enlist after Pearl Harbor. So, too, was Sergeant Lou Grandin.

The case of the vanishing giant preyed on Grandin's mind throughout the war. On his return to the United States, he decided to pay one last visit to Madame Olga. The aged psychic was still alive but frail.

She told the ex-cop that the Perricone brothers had all died in the war – which was why she felt free to suggest a possible explanation for the death of Ugo Pavesi.

She drew out a yellowed vaudeville poster. There were the three Perricone brothers in the centre of the stage, Mario with Tony standing proudly on his shoulders. And on Tony's shoulders stood Giorgio, ripping a thick telephone directory to shreds in his big hands. The three would have made an impressive giant: Mario the planner, Tony the middleman, and Giorgio – with the huge, powerful hands.

Sherlock Holmes' Real Case

It was a murder case worthy of the cold, calculating detective powers of Sherlock Holmes. An elderly widow had been battered to death by a brutal murderer who had rifled through her files of personal papers and who had, inexplicably, stolen just one cheap brooch from her valuable collection of diamonds and other gems.

A tall, dark-haired man of about 30 had been seen by witnesses walking calmly away from the murder house in Glasgow. It had not taken long for Scottish policemen, acting under the pressure of public outrage, to arrest a suspect who was tried for the murder and sentenced to hang.

Twenty-four hours before the convicted man, gems dealer Oscar Slater, was due to meet the executioner, his sentence was commuted to life imprisonment. Although his life was spared, he still faced a grim existence of hard labour in prison until his dying day. Yet there were some lingering doubts about the case ... fears that Oscar Slater was no more than an innocent scapegoat.

But who could prove his innocence? Who could sift through the evidence with enough authority and thoroughness to overturn the verdict of a powerful court backed by the full might of the Scottish legal system? Sherlock Holmes, that's who – in the form of the creator of the fictional detective, author Sir Arthur Conan Doyle.

Conan Doyle was disturbed by the case of Oscar Slater when he read of the murder investigation and conviction in the scholarly legal work *Notable Scottish Trials*. The book outlined how, on little more than suspicion and circumstantial evidence, Slater had been found guilty of murdering 82-year-old Miss Marion Gilchrist at her home in Queen's Terrace, West Princes Street, Glasgow, on 21 December 1908.

Miss Gilchrist had lived the life of a virtual recluse in her home, attended only by a young maidservant, 21-year-old Helen Lambie, and seeing only rare visitors, mainly relatives. The spinster's only pleasure in life seemed to come from the loving care of her collection of diamonds, valued at £3,000.

On the night her mistress died, Helen Lambie had followed her usual practice of leaving the house around 19.00 to buy the evening newspaper. Miss Gilchrist remained inside, secure behind the double-locked doors of her home. The outer door, leading to the street, was held only by a latch which could be opened by a cord from inside the apartment if Miss Gilchrist recognized a visitor at the street door.

A few minutes after Helen left, downstairs neighbour Arthur Adams heard the noise of a heavy fall from the apartment above and went to investigate. The outer door was open but the double-locked apartment door was still secure. As he stood there puzzled, Helen returned with the evening paper and the couple unlocked the door and went in. Just as they entered the apartment, a tall, well-dressed man walked calmly past them and into the street. Inside, Marion Gilchrist was dead in the dining-room, her skull crushed.

While Adams went to raise the alarm, Helen Lambie ran the short distance to the home of Marion Gilchrist's niece, Mrs Margaret Birrell, and told her she had recognized the man who had walked from the apartment. But the niece, in a burst of outrage, told Helen Lambie she must be mistaken and she must not 'smear the man's reputation' in any statement to the police.

The police took only five days to produce some results to still the public outcry which followed the murder. They learned that gem dealer Oscar Slater, who lived not far from the murdered woman, had pawned a brooch of about the same value as the missing one. They also discovered that he and his young French mistress had fled from Scotland aboard the liner *Lusitania* using assumed names.

Police pursued the couple to New York where Slater was arrested and, protesting his innocence, agreed to waive extradition formalities and return to Glasgow.

Sir Arthur Conan Doyle

Oscar Slater's trial

At his trial the witnesses, with some hesitation, identified him as the mystery man. Slater, a German Jew, claimed: 'I know nothing about this affair, absolutely nothing.' But the jury found him guilty by a majority verdict. Slater suffered three weeks in the condemned cell before his reprieve.

The few doubts about Slater's innocence were carefully noted in the book which Conan Doyle read and it was enough to arouse his interest. He began to examine the case with the same fresh uncluttered mind that he had devoted to his fictional super-sleuth, Sherlock Holmes of Baker Street.

Three years after the trial, after careful study of the transcripts of the court proceedings and correspondence with witnesses, Conan Doyle caused an uproar with his book, *The Case of Oscar Slater*. In the same calm style as Holmes, he punched gaping holes in the prosecution case.

The brooch which had first drawn suspicion on Slater had been pawned three weeks before the murder. Slater, Conan Doyle pointed out, had fled with his mistress under assumed names because he wanted to give the slip to his domineering, grasping wife. Slater's own lifestyle, as a gambler and womanizer, had probably prejudiced the puritanical Scottish jury against him.

Conan Doyle demolished the conflicting evidence of witnesses, some of whom claimed that the mystery murderer had been clean-shaven, others who said he was bearded. And, drawing on his own forensic expertise, he pointed out that when Slater's entire wardrobe of clothes was seized in his luggage aboard the *Lusitania*, not a single trace of blood was found on any of them.

The 'Sherlock Holmes' investigation produced immediate demands for a re-trial or public inquiry. But the wheels of justice grind slowly. It took 18 years before Oscar Slater was released by the newly appointed Scottish Court of Criminal Appeal on the technicality that the judge at his trial had misdirected the jury. Slater was awarded £6,000 in compensation.

But Arthur Conan Doyle never published the final chapter of his important murder investigation. 'Sherlock Holmes' had proved Slater's innocence. But had he ever uncovered the real identity of the killer of Marion Gilchrist?

Shortly before he died in 1930, Conan Doyle revealed to a friend:

'I knew I had a difficult enough job in getting Oscar Slater freed. That was the most important objective I had to achieve. If I had tried at the same to lay the blame for the murder on the real guilty man, it might have prejudiced Slater's chances of release.

But I believe I know the identity of the real murderer, a man who was protected by the police because he was a prominent citizen who desperately wanted something from the private papers of Marion Gilchrist. He has gone unpunished. But it is more important to me that an innocent man is free. I am satisfied.'

Dead Men Cannot Talk

The liner *Georges Phillipar* was one of the best designed cruise ships afloat when she was launched by her French builders from the slipway at St Nazaire in 1930.

It took almost two years to fit out the 17,300 tonne (17,000 ton) ship to carry up to 1,000 passengers in sumptuous luxury in richly panelled cabins with comfortable, efficient air conditioning. And no expense was spared to guarantee their safety, with an automatic sprinkler system and the latest fire-fighting appliances.

Yet the fire which broke out on D Deck on the liner's maiden voyage, a round trip to China, spread with devastating speed, killing 53 passengers and sending the pride of the French liner fleet to the bottom of the Red Sea.

The commission of inquiry in Paris which later investigated the sinking of

Above: The liner *Georges Phillipar* on her maiden voyage,
a round trip to China. No expense had been spared in the design of this
luxurious ship.
Left: The *Georges Phillipar*, almost burnt out by the
mysterious fire in which 53 passengers died.

the *Georges Phillipar* could find no firm evidence that faulty electrical design had caused the blaze, or that the fire had been accidental. They left only a tantalizing, inconclusive hint ... that powerful international assassins had turned the liner into a floating fire-bomb just to kill one VIP passenger, a crusading French journalist.

Freelance writer Albert Londres had joined the *Georges Phillipar* in April 1932 in Shanghai for the return leg of its maiden voyage. He had spent almost a year in Indo-China on a gruelling and dangerous assignment and his carefully guarded notebook was crammed with information which would have caused public outrage against the profiteering industrialists of London, Paris and Berlin..

Millions of readers throughout Europe were waiting and wondering what scandalous subject the best-selling author would choose for his next devastating report. In his first book, *The Road to Buenos Aires*, published only three years before, he had exposed the vile white slave trade of young women from the brothels of Marseilles and Hamburg to South America. It earned him the undying hatred of the French and German vice kings.

Undeterred, Londres went on to expose a similar traffic in young European girls to the houses of pleasure in Shanghai, and followed this up with an investigation of the terrorist group who had assassinated the King of Yugoslavia on French soil.

Now he had completed his damning examination of the deadly arms trade in the Far East, where the Japanese Imperial armies were gearing themselves for an expansive war of aggression and the bandit Chinese war lords were slaughtering their own countrymen in their bloody battles to gain control of vast areas of China and Manchuria.

Word quickly spread among enthusiastic European publishers that Albert Londres was on his way home with a manuscript that would light a fuse underneath the European millionaire arms suppliers, the Merchants of Death.

Londres was safely installed in his cabin, working on the notes for his new book when the liner docked briefly at Saigon, the capital of French Indo-China, and took aboard more travellers, mainly French colonial officials and their families. With a complement of 800 passengers, the liner called at Singapore, Penang and Ceylon, en route for the Red Sea, the Suez Canal and the French Mediterranean port of Marseilles.

On the night of 15 May as Londres worked alone in his cabin, the other passengers gathered on deck for a dinner dance in the sultry evening air, admiring the twinkling lights of the Arabian coast and waving to the crew of the Russian tanker *Sovietskya Neft* which passed less than a mile astern.

Around midnight the master of the *Georges Phillipar*, Captain Anton Vicq, retired to his cabin, bidding goodnight to the last of the dinner-dance revellers who stayed on the starlit deck, sipping chilled champagne.

Two hours later he was roused by the officer of the watch who warned him that a passenger cabin on D Deck was ablaze. When he made an examination in portside Number 5 cabin, Captain Vicq noted that 'It was not a local accident, but a fire appearing to become general and widespread.'

As he retreated along the deck corridor to the sound of the alarm, Captain Vicq was confronted by Nurse Yvonne Valentin who screamed that her cabin, Number 7, was also engulfed in flames. Between the two, in cabin Number 6 on D deck, writer Albert Londres was unaware of the drama.

Trying vainly to contain the blaze, Captain Vicq ordered all portholes to be closed and stopped the liner's engines. Within minutes the flames had spread to the bridge and the captain gave the order to abandon ship.

As the lifeboats were lowered the radio operator broadcast a frantic series of sos messages. But his transmission was cut suddenly short when his radio failed and power from the generator ceased. Following his well rehearsed emergency procedure, the radio operator reached for the sealed locker which held an ample supply of spare batteries – the batteries were missing.

As passengers wrapped wet towels round their faces to fight their way through the blinding acrid smoke, Captain Vicq and his crew calmly organized the evacuation of the ship. All floating furniture which could be used as liferafts was heaved overboard and terrified passengers were helped over the stern of the liner into the warm still waters of the sea.

The brief burst of pleading on the ship's radio had been enough to summon a rescue flotilla to its aid, including the Soviet tanker, two British steamers, a Japanese cargo ship and two other ocean liners.

The task of saving the souls in the lifeboats and clinging to the rafts was carried out speedily and most of them were soon aboard the mercy vessels. The stricken liner burned for three days in a column of flame which could be seen for 60 km (40 miles). When the *Georges Phillipar* finally heeled over, she sank within two minutes.

But no trace was ever found of the body of Albert Londres who had been trapped in his cabin between the two sources of the sudden, unexplained fire.

Survivors reported that they had last seen him crawling through his cabin porthole, his precious manuscript held tightly under his arm. The man who knew too much was officially logged in the disaster list as drowned.

His notebooks and manuscripts drifted away in the ebb and flow of the Red Sea's tides. And seven years later, the wealthy and ruthless arms dealers, unhampered by the spotlight of Albert Londres's unfinished investigation, saw their staggering investment in munitions bear fruit when all of Europe was plunged into war.

The Green Bicycle Murder

The tragic death of pretty Bella Wright would have been written off as a fatal road accident if it had not been for the shrewd curiosity of a young country constable.

For when 21-year-old Bella was found dead on a quiet road near the village of Stretton in Leicestershire, with her bicycle lying on the grass verge, it added a terrible weight to the complaints of the locals who cursed the reckless and speeding drivers in their peaceful little communities.

The dead girl's face was deeply gouged and matted with blood. Gravel from the roadway was embedded in her face where she had pitched forward from her bicycle and struck the ground. She had obviously been run off the road by some ruthless motorist, the villagers insisted. It was July 1919 and clattering motor cars were not yet a commonplace sight in the quiet countryside. Their drivers, according to popular rural opinion, terrified the farm animals and were a mortal danger to peaceful cyclists and rambling pedestrians.

A cursory examination of Bella's body by a local doctor seemed to confirm that opinion. He concluded that something had caused Bella to lose control of her bicycle, throwing her into the road where she died of loss of blood and head injuries.

The local constable, however, had some nagging doubts. He went to search the scene of the road accident for any further clues to showing exactly how Bella had met her death.

As he poked around the grass verges on either side of the narrow road, the constable found the blood-spattered body of a dead carrion crow. But there were no tyre marks near the bird. He turned its body over with the tip of his boot and continued his search. A few feet away, where Bella's bicycle had lain, he found another object which caught his attention. It was a spent bullet, pushed down into the soft earth by the imprint of a horse's hoof.

A fresh examination of Bella's body showed the grim truth about her death. In the swollen blood-stained tissue below her left eye was a bullet hole. Hidden in the tangled mass of her hair was an exit wound. Bella had been shot clean through the head.

The police search switched from the pursuit of a hit and run driver to the hunt for a cold-blooded murderer.

The night before Bella died she had been on one of her frequent cycling jaunts, riding to the village postbox to send a letter to her sweetheart, a young sailor aboard a warship which was stationed 240 km (150 miles) away in Portsmouth. The pretty brunette who lived with her parents had made male admirers, but she only flirted with them. Her deepest affections were reserved for the sailor she hoped would soon ask her to marry him.

Bella had finished a long tiring night shift as a mill hand in a factory in nearby Leicester when she returned home on Saturday 5 July and slept until late afternoon.

After a quick meal when she woke she cycled off briskly to post her letter, telling her parents she might pay a visit to her uncle, a roadworker, who lived not very far away.

When Bella arrived at her uncle's cottage two hours later, she was not alone. As she went inside the cottage a sallow-faced man waited outside for her, seated astride his green bicycle.

Bella's uncle, George Measures, teased her about her strange companion. She smiled: 'Oh him, I don't really know him at all. He has been riding alongside me for a few miles but he isn't bothering me at all. He's just chatting about the weather.'

When Bella was ready to leave for home an hour later, her uncle glanced through the window and saw the man with the green bicycle was still waiting outside. 'Oh, I do hope he doesn't get boring,' Bella laughed coyly. 'I'll soon cycle fast enough to give him the slip.'

The man with the green bicycle grinned happily at Bella when she left the cottage and pedalled his bicycle to join her as they rode off together in the warm summer evening's air.

An hour later a farmer driving his cattle along the peaceful Burton-Overy road, found Bella's body. An inquest on the dead girl returned a verdict of 'murder by person or persons unknown'. The vital witness, the man with the green bicycle could not be traced.

But his bicycle was found, seven months later, when a barge skipper on a canal outside Leicester found that a line trailing from his boat had snagged on a piece of junk on the canal bed. The junk brought to the surface was the frame of a green bicycle. Policemen who probed the muddy canal bottom soon uncovered a gun holster and a dozen revolver cartridges.

One of the serial numbers on the bicycle frame had been hastily filed off. But another identifying number inside the saddle support led police to the local dealer for the bicycle maker and then to the identity of the man who had bought it ten years before.

The owner of the bicycle was railway draughtsman Ronald Light, a moody shell-shocked veteran of World War 1 with a fascination for guns. He had been invalided out of the Army and had lived in Leicester until six months after Bella's murder.

When police traced 34-year-old Light he had left his home in Leicester he shared with his widowed mother and taken a job about 100 km (60 miles away) as a school teacher in Cheltenham. He was arrested and brought back to Leicester to be charged with the murder of Bella Wright.

His trial began at Leicester Assizes in June 1920 and from the opening speech of the prosecution the circumstantial evidence was stacked mercilessly against Ronald Light. Witness after witness identified him as the man with the green bicycle and a young maidservant from Light's own home told how he kept firearms and ammunition in the attic.

The prosecution amply proved that Ronald Light had been the mystery man who cycled off with Bella just before her death. Light himself admitted filing the serial number off his bicycle and throwing it, with the holster and cartridges, into the canal a few weeks after the murder.

The only arguably weak point in the prosecution's case was the lack of motive. Bella had not been sexually assaulted or robbed. Even though Light denied killing her, claiming that they parted company at the village crossroads, the irrefutable testimony seemed certain to lead him to the gallows.

One other piece of evidence seemed to cloud the case, almost irrelevantly. The bullet found by the village constable had several marks on it. The marks were caused by it passing through the dead girl's skull and the crushing effect of the steel-shod horse's hoof which had ground it into the earth. There was even one mark which might have been caused by a ricochet.

When Ronald Light gave evidence in his own defence, he seemed at first to be damning himself. He admitted trailing around after Bella on his bicycle on the night of her death, pestering her for the use of a spanner and a pump because his own cycle had developed a loose wheel and a flat tyre.

He told the jury of his own sad and tortured mental history: how he cracked up after three years of savage war in the frontline trenches, and how he was classified as a shell-shock victim and sent back to England in the closing stages of the war for psychiatric treatment.

But the effect of his testimony on the jury was electric. In a firm clear voice, without a trace of hesitation or emotion, Light told the court: 'I was an artillery gunner in the trenches from 1915 to 1918 when I was sent home a broken man. I kept my holster and ammunition because they were wrapped in a bag attached to my stretcher when they took me from the front. The Army kept my service revolver.

'When Bella Wright was murdered I knew from newspaper reports the next day that she was the girl I had been with just before she died. I knew the police wanted to question me.'

Staring blankly and coldly into space, Light admitted: 'I became a coward again. I never told a living soul what I knew. I got rid of everything which could have connected me with her. I was afraid.'

The jury looked at the gaunt face of the anguished war veteran before they retired to consider their verdict. They returned three hours later and pronounced him 'not guilty'.

As Light walked from the court a free man, the sharp-eyed constable who had turned her death into a murder investigation, blamed himself for one flaw in his inspired detective work...

The body of the dead carrion crow in the field. He had kicked it aside with hardly a second glance.

Had the bloodied crow also been blasted by a bullet from the same gun which killed Bella Wright? Had the same bullet ripped through the crow in flight and found a second, innocent human target? Could the bullet have ricochetted from a tree and ended Bella's young life?

Without the evidence of the crow and perhaps of further bullets and footprints at the scene, no one would ever know. But it was not beyond the bounds of possibility that an amateur marksman had been taking potshots at the sinister black shapes of the carrion crows in the field beside the country road.

Was there somewhere a thoughtless gunman who knew his wild shooting had killed an unsuspecting girl and who had fled from the scene to keep his terrified secret? A gunman infinitely more cowardly than the shell-shocked, broken ex-soldier Ronald Light.

Double Dealing at the Dogs

The most spectacular swindle in the history of greyhound racing was pulled off at London's White City track on 8 December 1945. The perpetrators, who were never caught, got away with more than £100,000, a fortune at the time.

The swindle became apparent to the race fans as they watched the last event of the day. The second favourite, Fly Bessie, led at the first bend, closely followed by Jimmy's Chicken. Then, to the amazement of the 16,000 crowd, the dogs began to swerve drunkenly and lose ground. One by one, they started stumbling ... all except the rank outsider, a white hound called Bald Truth. He streaked home 15 lengths ahead of the second dog, with the favourite, Victory Speech, trailing in fourth.

No one was more amazed than Bald Truth's owner, Colonel B. C. 'Jock' Hartley, wartime director of the Army Sports Board. The dog had only been brought in as a late substitute and his £2 bet on it was prompted more by his heart than his head. He sat speechless as fans shouted and growled and track officials delayed making the official announcements. But there was nothing they could do. Number 4 went up in lights; Bald Truth the winner. Bets would be paid.

As far as Scotland Yard was concerned, however, the affair was far from over. Chief Inspector Robert Fabian was called in to investigate the coup, which had followed a series of minor frauds at tracks around the country. Slowly the pieces of the puzzle were fitted into place. The swindlers had used a dope called cholecretone, untraceable in pre-race examinations, but which had an alcoholic effect as the dogs heated up during a race.

Investigators decided that the culprit had crept into a disused kennel used to store straw and timber. Then, when all eyes were on the track during the penultimate race, he had crawled out, fed drugged pieces of fish to all the dogs except Bald Truth – the only white dog in the field – and returned to his kennel until the coast was clear. Meanwhile the rest of the gang were placing bets with bookies all over the country and on the course, bringing the price down from 33-1 to 11-2 by the start.

But that was all renowned sleuth Fabian of the Yard could discover. Despite the Greyhound Racing Association's offer of a £1,000 reward, the culprits were never caught.

A Fatal Flight

Two planes carrying 116 passengers mysteriously vanished in the Andes – and investigators believe both craft may have been hijacked.

Saeta Airlines Flight 11, with 59 passengers on board, left Quito, Ecuador, on 15 August 1976 on its 45-minute flight to the mountain city of Cuenca. It vanished without trace.

Two years later Saeta Flight 11 left with 57 people bound once again for

Cuenca. It passed over the same relay station as its 1976 namesake then vanished. Intensive searches found no signs of the aircraft or their passengers. But at a special hearing in Quito, five farmers and a teacher gave sworn statements that they saw the second flight suddenly veer from its normal southerly course and head north-east.

Major Carlos Serrano, president of Saeta, one of Ecuador's three domestic airlines, supported the theory that the two Vickers Viscount planes had been hijacked. He said drug smugglers may have been involved. 'They are the perfect planes for them,' he said 'They fly long distances, land on short runways and with the seats removed hold up to 12,000 pounds of cargo.'

Searches for the two planes involved the Ecuadorean Air Force and army patrols, a United States Air Force C-130 search plane and a helicopter with sophisticated laser reconnoitring devices. None of the searches were successful. And Commander Reinaldo Lazo, the United States Military Liaison Chief, said the C-130 crew had reached no conclusions after either of the week-long searches.

James Kuykendall, the Ecuador representative of the United States Drug Enforcement Administration, said his agency had found names of people with narcotics trafficking records on the passenger lists of the missing aircraft. He said his agency had no idea what had happened to the flights.

Saeta's Major Serrano, however, is more certain. He believes the passengers were pressed into service harvesting marijuana. The missing included 74 men, 36 women and 6 children – ranging from farm workers to doctors and lawyers.

Guillermo Jaramillo, a Quito lawyer whose 39-year-old son Ivan disappeared on the second flight, organized a committee of the grieving families to probe the mystery. Together with Saeta, they offered a $325,000 reward for information – without success.

Lord Byron

Were Byron and his half-sister, Augusta Leigh, lovers? The question has haunted generations of those intrigued by the romantic poet with the reputation of being 'mad, bad and dangerous to know'.

George Gordon, sixth Lord Byron, born on 22 January 1788, was the son of a handsome rake known to his family as 'mad Jack'. This same black sheep was also the father of Augusta. Byron's mother was a Scottish heiress called Catherine of Gight, a Celt with such a bad temper she once bit a piece out of a saucer. Augusta's mother was the wife of Lord Carmarthen who caused a major scandal by eloping with rakish Jack and marrying him after her divorce.

Brother and sister met for the first time in 1802 when Byron was fourteen and Augusta, nineteen. To the boy who suffered bitterly from awareness of his club foot and a tendency to stoutness, she seemed like an angel of understanding. Gentle, sensual, dark, with a beautiful curved mouth, she fitted exactly Byron's idea of a perfect woman. But of course she was forbidden fruit. She was also engaged to their cousin, George Leigh. 'Can't you drive this cousin of ours out of your pretty little head?' he begged her. But she went through with her plans, married the horsey Colonel Leigh and settled down to be a country wife in Newmarket.

As the years went by, however, and Byron grew to be one of the most handsome and fascinating men of his day, the two found themselves drawn to each other and their affection developed into an intense passion. Byron called her 'the one whom I most loved' and even confessed to his bride on their wedding night that no woman would ever possess as much of his love as his sister Augusta.

Byron had a miserable childhood and spent most of his life making up for it by indulging his passionate, sensual nature. When he was a boy his mother's moods of depression alternated with bursts of tenderness or furious temper. She once called him a 'lame brat' and the words seared his soul. He had a thoroughly Scottish upbringing in Aberdeen and was looked after by a Calvinistic nanny who taught him that all people were sinners, predestined to damnation, a harsh doctrine that also left its mark.

When he was ten his great-uncle, always called 'the wicked Lord Byron' because he lived as a recluse with a servant girl he had named 'Lady Betty', died and left him heir to the title. He also left him Newstead Abbey, a magnificent Gothic ruin of a place in Nottinghamshire with a sinister lake and a ghost. Byron loved it. His mother took him to live there and provided him with a pretty young nurse who added spice to her affairs with other servants by occasionally hopping into bed with the young Lord. 'My passions were developed early,' he recalled later. Too early, thought his mother, who dismissed the nurse and sent him away to school.

Byron's first real love was his cousin, Mary Chaworth, heiress of Annesley Hall, only a few fields away from Newstead. She was already 'promised' and cut him to the quick by saying in his hearing 'Do you think I could care anything for that lame boy!' He said the remark stayed in his heart like a splinter of ice and it certainly explained a lot of his ruthless behaviour to women in the future. When she married he missed a whole term at Harrow bcause he was so heartbroken. He wrote lines to her which began 'Well, thou art happy . . .' and it was years before he completely got over her.

He went from Harrow to Cambridge and threw himself wholeheartedly into the business of becoming a young rake. His mother was worried to death by his extravagance and his drinking. 'Ruined! At 18. Great God!' she exclaimed. But Byron had started to write poetry and that gradually became as important to him as other pleasures. Then, still inclined to stoutness, he began to follow a strict regime which he summarized as follows: 'Much physic, much hot bathing and much violent exercise.'

He emerged from this self-inflicted torture ready to make half the women in Britain swoon, giving the name 'Byronic' to a certain kind of male beauty. His figure was now slim and elegant. Dark curls clustered round his head, his grey eyes were fringed with long, dark lashes; his well-shaped mouth, cleft chin and smooth, pale brow combined to give his face a look of classic nobility.

At Cambridge, however, he had gained a reputation as a profligate and gambler and now he plunged headfirst into London life. 'I am buried in an abyss of sensuality', he informed his great and brilliant friend, John Cam Hobhouse', later to be Lord Brougham. But it is important to remember that Byron always liked to exaggerate his wickedness for dramatic effect.

His unfulfilled love for Mary Chaworth lingered on and he had failed to persuade his sister Augusta not to marry, so in 1809 he decided to travel in Europe and the Near East and forget them both. After a farewell party at Newstead Abbey he sailed from Falmouth with Hobhouse and did not return to England for two years.

Byron cut his teeth on various love affairs abroad, then once back in London decided to give himself up to his poetry. He only half-succeeded. His club foot, which he did his best to conceal, proved no obstacle to his success with the opposite sex. Women gazed instead at that pale face with its arrogantly sensual lines and were lost. Suddenly, he woke up one morning to find himself famous. On 10 March 1812 the first two Cantos of *Childe Harold* were published. The epic was greeted with near hysteria and sold like hot cakes. Some people tried to

Lord Byron

identify Byron with his hero and were convinced that he had a hidden life. Mounds of invitations arrived at his lodgings in St James's Street. It was said you could not sit down at a dinner table in London without hearing the constant repetition of his name.

Of course what most fascinated women was the hint of scandal about him. Behind the pale beauty many suspected darkness and mystery. He revelled in the notoriety, and no doubt derived much satisfaction from it. He had a keen sense of humour and satirical wit which permeated a great deal of his work.

One woman who literally threw herself at him was the wild, delicate hoyden Lady Caroline Lamb, daughter of the Earl of Bessborough. At her first meeting with Byron she turned on her heel saying that the very sight of that handsome face made her feel faint. They were introduced again at Lady Holland's and he was entranced by her huge brown eyes, short, tumbled curls and boyish figure. Her tantalizing first rejection of him, then the experience of meeting the pretty creature face to face, was a challenge Byron could not resist.

For a few months he was in love with her then, just as suddenly, cooled off. The wild extravagance of her passion had proved too much for him. He had awakened her sexually. 'The tumult, the ardour, the romance bewildered my reason,' she wrote after one lovers' meeting. She besieged him with her emotions and when they quarrelled tried to stab herself, first with a knife, then with a piece of broken glass. She exposed him to public ridicule and that he could not forgive. At the beginning of their affair he was telling her that her heart was a little volcano – 'It pours lava through your veins and yet I cannot wish it a bit colder' – and he assured her, 'I have always thought you the cleverest, most agreeable, absurd, amiable, perplexing, dangerous fascinating little being.' Before long, however, he was moaning, 'this dream, this delirium . . . it must pass away'. She sent him some of her pubic hair, asking for his in return. Her immodesty put him off even more.

When Lady Caroline's mother tried to persuade her to go to Ireland, hoping that with the sea between them the affair would come to an end, Caro asked Byron to elope with her. He took her back to Lady Bessborough as though she were a naughty child and in the end she had to settle for Ireland. From there she bombarded him with letters.

Byron did the only thing possible to stop Caroline pestering him. He took a new mistress, the Countess of Oxford, a beautiful bluestocking who believed in free love and was twice his age. He declared that the autumn of her beauty was preferable to another woman's springtime and when Caro wrote asking for confirmation of his love he replied: 'Lady Caro, our affections are not our own . . . mine are engaged. I love another. I am no longer your lover.'

In the midst of all this he met Annabella Milbanke. She, too, was a bluestocking, a clever, intellectual girl who specialized in mathematics, theology and Greek. She was only 20 but liked life to be orderly and systematic. Byron's friends tried to make him see that they were not even remotely suited, but he was in raptures about her 'nutbrown looks' and had no doubt added to the list of her charms the fact that she was an heiress. Annabella was quite bowled over by his famous looks, came to the conclusion that he needed saving from himself, and she would do the saving. He called her 'my princess of the parallelograms' and proposed. To his amazement, she refused him.

Suddenly Byron's half-sister, Augusta, arrived on the London scene. They had been writing to each other for years, a charming, lively correspondence that showed their affection. But in the hot summer of 1813 Augusta was bored, restless and dissatisfied. Living at Newmarket with her three daughters, she hardly ever saw her husband other than when he appeared for the races. She packed her bags and descended on Byron and he was reminded once again that his sister, with her dark, sensual grace, was his ideal woman.

Byron's whole life had been devoted to satisfying his sensations. Now, it is almost certain, he gave away to his desires once again and discovered the sensation of forbidden love. In her biography of the poet, Lady Elizabeth Longford says, 'Gradually, however, there was another sensation not so pleasant as the first – sexual guilt. Ill-treated by her husband, Augusta would do anything Byron wanted. It is as certain as these things can be that she was his lover. Her unthinking acquiescence in his crime must have increased his guilty torment.'

Augusta constantly dominated his thoughts and feelings. At last he could no longer bear the burden without telling someone else. Lady Melbourne seemed the ideal person. She had been acting as go-between for him with Annabella, but was a modern thinker and feminist. Byron told her how this love for his sister made all other loves seem insipid. Their intentions, he admitted, had been very different and when they failed to ȧdhere to them it had been due to her 'weakness' and his 'folly'. Lady Melbourne was appalled and told him so. Byron had some wild idea about going abroad and taking Augusta with him. Lady Melbourne implored him to go abroad by all means, but to leave Augusta behind.

When Byron celebrated his 26th birthday Augusta was heavily pregnant. For the moment only Lady Melbourne knew of his feelings and she dreaded to think what society would say if the 'truth' came out. The press had already described Lord Byron as 'a deformed Richard III, an atheist rebel and a devil'. What would they do if they found out about his relations with his sister?

Augusta gave birth to a daughter. Could he be the father? Byron himself, apparently, had doubts and he was never as fond of this child, christened Medora, as he was of Augusta's other children who were undoubtedly fathered by Colonel Leigh.

Lady Caroline Lamb

Ten months had gone by since he last saw Annabella Milbanke, proposed to her, and received her refusal. He decided he must try to lay the ghosts of past love affairs and commit himself to a decent marriage. Various candidates were put forward by well-meaning friends but he would not consider them. He became involved with the pedantic young bluestocking again and they drifted into a marriage which both were to regret bitterly.

Though he could be a sparkling and charming companion, he behaved abominably on the honeymoon, taunting Annabella with his love for Augusta and hinting that the child she had just given birth to was his.

Marriage was not as bad as he had expected. They had some pleasant times together at the Milbanke home at Seaham in the north of England, but Byron began to feel cut off, trapped, and insisted they move back to London. They collected Augusta on the way and Annabella, seeing brother and sister together, had her worst suspicions confirmed. Byron, torn apart by his conflicting emotions, behaved even worse than on his honeymoon. 'There were times,' Annabella wrote later, 'when I could have plunged a dagger into his heart.' Strangely enough his behaviour drew the two women together and Annabella began to have hopes that she could 'save' them both. 'His misfortune is an habitual passion for excitement,' she told Augusta.

When their daughter Ada was born Annabella began to suspect that debts, drunkenness and remorse over Augusta had driven Byron mad. He told her they could no longer afford to live in style in London and she was to go home to her parents at their estate in Leicestershire. They said goodbye for the last time on 14 January 1815. She could take no more and had come to the conclusion that she had fallen in love with Lucifer himself. The truth was, they were ill-matched from the start.

Byron himself seemed to accept her judgement, saying bitterly in one letter to her, 'It is my destiny to ruin all I come near.' Annabella eventually admitted to a confidante that her secret reason for parting with Byron was her growing suspicion of his incest. Augusta was pregnant again and this time people were giving voice to their suspicions. She could no longer stay for even short visits at Byron's house in Piccadilly. She went off to resume her duties as a woman of the bedchamber to Queen Charlotte, who would not have believed in such goings on, even if she had been told about them.

The separation of Byron and Annabella caused no little scandal. Female society turned against the poet, though women still peeped from behind their fans, around doors and lace curtains to catch a glimpse of him, and their hearts beat faster at a glance from those cool grey eyes.

It was under these circumstances that Byron boarded a packet for Ostend on 25 April 1816 and left England, never to return alive. He and Augusta said goodbye to one another wretchedly and in tears. They were never to meet again. He wrote her the exquisite lines beginning:

'Thou wert the solitary star
Which rose and set not to the last . . .'

His friend Hobhouse listened to him curse the hypocrisy and repressiveness of

English morality, which was driving him away and noticed that some inquisitive society women, disguising themselves as servant girls, had gathered on the quay to have one last look at the demon lover.

Byron travelled through Belgium and Switzerland in his dark green Napoleonic coach to join his friend, the poet Shelley, and his wife Mary at their hotel on the outskirts of Geneva. Also waiting for him was a hot-headed girl he hoped he had left behind in England.

At the eleventh hour before his departure Byron had become involved with 17-year-old Claire Clairmont, Mary Shelley's step-sister. She was an incurable romantic, jealous of Mary's elopement with Shelley and determined to catch herself a poet. She wrote to Byron, asking for a meeting and making it clear she was ready to be his mistress. The meeting took place somewhere in London during his last week in England. Byron had no intention of seeing her again but had unwisely given her the address in Geneva where she could write. She packed and hurried to Switzerland ahead of him.

Now the party was a foursome. He took the Villa Diodati on the Belle Rive of Lake Geneva while the Shelleys occupied a villa on the hillside above. He spoke of Claire as 'a foolish girl' but she was close to him for a brief spell and gave birth to his daughter.

Switzerland was a watershed in Byron's life. Stimulated by the company of the younger poet and by the drama of the mountains and lakes, he wrote his great poem *The Prisoner of Chillon*. When it was translated into German Byron was taken up by Goethe and his fame began to spread throughout Europe. He also climbed the Alps with Hobhouse and wrote the first two acts of his poetic drama *Manfred*.

For a time it was an idyllic life but Byron eventually made a move to end it for he did not want to be tied to Claire. He persuaded the Shelleys to take her home. He still encountered upper class English tourists in Geneva who stared at him 'as though a devil had come among them'. He wanted to get even further away from his homeland. Italy had a very strong appeal for him. He headed for Venice and the sun.

It did not take him long to find comfortable lodgings over a prosperous baker's shop. The great attraction of these premises was the baker's wife, Marianna Segati, with whom he fell 'in fathomless love'. Her husband saw no harm in her taking this English Lord as her lover, in fact he bragged about it. Marianna was a seductive, hot-blooded creature with large, liquid eyes, dark, glossy hair and the grace of a gazelle. She also had a fearful temper which she displayed when she thought her sister-in-law was trying to take her place in Byron's bed.

Rumours of her violent love for the poet travelled all over Venice and, naturally, shocked the resident English. Apart from the affair with Marianna his

Margherita Cogni

first few months in the city were comparatively respectable. He was entranced by its ancient narrow streets and canals and loved the Italian working people and shopkeepers whom he found natural, vivid and warmhearted. It was after he installed himself in the Palazzo Mocenigo overlooking the Grande Canale that he gave way to the excesses that impaired his health. The Venice Carnival, with its unspeakably dissolute entertainments, held him captive. Yet it was at this time that he wrote some of his finest poetry including the first Canto of *Don Juan* and *Manfred*, which contained some of his most profound thoughts about man's destiny.

La Segati was followed by baker's wife Margherita Cogni. He met her one day while he was out riding and was immediately drawn to the magnificent, 22-

year-old peasant, tall, strong, wild and beautiful. To keep her near him he employed her as housekeeper at his summer villa at La Mira on the river Brenta, seven miles from Venice. She, too, had a terrible temper and it was said she once took advantage of Byron's lameness and beat him in a fit of jealousy. Certainly after a few months he had had enough of her, but she refused to leave. When he finally managed to dismiss her, she threw herself into the canal from which she was rescued just in time.

This was the most dissolute period of his life. When he celebrated his 30th birthday in 1818 he was beginning to show some of the effects of his self-indulgence. He was said to have founded a harem which cost him £3,000. He boasted that it accommodated 200 women of every nationality, but he was probably exaggerating. He had become, in his biographer Lady Longford's words, 'a puffy Romeo, both comical and sad'. Yet his poetry flooded out to a disapproving world that could not help but recognize his genius, and in his debauchery he wrote one of the most beautiful lyrics in the language:

'So we'll go no more a-roving
So late into the night,
Though the heart be still as loving,
And the moon be still as bright.

For the sword outwears its sheath,
And the soul wears out the breast,
And the heart must pause to breathe,
And love itself have rest.'

At a reception held by the Countess Benzoni the 30-year-old Byron came face to face with the last love of his life. Nineteen-year-old Countess Teresa Guiccioli had been married for just three days when they met. Her husband was an elderly, eccentric landowner and the marriage had been one entirely of convenience. Byron was attracted by this striking Italian girl with golden hair, blue eyes, a fine complexion and magnificent bust and shoulders, but did not at the time foresee what the depths of his feelings for her would be. They discussed Dante together, rode on horseback under the great umbrella pines, strolled through scented gardens on balmy evenings. Soon he was writing to her, 'You have been mine and whatever is the outcome, I am and eternally shall be yours . . .' She called him 'mio Byron' in public, which was guaranteed to shock.

The Guicciolis moved to their palazzo in Ravenna and Byron was invited to rent the upper floor. He was not entirely happy about it, suspecting that the old man intended to spy on them. Nevertheless he moved in, bringing with him ten horses, for which he had been promised stabling, eight enormous dogs, three monkeys, five cats, an eagle, a crow and a falcon. After a few months he added five peacocks, two guinea hens and a crane.

Byron and his countess lived in a romantic trance. This time he was really in love. She brought such beauty and intelligence into his life that he was haunted by regrets that they had not met sooner. He quite clearly saw himself as an ageing Don Juan.

Count Guiccioli was well aware of his wife's affair with Byron but waited until he caught them together on a sofa one day before reading the riot act. He demanded she should give him up. Her answer was to ask the Pope for a separation. This was eventually granted to her and she went to live under her father's roof at the nearby Palazzo Gamba. Byron was left with her eccentric husband, the poet comically protesting that he could not possibly move out because of his vast menagerie!

Revolution was in the air and politics were soon to change all their lives. Teresa's family was well known for its sympathy with the oppressed poor. In 1821, after a fracas in which the commander of the papal troops was killed in the street in Ravenna, the Gambas, including Teresa, had to fly from the Pope's domain. Teresa left Byron in floods of tears, wondering if she would ever see him again.

Three months elapsed before he could follow. Shelley had visited him in Ravenna, finding him popular with the people there who knew he sympathized with their struggles. Byron told his friend that he was 'reformed, as far as gallantry goes'.

In October of that year Byron's travelworn Napoleonic coach rumbled out of Ravenna for the last time. He found a suitable house on the river Arno, near Pisa, only two or three minutes from where Teresa had settled with her family. They formed a new social circle, entertaining in style and giving dinners at which a mellowed Byron played host with wit and irony until the early hours of the morning. Perhaps it was just a shade too domestic, too cosy. When Lady Blessington visited him he told her, 'there is something in the poetical temperament that precludes happiness, not only to the person who has it, but to those connected with him'. To her he confessed his extraordinary presentiment that he would die in Greece.

Greece had been on his mind for some time. He was totally in sympathy with those who suffered oppression of any kind. By the beginning of April 1823 he was afire to help the struggling Greek patriots in their war of independence against the Turks. He did not dare tell Teresa that he was going to war, partly because he feared she would try to stop him. But the young countess knew well enough what was happening and she too had a presentiment that he would not return. Their last hours together almost broke her heart.

Byron was only 35 when he sailed from Genoa to Greece in July 1823 but his constitution was wrecked and his life force spent. When he landed on the beach at Missolonghi, resplendent in scarlet uniform, the Greeks hailed him as a delivering angel. But the enterprise to which Byron was committed was badly planned and ill-conceived. Missolonghi was set on a lagoon rich in malaria. Once the winter rains began the place became a disease-ridden mudbowl. His health weakened by the conditions, Byron had no strength left to fight the rheumatic fever that struck him in the spring following that appalling winter. The end came swiftly on Easter Monday, 19 April 1824 when he fell into a deep sleep after delirium. There were memorial services in every important town in Greece. In England, those who had considered him to be a demon lover, Lucifer incarnate, flocked into the streets as the cortège carrying his body made its way home for burial.

Who was Jack the Ripper? The elusive outlaw

A question that still baffles criminologists

In the late 19th century Britain was the greatest, most prosperous nation in the world, and London the greatest city. But one part of the capital lay like a festering sore on the face of the British Empire. The jumble of ill-lit, foul-smelling little streets known as the East End offered its inhabitants only degradation and poverty.

More than half the children born there died before the age of five. Women were old by the time they were 40. Men turned to drink, and often crime, as their only escape. Many women would sell their worn, raddled bodies for a few pennies. And it was these 'fallen' women – the 'unfortunates', as they were euphemistically known to more genteel society – who became the prey of the world's most infamous murderer. Even today, nearly a century later, the very name Jack the Ripper induces a feeling of horror in London's East End.

The Ripper's reign of terror was short. He first struck on a warm night in August 1888. And on a chill, foggy evening three months later he claimed his last victim. It is known for certain that he slaughtered at least five women, and some criminologists have credited him with 11 murders.

Why does this man who killed only a handful of people during such a short span of time continue to exert such a frightful fascination? Why is he still held in awe around the world long after he has joined his pathetic victims in death?

Is it because of the unknown? Because he came from the darkness and struck in the most brutal, bloody and bestial way? Because he stalked the grim, dark alleys and yards at the dead of night? Because he eluded one of the most efficient and sophisticated police forces of the day? Because he left a frightened city whispering his gruesome name and then disappeared forever, back into the darkness?

All that is known for certain about Jack the Ripper is that he was left-handed – this was deduced by the police surgeons who examined the grisly remains of his victims – and that he had at least some medical knowledge. He was probably a tall, slim, pale man with a black moustache. This was the description given by witnesses who saw someone scurrying away from the vicinity of several of the crimes. Each time, the man wore a cap and a long coat, and he walked with the vigorous stride of a youth.

Writers, scientists, psychologists, detectives of every nation have sought to discover the identity of this most ghastly of killers. But none has done so. And it is unlikely that anyone ever will. Even when the secret Scotland Yard files on the case are finally made public in 1992, they are expected to cast little new light on the riddle.

The story of London's most mysterious and ferocious mass-murderer began shortly after 5 am on the morning of 7 August 1888. A man, desperately hoping for a job of which he had heard, hurried down the stairs of the Whitechapel hovel in which he had a room. He was determined to be first in the queue but was halted in his progress by a bundle lying on the first-floor landing. He went to push the bundle out of his way, and then recoiled with horror when he realized that what lay at his feet were the bloody remains of a woman.

He forgot about the job and rushed off to alert the police. The woman was identified as Martha Turner, a 'lady of easy virtue'. Her throat had been slit, she had been stabbed several times and bestial mutilations had been carried out on her body.

There is some doubt whether this woman was, in fact, a Ripper victim. And, as the murder of prostitutes was no rare thing in those days, the case was soon shelved. But when a second, similar murder happened 24 days later, fear and panic began to sweep the mean streets of the East End.

On the night of 30 August, Mary Ann Nicholls, known as Pretty Polly in the sleazy pubs of Whitechapel, was desperate for the money for a doss-house bed. So, when a client approached her, she leapt at the chance of making a few coppers, which would perhaps leave her with something over for a couple of tots of gin.

The man drew her into the shadows. If she finally realized there was anything wrong, it was too late. Her end was swift. The Ripper put a hand over her mouth and dextrously slit her throat. Then the killer set about his savage butchery.

Some time later, a police constable passing the tiny, unlit courtyard thought he heard a scuffling sound. He paused uncertainly, his eyes trying to pierce the gloom. As he moved forward, his foot slipped on something wet. It was blood, and the gory trail led him to the mutilated body of Mary Nicholls.

Had the constable disturbed the Ripper? If so, it was the nearest the police ever came to him at work.

A white-faced detective, sickened after examining the body, told a newspaper reporter: 'Only a madman could have done this.' And pathologist Dr Ralph Llewellyn told the coroner: 'I have never seen so horrible a case. She was ripped about in a manner that only a person skilled in the use of a knife could have achieved.'

The Ripper waited just a week before he struck again. His prey was 'Dark Annie' Chapman, who was dying of tuberculosis when she was hacked down. When she was found in Hanbury Street by a porter from nearby Spitalfields Market, her pitifully few possessions had been neatly laid out below her disembowelled corpse.

Rumours swept Whitechapel. One was that the Ripper carried his instruments of death in a little black bag – and so any innocent passer-by seen carrying such a bag was immediately chased by the crowd. Another rumour was that the Ripper was a foreign seaman. So any stranger with a foreign accent in Whitechapel had to be careful of what he said. Some had it that the killer was a Jewish butcher – and latent anti-Semitism, already simmering because of the influx of Jewish immigrants fleeing the Russian and Polish massacres, began bubbling to the surface.

An even wilder theory, popular in the most squalid areas, where there was no love lost between the inhabitants and the police, was that the killer was a policeman. How else, it was asked, would he be able to safely prowl the streets at night without creating suspicion?

The growing fear developed into irrational anger. And the spark needed to set the flames of panic coursing through Whitechapel came on the morning of Sunday, 30 September. As church bells chimed at eight o'clock, a constable on his way home spotted a white-stockinged leg projecting from a factory gateway. He had found the body of Elizabeth 'Long Liz' Stride.

It seems that the killer had been disturbed in his work – for the body of Long Liz was not mutilated – and that, to satisfy his frustrated bloodlust, the Ripper had struck again that same night. It was during this killing that he left what may be the only positive clue in his reign of terror. Just 15 minutes' walk from where the body of Long Liz was discovered lay the bloody remains of Catherine Eddowes. From her body, the most terribly mutilated so far, a trail of blood led to a message scrawled in chalk on a wall: 'The Jews are not men to be blamed for nothing.'

Did this mean that the Ripper was a Jew who, driven beyond endurance by persecution, had struck back at the only victims he could find? The message, a vital piece of evidence, was never studied properly. Sir Charles Warren, head of the Metropolitan Police, perhaps fearing a violent backlash of hatred against the Jews, ordered the chalked message to be rubbed out and kept a secret.

Two days earlier, a letter had been sent to the Central News Agency in Fleet Street. It read:

Dear Boss, I keep on hearing that the police have caught me. But they won't fix me yet . . . I am down on certain types of women and I won't stop ripping them until I do get buckled.

Grand job, that last job was. I gave the lady no time to squeal. I love my work and want to start again. You will soon hear from me, with my funny little game. I saved some of the proper red stuff in a ginger beer bottle after my last job to write with, but it went thick like glue and I can't use it. Red ink is fit enough, I hope. Ha, Ha!

Next time I shall clip the ears off and send them to the police just for jolly. The letter was signed Jack the Ripper, the first time the name had been used. And the killer of Catherine Eddowes had indeed attempted to cut off her ears . . .

The rumours continued to spread. The killer was a mad doctor. He was a homicidal Russian sent by the Czar's secret police to discredit the London police, because they were not taking enough action against emigré anarchists. He was a puritan, obsessed with cleansing the East End of vice. He was a crazed midwife with a murderous hatred of prostitutes.

But still nobody was any nearer to naming the Ripper. And, on 9 November, he struck again. Mary Kelly was unlike any of the other victims. She was younger – only 25, whereas the others had been in their 40s – blonde and attractive. The last person to see her alive was George Hutchinson, whom she had asked for money to pay her rent. When he said he could not help, she approached a slim, well-dressed man with a trim moustache and a deer-stalker hat. . . .

Early next morning, a man named Henry Bowers knocked impatiently at Mary's door for her unpaid rent. Finally he went to the window of her room and pushed aside the sacking curtains. The sickening sight within made him forget all about the rent and sent him running for the landlord. Later, he was to say: 'I shall be haunted by this for the rest of my life.'

With Mary Kelly's death, the Ripper's reign ended as suddenly and mysteriously as it began.

Today we are no nearer than ever to discovering his identity. If the style and spelling of his messages were genuine and he was a poor, badly educated man, where did he obtain his medical expertise? If he was wealthy, how did he know the back streets and slums of Whitechapel so well that he could melt into the shadows as expertly as a native?

Two convicted murderers claimed to be the Ripper. One, who poisoned his mistress, said when arrested: 'You've got Jack the Ripper at last.' But there is little evidence to suggest that he was telling the truth. The second cried out, as the trap door of the gallows opened: 'I am Jack the . . .' But it was later proved that he was in America when the Ripper crimes were committed.

Some members of the police force were sure they knew the identity of the Ripper. In 1908, the assistant commissioner of police said flatly: 'In stating that he was a Polish Jew, I am merely stating a definitely established fact.'

But Inspector Robert Sager, who played a leading part in the Ripper investigations and who died in 1924, said in his memoirs: 'We had good reason to suspect a man who lived in Butcher's Row, Aldgate. We watched him carefully. There was no doubt that this man was insane, and, after a time, his friends thought it advisable to have him removed to a private asylum. After he was removed, there were no more Ripper atrocities.'

Even Queen Victoria's eldest grandson has been named as a suspect. He was Prince Albert Victor, Duke of Clarence, who, if he had lived, would have become King when his father, Edward VII, died.

A contemporary print of 'vigilantes' watching for Jack the Ripper suspects.

Perhaps the two most intriguing solutions are the two most recent. Author and broadcaster Daniel Farson points his finger at Montagu John Druitt, a failed barrister who had medical connections and a history of mental instability in his family. Farson bases his accusation on the notes of Sir Melville Macnaghten, who joined Scotland Yard in 1889 and became head of the Criminal Investigation Department in 1903. Macnaghten names three main Ripper suspects – a Polish tradesman who probably hated women, a homicidal Russian doctor, and Druitt. Finally, police decided that Druitt was the murderer. A few weeks after Mary Kelly's death, his body was found floating in the River Thames.

Writer Stephen Knight proposes the fascinating theory that three men were responsible for the Ripper murders. He says that a royal physician, a coachman and an artist committed the crimes. Their motive was to silence a gang of prostitutes who had concocted a plan to blackmail the royal family about the secret marriage of the Duke of Clarence. The resulting scandal, it was feared, might lead to possible revolution. So a tortuous plot to murder the prostitutes was worked out by members of the royal family, Prime Minister Lord Salisbury, police chiefs and freemasons.

The East End of London is changing now. High-rise blocks replace the mean little houses. The streets are well lit, the public houses respectable. The people are relatively prosperous. But however much the East End changes, the ghost of Jack the Ripper will haunt its streets until the end of time.

The Enigma of Nuremberg

The teenage boy who appeared from nowhere, staggering through the streets of Nuremberg, Germany, on Whit Monday 1828, acted as if he was injured or drunk.

He walked unsteadily up to a complete stranger, a local cobbler, and gave him a letter addressed to the Captain of the 6th Cavalry Regiment, then stationed in the city, and mumbled repeatedly: 'I want to be a soldier like my father was.'

The cobbler helped the boy to walk with difficulty to the police station where the lad waited until the cavalry officer was summoned. At the police station the letter was opened and the senior police officer and the cavalryman read the poignant and bitter message.

The letter explained: 'I send you a boy who is anxious to serve his king in the Army. He was left at my house on 7 October 1812, and I am only a poor labourer. I have ten children of my own to bring up. I have not let him outside since 1812.'

With cruel indifference, the letter added: 'If you do not want to keep him, kill him or hang him up a chimney.'

The letter was unsigned and the police and the army officer sadly assumed that the 16-year-old boy, abandoned as a baby, was still unwanted. The scrawled message seemed to explain his peculiar behaviour, unable to walk properly on feet as soft as a baby's and with an infant vocabulary of only a few words. But the lad could write his own name in a firm, legible hand – Caspar Hauser.

The jailer in Nuremberg was fascinated by the boy and kept him in a room in his own quarters where he could watch him through a secret opening. It took him only a few days of careful observation before he decided that Caspar was neither a born idiot nor a young madman. With loving patience, the jailer, using sign language, taught Caspar to talk, noting how quickly and eagerly the boy began to learn new skills.

Within six weeks the burgomaster of Nuremberg had been summoned to the jail to hear the first halting details from Caspar of his wretched life.

All Caspar could remember was being kept in a small cell, about 1.8 m (6 ft) long, 1.2 m (4 ft) wide and 1.5 m (5 ft) high. The shutters on the window of the cell were kept permanently closed and he slept in threadbare clothes on a bed of straw. He saw nobody and heard virtually nothing all the years he was there, living on a diet of bread and water he found in the cell when he awoke each day. Sometimes, he revealed, the water tasted bitter and made him fall asleep. Every time this happened, he woke up to find his hair had been cut and his nails trimmed.

After years of isolation, Caspar recalled, a hand reached into his cell from behind and gave him a sheet of paper and a pen. The hand guided him each day until he could write his name and repeat the phrase: 'I want to be a soldier ...'

One morning his cell was unlocked and he was taken out into the street, into daylight and the company of other people for the first time in his life. It was the first time, too, that he wore shoes.

In the confusion of unfamiliar sights and sounds, Caspar remembered nothing until he found himself in Nuremberg with the letter in his hand.

The boy's story touched the burgomaster and the people of Nuremberg and soon young Caspar was 'adopted' by a Professor Daumer who began the task of educating the teenager into the ways of the world around him.

In a few months Caspar was transformed from a stumbling retarded child to a bright intelligent young man. With his mysterious background creating a

Caspar Hauser

buzz of excitement in his new home town, he became a much sought after guest in the homes of curious philosophers and wealthy intellectuals. And Nuremberg society soon began to remark on Caspar's startling physical resemblance to the members of the families of the grand dukes of Baden, the rulers of the province. Rumours abounded, the most popular being that Caspar was of noble birth and that his childhood isolation had been heartlessly planned to prevent him succeeding to power as a Baden prince.

At the time of Caspar's birth, two of the princes of the Baden family in direct line of succession had died in mysterious circumstances. The people of Nuremberg were convinced that Caspar Hauser was an unwanted son of the royal family, born to the Grand Duke Karl and his wife the Grand Duchess Stephanie.

Grand Duchess Stephanie had indeed given birth to a child sixteen years earlier, but she never saw the baby. Scheming palace doctors had told her that her baby had died soon after birth of cerebral meningitis, a diagnosis confirmed by a post-mortem examination.

And when Grand Duke Karl became seriously ill in 1829, he had no son and heir to succeed him.

Caspar, by that time, had been in Nuremberg for a year, living with Professor Daumer and growing in reputation as a personable, intelligent young man of distinct ability and culture.

As the Grand Duke's health failed, in October 1829, Caspar's already bitterly unhappy young life was almost ended. He was attacked and stabbed by a masked assailant in the basement of Professor Daumer's house, but he survived his wounds.

The following year the Grand Duke died and the royal succession passed to another line of the family, the sons of the Countess of Hochberg.

A few months later an eccentric English nobleman, said by many to be a friend of the Hochberg family, appeared in Nuremberg to petition the courts to become Caspar's guardian in place of Professor Daumer. Philip, the 4th Earl of Stanhope, won his court plea in spite of local opposition. And so, out of public sight, another period of isolation began for the wretched Caspar. He was taken away from his new found friends in Nuremberg on Lord Stanhope's orders and lodged with a surly Protestant pastor in the town of Ansbach, 20 miles away.

With Caspar safely out of the way, Lord Stanhope lost interest in his new foster son, leaving him to his miserable existence with Pastor Meyer.

On 11 December 1833 Caspar, then 21 years old and working as an apprentice bookbinder, was returning to his dismal lodgings through a park when he was stopped by a stranger. The man asked his name and when Caspar replied, he stabbed him repeatedly. Badly wounded, Caspar staggered back to Pastor Meyer's home. But the preacher never informed the police, cruelly taunting Caspar that he had inflicted the wounds himself to get attention. Three days later Caspar Hauser died in agony.

Hearing of his death, the Grand Duchess Stephanie was reported to have broken down and wept, sobbing that she believed the young man had really been the son she was told had died in infancy.

But none of his friends or the German courts could ever prove the background of the boy with no history and no future. They could never solve the riddle of who had locked him away for the first 16 years of his hopeless life, or who the mysterious assassins were who finally succeeded in killing him.

The boy who came from nowhere was buried in the churchyard at Ansbach. On his tombstone was the simple epitaph: 'Here lies Caspar Hauser, enigma.'

Chapter nine

MYSTERIES OF MANKIND

They are loved, loathed, feared, despised and even worshipped; 'human beings' whose appearances and natures often conspire to defy that very description. They are called freaks or misfits, they are exhibited, exploited, applauded and even laughed at, sometimes they are shut away from the world. But, however odd, they *are* human beings, unfortunate victims of the mysteries of mankind.

The Elephant Man

'**S**tand up!' The penny showman barked his command. And from a darkened corner of the room, what had appeared to be a pile of filthy rags began to stir. Slowly, an inhuman-looking shape began to rise in the gloom, discarding the tattered blanket under which it had cowered. A stench of decaying fruit filled the air as the figure laboured to pull itself to the limit of its bowed height.

Joseph Carey Merrick finally stood quite still. In the dimness of the old shop, once used by a greengrocer, he cast a strange, unnerving shadow; a hideous, nightmarish caricature of a human being, or of something only half-human. He appeared to have the legs and body of a man. But his head, face and one arm were so grotesquely distorted that they seemed to represent the profile of a wild beast with a long, pendulous trunk. Joseph Merrick, the wretched, stooping, sideshow attraction in the hired shop at No. 123 Whitechapel Road, London, was the Elephant Man.

Outside the shop, opposite the famous London Hospital, a garish, painted poster advertised the most famous of all freaks exhibited in sensation-hungry Victorian England. And such was Merrick's monstrous appeal that his penny showman master was able to charge a handsome tuppence-a-peep at his prize specimen. The Elephant Man was big business.

In 1884 a young and ambitious surgeon from the London Hospital crossed the road one day to investigate beyond the lurid poster which had caught his eye from an upper window. Frederick – later to become Sir Frederick – Treves, wrote of the freakshow billboard:

'This very crude production depicted a frightful creature that could only have been possible in a nightmare. It was the figure of a man with the characteristics of an elephant. The transfiguration was not far advanced. There was still more of the man than of the beast. This fact – that it was still human – was the most repellent attribute of the creature. There was nothing about it of the pitiableness of the misshapened or the deformed, nothing of the grotesqueness of the freak, but merely the loathing insinuation of a man being changed into an animal. Some palm trees in the background of the picture suggested a jungle and might have led the imagination to assume that it was in this wild that the perverted object had roamed.'

Inside the shop Treves caught his first sight of the Elephant Man. The pathetic Merrick, then aged 21, was stripped naked to the waist, bare-footed and wearing only a ragged pair of trousers several sizes too large for him. A hip disease had left him lame and he was only able to stand upright using a

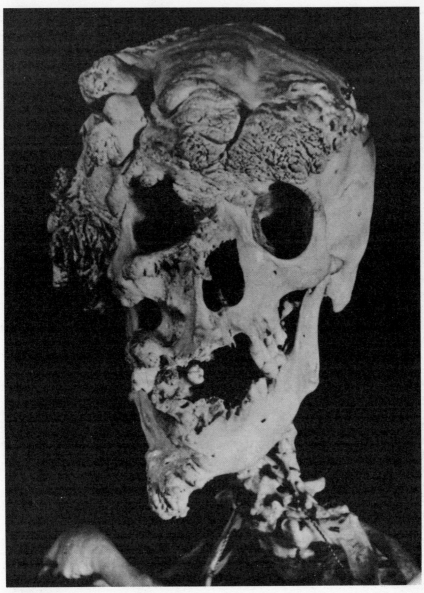

Joseph Merrick's deformed skull

stick. A huge, bony growth had enlarged his head to the thickness of a man's waist, almost hiding one eye, and a second gnarled growth had twisted his mouth into a trunk-like shape. Treves described the face as totally expressionless and wooden, like an ugly native idol. Both legs and one arm were swollen, misshapen and useless, ending in hands and feet no better than paddles, with fat, stunted fingers and toes. In stark contrast, one arm was perfectly formed with smooth skin and a delicate, sensitive hand. A colleague of Treves later said of Merrick: 'The poor fellow . . . was deformed in body, face, head and limbs. His skin, thick and pendulous, hung in folds and resembled the hide of an elephant – hence his show name.'

Little is known of the early life of Merrick, who seemed to have appeared from nowhere as a freak-show horror in London's East End. According to his birth certificate, however, he was born on 5 August 1862, the son of Joseph Rockley Merrick and Mary Jane Merrick, at 50 Lee Street, Leicester. His mother was a cripple, the family home was a slum and, shortly after his birth, Joseph Merrick was abandoned to an orphanage. For as long as he could remember, he had been exhibited as a freak, passing from one keeper to another and from one peepshow to the next. He could speak, but his appalling facial deformities made his words barely intelligible.

The only life he had ever known was in a fairground booth as an object of derision, revulsion or sneering humour; so near to the laughing, cringing crowds to whom he was forced to display his body, yet so far removed from a normal existence. It is known that Merrick could read, but the only books he was ever given were a bible and cheap romantic novels. He was childlike, naive about worldly matters. His idea of pleasure was to lock himself away in a shuttered room.

After much persuasion, Treves managed to prise the Elephant Man away from his keeper. Showman Tom Norman agreed to allow the surgeon to examine him. The examination took place – but just 24 hours later police closed the Whitechapel Road show and Merrick and Norman vanished. Merrick fled to the continent and a string of new masters. But in towns all over Europe, exhibitions of the Elephant Man were being banned and censured as being degrading. Eventually, in Brussels, he ceased to be a viable asset. His latest master robbed him of his savings, gave him a railway ticket to London and washed his hands of him. Merrick was alone, unwanted and penniless; a bizarre, cloaked figure who hid his face with a huge cap pulled well down to avoid investigation by suspicious and untrusting strangers.

Treves, in an essay on the life of the Elephant Man, wrote of Merrick's voyage home: 'The journey may be imagined. Merrick was in his alarming outdoor garb. He would be harried by an eager mob as he hobbled along the quay. They would run ahead to get a look at him. They would lift the hem of

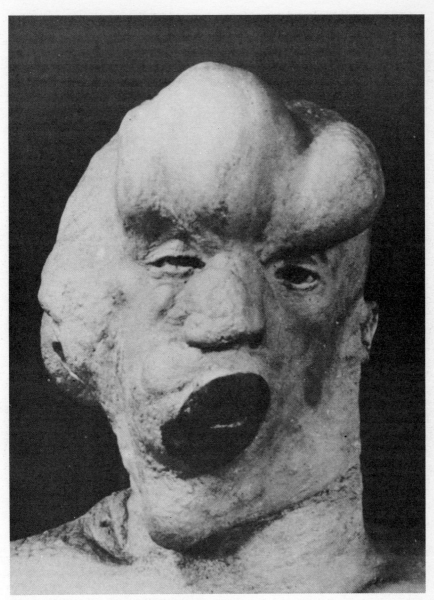

Reconstruction of the Elephant Man's face

his cloak to peep at his body. He would try to hide in the train or in some dark corner of the boat, but never could be free from that ring of curious eyes or from those whispers of fright and aversion. He had but a few shillings in his pocket and nothing to eat or drink on the way. A panic-dazed dog with a label on his collar would have received some sympathy and possibly some kindness. Merrick received none.'

Somehow, amazingly, Merrick managed to make it to London's Liverpool Street Station, where he was found, terrified, exhausted and huddled in the darkest corner of the waiting room, by a policeman. He was clutching his only remaining possession – Frederick Treves' business card. Treves was called for, and was able to usher the creature he immediately recognized through a gawping crowd and into a cab to the London Hospital. There he hoped to provide a permanent refuge for Merrick, despite a hospital rule against taking chronic or incurable cases. Treves succeeded in persuading the hospital's management committee to make an exception, and so began the second life of the Elephant Man.

In a letter to the *Times* newspaper, the hospital management committee immediately launched a public appeal for funds. Within a week, enough money had been raised to keep Merrick there for the rest of his life. A self-contained suite of two isolation rooms was allocated to him. Treves was now able to begin the long and arduous task of trying to rehabilitate him. Slowly, he learned to understand Merrick's speech. And then he made a discovery which was to add a new, tragic twist. In most cases of such extreme physical deformity, Treves believed, there was an accompanying lack of intelligence and understanding which helped lessen the subject's awareness of his appearance. In Merrick's case, he had been blessed – or perhaps cursed – with a sensitive, intelligent mind, fully aware of his appearance and desperate for affection.

Treves wrote: 'Those who are interested in the evolution of character might speculate as to the effect of this brutish life upon a sensitive and intelligent man. It would be reasonable to surmise that he would become a spiteful and malignant misanthrope, swollen with venom and filled with hatred of his fellow men, or, on the other hand, that he would degenerate into a despairing melancholic on the verge of idiocy. Merrick, however, was no such being. He had passed through the fire and had come out unscathed. His troubles had ennobled him. He showed himself to be a gentle, affectionate and lovable creature ... free from any trace of cynicism or resentment, without a grievance and without an unkind word for anyone. I have never heard him deplore his ruined life or resent the treatment he had received at the hands of callous keepers. His gratitude to those about him was pathetic in its sincerity and eloquent in the childlike simplicity with which it was expressed.'

Gradually, under the care of Treves, Merrick progressed. Yet he remained haunted by one nagging doubt. He could not understand, or believe, that his stay at the London Hospital was to be permanent. 'When am I going to be moved?' he asked Treves, 'and where to?' Pathetically, he asked that if he had to be moved, could it be to a lighthouse, or an asylum for the blind, where at least he would be free from the ridicule of his fellow men. Slowly, Merrick's health began to improve and his confidence grew daily. 'I am happier every hour of the day,' he told Treves, an expression of joy which prompted the gifted surgeon to try a further experiment.

Treves persuaded a young lady friend to visit Merrick and spend some time talking with him. The girl agreed. As she walked into Merrick's room, she smiled and held out her hand. Merrick bowed his heavy head and wept. His tears, though, were not in sadness. He was still a young man of only 23, with a tender feeling for anything beautiful. And it was the first time in his life that a beautiful woman had smiled at him, or even taken his hand.

That poignant moment proved to be another turning point in Merrick's life. His fame began to spread far beyond the hospital walls and many people became eager to meet the celebrated Elephant Man. They were allowed to do so, provided they behaved as guests and not sensation-seeking sightseers. Soon, Merrick's hospital suite was decorated with signed pictures of Victorian socialites who flocked to see him. But his greatest joy was still to come . . .

It came on the day he was visited by his most important guest, the Princess of Wales (later Queen Alexandra). She made a special visit to take tea with Merrick. That visit was the first of many, and Treves later wrote of the Elephant Man's Royal appointments:

'The Queen . . . sent him every year a Christmas card with a message in her own handwriting. On one occasion she sent him a signed photograph of herself. Merrick, quite overcome, regarded it as a sacred object and would hardly allow me to touch it. He cried over it, and after it was framed had it put up in his room as a kind of icon. I told him that he must write to Her Royal Highness to thank her for her goodness. This he was pleased to do, as he was very fond of writing letters, never before in his life having had anyone to write to. I allowed the letter to be dispatched unedited. It began "My dear Princess" and ended "Yours very sincerely". Unorthodox as it was, it was expressed in terms any courtier would have envied.'

As the Elephant Man's life began to blossom, there were, more and more frequently, expeditions outside the hospital. A famous actress of the period arranged a private box for him at the Drury Lane Theatre, where Merrick was allowed to use the Royal entrance. There, with a screen of nurses in evening dress in front of him, Merrick watched, transfixed, as a troupe of pantomime players took to the stage. He was deeply impressed, if confused. It did not occur to him that the performances he was watching were not part of real life. Long after his visit, he spoke of the characters portrayed as if they were real people and as if the show he had seen was still going on.

Once, he was allowed to visit Treves' own home, where he gaped in astonishment at every room. He had read descriptions of furniture-filled homes, but he had never been inside a real house. The safe refuge of a gamekeeper's lodge was also found, so that Merrick could enjoy trips to the country. Peeping from a freak show caravan on his earlier travels, he had often seen trees and fields, but he had never before actually walked in a wood, or picked a flower. Merrick's stay in the country became an immensely happy period in his life. He wrote to Treves in ecstasy, enclosing daisies, dandelions and buttercups; simple flowers, but to him rare and beautiful objects. In his letters, Merrick told how he had seen strange birds, startled a hare from her form, made friends with a fierce dog and watched trout darting in a stream.

After a few weeks in the country, Merrick returned to the hospital, happy to be 'home' with his personal possessions. More and more he tried to become like other human beings. But his deformities, if anything, became worse. A report later revealed his continuing tragedy:

'The bony masses and pendulous flaps of skin grew steadily. The outgrowths from the upper jaw and its integuments – the so-called trunk – increased so as to render his speech more and more difficult to understand. The most serious feature, however, in the patient's illness was the increasing size of the head ... The head grew so heavy that at length he had great difficulty in holding it up. He slept in a sitting or crouching position, with his hands clasped over his legs and his head on his knees. If he lay down flat the heavy head tended to fall back and produce a sense of suffocation.'

One night in April 1890, Joseph Carey Merrick, the Elephant Man, was found dead in his bed. He died because of his desperate desire to be like other people. And, in a desperate, fateful last experiment, he tried to sleep flat on his back.

After Merrick's death, it was Treves's painful duty to dissect the Elephant Man's body and eventually remount his bones into the appallingly misshapen skeleton which remains today. It must have been an agonizing task for the skilled surgeon, who had grown so close to his strange patient. Yet, of the man he once described as 'the most disgusting specimen of humanity' that he had ever seen, Treves was finally to write this epitaph:

'As a specimen of humanity, Merrick was ignoble and repulsive; but the spirit of Merrick, if it could be seen in the form of the living, would assume the figure of an upstanding and heroic man, smooth browed and clean of limb ... and with eyes that flashed undaunted courage.'

Sisters of Mystery

Twins Greta and Freda Chaplin are Britain's sisters of mystery. A quirk of nature has created them totally identical in mind, body, behaviour and even emotion. They are absolute mirror images of one another; living so perfectly in unison that they sometimes conjure up the idea that they might have been cloned in the style of only the wildest of science fiction fantasies.

They have been called 'The Terrible Twins', 'The Pests', and various other names in a blaze of newspaper publicity which has driven them into deep retreat from prying eyes. And, as though they were singing a duet, they say together with impeccable timing: 'We want to get away from people staring at us, laughing at us . . . the unkindness.'

It is true that their bizarre, unrequited love-in-tandem for a Yorkshire lorry driver landed them in a courtroom and at the centre of controversy. But, equally, they have become victims too; time-warped back to the days of the Victorian peep show by a new public lust for the true freak.

Greta and Freda, 39, spent six weeks in jail between May and June 1981. They were sentenced after a series of court warnings to stop their 20-year pursuit and harassment of 56-year-old near neighbour Ken Iveson, the unwilling object of their dual passion. Medical experts called to give evidence admitted that they were completely baffled by the twins' exact physical and mental make-up, let alone their illegal duplicity. The judge who sentenced them released them two weeks early 'as an exercise purely of mercy.'

Lorry driver Iveson, who lived near the twins in Moore Avenue, York for many years, later explained: 'Wherever one went, the other was walking behind. They never played with the other kids in the street when they were young. My trouble with them began when I ticked them off for throwing torn newspapers into my parents' garden. After that, they were always hanging about me and pulling faces at me. Their obsession grew and grew. They followed me everywhere, popping up from behind walls.'

Into adulthood, the infatuation followed, until a mighty legal hand fell at the same time upon the shoulders of Greta and Freda. Now they live together in a hostel in York, maintaining their remarkable double act.

They have always worn the same clothes, even to the extent as schoolgirls of swopping a sock each if their mother sent them out in different coloured pairs. And, uncannily, they burst into tears at the same time at the slightest hint that they might ever be separated. They sob: 'Nothing will ever make us hate each other. We will always do everything together.'

On the twins' release from prison, a social worker gave them each a bar of soap as a present. The bars were different colours, so they cut each in two and swopped halves. Their eating habits are identical. They have been seen to put food in their mouths simultaneously and finish their meals at precisely the same time. Their powers of telepathy, explored to the limit of current understanding, remain as mysterious as their facsimile lifestyle. Sometimes they speak in unison. Sometimes one begins a sentence and the other finishes it.

Dr Wilfred Hume, of Leeds University Department of Psychiatry, who has studied Greta and Freda at length, has said: 'I have never come across anything like this case. They are very dependent on each other. And now they have got to this stage in their lives it is unlikely they will change. The only problem is going to come when one of them dies. The remaining one would either cope, eventually, after a period of stress, or, perhaps more likely, die very shortly afterwards.'

Following their release from jail, Greta and Freda reported to a local hospital every day for occupational therapy. Their efforts would include flower arranging or handicrafts, and very often their work was identical.

The twins still do their shopping together; carrying their identical purchases home in identical plastic bags, from the same local supermarket. According to their social worker at the hostel: 'They are free to walk away from here whenever they choose. But they don't want to go. They do absolutely everything together. I have never seen them apart.'

In a frank interview with the London *Daily Star*, Greta and Freda have spoken of the strange mental bond that ties them together like inseparable Siamese twins. At school, they say, they always insisted on sitting together, and would scream if any teacher tried to separate them. And, speaking virtually always in unison, they add: 'We have always been like this, all our lives. Speaking together just comes naturally to us. We do everything together; dress the same, have a bath together and we like the same kind of food. We go everywhere together. We are never apart.'

Sadly, and almost like fairytale caricatures of themselves, they explain public reaction to them: 'People are always looking at us, laughing in the street. But they hadn't better say anything. No they hadn't better. No they hadn't better. People have been hurtful and unkind to us. We want to find a place of our own to live together. We must be together. Nothing interests us much. We are only happy together.'

Dr David Westbury, of Winterburn Hospital, Tees-side, who has also studied the twins in depth, says: 'There is certainly no medical explanation or medical solution. All that can be done . . . has been done.' Which means that Greta and Freda Chaplin must remain, together, sisters of mystery.

Greta and Freda Chaplin

Maurice Tillet

The Hideous Wrestler

Maurice Tillet born in France in 1910, was a gifted, highly intelligent man who could speak 14 languages and turn his hand adroitly to virtually anything he chose. He could have had the pick of any career he wanted and, if ever the phrase applied to one man exclusively, the world really was his oyster.

Then tragedy struck. When he was in his twenties, he developed acromegaly, a rare and horrific disease which causes bones to grow wildly and uncontrollably. From an early age, it tends to turn infants into fast-growing giants. Yet at his stage in life – a life which had been so rich in promise – it turned Tillet instead into a hideously deformed parody of a human being. Within months, he had changed from a smart, reasonably handsome whizz-kid, as we would have known him today, into a grotesque distortion of a young man, frightened even to venture into public gaze.

In search of a new identity to fit his chronic disfigurement, Tillet fled to America, where he cashed in on his shattered appearance in the only way he could, by becoming a professional wrestler, billed as a fearsome, freak ogre of the ring. He was an instant success, an ironic comparison with the time when his life could have meant so much more to him. Spectators roared with delight as he – cast as a wrestling 'baddie' – grappled with other men for a living.

He resigned himself to a friendless, lonely existence, even shunning the charity of others who took pity on his misshapen form. Bones jutted into awkward positions all over his body, twisting it into what resembled a huge, anomalous mass. In the ring, he resembled some kind of nightmare contortionist as his body was so badly afflcted.

Yet Tillet himself remained a gentle giant, with the inner soul of a poet, scholar and serious man. And a few people did, somehow, manage to befriend him. One was businessman Patrick Kelly, to whose home in Braintree, Massachusetts, Tillet was often invited. Together, the two would play chess and, in rare moments of self-pity, Tillet would raise his deformed head and moan: 'How awful it is to be imprisoned in this body.'

In 1955, Tillet died. In his memory, Mr Kelly had a death mask of his tragic friend made, which he placed on his library desk. It was to mark the last of their chess games: games the two had enjoyed so much, and which had spawned a bond of friendship between a businessman and a monster.

In 1980, 25 years after Tillet's death, the games began again. This spine-chilling twist to the tale came after Mr Kelly had installed a computerized chess machine, against which he frequently played, beside the plaster cast of Tillet's head. Late one evening, the computer deviated from its programmed patterns of play and used an 18th century opening invented by a French master – a gambit the long-since dead Tillet had used consistently.

'I played out the game, and the next morning noticed that the computer was not plugged in,' says Mr Kelly. 'But I thought nothing of it at the time. Yet a few weeks later the computer used a similar opening – and again it was not connected to any power supply'. Electronic engineers made a painstaking check of the system for Mr Kelly – and discovered to their astonishment that the computer could operate without electricity as long as it was close to the death mask of the long-forgotten Tillet. Puzzled, the businessman had the plaster cast X-rayed, only to affirm the fact that it was, indeed, solid plaster.

Only one, haunting answer could remain; the ghost or, perhaps, the sensitive, gentle soul of the hideous wrestler had returned to the place and the pastime he had enjoyed the most in his tortured life – playing chess with his best friend.

Mr Kelly firmly believes this is the case, and accepts that if the unplugged computer does not work for a period of days, Tillet's spirit is absent. 'When I want a game,' he says, 'I set up the pieces without plugging the set in. If there is no response, I know that Maurice is not with me for the time being . . .'

The Faceless Child

The little girl called Alice was just a few weeks old when she was rejected by her mother. The infant was considered to be too much of a burden and the poor woman made the heart-rending decision that she would never be able to cope with her or help her in later years to lead anything like a normal life. For Alice was born without a face.

She had come into the world suffering from one of nature's rarest and most cruel aberrations, a birth defect known as bilateral cleft face. Her eyelids were on the side of her head, yet she had no eyes; where her mouth should have been there were only small holes opening into soft mucous membranes; she had no nose; the very shape of her skull was distorted. She had severe problems simply breathing; she could only be fed through a tube inserted into her neck. It seemed that whatever future the stricken baby might have would be a nightmarish one in a sightless, shuttered world as far removed from an ordinary life as it might be possible to imagine.

Alice's first good fortune came when a nurse, Thelma Perkins, at the University of Tennessee Hospital in Knoxville where she was born, fell in love with the tragic infant and, with her husband Raymond, became her legal guardian. Thelma said: 'Alice was only one hour old when I first saw her . . . and I cried that any little baby should be born like that.'

Astonishingly, apart from the appearance of her face, her breathing problems and the difficulties attached to feeding her, Alice was healthy. Today, at the time of writing, she is 6 years old – and beginning to reap the benefits of her second stroke of luck which is, against all the odds, helping her learn to lead a life which, though it may never be perfectly normal, is far removed from the tortured existence it seemed she had been destined to lead.

Dr John Lynch, a plastic surgeon at the Vanderbilt Hospital saw her plight and is now, in a series of remarkable operations, rebuilding her face. He is pioneering advances in what he says is only the seventh documented case of bilateral cleft face in medical history. But it is a slow, delicate and nerve-racking process, fraught with uncertainty and the natural impatience of Thelma and Raymond Perkins, who are awaiting official clearance to adopt Alice as their own child, to see her progress.

Alice has undergone 11 painstaking operations so far and now has gums, teeth – which could not previously grow inside her disfigured mouth – and a nose which has an artificial bone taken from one of her ribs. Because no grafted-on nose could grow with the rest of her, Dr Lynch has given her an adult-sized one. Her mouth has been totally reconstructed, and Alice, having quickly learned how to move her tongue and jaws, has begun to eat semi-solid food; the tube attached to her oesophagus having at last, mercifully, been rendered useless.

Dr Lynch has also strengthened and completely reshaped Alice's skull and moved her eyelids to the correct positions on her rapidly changing face. The surgeon estimates that he will be required to perform a whole string of operations until she is 18 years old, by which time, he believes, Alice will be able to step out into a brave new world, with a completely new – and, he says, perfectly normal – face.

The total cost of the surgery will be about 300,000 dollars. The state of Tennessee has already contributed in excess of 60,000 dollars and the United Brotherhood of Carpenters and Joiners, of which Raymond Perkins is a member, has raised 23,000 dollars from members across the country. Fund-raising efforts are continuing, and thanks to the overwhelming generosity of public bodies and private citizens, Alice seems certain of her previously unthinkable bright prospects for the future.

For the time being, though, she is progressing by leaps and bounds. Although she is, of course, blind and still has a few problems with her mouth, she is learning at a fantastic rate. She can talk, following continued help from speech therapists and has been enrolled in a special education class. 'She has even learned to sing a little bit,' says her proud foster mother.

The use of skilled plastic surgery to correct and improve hideous facial deformities may sound like 20th century 'miracle medicine', yet such surgery, although obviously nowhere near as sophisticated, was being performed almost a century ago. The *International Medical Magazine* of Philadelphia reported a case in its issue of February 1894, in which a 72-year-old man with an enormous, disfiguring facial growth with an estimated weight of two pounds was rid of his deformity by plastic surgery.

In 1892, Dr J. P. Parker of Kansas City restored the missing bridge of a patient's nose by transplanting the bone and tissue of the second joint of his little finger in a then quite unique 'plastic operation'. Yet such surgery in those days was a rarity and for generations, tragic characters such as the Elephant Man were forced to live with their dreadful deformities. It is only relatively recent development that has enabled such savagely afflicted victims such as David Lopez and little Alice to look to the future with hope.

The hunchback of Memphis

In January 1982, a strange, appallingly bowed intruder snatched a teenage girl from the home of her wealthy parents – and, in a macabre re-enactment of the story of Quasimodo, the Hunchback of Notre Dame, took her to live with him in a filthy, secluded church attic.

After Leslie Marie Gattas, aged 15, was finally set free by her hideously stooping captor, police in America launched one of their most incredible manhunts ever, for the 'Hunchback of Memphis'. They have named their suspect, who is still at liberty, as a man called Ernest Earle Stubblefield, a 270-pound giant whose back is permanently bent by a terrible disfigurement.

Allegedly, the lonely, tormented hunchback treated young Leslie as an adopted, though trapped, daughter throughout her terrifying ordeal. By day, they slept in a tiny crawl space in the attic. By night, the hunchback would take his treasured victim down into the church itself, or even outside for walks. Memphis cops later revealed that they played gackgammon, watched a television which the hunchback had installed in the attic and lived on food stolen from the church refrigerator.

Says Leslie: 'He was a very lonely man. He treated me well, but all the time he knew that my only thoughts were on how I could escape. He didn't touch me or harm me physically in any way. In a sense I feel great pity for him, because his mind must be incredibly mixed-up. He has the appearance of a monster, yet although what he did to me was terrible, I am not sure that he is the evil ogre the world now thinks he is.'

Carolyn Browder, a close friend of the Gattas family told an American newspaper of the bizarre night that the twisted hunchback climbed through a house window and got into the bedroom where Leslie lay sleeping.

He tied her up and drove her through Memphis to the Christ United Church in the Gattas family car, which he had stolen. It was 12 hours before Leslie's family called the police, thinking that she had simply wandered off with a girl friend who was also missing from her home at the time.

During her four-month kidnap ordeal, Leslie tried desperately to summon rescue by dropping concealed notes around the church whenever she was taken out for moonlight walks by her hunchback captor. But, ironically, the church pastor, Reverend Gerry Corlew, dismissed the scribbled pleas for help as the work of cranks. At one stage, police actually searched the attic, as they turned the city of Memphis upside down in their hunt, but they failed to look in the camouflaged crawl space where Leslie and the hunchback lay hidden.

Leslie was finally rescued in April by two maintenance men who were armed with an axe-handle and a table leg, hoping to catch vandals or youngsters trying to steal church possessions. They spotted Leslie and her hunchback tormentor on one of their bizarre midnight prowls. One of the men, 55-year-old Milton Bennett, recalls: 'We couldn't believe our eyes. But we knew instantly that it was Leslie being held by the hunchback because there had been so many pictures of her in the local newspapers while the police search was being carried out.

'My partner and I immediately went for the hunchback. I managed to get him with one blow on the back of his neck with the table leg I was carrying. He was just like a wild animal. He never said a word. But he was hurt, and when he saw that we were prepared to use our weapons again, he just backed off and fled. He was so fast, we didn't stand a chance of catching him.'

Leslie later identified the 42-year-old Stubblefield as her strange, almost pathetic kidnapper from police 'mug shot' photo-files. Fingerprints taken from the church matched up – and the search is still going on for the now-identified 'Hunchback of Memphis', whose ex-wife, Ann Clarke, of Haleyville, Alabama, says: 'He has always been obsessed with violence and religion, possibly as some kind of unaccountable result of his deformity. He had wanted to take our daughter Patti, who is 17, to live with him in Memphis, but I would not allow it. When I heard of the kidnapping I realized that in his twisted mind Leslie had become a kind of surrogate replacement for her.'

Hunchbacks are a much rarer sight nowadays than they once were, mainly because most cases are not so severe that the bone disorder cannot be treated.

One of the most incredible stories concerning these figures, now immortalized by Hollywood horror films, unfolded on 13 July 1842 when 60 hapless hunchbacks were thrown into jail in London as police scoured the city for the misshapen wretch who had attempted to shoot Queen Victoria as she rode in her carriage with King Leopold of Belgium. The innocent freaks were eventually freed when hunchback John William Bean was arrrested and sentenced to 18 months in jail – a light sentence because his gun had only been loaded with pieces of clay pipe.

Hunchback dwarf

How many scholars realize that the great essayist Alexander Pope suffered the ignominy – as, indeed, he is known to have thought it was – of being a freak twice over? He was, in fact, both dwarf and hunchback, standing barely four feet tall and with an atrociously bowed, stooping body. Of his appalling afflictions, however, he is never known to have complained.

The Devil Boy

It is difficult to imagine the depths of suffering to which a two-year-old child can sink. Yet, when he was rescued by a group of nuns in 1976, it was the first time in his tortured little life that David Lopez had ever experienced an expression of love.

His home, in a village deep in the Peruvian rain forests, was a wooden cage through whose bars pitying adults would occasionally feed him morsels of food before turning away in horror. His very survival depended on such irregular acts of charity from a native community to whom he was a living curse or 'devil boy'; a human punishment meted out to them by some hidden, potent force.

The reason behind their cruel, superstitious imprisonment of an infant was simple; baby David was born without a face. He had no mouth or upper jaw, no lips or nose. And, as time went by, it appeared that his remaining features were being relentlessly eaten away. Had he not been discovered by those travelling sisters of mercy, David Lopez – a random name with which he was later christened – would almost surely have faced a lonely, agonizing death.

Instead, he plays today with little boys his own age, goes out shopping with his adoptive mother, absorbs, bright as a button, all that he is taught and enjoys a life a world away from the nightmare he once knew. At the hands of a skilled and dedicated surgeon who is literally rebuilding his face, David has emerged from his ordeal into what is indeed a brave, new world.

The first real glimmer of hope came when a social worker at the orphanage in the Peruvian capital of Lima where David was first taken remembered seeing a televised interview in which top Scottish surgeon Ian Jackson spoke of the enormous challenge of correcting facial deformities in children.

Cutting through a mountain of red tape, the orphanage managed to organize a passport for David to travel to Britain and a visa for him to stay in the country as long as he needed. Two airline companies responded to an appeal by providing him with a free first-class flight.

Ian Jackson, whose wife Marjorie and their four children immediately agreed that David should live with them as a member of the family, offered to perform a planned series of delicate operations completely free of charge. An appeal fund organized by church officials and local newspapers, to cover the cost of National Health Service facilities for David's treatment at Cannies-burn Hospital, near Glasgow, raised more than £50,000. Despite seemingly insurmountable difficulties, in little more than a year since he was found cowering in his prison cage, David Lopez was on the verge of being re-born.

To begin with, the prospect of surgery threw up alarming complications. In an interview two years after he began work rebuilding David's face, Ian Jackson said: 'I asked myself if David knew whether he was being punished or helped because he was too young to realize what was going on. He developed chest problems, so I had to suspend surgery for quite a while.

'Some day, David may curse me for not leaving him to his fate in the jungle, but I just hope I am giving him a chance, giving him a face that will be acceptable. He will have to take it from there. David will never be considered handsome, but surgery can give him a face that will allow him to lead a normal life. He has the opportunity to develop and I think he will come out on top. He is a bright, warm and intelligent little boy.'

Initially, it was difficult to determine whether David's face had been mauled by animals or if he had been the victim of a horrendous disease. In fact, his disfigurement was the result of a rare disease called noma, a condition caused by malnutrition which usually eats away at the corners of a victim's mouth. In David's case, the disease had become rampant, relentlessly devouring his jaws, nose and upper lip. When found, he was unable to talk and responded only to a few words of Spanish, the native tongue of the South American Indians.

With the trusting, innocent love of a child, David soon accepted Ian Jackson and his wife as 'mum and dad'. A Spanish-speaking tutor was hired as he began to settle into what to him was the unknown world of the family. But there was still the problem of the tiny girl at the play school, who refused to play with 'the boy with the funny face' and holidaymakers who took their children away from the beach when David arrived to build sandcastles.

Said Ian Jackson: 'Children are straightforward and honest when confronted with people who are disfigured. They make a casual remark out of innocent curiosity, but within five minutes they have forgotten about it and accept the person. David knows he doesn't look like other children. We have explained the matter to him and now he is so accustomed to being regarded as normal that he wonders why anyone bothers to remark on his face.'

On one occasion, the surgeon continued, David was in a sweet shop, and heard the shop-keeper remark about his 'terrible face' to a customer. 'David stood behind the counter, put his thumbs up to his ears and started to waggle his fingers. He regarded it as a huge joke. To him, waggling his fingers and poking out his tongue is really pulling a terrible face. He's a tough, independent little kid. David stands up for himself and really considers himself to be a member of our family. We treat him just like we treat our own children. When he is naughty, he gets spanked, just like my own son and daughters. David accepts that as natural, and that's the way it should be. He gets his fair share of cuddling, and he appreciates the fact that we don't hide him away. When the whole family goes out shopping or on a picnic, he comes with us. We have so forgotten about David's face that sometimes it takes a moment's thought to understand why strangers are staring at him.'

David has already undergone dozens of operations in which the tips of his ribs have been cut away and transplanted inside the fragile tissue of his face to form his upper mouth and nose. And, in a series of intricate skin graft operations, tissue has been transferred to his face to cover his newly-built, man-made features. One day, that gaping hole in the middle of his face will be gone forever.

Meanwhile, his home life too is being lovingly moulded. Marjorie Jackson says: 'The family has taken David to its heart. Everyone does if they take the trouble to get to know him. When he first arrived, he couldn't, or didn't want to, communicate at all. David must have known from his earliest moments that he wasn't like other children. Before we could win his trust he had to get over whatever had happened to him in the jungle. Because of the damage to his face he couldn't attempt to speak, but we soon realized how quick and intelligent he was. We had a worrying time when he first started play school, but only one of the children reacted badly.

'He makes friends quickly among other children. It is only grown-ups who present problems. I get very angry when adults approach to tell me that I shouldn't allow him to be seen outside the house because he is so ugly. They are the ugly ones. They refuse to understand the needs of a boy like David. He can be tough and boisterous and too energetic at times. When he gets together with our son Andrew the pair of them wrestle on the floor and play rough games of football in the back garden.

'But we don't wrap him in cotton wool. All we try to do is make sure he doesn't get any bruises or cuts which will hold back the healing of his surgery.'

Surgery which is transforming the face of a dark-complexioned, piercingly dark-eyed little boy from a jungle prisoner of hate into a happy, affectionate fellow who can face the world with dignity, pride, and a fiercely independent courage born from love.

Shepherd boy genius

The son of a shepherd, Vito Mangiamele astounded experts at the French Academy of Sciences with his mathematical wizardry when they examined him on 3 July 1839. Learned scholars were speechless when Sicilian-born Vito was able to calculate the cubic root of 3,796,416 in his head in the lightning time of just 30 seconds. He was 11 at the time.

The Limbless Wonder

An elderly nurse gently cradled the newborn infant in her arms and quietly wept as she whispered: 'Ah, the poor little thing. God will take him and it will be all for the best.' It was the first prophecy in the life of Arthur MacMurrough Kavanagh.

He was born, on 25 March 1831, into the ancestral home of Boris, County Carlow, amid vast estates in Southern Ireland whose owners through eight centuries had helped shape the country's history. His mother was Lady Harriet Margaret Le Poer Trench, second wife of Thomas Kavanagh, MP, a descendant of the Kings of Leinster. Yet, though high society had been eagerly awaiting the infant's arrival, there was no rejoicing when Arthur came into the world. No dreams or hopes for a baby boy whose life of pomp and privilege would be beyond question. Only the heart-rending words of the family nurse.

Fortunately, however, her prophecy proved wrong. Arthur lived 58 years, becoming one of the most famous characters in an already glittering dynasty, proving himself an accomplished sportsman, horseman and hunter and, eventually, an adroit and respected politician. Indeed, he was one of the most remarkable characters of the 19th century, which was truly amazing, for he was born without limbs.

Where his arms should have been, there were only two little stumps a few inches long. There were no legs at all. But such were Arthur's achievements, that it was said there was only one sad thing about him; his deep blue eyes. And such was his fighting spirit, that he never once displayed an inferiority complex.

He taught himself to write 'in a good hand' by gripping a pen between his teeth. He developed a keen intellect, shining as a youth in academic studies. But from an early age, he derived his greatest joy from his skill as one of the most able horsemen in Ireland, rarely missing a local hunt meeting. By leaning his broad shoulders forward, he could grip the reins with his two arm stumps, while strapped onto the horse in a specially-made chair saddle.

Once, he cheated death when his horse bolted while riding in a deer park near Boris. The horse galloped wildly and Arthur's strength began to wane, as he tried desperately to rein in the terrified beast with his two arm stumps. In act of incredible courage, he set it at a seemingly-impossible obstacle, a high brick wall surrounding the estate. As the animal reared, Arthur's saddle device slipped and he was thrown off onto his head. Several hours later, he was found, lying unconscious, by a member of his family.

Arthur trained himself to be a crackshot, using a gun without a trigger guard. He was able to hold the weapon under his left arm stump and squeeze the trigger with the other. He became a skilled yachtsman and a good angler, fishing from a boat or even on horseback. On one of his many travels around the world, he once went deep-sea fishing in the Arctic Circle. He excelled academically and artistically too, becoming a trained draughtsman and a talented painter.

When he was just 15 years old, Arthur, the Limbless Wonder, set out on an arduous tour of Africa and the Middle East as part of his education. Later he became one of the most travelled men of his time, covering vast distances on horseback or being carried by servants.

Once, while sailing down the Nile, Arthur nearly drowned. As his boat rolled suddenly, he was thrown from the deck and was in danger of being crushed by a second vessel alongside as he plunged into the water. None of the party on his boat had witnessed his fall overboard, but an Arab on the riverbank dived in to reach him and managed to bring him ashore. He at first appeared to be dead, but was miraculously revived by artificial respiration.

Only months after Arthur returned from his spectacular youthful adventure, he was planning his next and most ambitious foray. With his tutor, the Reverend David Wood, and his eldest brother Thomas, he set out to travel from Sweden to India on horseback. Their journey was to take them through Finland, Russia, along the Volga, over the Caspian Sea into Persia and, eventually, across the Persian Gulf and into Bombay. It was a three-year expedition which carried Arthur through the ordeals of semi-starvation, bitter winter climates, maddening desert heat and illnesses and hardships that would have proved insurmountable to a lesser man.

In November 1849, Arthur's party met a Persian Prince, whose palace became a temporary home after Arthur developed a fever. He awoke one morning to find himself being nursed back to health by an old black slave in the prince's harem, and spent his convalescence in the ladies' quarters!

In January 1850, he set out again, and once more narrowly cheated death.

Legless acrobat

Legless acrobat Eli Bowen, whose feet were joined straight onto his hips, became a sensation in the early 1900s when he left his home town of Ohio to join the famous circus 'The Greatest Show On Earth' in London. He was able to perform tumbling tricks and nimbly balance at the top of an unsupported pole. By far his most popular act, however, was a joint tandem ride with his geart friend Charlie Tripp – the incredible 'Armless Wonder'!

While crossing 'Old Woman's Pass', the highest in Persia, his horse Jack stumbled and the mule ahead, carrying the party's canteen equipment, struck a rock and vanished over the side of a hidden precipice with a sheer drop of hundreds of feet. A year later, Arthur arrived in Bombay, where he instantly took up a new sport: tiger hunting! He went out in search of big game strapped into the howdah on an elephant's back.

Tragedy struck Arthur's bold expedition when his brother Thomas died of consumption in December 1851. With only 30 shillings left, Arthur was forced to take his first job, at £400 a year, with the East India Company, as a horseback dispatch rider carrying urgent messages. He stayed in employment at Aurumgabad in the Poona district for a year, until he was recalled to Ireland after the death of his elder brother Charles.

Arthur now succeeded to the fabulously rich family estates. And, on 15 March 1855, he was married to his cousin, Frances Mary Leathley, at the home of his aunt in Dublin. The couple had four sons and three daughters. He began on various ambitious local schemes: replanning and rebuilding the entire village of Boris, and opening a railway branch line linking it with the nearby hamlet of Ballyragget, the girlhood home of Anne Boleyn. His new-found flair for civic projects propelled him to further success – as a politician. In 1866 he was elected Member of Parliament for County Wexford, with a majority of 759 votes. In the General Election two years later, he was returned as MP unopposed.

The Limbless Wonder made his maiden speech in the House of Commons from the Opposition benches during a second reading of the Ireland Poor Law Amendment Bill. And to this day he remains the only MP who has ever voted in the House without getting up from his seat to go to the division lobby. Arthur eventually lost his seat in 1880, but was honoured with the appointment as Lord Lieutenant of County Carlow.

Arthur died, after three years of illness, on Christmas Day 1889, and was buried in the small, ruined church at Ballycopigan. His family name lives on, as does the remarkable memory of Arthur MacMurrough Kavanagh himself – the Limbless Wonder who conquered every challenge with a courage which would still humble many able-bodied men.

Say cheese

Say cheese! An amazing man, known only as 'Black Diamond', who was exhibited in Philadelphia in the 19th century, had plenty to smile about as he coined a small fortune from freak show appearances. A rare affliction known as congenital macrostoma had left him with a mouth so abnormally large that his speciality act was to stick both his fists in it at once.

Freaks of Nature

There are times when a threshold of horror and revulsion is crossed; times when a human freak has to bear, no matter how tragic or pitiable the circumstance, the description of monster. Far beyond the realms even of Edgar Allan Poe, there exist, and have existed, human beings who, by all the laws of nature, should have no rightful place on earth.

Today, a skull is on exhibition at the Royal College of Surgeons in London. It is a skull of two heads which belonged to a child born in Bengal, India, in the last century. The child had been born with a second, supernumerary head, perfect in every feature – eyes, nose, mouth, ears and so on – fused to his own. The heads were joined so that one was actually on top of the other, facing upwards. As an infant, this two-headed boy narrowly escaped death after the midwife who delivered him hurled the nightmarish form in her trembling hands onto a fire.

The child monster survived, and lived for four years. Each head had its own separate blood vessels, brain and, by all accounts, sensibility. The supernumerary head, although firmly fixed in its parasitic position, displayed movement. If its 'host' – and however ludicrous that may sound, it is the only description that seems to fit – was given milk, it would salivate from the mouth. A venomous snake bite killed the boy in infancy, so it can only be left to the imagination to wonder what almost-surreal path his double-headed life would have taken.

His case is, however, not unique. Despite being able to draw only from lay reports, the Victorian medical test *Anomalies and Curiosities of Medicine* does, however, repeat this fairly well documented description:

'One of the weirdest as well as most melancholy stories of human deformity is that of Edward Mordake'. He was heir to one of the noblest peerages in England, yet he never claimed the title, and killed himself at the age of 23. He lived in total isolation, refusing the visits even of the members of his own family. He was an accomplished young man, a profound scholar and a gifted musician. His figure was graceful and his natural face quite handsome. But upon the back of his head was another face, that of a beautiful girl, 'lovely as a dream, hideous as a devil'. The strange parasite face was a mask, occupying an area at the back of the skull, yet exhibiting signs of malignant intelligence. It would sneer and smile while Mordake cried. The eyes would cunningly follow the movements of visitors and the lips would gibber. No voice was audible, but Mordake swore that he was kept from sleeping by the hateful whispers of his 'devil twin', as he called it, 'which never sleeps but talks to me

Pascal Pinon, aged 40 from Lyon, France

forever of such things as they only speak of in hell. No imagination can conceive the dreadful temptations it sets before me. For some unforgiven wickedness of my forefathers I am knit to this fiend – for a fiend it surely is. I beg and beseech you to crush it out of human semblance, even if I die for it.' Such were the words of the hapless Mordake to his physicians.

Despite the close attention of family and doctors, he managed to poison himself, leaving a letter beseeching that the 'demon face' be destroyed before his burial, 'lest it continued its dreadful whisperings in my grave'. He also requested that he be interred on waste ground, without stone or legend to mark his grave.

Quite distinctly apart from Siamese twins, there have been recorded cases of joined infants sharing a single set of limbs. The much-exhibited Tocci brothers, who were born in Turin, Italy, in 1877, each had perfectly formed heads and arms. But below the chest, where they were joined, there was only one pair of legs. It was as if two children were growing up from the base of a single child. The twins, christened Giovanni-Batista and Giacomo, could each control a single leg. Walking was impossible, yet the twins' sensations and emotions above the waist were quite separate and they are believed to have lived well into adulthood.

In Montreal, Canada, in 1878, the case of two female twins, Marie and Rosa Drouin, who shared a single trunk was reported by doctors. Their two upper bodies apparently formed a right-angle to one another. According to one report 'Marie, the left-hand child, was of fair complexion yet more strongly developed than Rosa. The sensations of hunger and thirst were not experienced at the same time, and one might be asleep while the other was crying. They were the products . . . of a mother of 26, whose abdomen was of such preternatural size during pregnancy that she was ashamed to appear in public.' Another case of a single-trunked, double-bodied child is that of the sisters Ritta-Christina, as they were simply known, who were born as Sassari, near Sardinia, on 23 March 1829. As the twins grew into infants, Ritta developed a sad, melancholic character and feeble health while Christina thrived and seemed to be full of happiness.

Monster girl

A two-headed French girl caused a sensation before her death at the age of 12 in 1733 when scientists at the Académie Royale des Sciences in Paris discovered that the supernumerary head could transmit feelings of pain to its partner. When the extra head was pinched, the girl winced and began to cry, with tears streaming down the cheeks of her normal head.

Lazarus-Joannes Baptista Colloredo

Their impoverished parents quickly overcame the traumas of the 'monster-birth' and travelled to Paris hoping to earn a fortune exhibiting them. Forced to stage shows secretly because of prevailing public opinion against such supposedly horrific sights, their clandestine exhibitions were eventually banned by the French authorities and they were soon returning home, penniless once more. The twins did not last long; Rita, the more sickly of the two, expired first and Christina, who had been suckling at her mother's breast, suddenly relaxed and died seconds later with a sigh. Leading physicians anxious to chronicle their case managed to perform a post-mortem examination before the pathetically deformed, mutant body was burned by order of the authorities.

Rare cases of babies born with three heads have been recorded. One such 'monster' was described by a leading expert in deformities in Catania in 1834. Atop an otherwise perfectly normal body, two necks grew from the child. One bore a single head, while from the other grew two further, well-formed heads. All three, it is claimed, functioned normally.

Cases of lifeless, parasite half-bodied growing from otherwise normal people fascinated peep show audiences all over Europe for centuries. One of the most famous was Lazarus-Joannes Baptista Colloredo, from whose trunk hung the upper half of a second body, thought to have been that of a 'twin' which never knew life. Colloredo, born in Genoa in 1617, reached adulthood, carrying his second torso, which seemed to grow out of his stomach, with him to circuses and shows throughout the continent. There were occasional signs of movement in the parasite body, which seemed at times to be trying to breathe. Saliva constantly dribbled from its open mouth, yet its eyes never opened. More common than this extreme example, though, are cases of men and women with three and even four legs.

The Three-Legged Man

When he died in hospital in Jackson, Tennessee on 22 September 1966, Francesco Lentini had created a bizarre record; at 77, he had become the longest-living man ever with three legs.

Lentini, who was billed in later life as the 'Three Legged Wonder', was born at Rosolini, near Syracuse, Sicily, in 1889. His well-to-do parents had twelve other children, five boys and seven girls, who were all shaped perfectly normally. But Lentini, from birth, had an extra leg jutting from the right side of his body. Doctors said it could not be removed surgically, for fear of death or paralysis, and the young boy, condemned to life as an oddity, became, very understandably, chronically depressed and embarrassed as he grew older and more aware of his disability.

When he was seven, his parents took him to an institution for severely handicapped children, where he saw blind, crippled and atrociously deformed youngsters far worse off than himself. 'From that time on,' he cheerfully said later, 'I never complained. I think life is beautiful and I enjoy living it.'

A year later, the family moved to America, where eager circus masters and dime arcade bosses constantly besieged Lentini's father, begging to be allowed to exhibit the boy. His parents refused, insisting that he finish his schooling undisturbed. By the time he did eventually join the Ringling Brothers circus act, Lentini was actually perfectly fluent in four different languages.

Later, he toured with Barnum and Bailey, the Walter Main Circus and Buffalo Bill's Wild West Show in addition to running his own carnival sideshow. He could walk, run, jump, ride a bicycle or a horse, skate on ice or rollers and drive a car. He could not walk on his third limb, however, because it was two inches shorter than his other two but he did learn to kick a ball with it, and developed a wry sense of humour about his abnormality. He would use his third leg as a stool, joking that he was the only man who carried a chair with him everywhere! He claimed he ate 15 per cent more than other men to feed the leg. And he insisted that it was a vital aid when he went swimming, acting as a rudder. Even buying shoes was no problem. He quipped: 'I always buy two pairs and give the extra left one to a one-legged friend!'

Lentini married and had four perfectly normal children. He lived for many years at Weatherfield, Connecticut, moving to sunny Florida in his old age. But he never stopped touring the country and was on the road with the Walter Wanous Side Show when tragically he fell ill and died shortly afterwards.

What was the third leg? As in many other cases, doctors said it was an incomplete Siamese twin. They believed Lentini's mother could have been carrying identical twins, but instead of dividing into two equal parts, her egg only part-divided, leaving Lentini with just the leg of the brother he never had, attached to the base of his spine. According to modern doctors this theory is generally accepted as feasible.

The Four-Legged Woman

The Four-Legged Woman

Another famous multi-limbed freak was Louise L. (her true identity was kept a closely-guarded secret) who toured 19th century France as 'La Dame à Quatre Jambes' – the four-legged woman.

Louise was born in 1869 with two extra, atrophied limbs hanging between her own legs. She always claimed to have feelings in the misshapen limbs, which were about two feet long in adulthood, apart from the feet. Again, doctors believed that the extra legs belonged to a Siamese twin which was never born. Louise, who by all accounts coined a small fortune on the circus circuit, never seemed bothered in private life by her supernumerary appendages. She married and, in the space of three years, gave birth to two perfectly-formed daughters.

Laloo And Others

A dime museum freak who became known only as Laloo, actually had two extra legs, two extra arms and a deformed trunk growing out of his chest. Laloo, who was born in Oudh, India, became famous throughout America in the latter part of the 19th century. And, despite the fact that the parasite body which grew from his was undoubtedly that of an unborn twin brother, he pandered to the whims of peep show managers who dressed it in female clothes to add extra titillation for audiences. A counterpart of Laloo's, who was being exhibited in London around the same time, was a Chinese man known as A-Ke. Casts from his skeleton exist today, and reveal that he had a part-mature foetus growing from his chest, with two arms, two legs and a short trunk.

Duplication of various organs of the body is quite a common occurence – and one which was heavily exploited during the peak of the peep show's popularity in the 19th century. In this area, the sex organs were of special interest to legions of voyeurs in Victorian England; to whom men such as Jean Baptista dos Santos became legendary. It needs little imagination to explain why their following was so large.

Extra ears form the most common casebook; in one 19th century survey of 50,000 children, 33 were found to have at least one additional auricle. An 1870 report in the *British Medical Journal* describes a baby boy born with two perfectly normal ears, plus three extra ones on the right side of his face and two more on the left. By way of home-grown diagnosis the boy's mother claimed that she had been startled during pregnancy by the sight of a child with hideous contractions in the neck!

Double hands have been recorded, as have cases of cloven feet; one 19th century charwoman said her extra hand made an ideal floor rest while she scrubbed away with her other, normal hand, though she maintained that it was less powerful. Multi-fingered hands are common too.

On 16 August 1936, the *Times* newspaper in London carried this report from Mexico City: 'A boy, Modesto Martinez, was born with twenty-five fingers and toes to a family of farmers who have a ranch near Jalapa, capital of Vera Cruz state. The infant has seven fingers on his left hand, six on his right hand and six toes on each foot. An elder brother, Pedro, has twenty-three digits.'

Among the most tragic of all humans are those born with no limbs at all. Indeed, the tremendous courage with which some people, such as 'Limbless Wonder' Arthur Kavanagh, overcome this indescribable burden, is truly inspiring. Today, unhappily, we are well used to the sight of infants born without limbs, an awesome legacy of the Thalidomide drug disaster. Yet many youngsters born limbless have managed to achieve incredible mobility, have learned to write, paint and even play musical instruments in the face of their deformities.

One parallel case of more than a century ago is that of the so-called 'Turtle Woman of Demerara', about whom an article appeared in the medical journal *The Lancet* in 1867. Her thighs were barely six inches long and her distorted feet grew directly from them. Her right arm was a mere stump yet her left one, although grossly misshapen, hung the full length of her body, giving her a bizarre, unbalanced appearance. When she walked, if you can call it that, her strange and stunted ambling gait resembled that of a turtle making slow progress on its route.

She attributed her mutations – as seemed the vogue in those days – to the fact that her mother was frightened during pregnancy by a turtle. Astonishingly, when she was 22 years old, the Turtle Woman gave birth to a normal-sized baby daughter totally free from deformity. She later died of a sex-related disease in the Colonial Hospital.

In contrast to putting limbless yet courageous people on a pedestal in the non-physical sense, in the past this has happened quite literally. The celebrated Violetta, the Victorian 'Trunk Woman' was exhibited on a velvet-topped stand. However sick and degrading that may sound today, she was said – as indeed can be seen from photographs – to have been remarkably pretty and even graceful, with beautifully styled hair and a string of pearls adorning her finely dressed torso.

The Back-To-Front Man

Italian grocer Emilion Guastucci is a walking medical marvel – and that fact once saved his life. Doctors say that there isn't another man in ten million like him. For every organ in his body above the hips is, simply, the wrong way round!

The 63 year old grandfather from Lucca, near Pisa, was born with his heart on the right, his liver on the left, his spleen on the right and so on. Internally, he is a total mirror image of what he should scientifically speaking, look like. It's a good job he is. For, during World War II, when the advancing German Army took over his home town, every remaining healthy man was sent to fight in Russia or Africa.

But when Nazi doctors witnessed Emilion's X-rays, which baffled them completely, they were in a quandary. Should they send him to the front line or deem him unfit for active service? A senior officer reached the decision that he had such a bizarre condition that he could not possibly be allowed to join the fighting and ordered that he should be sent to a hard-labour camp, close to the Austrian border.

What the invaders had not realized, however, was the face that despite his bizarre back-to-front structure – for which medical experts can still not give nor even propose a logical reason – Emilion was, in fact, a perfectly healthy individual.

Within weeks, he managed to escape from incarceration and, calling on almost superhuman reserves, evaded gun patrols to walk home. Emilion was then sheltered from retribution by friends and family and, despite a few heart-stopping moments – felt on the right side of his body, of course, – was never recaptured. From the end of the war, he determined to live life to the full and make his living in the grocery business. Even today, the customers to whom he serves pasta, cheese and bread comment on his peculiar condition and joke: 'Another few slices, please, from the man in ten million.'

Medically, Emilion has a condition called *situs viscerum inversus,* very few other recorded cases of which are to be found around the world. Yet he still enjoys a perfectly normal, ordinary existence. He has two children, a son and a daughter, plus several grandchildren, all of whom are perfectly normal. He says: 'I don't feel any different from anyone else in Italy, even though they first discovered that I was built back-to-front way back in 1933, when I went for my army call-up medical.

'You should have seen the look – an expression you wouldn't believe – on the doctor's face when he discovered that I was not standing back-to-front, or performing some sort of stunt, behind his machine. The German specialists at first simply refused to accept my condition. They didn't believe it was possible.

'It took a series of five more X-rays, before five different doctors until they were finally convinced of the truth. Although I had guessed as much, I was almost as astonished as the doctors at the results of the X-rays. I had always thought that I might, perhaps have been wrongly proportioned – you can't after all, miss a heartbeat on the right instead of the left side of your body – but I never began to realize the full extent of my back-to-frontness.

'All I can really add is that, if God chose me to be different, and created me the wrong-way-round – for some purpose I, certainly, have never been aware, then so be it. I'm in perfectly good health, and I've never really had a problem with illness. So, perhaps, I can even recommend being born back-to-front!'

While Emilion Guastucci may be the original back-to-front man, the circus world and the peep shows of old were delighted when they could recruit those inside-out and upside-down human body tumblers who were expert contortionists and, to give them the medical name in which the Victorians delighted, dislocationists.

Towards the end of the last century, one of the most popular of these characters was the Englishman Wentworth, who, while still performing in his seventies, claimed the title of the world's oldest-ever contortionist. His most popular act was to shut himself, along with six empty soda water bottles in a box measuring a mere 23 by 29 by 16 inches. As he curled his still agile and amazingly flexible body round the bottles, he was packed so tightly in that the lid could be slammed shut on the box. Wentworth even coined a special name for his speciality act: 'Packanatomicalization.'

American contortionist Charles Warren became known as the 'Yankee dish-rag' because of the amazing way in which he could twist his flexible muscles and double joints into virtually any conceivable position. By the tender age of 8, he had joined a travelling troupe of acrobats and strolling performers and within a few years he had tuned his body so perfectly that he could make tiny areas of muscle stand out like a string or perform in a variety of bizarre ways. He was able to contract muscles in his stomach in such a way that vital organs, at will, could be make to bulge out. He could even control the bones of his body to such an extent that, barely moving, he could dislocate his own hip before simply clicking it back into place again. Without any undue effort he could contract his chest to 34 inches and expand it to 41 inches. Warren, a strict teetotaller who weighed in at 150 pounds, could even fool medical experts into believing that he had broken joints or that he had twisted or pulled muscles. He was the father of two children, both of whom could dislocate their hips without breaking into a sweat!

A Frenchman sprang, or rather coiled and twisted, his way to fame around 1886 in his homeland. He was known simply as The Protein Man. He could make his body so completely taut and rigid that hitting him with a hammer had the same effect as trying to bash a concrete wall. Even muscles which in ordinary people are involuntary, he could exercise at will. And he had such power over his body that he could twist himself into what were, in effect, three-dimensional caricatures of figures such as a gnarled old city alderman or a lean and hungry young student.

A leading French scientist who made a detailed study of the Protein Man also discovered that he could totally shut off the blood supply to either side of his body. In other words he could give himself a half-anaemic look by 'switching-off' the supply to the left side of his body and then, in rotation, do the same thing to the right side. The scientist ascribed this weird phenomenon to his ability to control his muscles perfectly.

In Washington in 1893, a man named Fitzgerald claimed his sole source of income was from exhibitions at medical colleges around America. He could simulate every conceivable bone dislocation and became a walking encyclopaedia on the science of pathology. He even claimed to be able to display varying degrees of dislocation which might occur in patients depending what kind of accident had befallen them.

Freak Senses

It is often said that if one human faculty is impaired, the body compensates by sharpening the rest of the senses. In the 19th century, after she was struck deaf, dumb and blind, a girl called Helen Keller became the world's most baffling medical oddity, because she could distinguish colours simply by touching them and people simply by sniffing them.

She was examined by doctors and public audiences, who marvelled not only at her incredibly developed freak senses but also her remarkable courage. She became famous across America as 'the girl with eyeless sight', and, in a tremendous victory over her own infirmities, managed to succeed in gaining several university degrees.

Helen Keller had been a perfectly normal, happy little girl at her family home in Alabama until tragedy struck when she was 19 months old. She contracted a virulent fever which gave her delirium, convulsions and a raging temperature which doctors were convinced would kill her. After three days, however, it became apparent that she *would* survive against all the odds – although joy quickly turned to heartbreak again when her parents were told that the ravages of the fever would leave their bright-as-a-button little girl permanently deaf, dumb and blind.

Until she reached the age of 8, Helen's mother and father nursed and cared for her as best they could – though it soon became obvious that they were unable to educate or even discipline her; she had developed into a physically strong girl given, occasionally, to violent temper tantrums. Their situation was desperate; their sense of love and loyalty made them reluctant to send Helen to a home where she would have been cared for but, more than likely, would never have progressed.

It was at that stage that a Miss Sullivan from the Perkins Institute for the Blind in South Boston became interested in Helen, and determined to try to teach her to manage simple day-to-day tasks and how to behave. It soon became apparent to Miss Sullivan that Helen had a bright and agile mind and, with the help of another teacher, Sarah Fuller, Helen began to absorb a little and then a lot of information about the world in which she had previously been a total stranger.

Miss Fuller, an expert in speech therapy for the deaf, began by teaching Helen the manual alphabet – spelling out letters and words on the palm of her hand. Slowly, the silent and incomprehensible darkness which had enveloped the tragic little girl began to fade away. Helen began to learn more and more quickly, until she was able, using the hand signals she had mastered, to tell Miss Fuller what she wanted to do next. She wanted to learn how to speak. Miss Fuller was delighted.

Despite the disapproval of Helen's parents, Miss Fuller began the lessons which would eventually lead the little girl into a life where she would constantly be in the public eye; where crowds would gaze in awe and admiration at a curiosity whose achievements almost defied belief.

Helen's first lesson lasted two hours and involved tracing her fingers, tentatively at first, around the outline of Miss Fuller's face, mouth and neck. She discovered every part of her patient teacher's mouth, tongue, teeth, lips and palate until she understood how vital they all were for the power of speech. Miss Fuller then began to shape Helen's own mouth for making basic vowel sounds and placed the eager child's hand on her windpipe so that she could feel the vibrations. Next, she placed Helen's fingers on her tongue, so that she could feel the movement it made when she uttered a noise. The teacher was astounded when Helen's hands flew to her own mouth and throat and repeated the sound she had just made so perfectly that it could have been an echo.

Six years after making that first sound, Helen Keller could speak. Despite the fact that she still could not see or hear, her remaining senses, unaccountably, became so finely attuned that she actually learned to 'feel' colours. The only way she could explain this incredible freak phenomenon was by saying that to her sensitive fingers, different colours seemed to radiate different forms of energy which she was capable of picking up. Later, this remarkable eyeless sight enabled her to appreciate the rich colours of an oil painting; she could 'see' with her fingertips the magnificent hues of a sunset on canvas just as others could see them with their eyes.

Helen also developed an acute, unerringly accurate sense of smell; where normal people so easily distinguished friends and relatives simply by looking at them, Helen could detect them with her nose. When upset, she would run to her mother simply by following the scent! Throughout her life, she could uncannily sense which of her friends or colleagues were in the room with her before they made themselves known by using the manual alphabet.

Her nimble mind helped her earn several university degrees and in her twenties Helen became the talk of America, with a series of tours, public meetings and lectures which she gave in the hope of helping others like herself. Hands, nose, speech and intuition turned her into a celebrity – and a sensation in the medical world. With true dignity though, she never joined the garish and crude peep show circuit, preferring to tour independently and use her special gifts to try to open up a new world for others in darkness and despair.

Eyeless Sight

The miraculous freak phenomenon of eyeless sight – despite the incredible levels of awareness to which Helen Keller took it – is, in fact, centuries old. British scientist Robert Boyle reported the case of a 17th century man, John Vermaasen, who was totally blind in both eyes but could, nevertheless distinguish colours. Using ribbons placed between his fingers, Vermaasen accurately identified every colour, explaining that black had the same feel as very coarse sand or the points of needles, whereas red felt as smooth as silk. Strangely, this freak sense was particularly acute in Vermaasen's thumbs and seemed to be heightened when he had been fasting.

Kuda Bux was a quiet, unassuming Kashmiri man who, although not blind, supplied powerful persuasion to the medical world that eyeless sight – or extra-retinal vision as it has since become known – is a freak sense possessed by certain people.

Skilled in the art of Yoga after years of intensive study of the mental powers required to use it, Bux gave stage performances of eyeless sight all over the world during the 1930s. He vowed that his ability to distinguish colour and perform skilled feats while totally blindfolded was genuine, and in 1934 his claims were put to the test by a panel of medical experts and scientists. They blindfolded him by putting lumps of dough on his eyes and then wrapping them in metal foil and several layers of gauze and woollen bandage. When they were finally satisfied that there was no possible way that he could use his eyesight, they placed books in front of him, from which they asked him to read. Bux then astounded the panel by giving a faultless performance.

A similar investigation into his powers was carried out in Montreal, Canada, in 1938. The result was the same – flawless. Further proof of his ability to use extra-retinal vision came in September, 1937 in Liverpool when, balanced on a narrow ledge, blindfolded as before and 200 feet above the ground, he walked the entire length of the roof on his precarious perch with ease. Touring in America in 1945, he astonished onlookers by again demonstrating his powers by riding a bicycle blindfolded through the busy traffic of New York's Times Square.

Another remarkable eyeless sight case is that of Laura Dewey Bridgman, born on 21 December, 1829, who was left deaf and totally blind in her right eye, with only very slight vision in her left, at the age of 2 after contracting scarlet fever. Like Helen Keller, Laura was exceptionally bright, and quickly surpassed all her classmates at the Massachusetts Asylum for the Blind.

Her finely developed sense of touch included a peculiar sensitivity to vibration – and she could even 'hear' music with her fingertips. Her musical digits enabled her to tell the difference between a full and a half note, a feat which many people who can hear are incapable of doing. She even developed her sense of touch through her feet. She was able to detect the comings and goings of people by picking up vibrations in the ground.

The astonishing case of a totally blind Brooklyn woman, Mollie Fancher, who claimed to have an eyeless sight sense in the top of her head, was reported in 1893. Doctors were completely baffled by the way she could read an ordinary book – in light or darkness – simply by running her fingertips across the printed page.

Amazing Memories

The machinations of the mind all add up to a mystery for most of us. And usually, the sum total of our mental arithmetic amounts to a struggle to tot up the addition of a restaurant bill. But for some people, being a mastermind is simply child's play.

Little Oscar Moore first demonstrated his powers when he was just 3 years old. Born to poor parents at Waco, Texas on 19 August 1885, Oscar became the sole attraction of the city's Central Music Hall, where the awesome assembly of brainpower focused its attention on his remarkable skills.

The toddler was not only super-intelligent, but he could also soak up information so swiftly that his mind had become an encyclopaedic marvel before he was even able to walk. It is rare to find a case of total memory recall coupled with genius. It was even rarer in Oscar's case, for he was blind.

A likeable, affectionate little boy, Oscar quickly won the hearts and minds of his intellectual mentors, establishing an easy rapport with men who despite years of study and devotion often struggled to keep pace with his darting, probing brain. Way before his teens, he was to become not simply university material but a rival in genius to the most learned men of any country. Exactly what freak of nature caused his incredible mental prowess remains a mystery, but it is an aberration which has been repeated on a number of occasions throughout the centuries.

Eight years before Oscar was bewildering the best scholars America had to offer, an 11-year-old boy was found wandering the streets of Marseilles in France with a trick monkey on his back, a begging bowl in his hand and a neat line in patter. There was, however, more to unkempt little Jacques Inaudi that met the eye. One of his favourite money raising ruses was to bet strangers that he could solve any mental problem they cared to set him. It never failed, for behind the beggar-boy façade, Jacques was capable of what today would be computer-speed reaction in answering mathematical mind-benders.

Memory man

The world's most incredible 'Memory Man' is Mehmed Ali Halici of Ankara, Turkey who, on 14 October 1967, recited an astonishing 6,666 verses of the Koran by memory in six hours. Mehmed's perfect recall was monitored by half a dozen leading academics who verified his claim to a world record.

Mini-mastermind

A little Korean boy called Kim became the mini-mastermind of the world after he was born on 7 March 1963, to parents who were both university professors born on the same day in the same year at exactly the same time. Baby superbrain Kim understood integral calculus at the age of four and mastered four languages before starting school. His IQ has been calculated at 210. It was not previously thought possible to exceed 200.

Jacques' rare talent quickly drew the attention of a well-to-do resident of Marseilles who, astonished by the boy's intelligence, took him to Paris for examination by the city's famous Anthropological Society in 1880.

There, he confounded the leading lights of the academic world by solving in less than ten minutes in his head a multiplication of numbers running into trillions by numbers running into billions. When asked exactly what process he had used to arrive at the correct answer, it was discovered that he worked backwards in his head from left to right instead of the usual right to left method which most people use either in their heads or on paper. Under the wing of scholastic luminaries the future for little Jacques, the former street urchin, was secure. But, in his thirst for knowledge, his first request was not for weighty mathematical tomes or a set of problem equations; he asked if he could first learn to read and write!

One of the leading adult mental arithmetic freaks of the era was America Rube Fields, from Johnson County, Missouri, who was described as a 'shiftless, idle fellow' who during his childhood had refused to go to school on the grounds that education would turn him into 'as big a fool as other people.' In his forties when first pounced on by academics keen to unlock the secret of his mental abilities, Fields is said have been able to answer any mathematical problem in less time that it took to ask it. One report at the time said: 'Give Rube Fields the distance by rail between any two points, and the dimensions of a car wheel, and almost as soon as the statement has left your lips he will tell you the number of revolutions the wheel will make in travelling over the track. Call four or five or any number of columns of figures down a page, and when you have reached the bottom he will announce the sum.' His answers were quick and sharp, seemingly by intuition. Fields himself could not give any explanation for his uncanny power. Despite offers, Fields steadfastly refused to go on public exhibit for circus or peep show bosses anxious to acquire his talents, although he did earn occasional money from attending scientific conferences and the like.

Modern day memory masters include Dutch born Willem Klein, who holds the world record for the fastest extraction of a 13th root from a 100 digit number in 1 minute 28.8 seconds at the National Laboratory for High Energy Physics in Tsukuba, Japan, on 7 April 1981.

Indian-born Mrs Shakuntala Devi lived up to her name of the 'Human Computer' when she came up with the answer of a multiplication of two 13-digit numbers chosen at random by the Computer Department of Imperial College, London, in an astonishing 28 seconds on 18 June 1980. The size of the problem can perhaps best be gauged by her correct answer: 18,947,668,177,995,426,462,773,730.

On the world's accepted indeces for intelligence quotients 150 represents genius level. Only one person in 10,000 has an I.Q. above 160. In terms of national averages, Japan leads the world with 106.6. The British national average is around 100.

From brain power to the brain itself (though it doesn't naturally follow that big-heads are egg-heads!) Largest brained characters in history include Oliver Cromwell and Lord Byron, though the heaviest verified weight of a human brain was that of a 50 year old male which was gauged at 4 pounds 8.29 ounces by Dr Thomas F. Hegert, Chief Medical Examiner for District 9 of the State of Florida on 23 October 1975. The smallest brain ever recorded was that of writer Anatole France (1844-1924) which barely tipped the scales at only 4.126 ounces.

Amala and Kamala

Deep in the heart of India, the terrified and deeply superstitious villagers of Midnapore made an impassioned plea to the travelling missionary who had just arrived in their small community. They begged him to exorcise the evil spirit of a dreaded 'man ghost' and rid them forever of the nightmarish ghoul which seemed to stalk them like a wild, savage beast.

On 17 October 1920, the Reverend Joseph Singh, perhaps seeking only to allay the imagined fears of simple minds, agreed to lay their supposed phantom. With a posse of nervous villagers, he was led to a series of holes in a clearing, from where it was believed the mysterious spectre appeared. He

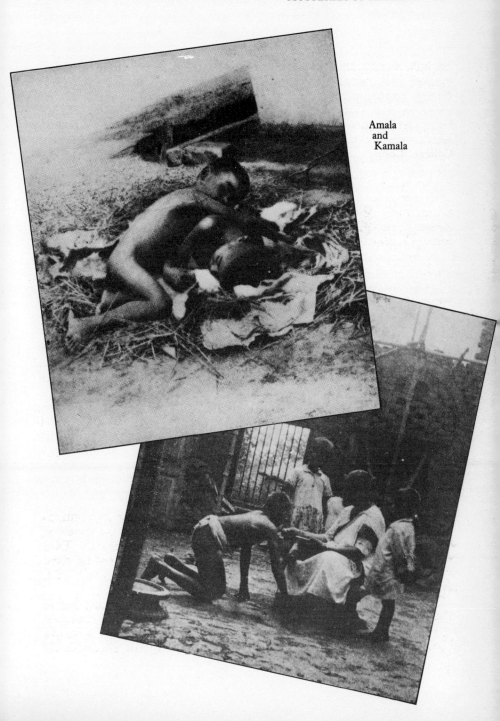

Amala
and
Kamala

waited there for several hours with the terrified villagers keeping their distance. The Reverend Singh's diary records what happened next:

'All of a sudden, a grown-up wolf came out from one of the holes. This animal was followed by another of the same size and kind. The second one was followed by a third, closely followed by two cubs . . . one after the other. Close after the cubs came the ghost – hand, foot and body like a human being; but the head was a huge ball of something covering the shoulders and the upper portion of the bust, leaving only a sharp contour of the face visible, and it was human.

Close at its heels there came another awful creature like the first, but smaller in size. Their eyes were bright and piercing, unlike human eyes.'

What the Reverend Singh was describing, and what the fearful had thought to be a 'man ghost' was, in fact, two little girls who had been abandoned by their mother and raised from infancy by a she-wolf. The Reverend Singh was witnessing what still remains the only properly-documented case of feral children being brought up by an adopted animal mother.

As soon as the Wolf Girls of Midnapore had emerged, snarling and on all fours, from their cave, the entrance of which was almost camouflaged by a termite mound, the petrified villagers killed their she-wolf guardian. The youngsters themselves were rescued by the Reverend Singh, who managed eventually to take them to an orphanage, where he christened them Amala and Kamala.

The two little girls could run swiftly on all fours, but were unable to stand up. They ate only milk and raw meat, lapping and tearing with sharp teeth like the wolf cubs they had been raised with. They could not talk or laugh, yet their sense of smell was acutely developed, like the natural hunters their she-wolf mother had been teaching them to be.

Their exact ages could only be guessed at, but it was thought they were about seven years old when they were discovered. Their only gestures were those of wild animals and their sole reaction to the human society into which they were thrust was one of utter bewilderment. It was hardly surprising that Amala survived in captivity for only a year. When she died, her sister, ironically, displayed her first human emotion. Kamala cried two tears.

Slowly, Kamala began an almost imperceptible metamorphosis from wolf cub to human being. Eventually, she learned to stand upright, eat cooked food and speak a few words. By the time she died, nine years later, she had a vocabulary of 30 words. She was thought to have been about 16, but with the mental age of a three-year-old. Although she had been almost totally animal when found, her genetic adaptability had been quite remarkable. Little Kamala died a human being.

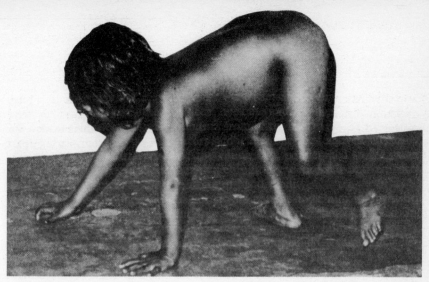

Tissa, brought up by monkeys in Sri Lanka

More Children of the Wild

Human freaks from the wild, like the Wolf Girls of Midnapore, have not only fired the imagination for centuries. They have sparked the seemingly never-ending search for man's lost elusive ancestor – the Missing Link. During the early 1880s, a much-exhibited female freak rocked the medical world, and, in fact, was widely accepted as the living proof of Darwin's theory.

Krao, a native of Indochina who shot to fame all over Europe, was indeed a bizarre, misshapen creature, appearing to be half-ape, half-human, with a thick covering of hair on her face and what appeared to be a mane running down the back of her neck. According to reports at the time, she displayed 'extraordinary prehensile powers of feet and lips' with the ability to pick up very delicately the most fragile objects with her toes and contort her mouth into amazing, monkey-like expressions.

One observer wrote: 'When annoyed, she throws herself to the ground, screams, kicks and gives vent to her anger by pulling her hair in a very peculiar way.' It seems, however, that Krao's rantings were more like those of a petulant, tantrum-throwing child than of a so-called 'Missing Link'. For she was, indeed, only seven years old when she was first exhibited as a peep show attraction.

Other claims to wild fame by human freaks have proved to be enormous, though entertaining, frauds in the mould of master showman and peep show trickster Phineas T. Barnum. For example, the Wild Men of Borneo, two ferocious-looking and incredibly strong midget brothers who became a huge attraction across America, were neither wild nor from Borneo. They were christened Hiram and Barney Davis, though later changed their names, for the sake of their show, to Plutano and Waino. And, far from tearing apart unwary Western sailors who landed in their far-flung territory, they were apparently born in either Connecticut of Long Island.

Zip The Man Monkey, another freak exhibited by Barnum from the mid-19th to early 20th century, may have appeared to be a savage, neanderthal monster with his close-shaven head topped only by a hard, horny knoll of hair. But it is likely he was actively encouraged to grunt and act like a wild beast, rather than let anyone begin to guess that he might just be a simpleton, born to a poor Negro family in Brooklyn.

Such harmless, manufactured stories, designed to enhance the crowd-pulling potential of what, after all, really were human freaks, fail to detract from recently documented cases of wild men and boys.

In 1973, a youngster was found in the jungles of Sri Lanka who had apparently been adopted by a family of monkeys. When discovered, he was about ten years old. He could neither speak nor stand up. Yet, like the Wolf Girls of Midnapore half a century before, he was able to run swiftly on all fours and could use his hands and feet to cling and pick up objects with remarkable skill. Is he another example of the true feral child?

And as recently as May 1982, staff at a hospital in Kenya, East Africa, were shocked to find a new arrival scavenging for scraps in their backyard. The hairy, grunting being on all fours is slowly being 'tamed' by medical experts who reckon him to be aged about 20. They are convinced he is truly an example of that rare phenomenon, a human freak from the wild.

Many tales of genuine finds of true wolf-children must have brought the story of Romulus and Remus to life in the sensation-hungry 19th century. One of the strangest was reported in *Chambers' Journal*. It told how a boy in India was actually captured from a roaming pack of wolves with whom he seemed to be totally at ease; hence captured rather than rescued.

It was discovered that the child's parents had mysteriously 'lost' him while he was a babe-in-arms and there was a great village celebration when the family was re-united. Joy turned to horror, however, when the wolf-boy's mother and father tried to coax him back into the normal routines of any family home. He was found to be troublesome and virtually impossible to control – just like a caged wild beast, in fact.

Often during the night, the boy would wail and moan in a guttural, animal cry for hours and hours on end. When dusk had fallen, it became a nightmare time for his parents and brothers and sisters who had so eagerly opened their arms on his return. It is claimed that one moonlit night, the boy's feral screams attracted two wolf cubs who had been prowling near his home. He had been tied by the waist to a tree by superstitious villagers and his plaintive wails were thought only to have been cries of anguish at his predicament. However, by the light of the full moon villagers swore that they saw the two cubs gambolling around the tree trunk where the little boy was held captive. Uncannily, it was as if they all knew each other – and the cubs only departed as day was about to break.

According to the report, the wolf-boy did not survive long. He never spoke and never displayed any signs of human intelligence. In another case from around the same period, a boy who had allegedly lived with a wolf pack for six months after being snatched from his home by the she-wolf, only had one desire when he was at last found by his frantic mother: to return to the wild. He would growl and snarl if upset and would eat any scraps of food, especially meat which he would devour in an animal fashion, that was thrown to him. He could drink a full pitcher of milk in one single gulp, and refused to wear any clothes, even during the most bitter winter weather. He showed a great liking for bones and would gnaw at them with canine relish for hours. He could not speak a single word. He was ugly, filthy and was constantly trying to escape from the human world which he totally rejected.

In many cases of purported wolf-children, the youngsters were found to have hard, calloused layers of skin on their elbows and knees as a result of going around only on all fours. The *Zoologist* magazine of March 1888 related six such cases. In one, the boy concerned could only understand sign language, yet had an acutely developed sense of hearing.

Another curious account is that of two children in the orphanage of Sekandra, near Agra in India, who were discovered living among wolves. One was found by a trooper on a mission for a local native governor. He was passing alongside the bank of a river around noon when he was astonished to see a large female wolf leaving her lair followed by three cubs and an infant boy.

The boy scuttled along with his adopted 'family' of beasts on all fours – and when the trooper tried to catch him, he ran as fast as the cubs and was able to keep up easily with the she-wolf. The trooper returned to the nearest village to seek help to rescue the boy and a team of willing hands was recruited to dig the youngster out of the den into which he had so nimbly raced. Though still little more than a toddler, the boy struggled desperately to free himself when the rescue team snatched him from his 'home'.

As they forcibly carried him back to civilization, he lunged and tried to bolt for every hole or gully that was passed. Later, when he was confronted with adult people, he was petrified, but when he saw other children, he snarled at them ferociously, trying to attack and bite them. Back at the orphanage, he totally rejected cooked meat but drooled at the sight of raw flesh and bones, hiding all his food under his hands the way a dog holds his paw over his meat.

The story behind the second so-called wild child at the orphanage in Sekandra is equally bizarre. The little boy in question this time was, it is claimed, carried away by a she-wolf in March 1843, after his Hindu mother had left him in a sheltered 'safe' spot near the rice field.

For a year, there was no sign of the child, and his heartbroken parents were forced eventually to give him up for dead. Suddenly, however, a wolf, followed by her litter of cubs and a strange, small ape-like creature were sighted about ten miles away from the village where their son had mysteriously vanished.

Villagers gave chase to the strange-looking creature and, on catching him after a breathless chase, recognized him from a small burn-mark on his knee to be the boy who had gone missing from beside the rice field. His elbows and knees had become hard and horny as a result of moving around on all fours. He would not eat anything apart from raw meat and could never be taught to speak. His only form of communication was a strange, muttering growl.

Despite being sent away from his real parents, the boy never even made an effort to adapt to a human way of life. In the winter of 1850, he made several unsuccessful attempts to escape and in the following spring he made it to freedom and the jungles of Bhangapore.

The Curse of Youth

His hair was white, his skin gnarled and wrinkled, and the varicose veins stuck out on his arms and legs. When he walked, his shoulders had the droop of a tired, aged man. He was so weak, he could barely talk. It came as no surprise to family, friends and neighbours when, inevitably, Charles Chesworth collapsed and died of old age. He was seven.

When he was born, to perfectly normal parents in a Staffordshire village, the baby had appeared to be perfectly healthy and ordinary, apart from minor imperfections in his shoulder and bottom jaw. But by the age of three, he began to develop with frightening speed. Within 12 months, he reached sexual maturity and began to grow a beard. Over the next three years, until his death on 14 March 1829, he withered away into old age and senility.

Gazelle boy

The Gazelle Boy, a supposedly feral child, was caught, with incredible difficulty, in 1967 running with a herd of wild gazelle in the Arabian desert. According to a letter to *John Bull* magazine, those most graceful animals had brought him up, and he could match their incredible bursts of speed on his two legs.

Doctors are still baffled by the rare, startling disorder which causes young children – even newborn infants – rapidly to develop the characteristics of adults and sometimes die of old age at a time when they should normally just be reaching puberty. Little boys, some as young as 2 or 3, have been known to grow beards, speak in deep voices, feel sexual desires and exhibit the body hair of men.

Girls have sometimes had the physical characteristics of women at an even younger age – as early as 6 months. They menstruate, grow breasts and, by the time they should simply be toddlers, are capable of bearing children of their own. They are victims of precocious development, a disease caused by a massive imbalance of hormones in the body.

In recent years, doctors throughout the world have been forced to stand helplessly by while the devastating disease speeds up the ageing process of its little victims, often resulting in death after only a few years. In one case, a little girl became a feeble, arthritic, bedridden old woman while her parents watched in horror. New hormone treatments are being tested in places such as the US Government's National Institute of Child Health and Human Development. But the disease itself has been recorded as far back as the days of Ancient Rome.

Brewster's Journal of 1829, recording the case of Charles Chesworth, says: 'At the age of 6, he was 4 feet 2 inches tall and weighed 74 pounds. In all respects, he was as well developed as any adult'. Louis Beran, born on 29 September 1869 at Saint-Gervais, France, was so tall, strong and mature at the age of 6 that he shunned other children and, according to a local physician, 'helped his parents in their labours, doing the work of a man'.

Nineteenth-century dime museums across America put on show a 'Man-Boy' who, at the age of 15 months, weighed almost 7 stones and displayed all the signs of maturity of a youth many years older. The 'Man-Boy', who was said to have been a phenomenal size at birth, died after only a few years – years which had turned him into a hideous old man – on Coney Island. At about the same time, the French physician Desbois recorded the case of

Dental display

Polish strong man Siegmund Breitbart gave a dazzling display of dental power on 27 November 1923, when, using only a bit between his teeth, he controlled the reigns of a team of horses pulling a wagon containing 50 people through the streets of Washington DC. Breitbart said he performed the incredible stunt to draw publicity to his circus show, which had just rolled into town!

Tattoo you

Britain's most decorated man is Wilfred Hardy, of Huthwaite, Nottinghamshire, who has covered an eye-catching 96 per cent of his body with tattoos and has now started on his cheeks, tongue, gums and eyebrows. The most tattooed lady is Mrs Rusty Skuse of Aldershot whose husband, who always had designs on her, has covered 85 per cent of her in patterns.

---

another 'Man-Boy', aged 11, who, during one period of his kaleidoscopically fast maturing process, shot up an astonishing 6 inches in 15 days.

The Victorian tome *Anomalies and Curiosities of Medicine* describes 'a boy of four years and three months who was 3 feet 10½ inches tall and weighed 54 pounds'. His face was like that of an adult and his sex organs were fully developed. However, mentally he was dull, quite obstinate and self-willed. He was not different to other children until he was three after which his voice began to break and his sexual organs developed. Another medical publication tells of a boy born at Willingham, near Cambridge, in 1741, who showed signs of puberty at the age of 12 months. When he died four years later, he had the appearance of an old, senile man.

Exceptionally precise measurements were made during a close study of young Philip Howarth, who was born at Quebec Mews, Portman Square, London on 21 February 1806. Within a year, he had lost his babyish roundness and become awkward as his limbs began to grow like those of a boy much older. Before he was 3, his sex organs developed and his voice broke.

At the age of 3, he was 3 feet 4½ inches tall and weighed 51¼ pounds. His thigh measured 13½ inches round, his waist 24 inches and his biceps 7 inches. He was reported to be 'clever, very strong and muscular,' despite being terribly ugly as a result of the disease that seemed to be racing him through life. By all accounts, however, the ageing Howarth did survive at least into early adulthood.

After dozens of similar cases over the centuries, many of which have ended so tragically, doctors in America are now experimenting with a synthetic hormone which they believe may succeed in arresting precocious development. A team at Massachusetts General Hospital, led by Dr Gordon B. Cutler Jr, is working on the drug, which is thought to be able to block production of sex hormones. It is hoped to be able to use it on children, who would undergo a course of the drug before it was withdrawn at the appropriate time to allow puberty to occur normally.

A Ripe Old Age

If it is the curse of youth to die prematurely of old age, then it must be a blessing of life for those who do live to a real ripe old age. Longevity is something almost everyone hopes to attain, whether we like to admit it openly or not.

Quite remarkable claims to old age litter the history books, many of which seem unlikely. The bounds of credulity were stretched to absurd limits even as recently as 5 May 1933, when a news bureau quite solemnly released a story to the world, with a Peking dateline, about the death of Li Chung-yun who was purported to be the oldest man on earth. The agency claimed that he was no less than 256 years old when he died, having been born in 1680 which really is very difficult to believe!

Genuine error, deception and even outright fraud symbolise many of the claims of super centenarians of the past. Freak show exhibitors of such alleged characters almost always added the first number that came into their heads onto the true age of their wrinkled and gnarled showpieces.

Celebrated centenarians of the past have been discovered not to be just one person at all, but the sum total of years of a father and son who shared the same Christian name. It is only comparatively recently that official censuses throughout the world have begun to properly chronicle birth certificates to establish true ages.

The greatest properly authenticated age to which a human has lived is, at the time of writing, 116. Shigechiyo Izumi, who lives on a Japanese island 820 miles south-west of Tokyo, was born there on 29 June 1865 and was recorded as a 6 year old in his country's first official census in 1871. Today, he watches television and advises that the best way to lead a long life is, simply, 'not to worry!'

The oldest authenticated centenarian in Britain, which currently has a population of around 4,000 hundred year olds, was Miss Alice Stevenson, who died in 1973 with the distinction of being the only Briton ever to have birth and death certificates 112 years apart.

One of the most baffling recent cases, far removed from the clear-cut issue of Miss Stevenson, was that of Charlie Smith of Barlow, Florida who, in 1955 managed to obtain a social security card after claiming to have been born on 4 July 1842.

Smith said he had grown up as a child in Liberia and had no documentary proof of his birth. His card was issued, however, with the US Department of Health, Education and Welfare adamantly refusing to disclose their sources of information about his age. Smith, fully accredited, was thus able to claim to be celebrating his 137th birthday on 4 July 1979, just three months before his death. It was only quite recently that county records in Florida turned up a marriage licence for him from 1910, showing his age to be 35 then. After exhaustive research, it was finally decided that he died roughly two months short of being a true 100 years old.

Perhaps the centenarian feat which was against more odds than any other was that achieved by identical twins Eli and John Phipps, born on 14 February 1803 in Affington, Virginia, who both lived to be more than 108 years old. The chances of that happening again are calculated at an astonishing 700 million to one. The oldest twins in Britain have been Robert and Mary Beau, who celebrated their 100th birthday on 19 October 1973. Mary, now Mrs Simpson, lives in Etton, Cambridgeshire. Robert died before the end of 1973. The oldest triplets ever to live on record were Faith, Hope and Charity Caughlin of Marlboro, Massachusetts, who were born on 27 March 1868 and all lived for at least 93 years.

In many cases, claims to fantastic longevity seem all the more spurious nowadays in the light of investigations in Sweden, which is the only country in the world to officially investigate the death of every claimed centenarian. So far, the Swedish Government has not verified one single case of anyone living over the age of 110. Longevity claims for entire races or creeds, such as the Brahmin priests of India or the ancient Greeks and Chinese are steeped in myth, folklore and mystery, with not a scrap of evidence that such occurrences are scientifically possible.

There are, however, suggestions that a Yorkshireman named Henry Jenkins just might have lived to the fantastic age of 169 which was, on his death in 1670, widely enough believed to earn him a place in history. Chancery registers were said to have 'proved' that he had appeared in court, sworn an oath and given evidence in a trial 140 years before he died. There is a further record which reveals that he appeared in court again to give evidence at the age of 157. In old age, Jenkins is said to have been able to recall the Battle of Flodden Field of 1513, which was fought when he was barely 12 years old. It is also claimed that he was in such good health that even after he passed his 100th birthday he was able to swim against the strong current of a fast-flowing stream.

Another celebrated English super-centenarian was Thomas Parr who later became known as 'Old Parr'. He was a poor farmer's servant who was born in 1483. He is reported to have lived to the grand (possibly grandiose) old age of 152. And, although he was a batchelor until he was 80, he certainly seems to have lived life to the full and made up for lost time after that. For, shortly after he became an octogenarian, he took his first wife, who lived, as his wife for 32 years before she died. Eight years later, at the age of 120, untiring Thomas took the plunge again and re-married.

It is claimed that old Thomas lived not only an extraordinary marital life, but was also an indefatigable labourer, toiling ox-like in the fields until he was 130, at which age he was said to still be able to thresh with quite dazzling speed. News of his incredible life reached London, and it is said that a succession of noblemen who visited his humble abode finally persuaded him to visit the capital for an audience with the King.

It was that journey, or rather the excitement of it, which is thought to have hastened Thomas's death. Huge crowds had gathered to greet him as the carriage in which he travelled pulled up at the gates of the palace. In the royal court, the King and all his acolytes were reported to have been amazed by his intelligence, speed of thought and dexterity. Within a year of his rise to stardom, however, old Thomas was dead.

A surgeon who examined his body found that all his organs were in a perfect state; his bones had not even ossified as is usual in the extremely aged. The surgeon could not find the slightest cause of death, and so finally decided that the high life killed him. His impression was that good treatment and being over-fed in London had caused his demise.

A monument in Westminster Abbey today still marks the memory of old Thomas Parr, whose great-grandson, it is claimed, emulated his celebrated forbear's centenarian stand and lived to the age of 103 in Ireland, where he died during the 19th century.

Nature is the great natural re-cycler of our world. And perhaps that's what accounts for the amazing case of a German magistrate, who died in 1791 reputedly aged 120, who really got his teeth stuck into life. In 1787, after spending years of difficulty trying to chew his food in a toothless mouth, he was astonished to discover that, at the age of 117, eight new teeth had begun to grow. Delighted with his new set, his happiness turned to sorrow when, six months later, they all fell out. Within days, however, yet another new set of eight teeth began to grow in their place ... and the long since retired old legal eagle lived out the rest of his days with a happy, toothsome grin!

Another hale and hearty super-centenarian was Anthony Senish, a farmer in Limoges who died in 1770 aged 111. According to reports, he toiled in his fields right up to his demise and still had the strength and determination of a carthorse. Considering the frailty which usually accompanies old age, it was his quite incredible boast that he had never shed a drop of blood or touched a drop of medicine in his entire life. He still had a full head of hair and excellent vision. He attributed his longevity to his staple diet of chestnuts and corn.

Which naturally raises the question asked all the time of centenarians today: Just how do you keep young and beautiful at such a ripe old age? It is a question which has prompted some entirely unexpected and very surprising answers.

An Englishman called William Riddell who is said, although there is no precise verification, to have lived to 116, swore all his life by the bottle. He adamantly refused to ever touch a drop of water, quenching his thirst instead with brandy. Every day he quaffed a tot of varying size and was convinced that the booze kept him bounding along in good health. Thomas Wishart of Annandale, Dumfries, who died in 1760 aged 124 said he had chewed tobacco every day of his life since he was 7 years old. He explained that his father had introduced him to the weed at such a tender age to suppress his hunger while he was shepherding the animals alone for hours on end in the mountains.

John de la Somet of Virginia, who lived until 1766, actually smoked himself to death . . . for an alleged 130 years! He claimed that inhaling smoke worked wonders for his system and agreed perfectly with his constitution. In fact, he insisted, the more he smoked the better he felt. The British Medical Journal recorded the case of a physician called Dr. Boisy from Havre who lived to be 103. He was still doing his daily rounds until his death and lauded the medicinal effects of both alcohol and tobacco, being a smoker and imbiber himself of no mean standing. Another centenarian surgeon who lived around the same time found his elixir of life in the port bottle, which he uncorked and half-drained daily.

Another 'grand old man of medicine', Dr R. Baynes of Rockland, Maine, believed that quite the reverse was true. A strict teetotaler, he even condemned the drinking of tea! He lived on a strict vegetarian diet until his death at around the turn of the century, aged well over 100, drinking only water, milk or occasionally chocolate and banishing even potatoes from his frugal diet.

Apart from his rigid dietary habits, Dr Baynes harboured another theory for his longevity – the avoidance of beds! He refused to sleep on a bed, or even a mattress on the floor from the age of 50, preferring instead a less comfortable slumber on a reclining iron chair, over which he spread a few blankets for warmth.

There are many instances of centenarians surviving on incredibly frugal fare. Scotland abounds with stories of the over 100's who have lived on porridge alone.

In Germany, a labourer called Stender who toiled in the Holstein region until his death in 1792 at the age of 103, was said to have survived in the latter stages of his life entirely on oatmeal and buttermilk. The virile Baron Baravicino de Capelis, who married four times, his last wife bearing eight children, became the oldest man in the Austrian Tyrol in the eighteenth century on a completely meat-free diet of eggs, tea and sweet cordial which sufficed him until he died aged 104.

The Zombie Girl

In 1936, a ragged, wretched woman was found wandering aimlessly, as though in a trance, around the roads skirting a modest farm. She appeared to have totally lost the power of speech and she cringed fearfully under a tattered cloth she was carrying if anyone approached.

When she was taken to hospital for care and treatment, she prompted this incredible description from an American photographer: 'The sight was dreadful. That blank face with the dead eyes. The eyelids were white all around the eyes as if they had been burned with acid. There was nothing you could say to her or get from her except by looking at her, and the sight of this wreckage was too much to endure for long.'

The poor, inhuman woman was finally identified as Felicia Felix-Mentor. The farm around which she had been found roaming was that of her brother. But how she came to be there, and in such a bizarre state, was a mystery. For medical records revealed that Felicia Felix-Mentor had died of a sudden illness and had been buried twenty-nine years previously.

Her strange case, documented and photographed by the American Zora Hurston, has baffled the world everywhere apart from anyone who knew, was related to or, indeed, lived in the same country as Felicia Felix-Mentor. To the people of Haiti there has always been a simple, spine-chilling answer to why this freak-woman seemingly rose from the dead.

They say she was a zombie. One of the walking dead brought back to enslaved life by Voodoo, the bizarre and fabled religion of which horror films are made but which still, today, is a feared belief of, astoundingly, more than 90 per cent of the Haitian population.

Successive tyrants 'Papa Doc' and now 'Baby Doc' Duvalier have surrounded themselves with a fierce private army known as the *tontons macoute*; a *tonton macoute* being a travelling voodoo magician. Beneath the hocus-pocus, however, lies more than a show of strength and a convenient means of suppression of superstitious subjects.

In his book *The Invisibles*, British anthropologist Francis Huxley tells of a so-called zombie who was seen in his own village in 1959. In a state of shock, apparently, the zombie was taken to a police station, where local officers would have nothing to do with him. In the street, a stranger gave him a glass of salt water and he then managed to stammer his name. His aunt, who lived nearby, positively identified him. According to her, he had died and been buried four years previously.

Haiti has bred other, less reliably-documented accounts which seek to

A Haitian Zombie ceremony

explain appearances of wildly staring, automaton-like human freaks; supposedly raised from the dead by bokors, or voodoo sorcerers, who claim to weave
evil spells over corpses, turning them into mindless, re-born slaves.

Another, latter-day description of an alleged encounter with a zombie, by a
man called William Seabrook, makes blood-curdling reading: 'The eyes were
the worst. It was not my imagination. They were in truth like the eyes of a
dead man, not blind, but staring, unfocused, unseeing. The whole face, for
that matter, was bad enough. It was vacant, as if there was nothing behind it.
It seemed not only expressionless, but incapable of expression. I had seen so
much previously in Haiti that was outside ordinary, normal experience that
for the flash of a second I had a sickening almost panicky lapse in which I
thought, or rather felt, "Great God, maybe this stuff is really true ..." '

What would seem, to any outsider, to be superstitious mumjo-jumbo, is
treated with deadly seriousness by the bokors and their disciples in the
former French slave colony that is Haiti today.

But what really did happen to Felicia Felix-Mentor and others like her?
Could she – and so many more – simply have been people buried alive after

being drugged into a death-like, catatonic trance and then recovered from their graves to be seen later, wandering aimlessly around, ghoulish, freak aberrations of human beings?

Perhaps relevantly, Article 246 of the Old Haitian Criminal Code states: 'Also to be termed intention to kill is the use of substances whereby a person is not killed, but reduced to a state of lethargy, more or less prolonged, and this without regard to the manner in which the substances were used or what was their later result. If following the state of lethargy the person is buried, then the attempt will be termed murder.'

In the case of Felicia Felix-Mentor, 'more or less prolonged' was, or might have been, 29 years. Is that really what could have turned her into a freak from an unimaginable nightmare ... a zombie girl?

Six Year Fast

In a shuttered room a frail teenage girl wakes, stirring only slightly between crisp, white sheets. In the street outside, the new day's visitors have already arrived and wait, patiently and silently, to be called to her bedside.

One by one, or occasionally in small family groups, they are eventually ushered from daylight into the still-dark room. Slowly, as if to conserve every possible ounce of energy, the girl raises her head to observe, as she has done many thousands of times, the latest pilgrims who hail her as a saint.

Since Christmas 1975, the worshippers, the miracle-seekers and the simply curious have been flocking to the tiny Portuguese town of Tropeca, where 18-year-old Maria Vierira, her face a deathly-white mask, lies awaiting the audiences with her humble followers. Since Christmas 1975, Maria has apparently neither eaten nor taken a single drink of water.

Her incredible fast has been verified by completely mystified medical experts, who say she should have died within a month. Yet the fragile girl, who is not only defying all laws of nature but is also claimed to have immense healing powers, explains her survival by saying that she saw a holy vision. 'I talked to Jesus and the Holy Mother,' she says. 'They told me to help the poor people. They said I didn't have to eat any more, so I don't. They said they would provide and that I should have faith.'

Faith has drawn busloads of pilgrims from all over Portugal to the modest home where Maria lives with her parents, entombed always in her darkened, shrine-like bedroom. At first, her family were outraged by her refusal to take any form of sustenance. Says her mother, Elena: 'We even sat by her room for days trying to catch her sneaking food – but we never did.' Now her parents believe she has been blessed by God. Like priests and doctors who have closely examined and scrutinized her, they can find no logical, earthly reason why she should still be alive. One specialist from Oporto, who has verified Maria's total lack of intake of food or water, discovered that her average weekly urine output is a mere 50 cubic centimetres, or only 5 per cent of the average 1,000 cubic centimetres of a normal human.

In the face of such medical evidence, however, at least one priest in Tropeca disbelieves Maria's startling condition and claims. Father Enrice Joso says: 'She looks like an epileptic and I think the trances she has are epileptic fits.' More sinisterly, he adds: 'I think her mother has taken her to witches.' This alarming verdict is not, though, shared by Father Joseph Mauel, from nearby Oporto. He insists: 'From a human point of view anything is possible on a spiritual level.' Indeed, time and again, cynics have been confounded by the skeletal form of little Maria, who always maintains that her fast is on holy ordinance to save the world's sinners.

Her neighbours in Tropeca have been amazed by her fantastic healing powers. One, Evelina Menezes, recently told a North American newspaper: 'I have seen her heal people ... lots of them. I saw one man carrying a child who could not walk. They went into Maria's room, and when they came out the child was walking.' Another neighbour spoke of the hordes of pilgrims 'who come to be blessed by our saint ... some even crawling on their knees.'

Maria's mother tells how her daughter goes into a trance when she is healing: 'Her face becomes just like Christ's Her eyes are surrounded by dark circles and there is a crown of thorns on her head. Her face gives off a glow.'

Thousands of pilgrims have claimed to have witnessed a strange radiance being emitted from Maria's body and many attest to her seemingly divine ability to heal even the supposedly incurably sick.

No food

Doctors were completely baffled by the case of a 19-year-old girl, who became known as the 'Market Harborough Fasting Girl' after the name of her home town. She supposedly ate literally nothing between April 1874 and December 1877, when she died after surviving only on occasional doses of morphine, with neither food nor drink passing her lips.

Of her own destiny, the fragile waif of a teenager who is herself a medical miracle, has remained silent. Christmas 1981 marked the sixth year of her fast and, though she certainly grows no stronger, she is far from immobile. Her movements are slow, for her strength is slight, yet she remains totally articulate and determined to continue what she believes is her divine mission. Meanwhile, pilgrims still descend in their thousands and despite the fact that by now, had they willingly handed over money, Maria could have moved to far more opulent surroundings, she has refused to accept a single payment and remains in her rather austere family home guided by her religious vision. For she says she has no need of food or water, or other worldly things.

Young Mothers

On 13 July 1982, a girl of 10 was recovering in hospital after giving birth to a 4 pound 8 ounce baby. Both were said to be 'quite satisfactory.'

The unnamed girl was taken to hospital in Houston, Texas on a special flight from a country town in the east of the state for the delivery, which doctors had predicted would be premature. Immediately after the birth, cagey staff at the Hermann Hospital refused to say whether the infant was a boy or a girl or – honouring a request of total secrecy by the girl's guardian – give any other details.

The case is far from being unique, however. The world's youngest-ever mother was Linda Medina, a peasant's daughter from the Peruvian Andes, who was flown to Chicago for hospital treatment in 1940 when she was six years old, and her baby son was aged 15 months. Linda suffered from the disease which can kill youngsters from 'old age' by speeding up their ageing process to a phenomenal rate.

She was sent to America to be treated by Dr Karl John Karnaky. How she became a mother at such an incredibly early age remained a mystery to specialists. Her superstitious parents could only offer Indian folklore reasons; her mother Donna Loza said she had been bitten by a snake with curious powers over women and her father said that she had bathed in an enchanted mountain lake known as the 'pool of birth'.

As the photograph here shows, 9-year-old Venesia Xoagus was feeling well

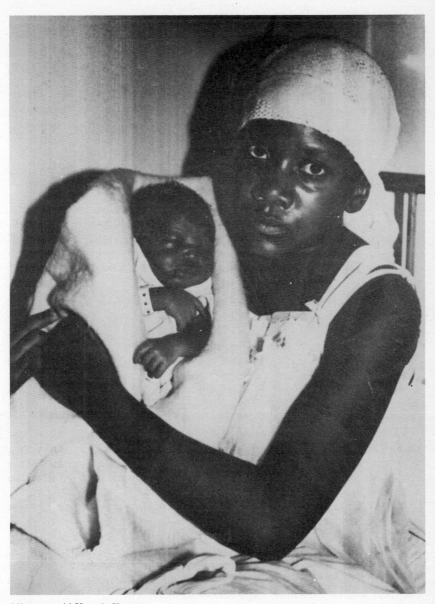

Nine-year-old Venesia Xoagus

enough barely a week after giving birth to a baby boy at Otjiwaronjo Hospital in Southern Africa, to pose with the infant. In July 1980 she became the youngest mother ever to give birth in that entire continent.

The oldest mother on record is Mrs Ruth Alice Kistler, born at Wakefield, Massachusetts on 11 June 1899, who gave birth to a daughter, Susan, at Glendale, near Los Angeles, California on 18 October 1956, when she was 57 years and 129 days old. In Britain, Mrs Winifred Wilson, of Eccles, Greater Manchester, had her tenth child, a daughter she christened Shirley, when she was 55 years and 3 days old on 14 November 1936.

There is an unauthenticated report that a septuagenarian gave birth in the Welsh town of Clwyd on 15 May 1776, in her 46th year of marriage. But, it is claimed, the baby boy who would have been 72-year-old Mrs Ellen Ellis's 13th child, was stillborn.

A Man Becomes a Mum

Young soldier Nochmen Tenenbaum served with great distinction in the Polish Army, earning bravery medals for rescuing several people from drowning and earning promotion to sergeant. But, after he was demobbed at the age of 24, he discovered that something quite startling was happening to him. He found himself gradually changing into a woman. A year later, in 1936, doctors and nurses at a Warsaw clinic were astonished when Tenenbaum, still wearing his men's clothes, asked to book a private room – because he was pregnant. He was admitted and, shortly afterwards, gave birth to a healthy, bouncing, 9-pound baby. The amazing incident is believed to have been the first time that a person who has changed sex has become a mother.

Other startling sex changes were happening in Britain at around the same time when two sets of sisters became brothers within four years of each other. Marjory and Daisy Ferrow grew up as girls in the seaside town of Great Yarmouth, Norfolk. But when they were 13, according to newspaper reports: 'they both developed characteristics that made them hold aloof from other schoolchildren, and eventually forced them to sacrifice scholarships which they had won to Yarmouth High School for Girls.'

The family left town for a few years. And when they returned in August

Man gives birth

'Man Gives Birth' is a headline editors throughout the world would love to put in their newspapers. It has, in a manner of speaking, already happened. On a number of occasions, males have been born with the foetus of a twin in their own bodies. In one famous case in Mexico City a huge tumour on a baby boy's back was opened, to reveal a crying, perfectly healthy infant.

1939, Marjory had become pipe-smoking Mark Ferrow and Daisy had become David. It was believed at the time to be the first instance of two members of the same family changing sex. Then, in 1943, a tragedy brought a similar case to light.

Mary Weston lived with her sister Hilda at Oreston, near Plymouth. She was a superb athlete and a key member of Britain's Olympic team, having been women's national champion javelin thrower in 1927 and having won an international shot-putting title in 1934. Two years later, she became a man and changed her name to Mark. In 1937, Mark married Alberta Bray, a 20-year-old blonde who had been a girl friend, first of Mary and then, of course, of Mark, for years.

Hilda's life also changed, but with no such happy ending. Operations at Charing Cross Hospital were suggested when she tried to register for national service in one of the armed forces and, though she changed her name to Harry, depression after the operations proved unbearable. Harry hanged himself from a tree, aged just 26.

Ronnie Rigsbee was born a boy at Durham, North Carolina, in 1944. But by the age of 6, he had begun to realize that he was very different from his playmates. 'I always associated with girls,' he recalled later. 'I couldn't understand why . . . but I just felt that I should be a girl.' After he joined the US Navy at the age of 17, Ronnie was comforted and told that his disturbed feelings were just 'a passing phase'. It was a phase that stayed with him, however. For in 1970, when he was 26, a leading New York doctor began a series of operations which eventually turned Ronnie Rigsbee into Susan Janette Fontaine.

She took a job as a barmaid, but quickly discovered that she had swapped one set of problems for another. She was raped, which added to her turmoil and mental anguish, and tried to commit suicide several times. After one attempt, a sympathetic nurse befriended Susan and took her to church. 'I realized I had made a terrible mistake,' she said, 'if God had made me male when I was born, then He intended me to be male.'

Dying of old age

This five-year-old little girl, who weighs only nine pounds, suffers from the rare and tragic disorder which speeds up the ageing process. As yet, there is little that doctors can do to help sufferers.

In November 1980, Susan's breasts were surgically removed, and Ronnie Rigsbee emerged from hospital to become a croupier at a Las Vegas casino. Through years of unease and confusion, he now says that he is finally completely happy to stay the way he is. He knows he will never be able to have a normal sex life, but he says: 'I feel it is loving and caring that are important. I am finally at peace . . . I have found myself at last.'

Sex changes, or, rather, stories about them, may seem well suited to some of the more salacious newspapers. But it is worth recounting that they began to attract intense medical interest more than a century ago. One of the best documented cases is that of Catherine/Charles Hoffman, who changed sex in 1870 at the age of 46. Catherine/Charles had lived with a male lover for 20 years, before marrying a woman. It is highly likely that Catherine/Charles was a true hermaphrodite – a double-sexed human. Hermaphrodites were extremely rare, highly-prized oddities in Victorian times, drawing the attention of leading doctors and freak experts all over the world. It is extremely doubtful whether any were actually exhibited in public, other than perhaps at the sort of underground 'fringe shows' which sometimes sprang up in an area overnight before moving on to evade the ever-following arm of the law.

One story of a true hermaphrodite, which bears repeating as an illustration of the mental anguish which must torture so many human freaks, is that of Marie-Madeleine Lefort, who checked into the Hôtel-Dieu, a public hospital in Paris, as an old man aged 65 suffering from chronic pleurisy. He was bald and had a long, flowing beard. In terrible health, he moaned to hospital staff of having led a miserable existence, barely scraping a living.

It was only when an autopsy was performed two months later, after the old man died, that hospital staff realized the full extent of the misery he had been through. They discovered him to be the same person who had been examined by an eminent panel of doctors at the age of 19, as a girl. His condition as a hermaphrodite had totally confused him and he had told the hospital staff that though he had only had the feelings of a man for 16 years, he was puzzled about why he had been taken for a girl when young. He was, of course, both!

General Tom Thumb

Never even from the legendary land of Lilliput could have come a figure quite so amazing as Charles Sherwood Stratton. He was a most rare human being; not dwarf, but a true midget – a perfectly proportioned person in miniature. He real name may sound unfamiliar, but the baby who was born on 4 January 1838, lager achieved worldwide fame as the most celebrated freak who ever lived – General Tom Thumb.

He became the jewel in Barnum and Bailey's collection of human oddities, the darling of the Palace of Queen Victoria and three-quarters of the way towards being a millionaire. In a blaze of publicity, he married a midget woman and, in moments of great pomp and pride, became a close confidante of the Duke of Wellington.

Stratton had been a normal enough – even strapping – infant, weighing in as he did at birth at 9 pounds. But, remarkably, he remained at exactly the same weight until he was 5 years old. His height at that age was a diminutive 2 feet 1 inch. With such a medical marvel on their hands, his parents did what to them and to hundreds of other mothers and fathers in the early part of the 19th century was a perfectly natural thing to do. They put their little boy on public exhibition.

News of the amazing midget's shows in Bridgeport, Connecticut, travelled far and wide until it fell upon the ears of Phineas T. Barnum's half-brother Philo. The master showman reacted like greased lightning; within hours he tracked down the little fellow and signed him on the spot to work for three dollars a week.

With his usual passion for overkill and hype, Barnum re-christened the tiny toddler 'General Tom Thumb' and billed him as a 'dwarf of eleven years of age, just arrived from England'. Barnum was determined that his prize capture should be taught to enrapture audiences by being 'autocratic, impudent and regal', and set about schooling him day and night in the wacky ways of the peep show world.

General Tom Thumb's first public appearance was marked by his strident, almost pompous recitation of one of Barnum's pun-ridden monologues. The little midget portrayed himself as an arrogant, barking bombast – and the public loved every second. He was coached in a variety of garishly-costumed roles by Barnum, including Cupid, Napoleon, Yankee Doodle Dandy and a semi-naked gladiator, and the paying punters couldn't get enough of it.

As word of the thumbnail-sized General's performances spread, people flocked from miles for the privilege of attending his shows. He quickly

Mr and Mrs Tom Thumb

established himself as Barnum's most inspired acquisition and indeed became something of an ambassador for the great showman. Literally overnight, he became the talk of New York and, less than a year later, the toast of London during an incredibly successful tour in England. A delighted Queen Victoria, who stood barely 4 feet 11 inches tall herself, summoned him to give three Royal Command Performances at Buckingham Palace, where he soon earned the nickname 'Pet of The Palace'. The Queen is said to have been most definitely amused by the little manikin's strutting and strange antics.

General Tom also became a good friend of the Duke of Wellington, who was another great fan of his. It is claimed that during one Palace performance in which he was playing Napoleon, the Duke asked him what he was thinking about. 'Sir,' he replied, 'I was thinking of the loss of the Battle of Waterloo!'

For every show, Barnum always billed General Tom as being six years older than he actually was. Advertised as 30½ inches and 18 years old, he was in fact, only 12. By maturity, his height had reached its miniscule peak of 3 feet 4 inches. In adulthood, he was a singing, dancing story-teller extraordinaire. Decked in splendid costumes and with a neatly-trimmed, military-style set of whiskers, he became a little living legend.

When Tom decided to marry a midget woman, Lavinia Warren, who was almost exactly the same size as himself, Barnum decreed that the wedding was to be a razzle-dazzle showbiz affair with photographs, publicity and as much hullaballoo as it was possible to muster. It was a staggering success. Photographs of the half-pint-sized bridal couple together with their midget attendants were among the best-selling items in the early days of the camera.

General Tom and his bride settled down to make their fortune together, and at the height of their success, the much-loved midget couple had amassed a nest-egg topping three-quarters of a million dollars. They seemed destined to hit that magical million figure until Tom fell ill and, tragically, died of apoplexy in his home town of Bridgeport, Connecticut, at the age of 45. The little man went to his grave in the sure knowledge that he had conquered the world from the proud height of 3 feet 4 inches.

Dwarf race

One of the most astonishing races of dwarf people, who existed in the French Pyrenees for three centuries until the 1900s, was a clan called the Cagots, who were widely believed to have been the descendants of the inhabitants of a leper colony. One late 19th century medical report said 'They never exceeded 51½ inches in height, and had short, ill-formed legs, great bellies, small eyes, flat noses and pale, unwholesome complexions'.

Other Midgets and Dwarfs

The smallest human being who ever lived was Pauline Musters, a little midget girl from Holland who was exhibited as 'Princess Pauline'. The fragile creature, who weighed a mere 9 pounds at her heaviest, was 12 inches long when she was born at Ossendrecht on 26 February 1876. She never grew beyond 23½ inches tall and her vital statistics were 47-48-43 . . . centimetres! Her exact dimensions were recorded despite the fact that, as ever, her peep show bosses advertised her as being only 19 inches tall. Sadly, she became an alcoholic and, with a drink-weakened heart and also suffering from pneumonia and meningitis, she died at the age of 19 in New York on 1 March 1895.

Despite the fact that Lilliputian-sized freaks tend, like giants to lead shorter than average lives, there are records of two centenarian dwarfs – one of whom is still alive. Parish registers reveal that a woman called Anne Clowes from Derbyshire died in 1784 at the grand old age of 103. At her death she was only 3 feet 9 inches tall and a paperweight 48 pounds.

Susanna Bokoyni, a retired, Hungarian-born circus performer, celebrated her 103rd birthday at her home in Newton, New Jersey on 6 April 1982. She is just 3 feet 4 inches tall, and weighs a meagre 37 pounds. When she was born, way back in 1879, Susanna's father was confidently told by doctors that her chances of surviving were desperately thin. Yet she has proved the grim diagnosis utterly wrong. Sixty-seven of her incredibly active years were spent as a dancer. She performed all over Europe and eventually America as 'Princess Susanna' and became a noted circus and vaudeville artiste. During her travels, she became fluent in several languages other than her native Hungarian. She remains to this day in perfectly good health. Until she underwent a cataract operation as recently as 1978, she had never spent a day in hospital since the time a group of ashen-faced doctors peered into her cot and gravely shook their heads a century previously.

Entire races of miniature people have been discovered, the most famous being pygmy tribes such as the Obongos and Dongos of Central Africa, which has proved a rich hunting ground for freak-seekers with an adventurous thirst for the bizarre. Such tribes, which still thrive today in the dense bush of countries such as Zaire, often have many members of only between 3 and 4 feet high. Yet explorers beware: even the evil tyrant of Uganda, Idi Amin, was reluctant to venture too far into the domain of the men and women whose unerring accuracy with the poison dart is renowned as the shortness of their stature.

Count Josef Boruwlaski with his wife Isalina and their baby

In the latter part of the 19th century, an expedition to discover 'lost tribes' of wild-men dwarfs ventured deep into the jungles of Central America. In a previously unexplored region near the Isthmus of Tehuantepec, anthropologists found their elusive quarry and succeeded in bringing back to civilization – and the freak show – two Cotta tribesmen, midgets standing only 3 feet 6 inches tall.

Despite the success of such largely thrill-seeking missions, however, the *Guinness Book of Records* today states that the smallest documented tribe are the Mbuti pygmies who live near the Ituri river in Zaire. Proper records of the tribe reveal that the average height for men is 4 feet 6 inches and, for women, 4 feet 5 inches.

One of the most remarkable dwarf stories is presented in *Anomalies and Curiosities of Medicine* by Gould and Pyle. The eminent surgeons recount the tale of Geoffrey Hudson, the most celebrated English dwarf, who was born at Oakham in 1619. He was presented to Henrietta Marie, wife of Charles I, in a pie at the age of 8. He became her favourite pet freak and until his youth, he was said to be not more than 18 inches high. In his youth he fought many duels, one with a turkey cock. He was a popular and charming courtier, and proved his bravey and allegiance to his sovereign by accepting command of a Royalist company.

He once challenged a gentleman by the name of Croft to fight a duel, and shot his adversary in the chest after being ridiculed about his diminutive size.

Hudson himself met a nasty end. He was accused of being part of the Papist Plot and eventually imprisoned in the Gate House at Westminster. His enemies in politics had won. He died in prison in 1682 at the advanced age of 63.

Little Estelle Ridley was a midget who happily took one of the few forms of employment that was open to her, and became a figure of fun in a circus. Then, in the early 1870s, she devised an even better way of cashing in on her misfortune. Using cunning make-up and child's clothes, she was able to transform herself from a hard-living, foul-speaking 40-year-old woman into a pretty, innocent-looking 'little girl' called Fanchon Moncare.

With an accomplice called Ada Danforth, she regularly cruised between France and New York on ocean liners. Ada would explain to enchanted fellow passengers that Fanchon was an orphan whose parents had died in a fire. She would inherit a fortune and vast estates on her 18th birthday, but meanwhile she was in Ada's charge.

Fanchon would curtsey sweetly and skip off happily, clutching a china doll. And, at the end of each trip, she would dance gaily through customs still cradling the cherished doll, while Ada took care of the luggage. No-one ever dreamed of stopping the 'young child'.

Lilliputian inferno

There seemed nothing particularly sensational in the news item which ran in the New York press on 28 May 1911, about how 300 inhabitants of an entire village on Coney Island had, although unharmed, been made homeless by a fire which completely razed their small community, apart from the fact that all 300 were professional dwarfs and midgets and the village, which had been custom-built to suit their stature, was called, in fine movie style, Lilliputia!

But once the couple were in a hansom cab outside the dock, the sweet smile would fade to be replaced by a mask of evil. For in New York's bustling Chinatown, elderly Wing To waited eagerly, with a greedy leer creasing his wrinkled face. When the travellers arrived, the head of the doll was unscrewed and out poured a fortune in gems, stolen during their months in Europe.

The lucrative charade was only ended when Estelle, alias little Fanchon, fell out with an acquaintance over the affections of a professional New York gambler. Her rival in love went to the police in a rage, and a reception committee was waiting when the doll next arrived at the city dock. The midget was jailed for life, and later hung herself in her prison cell. Ada Danforth, the accomplice who was 10 years younger than the bogus 'little girl' in her charge, was sentenced to serve 20 years for acting as an accessory.

Lilliputian adults have, in the past, posed as babes-in-arms for rather more noble reasons. A dwarf named Richeborg passed unchecked to and from Paris during the French Revolution disguised as an infant in a nurse's arms. His were spying missions, for he had memorized and carried in his head top secret dispatches which were considered too valuable or too dangerous to be written down. Richeborg, who stood only 23 inches high, was never once suspected of being anything other than a tiny child. He died in Paris in 1858, aged 90.

Throughout history, dwarfs have not only been the court jesters, but also the close and trusted confidantes of kings and queens. Peter the Great of Russia, whose passion for the bizarre and often utterly distasteful included keeping the head of an unfaithful mistress pickled in a jar by his bedside to serve as a warning to her successors, also delighted in keeping a troupe of dwarfs for his amusement and entertainment. He was so delighted with his assembly of little people that in 1710, he threw a massive banquet for the marriage of his favourite, a male dwarf named Valakoff, to the female dwarf of Princess Prescovy Theodorovna. Later, dwarf marriages were banned in Russia because of supposed difficulties which might follow during childbirth.

Two dwarfs who did marry and build a huge family were Robert Skinner, who stood, at 25 inches, an inch shorter than his wife Judith. They had no less than 14 children, all of whom were perfectly normal, healthy, and eventually grew up to normal heights. Another popular theory which was current during Victorian times was that dwarfs were naturally more intelligent than people of normal stature. In 1868, a detailed post mortem examination was carried out on a dwarf who had lived to the age of 61 and was said to have been especially wise. Indeed, the examination did demonstrate that the weight of the dwarf's brain was one-nineteenth that of his body, whereas in a person of ordinary stature the ratio would be anything between one-thirtieth and one-fortieth.

Finally there was a troupe of dwarfs actually called 'The Lilliputians'. They performed throughout America in the late 19th century with great distinction as burlesque entertainers. The dwarfs, thought to have been gathered in Austria and Germany, were so good that they cost, apparently, a small fortune to hire!

Trumpet player

Matthew Buchinger was born in 1674. Although his flipperlike hands and feet were attached directly to his torso he could juggle, play the trumpet and bagpipes, and was reputed to be able to dance the Hornpipe. He was also married four times and fathered eleven children.

The Mighty Atom

Pint-sized Jorge Monteiro has earned the nickname 'The Mighty Atom' from cellmates at the Linho jail in Lisbon, Portugal, who are amazed as the little man's exploits – or, rather, 'sexploits' as newspapers all over the world have preferred to call them.

For although he stands only just over four feet tall and is something of a physical rake, Jorge managed to make love to 38 women while still behind bars! The diminutive Don Juan accomplished his incredible love trysts by simply squeezing through a wafer-thin gap in a dividing wall between the men's and women's sections of the prison.

Jorge was in jail in the first place for seducing 70 women and stealing their money in the time-honoured traditions of a deceiving Casanova. But he managed to escape after just four months – and then the story of his amazing prison love-ins began to emerge. Eventually, the elusive little man was recaptured, but even after a new trial in April, 1982, with Jorge on his way back to his cell, a Portuguese government official was forced to admit: 'He is just incredible. There is no way to stop him – even when we lock him up,'

During his second trial, Jorge had even had the impudence to brag to the judge of his adventures while incarcerated. 'What I did may have been wrong,' he did confess, 'but you have got to admit that it certainly was daring!' Prison officials who are baffled as to how any man could have got through the hole in the wall through which their miniature inmate seemed so easily to squeeze, decided after his latest trial that the only place for him was solitary confinement.

But a rueful jail official was forced to say: 'We can't keep him there for any length of time if he is behaving himself. Heaven only knows what he'll get up to again when we let him out. He's irrepressible. Women seem to adore him and for a man of such limited stature, he seems to be able to pack an awful lot of energy into that little frame.'

Meanwhile, some of the women he so cruelly deceived while at liberty have actually formed a fan club for him. And, while he may be known as the Mighty Atom inside the jail, outside his adoring followers call him 'Captain Rody'. That was one of the aliases the 40-year-old ultra-short super-lover used while posing as an army captain, an engineer and an insurance broker. One attractive 24-year-old divorcee fought back her tears as she told reporters: 'Let them say what they like about my Jorge, but to me he was always a perfect gentleman. His size is of no importance to me whatsoever. I will wait for him till he comes out of prison and fly to his arms – if he will have me.'

There was a rather nasty side to the pint-sized stud's passionate crime wave, however. Apart from seducing his doting victims before making off with money or jewellery he 'borrowed' from them, he also blackmailed those unwilling to part with their valuables with Polaroid photographs of their lovemaking. He was only caught after a number of them complained to the police. But even some of the women he most wickedly duped still hold the Might Atom close to their hearts.

One, from Lisbon, sighed: 'He is my little pocket dynamo and I shall always remember him. He was the perfect partner, always caring and always pandering to my every need, no matter how small. His size makes no difference at all. In fact, it makes him rather more endearing. I know that the things he has done are bad, but how could anybody feel angry at someone who is so sweet and adorable?'

With the flames of such unrequited love still burning so strongly for him, it seems unlikely he will ever abandon his favourite hobby. Even during his second trial, his female lawyer was forced to quit the case – because the Mighty Atom made a pass at her! It was a defence which, of course, in the end failed.

The little Portuguese folk hero received a jail sentence of 7½ years from the judge, who was totally unimpressed by his heartless hanky-panky.

Yet another of his 'victims' insisted, though: 'He is a legend and there will be lots of pretty girls like me waiting for him when he is eventually released. Jorge is just a little misguided, that's all. He really is one of the most gentle people I know and he would never, ever do or say anything hurtful to anyone.'

Four others had sat silently sobbing as the smiling, impeccably-dressed Mighty Atom stood in court while the full weight of justice was meted out to him: they were his wife and three children. 'I am happily married and have wonderful children,' he says. 'And I love them all ... '

The Mighty Atom will obviously be greatly missed.

Kids' heroes

These men created the stories and the dreams on which children for centuries to come will thrive. The endurance of their works is unquestionable. Yet the legendary Aesop, whose Fables are beloved the world over, was a dwarf. And Hans Christian Andersen, the Danish genius of fairy tales, was a human skeleton, so thin that he stuffed his shirt with paper before ever appearing in public. He was dyslexic too, and so dictated his stories to be inked by another, unknown, hand.

The King of Giants

Walking tall . . . that was Robert Pershing Wadlow, all-time King of the Giants. He towered head and shoulders above the freaks of which shows like Barnum and Bailey's were really made. From Goliath to the Fantasy Ogre at the top of Jack's beanstalk, giants and giantesses have fired public imagination as have no other examples of human hyperbole, alive or dead.

Wadlow remains the tallest accurately-measured man who ever lived. At the age of 22 when he died, he was a skyscraping 8 feet 11 inches tall – and still growing! When he was born in 1918 in Alton, Illinois, his mother and father, Addie and Harold, could have had no idea that the average-sized 8½ pound infant would rocket upwards in such an incredible way.

Up to the age of 2, his development was quite normal. Then, after a routine operation, and for no apparent reason, he began to grow abnormally fast. At the age of 5, he had a long way to look down on his kindergarten playmates from his lofty 5 feet 4 inches. Three years later, he was a six-footer. By 11, the tape measure was stretched to 6 feet 7 inches and just after he had started high school, at 13, his head was really in the clouds at 7 feet 1¾ inches. And he just kept growing and growing . . .

When he was only 9, he could carry his father Harold, who was by then the Mayor of Alton, up the stairs of the family home and down again with ease. But then, Mr Wadlow senior was, to his son, a diminutive 5 feet 11 inches tall!

Wadlow was half an inch over the inevitable eight-foot mark shortly before his 17th birthday. A keen sportsman, he was an invaluable asset to his school basketball team as he was able to shoot down into the basket each time he had the ball for a certain score. For his incredible height he was, however, never obese. By the time he was 22, shortly before his death, he tipped the scales at a little over 31 stones. But for a man who was little more than half an inch from being nine feet tall, he carried the weight extremely well, looking, if anything, slightly thin!

It was Dr C. M. Charles, Associate Professor of Anatomy at Washington University's School of Medicine in St Louis, Missouri, who helped keep regular, scientifically documented records of Wadlow's progress towards the heavens. He was assisted by Dr Cyril MacBryde, who actually measured Wadlow's final recorded height just 18 days before his death on 15 July 1940.

Wadlow had suffered from a badly infected right leg, which was aggravated by a poorly-fitting brace. Ironically, he died just a month before

Robert Pershing Wadlow

the discovery of penicillin – the one thing that could have saved him. Quite surprisingly for the tallest man who ever lived, Wadlow never once succumbed to the lucrative offers from peep show bosses which poured in. It is hardly surprising that they were so desperate to get their hands on him, for it was the usual practice of rogues such as Barnum and Bailey to exaggerate wildly the height of their giants on display in an effort to prise yet more money from audiences.

Wadlow preferred instead to lead a quiet life with his parents, brothers and sisters, all of whom were normal sized, and shunned public life save for occasional newspaper photographs on special occasions such as his 21st birthday, when he was pictured amid the relatives he dwarfed. Indeed, he is reported to have looked an extremely dignified figure; a bespectacled man with the look of a scholar. He was sartorially elegant too, being exceptionally fastidious about his smart, specially-made suits and shirts.

After he died, he was laid to rest in an enormous coffin, 10 feet 9 inches long and 32 inches wide. Ironically, half a dozen accurate models of him were made shortly before his death by the famous artist James Butler. Where in life he had turned his back on the gaudy glare of the peep show, those models today still tour the world stored in huge coffins which have to be loaded through the freight ports of aircraft.

One of the models stood for a time in the main street of Helsinki, Finland, where it caused huge traffic jams as people stopped to stare at the world's tallest man, if only in the form of an effigy!

More Giants and Giantesses

The tallest man ever to live in Great Britain was Irishman Patrick Cotter O'Brien (1760–1806), who measured an incredible 8 feet 1 inch. His skeleton today stands preserved at the Royal College of Surgeons in London, where its height was re-checked as recently as 1975. How it comes to be there is the result of a remarkable story.

Throughout his life in Bristol, where he eventually settled, O'Brien lived in morbid fear of a cunning surgeon called John Hunter, who became obsessed with the idea of getting his hands on the giant's skeleton when he died. Hunter openly pursued O'Brien, threatening that he would 'boil him in a large iron pot till the flesh came off his bones' unless he agreed to the request. O'Brien, who staunchly refused to give the surgeon permission to have his body when he expired, often complained of being 'hounded to death' and begged the medical man to leave him alone.

The giant was, indeed, tormented all his life by the surgeon's vow to have his body, and by the spies he sent out to report on his movements. At the age of 45, O'Brien found his health deteriorating rapidly and, knowing he was on his deathbed, paid a group of fishermen to take his body after he expired and sink it in the middle of the Irish Channel, with heavy weights attached.

His dying wish to evade the clutches of the surgeon was not granted. Hunter, who had already bribed every undertaker in the city to hand over O'Brien's cadaver, managed to find the fishermen through his spies and out-bribed them too. O'Brien's body did, eventually, land in Hunter's giant melting pot, where all its flesh was boiled off to leave the surgeon – and, centuries later, the Royal College of Surgeons – in possession of the unwilling giant's skeleton. That melting pot that O'Brien had lived in such fear of has, ironically, been preserved as a museum piece too.

In recent history, America has towered over the world as the country which produces the tallest giants. Of the nine men positively known to have stood at over eight feet tall, the five tallest have all come from the United States. That figure includes the world's tallest living man, Don Koehler, who measures 8 feet 2 inches. Don, from Chicago, is the son of tall parents. He was born, with a twin sister who now stands at a rather more average 5 feet 9 inches tall, in Montana in 1925.

Perhaps the most famous super-tall freak of the peep shows was the Chinaman Chang Yu Sing, who was known to the discerning voyeurs of Victorian England as the aristocrat of giants. Chang, who was never accurately measures but was believed to have stood almost eight feet high, was known to have a passion for gold, jewels and pearls. He also had a penchant for the very finest clothes, and would refuse to appear on stage unless he was suitably dressed in embroidered silk, red velvet or panther-skin.

It was a golden rule among peep show bosses that, as well as being encouraged to exaggerate about their height, giants and giantesses had in their contracts a stipulation that they were never to be properly measured. So most reports of tall people who went on exhibit must, at best, be held to be rather questionable. For example, the costumes of circus giantess Ella Ewing always included an extra-large headress, and she was advertised at various heights up to 8 feet 4½ inches. She was scientifically measured at the age of 23, when she stood at 7 feet 4½ inches, though it is believed likely that she attained a height of about 7 feet 6 inches before her death. Ella became

The Chinese giant, Chang, with his wife and attendant dwarf

famous as the 'Missouri Giantess' when, at the age of 21, she joined the Barnum and Bailey circus and toured all over America, appearing also for a short time with Buffalo Bill's Wild West Show.

Ella, who became as well known for her warm, affectionate nature as she did for her height, had had a normal childhood until the age of about 10, when suddenly she began to shoot up, much to her embarrassment. Her parents, who were poor farmers, tried hard to shield her from stares and jibes, but after only a short while she was forced to quit school to escape the cruel taunts of her classmates. Ella turned to local fairs and shows to earn a living, but never really achieved great success until she was signed up by Phineas T. Barnum. With the King of the Freak Shows, the Queen of Giantesses made a fortune and was able to provide enough money to help her parents, who loyally followed her wherever she toured.

Ella was also able to buy herself a 120-acre ranch near her home town of Gorin, Missouri. On the land, she built a huge house, specially adapted to her gargantuan needs, with 15-foot ceilings, 10-foot doors and 7-foot windows. All the furniture was likewise proportioned and she was able at last to live in a home where she never had to stoop or feel uncomfortable. She was known as a kind, witty woman, who entertained with a wealth of stories about her experiences on the peep show circuit, and was a much respected member of the community until her death, at the age of 40, in 1913.

Ella's dying wish was that she should be cremated, so that her bones would never fall into the hands of vandals or even surgeons. Her father, however, could not bear the thought of it – so he arranged for her to be buried inside a solid steel casket in a cement-filled grave, over which he placed a guard for several years so that, in death, the 'Missouri Giantess' could have the privacy she so desired.

The world's tallest living woman is 18-year-old Zeng Jinlian (pronounced San Chung Lin) who lives with her parents and brother in Yujiang village in the Bright Moon Community, Hunan Province, central China.

At the age of 16, she was accurately reported to be an astonishing 7 feet 10½ inches, but is now said to have easily topped the 8 foot mark and continues to grow!

Zeng started springing upwards at the tender age of four months. She was the same height as her mother – 5 feet 1½ inches – before she was 4, and by her 13th birthday was 7 feet 1½ inches of little girl! Her hands measure 10 inches, her feet 14 inches, and her last recorded weight was 23 stones 2 pounds. Zeng suffers from acromegaly, a disease which has caused so many giants and giantesses to die while relatively young, and she already tires so easily that she can only go out walking with the aid of her family, who struggle to support her enormous body.

The tallest ever Englishwoman, who was also an acromegalic, was Jane Bunford, who was born on 26 July 1895 at Bartley Green, Northfield, West Midlands. Her growth rate was perfectly normal until the age of 11, when she started mysteriously putting on feet and inches at a phenomenal rate after receiving a head injury. At 13, she looked down on her parents from the awesome height of 6 feet 6 inches. Because of the disease which bowed and bent her spine, she measured a 'mere' 7 feet 7 inches on her death, at the age of 26, on 1 April 1922. Had her back not been so crippled and curved, it is estimated that her true height would have been 7 feet 11 inches.

What happens when a giant meets a giantess and two hearts begin to flutter ... ?

It ended in marriage when Captain Martin van Buren Bates and Miss Anna Swan fell for each other. He was a towering 7 feet 2½ inches and she was actually three inches taller! The happy couple, who had travelled from America to England in a freak show, were wed at St Martin's-in-the-Fields on 17 June 1871.

They had already become immensely popular with Victorian England's keenest connoisseur of oddities, Queen Victoria herself, and the monarch was so delighted with them that she sent the bride a large ring and the groom an enormous watch as wedding presents.

After a huge wedding reception, which was attended by the Prince of Wales, and a tour of Scotland, they returned to the United States, where they made a fortune from freak shows before retiring to Ohio and a tailor-made home with 14-foot high ceilings and 8½-foot doors. One of their very first visitors was the midget Lavinia Stratton, then widow of the world-famous midget General Tom Thumb!

One of the most amazing dinner dates was widely reported in America in 1975, when 7 feet 2 inches tall giant Dan Gerber of Illinois called to escort 7 feet 5 inches tall giantess Sandy Allen of Shelbyville, Indiana.

Despite the close attentions of newspaper photographers anxious to record their soirée for posterity, the couple were determined that their date should be as normal as possible. After a visit to a local bowling alley, they set out for a restaurant where they discussed how much they enjoyed each other's company and how much they would both like to date again.

It's a bit rough on a young bachelor's wallet, though, when between them, he and his date manage to polish off 5 shrimp cocktails, 6 fillet steaks, a mountain of baked potatoes, two basketfuls of hot rolls, popcorn served in giant salad bowls and, for dessert, double helpings each of the following: ice-cream cake, pie and ice cream and banana splits!

If giant and giantess can be ideal partners, then so can a couple where, by dint of height alone, one partner really has to look down on the other! That's

Anna Swan's marriage to
Captain Martin van Buren Bates

Anna Swan with Admiral Dot, the smallest
man in the world at that time

the case with Mr and Mrs Max Palmer of Illinois, who represent the most extreme difference in the respective heights of a married couple.

At the time of their wedding Max stood a towering 7 feet 8 inches tall, while his bride Betty must have been sure she was entering into wedlock with a man she could look up to from her 4 feet 11 inches height, in high heels! Even with that little support there was an incredible gap of 2 feet 9 inches from the top of her head to the top of his. When another giant American, Henry Mullins, fell in love and popped the question, it was to a lady who stood 5 feet 3 inches tall to his 7 feet 6¾ inches, making a gap between them of more than 2 feet 3 inches. The couple met, according to Henry, when his bride-to-be went shopping in downtown Chicago, saw a sign saying 'Giant Sale' and decided to get one for herself!

Henry, who became a great music hall star, had changed his surname to Hite before launching out on a career which eventually spanned more than 30 years, so when he married he and his wife of course became Mr and Mrs Hite. Apart from his great sense of humour (and love of tall stories) Henry displayed remarkably nimble talents for a man of his height.

He was able to perform a quick-fire string of somersaults with the agility of an Olympic gymnast and he was a delightful tap-dancer in shoes which were more than 16 inches long. Despite his slender, well-proportioned frame, he was also something of a strong man, easily able to lift two men – one on each muscular forearm – and carry them around.

After he retired from the music hall, he became a travelling sales promoter for a meat packaging firm called Wilson's where fame followed him and he became known as 'Wilson's Giant'. He motored around in a specially customized car which had the front seat removed to make room for his incredibly long legs, enabling him to become his own back-seat driver!

Britain's tallest living man at present is 38-year-old Christopher Paul Greener who is a heady 7 feet 6¼ inches tall. Another Briton, Terence Keenan, is only a quarter-of-an-inch shorter, but, unhappily, he is unable even to stand upright. His growth rate was perfectly normal up to the age of 17, when he stood 5 feet 4 inches tall, but after that he began to shoot up skywards suddenly and abnormally.

Possibly the tallest giant who ever actually went on exhibition as a freak was a man named Machnov, billed as the 'Russian Giant', who drew enormous crowds in Victorian England. It is claimed that he attained the almost unbelievable height of 9 feet 4¼ inches, and indeed is also said to have had that height properly verified by medical experts, and not improperly exaggerated by circus masters and peep show bosses as happened in more than a few cases where the taller the giant was, the more certainty there was of a good day's takings.

Plenty of Pa

Jan Van Albert, one of the tallest men in the world, is pictured with his wife, who is five feet 7 inches tall, and their daughter.

Another much-displayed giant of the same era was Hugo, who was born in the Alpes-Maritimes and first appeared on show at the Paris Exhibition. At the tender age of 6, he was well over 4 feet tall, at 15 he had topped the six-foot mark by a clear 6 inches and, by the time he was measured at 7 feet 6 inches at the age of 22, he was still growing at the rate of roughly an inch every year.

Hugo had enormous bulk to go with his height, weighing-in at more than 31 stones. He completly dwarfed his parents; his father was only 5 feet 4½ inches tall, his mother 5 feet 6 inches, and it is not hard to understand why he needed a mammoth bed, 10 feet long and 5 feet wide, to ensure that he got a comfortable night's sleep.

Fantastic Fatties

Luke McMasters sticks to a simple daily diet; one-and-a-half pounds of cheese, two loaves of bread, three-quarters of a pound of meat, three pounds of apples and two pounds of oranges washed down by 14 pints of milk. Not surprisingly, Luke – better known to millions of British television viewers as the wrestler Giant Haystacks – lays claim to being one of the country's heaviest men at an incredible hulking weight of 40 stones. At a towering 6 feet 11 inches tall, his vital statistics are equally herculean; his chest measures 76 inches and he has a 64-inch waist. In his size 16 shoes, he stands a truly awesome, bearded figure.

Fantastic fatties like Luke have captured public imagination for centuries. Fat men and women have always been objects of curiosity and a vast number have exhibited themselves for profit. During the last century, nearly every circus and penny museum had its example. Several fat freaks have managed to make a considerable fortune out of their disability. From William the Conqueror, through Henry VIII, Louis XVIII, American President William Taft and Ugundan dictator Idi Amin Dada, fantastic fatties have also risen in public life to positions of enormous power to shape and control the destinies of others.

The fattest man alive today – indeed the heaviest recorded human in medical history – is Jon Brower Minnoch, a 41-year-old former taxi driver from Bainbridge Island, Washington. At times in his life, he has weighed

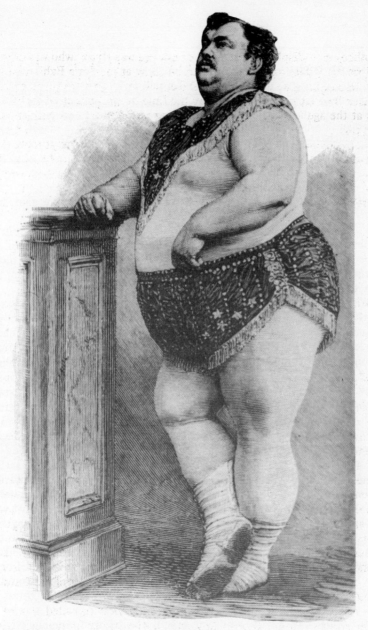

E. Naucke, born 1855, was reputed to be the biggest man in the world

Bonny baby

The bonniest baby ever to bounce into the world must have been tiny titan James Weir, who tragically died when only thirteen months old in 1821. According to the headstone on his grave in the Old Parish Cemetery, Wishaw, Strathclyde, Scotland, he was a staggering 8 stones in weight, 3 feet 4 inches tall and 39 inches in girth.

more than 100 stones. During periods of uncontrollable weight gain, he is claimed to have put on 14 stones in a single week.

Minnoch's unbelievable, ultra roly-poly frame landed him in hospital in Seattle in 1978, on the brink of death. It took 13 attendants simply to roll him over in bed. But after 16 months on an emergency crash diet of 1,200 calories a day, 6 feet 1 inch tall Minnoch was allowed home weighing what for him was a slimline 34 stones.

His problems still aren't over, however. In October, 1981, he was re-admitted to Seattle's University Hospital suffering from chronic weight gain and heart trouble caused by his obesity. The local fire department had to remove several doors as a 10-man emergency team struggled to get him out of his home. Doctors have still so far refused to reveal Minnoch's latest weight, which, at its 100 stone or more peaks can only be estimated by specialists.

America seems to have an image of producing the biggest of everything in the world – and that applies to fantastic fatties. In fact one city, Durham, North Carolina, has become the calorie capital of the country and earned itself the nickname 'Fat City, USA'. It all began 40 years ago, when Doctor Walter Kempner of Duke University pioneered a revolutionary fruit-and-rice diet. As waistlines shed inches, the success of his system spread as far and wide as the stomachs of his patients once did, and fatties from all over America began to roll into Durham. Today, unhappy fatties who are willing to pay up to £2,000 for a treatment course have to join a waiting list of 12 months to get into one of the city's four thriving slimming clinics. New York chef Anthony Milone, who in eight months of hard sweat managed to trim down from a chair-busting 36 stones 6 pounds to a much more comfortable 23 stones, declared: 'When I first came to Durham, I was so ashamed of the way I looked that I got up before dawn for a swim so that no-one would see me. When I went swimming near the end of the course I was the lightest guy there!'

Other super-fatties who, while not exactly turning into rake-like wraiths, have managed to slim down to more manageable sizes include an un-named

'Mr Big' who, after tipping the scales at 60 stones, was taken – by hoist – to a New York clinic where doctors, aided by a 15-strong team to move their patient, worked for three hours to cut more than 10 stones from his abdomen. A second operation on the mystery man, who previously had barely been able to walk because of his obesity, succeeded in removing a further 8 stones of flab from his body in October 1981.

It's certainly not rare for man to need mechanical help in lifting fatties. When Robert Earl Hughes from Monticello, Illinois, died, weighing almost half a ton, on 10 July 1958, he set undertakers a formidable task. Eventually, they decided that his coffin, a converted piano case, had to be lowered into its grave by crane. And on 21 July 1809, jovial heavyweight Daniel Lambert caused enormous headaches when he paid his last visit to the Waggon and Horses Inn at Stamford, Lincolnshire, and died in the ground floor bar. A whole wall and the ceiling had to be pulled down before he could be pulled out. Later, it took 20 pall bearers to carry the 52 stone 11 pound Leicester-born Lambert's coffin, which measured 6 feet 4 inches long and 4 feet 4 inches wide.

The only other Briton apart from Lambert to tip the scales at more than 50 stones was Glasgow-born William Campbell, who died, while working as a publican, at the tender age of 22 on 16 June 1878, weighing-in at 53 stones 8 pounds. The heaviest recorded Briton alive today is 47-stone Eric Keeling from Islington, North London. Eleven pounds at birth in 1933, Eric blossomed into an 18-stoner at the age of 13. His peak weight was attained in 1971, when he decided to try to reduce it by dieting. A couple of years later, he had already shrunk to just over 33 stones.

Some fantastic fatties attain such proportions that they actually fit the description 'human cannon-balls', being as wide, if not wider, than they are tall. One such was Mme Marie-Françoise Clay, a French beggar woman who lived during the last century. Although the date is obscured, it is known that at the age of 40, she was 5 feet 1 inch tall and was one inch greater in measurement around the waist. Her breasts were well over a yard in circumference and her arms were permanently elevated and kept away from

---

Heavy twins

The heaviest twins of all time were Billy and Benny McCrary, of North Carolina, who became professional tag-team wrestlers and bust the scales at a monster weigh-in in November 1978 at 743 pounds and 723 pounds respectively. Both sported 84 inch waists. Tragically, their gargantuan double-act ended in July 1979 when Billy died in a motorcycle accident.

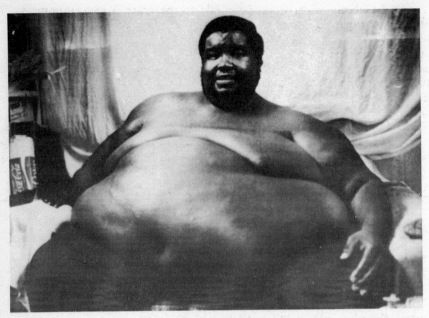

Photographed at a sideshow, Albert weighs 856 pounds

her body by a wall of fat. Astonishingly, she married at the age of 25 and bore six perfectly normal, healthy children. The whole family travelled on foot from village to village, Marie usually augmenting their meagure income from her husband's second-hand clothes barrow by begging at church doors and scavenging what she could. She must have been an incredible sight waddling along behind her husband. It was said that on top of her huge frame was a tiny head – and that her neck was totally obliterated from view by layers of fat.

The heaviest woman who ever lived was Mrs Percy Pearl, who died, aged 46, on 9 October 1972. Before her death, Mrs Pearl had searched long and hard around her home city of Washington for a pair of scales which could actually record her weight; most hospital scales only register up to 800 lbs (57 stones 2 pounds). Eventually though, it was discovered that she easily topped that at a hefty 62 stones 12 pounds. The heaviest-ever British woman was Muriel Hopkins, who registered 43 stones 11 pounds in 1978. Shortly before her death, on 22 April a year later, she had reportedly gone up to 52 stones, but – despite the lack of corroborative evidence – it is estimated, according to the *Guinness Book of Records*, that she more likely scaled around 47½ stones.

Extreme obesity right from the cradle to the grave is not uncommon. Records of super-fat babies reveal the case of a German girl who at birth weighed 13 pounds; at six months, 3 stones; at four years, 10½ stones; and at the age of 20, a toppling 32 stones. A little girl aged only 5½ who was exhibited at a meeting of the Physical Society of Vienna on 4 December 1894, tipped the scales at slightly more than 17 stones. She was just shedding her first teeth, but could only toddle like an infant due to her excess fat. The child, of Russian descent, was said never to perspire and was fed, it said, almost exclusively on cabbage, milk and vegetable soup!

Medical tomes are, indeed, littered with case histories of youngsters – like the 'Tompkins Child' or 'Baby Chambers' – who were born grossly overweight and remained that way through childhood, adolescence and adulthood. The question of whether such obesity is actually congenital still causes debate among leading doctors.

One man who is now single-handedly trying to shed the lifelong layers of fat which at one stage turned him into Cockney East London's celebrated 'King of the Fatties' is 58-year-old social club manager George Macaree, who once merited a Guiness Book of Records entry at a gargantuan 40 stones 4 pounds. George, unlike freak show figures of old who merely showed their bodies for gain, uses his famous frame to raise money for numerous charities, and is already well on his way towards a target of losing half his weight. After a year on a strict 500 calories a day diet, he has shed more than 10 stones so far. Soon he will have to abandon the special armchair which cost £500 to custom-build along with the specially-tailored suits to fit his 84-76-89 figure. But he says: 'I can now tie my own shoelaces whereas before I couldn't even see them. I tried 15 diets before I found the one for me. Now, I'm only allowed three meals a day! It's taken a lot of will power, but I'm proving it can be done.'

Hypnotist Alan Paige is offering other fantastic fatties the sort of cure that the freak show characters of old could never have dreamed of. Alan, from Newcastle, is offering British heavyweights 'fantasy island' package trips to Malta where they can eat and drink all they want, and still come home slimmer. The trick is that it will all be done under hypnosis and Alan, who revealed his tour plan in February 1982, says: 'They will believe they are tucking into steak and chips, when really the meal they will be munching away at is a salad. There's no secret mumbo jumbo about this. Hypnosis is the key.' And, for all fantastic fatties who are still sceptical, he pledges: 'If it doesn't work for any individual, I'll refund the money for the treatment.'

One wonders what Daniel Lambert, Marie-Françoise Clay and a whole heaving host of others would ever have made of that!

No chapter about fantastic fatties could ever be complete without a look at the amazing feats and eats of the world's most gluttonous trenchermen. Perhaps the hungriest of them all has been Edward 'Bozo' Miller, who daily consumes a staggering 25,000 calories.

Bozo, of Oakland, California, who was born in 1909, stands only 5 feet 7½ inches tall but weighs in at anything between 20 to 21½ stones depending on how peckish he's been feeling. He hasn't actually been beaten in an eating contest since 1931 and among his more astonishing feats was the record he established in 1963 by munching his way through 27 small chickens at one sitting.

The same year, Bozo, who boasts a bulging 57-inch waist, also set the world ravioli eating record of 324 with the first 250 swallowed in 70 minutes flat. If wanting to establish gluttony records sounds half-baked to you, don't try giving Peter Dowdswell, of Earls Barton, Northamptonshire, food for thought. He currently holds no less than 14 such records and when it comes to speed-eating he appears to be simply unstoppable.

His records, apart from five for beer and ale, include the following: 1 pound of Cheddar cheese in 1 minute 13 seconds, 1 pound of eels in 13.7 seconds, a 26-ounce haggis in 50 seconds, 22 meat pies in 18 minutes 13 seconds, 2 pints of milk in 3.2 seconds, 62 pancakes in 58.5 seconds, 3 pounds of potatoes in 1 minute 22 seconds, 40 jam sandwiches in 53.9 seconds, 3 pounds of shrimps in 4 minutes 8 seconds, 14 hard-boiled eggs in 58 seconds, 32 soft-boiled eggs in 78 seconds and 13 raw eggs in 2.2 seconds.

Peter would have had another record for prune eating to enter alongside his incredible list in the *Guinness Book of Records*, but for the fact that his time of 78 seconds to eat 144 of them was bettered by 13 seconds in 1978 by Douglas Mein. Generally, the bargees on the Rhine are reckoned to be the world's biggest eaters, averaging around 5,200 calories a day. In December 1972, however, the Federation of Medicine in New Zealand reported an intake of 14,321 calories over a 24-hour period by a long-distance road runner.

The craziest of all eating records must go to a bizarre Frenchman named Lotito, more appropriately nicknamed Monsieur Mangetout (Mr Eat-all) who, in 15 days between 17 March and 2 April 1977, consumed an entire bicycle, eating the frame as metal filings and stewing the tyres!

Records for such voracious eating, and also those for drinking, fail to even begin to compare, however, with the consumption of those people who tragically suffer from the rare disease of bulimia, a morbid desire to eat without stopping, and polydipsia, whose victims endure a pathological thirst. It is not unknown for bulimia sufferers to have to spend anything up to 15 hours solidly eating every day. One of the most extreme cases ever recorded was that of Matthew Daking, then aged only 12, in 1743. In the space of just 6 days he managed to eat an incredible 348 pounds 2 ounces of food.

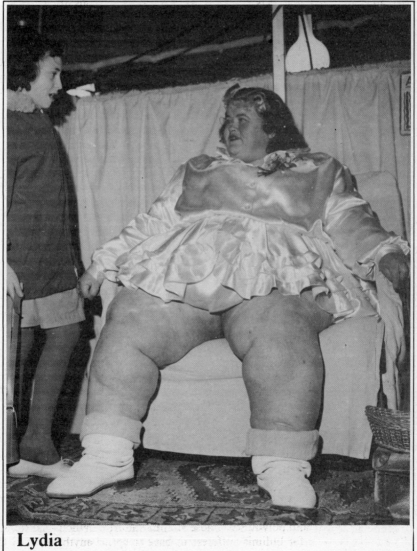

Lydia

Lydia, aged 23, from the Netherlands weighs an astounding 456 pounds. She is pictured here at a Paris fair in 1961.

A man from Johannesburg, Fannie Meyer, was claimed in 1974 to be drinking at least 160 pints of water a day, his incredible thirst apparently and inexplicably the result of a skull fracture. According to a further report four years later, he was managing to slake his thirst with 52 pints a day. Miss Helge Andersson of Lindesberg, Sweden, who was born in 1908, is reported to have drunk 40 pints every day between 1922 and January 1971, an astonishing total of 87,600 gallons during the period.

Hormone deficiencies can also produce unnatural obesity from an early age, producing the sort of 'Fat Boy' freaks who appealed to the Victorians but who lived, in some cases, in constant danger of suffocating themselves to death with their own fat. One such case was that of Carrie Akers, who, though she stood only 34 inches tall, weighed an astonishing 22 stones. And another fat woman, Miss Conley, who belonged to a travelling American circus, actually did smother herself in bed, by rolling onto her face. She was so gigantic that she couldn't turn on her back without help, and, on the night she died, there was nobody around to provide any assistance.

The Victorians discovered a condition, which they called adiposis dolorosa, which coupled gross obesity with other symptoms, such as a recurrent headache, and a painfulness quite different to the sort of discomfort experienced by other people who were simply fat. In one case, a woman whose age was believed to be 38 or 39, was found in June 1887 to be suffering from an inordinate enlargement of her shoulders, arms, back and the sides of her chest. The parts affected by adiposis dolorosa appeared, according to a report, to be elastic. In some places the fat seemed as though it were a writhing mass of worms under skin. Unlike normal cases of obesity, there was no muscular involvement in the condition and the skin was not thickened as it would be in an ordinary fat patient. This remarkable condition was accompanied by great pain whenever an affected area was touched. According to the report, the woman simply appeared to have extremely unsightly wobbling rolls of fat attached to various parts of her body which baffled all medical knowledge.

Little and large

The world's most amazing little and large couple were husband and wife Mills and Mary Darden. He weighed in at a staggering 72 stones 12 pounds, while she barely tipped the scales at a super-slim 7 stones. Despite their differences, it was a case of happy families, though, for Mary is said to have borne her heavyweight husband between three and five children before her death in 1837.

Strongmen

From Samson to Sandow to the children's fantasy character of the Incredible Hulk, now immortalized by television, feats of mighty muscular power by strong men and women have always fascinated us more feeble mortals.

Today's Olympic weight and power-lifters captivate TV audiences of millions with the jerks, squats and snatches that can raise loads in excess of five hundredweight. Circus strong-men still thrive in an era in which human competition rather than the mere display of freakish prowess is all-important.

Had Scotsman Angus Macaskill lived in the 20th century, he would undoubtedly have been among the leading contenders for that most elusive, often challenged and more often unofficially claimed title of the strongest man the world has ever seen. Born in the Outer Hebrides in 1825, he grew to be a giant of a man, standing 7 feet 9 inches tall in bare feet and with physical abilities to match.

Signed up in later life by the showman Barnum, he spent his early days as a dock worker-cum-fisherman. It is said that he could raise the mast of a fishing boat with one hand and was able to throw hundredweight sacks from the bottom of a boat right up onto the jetty with consummate ease. On a voyage to Nova Scotia, startled bystanders witnessed him carrying an enormous ship's anchor over one shoulder – a feat which is boldly recorded in the *Guinness Book of Amazing People* as 'the heaviest weight ever carried by a human being'.

Despite his enormous power, however, Macaskill was known as a gentle giant who steered well clear of public brawls and was shy of demonstrating his strength. When the champion heavyweight wrestler of Canada tried to provoke a fight with him, Macaskill decided that the only was he could avoid killing the man was to insist on shaking hands. As he gripped the Canadian's palm in a 'friendly' gesture, the wrestler's eyes began to bulge as he saw blood

---

Convict strongman

Prison exercise did Austrian convict Joseph Pospischilli a power of good. During incarceration in the fortress jail of Olen in the 19th century, he astonished his captors by balancing two gipsy dancers on a huge table with his teeth. When freed, he became a strong-man entertainer, earning a fortune touring southern Europe.

John Topham

Heaviest-ever

Twenty-five stone Olympic and professional weightlifter Paul Anderson, of Toccoa, Georgia, who became known as 'The Dixie Derrick', claimed the title of raising the heaviest weight ever lifted by a man on 12 June 1957, when he hoisted aloft an almost unbelievable 6,270 pounds on his back. The weight is the equivalent of two family saloon cars, or three entire football teams.

oozing from under his fingernails. Macaskill simply smiled politely and the stunned wrestler happily accepted his chance to back down.

The giant Scotsman was so strong that the incorrigible Barnum not only exhibited him, but also set him to work erecting big top tents. Macaskill used a 14-pound hammer – in *each* hand – to drive home the stakes. Other circus owners did their best to woo him away from Barnum and persuade him to become an all-in wrestler. But quietly-spoken Macaskill was content to stay where he was, doing the work of a dozen men for one man's wage!

Word of his Herculean feats in the Barnum shows was quickly picked up by royal freak enthusiast Queen Victoria, who summoned the Scottish Samson to Windsor Castle. The shy strong-man was so nervous at the prospect of meeting and amusing Her Majesty – who was almost three feet shorter than he – that he damaged the castle carpets by shuffling his huge feet. What did the damage were the two horseshoes he had welded on to the bottom of his boots!

Great strong-men throughout history have pitted their power against animals, cars, trains and supposedly immovable objects in incredible 'tug o' war' matches. 19th century Londoner Thomas Topham regularly won such matches using his teeth alone ... against two horses!

Topham, who stood a mere 5 feet 10 inches tall, could also lift, and hold in a horizontal position, a 6-foot long table – again using just his teeth. Holding a bit between those mighty molars, Topham's only real failure came when he lost yet another tug o' war, this time against four horses. He more than compensated for that, however, by turning to a different but equally exacting act – carrying a gigantic rolling pin, weighing 800 pounds, in his hands.

Another celebrated Victorian strong-man was Tom Johnson, a porter on the banks of the Thames who once doubled his workload by carrying out the duties of a sick colleague who could not provide for his wife and family. Johnson's job was to carry sacks of wheat and corn from the wharves to warehouses, and he was said to be so adept at carrying them that he could actually hurl them for several yards using the actions of a club-swinger.

When Johnson heard that the porters of Paris were used to carrying bags of flour weighing 350 pounds over their shoulders, he determined to outdo them three times over. Very soon he was able to carry three such sacks, with a combined weight of over 1,000 pounds over his shoulders with no apparent discomfort.

A more recent show of super-strength was that demonstrated by 40-year-old Belgian beefcake John Massis. On 19 October 1976, he must have shocked the world's dentists when, with his teeth alone, he pulled a British Rail locomotive and truck, together weighing an incredible 121 tons, along a level track at Park Royal, London. With the bit firmly between his teeth, he repeated the feat in Sweden two years later, this time pulling three railway carriages.

Massis can bend metal bars, bite enormous nails out of wooden blocks and lift a Fiat car into the air using only a harness attached to his jaws. He has lifted a staggering weight of 513 pounds from the ground with his teeth. But his most amazing stunt must have been the one he performed in front of television cameras in Los Angeles in 1979. Using only a bit between his teeth attached to a harness, he managed to prevent a helicopter from taking off.

Punjabi taxi driver Tara Chand Saggar is another modern-day master of muscle-power. And, like Samson, he claims that his enormous power comes from his long hair. In May 1972 at the age of 72 he decided to prove it. He walked into the offices of a Calcutta newspaper and, using a series of ropes to attach a board to his curly, brown locks, managed to lift a burly printer, weighing 143 pounds, a foot off the floor, using hair-power only.

Unfortunately, the rope knots gave way, and the recoil almost flung Saggar out of the office window. He apologized for the mishap and promised to return when his hair was longer and stronger. He did just that, barely two weeks later, and repeated the feat with total success, this time lifting a 165-pound printer off the ground!

Strongwomen

One claim to being the world's strongest-ever woman was made by 5 feet 11 inches tall Katie Sandwina, a housewife who found fame in John Ringling's freak circus in the early 1900s. Quite apart from making mincemeat of a 286-pound load in 1911 – which is recorded as the greatest overhead lift ever made by a woman – she also showed her strength

Katie Sandwina

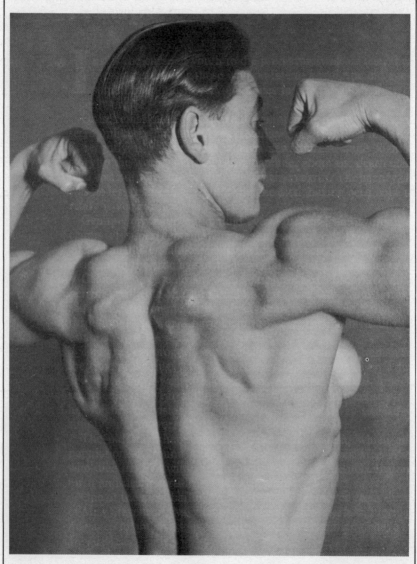

Ivy, photographed in 1930, was a champion wrestler and could lift a grand piano

by carrying a 1,200-pound cannon on her shoulder and performing military rifle exercises, using her 160-pound husband Max instead of a rifle!

The record for the greatest weight actually lifted by a woman belongs to Mrs Josephine Blatt, who raised an astonishing 3,564 pounds on her broad shoulders at the Bijou Theatre, Hoboken, New Jersey, on 13 April 1895. Among other famous strong women, from the period when freak shows were at the height of popularity, were the Frenchwoman Madame Elise and Miss Darnett, an English girl who became known as 'The Singing Stronglady'.

Madame Elise, who performed with her husband, was capable of lifting eight men with a combined weight of roughly 1,700 pounds. Miss Darnett, doing a back arch on the floor, could play the piano and sing while a platform, laden with a half-ton weight, was balanced on her chest, abdomen and thighs.

The Wolf Boy and other hair-raising freaks

In a land of 900 million people, little Yu Chenhuan is a medical marvel. When he was born in 1977, to peasant parents in the remote Chinese province of Liaoning, doctors were baffled by the long, silky hair which grew in a fine line down his spine.

They were certain it would quickly disappear. But instead, it kept on growing at a phenomenal rate, and within weeks covered Yu's entire body. Soon, his face was so hairy that he became known for hundreds of miles around as the 'Wolf Boy' and his astonished mother and father found themselves keeping his beard in trim in between bottle-feeding him. Despite a year of tests and experiments, Chinese scientists were forced to admit that they couldn't find a cure. Today, the hair still continues to grow. Yu, now a young boy, sports a full set of whiskers on his face and a dark, furry down still covers his entire body.

Bearded Ladies

Other hair-raising cases of extreme hirsuteness have exasperated the experts and amazed audiences all over the world – but none more so than those involving bearded ladies. The whiskers of Kentucky's famous bearded lady Janice Deveree, which earned her a fortune from dime arcades and peep shows, were measured as a flowing 14 inches at the height of her career in 1884, when she was 42 years old. A Swiss lady, Madame Fortune Clofullia, was showered with diamonds by Emperor Napoleon III who was delighted, much to the annoyance of the Empress, that she styled her beard the same way he did his. The fortunate Madame Fortune coined further riches when she joined Phineas T. Barnum's freak show circuit in America and drew more than 3½ million paying customers in just nine months.

Eventually she married an artist and had two children; first a girl and then a boy who became almost as hairy as she was Her son was, in fact, exhibited alongside her by Barnum, whose advertising posters declared: 'His body is

Yu Chenhuan

Annie Jones-Elliot appeared
with the Barnum and
Bailey Circus from
her childhood on.

Longest moustache

Holy whiskers! The world's longest moustache was cultivated by Indian religious man Masuriya Din. It sprouted to a staggering length of 8 feet 6 inches between 1949 and 1962. He is on the verge of being rivalled by New Delhi prisoner Karna Ram Bheel, who in 1979 was granted permission by his jail governor to keep the 7 feet 10 inch top-lip growth he hopes will eventually win him the record.

---

thoroughly covered with hair, more particularly over the shoulders and on the back; his face is fully surrounded with whiskers, fully marked and about half an inch in length, but of light colour. The child is strong and healthy and promises fair to astonish the reader.'

Perhaps the most astonishing thing about Madame Fortune's son was the fact that, under the showname 'Infant Esau', he was exhibited wearing dresses until he was 14 years old. This was typical Barnum hokum; not satisfied with a bearded boy, he did his best to dupe punters into believing that they were actually viewing a bearded girl!

One of the earliest recorded bearded ladies who was put on show was Rosine-Marguerite Muller, who became a celebrated 18th century circus attraction in her native Germany and died, with a thick beard and heavy moustache, in hospital in Dresden in 1732. A century later another bearded lady, Julia Pastrana, was so bewhiskered and hairy that she was billed as 'The Ugliest Woman in the World.'

Julia married her manager, a man called Lent, and their union is said to have been blessed (or cursed) with a daughter so akin to her mother in ugliness, that, at the sight of her, Julia was so distraught that she died soon afterwards. The bizarre story went on when Lent not only continued to exhibit her after her death – in mummified form – but also discovered another bearded girl, whom he persuaded to change her name to Pastrana, and displayed her as his wife's living sister.

Lent eventually married his new discovery and so established a record for himself as the only man to have wed two bearded women. Victorian physicians George Gould and Walter Pyle chronicled a 'curious case of a woman of 23 (Mrs Viola M.), who from the age of three had a considerable quantity of hair on the side of the cheek which eventually became a full beard. She was quite feminine and was free from excessive hair elsewhere, her nose and forehead being singularly bare. Her voice was very sweet; she was married at 17½, having two normal children and nursed each for one month.'

Luminous People

Electrical power is one of man's greatest creations. Harnessing it has given us unprecedented sophistication in both home and industrial life. But not all electricity comes from burning coal, gas or oil, from nuclear reactors or hydro-electric plants. Doctors and scientists have found yet another, confounding source – the human body itself. There are people who can glow in the dark and others who can disrupt – or mysteriously activate – electric currents.

Religious tracts have always told of auras or halos appearing around or over holy men. But there are also records of secular folk who shine and shimmer with no claim to ecclesiastical fame. A letter published in *English Mechanic* magazine in September 1869, related the tale of an American woman who, 'on going to bed, found that a light was issuing from the upper side of the fourth toe of her right foot. Rubbing increased the phosphorescent glow and it spread up her foot. Fumes were also given off, making the room disagreeable; and both light and fumes continued when the foot was held in a basin of water, or scrubbed with soap. It lasted for 45 minutes before fading away, and was witnessed by her husband.'

In May 1934, the astonishing case of Anna Morano brought leading doctors and specialists flocking to her bedside in Pirano, Italy. Signora Morano suffered from asthma. But no-one could begin to explain why, for several months, her breasts emitted a clearly visible blue glow while she slept. Her heart rate doubled while this happened, yet the glow was not caused by her sweat. Indeed she perspired only after each strange emission.

Three years later, two eminent British doctors documented the case of a female patient with breast cancer whose affected flesh gave off a light so bright that it could illuminate the hands of a watch several feet away in the dark. Infants, too, occasionally emit a soft, white radiance. One boy, born in Saint-Urbain, France, in 1869, was seen by witnesses to shoot luminous rays

---

Drip-die

The astonishing case of the 'Drip-Die Man' was reported in the *Medical and Physical Journal* of London on 25 February 1885. A 77-year-old-man, of previously good health, began to sweat profusely for no apparent reason, and continued to do so until he died of exhaustion after three months of continual perspiration.

from the ends of his fingers. The child, bathed in light when he died, also badly shocked all who tried to touch him. He was just nine months old.

Angelique Cottin was only 14 when her ten-week ordeal as an 'electric person' began in her home town of La Perrière on 14 January 1846. Objects seemed to retreat from her whenever she went near them. Her slightest touch was enough to send furniture careering across the room, spinning wildly or jumping up and down. No-one could hold onto anything already in her grasp. Compasses were sent wild whenever she was near. Yet this was no eerie poltergeist. Doctors could only attribute her unseen power to the fact that her heartbeat rose to 120 a minute in the evening, during which time her electro-magnetic power seemed to increase and centre, for no apparent reason, on her left forearm.

Jennie Morgan was another teenager to suffer what in today's cliché-ridden world of science might be termed 'High Voltage Syndrome'. During the 1890s, witnesses attest, actual sparks flew from her to nearby objects at her home in Sedalia, Missouri. Animals shunned her, and some people who shook her hand were knocked unconscious, supposedly by shock waves. In London, 20 years earlier, 18-year-old Caroline Clare had, according to record, been terrified when ordinary household cutlery stuck to her skin. Even the stays on her corset are said to have become magnetized.

The phenomenon of luminosity and super-static powers is not, of course, an exclusively female affliction. In 1889, doctors intensively studied the case of Frank McKinstry of Joplin, Missouri, whose feet stuck immovably to the ground when he became 'highly-charged'. And in 1890, Maryland scientists were completely dumbfounded by the wierd powers of Louis Hamburger, who could lift a 5 pound jar of iron filings with the tips of three fingers. Eight years previously, a Zulu boy was exhibited in Edinburgh, for giving off intense electrical shocks.

The 20th century too, has its share of electric people. In 1920, doctors at Clinton Prison, New York, published a paper reporting on 34 convicts who had suffered from botulinus poisoning. Amazingly, compasses could not work in their presence and metal objects simply moved – as if by some dark and mysterious form of auto-suggestion – away from them. Paper, also, seemed to be affected, and stuck to their hands. When they recovered from the poisoning however, the high-voltage symptoms seemed to vanish too.

Horns, Tails and·Noses

Horns, tails, nails and noses make up a truly oddball collection. But then, some of the World's Greatest Freaks are truly oddball characters.

Human horns, which have been known to grow to 11 inches long and 2½ inches in diameter, are far more common than is widely believed. Doctors in Mexico discovered a porter who hid a bizarre secret under his oddly-shaped red cap – no less than three horns sprouting at a lopsided angle from his forehead. In Paris in the 19th century, a woman identified only as the Widow Dimanche had a horn growing downwards from the dead centre of her forehead which was so long that it ended several inches below the level of her chin. Not surprisingly, to followers of the curious throughout the world she became known simply as 'Mother Horn'. In 1878, a Philadelphian doctor recorded the case of a sea captain who sported gnarled, horny growths from his nose, cheeks, forehead and lips. On several occasions, the 78-year-old mariner's horns appear simply to have dropped off, only for new ones to grow in their place.

In *Anomalies and Curiosities of Medicine*, Gould and Pyle report the case of a teenage girl, Annie Jackson, who lived in Waterford, Ireland, during the last century and grew hideously misshapen horns from her 'joints, arms, axillae, nipples, ears and forehead'. Modern studies have revealed that the growth of horns is far more likely to occur in women than men. Gould and Pyle also relate a case second-hand – which may be apocryphal – of a woman patient who had a scarcely believable 185 horns growing from her body.

Cases of congenital multi-horn growths on members of certain African tribes have been recorded, and legends of the lost Ju-Ju tribe of horned 'Devil Men' in Haiti remain today. However, serious doubt overshadows the so-called proof of their existence, which was the discovery of the remains of

Golden nose

Famous Danish astronomer Tycho Brae, after whom a huge Moon crater is now named, nosed his way into the world of freaks after his own nose was sliced off in a swordfight. Armed with bundles of money he had been given for research by the King of Denmark, he ordered surgeons to clamp on his face a brand new, specially designed one, made of solid gold. He wore it with shining pride till the day he died.

Central forehead

This picture was published in August, 1813, in a London magazine. The portrait was reputed to have been drawn in 1588 when the subject, Margaret Vergh Gryifith, was sixty years old. The horn, which was supposed to have been in the centre of her forehead, was four inches long.

Duck bill

Legendary Wild West lawman Wild Bill Hickock would hardly have inspired such fear as he did in bandits and gunslingers if his true nickname had ever leaked out. Close friends actually knew US Marshal James Butler Hickock as 'Duck Bill' because of his huge nose and freakish, protruding lower lip. After he was shot dead – ironically at Deadwood, South Dakota – on 2 August 1876, while holding a wild set of poker cards (aces and eights) the truth was finally revealed.

---

two shrunken, mummified figures with horns and hooves. The 'Devil' analogy was, however, certainly applied to horned men and women exploited throughout the world during the 19th century freak show boom.

Human tails are also not such a rarity as you might expect. Towards the end of the 19th century, a black child aged 8 weeks in Louisville began to grow a tail from the base of his spine which, within months, had grown to 2½ inches long with a base 1¼ inches in circumference. The tail, like that of a pig, was fleshy, with no sign of bone or cartilage running through it. As the boy – or 'Pig Boy' as he was cruelly dubbed – grew up, the tail seemed to cause him no problems whatsoever, so he kept it, despite the fact that even in those days doctors could probably quite easily have removed it.

In the early 1890s the most incredible tale of a tail emerged, when a travelling physician discovered a 12-year-old boy with a growth from the base of his spine which was an amazing 12 inches long. The youngster, from Cochin China, who became known as the 'Moi Boy' in medical circles, overnight became a world-famous oddity. Photographs of him appeared in the journal *Atlantic Monthly*. The 'Moi Boy's' tail, the longest ever recorded in a human being, was completely fleshy, without any trace of bone. Yet, just like an animal, he seemed to have perfect control over it.

Human noses, thanks in part nowadays to the party piece of the false nose, have become a vital part of the anatomy at least in cosmetic terms. Plastic surgeons now make a fortune out of performing 'nose jobs' on the rich and famous and even the deeply embarrassed yet less wealthy who have scrimped and saved in an effort to have their shame surgically removed or improved.

In the category of freak noses, there is really only one contender, 18th century Yorkshireman Thomas Wedders (or Wadhouse). His nose was 7½ inches long, and became the *objet d'art* on which dozens of contemporary illustrators focused their attentions. Graphic line drawings of simpleton – for that's what he was – Wedders and his nose still exist. Who knows what he could have achieved had he been born into the era of the freak show?

Romesh Sharma

Human nails can, of course, be grown to any length required – and Romesh Sharma, of Delhi, India has gone to great lengths to ensure that he has nailed a world record. From his picture, it's easy to see why: the curly, tusk-like nail on the thumb of his left hand would, if straightened out, measure an incredible 26½ inches.

Romesh set about getting himself into the record books from scratch. He was only 19 and still a student when his sister angrily told him that she was embarrassed to walk down the road with him because his finger nails were too long. Ashamed, Romesh scissored and filed away until his sister was happy. Back at college though, he found himself being chided once more, for giving in to her demands, and fellow students laid down the challenge: 'We bet you can't grow your nails long again.'

It was a challenge Romesh took up sharply. He agreed to let the nails on the fingers of his left-hand grow completely unchecked. Within four years that now-famous thumb had begun to curl itself in a perfect, if brittle, figure 'O'. In 1970, the curiosity with the crazy cuticles was beginning to receive such worldwide acclaim that he found himself the star exhibit in places as far away as Japan.

Shortly after appearing in the Land of the Rising Sun, where the distance from that moon-shaped crescent at the base of the nails to the very tip earned him a good sum, Romesh fell in love, and vowed to his young bride-to-be, as he had vowed to his sister, that he would cut his nails once more and forever keep them in trim.

This time, he broke his promise. Indeed, Mrs Sharma still waits today for the pledge to be honoured. At night in bed, her husband lies with his left arm dangling outside the sheets, lest he should roll over and crack the previous nails which have seen neither scissors, clippers nor file for 15 years. She helps bath him and buttons all his clothes for him – and she has long since grown

---

Tailed duke

The first Duke of Wellington, who as the Iron Duke became one of Britain's foremost statesmen and military leaders, could only ride on horseback using a specially adapted saddle with a hole at the rear to accommodate a small, bony, vestigial tail which grew from the base of his spine.

used to total strangers knocking at the door of their home to catch a glimpse of his claws.

Romesh, his wife and two children have, indeed, become celebrities in Delhi – a mystical, magical place where it is not unusual for spiritual devotees to seek the ultimate perfection of putting the world at their fingertips. There is one cruel cut, however. A religious man from the same country has inched ahead of Romesh's pursuit of the record.

Mr Shridar Chillal, of Poona, has grown his five left hand nails to a total length of 108½ inches. The aggregate length of the nails on the left hand of Romesh – despite that record-breaking thumb – is just slightly less than 100 inches. Now Romesh has set himself a new challenge; to cut through that record by growing his nails even longer. And he says: 'This time, I've got the blessing of my wife – and I'm determined to nail a new record!'